PETER GZOWSKI

PETER GZOWSKI

— A Biography —

R.B. Fleming

DUNDURN PRESS
TORONTO

Editor: Michael Carroll
Design: Jennifer Scott
Printer: Transcontinental

Library and Archives Canada Cataloguing in Publication

Fleming, Rae Bruce, 1944-
        Peter Gzowski : a biography / by Rae Fleming.

Includes bibliographical references and index.

ISBN 978-1-55488-720-0

1. Gzowski, Peter. 2. Radio broadcasters--Canada--Biography. I. Title.

PN1991.4.G97F54 2010   791.4402'8092   C2009-907440-0

2   3   4   5   14   13   12   11   10

 Conseil des Arts   Canada Council   Canada   ONTARIO ARTS COUNCIL
du Canada   for the Arts   CONSEIL DES ARTS DE L'ONTARIO

We acknowledge the support of the **Canada Council for the Arts** and the **Ontario Arts Council** for our publishing program. We also acknowledge the financial support of the **Government of Canada** through the **Canada Book Fund** and **The Association for the Export of Canadian Books**, and the **Government of Ontario** through the **Ontario Book Publishers Tax Credit program**, and the **Ontario Media Development Corporation**.

Care has been taken to trace the ownership of copyright material used in this book. The author and the publisher welcome any information enabling them to rectify any references or credits in subsequent editions.

J. Kirk Howard, President

Printed and bound in Canada.
www.dundurn.com

Dundurn Press
3 Church Street, Suite 500
Toronto, Ontario, Canada
M5E 1M2

Gazelle Book Services Limited
White Cross Mills
High Town, Lancaster, England
LA1 4XS

Dundurn Press
2250 Military Road
Tonawanda, NY
U.S.A. 14150

To Jeanie Wagner, who read each draft with care;
To Lois Smith-Brennan, who helped fund this biography;
To Frances Daunt, who listened, laughed, and encouraged;
And to Ron Rees, who understands the loneliness of long-distance writing.

Contents

The past is an empty café terrace.
An airless dusk before thunder. A man running.
And no way now to know what happened then —
None at all — unless, of course, you improvise

— *Eavan Boland, "The Black Lace Fan My Mother Gave Me,"*
Outside History

All remembrance of things past is fiction.

— *Ernest Hemingway,*
A Moveable Feast: The Restored Edition

Introduction:

"Never as Simply Heroic as We'd Like Them to Be"[1]

The only biographies worth writing are those whose subjects resemble fictional characters.

— Peter Conrad, The Guardian Weekly, *September 9–15, 2005*

For most of his restless, anxious life, Peter Gzowski lived inside his imagination. Inside that imagination, Peter was happiest. Right up to his death, his enthusiasm and curiosity were intact, as if the child in him had never completely grown up. Small wonder that two of his favourite guests on radio shows were W.O. Mitchell, whose most memorable character is a boy; and Paul Hiebert, whose poet-of-the-plains, Sarah Binks, exhibits a childlike naïveté. The naïf lives on the margins of society, from which vantage point he or she may observe and comment on the adult world. Small wonder, too, that throughout his adult life Peter identified strongly with Holden Caulfield, the rebellious, highly imaginative hero of J.D. Salinger's novel *The Catcher in the Rye*, which Peter had read soon after its publication in 1951.

In 1997, near the end of his long radio career, the sixty-two-year-old Peter said, "I'm still Holden Caulfield."[2]

Peter's imagination developed at an early age. He grew up in Galt, Ontario, a small city an hour or so southwest of Toronto. There, it was a park that sparked his imagination. Dickson Park, named for William Dickson, the founder of Galt, was located across the street from the upper duplex where Peter, his mother, and his stepfather lived. He loved to tell the story of a hockey game played on what he called *verglas*, the French word for fields of ice created when sleet covers snow, following which the temperature plummets overnight to create fields of ice. The tale usually began with one of his young pals firing the puck over the boards of the outdoor rink in Dickson Park. When the boy scampered to retrieve it, he discovered that his skates didn't pierce the surface of the ice-encrusted snow. Peter loved to recount how he and the other players followed the leader and fired infinitely long passes over the frozen snow as they soared "across roads, across lawns, racing down hills like skiers who never had to stop and out, out, into the country, by this time followed by every boy from our side of town who had skates — forty of us, fifty of us, soaring across the farmers' fields, inventing new rules to allow for fences in the middle of the playing area, and goals that might be half a mile apart: free, free as birds." In another version of the same story, as they skated miles and miles, the boys were "as untrammelled as birds in the clean crisp air." Peter concluded that version with a lament: "It is the freedom I remember, the freedom and the laughter, and I sometimes wonder if I, or my sons, will ever be that free again."[3]

"Where have all the fields of ice gone?" the adult Gzowski wondered, and added, in a burst of Gallic enthusiasm, *"Où est le verglas d'antan?"*[4] Where had all that carefree happiness gone? The story, in all its variations, owes a great deal to Peter's imagination, and therefore the listener or reader dare not ask how the boys managed to reach the fields surrounding Galt, since the park is today, and was when Peter was young, surrounded by streets of solid brick Victorian homes and wooden fences.

Peter once confessed that he never let "reality stand in the way of a good story."[5] In April 1982, shortly after the CBC announced he would be the next host of *Morningside*, Peter was interviewed by a reporter from the *Toronto Star*. He talked about his first summer job at the golf club in Galt. At age thirteen he sold cigarettes and illegal beer in the canteen, and he cleaned up the locker room. It was a terrible job, he told the reporter, and the hours were long. In fact, he said, it was exploitation of child labour. However, he told the reporter, picking up other people's wet towels had taught him a lesson. "I'm probably a little better about picking up my own towels in the locker room of the golf club so some kid doesn't have to do it." And he added, probably with a grin, "But I'm probably telling you a lie right now."[6] One of his favourite games on *Morningside* was called "Lie Detector," an idea lifted from Radio-Canada's *Détecteur de Mensonges*. Two panellists and Peter each made three statements, one of which was pure invention. The other two tried to guess which statement was the lie. One day, among his three statements, was the fiction that he had once scored a goal on Andy Moog, goalkeeper for the Edmonton Oilers.[7]

Because Peter lived inside his imagination, he was happiest in print and radio, which owe their existence to the imaginations of creator and audience, journalist and reader, broadcaster and listener. Peter always claimed to be a writer on radio. He thus combined the two most imaginative methods of mass communication.[8]

Radio is particularly magical. With words and voice, the broadcaster re-creates a world that exists in his or her mind. That world is transmitted to the listener by invisible waves. Once the waves reach a radio in a home, car, or office, each listener's imagination re-constructs the scene, not exactly the one imagined by the broadcaster, and not exactly the one imagined by fellow listeners next door or on the other side of the country. On radio Peter imagined the whole of Canada as one large field of ice. Each weekday morning the game began anew. On *Radio Free Friday* during the late 1960s, on *This Country in the Morning* during the early 1970s, and from 1982 to 1997 on *Morningside*, listeners, "as untrammelled as birds in the clean crisp air,"[9] happily followed Peter as he skated over those fields of ice that stretched across his frozen country.

Listeners loved Peter's persona, its mystery, its childlike curiosity, and its dark humour that hinted at vulnerability and anguish. He was a brother, a friend, or a helpful neighbour who chatted amiably over the backyard fence. He was the best kind of neighbour: there when you needed him, but never intrusive, for he rarely talked about himself. When he did, it was usually in a carefully crafted personal essay — a bulletin or billboard, he called it — which he read at the top of his radio shows. He was a great listener, and the questions he asked of guests seemed to emerge from the preceding answer, thanks to good scripts written by loyal producers, and thanks also to his agile, creative mind that never allowed the "greens," as they are called in media parlance, to dominate an interview. He even mumbled in half-sentences, as most of us do from time to time. His stammering, which was a carefully developed characteristic of his radio style, made him all the more human.

Born in 1934, Peter grew up listening to radio. He came of age during the 1950s, the decade in which CBC Television was founded. His career spanned the last half of the twentieth century, which was arguably the most creative fifty years in Canadian history. During that period, Canadians acted, painted, and sang as never before, and they wrote novels, poetry, histories, and biographies in great abundance. Publishing houses and art galleries sprang forth and flourished. The Canada Council for the Arts was founded in 1957. In the last half of the twentieth century, many Canadians grew interested in viewing, hearing, and reading about themselves.

Because of Peter, Canadians, or at least those who listened to him, watched him or read his articles and books, felt that they understood this country, so vast that it must be imagined to be real. Peter imagined his country into being, and he transmitted that country to his community of listeners, viewers, and readers. For francophones who listened to Peter, admittedly not a great many, (English) Canada was no longer a darkened stage without characters. Peter liked the expression, "As Canadian as it is possible to be under the circumstances."[10] And he saw himself as a creator and defender of that identity. Just as his ancestor, Sir Casimir Gzowski, had overseen the building of Canada's defence systems in the nineteenth century, Peter built his own Martello Towers at the CBC to ward off American cultural imperialism. Peter was so convincing that listeners wrote to him when he was leaving *Morningside* in 1997 to tell him he was the glue holding Canada together. When he died in January 2002, many Canadians shed a tear as if they had lost an old friend. He personified all that was good about Canadians, his mourning fans claimed. In a review of Peter's first *Morningside Papers,* Bronwyn Drainie noted that Peter's "radio persona seems to embody just about everything we like about ourselves as Canadians: humble but not grovelling, patriotic but not jingoistic, athletic but not superjock, cultured but not egghead."

Sir Casimir Gzowski in his Toronto mansion, "The Hall," at Dundas and Bathurst Streets. Especially in the eyes and nose there is a resemblance to Peter Gzowski, his great-great-grandson.

(Courtesy Trent University Archives, Gzowski fonds, 92-015-19, box 3, folder 6)

Because his career covered most of the last half of the twentieth century, a biography of Peter Gzowski is a memoir of his country during those decades. His journalistic career, beginning with *The Varsity* in September 1956, and ending with the *Globe and Mail* in January 2002, covered the period of eight Canadian prime ministers, most of whom he interviewed. It was also the second Elizabethan Age, and Peter even managed to interview Her Majesty. Or so he imagined. He was witness to the Quiet Revolution in Quebec and the growth of economic nationalism in the West. From the rise of state medicine to the decline of the patriarchy, Peter was there to comment, to resist, and to participate. Here was a man who was proud to call himself Canadian and who made millions of other Canadians realize that Canada was, in what he claimed was a Canadian expression, not a bad place to live.

Even though, in his memoirs, Peter twice hinted at a darker side, most of his fans, and a few of his colleagues, rejected the idea that behind that carefully honed persona, there was another Peter, an actual human being who was, as Sylvia Fraser wrote shortly after his death, a "troubled and a troubling man."[11] There were as many Peter Gzowskis as there are people who remember him. In fact, one person close to him admitted that there were days when she encountered a different Peter each time she ran into him. He was unpredictable. Michael Enright remembers being warmly invited to Peter's cottage at Lake Simcoe. "He had been very insistent that I go and very attentive in giving me the right directions," Enright noted. However, once Enright arrived at the cottage, Peter ignored him, preferring instead the company of eight or nine members of his inner circle.[12]

Peter was a complex man, full of contradictions. His affairs and flirtations with women were legendary, and thus his rather ambiguous notion of physical beauty is puzzling. Peter's eye was attracted to the naked male physiques of athletes, particularly hockey players such as Mark Messier, whose perfect body, which Peter had observed at close quarters in the Edmonton Oilers' dressing room, he described several times. On the opening page of *The Game of Our Lives,* Peter took note of the "handsome" Messier "with head thrown back, his eyes closed, his Praxitelean[13] body naked, one hand cupped over his genitals." In December 1981, Peter wrote that Messier had a body that "sculptors would kill for,"[14] and in 1984, on *Morningside,* he likened Messier's body to "a Grecian statue."[15] In *The Game of Our Lives,* Peter's descriptions of other Oilers players are sensuous.[16] None of this would be worth noting were it not for the fact that, in all his books and articles, there isn't a single description of a nude female body. In fact, he said once that he didn't enjoy looking at *Playboy* bunnies, whom he called "bovine." Instead, he preferred the rather wholesome models posing in Eaton's catalogues, models whose breasts and genitalia were suitably sheathed in bras and girdles.[17]

On air Peter was open and welcoming; in private he was carefully guarded. While most people considered him a success, Peter enjoyed dwelling on failure. Although he made it his life's work to reveal the inner workings of the Canadian political system and to uncover the psyches of writers and politicians, he thought it an act of high treason if a friend even hinted at his ruthlessly competitive nature. He was a man who loved giving advice on recipes, books, and politics, yet he loathed taking advice, and the few friends who dared to suggest that it was time to stop smoking were given the silent treatment for days. Peter sympathized with the downtrodden and the illiterate, yet only rarely did he associate with members of this lower stratum of society.

Although he played the role of Father of His Nation and Captain Canada, guiding his listeners through one constitutional crisis after another, he found it difficult to be a good father. One afternoon in 1983 his daughter, Alison, discovered Peter watching a television game show called *Family Feud,* a program that blended fact and fiction.[18] Peter's imagination was racing. He announced that he wanted to drive his family to Los Angeles where they could participate in *Family Feud.* Peter even imagined, according to Alison, "how we would learn to jump up and down with enthusiasm." Alison wasn't impressed, for she had already seen her father's imagination at work. When his wife and children objected, he "slammed a door in anger."[19] Peter had difficulty dealing with the real world.

On air Peter was usually a paragon of fairness. However, if a radio guest was of the wrong political stripe, and therefore didn't agree with Peter's definition of country or nation, he could grow petulant. He loved playing the part of the gregarious and generous host of golf tournaments that raised millions for literacy, yet in private he wasn't above cheating at golf and swearing at an opponent. Peter loved to direct and manage, but he had trouble dealing with managers at the CBC, and with Cabinet ministers in charge of the network.

How did this shy, awkward, sometimes mean-spirited man who sought, indeed required, constant encouragement from producers, partners, and friends manage to define and refine, sculpt and weave a vision of Canada so powerful that many people still believe in it? How did he gain the confidence of hundreds of thousands of Canadians to such an extent that they often poured out their hearts to him in letters? It was, in fact, these very contradictions, these conflicts, these ghosts, that made him one of Canada's best broadcast journalists. As psychotherapist Alan McGlashan once observed, "The depth of darkness into which you can descend, and still live, is an exact measure … of the height to which you can aspire to reach."[20]

Truman Capote put it another way: "Failure is the condiment that gives success its flavour." In fact, without failure, real or imagined, can there be success? Without darkness, can there be light? Without that acquaintance with the night, an artist risks producing books or paintings, radio shows or theatre, that are superficial. Peter was well acquainted with darkness, and that is one reason why many of his radio programs are still worth listening to, and why many of his longer magazine articles are worth rereading.

Why a biography? After all, surely Peter told the whole truth in *The Private Voice*, his memoir published in 1988. Ah, the lovely treachery of memoir! Had he intended that memoir to stand as definitive, why did he carefully preserve his personal papers which, after the publication of the memoir, he deposited, with no conditions attached, at Trent University Archives? Would he approve of a truthful biography? Probably, for he was always opposed to censorship of any sort. On June 1, 1963, in *Maclean's*, he damned managers and owners who forbade players to write about the darker aspects of hockey and baseball. In September 1981, he told students at the University of Guelph, "I oppose censorship absolutely. I don't want anyone else telling me not only what I can and cannot write or publish or broadcast, I don't want anyone else telling me what I can read or buy or attend — and I don't want them telling my children either." Publication of anything, even kiddy porn, was a right, he insisted.[21]

Furthermore, Peter loathed idealized figures such as Pa Cartwright in the television series *Bonanza*, the most popular TV western of the 1960s. Cartwright, played by Canadian Lorne Greene, was impossibly flawless, "kind, wise, courteous, strong, rich, loyal, honest, and fair to his sons," who, as Peter pointed out with a wink, never left home. The real West, Peter added, wasn't populated exclusively by courageous and heroic characters dressed in clean, well-pressed clothing. He preferred Dr. Ben Casey, the main character in a television series set in a hospital, for Casey was "rude, arrogant and believably human."[22]

In March 1984, during an interview on *Morningside* with Michael Bliss, Peter and Bliss discussed the latter's biography of Dr. Frederick Banting, whose private life was somewhat tortured but whose public life was full of honours, including a Nobel Prize for the co-discovery of insulin. "Are you at all troubled for taking this great Canadian figure … and showing that he had feet of clay?" Peter asked Bliss. There was pain in Peter's voice. And wasn't to do so a Canadian phenomenon, Peter continued, to denigrate our own accomplishments? Above all, Bliss explained, biography must be honest. Peter agreed, and the two men concluded that they continued to admire Banting, warts and all. In no way, Bliss and Peter concluded, did exposing this less attractive part of Banting remove him from the pantheon of Canadian heroes. Nor should this biography of Peter Gzowski.

— 1 —

"Some Drastic Shaking Up, Early in Life,"[1] 1934–1949

Families sustain themselves through self-deluding stories.

— Michael Billington, The Guardian Weekly,
January 27–February 2, 2006

The light was fading from the cold winter sky hovering over Dickson Park. Across from the park, in the windows of the houses along Park Avenue, warm electric lights began to glow. Evening meals were being prepared. In the park a boy was playing hockey on the small man-made rink. The boy was Peter Brown. In his imagination, he was a hockey hero, perhaps Gordie Howe or Howie Morenz or Maurice "Rocket" Richard. He was playing in the deciding game of the Stanley Cup playoffs. The score was tied. The imaginary crowd grew silent. The boy was mumbling something to himself as he skated around that rink by himself, stick handling, zigzagging, making the familiar rasking[2] sound of blade on ice. Imaginary teammates were skating alongside, watching his every move. The boy moved closer and closer to the net of the opposing team.

Peter Brown — the once and future Peter Gzowski — was playing two roles. As he raced down the ice to score the winning goal, he was also giving the play-by-play commentary of the game. Not only was he a star of the National Hockey League (NHL), but he was also Foster Hewitt, the voice of hockey in English Canada throughout much of the twentieth century. Hewitt cried out, "Here comes Brown down the ice. He shoots! He scores!"[3] The crowd went wild. They remained standing as the last seconds of the game ticked away. Peter Brown had scored the winning goal. He had won the Stanley Cup for his team. He basked in the accolades of the crowds that existed only in his imagination.

The hockey story is but one of many examples of Peter's vivid imagination. The young Peter was typical of creative people. He required solitude to create, but he loved and needed an audience to praise his art. "Writing at its best is a lonely life," noted Ernest Hemingway, one of Peter's literary heroes. For the boy playing hockey by himself, it was also important that his supper was being kept warm in the family duplex across the street.

Peter's mother, Margaret McGregor Young, and his father, Harold E. Gzowski, were members of prominent Toronto families. Margaret's father was James McGregor Young, a lawyer and law professor who was born in 1864 in the village of Hillier, Ontario, near Picton.[4] Peter liked to claim that the Youngs were "somehow related" to Sir John A. Macdonald, though when questioned once, his unconvincing response was that "Bay of Quinte Scots were all related."[5]

In 1906, at age forty-two, McGregor Young married Alice Maude Williams, who was born in Winnipeg about 1880. Maude Williams was a good friend of Mabel Mackenzie, daughter of William Mackenzie, millionaire president of the Canadian Northern Railway. Maude's sister, Jane, was married to Donald Mann, partner of Mackenzie.[6] In May 1900, Maude visited the Mackenzies in Kirkfield, Ontario, northeast of Toronto. In Mabel's visitors' book, Maude signed her name and contributed a poem, which reads in part "Kirkfield, I love thee / How can I leave thee / Without a frown."[7] While Peter invented connections with John A. Macdonald and with "Uncle" Stephen Leacock, rarely did he let on that he was a grand-nephew of Sir Donald Mann, the railway baron.

Peter's mother, Margaret, born in November 1909,[8] was one of three children of McGregor and Maude Young, who enrolled her in Toronto's Bishop Strachan School, a private institution for daughters of the wealthy. She also attended *le Manoir*, a private Swiss school, which Peter called a "lycée."[9] Afterward, according to Peter, she enrolled at the University of Toronto where she studied Latin, French, English, Spanish, history, and mathematics. There is a problem with Peter's story: no record exists at the University of Toronto that a Margaret Young ever registered as an undergraduate, and there is certainly no evidence that someone with that name graduated with a bachelor of arts.[10]

In 1972, Peter told Pat Annesley that his mother went on to attend the University of St Andrews in Scotland "because no Canadian university would accept her at age fourteen," and that at age nineteen she was awarded a master of arts from the same institution.[11] Records at St Andrews tell a slightly different story. In 1926, when she was sixteen, Margaret registered at St Andrews where she studied Latin, English literature, history, French, and philosophy. According to her records at St Andrews, Margaret, at age twenty, graduated in June 1930 and then returned to Toronto. Even during the Great Depression, the Youngs lived in fashionable parts of Ontario's capital.[12]

One contemporary of Margaret at Bishop Strachan offers another version of Margaret's story.[13] While a student there, Margaret became pregnant, something that good breeding and mid-Atlantic accents were meant to preclude. Is that why she left for Switzerland? Was attendance at the University of Toronto invented in order to account for some of those missing years? There is another curiosity: in the early 1980s, a resident of a Toronto nursing home on Cummer Avenue, east of Bayview Avenue, claimed to be a sister of Peter Gzowski. She might have been delusional, or she might have been a half-sister born to the teenage Margaret. In any case, Peter used to visit her.[14]

—•—

During the late nineteenth century, the Gzowskis of Toronto were even more prominent than the Youngs. Sir Casimir Gzowski was an engineer and contractor who combined innate talent with political and personal connections to become, by the end of his life, an esteemed man. Born in St. Petersburg in 1813 into minor Polish nobility, he participated in a revolt against Russian imperialism in Poland and was exiled to the United States. In the 1840s, he made his way to Canada West where he became superintendent of public works in the London district. He made a small fortune on railway contracting, land speculation, engineering projects, and businesses connected with railways. Sir Casimir was a founder of the Toronto Stock Exchange and the city's philharmonic society. His Toronto mansion, "The Hall," near the corner of Bathurst and Dundas Streets, was a setting for fashionable gatherings throughout the last half of the nineteenth century. Sir Casimir's friends and acquaintances included the political, business, and social elite of Canada and Britain. After fulfilling what H.V. Nelles, in Volume XII of the *Dictionary of Canadian Biography,* calls "the late Victorian Canadian yearning for a romantic hero," Sir Casimir died in Toronto in 1898.

His children married prominently and lived in large homes in leafy parts of Toronto. When Casimir S. Gzowski, son of Sir Casimir, died in 1922, he left a substantial estate valued at almost half a million dollars. Harold Northey Gzowski was a son of Casimir S. and grandfather of Peter, who called him the "Colonel," though he really was a lieutenant-colonel.[15] Harold N. was commander of the 2nd Divisional Engineers in Toronto, the successor to the militia unit raised by Sir Casimir to defend Canada against the Fenians. The Colonel graduated from the University of Toronto in 1903 in applied science. He served in the First World War as a major and worked on water filtration for the French Red Cross at Verdun. When Harold E., Peter's father, was born in 1911, the Colonel lived at 60 Glen Road in north Rosedale, Toronto's wealthiest neighbourhood. In 1927 the Colonel sent his only son to Ridley College in St. Catharines, Ontario. The stock market crash of 1929 made life less pleasant for many of the First Families of Toronto. Harold was pulled from Ridley, and the Colonel and his wife, Vera, along with son Harold and daughters Jocelyn Hope (Joy) and Vera Elizabeth (Beth), moved to more modest but still respectable accommodation at 63 Wells Hill Avenue near Austin Terrace and Casa Loma.[16] Vera, the Colonel's wife, taught school, and Peter's father tried to sell insurance policies for Canada Life Assurance.

During the 1930s, the Colonel's income was dependent on revenue from the Toronto Ignition Company, an Imperial Esso service station at 1366 Yonge Street, just south of Balmoral Avenue, close by the Atlantic & Pacific Tea Company. Across Yonge Street was the Deer Park Garage & Livery. The Colonel was also secretary-treasurer of the Queen City Bowling Alley. In the *Toronto Star* on January 26, 1979, Peter claimed that his grandfather invested in a gravel pit on Vancouver Island and once saved a Chinese employee from drowning, an unlikely story given the anti-Oriental mood of Canada at the time. At his gas station the Colonel, Peter wrote, "hired more men than he needed, and played darts with them in the basement." In other words, the service station made little money.

Vera Gzowski, the Colonel's wife, was one of three children of Judge Edward Morgan, whose daughter, Hope, studied singing in Paris. In an article in *Canadian Living*, Peter claimed that his grandmother and her sister once toured France, and that for the rest of her life, Vera pronounced English words of French origin as if they had never migrated across the English Channel. Peter didn't say whether Vera called her husband "le Colonel," *à la française.*

In his memoirs and elsewhere, Peter liked to claim that his parents were married "in one of those run-away deals" in Jamestown, New York.[17] In an interview on CBC's *Life & Times*, Peter added another detail, that his parents were divorced "almost before I was born." They lived together "barely long enough to produce me," he claimed in his memoirs. They were divorced "not long after I was born," he wrote in *The Morningside Papers.*[18] The story of the unwanted child who had forced his parents into an unsuccessful marriage was a figment of Peter's imagination. The marriage and birth were perfectly respectable. Margaret Young married Harold Gzowksi in May 1932 in Toronto, and their only son was born more than two years later.

Life insurance wasn't a hot seller during the Depression, so for the remainder of the 1930s, Harold left Toronto to look for work.[19] The Colonel and Vera Gzowski welcomed Margaret and young Peter to their house near Casa Loma.[20] During summers, mother and son lived in Prince Edward County in eastern Ontario near Picton, where McGregor Young owned a cattle ranch.[21] Years later one of Peter's adoring *Morningside* fans, who had grown up in a general store close to Picton, told him that she remembered "a little blond baby whose first name was Peter and whose last name we couldn't pronounce." When he learned to walk, his mother dressed him in a sailor's suit.

In 1937, Margaret was granted a bachelor of library science from the University of Toronto.[22] The next year she and Peter moved in with her

Harold Gzowski, Peter's father, during the Great Depression at Larder Lake around Christmas, mid to late 1930s. The photo was apparently taken by John Taylor, who, in 1987, when he sent it to Peter, lived in Breslau, Ontario.

(Courtesy Trent University Archives, Gzowski fonds, 01-004, box 1, folder 1)

father at 112 Rosedale Heights Drive near St.Clair Avenue and Mount Pleasant Road. By that time, Margaret was employed at the book department at Eaton's. Since government money for libraries, as for almost everything else, was in short supply, her choice of Eaton's may have been forced upon her by the Depression. In 1939, Margaret was listed with the Young family at 481 Summerhill Avenue near Yonge Street, south of St. Clair Avenue. In one of these houses, Peter conducted an experiment. "I remember one night," he wrote years later, "when I tried to see how close I could hold a candle to the curtains that billowed over my bed without setting them on fire." When the curtains caught fire, he cried out for help. As his hysterical mother and grandmother Young doused the flames, his grandfather Young, who used to sing Peter to sleep with Stephen Foster melodies, burst into rounds of laughter.[23]

Perhaps because of Harold's constant absence, his marriage with Margaret was terminated about 1938 when Peter was four.[24] In the 1930s, there was only one cause of divorce: provable adultery. The aggrieved spouse needed witnesses or a confession.[25] In *Life & Times,* Peter speculated that his mother always remained in love with his father even after she remarried, a story that may say more about the second than the first marriage. On the rare occasions when Margaret spoke to Peter about his father, she would tell Peter that he reminded her of Harold.[26]

Sometime in 1939, Margaret, and likely Peter, too, moved once again, this time to a house at 30 Edith Drive in the Eglinton Avenue and Avenue Road district of Toronto. In the *Toronto City Directory* for 1940, Margaret was listed as co-owner with Edward Feather, who, with a business partner, operated a sheet metal works at 198 Dupont Avenue near Spadina Avenue. Margaret, it seems, was searching for a surrogate father for her son, and also for a husband with enough income to provide a more secure living. Not once in his memoirs, books, or scores of articles did Peter mention Edward Feather.[27] Meantime, Peter's father enlisted to serve in the Second World War as a sergeant in the Royal Canadian Engineers. In London, on April 24, 1940, he married Brenda Raikes.[28]

—•—

Margaret's relationship with Edward Feather didn't last long. On Saturday, October 19, 1940, according to the *Globe and Mail*, "Mrs. Harold Gzowski" was married to R.W. Brown of Galt at the home of Margaret's aunt, Lady Mann,[29] a marriage that, according to Peter, was arranged so that his mother could be certain Peter would have a roof over his head and food on the table. Present at the large red-brick house at 161 St. George Street,[30] a few blocks north of Bloor Street, were the bride's parents, as well as the Colonel and Vera Gzowski, Reg's two brothers and their wives, and, among others, members of the Kingsmill and Hancock families. After a honeymoon trip north, probably through Muskoka or the Ottawa Valley, Reg and Margaret Brown settled in Galt. Soon after his mother's remarriage, Peter's surname was changed to Brown, largely, he explained in his introduction to *A Sense of Tradition*, his book on Ridley College, "to avoid awkward questions."

Like many other towns in southern and southwestern Ontario at the time, Galt, whose population was about eighteen thousand, was home to a wide variety of manufacturing, including textiles, shoes, furniture, metal works, and machine shops. Reg Brown was sales manager of the Narrow Fabrics, Weaving, and Dyeing Co., which produced labels for towels, bedsheets, and shirts made in other small factories.

The war made housing scarce, and it was probably for that reason that the Browns rented the upper duplex at 24 Park Avenue, an attractive buff brick Victorian house on a street of well-tended lawns, shrubs, and flower beds. Dickson Park was across Park Avenue from number 24. The town itself was named for the Scot, John Galt, a member of the Canada Land Company, who was also a novelist and friend of the poet Lord Byron. Several acres in size, Dickson Park slopes gently toward the Grand River, which runs through old Galt, now the centre of Cambridge. From the upper duplex at 24 Park Avenue, Peter enjoyed a splendid view of the centre of Galt with its soaring church spires, solid Romanesque banks, and a neoclassical Carnegie Library, along with square-shouldered stone and red-brick factories that helped to make Galt secure. Over to the left, across the river, is the ponderous Galt Collegiate Institute, also made of local fieldstone. Galt was built by Scots stonemasons who longed for the "old country" and re-created it in the rolling, fertile lowlands of southwestern Ontario. Today, beautifully preserved, the centre of Cambridge looks much as it did when Peter was young.

Even as a child Peter was a great observer. In an article called "A Perfect Place to Be a Boy," written as part of an introduction to *Images of Waterloo County* (1996), Peter painted a picture of a young boy who enjoyed sitting in the second-floor bay window at number 24, fascinated by seasonal rituals in the park. Each September the Galt Fall Fair was staged there amid the brilliant fall finery of the surrounding trees. "A midway filled the baseball diamond and spilled over around the bandstand," he recalled, while "sheds and barns that stood unused for the rest of the year sprang to life." A menagerie of farm animals, from sheep to pigs, horses and cattle, filled the park. "In the autumn air," he continued, "the honkytonk of the midway barkers and the squeals of terrified rapture from the whirling rides mingled with the cries of roosters and the lowing of cattle, and the smell of candy-floss and frying hamburgers, mixed with the sweet aroma of the barnyard."

Halloween, Peter remembered, allowed for "soaping windows and ringing the door on the school principal's house before running madly away," as well as "standing on one side of the road while a friend stood on the other, and when a car came by pretending to pull on an imaginary rope." At a time when not every household had indoor plumbing, even in prosperous towns like Galt, an annual ritual at Halloween was knocking over an outhouse or two.[31]

Many of his memories of Galt, Peter claimed in an essay read years later on *This Country in the Morning,* were set in winter, and these memories included "a big dog that wouldn't stop chasing my sled. Soakers from a winter creek. Making angels in the snow. The way the snow matted in your hair and around the edge of your parka." He also recalled "nearly frozen toes and fingers, and the equally exquisite relief from a warming fire," as well as hot chocolate and sleigh rides and snowball fights. And, of course, those endless hockey games over *verglas* fields.[32]

In Galt, Peter was enrolled in grade one at Dickson School, located, like Park Avenue, on the west side of the river, about a twenty-minute walk south of Dickson Park. Even though he started grade one a bit late, he skipped one of the early grades, and thus spent slightly less than seven years at Dickson.[33] "They don't build schools like they used to," he mused on *Morningside* one morning in early February 1991, the day after he visited his old school. He talked about seeing a photograph of his old principal, "Pop" Collins," and he spied himself and classmates in a class photograph taken in 1944 when he was ten. As he gazed at himself and his classmates, none of whom he had seen for years, "a thousand memories" tumbled through his mind:

> Games of scrub and British Bulldog in the gravelled schoolyard, marbles and soakers in the spring, Mr. McInnis saying he could stick-handle through our whole hockey team backwards and Billy Parkinson saying no, sir, you couldn't, you'd put yourself offside, Valentine notes to Georgina Scroggins, the smell of wet wool in the cloakrooms, cleaning the brushes on the fire escape, singing in the massed choirs on Victoria Day at Dickson Park, figuring out chess with Danny VanSickle — who plays bass with the Philadelphia Symphony, I think — Miss Zavitz's grade two, Christmas concerts, VE day when we wove crêpe paper through the spokes of our bike wheels — I in Dickson's blue and gold — and rode downtown and ...

He stopped mid-sentence, for he suddenly recalled that, during those idyllic years, Galt was a wartime city where WRENS marched and airmen from around the empire trained by flying over Dickson Park. There were war bonds, Victory gardens, and rationing. Children collected milkweed pods and the silver wrapping in cigarette packages. Peter learned the difference between a Messerschmitt and a Spitfire, and he and his mates played war games.[34] "My own most vivid memory of World War II," Peter once wrote in *Maclean's*, "is about riding my decorated bike in a parade to celebrate V-E Day."[35]

During any distant war, life on the home front goes on almost normally. Such was the case, apparently, in Galt during the Second World

War. People played ball games in the park, and during the annual Galt Fall Fair, young people, but surely not Peter, hopped the fence surrounding the park in order to avoid the admission charge. Lois, one of Peter's *Morningside* listeners, recalled the gangly boy she used to glimpse through the boards of the back fence as she rode her bike down the lane, past the large bush of yellow roses that pushed through the fence at 24 Park Avenue.[36] Jeanette, another schoolmate, remembered Peter's beautiful blond hair and flawless olive complexion. Photographs verify that he was an attractive young lad. In most, Peter appears content, though in one he seems a bit overawed by his tall, well-dressed mother. As he peers up admiringly at her, as if waiting for some sign of recognition, she ignores him. With a slight and knowing smile on her round, attractive face, she is more interested in the camera and perhaps in the person taking her picture.

Photographs of Peter's stepfather and Peter together either were not taken or have not survived. Uncle Reg, his nieces recall, could be difficult. He was a man of silences. Ed Mannion, whose family lived near the Browns, recalled Reg as rather brusque and difficult. Although Peter and Reg were never close, Peter admitted that Reg did, on occasion, slip over to the ice rink to watch his stepson play hockey, and perhaps to remind him that it was suppertime. In fact, on one occasion Peter called his stepfather "a very nice, decent man." It was Reg who drove Peter, at about age twelve, to the family doctor when he was hit on the forehead by a stray puck, which, Peter claimed, had left a scar that "still creases my forehead, and which I still finger proudly when I stare in the mirror and think of the mornings in the winter sun." It may have been Reg who encouraged Peter to hunt. In "The Pleasure of Guns," an essay read on *This Country in the Morning*, Peter related an incident that happened when he was thirteen. "I shot a groundhog once," Peter told his listeners, "and then I went and picked it up, and that was enough for me."[37]

Peter was on good terms with his step-cousins who lived nearby. One night, when he slept over at their house, he shared a bedroom with Shirley Brown. She was ten and he was six. The future broadcaster talked and talked well into the wee hours of the morning. Unknown to Shirley at the time, Peter had a childhood crush on her. An only child, Peter seems to have longed for conversation. From an early age, he loved to communicate. "When you're the only pea in the pod," observes journalist and memoirist Russell Baker, "your parents are likely to get you confused with the Hope Diamond. And that encourages you to talk too much."[38]

In his memoirs, published in 1988, Peter paints a sunny picture of the town. However, in 1982, during the first season of *Morningside,* he inadvertently revealed that there had been shadows. In an interview with Alice Munro, the fiction writer talked about Poppy Cullender, a character in her short story "The Stone in the Field." Poppy was thought odd because he was single, and because he collected antiques. Poppy and the narrator's mother were partners in an antiques business. Peter asked Munro to read from the story.

"There were farmhouses," Munro read, "where Poppy was not a welcome sight." Children teased him, and not a few women locked the door as he approached, his eyes rolling "in an uncontrollably lewd or silly way." He usually called out "in a soft lisp and stutter, 'Ith anybody h-home?'" In 1969, years before the government of Pierre Trudeau decriminalized homosexuality in Canada, Poppy went to jail for making harmless overtures to two baseball players on the train to Stratford.

At the end of the reading Peter suddenly blurted out that there was a Poppy Cullender in Galt. Immediately, he began to distance himself from that odd, unnamed man of his childhood. "He wasn't close to me," Peter insisted. "I didn't know him." Just to make sure that there was no parallel with Munro's story, he added, "He wasn't friends with my mother."[39] It was an oddly defensive statement, especially for a man who painted himself as sympathetic to underdogs. Nowhere in his memoirs or elsewhere does this Poppy-type man appear, except in *The Morningside Years,* published in 1997, which includes the transcript of the interview with Munro.

Each summer Reg and Margaret Brown drove Reg's Oldsmobile coupe[40] to the Gzowski compound on Lake Simcoe near Sutton, Ontario. Peter's grandfather had purchased the lakeshore property from the Sibbald family around 1920. Reg and Margaret sometimes stopped for a visit and occasionally stayed overnight. Their purpose was to leave young Peter for the summer under the watchful eye of his grandparents.

Peter always remembered the Colonel with affection. He was the only respected male authority in his young life. During part of one summer, so Peter once claimed, he attended Camp Nagiwa, a camp for boys on Ontario's Severn River[41] where, perhaps, he imagined himself participating in campfire singsongs, long hikes, and canoeing. If indeed he had ever attended a summer camp, it wasn't Nagiwa, which wasn't founded until 1954.[42]

In Galt, Margaret was able to put her library degree to good use. At the public library she became the children's librarian. Years later several of Peter's listeners wrote to him about the librarian they adored. Not only did she read to them, but she also allowed them to stamp return dates on borrowed books and to re-shelve returned books.

"Mother felt out of place in the Presbyterian stone town of Galt with its knitting mills and metal works," Peter once noted. Her tastes were different from those of the average resident. She read Dorothy Parker, F. Scott Fitzgerald, and W.B. Yeats, and she spoke French. She also enjoyed jazz. And she took a fancy to mixed-doubles badminton. Margaret joined the local club, whose members played in the auditorium of the Galt City Hall on Main Street, a couple of blocks uphill from the Carnegie Library. There is a photograph, taken not long before her death, of Margaret posing with fellow members of the club. While the others look relaxed and happy, Margaret appears uncomfortable as she stands beside her badminton partner. Years later one of the players mailed Peter a copy of the photograph clipped from the local Galt newspaper. Peter kept the clipping on his desk at the main CBC building on Jarvis Street. One day, in May 1992, he showed it to Marco Adria, who was interviewing him. As he examined this photograph, Peter speculated, "Mother would not have been happy in the badminton club."

Inside her "confining" marriage, Peter noted, his mother "chafed and strained."[43] On an episode of *Life & Times* filmed in 1997, Peter remarked that Margaret was "very funny, very quick and ... very naughty." Very naughty? What did he mean? That was the closest he ever came to acknowledging what appears to have been an open secret in Galt in the

1940s. One of the other people in the photograph of the badminton club offered a slightly different interpretation. "I admired her for her appearance and poise," she recalled, "but not for her behaviour." It seems that Margaret and her badminton partner were "more than friends."

Alice Munro knows that in small towns there is rarely, if ever, a quiet affair. In her book *Open Secrets*, there is a story called "Carried Away," which features a small-town librarian who favours a dark red blouse and has lips to match. "You could not say with any assurance that she had a bad reputation," notes the narrator. "But it was not quite a spotless reputation, either." Like Peter's mother, Louisa the librarian once worked in the book department at Eaton's. Louisa was rumoured to have had affairs with travelling salesmen.[44]

During the interview with Marco Adria in 1992, Peter seemed artfully ignorant of the extramarital relationship. However, on school playgrounds children are prone to gossiping and teasing. The children who mocked Poppy Cullender in that other Munro story were typical of children everywhere. Peter's use of the code word *naughty* on *Life & Times* suggests that he did know about his mother's alleged affair. That his stepfather probably knew about it may explain why some people found him difficult.

In 1946, when Jack Young, Margaret's cousin, was studying at the University of Western Ontario in London, he visited the Browns one weekend. He slept in Peter's bedroom. That weekend Peter was "sleeping over" with a friend. On Saturday afternoon, the two boys "burst upon the scene like gangbusters." They had just been thrown out of the matinee of a local theatre and were "quite pleased by the notoriety."[45] No doubt they were indulging in typical matinee fare: a western or perhaps Abbott and Costello, two of Peter's favourite comedians.[46]

Almost immediately upon arrival, Young felt tension in the household. Margaret arranged a bridge game. She invited a male friend to join them. The friend mistook Jack for Mac, Margaret's brother. "I remembered Reg's indignation at such a thought," Jack told Peter in 1996. Jack and Margaret were partners, and they won all evening. The next day before he boarded the return train to London, Jack and Margaret had a walk in a nearby park. "I still remember the English tweed suit she wore," Young told Peter, "and her 'sensible' walking shoes. It was a beautiful, crisp, fall day." Margaret talked about her son and described him as "an extremely bright boy bordering on genius." She was certain that Peter would be a success.

In addition to books and bridge, Margaret also indulged in alcohol, cigarettes, and fine clothing, the accoutrements of the liberated woman of the 1940s. Because nylon stockings were made scarce by the war, Margaret took to staining her long legs "a silken brown," and her young son, sitting on one of the twin beds in his parents' bedroom, sometimes watched her as she carefully painted a faux seam on each leg "from her heel to the back of her knees."[47] For one of her photographic portraits, she wore a beautiful fur stole draped around her elegant shoulders. She enjoyed trips to Toronto where she dined at the fashionable Arcadian Court at Simpson's department store, high above the intersection of Queen and Yonge Streets.

Fascinated by drama, Margaret became active in the Galt Little Theatre. For *Love from a Stranger*, a murder-mystery produced for the 1946–47 season, she was assistant director.[48] In another production Peter played the role of his mother's son. Margaret also performed in Noël Coward's *Blithe Spirit*,[49] a play about love the second time around.

The boy and his mother were always close. In those days, the biannual arrival of Eaton's catalogue was always a time of excitement at farms and in small towns across Canada. The catalogues were full of colour photographs of toys and clothing and household wares that stimulated the imagination, especially during the Second World War when many goods were rationed. Peter always retained happy memories of snuggling up against his mother as they examined the catalogue page by page.[50]

During one Christmas holiday, Peter folded gift boxes at Brown's Jewellery Store on Main Street. Owned by the father of his good friend, Tom Brown,[51] the store was located just up the street from the Carnegie Library. The money he earned bought a Christmas gift for his mother, perhaps something from the elegant jewellery shop decorated with two large, attractive urns imported from Japan by earlier generations of Browns.

—•—

The boy was mad about hockey. One winter his mother dressed him in a scratchy white turtleneck with dark blue cuffs and waistband, which had once belonged to her brother. The sweater kept her son warm during bone-chilling mornings when he insisted on "slipping down the hill to the hockey rink before decent people were up."[52]

"I can feel that turtleneck now, rough and itchy under my ears," he told *Morningside* listeners one day when he was introducing novelist Roch Carrier, well-known for his story about ordering a Montreal Canadiens sweater from Monsieur Eaton, who, instead, mailed the boy a Toronto Maple Leafs sweater.

Peter was so busy playing hockey in the park that he failed to catch a glimpse of the sixteen-year-old Gordie Howe, who was in Galt during the 1944–45 season as a member of the junior farm team of the Detroit Red Wings. At least that's what Peter claimed in an article in 1965.[53] Fifteen years later he told fans of the Edmonton Oilers that, as a boy, he had indeed seen Howe in uniform, and he repeated that version of the story in *The Game of Our Lives*. He also bragged that, when he was about eight, Harry Lumley threw him over his shoulder into the local swimming pool. Eight years older than Peter, the young goaltender played for the farm team of the Red Wings, and therefore, like Howe, he may very well have been practising in Galt during the summer of 1942. In *The Game of Our Lives*, Peter's imagination embroidered the Lumley story. Lumley was joined by fellow hockey player Marty Pavelich, and Peter was thrown into Willow Lake along with a whole gang of his friends.[54]

Radio, the only broadcast medium then available in Canada, was a means of escape for Peter. It also helped to develop his imagination and taught him to listen. "Writers have to cultivate the habit early in life of listening to people other than themselves," claims Russell Baker.[55] In his memoirs, Peter mentioned Abbott and Costello, Jack Benny, and other American radio entertainers, as well as CBC personalities such as the Happy Gang, Mart Kenney, and Lorne Greene. He also enjoyed radio drama. As she ironed on Monday evenings, Margaret listened to *Lux Radio Theater,* produced by Cecil B. DeMille, and Peter was there with her. He also began to pay attention to dramas produced by CBC Radio.[56]

Until 1952, when Canadian television first aired, most Canadians had only *heard* hockey games, unless they were lucky enough to obtain tickets to games at Maple Leaf Gardens, the Forum in Montreal, or Detroit's Olympia. Listening to hockey games on radio was an excellent way to develop the imagination. As the play-by-play was described by Foster Hewitt, the listener had to picture the players moving out of their own zone to stickhandle and pass into the opposition's zone.[57] Like most boys his age, Peter supplemented his imagination by collecting photographs of National Hockey League players, courtesy of Beehive Golden Corn Syrup, whose labels, when mailed to company headquarters, brought an autographed photograph of a favourite player. Peter also filled scrapbooks with articles about hockey and photographs of players clipped from Galt's *Daily Reporter,* which he delivered six days a week. He may also have clipped articles and photos from the *London Free Press* and *Liberty* magazine, both of which he delivered for a short time. At about age eleven he heard Syl Apps, a native of Galt, speak at the annual hockey banquet in Galt.

During the 1945–46 season, Peter first witnessed an NHL game. Gregor Young, his favourite uncle, was a returned soldier who found work in the advertising department of Imperial Oil, sponsor of the hockey broadcasts. The company gave Young two tickets. Uncle and nephew were ushered up to the Gondola, the large broadcast booth floating high above the ice of Maple Leaf Gardens. Peter was thrilled to sit close to Foster Hewitt, whom he could see through soundproof glass. Peter and his uncle were handed earphones that allowed them to listen to Hewitt as his voice went across Canada and Newfoundland. The excitement at being in the Gardens, and so close to Hewitt, as well as the unaccustomed height above the ice, made Peter nauseous. "I tore my earphones off in a moment of frenzy," he recounted in his memoirs, "and banged them on the shelf. The impact echoed through Foster's microphone and out to hockey fans in Canada and Newfoundland and on the ships at sea." In reality, of course, Peter's earphones did no such thing. Otherwise Hewitt and listeners from Vancouver to St. John's would also have picked up every word of conversation between Peter and his uncle. Ten years later Peter varied the story by claiming that he had assisted Hewitt that evening.[58]

Even as a child, Peter was passionate about golf, and Margaret and Reg encouraged him "to swing a sawed-off club at some old balls on the front lawn." When Peter was about ten, the Colonel also gave his grandson tips on golf. "Pr-r-retend there-r-re's a big spike r-r-running r-r-right up your ar-r-rse and out thr-r-rough your-r-r head, laddie," the Colonel would tell Peter. In his sports column in *Saturday Night* twenty years later, Peter explained that his grandfather trilled his r's because his ancestors were Polish.[59] Under his grandfather's tutelage, Peter soon learned to break eighty. "That summer," he noted in an article in *Saturday Night* in 1966, "I entered myself in the qualifying round for my age group in the Ontario Junior Tournament." On the day of the tournament, he rose early in order to practise. "Around mid-morning," Peter recalled, "the other young players from my hometown came to drive me to the Cheddoke course in Hamilton." Peter even brought his own caddy, the only player to do so.

In June 1947, Peter graduated from Dickson Public School. That summer of his thirteenth birthday he worked at the Waterloo Golf and Country Club in Galt for two dollars a day, fourteen hours a day, seven days a week. Early each morning he rode his bike to the club where he cleaned the shower room, gathered up soggy towels and beer bottles, and emptied ashtrays. In the canteen, he sold coffee, cigarettes, and chocolate bars. On Wednesdays he served cold beer to doctors and businessmen, including his stepfather, none of whom worried about circumventing the strict liquor laws of Ontario. Even the local police chief, so Peter once claimed, came into the canteen "to buy his illegal beer from me for 25 cents a bottle." On slow days, the club professional taught Peter how to play golf. When Peter biked home, still smelling of beer, his mother suspected that he had been drinking."[60]

—•—

Peter read widely. Among his favourites were Stephen Leacock's *Sunshine Sketches,* Ralph Connor's Glengarry novels, and Ernest Thompson Seton's *Two Little Savages.*[61] Peter also read *Chums, Boy's Own Annual,* Rudyard Kipling, Charles Dickens, Walter Scott, A.A. Milne, and William Wordsworth. Like students of his generation and the next, he probably memorized Canadian poets from Bliss Carman to Archibald Lampman and Duncan Campbell Scott, whose smoky hills, crimson forests, and lumbering potato wagons were iconic Canadian images. In Moose Jaw's *Times-Herald* in 1957, Peter's list of childhood favourites also included American novels such as *My Friend Flicka* and *Tom Sawyer,* as well as Captain Marvel comics. By age twelve, Peter had accumulated a large number of books, so Jack Young observed when he visited 24 Park Avenue in October 1946.[62]

The poems of William Henry Drummond, whose main characters were caricatured *habitants* speaking in fractured English, were on the curriculum at Galt Collegiate. In his memoirs, Peter claims that when he was in grade nine, Drummond spoke to a school assembly and read some of his poetry, which the adult Gzowski disparaged as "racist doggerel."[63] Since Drummond died in 1907, whoever it was who came to Galt Collegiate that day in 1947, it wasn't Drummond. At Galt Collegiate, Peter studied French, but like most Anglo-Canadians of his generation, and too many succeeding generations, he soon discovered that writing and reading a language didn't prepare him for the spoken version.

Peter's earliest extant piece of writing appeared in the 1948–49 edition of the Galt Collegiate Institute yearbook. In grade ten, he was a member of the junior basketball team. "When Kitchener came here unbeaten," reported Peter Brown, who stands in the front row of the accompanying photograph,

> [T]he juniors held them to a 28–26 game. Galt was
> beaten only when Kitchener scored with nine seconds
> remaining. In the season's finale, Guelph came to Galt.
> In one of the most thrilling games seen here in a long
> time, Galt came from behind to almost tie the score
> but did not have quite the remaining drive to overcome

a one-point lead. The score 22–21. The final analysis showed Bob Hoffman high scorer with 35 points, followed by Peter Brown with 26, and Jim Chaplin with 16. Jim Chaplin, a newcomer to the school, proved himself both an able captain and an excellent pivot man. Peter Brown — 10B.[64]

Puberty wasn't kind to the beautiful, olive-complexioned lad. Around the time of his short article, Peter developed bad acne, not only on his face but also on his back. The sores sometimes festered, and his nickname at Galt Collegiate was "Pus." Just when his hormones were beginning to rage, he became unattractive to females, especially at the beach. In his memoirs, he hints that he had sex for the first time in a barn somewhere near Park Avenue. Toward the end of his life he provided details. "The apple-cheeked daughter of a farm family on the edge of town" pinned Peter "to the barnyard sod and brought a hitherto unknown — well, unknown in someone else's company — feeling" to his loins.[65] There may have been few such encounters, and even that one sounds more like a scene from a short story.

Perhaps because of the acne, or maybe because he was a normal teenager, he began to rebel. In the fashion of post-war teenagers, he took to slicking down his hair with Brylcreem, possibly in emulation of Marlon Brando's anti-establishment characters, whom he probably observed during "wild nights," his phrase in an article in *Canadian Living,* at the local drive-in theatre. He also took to smoking clandestinely, though he didn't fool his mother. When she confronted him, he confessed. She pulled out her Winchesters, offered him one, and warned him not to smoke so slyly. At age fifteen it was, and is, not uncommon for a teenager to question standards and patterns and to challenge parents, teachers, and anyone else who upholds those standards.

Although Peter claimed in his memoirs that he was an abysmal failure at Galt Collegiate,[66] a decade after the publication of those memoirs he painted a more optimistic picture. In 1998 he was interviewed by a staff member of *Professionally Speaking*, the magazine of the Ontario College of Teachers. In "Peter Gzowski's Remarkable Teachers," Peter recalled two remarkable English teachers. Helen Rudick "had a naughty turn of mind," Peter told the interviewer from *Professionally Speaking*. She loved to embarrass the boys in her classes with double entendres. The other remarkable teacher at Galt Collegiate, Peter added, was "a wonderful man named Frank Ferguson.... He so obviously loved the works he taught, that you would put your own natural aversion to Shakespeare aside and say, 'If he can get this enthusiastic it must be something.'"[67]

When Ferguson first heard Peter's voice on radio in the late 1960s, he wrote several of what Peter called "wonderful, erudite, funny, and occasionally scolding, hand-written letters done in fountain pen on small white stationery ..." In 1984, Ferguson told Cambridge's *Daily Reporter* that Peter had been an "an excellent debater" who always enlivened a dull discussion.[68] Ferguson was still alive in December 1989 when Peter was in Cambridge to sign copies of his latest *Morningside Papers*. At that time Ferguson told a reporter with the Cambridge *Times* that Peter had been "one of the most interesting students," full of ideas and arguments, and "bent on keeping things stirred up. He was outgoing, bright and friendly, interested in sports, interested in politics, interested in darn-near everything."[69]

Too often Peter suppressed happy memories. He even admitted as much concerning his period in Galt. "Under the scar tissue of the memories I've tried to shut out are happy times," he wrote near the end of his life.[70] Throughout his life, happiness was often snuffed out by unhappy memories, as if he preferred it that way.

Ernest Hemingway once told John Dos Passos that an unhappy childhood was often a precursor to a writing career. In the preface to *The Selected Stories of Mavis Gallant*, Gallant notes that the impulse to write, and the stubbornness to keep going, may be due to "some drastic shaking up, early in life." In Peter's early life, there was much shaking up, real and imaginary. To the normal insecurities of childhood were added unstable adult relationships, shifting domestic arrangements, adjustments from big city to small town, and the curse of acne: in other words, the very sort of instability that, according to Gallant, "unbolts the door between perception and imagination and leaves it ajar for life." Childhood flux, Gallant adds, often fuses "memory and language and waking dreams."

The novelist John Le Carré explains creativity in a slightly different manner. Le Carré's father was, like Harold Gzowski, charismatic and unreliable. "If you've been brought up in that anarchic situation by a maverick dad," LeCarré once mused, "as a boy it deprives you of your self-pride, it makes you conspire in your mind about getting even with society." LeCarré chose to get even by using his imagination.[71] So did Peter, it would seem.

In August 1968, in his hurried, almost illegible, handwriting, Peter quoted the novelist Jean Rhys: "If you want to write the truth, you must write about yourself." To underscore the absolute necessity of being true to oneself, he underlined *must*.[72] Two decades later, in his memoirs, he argued that "the only honest writing anyone can do is about himself." If the child is father of the man, then it was almost inevitable that the man who grew out of that highly imaginative childhood in Galt would be creative, curious, and constantly in need of encouragement from friends, colleagues, and lovers as well as from brandy, Scotch, and Winchester cigarettes.

— 2 —

"Don't Try to Be Something That You're Not," 1950–1956

Though acne neither kills nor cripples,
it can leave mental and physical scars for life.

— Maclean's, *June 17, 1961*

It was an ink fight, Peter claimed, that made him feel at home at Ridley College, a private boys' school in St. Catharines, Ontario. During the early 1950s, ballpoint pens were just coming into use.[1] More widely used for letters and note-taking was the fountain pen, which sucked up ink from small glass bottles set into specially designed holes on each student's desk. When pumped full, these pens could be made to gush ink over a considerable distance. One evening during a study period, Mr. Cockburn, the master in charge, stepped out for a couple of minutes. Shiggy Banks launched a stream of ink at Jimmy Conklin. Sitting midway between the two, Peter was sprayed by tiny drops of blue ink. Soon the room erupted into a general melee. In his introduction to *A Sense of Tradition,* a book celebrating the centenary of Ridley College, Peter was at his best in re-creating the battle, complete with literary and cinematic allusions: "By now, hostilities are spreading. Incidental skirmishes break out on the perimeter. Pens dip to inkwells. Pump, load, slurp, fire. No one is safe. The air is wet with ink. Faces, white shirts, brown desks ... everything is spattered with blue Rorschach stains and arpeggios of polka dots." It was a slugfest straight out of a Roy Rogers movie, imagined Peter. "And I am in the thick of it," he continued, "happily splashing, happily splashed. I drench Freddy Lapp. Harry Malcolmson drenches me. Norrie Walker hits a double — Bob Broad and John Girvin with the same roundhouse swing. Broad gets me. I go for Walker. By the time that Mr. Cockburn returns, the damage is done. We are the sons of Harlech, drenched in woad." After cleanup the boys returned to their rooms. Finally, Peter felt that he was one of the boys.

Like the story of skating endlessly over fields of ice, or the tale of Peter's scoring the winning goal in the seventh game of the Stanley Cup, the ink fight owes much to Peter's imagination. Its rise and fall, its suspense, climax, and denouement are the characteristics of a good short story. Today Norris Walker, who scored that double, has no recollection of the incident. Others have only vague memories, some of them no doubt created by Peter's account in *Sense of Tradition*. In his fertile imagination, Peter converted the rudiments of a fight into a story whose theme is the quest to belong. Ink and battles were fitting metaphors for Peter. Throughout his working life he created articles and stories with ink, he fought battles with ink, and it is in ink that he has left a legacy in articles, books, letters, and the scripts of his radio and television shows.

According to Peter, the road to this private boys' school in St. Catharines was paved with loneliness and failure. Christmas 1949 wasn't a happy time for the fifteen-year-old. The results of his Christmas exams at Galt Collegiate, he claimed, were disastrous. During the autumn of 1949, he had spent too much time sipping lemon Coke at Moffat's or "trying to make a pink ball" at Nick's. Peter's version of his problems bears a striking resemblance to the story told by his favourite fictional hero, Holden Caulfield. "I wasn't supposed to come back after Christmas vacation," Caulfield tells readers of *The Catcher in the Rye,* "on account of I was flunking four subjects and not applying myself and all."[2] On Boxing Day 1949, Peter headed for Toronto. There are, of course, several versions of the event, including one told by Peter, that, like Holden Caulfield, he ran away from home, his belongings in a bandana.[3] More likely, he was driven to Toronto, perhaps by his mother and stepfather. He often visited his grandparents and his father on weekends. Soon the Gzowskis made arrangements to send the boy to a private school where he might improve with stronger discipline. No doubt they talked it over with his mother and stepfather. It was Peter's father, Harold, who made arrangements with J.R. Hamilton, the headmaster at Ridley.

The college had long Gzowski connections. In the late 1880s, Sir Casimir Gzowski had joined with other wealthy Torontonians to buy an old sanitarium called Springbank in St. Catharines. It became the college's first building and was used until it was destroyed by fire in 1903. Two of Peter's great-uncles had been among the first boarders at Ridley when it opened in September 1889. Peter's father had also enrolled at the college midway through high school in September 1927 at age sixteen.

The Gzowskis bought Peter appropriate Ridley attire — grey flannel slacks, white shirts, and a blue blazer. It was Harold Gzowski who suggested that Peter revert to "Gzowski." His delighted grandmother sewed tags bearing the name PETER JOHN GZOWSKI into his new clothing. Shortly after New Year's Day, Harold borrowed the Colonel's Morris Minor to drive Peter to St. Catharines along a snowy Queen Elizabeth Way (QEW). Peter always recalled passing the stone lion west of Toronto, unveiled in 1939 by Queen Elizabeth, consort of King George VI, as part of the official opening ceremonies of the QEW.[4]

Soon after arriving at the lovely campus, whose mix of Queen Anne, early Georgian, and perpendicular Gothic emulated Eton and other private boys' schools in Great Britain, "Peter John Gzowski" signed the student registry. He was number 3084, which meant that he was the 3,084th student to register at the college since its founding. Although "Brown" was banished from his name, there is a Brown family story that Reg Brown helped to pay for Peter's education, a story with credibility, given the pinched financial circumstances of the Gzowskis. In his memoirs and his introduction to *A Sense of Tradition*, both published in 1988, Peter paints a picture of a bewildered, lonely boy of fifteen surrounded by strangers already familiar with Ridley routines and regulations and already adept at "swapping lies about life at home." As boys rushed back to their dorms after being dropped off by parents, Peter "stood bewildered in the dark hall of Dean's House," which was the college's oldest surviving residence, opened in 1909. The other residents knew not only one another's names but also nicknames, proof that they belonged, and that he did not.

Peter was exaggerating his loneliness, for he really hadn't been dropped into a completely alien environment. He already knew Jim Chaplin, who had been the captain of the Galt Collegiate basketball team, whose members, including Peter, had played at Ridley. Ten years later, in an article in *Maclean's* on April 22, 1961, Peter admitted that, even before he arrived at Ridley, he already knew several of the boys there.

Understandably, Ridley rituals were new to Peter, from Latin grace to "houses" without kitchens, as well as chapel, caning, and "masters," who he quickly learned to call "sir." He soon realized that he was living not far from battle sites of the War of 1812. He could walk the route of Laura Secord when she warned the British officers and Canadian militia that the Americans were coming.[5]

At Galt Collegiate, Peter had "wriggled out of Latin," but at Ridley he was "grinding out" his Latin verbs. Master J.F. Pringle, who taught English literature and composition, kept Peter in line. A wounded veteran of the Great War, Pringle was "occasionally morose," Peter told *Professionally Speaking* in 1998, "but also very sharp and quite a pleasure to be around." In both his memoirs and in *Professionally Speaking*, Peter noted that Pringle inspired him "to write clearly and well." In fact, Peter was "something of a star" in Pringle's composition class, except on one occasion when Peter wrote "a stream of consciousness piece." Pringle "kicked the living Jesus out of it" by making "caustic comments" and giving Peter a failing grade. "What he meant to me," Peter concluded, "was don't be pretentious. Don't try to be something that you're not."[6] Pringle was no doubt vexed at Peter when the English teacher read a poem that alluded to Jesus Christ, and Peter asked if this wasn't the same J. Christ of New Testament fame. One of his classmates remembered that Peter asked the question with a slight stammer, which later, on radio, became one of his trademarks.

Peter was a great disappointment to the choirmaster, who assumed that the son would have inherited his father's melodious singing voice. "Poor Sid Bett," Peter recalled. "It was as if Howie Morenz Junior had showed up at hockey camp and couldn't skate." Although off-key, Peter loved to sing hymns — his favourite was "Jerusalem" by William Blake. He was also a disappointment to his French master, for he was a year behind in French and never did catch up.

For anything not terribly important like shining shoes and knotting ties, he found ways to fake it. He quickly learned "where to slip down the Hog's Back for a butt before dinner." Peter also smoked in the communal showers, where headmasters were unlikely to patrol and where the smoke was camouflaged by mist. He was caught at least once and was strapped by a member of the staff. Within the first six weeks, Peter had served an hour's detention for saucing a duty boy. He wrote home with the latest hockey scores and with a request for more money to buy things at the tuck shop. Peter skated on the Ridley rink, played squash, and lay awake at night "thinking of the girls I left behind."

Probably for the first time, Peter met an African American, a boy called E. Abelard Shaw. In 1961, Peter wrote about Shaw in *Maclean's* in an article called "My First Negro." "His features were Negroid all right," Peter wrote. "He had tight curly hair and a wide, flat nose and full lips that were almost always curved in an enigmatic smile." In the article, Peter called him Fuzzy-Wuzzy, which is what Rudyard Kipling called Sudanese warriors, not as a compliment, in a poem of the same name. The son of a dentist from Brooklyn, New York, Shaw was admitted to Ridley in spite of an unofficial colour ban. He was an outsider for other reasons: he didn't smoke, he didn't play pinball, and he suffered from body odour, as Peter mentioned twice in the article.

Worse, Shaw refused to take part in the Battle of Ridley. "He even kept his inkwell covered so that no one else could fill up at his desk," Peter wrote in the *Maclean's* article. And when the master returned to find the inky mess, Shaw even announced that he hadn't participated. In the *Maclean's* article, Peter's discomfort is palpable as he recalled his view of Shaw during the early 1950s, especially in a sentence like "I was no more convinced that Shaw wasn't fit to be my friend than I would have been if he wore crutches." Peter usually wrote in a much clearer, simpler style. Two negatives and the conditional tense of the verb make for a rather convoluted, worried sentence.

During the late 1980s, when Peter came to write his account of the ink fight in *A Sense of Tradition*, Shaw had vanished completely from the narrative. Perhaps he didn't fit neatly enough into the theme of belonging. While Peter would eventually become one of the gang, Shaw was never completely accepted, even when he lost a heavyweight boxing tournament and was awarded a trophy for trying.

Peter had the good fortune that his roommate was John Girvin, who had also transferred to Ridley in early January 1950. At first neither boy wanted to be at Ridley, but they soon adjusted. Girvin was not only an excellent scholar but also a fine athlete. While never as skilled as Girvin, Peter loved sports. In the pages of *Acta Ridleiana*, one glimpses Peter in the various stages of his two and a half years at Ridley. Soon after arriving, he joined the basketball team. In a team photograph published in *Acta* in March 1950, Peter stands in the back row, tall and gangly, looking a bit lost, as if he hasn't quite settled in to Ridley routines. His face shows a touch of acne. He is one of the tallest on the team. A year later, in March 1951, the basketball photograph shows a rather forlorn Peter, the acne on his face more pronounced and clearly visible on his shoulders. At age sixteen he is no longer among the tallest. And he no longer stands tall. What happened between these two photographs helps to explain the change.

On Thursday, August 24, 1950, after a two-week hospitalization, Margaret Brown died. Peter claimed that no one had told him of her illness. The news came as a shock. Margaret was only forty. In announcing her death, Galt's *Evening Reporter* of August 25 listed her relatives as Reg Brown, Peter, the late McGregor Young, Margaret's mother, her sister, Jean Rowe and her brother, Brigadier Gregor Young, all of Toronto. Harold Gzowski received no mention.

Her funeral was held on Sunday, August 27, at Little's Funeral Home in Galt. The next day the *Reporter* noted that Harold had helped to carry his ex-wife to her grave at Galt's Mount View Cemetery. The papers, of course, didn't report the cause of her death, but the town was already speculating. In small towns, neighbours not only know of excessive

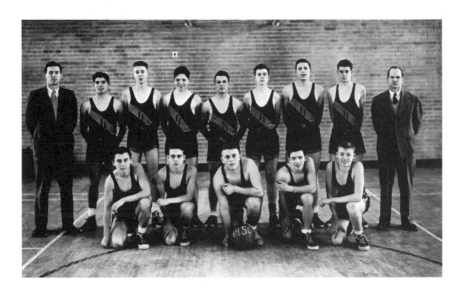

Ridley College basketball team, March 1950 — Peter in back row, second player from left.

(Courtesy Paul Lewis and Ridley College Archives)

drinking but exactly where in the house the drinker hides half-empty bottles. In hushed tones, the townsfolk talked of cirrhosis of the liver. At the funeral and afterward at the tea, Norma Brown, sister-in-law of Reg, noticed the abandoned sixteen-year-old, silent and slouching in a corner. Peter seemed a pleasant young man, she thought, but perhaps because he was shy, and no doubt overwhelmed by grief, he kept to himself. His mother's death, "and the years of loneliness and unfulfilment that led up to it," he wrote in his memoirs almost four decades later, "scarred my soul more than the acne marked my skin. I miss her still."[7] The memory of her brought tears to his eyes on CBC's *Life & Times*.

When he returned to Ridley in September 1950, Peter didn't grieve. At least outwardly. In fact, some of his mates there can't recall that he even mentioned his mother's death. It wasn't the manly thing to do. After all, Ridley, like all private schools, taught Peter muscular Christianity. A man wasn't expected to show his emotions, and young men and boys were governed by expressions such as "take it like a man."

However, Peter remembered his Ridley years as "three of the best years" of his life. No doubt student shenanigans helped take his mind off his grief. He reported in a *Maclean's* article of 1961 that one day, or more likely one night, a group of boys carried the history master's tiny English car up to the second floor of the building where they took their classes.

College sports were also a welcome diversion. In the autumn of 1950, he was an alternative for the Ridley football team, and in one photograph he stands with other alternative players in Varsity Stadium in Toronto. Behind them is a view of Bloor Street. He was determined to make it to the first team. During the summer of 1951, he practised throwing footballs. When he returned to Ridley in September, he so impressed the coach that he was asked to play quarterback on the first football team. In the team photograph, Peter is standing in the back row on a chilly November day in 1951. He sports a broad grin. John Girvin is in the photograph, and so, too, are Jim Conklin and Jack Barton. Headmaster Hamilton sits in the centre. The quarterback holds a football marked 1951. Around his neck Peter is wearing a sling that holds up his right arm. In the *Globe and Mail* of December 22, 2001, he offered an explanation. During tackling practice, he had crashed into John Girvin, a collision that resulted in a broken bone in Peter's right hand. Years later, in a column for the *Toronto Star*, he upped the ante by claiming he had broken two bones in his hand. In an article in *Saturday Night* in January 1965, he claimed that, while playing football, he had broken a bone in his foot. Soccer was less strenuous, and *Acta Ridleiana*, the Easter 1951 issue, shows Peter and ten other members of Dean's House Soccer Team.

Ridley was, however, more than just pigskin, broken bones, and books. The Midsummer 1951 issue of *Acta* depicts a group of partying boys, all smiling and laughing, especially Peter, who throws back his head, closes his eyes, and laughs harder than anyone else. *Acta* published a few of Peter's short articles. In the Easter 1951 issue, he argued in favour of Sunday sports. "Self-righteous dowagers and demagogues have slandered the very name of Sunday sport, crying piteously that it is heresy and sacrilege," he wrote in a self-confident style with an overlay of pretense. He believed that "Sunday afternoons should become a

Autumn 1950 alternatives for the Ridley College football team at Varsity Stadium on Bloor Street in Toronto, Peter in the middle.

(Courtesy Paul Lewis and Ridley College Archives)

Canadian institution, something to be proud of like maple trees," adding that since gas stations and drugstores were allowed to remain open on Sundays, why not sports stadiums? He quickly put paid to the argument that Sunday sports would lead to Sunday movies, grocery stores, pool halls, and beer parlours. He was a bit ahead of his time — Premier Leslie Frost, municipal politicians, and indeed a majority of Ontarians weren't ready to follow Peter's advice.

On May 4, 1951, the Ridley Sixth Form (grade twelve) held a debate: "Resolved — that a camel makes a better house pet than an elephant." Master Pringle was the "speaker" or moderator. Peter, who debated under the title "an Honourable Member from the Orient," argued for the negative. He informed the audience that "the elephant was a great animal," and threw in "numerous quotations" to prove his point. He had prepared carefully and possibly had consulted an encyclopedia and some of the other books in the school library.[8] When the debate began, the audience was evenly divided, but Peter's argument persuaded them to vote in favour of the elephant.[9]

In the Christmas 1951 issue of *Acta*, P.J. Gzowski's "Term Diary" for the previous autumn term appeared: "September 12, Here we go again." The next day, he reported, the football squads started to work out. The day following, his comment was "Oh my aching joints." On October 5, "Peter Sutton's hula girls amuse us greatly — very educating." On October 19, when a rival football team defeated Ridley 33–12, he wrote "Pardon the tear-smeared page," adding that a "very interesting liquid air lecture consoles us somewhat." He was pleased to report on October 29 that a jukebox had been installed at Gene's confectionary store near the campus.[10]

One of Peter's last articles at Ridley was entitled "Some Hints on Memory," an amusing, self-deprecating short essay that provided tips on how to remember things. Licence numbers were memorable if broken into meaningful pairs of numbers, giving an age, a year, and so on. To remember laundry day, Peter tied a handkerchief around his wrist on Sunday evening. The following Thursday, when it began to smell, it was laundry time. "I have noticed," he wrote, "that some boys around the School have tried to accomplish the same thing with a shirt or a pair of socks but I find the handkerchief less offensive." His final tip was to set important dates and events to rhyming couplets. His first verse was about the upcoming Mother's Day: "Though she may be far away / Please remember Mother's Day," lines both poignant and cheeky. The second verse was advice on how to avoid getting caught smoking: "Prefects check at half past ten / Then they go to sleep again. / Remember they are in a rut: / Eleven o'clock's the time to butt." And his third verse was how to get back into one's room after curfew. He bragged that even his roommate, whose name he couldn't recall, complimented him on his memory. He was so proud of this article that, more than thirty-five years later, he included it in *A Sense of Tradition*.

That he had become more self-confident and slightly cocky during his last year at Ridley shows in his writing style and ironic attitude. The March 1952 photograph of the first basketball team reveals a young man who is no longer the confused boy who cowered at Dean's House two years earlier. At seventeen he seems more relaxed, the scars of acne no longer an overwhelming problem. His upper body muscles are developing, and he is becoming quite the handsome, self-aware lad.

Peter's accounts of a trip to a bar on the American side of Niagara Falls also revealed a cocksure nature. In Ontario the legal drinking age was twenty-one; however, it was eighteen on the American side of the border. One version of the story appeared in an article written by Peter in 1970 for *Saturday Night*. After chartering a bus to Niagara Falls, Ontario, several of the boys from Ridley walked over the international bridge, spent time in a bar, and got drunk. Others only pretended to be drunk, for they didn't want to be teased for not drinking. Two or three honest, sober boys were ostracized. In retrospect Peter admired their honesty but carefully avoided explaining his own role in the incident. The reader might be tempted to guess that he was one of the young men who merely faked inebriation. There are, naturally, many variations of the drinking story.[11]

There was one episode, however, for which there is only one version, because Peter never wrote about it. One dark evening, probably in his last year at Ridley, Peter was returning to the college. He was desperate for another smoke. He had a cigarette but no match. In the dim light of a street lamp, he came upon another solitary walker. "Gotta light?" he asked the man. The man reached into his pocket, pulled out a penny match packet, and proceeded to light a match. Mere inches apart, their faces glowed in the amber light of the match. As Peter sucked at the end of the cigarette, the man quietly asked "Wanna fuck?" Peter dropped the cigarette and ran. He reached the college dorm, tore up to his room, and was so agitated that he couldn't speak. "What's the matter, Peter?" asked John Girvin. It took Peter several minutes to calm down enough to recount the episode. Girvin never forgot that night. Peter, apparently, did, for in *Canadian Living* in March 1998, he wrote a loving article about Girvin called "Chums by Chance," in which there is no mention of the proposition on the bridge. Instead, Peter recalled only that each night he and Girvin "would lie awake in our room and talk of girls, dreams and home."

Strangely enough, in the first *Morningside Papers*, published in 1985, Peter and his editors decided to include a short chapter called "The Closet," which consists of two letters, both of them on the subject of gay men. Coincidentally, St. Catharines and a boarding school play roles in each letter, which were sent to Peter after two people, strangers to each other, had heard a *Morningside* interview with novelist Howard Engel, on the subject of a gay man in St. Catharines who had committed suicide when he discovered his name on a police list of men who had enjoyed sex in a public toilet. Of course, it is improbable, after more than thirty years, that the man in St. Catharines who committed suicide was the same man Peter had met on the bridge about 1952. The first letter in "The Closet" was from a married man, the father of two children. To all appearances, he told Peter, he was happy. He did have, however, a dark side. "I want anonymous sexual encounters," the man confessed. "They *must* be anonymous because I just cannot afford them being anything else." From Duncan, British Columbia, came a second letter that told of a gay teacher in an unnamed boarding school who was forced to resign. Peter made no comment.

Peter graduated from Ridley in June 1952 with honours. He was awarded the Kelly Matthews Memorial Prize for mathematics, physics, and chemistry; received the Julian Street[12] Prize for prose; and cadet platoon number four, of which he was the sergeant,[13] won second prize. Peter also won the William H. Merritt Prize for public speaking, a prize that caused a bit of controversy. Each year the winner repeated the speech to the Rotary Club of St. Catharines. His topic was a comparison of American culture to human waste. American culture, he contended, developed at the same time as outdoor facilities moved inside and as toilet paper replaced stiff, glossy pages from shopping catalogues.[14] As human waste grew more sanitized, American popular culture grew more insipid, proof being the movies of Shirley Temple and the Andy Hardy films of Judy Garland and Mickey Rooney.

In the end, Ridley authorities did allow their best public speaker to address the Rotarians, whose reaction went unrecorded. Peter was also awarded two university scholarships. In a photograph of Upper School prize winners, Peter looks proud as he poses in shirt, jacket, and tie, in the back row, with other prize winners, including John Girvin, on Peter's left, as well as Jim Chaplin, R.K. "Shiggy" Banks, Andre Dorfman, and other bright young adults ready to face the world and to make their contributions to it.

Peter remembered his years at Ridley with great affection. "I belonged. I was a part of something in a way I have seldom been since," he wrote in the *Toronto Star* on November 28, 1978. Even though he claimed that his year as editor of *The Varsity*, 1956–57, and his months as city editor of Moose Jaw's *Times-Herald*, were also his happiest, there is no doubt that the high standards and strict discipline of the private school left a lasting impression, as well as many topics for books and articles. To be at his creative best, Peter always required imposed discipline.

A teenage Peter with sign
THIS STRUCTURE IN
DISREPAIR. PERSONS USING
IT DO SO ENTIRELY AT
THEIR OWN RISK, *perhaps
on a construction site?*

(Trent University Archives, Gzowski
fonds 92-015/1/34/Photographer:
Michael Gillan)

In September 1952, Peter entered the University of Toronto. By that time, the young adult, less self-conscious, was beginning to cope with the scars of acne. What he couldn't handle was the lack of Ridley discipline. Years later he told a reporter that he wasted time playing crap games with taxi drivers. He drank at the King Cole Room in the Park Plaza Hotel and attended parties at his frat house, Zeta Psi, at 118 St. George Street, just north of Harbord Street on land now occupied by the Thomas Fisher Rare Book Library and the university's archives.

One autumn weekend the University of Western Ontario football team was playing at Varsity Stadium in Toronto. John Girvin, a member of the Western team, visited Peter, who took him over to his frat house and showed him his initiation scar. Zeta Psi had welcomed Peter in typical fashion by imprinting its insignia into his arm with a branding iron.[15] Since he was under oath to keep the practice a secret, his fellow frat members, including Scott Symons, weren't pleased. According to Symons, Peter was "a real asshole."[16] It might have been at this time that Peter bragged to Girvin that he wasn't going to read any assigned texts until just a few weeks before final examinations. Already, it seems, he had developed an ability to assimilate books by skimming them. He managed to scrape through his first year with a C-minus. Ironically, as editor of *The Varsity* four years later, one of Peter's first pieces of advice to new students was to avoid cramming just before exams.

According to the university directory of staff and students for 1952–53, during his first year, Peter lived at 73 St. George Street in a house once inhabited by Sir Daniel Wilson (1816–1892), who was associated with the University of Toronto from 1853 to 1892 and was president of the institution from 1889 to 1892. During most of his four decades in Toronto, Wilson had been a friend and colleague of Sir Casimir Gzowski.[17]

The *Toronto City Directory* gives a second address for Peter in 1952 at 32 Tranby Avenue, a street running west off Avenue Road between Bloor Street and Davenport Road in the district known as the Annex. In the 1950s, its attractive brick Victorian homes were being broken up into apartments and rooms. On the upper two floors of a handsome semi-detached, three-storey red-brick house[18] lived Peter's father. It was to this house that Peter escorted Girvin to meet his father during that football weekend. Peter may, in fact, have stayed there on weekends while visiting Toronto from Galt during the late 1940s and on weekends away from Ridley College in the early 1950s. He admitted that possibility when interviewed by Marco Adria in May 1992, though he probably didn't want to be too precise, for he always liked to claim estrangement from his father.

By 1952, Brenda (Raikes) Gzowski had obtained a divorce and had returned to England. Girvin remembered meeting a woman whom Peter called his "stepmother."[19] In 1952, "Mrs. Camilla Gzowski" was the co-owner of 32 Tranby. Camilla ran Harold's office, probably from a room in the house on Tranby. Harold sold awnings. In the 1950s, aluminum awnings were all the rage with suburbanites in North York, Scarborough, and all those other post-war residential developments. Camilla may have brought money to the marriage and invested it in the house and business. The co-owner of the house was James B. Drope. Peter claimed that Jimmy was a bootlegger. In the city directories, he is listed as a "manufacturer's agent," who may have bought home-distilled liquor from "manufacturers" and resold it tax free. The strict liquor control laws of Ontario during the days of Premier Frost encouraged bootleggers, who had no difficulty finding customers. According to Peter, Drope had once spent time in the Guelph Reformatory. While Jimmy stayed at the house for several more years, Harold and Camilla, according to city directories, seem to have moved on by 1953.

In order to earn tuition money, during the summer of 1953, Peter worked in northern British Columbia on the construction of a power line to link Kitimat's aluminum refinery with Kemano, a hydro-electric station forty-five miles inland.[20] Some forty years later, in an introductory billboard or essay on *Morningside,* Peter talked about his work at Kitimat. His fellow workers, he told listeners, came from across Canada and around the world, from Newfoundland, the Prairies, Quebec, Portugal, Finland, and Saudi Arabia. "I was eighteen," he went on. "After writing my first-year exams, I had taken a bus to Vancouver and signed on for the float-plane north." He lived in a tent with a wooden floor, he fed cookies and sweetcakes to black bears, and once, by using an orange as bait, Peter's tent mate coaxed a bear into the tent. The food was good but the work was tough, the hours long, and the weather wet. While wearing his "blue university windbreaker, class of 5T6," he operated a shovel with a nine-foot handle that mulched out the footings of the power line. In a big recreation hall, if the men didn't like a particular clip during one of the free movies, they stomped so loudly that the projectionist was forced to put on the next reel.[21] Behind the hall was a gambling tent. Years later a *Morningside* listener reminded Peter that Bertrand Bélanger from Arvida, Quebec, had taught workers French three days a week, and that each Friday fresh meat, milk, and vegetables arrived by boat at the Hudson's Bay Company store. Another *Morningside* listener, who had been in Kitimat in 1953, remembered "a young clean-cut and friendly feller with the same name as yours ... always very friendly and polite with us emigrants."[22]

After the residence at 73 St. George Street was razed in 1953 to make way for a new men's residence, the occupants were relocated temporarily on Grenville Street near the corner of Bay and College Streets, and that was where Peter lived during his second year at the University of Toronto.[23] Apparently, he did little academic work. During the summer of 1954, he worked as a surveyor on railway construction in Labrador. It was perhaps his father who got him the job, or who inspired him to go to Labrador. Harold had also worked on railway construction from Sept-Îles north into Labrador, and that may be where he met his third partner, Édith.

Nine years later in *Maclean's*, Peter wrote two articles (November 2 and 16, 1963) about working on the Quebec, North Shore & Labrador Railway, built to carry iron ore from Knob Lake, Labrador, 300 miles south to Sept-Îsles. Like all the workers, he was treated, he claimed, like a serf by the construction company. He slept in filth and ate dismal food. By far the biggest problem were the blackflies, which feasted on the construction crews and the surveyors, even though the construction company sprayed the work areas from an airplane and doled out gelled repellents, which, Peter speculated, may have contained DDT. Even on the hottest days, Peter and the other workers kept their shirt sleeves rolled down and their pant legs tucked into their socks. "Everyone I saw," Peter wrote in *Maclean's* (November 16, 1963), "was bitten behind the ears, down the neck, in the belly." A bulldozer operator, who had to keep both hands on his machine, suffered a nervous breakdown because of the flies.

There was one great pleasure, Peter recalled, and that was fishing in the Moisie River. Since it was so easy to catch the plentiful salmon, as well as trout and pickerel, Peter grew bored with fishing and turned to magazines such as *True, Ace Detective,* and whatever else he found in the camps. He also played poker.

What he failed to mention in *Maclean's* was his experience in a gay bar in Montreal while he waited for his train to Sept-Îles. In his papers at Trent University Archives, he left a document, perhaps a rough draft of an unpublished article, which describes the incident. Because he wanted a taste of the wicked side of Montreal, he didn't tell his Gzowski relatives that he was in the city. At Central Station, while picking up his train ticket, he met "a short man not much older than I," who was going to Labrador as a cook. The two men adjourned to the beer parlour in the Mount Royal Hotel near Peel and St. Catherine Streets, and ordered a quart or two of beer. It took Peter a while to recognize that they had entered a bar frequented by gays. To use Peter's term and the one employed in the 1950s, it was a "queer" bar. At almost twenty he was tall and broad-shouldered with slim hips. He would have been noticed the moment he entered the bar. The young cook introduced Peter to some of the other customers. Two men joined Peter and the cook at the table and carried on a dialogue in French. Occasionally, they looked at Peter and smiled. He grew uncomfortable. When he announced that he had to go, the cook told him that one of the men, Gilles, wanted to take him out for dinner. Peter responded by throwing a couple of dollars onto the table and walking out. He ate by himself in a steak house and wandered the streets until the train left at midnight.[24] Inevitably, he ran into the cook at the construction site, but in the unpublished article he doesn't say whether he ever again communicated with him.

Surely, however, Peter couldn't have been as naive as he depicts himself in the unpublished document. In fact, Harold Gzowski once introduced his son to "a certain wicked adult institution" of Montreal, so Peter recounted one morning when *Morningside* was broadcast from that city in 1984. Peter didn't give the year, but the visit was perhaps soon after the death of his mother. Did Harold take him to see Lili St. Cyr, the famous stripper, at the Gayety Theatre on St. Catherine Street near St. Laurent Boulevard? Or did his father introduce Peter to a brothel? Peter concluded his *Morningside* account by telling his listeners: "This city excites me, and marks moments in my life."

—•—

In the early autumn of 1954, Peter was back in Toronto. He probably didn't even bother to register at the University of Toronto.[25] For a short time, he worked for the Hydro-Electric Power Commission of Ontario, probably on St. Lawrence Seaway construction. In October he spent a few days at his paternal grandparents' apartment at 39 Rosehill Avenue near Yonge Street and St. Clair Avenue, where they had lived in a small third-floor flat since the late 1930s. Once the devastating floods caused by Hurricane Hazel had receded, Peter boarded a train for Timmins to work at the *Daily Press*. The job was the result of knowing Ed Mannion, who had once played badminton in Galt with Margaret Brown. Mannion was at the Toronto headquarters of the Thomson chain located on the top floor of the Bank of Nova Scotia skyscraper at King and Bay Streets. A friend of Margaret's in Galt had telephoned Mannion to ask him if he could find a job for Peter. Mannion discovered that the Timmins paper needed an advertising salesman. Although Peter had little interest in selling ads, the job allowed him the vicarious pleasures of deadlines and printers' ink.

Over beer at the Lady Laurier Hotel, he pestered reporters and editors to let him become a reporter. Robert Reguly obliged. Peter's first published piece was a five-paragraph report on a speech delivered at the Beaver Club of Timmins. The only problem, Peter admitted in his memoirs, was that he hadn't written it. Yes, he had typed it, but it had been dictated by Reguly.[26] Why? For the simple reason that, when Peter arrived in Timmins, he couldn't write in a good journalist's style.[27] In Timmins he memorized the *Canadian Press Style Book*, which taught him that *accommodate* has two *c*'s and two *m*'s; that *infer* means something different from *imply*; and that *unique* is absolute.[28]

Peter and Reguly rented suites in the Sky Block, a small apartment house featuring shared toilets, one for every four suites, and hot plates in each tiny suite. Once a week, Peter, Reguly, Chris Salzen, and one or two other reporters adjourned to the Finn Boarding House, where for eighty cents they could eat all they wanted. The only problem was that if they didn't arrive early the meat was gone and they had to dine on potatoes. Occasionally, reporters adjourned to the Riverside Pavilion across the river in Mount Joy Township. "The Pav" was an illegal booze joint and dance hall. Customers brought their own liquor, and the club provided the mix. It was frequented by, among others, the mayor of Timmins and a local priest known as the Black-Robed Bandit, who, according to rumour, was a part owner of The Pav, whose chief purpose was to act as a pickup joint. Most of the men left with a woman, but never Peter, who was overly shy.[29] His story, recounted in a radio essay on *This Country in the Morning*, about "trying to get a goodnight kiss when it was fifty below and walking home across a northern Ontario town because the buses had all stopped running,"[30] should be taken with a grain of salt.

Soon Peter was in charge of the cultural beat of the *Daily Press*, with help one evening from a "pretty piano teacher." Over drinks at the Empire Hotel, she helped him write a music review, with near disastrous results when they reviewed a performance by Jeunesses Musicales du Canada without having heard the concert. The youth orchestra hadn't been able to make it to Timmins through a snowstorm. Peter caught the review just before it went to press.[31] This story has variations. In an article in *Saturday Night* in 1968, Peter claimed that he had taken the "pretty young piano teacher" with him to a recital in South Porcupine "to make sure that I didn't deliver an incisive analysis for the next day's paper on a piece the visiting artist neglected to perform."[32]

Peter always loved acting, onstage or off. He was active in the Porcupine Little Theatre in Timmins, and in his memoirs, he claims that he reviewed a play — perhaps *Springtime for Henry* — in which he had a part. In *The Man Who Came to Dinner*, produced in the spring of 1955, Peter had the starring role of Sheridan Whiteside, the outlandish and witty radio broadcaster from New York City. Whiteside is invited to dine with industrialist Ernest W. Stanley, a role played by Chris Salzen. Denise Ferguson, whose acting career later flourished, also had a role. Just before Christmas, Whiteside slips and injures his hip in front of the Stanley house. He makes two things clear: that he intends to remain in the house until his hip is healed, and that he is going to sue Stanley. From his wheelchair, he insults everyone, including the local doctor.[33]

Are actors drawn to roles that suit their personality? Did Peter even then long to become not only a good journalist but also a witty, famous, and curmudgeonly broadcaster? Is it possible to imagine one-self into reality?

April 1955, Chris Salzen standing, and Peter as Sheridan Whiteside, the crusty journalist in the Timmins Little Theatre production of The Man Who Came to Dinner.

(Courtesy Chris Salzen)

Peter also enjoyed performing solo. One day he did a skit for the local Rotary Club. The script had been sent to the club from headquarters. Most of the script had been recorded earlier on a big tape recorder, and Peter acted as the live narrator who happily bridged the gaps between the various recorded scenes. The play was really meant for radio, but the narrator, much to the amusement of the Rotarians in Timmins, brought it to life on the stage.[34]

Inspired perhaps by his acting career, by the Canadian Players' touring version of George Bernard Shaw's *Saint Joan,* and by CBC Radio drama, broadcast from Toronto and picked up by CKGB, a CBC affiliate one floor above the *Daily Press* office in Roy Thomson's attractive art deco headquarters,[35] Peter co-wrote a radio play called *Christmas Incorporated.* Its characters include Paul, an unhappy businessman; Chris, a stranger; Paul's wife, Kay; and Paul's young daughter, Jill. On

Christmas Eve, Paul meets Chris at the Empire Hotel and invites him home for dinner. At midnight Chris leaves. A few minutes later Kay's brother, George, arrives, inebriated as usual. He surprises his sister and brother-in-law by announcing that he is going to quit drinking. On his way to their house, George tells them, he passed a sleigh and eight tiny reindeer hovering in the air. He saw a man climbing a rope ladder into the sleigh. The identity of their departed visitor slowly dawns on Paul and Kay. Chris is a combination of Santa Claus and Christ. A children's choir sings "O Come All Ye Faithful." Paul and Kay go upstairs to get Jill so that she, too, can listen to the singing. Before they turn on the tree lights, they wish one another a merry Christmas.

Peter was no doubt influenced by movies such as *It's a Wonderful Life* (1946), *Miracle on 34th Street* (1947), *A Christmas Carol* (1951), and other cinematic morality tales that portrayed the triumph of generosity and love over greed and materialism. The play, which bears the marks of two young and earnest playwrights, incorporates themes that later grew in importance: Peter's indifference to materialism and personal appearance; his battles with alcohol and depression; and his strained family relations. Peter must have been thrilled when the play was broadcast on CKCL, a bilingual radio station a couple of blocks from the Thomson building.[36]

In his memoirs, he confessed (or bragged) that he had faked a photograph. In the spring of 1955, he was sent out to a raging fire near Timmins. On the edge of the fire was a spruce tree with a sign that warned about the dangers of forest fires. Nearby was another sign about the dangers of smoking. He moved the second sign to the lone spruce tree, just under the first sign. The only problem was that his tree "stood in unspoiled symmetry, a cool green sentinel amid the onrushing inferno," so the young reporter plunged a pine branch into the nearby fire and ran back to his tree with the burning torch. The tree caught fire, and he got his picture. He rushed back to develop the photo. It appeared in the Timmins paper under the headline "Do Not Set Out Fire Without Permit," but with "Daily Press Photo" not "Pete Gzowski" as the photographer. On May 24, 1955, when the photo appeared on the front page of Toronto's *Telegram*, it was attributed to Don Delaplante. Might one

assume that not only did Peter fake the photograph but that he con-
cocted the whole story about the authorship of the article? As he noted
in his memoirs, he never let reality "stand in the way of a good story."[37]

Nevertheless, Peter claimed that the photograph, which won an
award, was his ticket to success. In announcing his promotion, the
Timmins paper claimed that "Pete" had been at the University of Toronto
for two years and that he had studied philosophy and English. No doubt
Peter had fed the paper that rather optimistic account of his studious
university career. When he was promoted to the position of reporter at
the paper's Kapuskasing bureau, his articles began to appear in both the
Kapuskasing Weekly and the *Daily Press*. On Wednesday, August 3, 1955,
under "Pete Gzowski, Staff Writer," he wrote about yet another raging
forest fire, but this time from a point high above in a Lands and Forests
Otter aircraft. He also wrote about teenage figure skaters at practice in
Porcupine during the hot summer of 1955, about water fluoridation in
the township of Tisdale, and on the possibility of the National Ballet
of Canada performing in Porcupine. Peter visited an art exhibition in
Porcupine, and one week he produced a humorous issue under the headline "Too Much Bad News Printed? Here's Something Cheerful," in
which the unnamed staff writer of the *Kapuskasing Weekly*, no doubt Pete
Gzowski, printed only good news. He reported, for instance, that Bruce
MacDonald had just celebrated his birthday.

Peter was always full of mischief. One snowy day, while out for a
walk with Chris Salzen, he passed a public school during recess. He
started shouting, "Monsters, beasts," and threw snowballs at the children. Delighted, they returned fire. One day, just before Christmas
1954, Reguly, Salzen, and Gzowski were quaffing beer at the Lady
Laurier when Peter came up with a brilliant idea. Why not adjourn
to the Metropolitan Stores outlet, one of a chain of discount department stores, where they would sing Christmas carols? That way, Peter
explained, they could brag that they had sung at the Met. They did, and
they bragged for weeks afterward. Never once, apparently, did he allow
his fellows to see inside his bright mind. Years later, when Chris Salzen
first heard Peter on CBC Radio, he was surprised at just how bright his
former colleague could be.

In September 1955, probably somewhat reluctantly, Peter returned to the University of Toronto. The university directory notes that he stayed at 12 Walmsley Avenue in the Yonge and St. Clair area — in other words with his grandmother Young. The directory also notes that he was in his second year, which means that he actually failed his first attempt at a second year in 1953–54. To help pay for his tuition, he worked as a part-time reporter for the *Telegram,* which hired him to write about crime and punishment on the police beat. From 1:00 a.m. to 9:00 a.m., he sat at a desk at police headquarters at 149 College Street, just west of Bay Street, where he monitored police radio reports and checked precincts, fire halls, and emergency wards. At the end of the shift he sent stories by taxi to the *Telegram,* with a duplicate to the *Toronto Star.* Each morning at 9:00 a.m., as he shuffled along College Street to the nearby campus, he imagined himself as the actor Leslie Howard, "wan and dreamy," a volume of Dylan Thomas under his arm. His salary of $55 per week also paid for beer at the King Cole Room and for any entertainment in his "dingy basement" apartment on Tranby Avenue. He may have made arrangements with Jimmy Drope to sublet the basement flat for occasional use when Grandmother Young's rules might have been too restrictive.

As a general reporter for the *Globe and Mail,* Robert Fulford was sometimes assigned the police beat from early Saturday morning to Sunday afternoon. In his memoir *Best Seat in the House,* Fulford recalled that Peter once arrived at police headquarters with a book of poetry by John Milton. When Fulford asked him if he enjoyed Milton, Peter replied, "'Hell, no. It's on the course.'" Fulford concluded quite rightly that Peter was camouflaging his intelligence in order to be considered one of the boys.[38]

That year Peter was also the managing editor of *Gargoyle,* the monthly magazine published by students of University College, the non-denominational college of the university. On February 8, 1956, *Gargoyle* published an article by "Pete Gzowski." Leon Major was directing rehearsals for the musical *Kiss Me Kate,* starring Donald Sutherland, the twenty-year-old native of New Brunswick.[39] Interviewing Major, noted Pete Gzowski, in one of his more contrived similes, was "like trying to play gin rummy with a tongue-tied auctioneer."

During the summer of 1956, Peter joined Clyde Batten in publishing a weekly called *The South Shore Holiday*, which reported on the cottage areas and towns along the east side of Lake Simcoe from Beaverton to Keswick. The publication was based in Jackson's Point, probably at Betlyn, the Colonel's summer home. In the first issue of May 18, Batten and "Peter J. Gzowski" introduced themselves in an article entitled "This Paper's Editors Young but Very Eager." Journalism was Peter's "one true love." If all went well, he would graduate from the University of Toronto the next year. The issue also included an article called "Shooting the Wedding," an amusing look at nuptial photography by Alf Brodie, who called himself "the voice of the Beaverton Bandwagon."

The South Shore Holiday was printed each Thursday at the offices of the *North Toronto Herald* on Yonge Street, following which Gzowski and Batten drove it up to numerous general stores along the lake. The weekly published Peter's reviews of plays produced at the nearby Red Barn Theatre, and the pair "borrowed" articles from the Toronto papers. By altering the byline and the opening lines, they managed to get away with plagiarism. When it became obvious that *The South Shore Holiday* wasn't going to pay the cost of university tuition, it folded. Batten and Gzowski forgot to tell Alf Brodie, who, according to his daughter, Judy, was left "high and dry."[40] Brodie's diary talks only about Batten, as if he were the real star of the weekly.[41] Peter finished the summer working on the St. Lawrence Seaway construction.

By the mid-1950s, the inkwell and the fountain pen had almost vanished from everyday use, replaced by the more convenient ballpoint pen. For the rest of Peter's life, ink was his mainstay, whether the pen or the ink-imbued ribbon of a typewriter, the printer's ink of newspapers and books, or the ink cartridge of a computer printer. Beginning with those rather earnest, sometimes witty short pieces in *Acta Ridleiana* in the early 1950s and ending with Peter's final article in the *Globe and Mail* in January 2002, he expressed his opinions and developed his imagination with the help of that bluish-black liquid that was sprayed and pumped so dramatically at Ridley one raucous evening in 1950, the night when he finally felt that he belonged. If the pen is indeed mightier than the sword, it is the ink in the pen that deserves the credit. Even more important is the intelligence and wit of the person holding that pen or pecking at a keyboard.

— 3 —

Not Paris Nor London, but Moose Jaw and Chatham, 1956–1958

Maybe each human being lives in a unique world,
a private world, a world different from those inhabited
and experienced by all other humans.

— *Philip K. Dick*, I Hope I Shall Arrive Soon

Upon his return to the University of Toronto in September 1956, Peter was elected editor of *The Varsity*, the campus newspaper whose offices were in the basement of the old Stewart Observatory in the quadrangle adjoining Hart House and the University College building. Peter was the outside candidate who defeated Michael Cassidy, the insider.[1] He may have had the support of Clyde Batten, a former editor of the paper, as well as that of Art Cole of the *Telegram*.

In one of his first editorials, Peter announced that in "this vastly monotonous world, it is the duty, not the right, of the undergraduate to have a good time." When he took over, the paper was biweekly. Soon it became a daily paper, published each weekday morning. Among the paper's reporters in 1956–57 were John Gray, Liz Binks,[2] Michael

Cassidy, Ed Broadbent, Howie Mandel, and Hagood Hardy. During Peter's tenure, Wendy Michener,[3] his immediate predecessor as editor, contributed an occasional article, as did Clyde Batten.

Under Peter, coverage of the arts was superb. The editor and staff reviewed musical performances by Jon Vickers, Herbert von Karajan, and John Charles Thomas; theatre at venues such as the Crest; and films such as *Giant* and *Baby Doll.* The paper also reviewed books. On November 26, 1956, Peter referred readers to a review, elsewhere in the paper, of *New Voices,* an anthology of writing by Canadian university students. He reviewed Canadian drama shown on CBC-TV, drama that he thought superior to anything on American television. Peter also noted that Canadian actors such as Don Harron and Christopher Plummer were doing well on Broadway, the result of good training in Canada. The paper reviewed a show of paintings by the young Michael Snow, and it featured a photograph of Charmion King, Amelia Hall, and Kate Reid, who were rehearsing Anton Chekhov's *Three Sisters.* There were reviews of performances by Glenn Gould and Maureen Forrester, and Peter promoted the Hart House Orchestra Association, which was experiencing financial difficulties. On Friday, October 5, 1956, Peter reviewed *Macbeth,* one of three Shakespearean plays that the Old Vic was staging at the Royal Alexandra Theatre. Peter's review, entitled "Ye Ballade of Macbeth ye Knife," took the form and rhythm of the theme from Bertolt Brecht and Kurt Weill's *The Threepenny Opera,* written in 1928 and made popular by Weill's wife, Lotta Lenya:[4] "In the courtyard, hacked to pieces / Lies Macduff's lamented wife / With her nephews and her nieces / Compliments of Mac the Knife." Peter liked the Old Vic's interpretation.

On Tuesday, October 9, the editor chastised university students, and Canadians in general, for being afraid of their own opinions, and he called the University of Toronto student government "anaemic and lacklustre." Inspired by Allan Fotheringham, editor of *Ubyssey,* the student newspaper at the University of British Columbia, Peter sent John Gray and Iain Macdonald, *The Varsity*'s cartoonist, over to Queen's Park to steal Premier Frost's black homburg. Other young editors emulated Fotheringham and Gzowski, and Prime Minister Louis St. Laurent, opposition leader John Diefenbaker, and Charlotte Whitton, the colourful mayor of Ottawa, also lost their hats, which, like Frost's, were auctioned for charity. Perhaps inspired by *New Yorker* cartoons, Peter commissioned Macdonald to draw a cartoon of a waiter carrying a tray with a Benedictine friar on it. "You ordered a Benedictine, sir?" the waiter asked the diner. It was a cartoon that Peter had always wanted to see, and he published it immediately.[5]

During Peter's tenure as editor, the Hungarian rebellion was suppressed, which gave him a chance to preach against Soviet aggression. In an editorial on Thursday, November 1, 1956, he was furious that the Student Administrative Council (SAC) was slow to support the uprising.

Peter loathed censorship of any kind. He chastised George Hees for suggesting in the House of Commons that John O'Hara's novel *Ten North Frederick* be banned in Canada. "The novel, incidentally, is highly enjoyable," the editor teased Hees. Peter decried Ontario's arcane drinking laws and the Liquor Control Board of Ontario, which he dubbed "Les Frost's pharmacy." He was highly supportive of the exchange, then in its infancy, between students of l'Université de Montréal and the University of Toronto, and he published a few articles in French during the Quebec university's visit in the autumn of 1956. In one issue, he got into trouble when he claimed that the *Telegram* would be, of course, pro-Israel during the Suez crisis, in order to protect its Jewish subscription list. On Tuesday, November 20, 1956, he took on the Massey Commission's recommendation that a "Canada Council" be established. "Frankly," Peter wrote, "we dislike the notion of 'Canadianism' in culture as in politics." He didn't object to support for the arts, but he feared that the name "Canada Council" implied cultural nationalism, and, even worse, conservative nationalism. Was the council established in order to reinforce the status quo? he wondered. How would such an organization deal with a biographer of anti-establishment figures such as Louis Riel, Joseph Brant, and William Lyon Mackenzie?

In October 1956, Peter made his radio debut on CJBC, one of the CBC's two English-language radio stations in Toronto. He made an appeal for funds to help move American-made I GO POGO buttons through customs. The buttons, designed to promote a Pogo-for-President campaign, of which Peter was manager, satirized the American presidential election underway at the time.

In January 1957, Michael Cassidy and Peter travelled to Ottawa to report on the Progressive Conservative leadership conference. Peter's observations and analyses of the successful candidate were astute. He saw in John Diefenbaker a strange combination of evangelical preacher and working man. When Cassidy and Peter crashed a luncheon, the latter noted that, as the new leader of the opposition approached a supporter, "his right hand went out with a reflex that would do an athlete proud and it began to pump almost before contact." While Peter was impressed with Diefenbaker's speaking ability, he hinted that the man was nothing more than an impressive speaker and a glad-hander. Several years before Peter C. Newman said so in *Renegade in Power*, Peter realized that John Diefenbaker was contrived, devious, and somewhat shallow.

Later, in February, Peter complained about too much royal news in the media, and the same month he lost his job with the *Telegram* when he editorialized against the paper and its rival the *Toronto Star*, accusing them of trial by headlines. During the 1950s, the two dailies furiously competed, and in order to sell papers they sensationalized the news. One day both papers published a photo of seventeen-year-old Peter Woodcock, charged with the rape and murder of a five-year-old girl. In lurid headlines, they called him a murderer. The *Telegram*'s city editor, Art Cole, fired Peter for using *The Varsity* to criticize his paper.

"From their ivy-covered strongholds," Peter later recalled, "Canada's liveliest newspapers aim a barrage of spoofs, puns and vitriol at a world that notices them only when they're in hot water. Fortunately they usually are." He liked *The Varsity*'s satirical sauciness, and he was proud to add his name to a list of Canadians — Bliss Carman, Nathan Cohen, Earle Birney, and Stephen Leacock — who had written for university newspapers.[6]

The Varsity was published by SAC, whose offices were on the main floor of the old observatory, just above the offices of the newspaper. Tom Symons, chair of SAC at the time, soon realized that the new editor of *The Varsity* was a complex individual. In September 1952, Peter had arrived at the university well-scrubbed, the result of two and a half years of strict discipline at Ridley College. He soon became, in Symons's words, "freighted up." He was a mixture of opposites: he envied the established, wealthy families of Toronto, and yet he mocked them and their power.

Soon he developed an unprepossessing persona, that of the professional student, and he made a cult of it.[7]

In his memoirs, Peter admitted to being a poseur. He saw himself as the hero in a movie, and one can only speculate what kind of movie — perhaps a film noir from the 1940s set in a cluttered newspaper office whose windows sported weighty venetian blinds as well as a clanging upright telephone that brought the chain-smoking editor news of the latest horrific murder in a Toronto ravine. Was that book carried under his arm as he loped along College Street toward police headquarters not so much John Milton or Dylan Thomas as Dashiell Hammett, the American crime writer who wrote scripts for film noir movies? Peter also claimed to have been influenced by Damon Runyon of *Guys and Dolls* fame, the Broadway musical about horse races, bookies, and salvation.

During lectures, Peter declared, he turned up his collar, and with a cigarette dangling from the corner of his mouth, took lecture notes using thick 2B pencils on "crumpled pads of *Tely* copy paper." If it is true, as he alleged in his memoirs, that he wrote not a single essay and attended few classes that year, his story about showing up at lectures looking like a newspaper reporter probably owes much to his imagination.

Peter's term as editor of *The Varsity* ended in March. That month Cathie Breslin[8] interviewed him, and on the fourteenth her article appeared in *The Varsity*. "The motto 'wine, women and song' was around for several centuries," Breslin noted, "before Peter came along to justify it." Breslin claimed that Peter could dash off an editorial in half an hour, and that his interests were wide, from politics to poetry, prose, theatre, women, alcohol, and newspapers. While he had pretended to Robert Fulford that he read only what he was forced to read, Peter told Breslin that he had read each and every book in his personal library, some 250 books, from skin novels to economic dissertations to the *Oxford Book of English Verse*. That year he had found time to dash off a children's book on the subject of bread, commissioned by Christie's Breads of Toronto. In between, according to Breslin, he was the ringleader of most of the campus escapades.

All life for the outgoing editor was drama, Breslin wrote, and Peter could regale an audience for an hour with something as ordinary as a trip to the cleaners.[9] "When he sweeps into a room, arms waving, coat flapping, eyes a-glitter," Breslin continued, "you know that something is going to happen. And it does." She also noted that his rich construction camp language sometimes shocked junior reporters. Soon he would be leaving for the West where he would become, in Peter's words, "the youngest goddamn city editor in Canada."[10] Breslin concluded her article by calling Peter a "helluva fine newspaperman."

Peter wasn't, however, a "helluva" fine student. His final year was a complete miss, academically speaking. In fact, his clipping file at the university archives indicates that he never enrolled that year. And the student-staff directory for 1956–57 makes no reference to a Gzowski, Pete or Peter or Peter J. Four decades later Peter blamed his early departure from the University of Toronto on lack of money.[11] However, he wasn't going to graduate, anyway, so why stick around when he was presented with an attractive opportunity out west?

If he didn't learn much philosophy and English that year, he did learn journalism. Student newspapers were de facto schools of journalism at a time when the profession was learned by legwork and tapping out stories on an old typewriter. "There is much to be said," Peter reminisced years later, "for learning by doing, and having a place to make mistakes on your own." He belonged to the last generation of journalists to learn on the job, the last to acquire the skills of the trade by an age-old apprenticeship system that dated back at least to 1665 when the *Oxford Gazette,* considered to be the first English-language newspaper, was founded. Under that tried-and-true system the student apprentice learned by emulating seasoned journalists, by making mistakes, and by correcting those mistakes under watchful eyes.

In his last issue of *The Varsity,* Peter wrote an open letter to Michael Cassidy, the new editor. He had two pieces of advice. First, never underestimate your own power as editor, for *Varsity* editorials were widely read not only on campus but also in the offices of the large newspapers downtown. And second, never overestimate your power, for an editor must not sit in judgment too often, though he shouldn't be afraid to write what he thinks. It was good advice.

—•—

Like the Timmins and Kapuskasing papers, Moose Jaw's *Times-Herald* was part of the Thomson chain. Perhaps someone in Timmins had told Peter about the opening, or maybe he saw an advertisement. Ed Mannion might have put in a word for him. Ron Brownridge, the *Times-Herald*'s managing editor, travelled to Toronto for interviews. He chose Peter. On Sunday, March 17, 1957, Peter boarded a Canadian Pacific Railway train at Toronto's Union Station.

When Peter arrived in Moose Jaw, he found a small apartment in a house at 1142 Grafton Avenue, a two-storey, hipped-roof frame house on the city's south side. Nearby stands the magnificent St. Joseph's Roman Catholic Church, whose soaring spire and crucifix overlook the city from the rise of ground that is the city's south end. Inside the church there is a beautiful statue of St. Joseph. Carved from a piece of wood about six and a half feet high, the statue was installed in the church shortly before Peter's arrival. Located stage left of the high altar, St. Joseph hews a log with an adze. St. Joseph the workman is a Canadianized version of the stepfather of Jesus Christ, whose teenage years, one can only imagine, must have been as trying for Joseph as Peter's were for his own stepfather.

Although Peter's colleagues and friends assumed that he was always an agnostic, he used to kneel in prayer in front of St. Joseph. On August 17, 1982, when a long-time resident of Moose Jaw heard an announcement on CBC Radio that Peter was returning to radio, she wrote to Peter. "My first time seeing you," she told him, "was at St. Joseph's Church every week day before noon, praying before St. Joseph's statue, you in the front pew and I in the back." She could still picture the young man turning his head slightly left toward the high altar. "What a nice, devout young man," she added.[12] Surely, there is no doubt that, during his short time in Moose Jaw, Peter exhibited some sort of religious faith. Or did he perhaps agree with one of Mavis Gallant's characters that St. Joseph was "the most reliable intermediary he could find"?[13] "Religious feeling cannot be disproved," argues the fictional William James in Colm Tóibín's novel *The Master*, "since it belongs so fundamentally to the self."[14]

After morning prayers, Peter shuffled down the main thoroughfare to the newspaper office on Fairford Street and made his way to his desk, a large U-shaped piece of plywood topped with mottled green arborite.[15]

The desk gave the new city editor a good view of the entire newsroom. In order to look more mature and to impress colleagues in Moose Jaw and Toronto, Peter donned horn-rimmed "respectacles."[16]

It was a zesty moment in Saskatchewan. In the House of Commons in Ottawa, Prince Albert's John Diefenbaker was displaying his rapier wit and prosecutorial style. In the same House in 1956, Ross Thatcher, MP for Moose Jaw and district, had deserted the Co-operative Commonwealth Federation (CCF) to join the governing Liberals. He attacked Saskatchewan Premier Tommy Douglas's policy of creating Crown corporations to manage the province's economy. During the 1957 federal election, Douglas challenged Thatcher to a debate, which took place at Mossbank near Moose Jaw on May 20, 1957. The next day Peter's article, headlined "Great Mossbank Debate Was a Memorable Clash," appeared on the city page of the *Times-Herald.* Douglas had accused Thatcher of "misrepresentation and maligning of the province of Saskatchewan." Thatcher shot back that the only hides tanned in the provincially owned tannery were those of the Saskatchewan taxpayer.[17] Seven years later, in an article in *Maclean's*, Peter recalled the bitterness of the debate during which the usually witty Tommy Douglas "lunged bitterly and personally at Thatcher."[18] In 1988, however, Peter had changed his mind. In his memoirs, he claimed that political debates in the Prairies were infused with decency.

As city editor, Peter's task was to assemble local news, which included municipal council meetings, obituaries, and accidents. A Moose Jaw man was found guilty of murder in May, city teachers were granted a raise, and firefighters wanted one. At the Moose Jaw Public Library circulation was up but children were reading less. The Saskatchewan section of the Trans-Canada Highway was completed in August, and on September 5, nineteen-year-old Colin Thatcher, "Student of the Week," who was learning the "tricky" art of ranching on the family ranch at nearby Caron, was planning to enrol in animal husbandry at Iowa State College.[19] Each Saturday the city page included a column called "Town Talk," which consisted of about a dozen short pieces of local news, two or three sentences each. On May 25, the city editor noted that Moose Jaw–born Joseph Schull, an established radio and television playwright, was about to have an article published in *Weekend Magazine* on the subject of a sailing ship launched in Saint John, New Brunswick, in 1851. "How about writing about home, Joe?" Peter advised. On June 15, "Town Talk" asked the following: "Isn't it about time that something was heard from Ottawa about the proposed new post office building?"[20]

The city editor was always interested in politics. On Saturday, June 8, 1957, under the headline "Election Victors: Liberals but Tories Will Gain Seats," Peter predicted that the government of Prime Minister Louis St. Laurent would be re-elected the following Monday. After more than two decades of Liberal rule, most Canadians had only vague memories of the last Conservative government, that of R.B. Bennett, who had been defeated in 1935 when Peter was too young to remember. On election Monday, Peter wrote, "In the proudest sense of the word, I became a citizen today. I did it by standing in the curtained-off corner of a Grafton Avenue living room, by marking a simple X on a slip of paper." The polling booth for Peter's part of town was in the living room of Mrs. Richard Bolton of Grafton Avenue, and the deputy returning officer was Tom Kearney. As Cathy Breslin had noted in *The Varsity*, Peter could make a trip to the dry cleaner sound interesting. "Mr. Kearney tore a green ballot from one of his books of 100 and handed it to me," Peter wrote. "He gestured toward the curtained corner, where a bright light illuminated the small table." Peter stepped inside, drew the curtain, read the ballot, "and with two quick strokes of a soft pencil," exercised the right that "my forefathers earned through bitter bloodshed and years of turmoil." In one sentence, Peter slipped effortlessly from fact into fiction. Was he implying that his forefathers were men such as Samuel Lount and Peter Matthews, hanged for participating in the Rebellion of 1837 in Upper Canada? Were the Youngs somehow related to William Lyon Mackenzie or to Louis-Joseph Papineau? Or did Peter believe that Casimir Gzowski's revolt against tsarist rule in Poland, also in the 1830s, had led to Peter's freedom to exercise his democratic rights on that overcast Monday in 1957? Most readers, of course, would never have questioned their city editor and his enchanting prose.

After chatting with Kearney, Peter checked out the poll at Central Collegiate and then headed to his desk where he pounded out the evocative article on his typewriter. "In later years, no doubt," he wrote in a concluding paragraph, "I will have the right to vote in many more elections. On those future election days, perhaps I will feel some of the same thrill that tingled today as I cast my first vote. But no matter how this year's election turns out, it will be a long time before I forget the thrill of the day I became a citizen."

Other topics that interested the city editor were the children who performed at the Moose Jaw Music Festival (March 27) and the discovery near Moose Jaw of about two hundred primitive tools used by First Nations centuries earlier (March 30). Peter was in favour of a roller skating rink, which would, he predicted, lower the juvenile crime rate (May 18). "If today's teenagers were examined closely," Peter wrote on June 1, "I'll wager they would emerge as actually a more sober and thoughtful group than many a generation before them." He then suggested a Teenagers' Week in order to highlight their positive character and deeds.

In June the *Times-Herald* published a supplement, edited by Ron Brownridge, on the subject of oil. Peter contributed an article on the history of oil in Saskatchewan, which began, he claimed, 277 years earlier when the Hudson's Bay Company acquired fur and mineral rights to the vast area known as Rupert's Land. The article combined first-hand observation with a wide range of secondary sources.

Peter was always a great reader. Years later Murray Burt, a New Zealander who had arrived at the *Times-Herald* in November 1956, recalled the pile of books that grew with each passing week beside Peter's bed. (Burt also remembered a pair of panties draped over those books.)[21] Louise, the assistant women's editor and a neighbour who sometimes gave Peter a ride to work, also recalled piles of books in his messy bedroom.[22] He read well into the night. On May 25, 1957, in an article headlined "Reading Really Isn't So Bad as Some Would Make It Out," he announced: "I am a bookworm and proud of it!" When he was a teenager, he explained, there wasn't any television;[23] he and his peers relied on books for information and entertainment. "Anyone who grows up without meeting *Winnie-the-Pooh* and *Dr. Doolittle, Huckleberry Finn* and *Black Beauty* is not growing up fully," he argued. "A bookworm," he added, "even a mild one, makes friends during his larva stage that will remain with him longer than all the human butterflies he will meet in real life." Television, he concluded, would never take the place of books.

Laughing eyes gave the impression that Peter was constantly flirting. Women who found him seductive always recalled those lovely eyes, which gazed intently at anyone who was telling him something intriguing. "People are drawn to him like magic," a female colleague once noted.[24] In Moose Jaw there were parties and attempted seductions. In his memoirs, Peter claimed that he had tried to make it in the stubble with the attractive assistant women's editor. Almost half a century later, Louise could only laugh. "He never got to first base with me," she asserted, "though he did think of himself as Don Juan." Peter and the other men at the paper treated Louise to her first drink in "The Winston" on seedy River Street. (The women's editor, of impeccable moral standards, wasn't invited.) "We partied too much," Louise recalled, laughing again.

Murray Burt never forgot Peter's demonstrations on how to drink tequila properly — by rubbing the rim of a glass with lemon juice and shaking salt over it. In his memoirs, Peter recalled drinking lemon gin at midnight in a field near Moose Jaw and quaffing beer on Saturdays at the Harwood Hotel until closing time. "He loved to brew," one of his compositors at the newspaper remembered. In fact, Peter made it a habit to head over to the Harwood, a five-minute walk from the *Times-Herald* building, each and every weekday. At the corner of Fairford Street and First Avenue, midway between the newspaper office and the hotel, is the handsome Romanesque city hall. Sheila Thake, who had arrived in Moose Jaw from England about a month before Peter, worked for the city. From her desk, located near an upper window overlooking the street, she used to watch Gzowski and Burt as they strolled toward the hotel after the next day's paper had been composed around 3:00 p.m. Gzowski's height, about six foot four, made Burt's five foot six appear even shorter. Sheila was reminded of the cartoon characters Mutt and Jeff, published each day in the local paper.[25]

"He was a marvellous editor," Burt recalled years later. As a reporter, Burt's writing was subject to the city editor's red pen. Peter gave Burt the "first inkling" of what was good and, of course, what was bad in his writing. He could be hurtful when he didn't like a piece. Like many other journalists,

Burt gives Peter the credit for his career in journalism. One day Murray wrote a short article about Mel Crighton, the popular caretaker of King George School. As he approached seventy, Crighton was being forcibly retired, even though, as Burt pointed out, he was younger than either Prime Minister Louis St. Laurent or President Dwight Eisenhower. The teachers wanted to keep him for another year. Burt quoted a local physician who hated to see healthy people pushed into retirement.

Burt finished the article rather quickly and worried about what the city editor might say. As Burt watched, Peter read the piece in silence. Suddenly, Peter bounded from his chair. "This is marvellous! This is marvellous!" he shouted as he strolled around his U-shaped desk, past the desks of fellow reporters, and into the next room where the wire editor's desk was located. He was yelling so loudly that the typesetters in the basement stopped composing. "Hey, listen to this," Peter ordered. "At least two of the trustees were strongly in support of granting another extension. Tom Warner said some men at seventy can do as much work as men in their forties. Tom is seventy-three." When Peter finished reading the article, he sent the piece "down the tube" to the typesetters. Under the headline "To Retire or Not to Retire, That Is the Caretaker Question," the article appeared on the city page the next day, Saturday, May 25. For the young New Zealander, there could have been no greater encouragement. From that moment on, Burt knew he could spend his life in journalism, which he did as editor of the *Times-Herald*, St. Catharines' *Standard*, and finally the *Winnipeg Free Press*. To edit well, one must display self-confidence. Peter knew he was good. Even in Moose Jaw, according to Burt, Peter was "aware of his potential."

Peter was always unconventional and impulsive. During the long, hot, and dry Prairie summer of 1957, he came to work in sandals. Sans socks, of course. One afternoon, in an act of bohemian indifference, he retired to a corner of the Regal Room at the Harwood. Wearing what appeared to be a pajama top, he took out an electric shaver from a pocket and proceeded to shave. On another day, when Peter discovered that Burt was quite a sailor, he nagged the reporter to teach him sailing. The problem was finding a sailboat. Finally, Burt discovered that the local sea cadets had one. Murray and Peter went sailing just once on Buffalo

Pound Lake, and certainly not enough for Peter to claim, as he does in his memoirs, that he had learned to sail on the Prairies.

Soon after arriving in Moose Jaw, the new city editor drove to Swift Current to attend a performance by Douglas Campbell's Canadian Players. During intermission, he overheard an audience member remark, "This is just as good as anything you can see in New York. It sure beats the movies." He recounted that story on Saturday, May 11, in an article headlined "Theatre Would Assist Talent and Contribute to the City," in which he urged the formation of a community theatre group in Moose Jaw. "Live theatre," he wrote, "even at its worst, sure does beat the movies." He enjoyed the experience of watching "flesh and blood actors actually speaking their lines." Furthermore, Peter contended, local theatre often prepared local talent for the larger world in the big cities. All that was needed now was for someone to call a meeting.

In another part of the same edition, Leone Wellwood, executive director of the YMCA, who had probably discussed the subject with Peter, placed a notice in the paper announcing a meeting the following Monday evening, May 13, at the Y, across Fairford Street from the Harwood and more or less on the site of today's casino. Peter attended, as did Sheila Thake, Duane Campbell, and others. The next day on the city page Peter introduced the new Moose Jaw Community Players. He announced that he was a member of a committee of four charged with developing local theatre.

During a second meeting, two weeks later, the Players decided to present an evening of three one-act plays in November. At the third meeting, on Monday, June 3, prospective directors were asked to present outlines of plays. Duane Campbell's choice was *Suppressed Desires*; Marv Balabuck's was a "Judgement Day" comedy called *Rise and Shine*, which would star members of the nearby air force station;[26] and Peter's choice was J.M. Synge's *Riders to the Sea*, one of the greatest one-act plays. His choice suggests that he was a fan of serious theatre. The themes of *Riders to the Sea* are motherhood, death, and memory. At one of the first meetings of the Community Players, Peter had summarized the plot of *Riders*:

an Irish mother longs for eternal rest after she buries the last of her six sons, who, like her husband and first five sons, had drowned in the sea. With Peter the roles were reversed, for it was he who was in mourning for his lost mother.

On May 28, the day after the second meeting of the Players, Peter scanned Regina's *Leader-Post*, perhaps while sitting at his U-shaped desk at the newspaper office or in the Ambassador Restaurant on Main Street, which was popular for coffee breaks. He turned to the city editor's page. No doubt he always checked to see what his counterpart in the provincial capital was doing. There, up in the far left-hand corner, directly under an ad for Capital Cab Ltd., was the photograph of a fetching young woman with long, silken hair and large, attractive eyes. Her pose and poise gave her the look of a Loretta Young, a Gene Tierney, and several other beautiful Hollywood stars of the day. Jeanette Lissaman of 2925 Fourteenth Avenue, a respectable middle-class area of Regina,[27] was about to be presented with the Regina Little Theatre's Zarek trophy for "outstanding contribution to scenic design during the past season." She had good ideas, recalls Cal Abrahamson, president of the Regina Little Theatre. Although shy at first, once she grew familiar with Abrahamson, Jeanette wasn't afraid to speak her mind.[28] The play for which she had designed seventeen sets was a foretaste of her twenty years with Peter. A satire of society women in the New York of the 1930s, *The Women* by Clare Boothe Luce deals with the reaction of a group of women to one of their friends whose husband is having an affair.

One can imagine Peter saying, "That's the woman I'm going to marry!" For a man who lived much of his life through one medium or another, it seems fitting that he should meet his future wife through a photograph in a newspaper. Peter may have called Cal Abrahamson, whom he already knew through a writers' group, to get the number. Peter was now interested in doing a story on *The Women*, and particularly on the designer of its multiple sets.

In his memoirs, Peter mentioned the photograph in the *Leader-Post*. "I tracked her down," he remembered. "I asked her for a date, and suggested the following Friday, July 13, my birthday." He claimed that he had first talked to his future wife only a few days earlier.[29] Not really.

Their first meeting had been a month earlier in Moose Jaw. It was Peter, surely, who invited Jeanette to speak to the Moose Jaw group. What better way to meet the prize-winning designer? On the city page of the *Times-Herald* of June 14, 1957, someone, most likely Peter, reported that three members of the Regina Little Theatre Group were coming to Moose Jaw the following Thursday to lecture on "various aspects of amateur dramatics" at the next meeting of the city's Community Players. He was so excited that he misspelled his future wife's first name, and he even had the wrong day — it should have read "Tuesday." The Regina threesome, Peter noted, would be Jim Young, production manager of the Regina Little Theatre; Mary Toombs, regional representative of the Dominion Drama Festival; and "Jeannette" Lissaman, whose topic would be set design. She had been giving similar lectures around the province for the Saskatchewan Arts Board.

On Tuesday, June 18, the three did indeed speak at the Moose Jaw Y, as reported in the *Times-Herald* the next day. At the top of the article are photographs of the speakers. Jeanette Lissaman, a stylish silk scarf (Hermès?) artfully arranged around her shoulders, holds up a poster-size sketch of a stage set. "Remember the sightlines," she told Peter and the rest of the audience.

Peter expressed great interest in the complicated sets for *The Women*. At some point Jeanette invited Peter to attend a dress rehearsal later that summer. In August, Peter attended all three performances of *The Women*. By that time, he was courting Jeanette. He made regular trips into Regina in an old station wagon that belonged to the *Times-Herald*. Once the newspapers were delivered, usually by 4:00 or 5:00 p.m. each afternoon, the station wagon, which was used to drop off papers for distribution by delivery boys, was available to the staff.

By the time he saw those three performances, he would have learned that Jeanette was from Brandon, Manitoba, where her father, Reg, was a well-to-do building contractor and realtor. Reg was also the Progressive Conservative Member of the Manitoba Legislature for Brandon, southwest of Winnipeg, a riding he represented for seventeen years beginning in 1952. He was also a member of the board of directors of Brandon College and a director of the Manitoba Hydro Board.[30] When Reg

Lissaman died in August 1974, the *Winnipeg Tribune* noted that he believed that "the least government was the best government," a political ideology that Peter espoused in the 1950s and 1960s.

Jeanette, or Jennie,[31] as her friends called her, was the middle of three daughters. She was born on July 13, 1933, and was therefore exactly one year older than Peter. During the mid-1940s, as a member of the Brandon Canadian Girls in Training, a Protestant organization that promoted Christian values and leadership, Jennie, for what it's worth, used the word *bif* as a substitute for "outhouse" or "public toilet," or so Peter claimed in 1965.[32] At Brandon College she graduated at the top of her class in physics and mathematics, for which she was awarded the E.J. Keddy Scholarship. At the University of Manitoba in Winnipeg she enrolled in the Faculty of Engineering and Architecture. Her specialty was interior design, including stage design. She was president of the Alpha Delta Pi sorority and was active in volleyball, basketball, and rifle shooting. In 1953 she was chair of her class's skit for *Varsity Varieties,* the university's annual stage show. She was also active in the Young Progressive Conservative Club. In the university's *Brown and Gold* yearbook, she announced plans to work in the United States at least for a while. Accompanying the mini-biography was a photograph of the graduate, wearing a mortarboard, gown, and heavy horn-rimmed glasses. She was always self-contained, according to Margaret, her roommate. She revealed little about herself.[33] When Louise, the assistant women's editor, met Jennie at Peter's overstuffed room on Grafton Street, she wondered what the two had in common — this quiet, shy, attractive woman and the ebullient, enthusiastic journalist who flirted constantly. When Peter met her, Jennie was working in Regina for H.K. Black & Associates, an architectural firm. One of her projects was the interior design of the new Murray Library at the University of Saskatchewan in Saskatoon.

Later that summer Peter acquired a very used green Austin "rag top," which took him on trips eastward to Regina across the newly completed Saskatchewan section of the Trans-Canada Highway through what he called the "changing, moody plains."[34] Jennie and Peter went to the movies, including no doubt the drive-ins around Regina and Moose Jaw.[35] They may have attended the Eighth Annual Mardi Gras held in

Temple Gardens Dance Hall about a decade before Peter first saw it. Acrylic by Yvette Moore.

(Courtesy Yvette Moore and Yvette Moore Gallery, Moose Jaw, Saskatchewan)

September at the Temple Gardens Dance Hall on Langdon Crescent. On Tuesdays the dance hall featured waltz music; on Fridays, big band music; and on Saturday evenings, the most recent dance crazes.

On drives to Regina, Peter began to appreciate the subtle landscapes of the Prairies — the marvellous pale greens, browns, mauves, and yellows, as well as the sharp blue of the big sky. Peter carried this landscape with him throughout his life in his imagination and also in a small collection of Prairie art. He always had an eye for landscape and setting, and his eye for colours and shapes was acute. He was, after all, an artist himself, whose canvases were radio and the printed page.

So quickly did he imaginatively absorb the Prairies around Moose Jaw that people in Toronto assumed he had actually been born and bred there. In speeches and magazine articles and in his memoirs, he liked to say that Saskatchewan was "the most Canadian of all provinces."

And he liked to boast that he shunned Paris and London, even Zagreb, Yugoslavia, in favour of Moose Jaw. Never once in all his prose, radio essays, and television interviews, however, did Peter repeat what he once told Jennie, that if any city deserved the title of asshole of Canada, it was Moose Jaw.[36] In his defence, the Moose Jaw of 1957, like most Canadian cities, was pretty rugged.

In later life, Peter idealized the Prairies. And this was perhaps because he began to view the Prairies through the eyes of W.O. Mitchell, whom Peter had first encountered in 1957 via the writer's novel *Who Has Seen the Wind*, published ten years earlier. At the same time Peter seems to have been completely unaware of another author whose novels investigated the psyches of Prairie people more deftly than did Mitchell's. By 1957, the year that Peter discovered *Who Has Seen the Wind*, Sinclair Ross's *As for Me and My House*, which had been published in 1941, was being hailed as a Canadian classic.

Ross's mother spent her last years in Moose Jaw. When she died, in early October 1957, her son spent several days in Moose Jaw in order to arrange and attend his mother's funeral. While Kate Ross's death was noted in the obituary section of the *Times-Herald*, the city editor was, it seems, completely unaware that an important writer was in town for the funeral. Surely, Peter, ever on the watch for a good story, read the obituary notices. However, on Wednesday, October 9, the day of Kate Ross's funeral, Peter was more interested in the fact that John David Eaton, scion of the wealthy Eaton clan, had just visited the family store in Moose Jaw. One of the greatest of Prairie writers came and went without being noted.

Like most white Canadians at the time, Peter overlooked the treatment of people now called First Nations. A few years later, however, he did make amends when he wrote an article in *Maclean's* about the shoddy treatment of Natives in an article called "This Is Our Alabama," in which Peter compared Canadian Natives to "Negroes" in the American South.

In Moose Jaw the Community Players' rehearsals took place in Pat and Betty Styles's basement suite at 1104 First Avenue NW. Sheila Thake had a small part in *Riders to the Sea*. Years later, as Sheila Phillips, she recalled that Peter began enthusiastically as a director but didn't stick around to see the play through to opening night in November 1957 at the Peacock Auditorium in the city's collegiate. J.M. Synge was upstaged by Jennie Lissaman. As winter set in, Peter suddenly resigned from the newspaper. In his memoirs, he gives no reason. According to co-workers, he was competent and got along well with his staff with one exception — a crusty veteran of the Second World War. One of his colleagues, a printer who worked with him on composing the paper, remembered that Peter had applied for the job of managing editor when Ron Brownridge announced he had accepted a post at the *News-Chronicle* of Port Arthur. Peter was told by management that he was too young and inexperienced. "What does it matter if I'm only sixteen," he replied in disgust, "if I can do the job?" Management chose a young American. When in time he proved to be incompetent, Murray Burt took over.[37]

Jennie and Peter drove eastward across the Prairies, stopping en route in Brandon to announce to the Lissamans that their daughter was going to spend the rest of her life with a young, unemployed journalist from Ontario. From Brandon they continued eastward and crossed into the States. The Austin broke down somewhere in Michigan. Eventually, they reached Toronto.

Peter hoped to join Clyde Batten in the publishing of a weekly magazine. The idea never got past the discussion stage, however, for Peter soon landed a job with another Thomson newspaper, Chatham, Ontario's *Daily News,* even though Roy Thomson, president of the chain, was none too pleased with Peter's "fickleness" at the *Times-Herald.*[38]

In Chatham, Peter was appointed city editor. Jennie and he took up residence in an apartment on Wellington Street West and First Avenue in a one-storey cottage that had once belonged to the Ursuline Sisters of Chatham, a fact that led to some teasing. Soon Peter met Darcy McKeough, whose grandfather, A.C. Woodward, had owned the *Daily News* until 1922. Apparently, Jim Chaplin had telephoned McKeough to tell him that Peter was in Chatham. McKeough and Peter went out for dinner, and Darcy arranged an interview for Jennie with an architectural firm.

On Saturday, February 14, 1958, Jennie and Peter were married in the chapel of the University of Toronto's Wycliffe College on Hoskin

Avenue, just west of Queen's Park. This theological college, named after John Wycliffe, the fourteenth-century clergyman and translator, was founded in 1877 by members of the evangelical branch of the Church of England. Casimir Gzowski had been a promoter and benefactor of the college and one of its first trustees. Later he served as chairman of the College Council. His son, Casimir S. Gzowski, also played a prominent role in the founding of the college. The chapel itself, where the wedding took place, dates from 1891.

The bride was given away by her uncle, William Seibel, of Ancaster, Ontario. Her maid of honour was Clyde Batten's wife, "Mrs. C.C. Batten, Jackson's Point." The bride and her attendant were described as "pretty" in lace and satin and nosegays. There was a noticeable absence of fathers. However, Reg Lissaman did send $500 as a wedding gift. Margaret Brown was named in the article as "the late Mrs. Gzowski." Clyde Batten was the only usher, and the best man was Ron Brownridge, who had driven down from Port Arthur. The presiding clergyman was the principal of Wycliffe, the Reverend Ramsay Armitage. At the reception, held in Clarendon Hall, Jennie's mother and Peter's grandmother Gzowski stood in the receiving line.

Peter and Jennie's wedding photo as it appeared in Chatham's Daily News *on February 18, 1957.*

(Courtesy Chatham-Kent Public Library)

On their honeymoon, Peter liked to boast, their first child was conceived.[39] As the old saying goes, babies usually take nine months, but with the first one you can never be certain. Peter Casimir Gzowski was born on October 22, 1958, less than nine months after the wedding. It is entirely possible that he was conceived during the honeymoon, though, since the couple had been living together in Chatham for several weeks, Peter's romantic conceit is probably another flight of fancy.

Peter didn't spend all his honeymoon lovemaking. He took time out to write an article about the wedding, which appeared on February 18 in Chatham's *Daily News*. Accompanying it was a photograph of the happy couple, Peter giddy and boyish, sans "respectacles," and Jennie, peering heavenward and giving the impression of being rather tired of all those nosegays. In the article, Peter claimed he was a graduate of the University of Toronto.

The creative city editor was soon back at his desk. On February 27, he wrote about the Chatham Little Theatre workshop. The cast for *Sabrina Fair* included the young and beautiful Sylvia Fricker, a few years before her last name changed to Tyson. It was probably also Peter who reported on the drama club at the Chatham Collegiate Institute. Although there is no evidence that he acted or directed in Chatham, he did attend Little Theatre productions, according to Darcy McKeough, who was a member. Peter also acquired review tickets from theatres in Detroit such as the Schubert, the Cass, and the Fox, and invited McKeough to accompany him a few times.

On March 6, 1958, "Peter Gzowski, News City Editor," wrote a piece entitled "Huge Chatham Crowd Hears Prime Minister." Having governed with a minority of seats since the previous June, Prime Minister John Diefenbaker had called an election for March 31. About three thousand people packed the Chatham Armoury, and another six hundred stood outside, making it, by Peter's count, "the biggest crowd to attend a political meeting in Chatham since the heydays of the 1930s." Since most of the articles about the city were published without a byline, one can only assume that it was Peter who covered events such as city council meetings, construction of a new Roman Catholic church, and rotting garbage in the city. He was probably the journalist who wrote stories about bootlegging, a fatal car accident, and vandalism at the local bus terminal.

Later, in March, Peter was promoted to the post of managing editor,[40] thus making him, along with Pierre Berton, one of the youngest managing editors in Canada. He was now in charge of editorials, one of which, on April 11, 1958, was headlined "Shooting at the Moon," which commented on President Eisenhower's recent statement that soon the Americans would be sending unmanned probes around the moon. In 1958, Americans were still recovering from the surprise *Sputnik* that the Soviets had lobbed around the Earth the previous October. On May 1, 1958, the editor wrote about the difficulties Prime Minister Diefenbaker was having passing bills. On the same day, Peter pointed out that the Red Ensign was the official flag of Canada and had been since 1945. So why all the fuss over a new flag? he wondered.

Winn Miller knew Peter in Chatham. Her father, Victor Lauriston, was a long-time journalist on the *Daily News,* and she herself was the Chatham correspondent for the *London Free Press.* According to Miller, Peter had good ideas and high ideals, and he was always community-minded. He wanted to hire Miller away from the London paper. To do so he tried to convince the Thomson organization to pay her two salaries, since he knew that one salary alone wouldn't match what the Siftons were paying her in London. There was no deal, but Miller got to know Peter. "The man had so much personality," she recalled years later. "You just couldn't believe it." She even got away with giving him a lecture on the evils of smoking.

After a few months in Chatham, Peter was offered a job at *Maclean's.* At that time the magazine was the most important window on Canada, and its journalists were among the best. No doubt he was pleased to be rid of Chatham society, which he considered "pretty closed."[41] It didn't matter that Jennie was making arrangements to join the architectural firm of Joe Storey. In 1958 there was no option for her but to move with Peter. Like many other talented women of her generation, Jennie was limited to domestic duties and to loving, honouring, and obeying the head of the household. She "girled" and "boyed," as Peter called the birthing process,[42] and she tended to the growing family, which allowed Peter to take pleasure in the joys of fatherhood, a fulfilling career, and an extramarital life. Peter was on his way to the top.

— 4 —

The Dangerous Temptation of
Prediction, 1958–1962

*It is now an inescapable fact that we are headed
toward separation into two countries.*

— *Peter Gzowski, "Conversations with Quebec's Revolutionaries,"*
Maclean's, *September 7, 1963*

Soon after the twenty-four-year-old Peter bounded into the offices of
Maclean's, the day after Labour Day 1958, he boasted to June Callwood,
and to anyone else at *Maclean's* who noticed him, that he would be a published novelist by age thirty. He may have been attempting to emulate
Ralph Allen, the magazine's editor, who had written several successful
novels.[1] Allen had taken note of Peter when he was editor of *The Varsity*.
While in Moose Jaw and Chatham, Peter had bombarded Allen with
short pieces and story ideas. During the summer of 1958, Allen had
called Peter in Chatham to offer him a job as one of eight assistant editors at *Maclean's* at $6,000 per year.[2]

Allen soon became Peter's "most important idol," and long after
Allen's death, Peter wrote almost nothing, he claimed, without feeling

that Allen was peering over his shoulder.[3] As editor of *Maclean's* from 1950 to 1960, Allen insisted on detailed outlines and multiple drafts before he accepted an article for publication. Delete the writing of which you are most proud, he used to tell his staff, for pride was a sure sign of self-indulgence. He required his writers to adhere to his formula: a lead or introduction followed by a sub-lead or hook that captured the reader. A series of anecdotes and expositions were to follow. If the article was a profile, at the halfway point the writer provided details such as the subject's birth and childhood. The conclusion of all articles, Allen told his staff, should be "succinct and tangy."[4] Allen was ruthless. "This is bullshit," he often scrawled beside a flatulent sentence. However, there was one piece of advice that Peter didn't absorb from his mentor: "Never stick your pecker into the payroll."

Peter began as a researcher for and contributor to the brand-new "Preview" section, which was printed in "the yellows," the outer section that wrapped around the much larger "white" section where the "feature" articles were published. Much in the manner of a newspaper, the yellows allowed the magazine to report and comment on current events and to speculate about the future. These short pieces usually bore no byline. In 1958 and 1959, "Preview" topics included a piece about the benefits of a four-day work week, and news of a new granting program to make films based on Canadian novels such as Mordecai Richler's *Son of a Smaller Hero*. The Alaska Highway was to be extended to Fort McPherson, Northwest Territories, and golfing was the coming rage. Velcro would replace the zipper, and faster skates might speed up hockey, a piece that bears the Gzowski style in lines such as "The blistering speed of Howie Morenz has long been a cherished dream for red-blooded Canadian boys."

At *Maclean's*, Peter was working with some of the best journalists in English Canada, including Peter C. Newman, June Callwood, Trent Frayne, Farley Mowat, and Bruce Hutchison. Soon Peter was promoted to Ken Lefolii's old job of copy editor, following which he became "Preview" editor. He made use of his wide array of friends across the country, including Harold Horwood from Newfoundland; Murray Burt from Moose Jaw; Don Gordon, son of the president of Canadian National Railways; Charles Taylor, son of tycoon E.P. Taylor; and Fred

Kerner, a publishing executive in New York who had once been a reporter in Saskatoon.[5]

Peter used the telephone to keep in touch with his stringers, and occasionally met them in person. For instance, in September 1959, he attended Murray Burt's wedding in Regina, which coincided with Peter's first trip to the Mackenzie Delta. Peter flirted with one of the bridesmaids, and he and the bride entertained guests with piano duets.[6] In the "Preview" section, the first short article to bear Peter's name was published on October 11, 1958, on the subject of a beer strike in Ontario. He challenged the contention of teetotallers that if alcohol were prohibited, money spent on booze would flow to better causes. Not true, Peter argued. Money not spent on beer would gravitate toward spirits and wine.

He also wrote feature articles for the white pages. His first, published on January 31, 1959, was called "The Gay and Gusty World of the College Press." Canada's twenty-three university newspapers, among them *The Varsity*, were, he noted, among "the last outposts of a flamboyant, crusading brand of journalism." His second feature, published on May 24, 1959, was called "What's It Like to Have a Famous (but Forgotten) Ancestor?" Its subject was, of course, Sir Casimir. On October 10, 1959, in "How Innocent Card Players Become Bridge Fiends," Peter wrote about bridge, one of his passions. "A million Canadians play a game called contract bridge," he wrote. "But it's much more than a game to a few thousand addicts, some of whom have thrown up promising careers to concentrate on one of the trickiest, most demanding mental exercises man has ever devised."

In the November 7, 1959, issue, "Preview" included several short speculative pieces on the 1960s. June Callwood predicted a decline in moral standards and an increase in both materialism and public displays of emotion. Ken Lefolii predicted that Polynesian could replace Chinese as the "ethnic" food of choice, while Barbara Moon foresaw flat-screen televisions mounted on walls showing up to ten channels. Peter wrote on cities of the 1960s. Winnipeg would experience a "controlled boom," and Ottawa would become a "modern Athens." On November 21, 1959, "Preview" predicted that automation would cause job losses in the postal system, and that in all provinces except Quebec, movie censors would allow more overt sex and frank language such as *bastard* and *bitch*.[7] On December 5, Peter Newman predicted that Canada would have both a national anthem and a flag by 1967, and that either Toronto or Montreal would host the world's fair in 1967. "Preview" also predicted that E.P. Taylor's colt "Victoria Park" would soon be an all-time great racing horse. (Did Charles Taylor send that one to Peter?) Two weeks later "Preview" notified anyone with a distinguished ancestor to get in touch with George W. Brown, who was collecting names for the first of up to twenty volumes of the *Dictionary of Canadian Biography*. In the issue of December 19, 1959, in the "Backstage" portion of the "yellows," Peter wrote about religion. Did the recently discovered Gospel of Thomas throw doubt on the four gospels, and on the "truth" of the pronouncements of Jesus Christ?

On January 16, 1960, Peter's first profile, "Ross McLean, the TV Star You Never See," was published. It was the first of Peter's long articles to venture away from familiar topics like family, student newspapers, and card games. One of the most acclaimed executive producers of his day, McLean worked in the CBC's Public Affairs Department. McLean, Peter wrote, "has brought the flair of show-biz to the often-dull realm of televised talks and public affairs." In shows like *Close-Up* and *Tabloid*, McLean had made stars of Max Ferguson, Joyce Davidson, and Pierre Berton.

By using code words, Peter's article hinted at a closeted side. McLean was a bachelor. His conversation was "spangled with epigrams of the Oscar Wilde school." His voice seldom lost "its hesitant, prepared quality or its wit." He dressed "meticulously" in a well-tailored dark suit; he carried his tall frame "stiffly"; he lived in a "swanky" area near Avenue Road and St. Clair Avenue; and he drove a shiny black Thunderbird. McLean was a "very complicated man," to use Peter's phrase.[8] Quite clearly, Peter was uncomfortable with McLean. In the 1980s, he was still trying to come to terms with the man. In a draft of his memoirs, he described McLean as "shy ... and easily wounded, but like a lot of shy people he seemed curiously insensitive to the effect his barbed words could have on others." The line is a good one, but it never made it into the published version of the memoirs, for Peter crossed it out, perhaps because he realized that the description suited not only McLean but himself, as well.

Throughout 1960, Peter remained as "Preview" editor and continued to keep in touch with his stringers across the country, urging them to come up with breaking and slightly unusual stories. Peter often called Murray Burt in Moose Jaw. "Got anything today, Murray?" Peter would ask. Peter was especially pleased if the news came from an unusual-sounding place like Elbow or Bienfait, pronounced *Beanfate*. In the "Preview" of Saturday, April 9, 1960, Burt predicted that if the CCF government of Tommy Douglas were to win the upcoming Saskatchewan election, it would embrace the British model of health insurance. In the same issue, "Preview" published a short piece, no doubt by Harold Horwood, on the growing reputation and price of Cape Dorset carvings and prints. On May 21, 1960, "Preview" included a paragraph on the dangerous rise in smoking, its link with cancer, and the worrisome fact that 80 percent of adults started smoking in their teens. (Did the "Preview" editor write this piece?)

One spring weekend in 1960, Peter and Jennie flew to New York. In an article that appeared in the July 2 issue, Peter began by claiming that Jennie and he had known the city for years by way of photographs and movies.[9] They posed for photographer Frank Wolfe, a New Yorker hired by *Maclean's* to record the visit. Several of Wolfe's photographs were published with the article, including one of Peter and Jennie looking down into Central Park from the balcony of their hotel. Another photograph shows them inside the Guggenheim Museum. Peter had his photograph taken while lighting a cigarette in Times Square, which he thought "garish and sleazy."

On the Thursday evening, Jennie and he arrived early at the Broadway production of *A Thurber Carnival*. In the lobby, they tried to guess the professions of fellow patrons. One distinguished grey-haired man they took to be an unsuccessful author. Next day they window-shopped at Tiffany's, after which they had lunch with Fred Kerner. In the afternoon, they headed over to the Algonquin Hotel to see the Round Table made famous by, among others, Dorothy Parker and Robert Benchley. They had already had a Dubonnet for lunch. At the Algonquin they ordered gin and tonic. Later, at a seafood restaurant on Third Avenue, they drank a "dreadful" rosé from Ohio. That evening they declared

The Threepenny Opera so dull that they left early, hand in hand, to stroll through Greenwich Village. At the White Horse Tavern, once a favourite drinking spot of Dylan Thomas, they drank a stein each of beer and porter, followed by draft beer in another bar. At a bookstore that was open until 4:00 a.m. they bought two volumes of Irving Layton's poetry, and a book of East Indian recipes.

On Saturday they rode to the top of the Empire State Building, and that evening, they took in *The Miracle Worker* starring Anne Bancroft and a young Patty Duke, playing Helen Keller. Peter declared the play "an evening of wonder." On Sunday morning, they spent an hour at the Metropolitan Museum of Art on Fifth Avenue on the east side of Central Park, where they viewed Rembrandts and El Grecos, as well as Auguste Rodin's *The Thinker*, whose "rippling back" Peter admired at such length that Jennie had to nudge him on. They walked the short distance north to the Guggenheim. Peter declared that only two paintings, a Paul Klee and an Amedeo Modigliani, were worth their time.[10] He dismissed the Guggenheim's collection of Abstract Expressionists as nothing but "great gobs of brown on black and little burned things or bold, bare patterns of primary colors that bored us at a glance."[11] Afterward, they headed for Idlewild Airport. Their taxi driver happened to be the father of Jerry Orbach, one of the stars of *The Threepenny Opera*. Orbach senior labelled Canadians "cheapskate" tippers. Although Peter seems to have enjoyed New York in 1960, eight years later he declared the city rather dull.[12]

Back at his desk at *Maclean's*, Peter continued to work on "Preview." On July 16, he chose to include another article about attempts to ban smoking in public places in Vancouver. Meantime, according to the same "Preview," Canadian Robert Goulet was scheduled to join Richard Burton and Julie Andrews in *Camelot* in October at Toronto's new O'Keefe Centre. One section in "Preview" was called "The Mailbag," which on August 27, 1960, printed a poetic letter whose first two lines, inspired by Joyce Kilmer's "Trees," read "I think that I shall never see / A sadder sight than my MP." It was written by a twenty-one-year-old from Baie-Comeau, Quebec, who signed his name M. Brian Mulroney. He was responding to an article by Peter C. Newman, in which Newman had argued that $10,000 was too low an annual salary for MPs.

During the last four months of 1960, three feature articles by Peter appeared in *Maclean's*. In October, "The Prisoner of Bordeaux," based in part on the book *Scandale à Bordeaux* by Jacques Hébert, focused on Robert Sauvé, a twenty-year-old who had spent three and a half years without trial or treatment in the mental wing of Montreal's Bordeaux Prison, a wing that was infested with cockroaches and rats, and homosexuals who, according to Peter, brazenly committed "unspeakable acts." In the second part of the article, Peter did a short profile of Hébert. After working at *Le Devoir* from 1951 to 1953, Hébert had founded and edited the weekly tabloid *Vrai*, in which he defended underdogs. Hébert concluded that Sauvé's greatest crime was daydreaming. He assembled a committee of nine lawyers, including Frank Scott and Pierre Trudeau,[13] who managed to free Sauvé.[14]

Peter's article, "The Raffish Tradition of the College Football Weekend," appeared in the last issue of *Maclean's* of 1960. Its subject was the championship game of the university football season.[15] In 1960, McGill played against the University of Toronto. Much of the article was written in half-sentences such as "One girl knitting and chewing gum." And "Band comes through leading conga line. Very Scott Fitzgerald … Band leaves. Car grows quiet." Perhaps Peter was attempting to imitate the speaking style of university students. He travelled to Montreal so that he could return to Toronto on a special train with the McGill players and fans. Along for the ride was the McGill soccer team, one of whose members, Peter noted, looked like Robertson Davies, who had just been appointed lecturer at the University of Toronto's Trinity College. As students sang "When the Saints Go Marching In," Peter spotted a politician necking with two students.

Next day, at the pre-game parade, Peter stationed himself behind Claude Bissell, president of the University of Toronto and recently appointed chair of the Canada Council. Immediately in front of Bissell, four soldiers in nineteenth-century uniforms fired an antique cannon. "I hate bangs," Bissell muttered as he moved backward toward Peter, who later slipped over to the Park Plaza for a beer. At the tea dance following the game, photographer Tom Davenport snapped Peter dancing with a baton twirler whom Peter described as "a pretty blonde in blue and white with bare legs and high white boots with tassels."

When the music grew agitated, Peter went home "for dinner." At 1:30 a.m.! "Decide I should have brought my wife," Peter later commented. Obviously, Jennie wasn't amused.

Meantime, the "Preview" of October 22 dealt with topics of great interest to the editor. Would Toronto vote in favour of Sunday movies on Monday, December 5, when the question would be included in the municipal election? The same "Preview" predicted that wealthy golfers would soon be building private clubs, now that golf courses were being inundated by ordinary people. And Native reserves, according to the "Preview" of October 22, would soon be losing their "slummy look" thanks to a government-sponsored housing scheme of mortgages and two-bedroom bungalows easily assembled for $3,000.

With Peter C. Newman, Peter contributed to a four-section report on rising young Canadians. "The Stiffening Spine of a Soft Generation" appeared on March 25, 1961. Among the fourteen successful young people were M. Brian Mulroney and Adrienne Poy, whose short story "Ring Around October" was included. Their generation, Peter noted, suffered from malaise and boredom brought on by too much comfort.

The second week of July, Peter flew north "to tell all our readers what forest fires are," or so he informed Mordecai Richler, who, from London, England, was sending Peter the odd piece for "Preview," including one on the cartoon figure Huckleberry Hound. Richler had also mailed the Gzowskis a used crib. In the shipping, "someone — a Jew, likely — lost the hardware," Peter joked.[16] On September 9, *Maclean's* published Peter's "1961: Summer of the Angry Forest Fires." He described the dramatic progress of a fire near Sioux Lookout in northwestern Ontario. "A fire can cross water," explained Peter, "jump the firelines, cut across its path and kill who or what is standing where the end of its moving blowtorch touches the earth."

In early 1961, "Preview" included an article on Dominion archivist W. Kaye Lamb and the fifty-two miles of history at the National Archives in Ottawa (January 28). There was also a piece on Bruce Kidd, the young runner who was resisting offers to attend an American university (February 25). On March 25, 1961, "Preview" mentioned Bell Telephone's problems with metal slugs replacing nickels at pay phones.

In April the "Background" section published a short piece on art. The University of British Columbia had just purchased a collection of Native art and artifacts for $10,000, and the provincial government had paid the astronomical sum of $70,000 for a collection that included a hundred paintings by Emily Carr. In the issue of June 17, 1961, now that birth control pills for women were coming onto the Canadian market, "Preview" predicted an oral contraceptive for men.

In July, in the "Background" section, Peter reported on a recent survey that found that Quebec teens were far more individualistic than their Anglo counterparts. In August, "Preview" featured an interview by Peter C. Newman with the head of environmental research of Atomic Energy of Canada. Was the disposal of atomic waste a problem? Newman asked. Not really was the answer. In September, "Preview" published Michael Sheldon's tongue-in-cheek article suggesting that all of Canada should speak French and that a new flag should feature a large fleur-de-lis with the Union Jack in one corner. The same "Preview" contained an article with no byline, but it was surely Peter's. A doctor in Windsor, Ontario, had discovered that tolbutamide, a drug for diabetes, reduced the curse of acne. "Though acne neither kills nor cripples," the writer noted, "it can leave mental and physical scars for life."

Peter's last article (November 4) as "Preview" editor was on a Montreal subject. Earlier in 1961, McClelland & Stewart had published William Weintraub's *Why Rock the Boat*, a raucous satire of the newspaper business in Montreal. The reviews were flattering, except in Montreal. What really upset one city editor, even though he admitted that the practice was widespread, was Weintraub's observation that editors often suppressed stories unfavourable to advertisers. Peter liked the novel.

"Preview" had been a good experience for Peter. It showed him how to condense a story and forced him to look for stories of interest to readers. "Preview" may also have provided a model for his radio shows, which usually opened with a short, pithy essay or bulletin, often personal. In feature articles, Peter was developing into a mature writer. While he had begun with articles on *The Varsity* and Sir Casimir Gzowski, as 1961 drew to a close he was casting his net farther afield to catch topics such as prison reform and the rising generation.

—•—

In November 1961, Peter was posted to Montreal as the first Quebec correspondent for *Maclean's*. By that time, *Le Magazine Maclean*,[17] the French-language version of *Maclean's*, founded in the late spring of 1960, was beginning to raise the hackles of Quebec nationalists. It was already clear that the French version wasn't a voice of Quebec, in spite of a top-notch staff that included Pierre de Bellefeuille, Jacques Guay, and André Laurendeau, who was also editor of *Le Devoir*. In August, Premier Jean Lesage called the new magazine a mark of respect for Quebec culture, but pointed out that it wasn't really representative of Quebec culture. Peter's office was on Peel Street, where the French-language version was produced.

A short piece for the entertainment section of *Maclean's* called "The Bike Race That Has More Fans Than the Grey Cup" (December 2, 1961) was Peter's first article written in Montreal. Le Tour du St-Laurent, modelled on Le Tour de France, was in its ninth year. It attracted more than a half-million spectators along the route from Quebec City to Montreal and through the Eastern Townships. It cost about $15,000 annually, and its founder was Yvon Guillou, a Frenchman whose greatest concern was an infestation of performance-enhancing drugs! Almost a year later, in the issue of October 6, 1962, Peter's expanded article on the race appeared in *Maclean's* under the title "Ohé, les Gars du Tour du St-Laurent!" In translation it was published that same month in *Le Magazine Maclean*. Each evening the riders and their fans were entertained by stars such as Dominique Michel, who, Peter pointed out, was the wife of Camille Henry of the New York Rangers. The overall winner of the race was Aleksei Petrov, who, Peter claimed, was as handsome as Bobby Hull.

On December 16, 1961, A.J. Newlands "with Peter Gzowski" penned a feature called "What It's Like to Drive a Buick to Moscow," in which Newlands described a road trip from Great Britain to the Soviet Union where his wife and he were surprised to discover good roads, friendly people, and clean sidewalks. Peter, it seems, edited the article and probably rewrote it.

Soon after the Gzowski family settled into a house on Snowdon Avenue in Notre-Dame-de-Grâce (NDG), Peter took the train to Quebec City to learn French. While Peter's French improved only marginally, he began to understand the resentment created each time that French Canadians/Québécois were forced to listen to and speak English. He concluded that if he had to live in a second language "in order to compete on equal terms with everyone around me," he, too, might become a separatist.[18] The resultant article, told with good humour and humility, was published in *Maclean's* on January 27, 1962.

Peter quickly picked up the currents of change in French-speaking Quebec. In the "Background" section of the December 16, 1961, issue of *Maclean's*, he wrote a short piece called "Why the Separatists Aren't Ready to Separate — Yet." The month before, he had attended a Laval University Conference on Canadian Affairs where panellists André Laurendeau, René Lévesque, and Gérard Pelletier, seated next to Eugene Forsey and Doug Fisher, complained about the absence of bilingualism in Ottawa and the fact that federal government cheques were issued only in English. At one point Lévesque told the young, enthusiastic audience that English Canada needed French Canada more than the latter needed English Canada. While surveys concluded that only a minority of Québécois opted for independence, Peter warned that if grievances were allowed to simmer, more and more French Canadians would support the idea of an independent Quebec.[19] The article was translated and published in *Le Magazine Maclean* in January 1962 as "J'ai découvert les racines du séparatisme."

On February 24, 1962, Peter's "Quebec Report" dealt with the move to secularize education. The leading organization pushing for a more "neutral" education was Mouvement laïque de langue française, composed mostly of francophone parents who were worried that their children were learning too much about the Church and not enough about modern, secular society. To examine the issue, the Lesage government had established a commission. "Things don't change *that* fast in Quebec — even in the 'quiet revolution,'" Peter noted. This was his first printed use of the phrase. The term was in the air, and good listener that he was, he picked it up. Years later he was credited with inventing the phrase, which he denied. It was coined by Brian Upton, a reporter for the *Montreal Star*. After Upton and Peter talked in Montreal in 1961, Peter had absorbed the phrase.[20]

In March 1962, Peter used the term again. Prime Minister John Diefenbaker was perceived by Québécois as unsympathetic to their aspirations. He massacred the French language; he refused to establish a royal commission to study bilingualism; and he didn't appoint a Quebec lieutenant. Peter understood that Diefenbaker failed to understand the Quiet Revolution and the determination of Québécois "to take a full share in Canada's future." Hence, the politician to watch, Peter advised, was Réal Caouette, the leader of the Créditistes, a party that had won safe Liberal seats in the 1958 election and that threatened now to take seats away from the Conservatives. Even though Liberal leader Lester B. Pearson wasn't much more popular in Quebec than Diefenbaker, Peter predicted that, in the next federal election, the Liberals would win as many as sixty seats in the province. He was right. In the federal election of 1962, the Conservatives' huge majority was reduced to a minority, in good part as the result of the rise of the Créditistes. To explain the Créditistes to English Canada, Peter interviewed Caouette. "A Strongman's Road to Power" appeared in *Maclean's* on July 28, 1962. There was no French version in *Le Magazine Maclean*. Quebec already understood the Caouette phenomenon.

For the "Quebec Report" of May 5, entitled "The Astonishing Success Story of French Publishers: Now They Can Make Money on Books They Don't Sell," Peter talked to Jacques Hébert, whose Éditions de l'Homme published bestsellers that were helping to inspire the Quiet Revolution, a term Peter used twice without capitalization in the short article. Hébert's stable of books included Jean-Paul Desbiens's *Les insolences du Frère Untel*, which attacked the public school system run by the Roman Catholic Church; and Marcel Chaput's *Pourquoi je suis séparatiste*.[21] The annual Salon du Livre de Montréal, which had begun modestly in 1959, boasted eighty-eight exhibitors in 1962. Québécois were eager to read about themselves.

In his "Quebec Report" of June 2, 1962, called "GOING: The Supporters of the Separatist Movements," once again Peter predicted the decline of separatism, whose principal leader, Marcel Chaput, was becoming more and more isolated. The previous April, Peter pointed out, *Cité Libre* had devoted an issue to separatism, including an article by Pierre Trudeau, who derided the totalitarian spirit of some separatists, the anti-semitism of others, "and, in all of them, the worship of generalizations and economic incompetence."

On April 7, 1962, in the "Background" section of "Preview," Peter's short piece focused on the St. Lawrence Seaway. In "To Open an Ice-Bound Seaway, Just Blow Bubbles," he discussed the possibility of extending the navigable period of the seaway by using an air compressor to force the warmer bottom layer to mix with the top colder layer, thereby melting some of the ice. On July 28, 1962, Peter's article "Are New Dailies Impossible? *Le Nouveau Journal's* Short, Sharp Life Says Yes" dealt with the demise of a rival to *La Presse*. And on September 8, 1962, his "Progress: Twelve More English Canadians Are Learning French" praised l'Université de Montréal's new course designed to make a dozen anglophones and the same number of francophones bilingual.

Peter also dealt with the arguments for and against the nationalization of hydro companies. On August 11, 1962, he reported that "Lévesque promised to make all of Quebec's power public." Peter predicted that René Lévesque might form a new party of the left. In his last "Quebec Report" (October 20, 1962), Peter continued to deal with the topic of the possible nationalization of eleven hydro companies. The issue was central to the upcoming provincial election, called for November 14. Once again he used the term *quiet revolution*, by now a cliché, he admitted, but an apt one to describe "the change that has swept through every facet of Quebec life from movie censorship to education, from the Church to the daily press, from high finance to the consumption of alcohol." And the mainspring of this change, Peter argued, was the provincial government. Of course, as he pointed out, by reforming the corrupt methods of former Premier Maurice Duplessis, Jean Lesage had denied his Liberals the spoils of office such as liquor licences and road construction contracts. Alienated Liberals, Peter predicted, might turn to Daniel Johnson, leader of the opposition Union Nationale.[22]

It didn't take Peter long to realize that one of the sore points among French-speaking Montrealers was Westmount. In "Westmount," Peter wrote about the wealthy city within a city. The article appeared in *Maclean's* in September 1962, and the month following in *Le Magazine Maclean*, where its title, "Westmount l'immutable," emphasized the seemingly permanent nature of the Protestant-Jewish enclave whose thirty-two thousand residents, less than 1 percent of the population of Quebec, controlled a good portion of the province's economy. Taxes were low, while services and political integrity were high. But don't look for *The Catcher in the Rye* in the Westmount Library, Peter warned, at least not on the open shelves. "It deals with homosexuality," a librarian had quietly explained.

Peter was one of the first English-speaking journalists, perhaps the very first, to write profiles of rising stars such as Pierre Trudeau, newly appointed as a law professor at l'Université de Montréal. In English Canada in 1961, Trudeau wasn't much known. While working on his article on Bordeaux Prison, Peter had encountered Trudeau's name, though perhaps not for the first time, for Trudeau and Blair Fraser had covered the March 1958 federal election for the CBC. Although Peter never wrote about that coverage, he had no doubt watched the results on television in Chatham.[23]

On December 15, 1961, when Peter arrived at the art-filled Outremont home of Grace Trudeau, Pierre poured Peter a triple Scotch while the abstemious law professor opted for mineral water. The resulting article, "Portrait of an Intellectual in Action," shows Peter at his best. The style is lyrical, the research meticulous, and the explanation of the complex nature of Quebec politics impeccable. "In a civilization where the influence of the thinking man is generally confined to his advice on filters for cigarettes," the article began, "Quebec stands out as a place where the intellectual had some part in a recent and vital political victory — the toppling, in June 1960, of the Union Nationale regime." Peter quite correctly gave some of the credit for the victory of Jean Lesage's Liberals to the small group of intellectuals who had been publishing *Cité Libre* throughout the 1950s. He also admired Trudeau's sense of fun, his mischief, his daring. Trudeau had thrown snowballs at Stalin's statue in Moscow in 1952, he had performed a somersault in Shanghai in 1960, and he had once tried to row from Florida to Cuba. Peter wrote that Trudeau enjoyed challenging flawed ideologies such as that of Premier Duplessis, or Quebec nationalism and separatism. Perhaps in some countries, Trudeau explained to Gzowski, separatism was an option, but not in Canada, which for most of the twentieth century had been creating a multinational state. "The hope of mankind," Trudeau added, "lies in multinationalism."[24] The article was published in *Le Magazine Maclean* as "Un capitaliste socialisant: Pierre-Elliott Trudeau." In English, Trudeau's intellectual qualities were underlined by the title; in French the contradiction in ideologies was more important.

Peter's third profile of an important figure in the Quiet Revolution was called "The Cardinal and His Church in a Year of Conflict." Published on July 14, 1962, it dealt with Cardinal Paul-Émile Léger and the changing role of the Catholic Church in the new Quebec. Peter knew how to hook the reader. "The French and Catholic people of Quebec," the article began, "in their by now famous quiet revolution, are changing faster than any group of people on this continent." One of the leaders of this change was the archbishop of Montreal, Cardinal Léger, who was supported by bishops in Ottawa and Quebec City but opposed by bishops in Quebec's smaller cities. To advise him, Peter pointed out, the cardinal had surrounded himself with bright, well-educated young priests who were connected with universities and the labour movement. While he wasn't in favour of dissolving the Church's role in education, Léger encouraged greater lay participation. The article won Best Magazine Article of the Year. As usual Peter was prescient. Only decades later did historians understand how the Quiet Revolution marked "a sustained attempt to enhance and strengthen, rather than weaken and ultimately sever, the relationship between Catholicism and Quebec society."[25]

While living in Montreal, Peter also wrote about non-Quebec topics, including a couple of short pieces on television. On April 7, 1962, he turned to a medical topic of relevance to him. In "Why Doctors Now Study Your Mind to Treat Your Body," Peter wrote about psychosomatic medicine, which was a new approach to healing the body by treating the mind. Accidents, some doctors claimed, can be caused by inner turmoil, and so, too, venereal disease. Peter explained that "indiscriminate promiscuity is symptomatic of emotional disorder and therefore VD has clear psychic components." And "diseases of the skin," he added, "provide the most straightforward examples of the psychosomatic effect." He quoted a doctor who claimed that "eczema is a disease which occurs in emotionally insecure individuals."

Two weeks later *Maclean's* carried Peter's "The New Women in Politics," a study of Judy LaMarsh and Pauline Jewett, two rising females. On August 11, 1962, Peter's topic was John Turner, a "man to watch." In the federal election of June 18, 1962, the thirty-three-year-old bachelor, who had danced with Princess Margaret in 1958, had won the Montreal riding of St-Laurent–St-Georges. Turner would, Peter predicted, be a candidate for prime minister "sometime after 1970." Peter's last feature article written and published while in Montreal (*Maclean's*, November 17, 1962) was focused on Canada's young athletes such as Harry Jerome and Bruce Kidd, who would soon be competing in the next Commonwealth Games in Australia.

Peter liked Montreal immensely, he told Mordecai Richler, but was getting tired of saying so. While he didn't like Montreal smoked meat, Peter informed Richler that he was fond of chopped liver and fresh bread, as well as Quebec's gallon jugs of wine, which helped him, he joked, "to stay drunk all the time." Peter may even deserve some of the credit (or blame) for Richler's articles and books critical of Quebec nationalism. While it was Richler's idea to write something trenchant about Quebec, it was Peter who encouraged the idea. "Whyinhell," he wrote to Richler on December 15, 1961, "don't you write a piece called Why I don't like French Canadians?"

During his year in Montreal, Peter revelled in the freedoms of the lively, cosmopolitan city. Since the Montreal International Film Festival, founded in 1960, wasn't allowed to cut films, according to agreements with the films' international directors, the festival helped to change censorship laws in the province. One night, at 1:00 a.m., Peter was able to view an uncut version of François Truffaut's *Jules et Jim*. The city's bar scene was vibrant, too. One weekend Cathy Perkins, on assignment with *Chatelaine*, joined Peter for dinner, after which they drifted into a bar where the great rock-and-roller Bo Diddley was performing. With the

A tender moment shared by Peter and his daughter, Alison, in 1964 as captured by photographer Lutz Dille.

(Courtesy National Gallery of Canada, Ottawa)

filmmaker Donald Brittain, Peter attended horse races at Blue Bonnets Raceway.[26] While Peter explored, observed, and wrote, Jennie was at home tending to three preschool children: three-year-old Peter C.; two-year-old Alison; and Maria, born in August 1961.

Like most of his articles published in *Maclean's*, the score or more articles written while Peter was Quebec editor are as relevant today as they were when he first wrote them. They are among the best portraits in English about the province/*pays*/*nation* during its Quiet Revolution. Peter's only challenger for the title of best anglophone eye on the rising Quebec was Scott Symons, who had already written extensively in French in *La Presse* about the post-Duplessis political and cultural revolution he had witnessed between the autumn of 1960 and the summer of 1961.[27]

Having gained that insight into Quebec, Peter considered writing a book about the province. He signed a contract, and once back in Toronto, carried out more research. The book was never published, and probably never written beyond an introduction. A good thing, too, for it is his *Maclean's* articles, so lyrical, so insightful and sensitive, that have stood the test of time.[28]

— 5 —

"You're Taking Too Much Goddamn Time,"[1] 1962–1964

Journalists become ordinary when they decide that the job isn't hard....
All his life, [Peter] had the courage, and the wisdom, to be scared.

— *Robert Fulford in Edna Barker, ed.,*
Remembering Peter Gzowski: A Book of Tributes

So successful was Peter as the Quebec editor that upon his return to Toronto the magazine's editor, Ken Lefolii, who had replaced Blair Fraser in July 1962, appointed Peter managing editor. At twenty-eight he was the youngest person to reach that important position. According to Harry Bruce, he was often brutal and sarcastic. When the magazine's journalists sat around a long table trading story ideas, the red-rimmed eyes of the managing editor remained expressionless. As more and more ideas were thrown out for discussion, Peter would silently push his hand through "his lank hair" and look sideways. A "shadow of distaste would cross his pock-marked face." Nevertheless, like most journalists who ever worked for Peter, Bruce deemed the new managing editor the best he ever knew, for he created a "yeasty office spirit" that brought out the best in writers.[2]

One of Peter's tasks was to solicit articles. On December 16, 1962, he wrote a newsy letter to Mordecai Richler. Peter wanted to hire Richler to do a regular television column for *Maclean's*, perhaps at $150 per piece, with a guarantee of twenty columns per year. *Maclean's* managing editor also thought he would be able to buy several of Richler's feature articles. Richler talked to Peter about going to Warsaw to do a story, and Peter encouraged him, for in that city lived several members of the Canadian Communist Party, including Fred Rose. The article might also deal with the intellectual and artistic life in Warsaw, Peter suggested, and he urged Richler to "come down pretty hard" on it. Too much of Canada's writing, Peter added, was the product of three men: Hugh MacLennan, Bruce Hutchison, and Pierre Berton. Canadian letters needed Richler's hard-hitting style. Meantime, he confessed to Richler that, after only a month back in Toronto, the city was getting him down. He would much prefer the Laurentian Mountains or anywhere else where he could write what he wanted to write and not have to spend his day purchasing pencils and "goosing the secretaries" at *Maclean's*.[3]

Richler was considering a move to Toronto. Finding a suitable home might be a problem, Peter warned, especially in downtown Toronto, though he and Jennie had managed to rent a three-storey house at 16 Washington Avenue, a short street running between Spadina Avenue and Huron Street, one block south of Bloor. All twenty-one houses on the street were owned by a man described by Peter as "one old kook" who was using several of them for storage. Once the "kook" discovered that Peter was a member of an old Toronto family (Peter must have told him!), and that he could afford to pay $175 per month for rent, he cleared out number 16.[4] Unfortunately for Jennie, the "son of a bitch" (Peter's phrase) failed to keep his promise to fix up the house, and Jennie had to scrape off old wallpaper. The "unhandiest man in town," as Peter described himself to Richler, was free to explore the area, which included the rooftop bar at the Park Plaza. He concluded his letter to Richler by announcing that it was time to go home. To help Jennie mind the children? No, to watch a football game. He sounds selfish, but Peter wasn't untypical of husbands, fathers, and bosses of the period.

Peter's year in Montreal had left a lasting impression. Although he was back in Toronto, his mind and heart remained in Canada's only cosmopolitan city at that time. His first feature article after his return was called "How I Nearly Learned to Ski in a Week," published in December 1962. The article reported on his attempt to learn to ski at Mont Tremblant. The first time that Peter fell, his sunglasses and, even worse, his cigarettes went skittering down the slope. Nevertheless, his powers of observation were keen. Young women wore stretch pants so tight that "if the girl has a dime in her hip pocket, you could tell if it was heads or tails." The French translation of the article, "Comment j'ai failli apprendre à faire du ski," appeared in *Le Magazine Maclean* in January 1963.

On April 6, 1963, *Maclean's* published Peter's "Young *Canadiens* Speak Their Mind." To research the article, Peter had returned to Montreal where he observed a panel discussion chaired by Gérard Pelletier. Ranging in age from mid-twenties to mid-thirties, the panellists were all federalists who demanded changes in the Canadian political system. Businssman Robert Demers predicted that French would soon become the language of business in Quebec. On English Canadians, journalist Jean David announced that he would be "bored to death to be an English Canadian." Madeleine Gobeil, a close friend of Pierre Trudeau, asserted that *les Anglais* were really not "good conversationalists."

In "Conversations with Quebec's Revolutionaries," an examination of the province's youthful and angry nationalists and separatists (*Maclean's*, September 7, 1963), Peter expressed surprise at the increased intensity of Quebec nationalism. Men such as Jean Lesage, Gérard Pelletier, René Lévesque, Léon Dion, and André Laurendeau, who had unleashed the Quiet Revolution only a few years earlier, were losing control. "It is now an inescapable fact," Peter wrote, "that we are headed toward separation into two countries." Accompanying the article was a second and shorter piece, unattributed but probably written by Peter, on the subject of five members of the Front de libération du Québec (FLQ), all charged with setting off bombs. The five — Gabriel Hudon, a designer; Yves Labonté, a salesman; Eugénio Pilote, a proofreader; and students Alain Brouillard and Mario Bachand — argued that violence was the only way to liberate Quebec.[5] As usual Peter had sensed the temper of the times and had written about it honestly.

Maclean's devoted an issue, that of November 2, 1963, to the question of Quebec nationalism and independence. Peter's article, "This Is the True Strength of Separatism," was based on the first-ever poll on the subject.[6] The previous summer he had helped to conduct the survey of a thousand people, 13 percent of whom had opted for independence, either through a referendum or by nominating separatist candidates in the next provincial election.[7] When asked which provincial politician most favoured separatism, most of those polled named René Lévesque, minister of natural resources in the Lesage government.

Peter also contributed short pieces to *Maclean's* on topics such as reactions in Quebec against the Quiet Revolution, especially against the anticlericalism promoted by *Cité Libre* and Mouvement laïque de langue française. His last short piece in the magazine appeared on October 17, 1964. In "Open Letter to French-Canadian Nationalists," Peter described his frustration at the ongoing political crisis in Canada. He was no longer so sympathetic, he admitted, to the constant stridency in Quebec. After all, he pointed out, French Canada had already won its revolution, and English Canada was now paying attention. On the other hand, French Canada seemed unwilling to listen to English Canada. "Virtually anything you can do in Quebec," Peter concluded, "short of killing people, can be done with the sympathy of at least a sizeable body of English Canadian opinion."[8] The open letter was translated and published in *Le Magazine Maclean* in November 1964. No one, least of all Peter, could have predicted that six years later those four words, "short of killing people," would take on new meaning.

As well as Quebec, Peter was interested in its neighbour, Labrador. In the November 2, 1963, issue of *Maclean's*, Peter's article "New Soft Life on the Last Frontier" compared the old and new Labrador. In Wabush, which was only three years old, Peter could enjoy an extra-dry martini on the rocks, snails, pea soup, beef tenderloin with mushrooms, fresh bread, and Mexican corn, all washed down by a bottle of Beaujolais. Wabush's malls, restaurants, and new houses made it no less comfortable, Peter thought, than the suburbs of any Canadian city. He and photographer Don Newlands stayed at the Sir Wilfred Grenfell Hotel where the hostess was "curvy" and the waitresses "pretty." The standard of living among construction men and miners was much better than it had been a decade earlier when Peter had worked on the railway from Sept-Îles into Labrador. In 1963, when Peter visited the company cafeteria, he discovered an appealing menu of fried chicken legs, corn on the cob, fresh bread, and ice cream. Nevertheless, the working men still had to put up with monotony and isolation and long days of work. "Life in the camps of the north," Peter wrote, "has some things in common with the life of Ivan Denisovich," the Siberian prisoner in Alexander Solzhenitsyn's newly translated novel *One Day in the Life of Ivan Denisovich.*

In the next issue, that of November 16, Peter wrote about the Quebec, North Shore, and Labrador Railway, in "Journey Down the Railway That Couldn't Be Built." Once Don Newlands and Peter had concluded their visit to Wabush, they travelled south from Labrador City to Sept-Îles on the railway Peter had helped to build. En route, he talked to the dining-car steward, a North Shore old-timer, who recalled the boom years of Sept-Îles in the 1950s when the construction companies found it next to impossible to keep women working in cafeterias and offices because prostitution paid so well. It was a sentimental journey, and Peter marvelled at the convenience of travelling southward at fifty miles per hour. "What a pleasure to be able to stretch back on a railway carriage seat," he noted in his best lyrical, romantic style, "and enjoy the scenery of a country whose beauty I had forgotten, first in the monotony and discomfort of camp life and then in the city years between."

Peter also continued to be keenly interested in the Canadian West, particularly Saskatchewan, where the NDP government of Woodrow Lloyd, successor to Premier Tommy Douglas, was defeated in the spring of 1964. Soon thereafter, Peter was in Regina to examine reasons for the defeat of a party that had pioneered state-supported hospital insurance and Medicare, and that in the 1940s and 1950s had created what was arguably the best-trained bureaucracy in Canada. Peter's "Report from the Changing Heartland of Canada," published in *Maclean's* on July 25, 1964, remains one of the most insightful articles on the province during the two decades from 1944, when Douglas was first elected premier, to 1964, when Ross Thatcher's Liberals gained power. Peter met most of the important architects of the CCF revolution, including Tommy

McLeod, who, along with Tommy Shoyama,[9] had helped to make the Douglas government the most innovative of its day. In 1956, in order to investigate agriculture and rural life, sociologist W.B. Baker had set up a royal commission, which, according to Peter, was the model for the federal government's Royal Commission on Biculturalism and Bilingualism, established in 1963. Peter admitted that, over time, the superb bureaucracy had grown too large, and voters had begun to feel that the right thing was being done for them "whether they liked it or not."

When Peter visited Saskatchewan in 1964, he was surprised to discover cocktail bars that hadn't existed in 1957, and he dined at three restaurants in Saskatoon and Regina that ranked with the best, in his estimation, in Toronto.[10] In a drugstore, he bought two copies of *Fanny Hill*, a novel that was banned in Ontario. He liked the handsome new Regina headquarters of the Saskatchewan Power Corporation, a building whose curvilinear form was an architectural wonder then, and he marvelled at the Wascana project, which, under the direction of internationally acclaimed landscape architect Minoru Yamasaki, would become, Peter predicted, an international showpiece. On Wascana Park, and so much else, Peter was more than astute. On a flat plain, Yamasaki was creating one of Canada's most attractive urban parks.

Natives of the Prairies drew Peter's attention, too. His *Maclean's* editorial on July 6, 1963, "Last Chance to Head Off a Showdown with the Canadian Indian," was a preamble to his feature in the same issue on discrimination and violence against Natives in Saskatchewan. In May 1963, a Saulteaux named Allan Thomas had been murdered in a village north of North Battleford. Most of the murderers were ordinary farmers and businessmen. "This is Canada's Alabama," Peter contended, and trouble was brewing. "If Canada can afford to spend $70 million on foreign aid," he argued, "we can afford to spend a small fraction more to prevent giving to the West and to ourselves another list of Birminghams and Little Rocks."[11] Once again, Peter was on the cutting edge, and it would take more than a few years for journalists and academics to catch up to him.

On May 2, 1964, under the title "Portrait of a Beautiful Segregationist," Peter wrote the first of a two-part feature on the Native activist Kahn-Tineta Horn, a beautiful twenty-two-year-old model who worked in

Montreal and lived on the Caughnawaga Reserve near that city. Horn was one of the first leaders to emerge from the Native community, and Peter was one of the first journalists to write about her. In speeches she scoffed at the so-called superiority of Western civilization. In "How Kahn-Tineta Horn Became an Indian," the second part of the article, published in the May 16, 1964, issue, Peter sketched a history of the Caughnawaga Mohawks and how the Horn family fitted into that chronicle.[12]

In March 1957, when Peter was heading for Moose Jaw, Cathy Breslin had claimed that he could regale an audience by describing a trip to the dry cleaners. In *Maclean's* of April 20, 1963, under the pseudonym Peter N. Allison, the names of his two eldest children, Peter entertained his readers by writing about a catalogue. His "Life in Eaton's Catalogue, or How I Wrestled My Uncle Ernest in My Medium-Weight Thermal Underwear" dealt with a catalogue that was first published in 1884 and that by the 1960s had grown to 40 million copies per annum, resulting in about fifty thousand orders each weekday. Peter loved the "slick, glossy handsomeness of the cover" and even the "sweet, and somehow secure" smell of a new catalogue. In these catalogues, Peter glimpsed Canadian identity: since their inception, Eaton's catalogues had always reflected "our way of life," and the products that they advertised, Peter argued, had helped to build Canada.

He concluded with a flight of fancy. Peter imagined that Jennie and he, along with his Uncle Ernest, were trapped at exactly 8:18 a.m. in Eatonia where they were doomed to play the role of catalogue models, including the two men who were dressed in thermal underwear, their right hands locked together in a test of strength. His fiction was a satire on the catalogue and the department store, both of which created the illusion that customers, if they ordered the items worn by beautiful models, could also achieve perfection and happiness. Even the images on the catalogue's television screens, Peter pointed out, were too perfect, as if someone had airbrushed the horizontal lines of black-and-white television sets during the 1960s. "It is still 8:18 as I write this and address it to Eaton's," he concluded. "What I want them to tell me is: How do I get out of here?"¹³ Although the imaginative world of Eatonia was told with humour, the ending strongly suggests Peter's discomfort with the increasingly materialistic world of the 1960s.

In magazine writing, and later during his radio career, Peter could move adeptly from the light-hearted to the serious. A month after his Eatonia article, he turned to the weighty business of crime and murder. On May 18, 1963, his topic was Hal Banks, "Canada's Waterfront Warlord." It was a brave article, for Banks, a notorious union leader, was known to employ violent tactics to maintain his iron grip on the Seafarers' International Union, and wasn't above knocking off an unsympathetic journalist or two. Under the title "Hal Banks, le héros des marins, un homme à battre?" the article appeared in *Le Magazine Maclean* in July 1963.

The *Maclean's* issue of September 21, 1963, saw Peter return to a lighter topic when his notes on the subject of the third annual Mariposa Folk Festival in Orillia, Ontario, were published under the title "Where the Boys *and* Girls Go." The fifteen thousand residents of Orillia were overwhelmed by the twenty thousand fans, including motorcyclists wearing black jackets, who had descended on the town made famous by Stephen Leacock. "This year's festival was a blast, man," Peter commented.

Two months later Peter was in a restaurant in Toronto when a waiter brought the news of the assassination of John F. Kennedy. He returned home to watch the terrible news with Jennie. When Peter C. returned from kindergarten, he found his father weeping. "I wonder if he remembers that that was the first time he saw his father weep," Peter later mused in a radio essay on *This Country in the Morning* on the tenth anniversary of Kennedy's death. "And I wonder if he can remember how I tried to explain to him why I was doing that.... I guess there are two things that I hope for the son who saw me weep that day," Peter added. "The first is that he will understand why. And the second is that if something should happen to him, the way it happened to all of us, that he will weep, too, and survive."¹⁴ Peter rarely revealed his tender, more vulnerable side in public.

In 1964, Peter's topics ranged from the national anthem to spectator sports. He argued, in an editorial on the search for a Canadian national anthem and a distinctive flag, against political correctness in old Canadian songs such as "The Maple Leaf Forever," whose lyrics were demeaning to French Canada. "Trying to rewrite one old song," he wrote, "is scarcely different from trying to rewrite the history from which it sprang." He thought that "O Canada" would do as a national anthem, provided that only the music was played, which would give sports fans a chance "to give silent thanks that we live in a land where everyone can pay homage to God *and* country the way he wants to."[15]

Spectator sports, from hockey to horse racing, sprinting, boxing, soccer, and lacrosse, were never far from Peter's mind. In 1964 he wrote about a dozen short pieces for the sports section of *Maclean's*. On February 22, 1964, his topic was racing: Northern Dancer was a promising, young racehorse in the stable of E.P. Taylor; and Bruce Kidd had just been beaten by an Australian at Maple Leaf Gardens.[16] For the April 4, 1964, issue, Peter wrote about watching the world championship boxing match between Sonny Liston and Cassius Clay on large-screen television. Peter wasn't amused. "Like wrestling," he wrote, "boxing will undoubtedly go on for a while, but I for one no longer care *who* is supposed to be the champ." The second part of the article dealt with the Vancouver sprinter, Harry Jerome, who, after several injuries and disappointments, was training for the Tokyo Olympics later in 1964. On July 25, 1964, Peter's topic was Canadian soccer — its rise in the Toronto of the 1880s, and its decline after the Second World War when Anglo-Saxon fans deserted the game. On August 22, he wrote about lacrosse in "How the Indians Are Leading One More Comeback for Our First National Sport." He predicted, correctly, that the sport would gradually attract more players and fans.

Peter was almost constantly in touch by cable and letter with Mordecai Richler. In early December 1963, he welcomed Richler's promise of a piece on highbrow clichés. Peter promised to include it in the "Argument" section of the yellows, and to pay Richler the standard $200 for any short piece. Two weeks later Peter announced to Richler that Jennie was pregnant with their fourth child. Before folding the letter, he stamped it with his special insignia, which he may have used, in the style of Ralph Allen, when condemning inferior work by his staff. The stamp read HORSE SHIT.[17]

On February 4, 1964, Peter told Richler that his piece on highbrow clichés probably wasn't, after all, right for *Maclean's*, though the final decision would be made by Ken Lefolii.[18] Peter answered a series of questions posed by Richler on the subject of prizes given for first novels, and also those awarded by the Quebec government for literature and political science. He assured Richler that he, Peter, was "not an active homsexual" [*sic*] but he refused to speculate on Nathan Cohen, Robert Fulford, Ken Lefolii, and Jack McClelland.[19]

Peter also kept in touch with W.O. Mitchell, one-time fiction editor of *Maclean's* and a continuing freelance contributor. In early March 1964, while visiting Toronto, W.O met Peter at an upscale bar. On March 11, 1964, once back in High River, Mitchell wrote to Peter asking if he could recall what story ideas were discussed. Mitchell was pretty certain that one of the pieces was to be entitled "How to Stop Smoking by Really Trying." The novelist promised to stay off martinis while writing the pieces.[20]

Clashes between owners and managers of magazines and newspapers, on the one hand, and editors and journalists on the other, occur from time to time. In late July 1964, claiming editorial interference, editor Ken Lefolii resigned from *Maclean's*. The dispute had been simmering for months, and Peter claimed it was one of his articles that had first riled management the previous March.[21] In "Maple Leaf Money Machine," published in *Maclean's* on March 21, 1964, Peter had quoted coach "Punch" Imlach. Instead of printing *fucking*, one of the coach's favourite words, Peter and Ken Lefolii had replaced the first four letters with a long dash. When Gerry Brander, the magazine's publisher, objected, Peter and Lefolii agreed on "— —," which fooled no one. In June 1964, when Ronald McEachern was hired as Maclean-Hunter's vice-president, tensions increased. McEachern and Brander decided not to publish an article by Harry Bruce about how a group of journalists had tried to circumvent a Toronto newspaper strike by printing, on their own, the three newspapers affected by the strike. McEachern pulled the article without consulting either Bruce or Lefolii.

Lefolii told the *Globe and Mail* that the cancellation was the last straw. No longer, Lefolii argued, was quality the most important criterion. Bruce's article was the third to be disputed.[22] According to Bruce today, his article may have been used by McEachern as an excuse to force the resignation of Lefolii, who had a way of rubbing management the wrong way. Although Lefolii knew that Floyd Chalmers, chairman of Maclean-Hunter Publishing Company Limited, preferred to be addressed as "Mr. Chalmers," Lefolii always addressed him as just plain "Floyd."

Nor was tact one of McEachern's strong points. On July 31, during a meeting with Bruce, Fulford, and Gzowski, as well as David Lewis Stein and Barbara Moon, McEachern called the yellow pages, of which Bruce was the editor, mere "filler." "I don't write fillers," the usually quiet Bruce blurted out, much to the surprise of Peter and the other journalists at the table.[23] At the same meeting Chalmers announced that, in order to attract more subscribers and advertising revenue, the company had no option but to please the reading public as well as the business community. "We are not running a Canada Council," lectured Chalmers. In other words, Maclean-Hunter couldn't continue to subsidize the money-losing magazine.

The dispute simmered into August. During the height of the crisis, McEachern, a short, stocky man with hair slicked back, and short, quick steps, tore out of Lefolii's office. He turned left, then left again, straight into the women's washroom. Wheeling around, he made a left turn and finally found the door to the stairs.[24]

"On the Friday before Labour Day, 1964," Peter wrote in *The Private Voice*, after he, Fulford, Moon, Stein, and Bruce had handed in letters of resignation, they ordered "a jeroboam"[25] of champagne. In Ralph Allen's old office, they posed for a camera, drank the contents of the bottle, smashed their glasses, and staggered up University Avenue to the roof bar of the Park Plaza.[26]

The imbroglio at *Maclean's* drew the attention of Edmund Wilson, the eminent American literary critic, thanks to a meeting, chance or otherwise, in the rooftop bar of the Park Plaza with Peter. In *O Canada*, his book on Canadian culture, published in 1965, Wilson chastised management and noted that "Mr. Gzowski and his associates succeeded in transforming *Maclean's* … into an outstanding journalistic achievement."[27]

The following October, Peter embellished his own role in the mass resignation. In *Canadian Forum*, his article "The Time the Schick Hit the Fan and Other Adventures at *Maclean's*" claimed that his piece about Punch Imlach the previous March had mentioned briefly that "Sixteen Leafs … recently lined up for a certain razor-blade ad — and got their fifty dollars each without even having to shave with one blade." He hadn't named the razor-blade company in question, but it was pretty obvious that it was Schick. Although the company didn't advertise in *Maclean's*, the article had put it off, and it threatened that it might never buy ad space in the magazine.

In the *Canadian Forum* article, Peter praised Ken Lefolii for never soliciting "the unadulterated support of advertisers."[28] Peter liked to think that his own resignation kept him aloof from corporate interference. Thus he preserved the mythology that he was a "competitive, self-contained actor who was quite immune to the contaminations of commercial, political, or even personal pressure." (Of course, how seriously dare one take the *Canadian Forum* piece? A few years later, in February 1970, when he testified before the Davey Commission on the mass media in Canada, Peter informed Senator Keith Davey that the *Canadian Forum* article had been meant in jest.)[29] In reality, Peter himself always followed the unspoken rule that a magazine, or later, his early radio shows, had to respect its corporate sponsors. All magazines, and all CBC Radio shows up to the mid-1970s, needed as much advertising revenue as they could find. Years later, Peter welcomed sponsorship money for his charity golf tournaments.

In December 1965, when he addressed journalism students at Memorial University in St. John's, Peter slammed both management interference and journalistic hypocrisy. Since publishers were, he claimed, members of the Canadian Establishment, *Maclean's* would never criticize Sam Bronfman, for fear of alienating Seagram's. Any sportswriter, he told them, who wrote the truth about Carl Brewer's resignation from the Maple Leafs earlier that year — that he "hates the guts of 'Punch' Imlach" — would never be allowed back into the hockey club's dressing room.[30] A few days later Peter joined Robert Fulford at the annual conference of

Canadian University Press (CUP) at the University of Alberta. No, he told reporters, he wouldn't speak about his resignation. However, he did lash out at reporters for self-censorship and at the power of the press. Even Peter C. Newman and Blair Fraser, he told reporters, had become too intimate with the Ottawa establishment. The headline over the article, as published in the *Toronto Star*, announced "Press Said Confused, Trivial,"[31] which sounds like Peter's own words.

Peter's last feature in *Maclean's* in 1964, though written no doubt before the mass resignation, was published on September 19, after Borden Spears was appointed executive director, a position that incorporated Lefolii's and Gzowski's old positions of editor and managing editor respectively. Peter's subject was golf. To write "Arnie Recruits His Canadian Army," Peter had returned to Montreal in late July to watch Arnold Palmer compete in the Canadian Open. During a pre-game practice, Peter joined "Arnie's Army," Palmer's numerous fans who followed the golfer from hole to hole. There were so many movie cameras, Peter complained, that they sounded "like a flight of swallows on a summer evening." He was vexed that one of those home movie cameras had captured an image of him. By 1964, Palmer had become such a mythological figure that Peter had difficulty realizing he was watching the flesh-and-blood player. Even when Palmer failed to win the Open that year, he graciously signed autographs. Palmer was Peter's ideal sportsman — skillful *and* magnanimous.

Unlike Palmer, Peter never learned to lose magnanimously. His competitiveness was so intense, Harry Bruce recalled shortly after Peter's death, that it verged on the offensive. Peter simply had to win, Bruce explained, whether at soccer, tennis, shooting baskets, liar's poker at the rooftop bar of the Park Plaza, handball, snooker, chess, Chinese checkers, Monopoly, poker, bridge, and all other card games. He smelled of ambition, as well as of cigarettes and brandy.[32]

Peter loved to win bar games played with Dennis Murphy, Susan Musgrave, Diana LeBlanc, and others. "Gzowski (or perhaps his estate) still owes me $320 for several backgammon victories at speakeasies around Toronto," Murphy once recalled. "He hated to lose and proved it by seldom paying debts." Peter had a baseball board game at the family home. Because he knew the game inside out, he always trounced Dennis, who grew to loathe the game.[33]

Each year staff members at Maclean-Hunter enjoyed a golf tournament. Rather than playing against par, players were paired off in match play, a bit like a tennis tournament. The event was staged over several weeks. One year, one of Peter's opponents was John Millyard, an editor of one of Maclean-Hunter's trade magazines. During the first nine holes on a course north of Toronto, Millyard had the edge. Peter wasn't amused, but he was certain to catch up and win.

On the eleventh or twelfth hole Peter hooked his ball into trees to the left of the fairway. The ball was lost, so Peter, following the rules of the game, hit a provisional tee shot. Now Peter was behind on this hole.[34] In silence the two men walked up the fairway to hit their next shots. Millyard addressed the ball for his second shot.

"You're taking too much goddamn time!" Peter shouted.

Millyard made another good shot. Peter hit his provisional ball fairly well down the fairway. The two men were now lying Millyard two, Gzowski four.

Peter disappeared into the woods. Was nature calling? A few minutes later he emerged, waving a ball he claimed to be the lost one. He announced that he was going to take a drop outside the woods for one stroke and play the lost ball instead of the provisional ball. Millyard knew that if the original ball had indeed been found, the rules for match play clearly stated that the ball had to be played from the point where it had come to rest, deep inside the woods.

"Now I'm lying three not four," Peter announced.

"But you've already played the provisional ball for your fourth shot," Millyard protested. "You can't revert to the first ball. The game has rules, you know."

Peter's face turned crimson. Once again he swore at Millyard, who quickly decided that discretion was indeed the better part of valour. So he let Peter break the rule. Peter lost, anyway. There was no post-game drink.

Always the novelist or short-story writer, a couple of years later, in one of his sports pieces in *Saturday Night*, Peter fictionalized the match.

"Peter" was working for "a large company" at the time. "All employees who played golf," he wrote, "had the day off in the spring, and the sixteen low medalists in that round then entered on a summer-long series of elimination matches." Suddenly, Peter's imagination kicked in. He had made it to the finals. John Millyard became "Good Old Charlie," a "nice fellow" from the accounting department. After fourteen holes, Peter had him four down. "All I had to do, in other words, was *tie* one of the remaining holes and I was the winner, the champion." Peter could taste victory. He imagined himself "humbly accepting the President's Trophy." However, on the nineteenth hole, Charlie sank a long putt to win the match.[35] In the fictionalized version, Peter's language is pure. Throughout the remainder of the summer, "Jennie," another character in the story, often awoke in the middle of the night to find "Peter" pantomiming his swing in front of a bedroom mirror. At other times "Jennie" was awakened by Peter's tossing and writhing as he mumbled, "Miss it, Charlie, miss it, Charlie."

"Oh, well," the real John Millyard reflected years later, "journalists are all — and I include myself — grave robbers and vultures who swallow experiences and regurgitate them in another form for fun and profit."[36]

Ironically, a few years later, Peter included "Ten Rules for Playing Golf" in *Peter Gzowski's Book About This Country in the Morning*. A good player never talks when others are hitting; nor does he cheat, for "golf is a game of honour." And by the way, Peter advised, a golfer should always enjoy himself.

On July 8, 1964, Harry Bruce turned thirty, and five days later, so did Peter. To celebrate what they called FOTT, the Festival of Turning Thirty, they began their toasts on the eighth and drank booze "harder than ever for five days in a row."[37] Also in 1964, the brilliant photographer Lutz Dille captured a more sober Peter in an intimate moment with his daughter, Alison, who peers over a banister at her father as he reaches up to touch her (see page 106). Peter's affection is palpable. It was a tenderness that he rarely, if ever, revealed in the corridors and offices of that impregnable concrete building at 481 University Avenue, the headquarters of the Maclean-Hunter empire.

— 6 —

A Sharp Eye on the World of Entertainment, 1964–1967

Canadians think like people who want, usually in vain,
all international sayings to end with a point about Canadians.

— Peter Gzowski, "The Global Village Has Everything
but Surprises," Saturday Night, *December 1968*

Ron McEachern, a man of few compliments, got it right when he called Borden Spears distinguished, professional, and intelligent.[1] Soon after taking command of *Maclean's*, Spears hired Peter as his television reviewer. No doubt Spears had noted Peter's interest in television, beginning when he was the Quebec editor for *Maclean's*. On January 27, 1962, Peter had examined a new technique that allowed Hungarian-born cartoonist George Feyer to draw cartoons from behind a screen, which allowed him to be invisible. His cartoons appeared to create themselves. In the entertainment section of *Maclean's* on March 10, 1962, Peter was vexed at the Canadian-content regulations imposed by the Board of Broadcast Governors (BBG). Because Canadian television was forced to show a certain number of hours of Canadian content, networks simply created mind-numbing quiz shows. Again, in the February 23, 1963, issue of *Maclean's*, in a review called "The Carnies on the Picture Tube,"[2] Peter blamed the BBG for the fact that much of the Canadian content on television was junk. In 1962, even Radio-Canada, Peter pointed out, was following BBG regulations with silly game shows such as *La Poule aux oeufs d'or.*

In the television section of "*Maclean's* Reviews" of March 9, 1963, Spears would also have seen Peter's review of the CBC Television show *Inquiry*, which he deemed the network's best public affairs show. Even after Peter resigned from the magazine, *Maclean's* published one of his television reviews, no doubt written before the mass resignation. Spears may have been scrambling to assemble his first issue, and, of course, he knew that Peter wrote astute reviews. In the September 1964 issue, Peter expressed surprise and disappointment that television had turned the Canadian Open into a dull experience. During the first part of the golf tournament, Peter had followed the players along the fairways of the Pinegrove Country Club near Montreal. To watch the final rounds, he located a television set. He was greatly disappointed. "One of my favorite sequences," Peter wrote sarcastically, "has the camera following a ball after it has been driven — up, up into the air and then bouncie, bouncie, as it rolls along the grass. What this is supposed to illustrate, I can't imagine." You would think, he wrote, that after so many years of broadcasting the game on television, "the networks would have learned a little about how to make golf interesting."[3]

Although Spears didn't hesitate to hire Peter,[4] he thought it best that his reviewer remain anonymous. Henceforth he was known as "Strabo," the Greek geographer who lived at the time of Christ. Peter claimed, perhaps incorrectly, that the name meant "squinter."[5] In any case, "Strabo" suited Peter's role as someone who squinted at a television screen in order to see around and behind the images presented on that screen.

Strabo's first television review appeared on February 6, 1965. In "TV's '7 Days' — Not a Gem in All That Muck," Strabo came down hard on the CBC's *This Hour Has Seven Days*, a current affairs show broadcast live each Sunday evening during the mid-1960s. *This Hour*, deemed Strabo, was raking muck for the sake of raking muck. And it failed "to raise or clarify a single legitimate national issue — unless one considers its bold stand against the corrosion of cars by salt." When Peter wrote that damning review, the two hosts were John Drainie and Laurier LaPierre, who had been chosen from a list of candidates that included Peter Jennings; Pierre Trudeau; Trudeau's future father-in-law, James Sinclair; and someone called Peter Gzowski.[6]

On March 6, 1965, in an article called "Why the Real Sports Fans Stay Home," Strabo discussed how television was changing the way fans viewed sports events. With the new tools of television such as instant replays, "stop-action," and the "isolated" camera, which could focus on an individual athlete, television viewers in the mid-1960s were beginning to enjoy not only immediacy but omniscience. Strabo argued that all this technology helped to make *Hockey Night in Canada* the most popular show on Canadian television.[7] Two weeks later Strabo wrote about *The Man from U.N.C.L.E.* and *Danger Man*, which used nonsensical dialogue and a plethora of James Bond–type gadgets to satirize the spy thriller genre. When Jonathan Miller, Johnny Wayne, and Frank Shuster, whom Strabo called "the three most accomplished satirists on TV," tried to satirize *The Man from U.N.C.L.E.*, they failed. "You can't spoof a program that won't take itself seriously," concluded Strabo.[8] On April 3, 1965, Strabo complained about commercial breaks. He chastised Bell Telephone for interrupting the mood of a show about Duke Ellington with silly commercials. Instead, he urged Bell to announce its sponsorship at the beginning and end of the program.[9] On April 17, 1965, Strabo again complained about the fact that television was trivializing the good, old parlour game called "Charades."[10] On May 1 he denounced stereotypes on television, specifically the nice "Negro."[11]

On June 19, 1965, *Maclean's* published an article called "How the 'Flush Test' Rates Your TV Habits." Although it bore no byline, the mischievous style seems like Peter's. In order to gauge viewer interest in Sunday evening shows, the magazine asked the Public Utilities Commission of Barrie, Ontario, to gauge the volume of water used during *Bonanza* and *This Hour Has Seven Days* on Sunday evening, April 2. *This Hour* came out the winner. In other words, fewer viewers of that show had wandered off to relieve themselves and flush their toilets.

Similar surveys in Saskatoon and Peterborough yielded the same results, the anonymous writer noted.[12]

In one column, Strabo admitted that he enjoyed American quiz shows such as *Call My Bluff* and *Jeopardy*, first broadcast in March 1964. Both were much better than what he called the "kindergarten pap" of Canadian quiz shows.[13] In another column, written after spending a sunny May afternoon watching ninety consecutive television commercials during the third annual Canadian Television Commercials Festival in Toronto, a grumpy Strabo complained that, no matter what the quality of the commercials was, the admen in the audience applauded.[14] In July, Strabo wondered, as he sipped gin and tonic on a summer evening, why he was presented with so many reruns of mundane TV programs. Why, for instance, did the CBC not replay its best shows from the 1950s, or even American dramas like *Marty* or the comedy shows of Sid Caesar?[15]

In his last column as Strabo, Peter wrote about one of his great concerns: that television might be robbing his children of the sense of wonder that he, as a boy, experienced whenever he met a "star" like Foster Hewitt or a hockey player like Max Bentley. Strabo informed his readers that he had never lost his childhood sense of wonder whenever a star hockey player (Eric Nesterenko?) or a well-known singing couple (Ian and Sylvia?) came to dinner. His children, especially the eldest two, seemed indifferent to stars. "To the generation born into the televised world," Peter contended, "there is scarcely any difference between someone's appearance on the television screen in the corner of the living room and his appearance in person."[16]

On September 18, 1965, Strabo became Peter (Strabo) Gzowski. Perhaps by that time Borden Spears no longer felt it necessary to hide the identity of his television columnist from Maclean-Hunter managers. In his coming-out column, Peter wrote a sarcastic piece called "Wow! Count Those Stars on the CBC." To introduce its new schedule, the CBC was sending "stars" like Catherine McKinnon, Norman DePoe, Gordon Pinsent, and Tommy Hunter to western Canada; and Maggie Morris, Knowlton Nash, and Warner Troyer to the Maritimes. "Guess that woke them up out there in viewer-land," Peter sniffed.[17] By October 2, just plain "Peter Gzowski" lamented the fact that on CTV, rival network to the CBC, youth culture seemed to be taking over in shows like *A Go Go '66*. Peter also excoriated CTV shows such as *Gomer Pyle, Jackie Gleason*, and morning cartoons. "As a grown-up," he concluded, "I expect to get a lot of reading done this winter."[18]

On November 1, 1965, Peter returned to *This Hour Has Seven Days*. Now he thought it was one of the highlights of the CBC's season. "For one thing," he noted, "it's lost its embarrassing, on-air fascination with itself — its self-congratulatory gloating over the week's mail and telephone calls; its self-glorifying promotion of programs yet to come." Furthermore, Patrick Watson was a far better co-host than John Drainie, and as long as Laurier LaPierre didn't try to sing, Peter would continue to like him, too. He admitted that he had once expected too much from the show. He had wanted more analysis. Now he understood that television's role was not to analyze but to transmit experience. Furthermore, Peter admitted, he was addicted to the show. It wasn't great journalism, but it was, he concluded, good television.

Two weeks later Peter was singing the praises of Peter Falk, who played a lawyer in *The Trials of Danny O'Brien*. Peter especially enjoyed O'Brien's flaws: he lied, cheated, and chiselled. Sometimes he lost cases, and he pursued his ex-wife almost incessantly.[19] On December 1, 1965, Peter was pleased with a new show, *Quentin Durgens, M.P.*, which, he thought, might even convince Canadians that "Canadian politics can be dramatic."[20] The star of the new show? None other than Gordon Pinsent, who, apparently, was becoming a real star.

On December 15, 1965, Peter excoriated shows such as *Hogan's Heroes* and *McHale's Navy* because they trivialized war.[21] On New Year's Day 1966, he gave out "Strabies" for the best and worst in television in 1965. Pierre Berton won for best improved performer, for he had "finally learned to listen to the people he's talking with." Gordon Sinclair, the popular and outspoken radio personality, won for best interviewer, and for the "sheer brass" of his questions on religion and income. For sports Peter liked Bob Pennington's commentary on soccer games. Pennington proved that it was possible to comment "in a reasonably normal voice, to be silent sometimes and sometimes even to criticize what's going on in the field without spoiling the viewer's enjoyment." Laurier LaPierre won Peter's award for the most perfect moment on live television: while introducing himself, he forgot his own name. Peter thought that CBC's coverage of the 1965 federal election, hosted by Norman DePoe, was "bungled," while CTV's coverage with Charles Lynch was "immaculate."[22] Peter also singled out *Singalong Jubilee, Quentin Durgens, M.P.,* and Wayne and Shuster's *Show of the Week* for special praise. He liked Beryl Fox's film reportage, particularly *The Mills of the Gods* (1965), one of the first films to criticize the American role in the war in Vietnam.

On January 22, 1966, Peter declared space shots on television dull and boring.[23] Two weeks later he thought the same of CBC-TV's news. At 11:00 p.m. each evening Earl Cameron merely read "someone else's words." Peter's point was that while the medium could be a powerful communicator, it was underused or misused. Where were the "interviews, films, cartoons, diagrams, maps, songs, skits, speeches," and so on? In other words, where was the visual content on CBC-TV's news?[24] On February 19, 1966, he defended the much-maligned spy series *Blue Light,* starring Robert Goulet, because the show was a serious interpretation of the detective genre. Now he had grown tired of satires of the genre such as *The Man from U.N.C.L.E.* and *Danger Man,* the very television shows, he admitted, that he had once liked. On March 5, Peter thought that colour television, which at the time was available only on American channels, was "a nice gimmick," but not much of an improvement over black and white. Peter was looking forward to *Batman* in colour, and so was Alison. "Imagine," she told her father, "Batman with green teeth and red eyes."[25] On April 2, 1966, Peter noted that, several years after the scandals of the 1950s, game shows were back in fashion.[26] Greed, uncomplicated by skill, he pointed out, was the emotion that seemed to appeal most to viewers.[27] Two weeks later Peter and his family were still having misgivings about colour TV, so he decided to return the rented set.[28]

On May 2, 1966, Peter debated whether it was better to watch hockey at Maple Leaf Gardens or live on television. On the one hand, he liked the way television brought the viewer both long shots and close-ups. On the other hand, he disliked some of the commentary, which failed to understand the subtleties of hockey. For instance, when Eric Nesterenko shot wide of the net, it wasn't necessarily a missed scoring opportunity. He might have been setting up a scoring chance by bouncing the puck off the boards to make it land in front of the net where a teammate was waiting to score.[29]

Two weeks later Peter was up in arms because CBC's president, Alphonse Ouimet, had fired Patrick Watson and Laurier LaPierre. Viewers, Peter pointed out, as well as some of *This Hour*'s guests, including René Lévesque and Pierre Berton, also protested, but in vain.[30] On June 4, 1966, Peter was fed up with the expression "would you believe that ...?" The expression, according to Peter, had begun as a joke on *Get Smart*, with a line like "The building is surrounded by 25 men. Would you believe it?" The other character in the show did not, so Smart, the bungling detective, pared down the number of men to twenty, then fifteen, then ended up with "How about two car hops and a nun?" Even Peter's tax accountant used the expression, as in "Would you believe that you owe ...?" It was a "pretence of fashionablity," deemed Peter, and those who used the expression were merely exposing their squareness.[31]

On June 18, 1966, in Peter's final column as television reviewer, called "The Vietnam War: TV's Epic Eastern," he slammed television coverage of the war. Dissenters were being marginalized, and Peter laid the blame on television, which gave too much time to the opinions of official Washington and almost none to young protesters. In place of debate, television showed specials on President Lyndon Johnson's ranch, and on Barbra Streisand and Frank Sinatra. "But on a cruel, ugly, sordid war," Peter railed, which was "sopping up the lives of thousands of young Americans, draining away billions of dollars, slaughtering innocents and innocence, what is here? One side of a many-sided picture."[32]

Peter's television reviews provide a window onto the world of the mid-1960s, a world that was being torn apart by war. His reviews also reveal his thinking on the nature of television as a medium. While most viewers were enchanted by its magic, and while most reviewers continued to review only content, Peter was beginning to examine the relationship of the media to its message. Marshall McLuhan, no doubt, influenced Peter.[33] Although McLuhan's *Understanding Media* wasn't published until 1964, just as Peter was beginning to write his TV reviews, articles by McLuhan had appeared beforehand. Since Peter read voraciously and assimilated information rapidly, *Understanding Media*'s explanation that form and structure of information determine meaning filtered into Peter's reviews. As Strabo, the skeptical squinter, he did indeed have the ability to see distant objects clearly. And, more importantly, to see through and around images near and far.

In addition to hiring Peter as a television reviewer, Borden Spears published several of Peter's feature articles. On November 16, 1964, "Do the Toronto Argonauts Lose on Purpose?" was published in *Maclean's* under the pseudonym Peter N. Allison. During the 1960s, the once-proud team, founded in 1874, usually finished last. Nevertheless, Peter remained a fan. What was compelling about the Toronto team, he wrote, was the fact that they always lost "marvelously," for they played with zest and enthusiasm right to the gend.

In "Geneviève Bujold to Stardom on a Cool New Path," published in *Maclean's* on December 15, 1965, Peter turned from sports to culture. For the article, he later admitted, he had interviewed the actress once only, over lunch in Montreal and while driving back to Bujold's home there. (The interview actually took place in Toronto.) His only other research, he confessed, came from a few clippings, and he had never seen any of her films. When next he met Bujold, she was rude. While writing some of his freelance articles, Peter later admitted, he had been more interested in money than quality. After all, he explained, he was paid the same fee, $600, no matter if he worked for weeks or days. One can scarcely blame him for shortcuts. He had no full-time job, and yet he had a growing family to support.[34]

The next month, January 1966, in "Dylan: An Explosion of Poetry," published in *Maclean's*, Peter turned to music. He had attended a Bob Dylan concert in Toronto's Massey Hall the previous November, and the show had changed his mind about rock and roll, which he had once judged "too loud, too boorish, too dull." To complete his research, he flew to New York where, in Greenwich Village, he listened to bands that blended classical music with rhythm and blues. His trip convinced him that this "New Music" was "the most vital, exciting art form in America," for it boldly mixed folk music, one of Peter's favourite genres, with 1950s hard-core rock as well as blues, jazz, and country. Dylan's innovation, Peter explained, was to add to New Music his haunting and poetic lyrics; these in turn gave voice to disenchanted youth and its preoccupation with racial injustice. The British music critic Kenneth Allsop was right, Peter concluded, to call Dylan "the most remarkable poet of the sixties."

During the mid-1960s, Peter collaborated with Trent Frayne on *Great Canadian Sports Stories: A Century of Competition,* which was published in 1965 as part of a series of books published in anticipation of Canada's centennial. Pierre Berton was editor-in-chief of the series; Frank Newfeld, art director; and Ken Lefolii, managing editor. In their generously illustrated book, Frayne and Gzowski covered sports from horse racing to figure skating to hockey. Among the short articles was one on Marilyn Bell's heroic swim across Lake Ontario in 1954, one on Tom Longboat's victory at the Boston Marathon in 1907, and one on Sandy Somerville's first-place finish in the American National Amateur golfing championship of 1932. While each chapter was the result of collaboration between the two men, the prologue was Frayne's, and Peter wrote the impressionistic epilogue entitled "The Changing Styles of Watching and Playing." Canadian pioneers, he argued, had little time for playing or watching sports. By Confederation, however, Canadians had become spectators. To celebrate Confederation on July 1, 1867, Torontonians took in a lacrosse match between the Toronto Lacrosse Club and Six Nations Natives from Brantford, Ontario. Spectator sports peaked between 1945 and 1965, but only hockey, Peter maintained, continued to attract spectators. Baseball was "a dead item in Canada," and boxing was "staggering against the ropes." Even Canadian football, he claimed, was at the end of a boom period that had begun in the 1930s. Horse racing, like hockey, drew crowds, but Peter wondered if it was only on-track betting that kept people coming to the races.[35]

However, there was some hope — as attendance declined, participation increased. "In 1965," Peter claimed, "more Canadians were engaging in sports more than ever, and their interests ranged from volleyball on Vancouver Island to skin-diving off Newfoundland." Sports equipment sales were up. So popular was curling that, he predicted, it might soon rival hockey as Canada's national game.[36] Golfing and sailing were increasingly popular. Skiing, too, was on the rise. Canadians had more leisure time, more expendable cash, and at the same time, Peter speculated, "the first excitement of televised sport" was wearing thin.

In the last half of his four-page text, Peter singled out Bobby Hull, who was, according to Peter, "indisputably the finest [hockey] player active in the game." Hull combined bits of his famous predecessors — "the speed of Morenz and the instinct for goals of a Richard to the strength and control of Gordie Howe." What Hull added to these qualities was "a sheer joy" in playing. According to Peter, he skated "with the abandon of a prairie twelve-year-old set free on a frozen river." Although he was "a remarkably clean and gentlemanly player," he sometimes belted the opposition "just for the thrill of the contact." And he derived his greatest pleasure, Peter thought, "from the pure motion and excitement of the game." Off ice, he engaged in farming, fast boats, and scuba diving "with the same swashbuckling enthusiasm" he brought to hockey.

To accompany the article, Peter chose a photograph of Hull standing nonchalantly against a background of an ice-blue sky. Photographer Horst Ehricht had taken the shot at thigh level looking upward to a bulging torso whose hands tenderly hold a fishing rod. The hockey star, as if unaware of the camera, peers at a distant object.[37] The photograph had already appeared in *Sports Illustrated* in 1961 where Peter must have seen it, and perhaps clipped it for future use. Copyright belonged to the photographer, but Peter never did seek permission to use it.[38]

After Harry Bruce had quit *Maclean's* in September 1964, he was appointed managing editor of *Saturday Night*. Almost immediately, Bruce hired Peter as the magazine's sport columnist. In the November issue, Peter gave seven reasons for scrapping the Olympics, including the fact that professionals were excluded, as were hundreds of millions of Chinese. To replace the Olympics, Peter suggested annual world tournaments focusing on specific sports.

In April 1965, Peter expressed his distain for professional boxing. In fact, he believed that Cassius Clay, the world champion, was "a publicist first and a fighter second," a premature judgment that he later modified. His sports column in May was a review of several books on horse racing — Trent Frayne's history of the Queen's Plate, published in 1959; Bert Clark Thayer's *The Thoroughbred*; and a collection of articles called *The Fireside Book of Horse Racing*. In June 1965, Peter was vexed because *Sports Illustrated* had refused to take a stand on the colour barrier that kept qualified "Negroes" from competing in the annual Masters Golf Tournament at Augusta, Georgia, an objection that was probably ahead of its time in sports journalism. In July he turned to soccer, which he had already written about in *Maclean's* two years earlier, and in much the same manner. He liked the "mosaic" quality of the game. In Toronto the most predominant flavour, Peter deemed, was Italian. In August he wrote about Bill Crothers's victory at the Toronto International Track Meet over Peter Snell, his greatest rival in the half-mile run. And in September 1965, the sports columnist was back to golf when he wrote about the Canadian Open of that year, starring Arnold Palmer and Jack Nicklaus, "golf's most exciting twosome." October found Peter arguing that "baseball is just as Canadian a sport as, say, golf." He even threw out the possibility that baseball was the only game played from Atlantic to Pacific in Canada.[39]

In November 1965, Peter's sports column for *Saturday Night* presented Barbara Long, a sultry twenty-eight-year-old New Yorker, whom Peter called "the most interesting sportswriter to appear on the scene in some time." She wrote for *The Village Voice*. Peter liked Long's "loose and easy" style of writing, and the fact that she always appeared to enjoy her subject matter. "She writes with a kind of cool," Peter explained, "that lets the essential humour of most sports shine through." She loved describing sexy male athletes. Long also wrote about a pool hustler, Nine-Ball Mike, for whom the game was "his whole identity, and he had to play every day." Peter's article was accompanied by a beguiling photograph of Long. He had never met the woman in person, but he seems to have fallen in love with her photograph, and with her "nice laugh" when he interviewed her during a one-hour telephone conversation. In the article,

Peter mentioned Norman Mailer, whose piece on the first Sonny Liston–Floyd Patterson fight had influenced Long. Peter also referred to Tom Wolfe, who once observed that Long's style was "a cross between H.L. Mencken and William Burroughs."[40] Peter concluded the article with the hope that he could convince Barbara Long to attend a hockey game, presumably in company with the sportswriter of *Saturday Night*.[41]

In January 1966, Peter wrote about the creation of a new trophy, the Vanier Cup, named after Governor General Georges Vanier. College football, too long ignored, according to Peter, would now gain a greater following.[42] In February, Peter was back to heavyweight boxing, which was becoming "more and more ludicrous." Since winning the world championship, Cassius Clay had never really been challenged.[43] In March, Peter sang the praises of Canadian sportswomen, and mentioned, among others, Petra Burka, who had recently won the world championship in figure skating; Marlene Stewart Streit and Sandra Post, champion golfers; Nancy Greene, Canada's best female skier of the day; and Elaine Tanner, one of the country's best swimmers.[44] Peter's topic in May 1966 was golf, and in June, baseball. Now he was down on the sport. "Poor baseball!" he opined, "It's become the cricket of the 1960s — a marvellous game to play, and an achingly boring one to watch."[45]

Peter's final sports column for *Saturday Night*, published in July 1966, was on volleyball. Two years earlier, soon after Jennie and he had purchased their Toronto Islands cottage,[46] a group of volleyball aficionados, friends, colleagues, and mostly fellow islanders had organized weekend volleyball tournaments. The court was located near the cottage of Harry and Penny Bruce. Among the players was a bank clerk who was also, according to Peter, "one of Canada's finest and most subtle poets" (Raymond Souster). There was a literary critic (Robert Fulford) who, according to Peter, never used his wit to demean a writer of little talent; a gentle, young mother (Elizabeth Amer); and a "devilishly handsome young writer, thought of by his friends as the sweetest and most evenly dispositioned of men" (probably Liz Amer's brother, Victor Coleman, poet and editor at one of Toronto's small publishing houses). David Amer was also one of the players. The Amers were so good-looking that the players assumed their marriage would last forever.[47] Although Peter doesn't describe a character who sounds like Harry Bruce, Bruce was indeed one of the regulars. Peter simply had to win. "Peter was one of those who, if the competition was good, wanted to play on till the stars shone and the ball disappeared in the face of the moon," recalled Bruce. After a poorly played or boring game, Peter skulked off, head held down in sulking disapproval. David Crombie, who was also one of the players, remembered Peter's zealous need to win.[48] In his article in *Saturday Night*, however, all that Peter recalled were "some highly enjoyable Saturday afternoons," and fellow players "leaping around in the sunshine ... arguing about what the score *really* was."[49]

In April 1965, Harry Bruce promoted Peter to the position of contributing editor of *Saturday Night*, where he joined the likes of Nathan Cohen, Robert Fulford, Ken McNaught, and Philip Stratford. The new position allowed Peter to write occasional feature articles in addition to his sports columns. In April 1965, his first feature was called "The B and B's Desperate Catalogue of the Obvious." In it Peter excoriated the Royal Commission on Bilingualism and Biculturalism, established in November 1963 by Prime Minister Lester Pearson to examine the perilous state of French-English relations in Canada. Chaired by newspaper editor André Laurendeau and university president Davidson Dunton, the commission was, according to Peter, a waste of $1.5 million dollars. The commission's first published report, which Peter called nothing but "committee think," informed Canadians what Peter believed they already knew — that French Canadians weren't happy with Confederation, and that English Canadians couldn't understand why. "The committee has laboured to design a horse," Peter concluded, "and has brought out the rough outline of a very expensive camel."[50]

Peter's next feature in *Saturday Night* was "The Awesome Cult of the Utterly Trivial," which began with "I wonder if everyone would mind not talking about homosexuals for a while," for he was becoming bored with "the homosexual problem." Every media outlet, he harrumphed, was discussing what was new with "the flits." An American magazine had even published a glossary of homosexual slang, and, especially irritating to Peter, the good, old word *gay* had been co-opted by homosexuals. He poured scorn on Susan Sontag, whose "Notes on Camp," published the year before in *Partisan Review*, had noted homosexual influences on camp, whose purpose, the New York writer pointed out, was to puncture middle-class artifice and pretension. "Homosexuals are in the vanguard of the fashionable, we're constantly being told," Peter went on, "and life for heterosexuals is just one constant struggle to keep up with what's new with the flits." The article was published in *Saturday Night* in June 1965, which was, ironically, the same issue in which Peter had boldly and admirably voiced his complaint about the Masters' banning of African-American players. Blacks, yes. Gays, no. For years to come, well past the time when intelligent people had begun to show some modicum of respect for sexual variation, Peter's mind remained firmly closed.

The following December, Peter was in Edmonton where Robert Fulford and he were the keynote speakers at the annual conference of Canadian University Press. Television, Peter predicted, would become the most exciting of all media, and he claimed that TV's coverage of baseball and football gave the viewer a better picture than if he or she were sitting in the stands.[51] Present at the conference was Dennis Murphy, chair of the Board of Publications of CUP as well as news editor of *Silhouette*, the student newspaper of McMaster University. Peter and Dennis became friends at the conference, and at least once, according to Murphy, they "closed the bar." In January 1966, after Murphy had read Peter's article on Bob Dylan in *Maclean's*, he sent Peter "a severe musical and poetic critique" of the article. More discussions over more drinks followed.[52] When Dennis became a police and court reporter at the *Hamilton Spectator*, the two men met in one bar or another where Peter would reminisce about his experiences on the police beat a decade earlier, as well as his months as city editor in Moose Jaw in 1957.

On Wednesday, May 18, 1966, the *Toronto Star* announced that Peter had joined the staff of the newspaper as entertainment editor. In 1966, Ralph Allen was managing editor of the *Star*, and it was he who made the appointment. Unbeknownst to Peter, he wasn't Allen's first choice. In his memoirs, *Running the Rapids*, Kildare Dobbs recalls that, in 1966, Allen invited him to become entertainment editor. In fact, Allen so admired Dobbs's work as managing editor of *Saturday Night* that he tried twice to convince him to join the *Star*. Dobbs wasn't interested in becoming a cog in the wheel of a large newspaper that had a reputation, according to Dobbs, of respecting a writer only until he or she became a staff member.[53]

Peter was already somewhat familiar with the inner workings of the *Star*, which, in September 1965, had published his three-part series on the threat to cottages on the Toronto Islands. In order to create a huge park, the Metropolitan Toronto Parks Department wanted to tear down the remaining 328 buildings, most of them summer cottages, privately owned but sitting on leased, city-owned land. While admitting self-interest, Peter pointed out that, after a previous round of demolitions, the number of visits to the islands had actually fallen. Obviously, visitors preferred the village atmosphere of the islands. Peter's argument against wholesale destruction of neighbourhoods was part of the new way of looking at cities. Urbanologists like Jane Jacobs preferred a more casual mix of land use. Through her books on urban development, Jacobs probably informed Peter's thinking. Her arrival in Toronto in 1968 would give further legitimacy to what was already taking shape in the city.

As the paper's new entertainment editor, Peter edited articles by Robert Fulford, by theatre critic Nathan Cohen, and by dance and music reviewer William Littler, whom Peter had enticed from the *Vancouver Sun*. Shortly after Peter took over, he called Littler. He had heard about the music critic through Nathan Cohen, whom thanks to a travel allowance from the *Star*, reviewed theatre across Canada. While in Vancouver, Cohen had admired Littler's music reviews. "How about it?" Peter asked Littler by telephone. "No" was the firm response. Peter began to offer bribes. The *Star* would pay more than the *Sun*. "Not enough," responded Littler, who didn't really want to leave Lotus Land. Peter raised the offer and mentioned how broadening Toronto would be. "More music here," he told Littler, "and you'd be closer to New York and Boston and Montreal."

Littler flew to Toronto and called Peter. "Come over to the island," Peter told him. Littler had never heard of the Toronto Islands. He found his way to Toronto's seedy harbour where he boarded a ferry. Eventually, he arrived at the ramshackle Gzowski cottage. At the *Star*, Littler became the longest-serving music and ballet critic in English Canada, and perhaps in the whole of Canada. Today he has nothing but admiration for Peter the editor, who, always in search of new ideas, pushed Littler and other members of the entertainment section to broaden their horizons, to take chances, and to remain restlessly curious.[54]

In addition to editing and writing his own articles on entertainment, Peter reviewed books that fell under the rubric of entertainment. One was George Plimpton's *Paper Lion*, a literary non-fiction study of football. Like other literary journalists, from Norman Mailer to Truman Capote, Plimpton placed himself in the midst of his story. Although not a professional player, he had trained for months, and played one game of football with the Detroit Lions. Peter admired the man for being "the world's greatest writer of experience for the sake of experience."[55]

For his first article as entertainment editor, on June 18, 1966, Peter drove to Detroit to spend an afternoon with The Supremes, the popular Motown trio. They showed Peter an impoverished section of the city called Brewster where they were buying derelict houses in order to renovate them and rent them to low-income families. Diana Ross and her two singing partners, who were about to perform at the O'Keefe Centre in Toronto, had grown up in poor parts of Detroit.[56]

In November 1966, the entertainment editor of the *Star* wrote a series of articles called "Pot in the Real World," in which he related the drug to artistic creativity. He traced marijuana's first connection with music to New Orleans in 1910 and showed its influence on jazz. Peter also pointed out that drugs had stimulated the imaginations of poets such as Charles Baudelaire and Samuel Taylor Coleridge. During the 1950s, pot did the same for Allen Ginsberg, and for The Beatles in the 1960s. Peter also dealt with the growing use of pot among white-collar businessmen. One of his researchers for the series was Barbara Frum.

These articles on pot bear more than a striking resemblance to an article called "In Defence of Pot, Confessions of a Canadian Marijuana-Smoker," published in *Saturday Night* in October 1965. The author of that article was "Peter Ludlow," which was, almost without doubt, one of Peter's pseudonyms; in it he evoked A.E. Housman's poem "When Smoke Stood Up from Ludlow." In the *Saturday Night* article, Housman's early-morning woodsmoke was transformed imaginatively into smoke from pot. In fact, if Peter Ludlow wasn't Peter Gzowski, Peter Ludlow might have sued Peter Gzowski for plagiarism, for many of the references — Baudelaire, New Orleans, enhanced music appreciation, and so on in the earlier article — were repeated in the *Star* articles. In the *Saturday Night* version, because Ludlow confessed that he was an "extensive" pot smoker, the pseudonym was necessary lest the author be charged with possession and use of an illegal substance.[57] In "Confessions," Peter Ludlow defended pot, which, he claimed, was harmless, and really nothing more than "a social activity." Ludlow also reported that he used to "turn on" in a yacht with all the hatches closed. The "heady and delicious" smoke stoned even the flies that rode on that yacht.[58]

His position as entertainment editor allowed Peter to revisit television. On October 19, 1966, he announced that a new series called *Sunday*, a public affairs show to replace *This Hour Has Seven Days*, would have five hosts, including Leonard Cohen and Ian Tyson.[59] A few days later, on October 22, Peter enthusiastically announced that the CBC would be broadcasting its first colour hockey game that evening. He had already seen three games in colour on NBC the previous spring during the Stanley Cup playoffs; these he described as "the most spectacular sports show" he had ever seen on TV, "as bright as ballet, almost more brilliant than life."[60]

Since Peter believed that "walking, respectfully approached, was a form of entertainment," he commissioned Harry Bruce, presumably recovered from his boating injuries, to write a weekly column on walking, to be published each Saturday in the *Star*. According to Bruce, the idea had originated one Saturday morning, a couple of years earlier, when he and Peter were working for *Maclean's*. On one Friday night at the top of the Park Plaza, they had drunk life to the lees. The next morning, slightly the worse for wear, they found themselves shuffling down Spadina Avenue in search of a soothing steam bath. "I have often noticed," Bruce once observed, "that your solid-gold hangover produces a mood of odd contemplation, a kind of reverent observation of things that you would normally not see at all." As they slouched past nineteenth-century red-brick houses, Peter mumbled, "I wonder why one of the dailies doesn't let some writer just wander around and write anything he likes about the streets of Toronto." Since Bruce was an editor at *The Canadian* magazine, published by the *Globe and Mail*, he thought it best to write for the *Star* under a pseudonym. The column appeared under the name Max MacPherson. The surname came from the street on which Harry and his wife, Penny, lived, while "Max" was chosen at random, though Harry liked the name so much that he named his next son "Max."[61]

In January 1967, Peter travelled to Charlottetown for the official opening of the Confederation Centre for the Arts. On January 28, his review of *Spring Thaw 1967* had few good words to say about the annual satirical review of Canadian history, politics, and mores. Peter thought the show "too flat, not musical enough" and that the sketches were "drawn-out." He hammered scriptwriter Don Harron for his bad jokes and for his portrayal of Laura Secord as a sexpot. On February 9, 1967, the entertainment editor reviewed *The Right Honourable Gentlemen*, a play about sex in high places. Director Sean Mulcahy had brought the play to the Central Library Stage at the corner of St. George and College Streets in Toronto. Set in London in the 1880s, it had enjoyed successful runs in New York and London. The play was based on a love affair that had brought down Sir Charles Dilke, who had been touted to succeed Prime Minister William Gladstone. As Peter pointed out, Dilke was the John Profumo of the 1880s, and the play, therefore, seemed appropriate for the 1960s when the career of Profumo was destroyed by revelations of country weekends with Christine Keeler and Mandy Rice-Davies, one of whom had been sleeping with a Russian military attaché in London. Peter liked neither the play nor the Toronto production. Much of the dialogue, he wrote, sounded as if it had been written "by a Victorian lady novelist with at least three names," and he found Mulcahy's direction lacking in "gusto and feeling." Furthermore, according to Peter, the actor playing Dilke "exudes all the emotion of a man whose cucumber sandwich has shown up soggy."

In March 1967, Peter suddenly resigned as entertainment editor of the *Star*. He had accepted the job, he explained, "not so much for the paper as for the man."[62] That man, Ralph Allen, had died from cancer the previous December. With no regular income, Peter accepted

Peter stands amid falling snow in front of Mrs. Kenny's Home Bakery, corner of Upper Queen Street and Bayfield Street, Charlottetown, on February 1, 1967. He was in the Prince Edward Island capital to review Spring Thaw. *The photograph is by* Toronto Star *photographer Frank Lennon (1927–2006), who five years later became famous as the man who snapped Paul Henderson's leap for joy after scoring the winning goal in the Canada-Soviet Hockey Summit Series.*

(Courtesy Trent University Archives, Gzowski fonds, 92-015, box 1, folder 34)

freelance contracts. For the Ontario government, he wrote a booklet called *Growing Up with Toronto*, in which he extolled the virtues of the increasingly cosmopolitan city with its Sunday movies, Italian immigrants, and a Henry Moore sculpture in front of an ultra-modern Finnish-designed city hall.[63] Peter also wrote a pamphlet for the federal government on the wise use of tax dollars, and penned captions for exhibits of the Centennial Train that travelled across Canada in 1967 to teach Canadian history and to promote unity.[64] Along with Ron Poulton, Joseph Schull, Ken Mitchell, Pierre Berton, and other writers associated in one way or another with Moose Jaw, Peter contributed to *Not Only a Name: A Long Love Letter from Hometown Moose*

Jaw, a mimeographed publication by Crocus House Publishers.[65] Peter wrote about the Canadian election in 1957, when he first voted.

Peter also wrote freelance articles for the *Toronto Star*. On March 22, 1967, when he reported on Nathan Cohen's honorary degree bestowed by Mount Allison University in Sackville, New Brunswick, he defended Cohen as a fellow curmudgeon.[66] During Cohen's recent illness, Peter added, even theatre people who had been "ripped" by him expressed concern for his health. On June 17, 1967, in a "Special to the *Star*," Peter returned to the theme of Canada's Natives. "Our Forgotten People — the Indians Remember Failures and Successes" was the result of a weekend excursion to Duck Lake, Saskatchewan, where he had attended a two-day jamboree that featured discussion, dancing, music, and drinking. In this piece, Peter witnessed the stirrings of First Nations' own quiet revolution. At Duck Lake, Natives were beginning to complain about the Indian Act, the Department of Indian Affairs, and residential schools. One Native discussed Marshall McLuhan with Peter.

Peter also freelanced for *Saturday Night*. In June 1967, his "Revelations in a Sheep Meadow" was a report on his Easter weekend trip to New York where, in Central Park's "Sheep Meadow," he was a participant-observer at a "love-in." He estimated that perhaps half the ten thousand or so participants were "turned on" by drugs such as pot, LSD, hash, and perhaps acid. "A lot of people," Peter reported, "looked an awful lot higher than I've ever seen anyone get on marijuana." His strongest impression was of silence and gentleness, even though by mid-afternoon the Sheep Meadow had become as crowded as Toronto's Canadian National Exhibition midway. Poet Allen Ginsberg was in attendance. One young man, dressed in flowing white robes, his head wreathed in banana leaves, fancied himself Jesus Christ. A group of two or three hundred people, who announced to watching police that they loved cops, began to kiss the police car. A rumour spread that baked banana skins, when smoked, were a turn on.[67] It was obvious that the thirty-two-year-old Peter felt young and groovy that day, and no doubt did more than just smell the smoke. Since he was in New York, there was no danger that he might be arrested by the Mounties for contravening Canada's drug laws.

In August 1967, in "Stratford's Midsummer Rites Wrong Our Theatre," *Maclean's* published Peter's review of the fifteenth annual Ontario festival. William Hutt as Nikolai Gogol's Government Inspector and Alan Bates as Richard III fell below Peter's standards. Hutt was too much the ham, and Bates played one of Shakespeare's most villainous characters "like something out of *Georgy Girl*," the popular British movie of 1966, which featured, among others, the same Alan Bates. After excoriating the festival's productions, Peter's critique broadened to include all theatre in English Canada. In fact, he added, Canada really had no indigenous theatre.[68]

Peter also tried his hand at freelance editing. In 1967, Jack McClelland was looking for an editor for Kildare Dobbs's proposed book on the Hudson's Bay Company. Dobbs and his illustrator, Ronald Searle, were convinced that a comic approach was best, a mix of fact and fiction that would convey the history of the fur company in an appealing way. McClelland, who knew that Peter was searching for work, proposed that Peter edit Dobbs's manuscript. Peter took Kildare to lunch at the rooftop bar of the Park Plaza. The meal consisted of numerous martinis washed down by a modicum of food. Peter began to explain exactly what kind of book he expected Dobbs to write. Dobbs staggered home and promptly wrote a letter that informed Peter that "he wasn't going to learn the subtle art of editing" at Dobbs's expense. Peter's equally irate reply was entitled "Without Prejudice." McClelland quickly intervened. During a multi-martini lunch at the Westbury Hotel at Yonge and Carleton Streets, the publisher told Dobbs that he didn't appreciate artistic quarrels. Another editor, the luscious, flaxen-haired bigamous wife of a prominent novelist, was hired. She and Dobbs, who married only one woman at a time, ushered *The Great Fur Opera*, as originally conceived by Dobbs, from manuscript to acclaimed book.[69]

Bridge, poker, and martinis atop the Park Plaza began to erode what little role Peter played as husband and father. By the mid-1960s, Peter and Jennie had five children. In addition to Peter C., Alison, and Maria, there was John (1964) and Mick (1965). Some of Peter's colleagues, even though most of them didn't know Jennie well, wondered how or why she tolerated a husband who devoted so much time to work and pleasure.

In the 1950s and 1960s, housewives were near the bottom of the class system, and "office wives" one step up. When Sylvia Fraser was hired at the *Star Weekly* in 1957, she was expected to be an accurate typist, to work for little money, and to correct the spelling of male writers. In order for her opinion piece about trapped housewives, "Housewives Are Self-Centred Bores," to be published, Fraser had to submit it under a pseudonym. "No matter how seriously you took yourself," Fraser noted, "you pretended you didn't."[70] Peter once told an "office wife," when she talked to him about moving from the *Toronto Star* to *Maclean's*, to stay home where she belonged.

One Sunday morning during the mid-1960s, in the midst of a marital quarrel, Peter grabbed his youngest child, a mere baby, and drove from North Toronto to Etobicoke to the home of colleagues at *Maclean's*.

"Did you bring the formula?" June Callwood asked. "And diapers?" Peter had no idea that babies took in food and liquids through one orifice and eliminated the processed remains through one or two others. June located pabulum and diapers that were once used on her youngest, Casey, born earlier in the 1960s.

"There was much gold in him," Callwood explained years later, "but you had to dig hard for it."[71]

At that time Peter had little more respect for his ancestors than he did for his wife. When the beloved Colonel Gzowski died at age eighty-four, Peter gave the Colonel's death scant, if any, mention in his columns, even though he dwelt on the deaths of his parents, Ralph Allen, John F. Kennedy, and later, that of Ross McLean. Once the Colonel was cremated and buried in St. James the Less Cemetery on Parliament Street in Toronto, he was forgotten, until 1987–88, that is, when he was resurrected for Peter's memoir. After her husband's death, the Colonel's widow lived on for a few years in an apartment on Bayview Avenue, also apparently forgotten by the grandson whose name, she once insisted, must remain Gzowski.

—•—

At the same time as Peter's marriage and career were in peril, the country, too, seemed about to implode. Mailboxes in Montreal were exploding. *Indépendentiste* parties were being formed. Quebec demanded equality or independence. In 1965, Peter wrote the lyrics and Ian Tyson the melody of a "Song for Canada," a tune with political and domestic overtones. In Peter's appeal to French Canada, one can imagine the heated discussions at home. "How come we can't talk to each other anymore?" the song begins. "Why can't you see I'm changing, too?" And "How come you shut me up as if I wasn't there? What's the new bitterness you've found?" The refrain, with its metaphor of "one single river rolling in eternity," is particularly appealing, especially when sung by Tyson, whose voice evokes the loneliness of the vast Canadian landscape. While the St. Lawrence River continues to roll seaward, and while the country remains together more or less, the two men and their spouses opted for separation not too many years after Peter penned that plea for unity.

— 7 —

"How Come We Can't Talk to Each Other Anymore?"[1] 1967–1970

I believe nationalism will become the great debate of the 1970s in Canada, so that by the end of the decade it will be difficult to be a Canadian and not be a nationalist.

— *Peter C. Newman, as Quoted by Courtney Tower in "The New Nationalism,"* Maclean's, *February 1970*

Finally, in mid-August 1967, Peter secured what promised to be permanent employment when he signed a contract at $35,000 per annum to become editor of the *Star Weekly*, the weekly magazine whose staff occupied one floor of the *Toronto Star* building on King Street, just west of Yonge. Its offices were washed "in shades of sepia, as in old photos," Sylvia Fraser recalled in a *Toronto Life* article published in 1996. Along a wall of windows, editors occupied brown cubicles, while the rest of the staff sat at rows of oak desks. The smell of cigarette smoke and the sound of clacking Underwood typewriters filled the room.[2] Like *Maclean's*, the *Weekly* was distributed nationally. Unlike the *Toronto Star*, the staid *Weekly* was losing money and readers.

When Peter was introduced to his staff, recalled Fraser, he slouched into his office "buttoned into a too-tight leather jacket — not the sexy Italian type with matching butt-smooth pants, but the tan suede sort usually teamed with jeans for roping cattle." His scruffy hair and unruly sideburns, his acne scars and heavy glasses, gave the impression of an awkward bear.

The important thing, Fraser remembered in a second article published in *Toronto Life* shortly after Peter's death, was that the staff at the *Star Weekly* was under the tutelage of one of the country's best editors. "Gzowski hooked writers with topical ideas baited with unabashed enthusiasm," Fraser recalled, and he always had a nose for significant and trendy stories. She praised Peter for urging writers to perform better than they ever imagined possible, and for "launching writers in unexpected directions." Harry Bruce agreed. "The best writing I have done in my life," he once told Gerry Brander, publisher of *Maclean's*, "was a direct result of Peter's being either one of my editors or, more often, my only editor." Bruce added that "Peter gets writers to perform better than they knew they could. He's a writers' editor."[3] Robert Fulford recalls that Peter brought the magazine to life "by developing some terrific new writers."[4] Over drinks Peter offered a position at the *Weekly*, for example, to the young and talented journalist Dennis Murphy of the *Hamilton Spectator*.[5]

On August 25, 1967, a few days after getting down to work as editor, Peter wrote to Mordecai Richler. "As I'm sure you read in the *London Times* last week, I have once again left the ranks of the unemployed and joined those of the (at least occasional) employers, and one of my first resolutions I made when I came here was to break my maiden[6] as a writer of letters to you." Would Richler consider contributing to the magazine, perhaps an excerpt from his novel-in-progress? In addition, Peter reported on his personal life and that of his friends. Ken Lefolii, busy with a book and a television show, had little time to play pool; Robert Fulford was about to return to Toronto from Expo 67; and Kildare Dobbs was living in Mexico. "We've had a great summer on the island," he added, "and I don't think Jenny[7] and the kids have ever been better." Peter concluded by hoping that the news was as pleasant in Surrey, England, "wherever the hell that is."[8]

In his letter to Richler, Peter made it clear that he was going to shake up the magazine's readership. He wanted to convert what was, in his humble opinion, a rather stodgy magazine into a "nationalistic magazine, speaking for and to the Trudeau generation." He intended to publish articles on pot smoking, venereal disease, and young single swingers who co-inhabited. Given that the country was just beginning to shake off decades of uncertainty, inferiority, and puritanism, Peter's intentions were daring. On October 23, he wondered if Richler could pay his own way to Ottawa to cover the Grey Cup game on Saturday, December 2. The only problem, Peter noted, was that the deadline for the piece would be two days later. Once again, in a letter dated November 10, Peter mentioned the tight deadline. "Does this frighten you?" he asked Richler. If so, Peter was pleased, for "Frightening you has long been an ambition of mine." Peter recommended that Richler get in touch with Peter Newman, but he thought that "the best, most charming, and genuinely funniest source on the whole Ottawa thing" was Newman's wife, Christina McCall, who was, according to Peter, "a hell of a good writer in her own right."[9] On November 20, Peter wrote that he hoped to use Richler's "anti-Jew piece," and he told the novelist that he liked his article on Canadian films so much that he would run it in January.[10] Once again he told Richler to introduce himself to Newman and McCall, who, like Richler, were invited to a party at the home of Bernard and Sylvia Ostry in early December.[11]

Early in 1968, Peter introduced a five-page review section called "of late," which discussed breaking trends and opinions. It included pieces by Richler on books, Robert Fulford on ideas, and Harry Bruce on personalities. In subsequent issues, Trent Frayne, following the death of a twenty-nine-year-old hockey player, wrote in favour of hockey helmets; Christina Newman discussed TV censorship of harmless jokes told by the Smothers Brothers; Keitha McLean wrote about Europe's new and lusty soap operas; David Lewis Stein dealt with violence in Detroit; and Harry Bruce wrote about heart transplants and the excessive power of doctors. Other articles dealt with the newly liberated woman, student power on campuses, and Quebec independence.

Peter always had an eye for the risqué. On January 27, 1968, a photograph of Sylvia Fraser, dressed in a revealing costume covered in sparkling sequins, accompanied her article on the Ice Capades. He loved tweaking noses in editorials. In one he advised candidates for the Liberal Party leadership, among them Pierre Trudeau, to avoid saying anything if they had nothing to say. Peter argued in another that Canada could very well survive without Quebec. He persuaded Pierre Berton to provide excerpts from his upcoming book, *The Smug Minority*, which examined the cozy relationship between business and government. On February 10, 1968, the first excerpt appeared, along with an interview with Berton conducted by Sylvia Fraser, who called Berton "Canada's No. 1 Celebrity." Two weeks later, "Why Our Schools Have Failed Us," another excerpt from Berton's *Smug Minority*, appeared. In the same issue, Sylvia Fraser wrote about Myer Rush, stock promoter and fraud artist, who had suffered the indignity of being blown up in bed. In the issue of March 2, Moses Znaimer, Walter Stewart, and Margaret Daly reported on crisscrossing the country in search of a new prime minister, and Mordecai Richler, while railing against "old and tired leaders," urged Liberals to choose Trudeau.

On February 21, Peter wrote to Richler to announce that one of the novelist's articles called "The Writer's Mail," probably on the subject of Richler's correspondence with fans and editors, just didn't work, at least for the *Star Weekly*. It wasn't funny, Peter thought, nor was it rude, and "it doesn't *tell* me anything." He added: "For Chrissake, I hate it when pieces don't work, and especially when I can see no way to *make* them work." In the same letter, he gave Richler some good news — that his piece on Ottawa politics had helped to boost sales of the magazine.[12]

In early March, the editor and the novelist had a testy exchange.[13] Apparently, Richler had used some of his *Star Weekly* material in the *New Statesman*. "Oh, golly, piss on this fucking shit," Peter wrote, and promptly assured Richler that he loved him. "I need you. *Canada* needs you." Then he added that the *Star Weekly* needed him.[14] In a subsequent letter, Peter told Richler that novelist Hugh Hood also wanted to write a piece on baseball in Montreal, which was about to gain a major league team to be called the Expos. Peter promised to give the topic to "whichever of you is nicer to me over the next few months." Immediately, he relented. "Oh, shit," he told Richler, "you can have it."[15]

In March 1968, Rolf Hochhuth's controversial play *Soldiers*, whose subject was the firebombing of Dresden in February 1945, was about to open at the Royal Alexandra Theatre in Toronto. The play depicted a calculating Winston Churchill, played by John Colicos, who was seen on stage making plans to destroy the beautiful and militarily unimportant city, which was full of refugees. The play also alleges that Churchill was responsible for a plane crash that killed the Polish prime minister, General Wladyslaw Sikorski. In the issue of March 16, Tom Hendry's article about the play, and about Hochhuth, who was in Toronto for the opening, was published in the *Star Weekly*. In 1968, while Toronto, like most cities across the country, was still enthusiastically naming parks, schools, and squares after Churchill, the decision of the editor of the *Weekly* to commission an article about the play was as brave and bold as the decision of "Honest" Ed Mirvish to allow the production to be performed in his Royal Alex Theatre, especially when London's National Theatre Board, a few months earlier, had cancelled the show before its scheduled opening.

On April 20, 1968, Peter's editorial discussed Canada's new and more relaxed divorce laws, which had been enacted by Pierre Trudeau in 1967 when he was minister of justice. To proven infidelity, the new laws added desertion, cruelty, imprisonment, and living apart for three or more years. Peter wasn't impressed. What about delays and waiting lists? he wondered. And he didn't like the provision that lawyers and judges were required to explore the possibility of reconciliation, which, Peter argued, would cause further delays.

In the issue of April 27, 1968, which featured a cover photograph of Pierre Trudeau and an article about the Liberal convention that had chosen him as leader and prime minister, Peter published Richler's review of *The Smug Minority*. "Muddleheaded" and "not sufficiently tough," opined Richler. The week following, Adrienne Clarkson was featured on the cover. Inside, an article asked "Why is one of TV's best shows buried in the daytime?" The show was Clarkson's popular and intelligent *Take 30*. In the same issue, David Lewis Stein wrote on violence in American cities, Jack Batten encouraged men to wear turtlenecks to work, and Peter wrote an editorial that called for Canada to leave the North Atlantic

Treaty Organization (NATO). The money saved, he argued, should be invested in underdeveloped nations.

During the first months of his tenure, Peter encouraged his journalists to write about anything from quiche to rebellious children. In May, Elizabeth Gray wrote about the slums of Montreal, Edna Staebler did an article on Mennonite cooking, and Mary Van Stolk wrote about why women have difficulty enjoying sex after being "denied sexual freedom in adolescence." In June there was an article on birth control. Margaret Penman wrote about a "lithe, sexy" John Saywell, academic and TV personality. On June 1, 1968, the editor devoted an entire issue to the promise of Canada. Articles that month focused on rising Canadian talent such as that of the soprano Judith Forst. In other issues, Margaret Daly wrote about June Callwood's arrest in Yorkville while helping street youth, Philip Resnick urged Canada to leave the North American Air (now Aerospace) Defense Command, and Bruce Kidd wrote about the pleasures of running.

In editorials Peter advised the CBC to divert money from its "physical distribution plant" into production of Canadian shows, especially those dealing with public affairs. He mused on the possible merits of a guaranteed income, and he questioned police use of mace to control crowds. In one editorial, he called the new prime minister a "man for today." On another occasion, he encouraged federal and provincial governments to establish student aid programs for university students, who, during the summer of 1968, were having difficulty finding jobs. He recommended that Canada adopt the au pair tradition of Europe to promote bilingualism. In "How to Be a Canadian," Peter urged Canadians to explore Canada.

After months of frenetic activity, Peter began to find the role of editor a bit taxing. "Some day I'm going to start a letter to you without apologizing," he told Richler on June 4, 1968, "for not having written it before." Peter listed the preoccupations of an editor — "promotion, circulation, budget, union problems (we're facing a fucking *strike* at the *Star*), and Grand Tours of Vancouver" to promote the magazine.[16] He lamented the fact that although the *Star Weekly* was much improved, its sales figures hadn't risen. With so much work, he explained to Richler, "I never get around to doing what it was I thought they brought me here to do. Like deal with writers. Or write reviews of their books. Or occasionally write letters to my friends, even." He was turning down Richler's last book review, but of course Richler would be paid the usual $100 per review. He was desperate, he told Richler, "to get something spinning around here, before all the turds in Saskatchewan write enough hate mail to engulf us forever."[17]

During the remaining months of his tenure, the magazine published an article on "Shirley Douglas — Tommy's daughter — and her husband Donald Sutherland, the film star." A photograph of the happy couple with their children, including Kiefer, appeared on the cover of the August 24, 1968, issue. Another article claimed to be the first to deal with businessman Paul Demarais, who at forty-one was, according to the *Star Weekly*, more powerful than E.P. Taylor. One article discussed children who were sniffing glue; another made the case for polygamy; and yet another, by B.C. novelist Paul St. Pierre, talked about the pleasures of hunting. Consumption and affluence, one article argued, were destroying the environment. Trent Frayne sounded off against the $20 million spent by Montreal, Toronto, and Hamilton to win the right to be the Canadian entrant in the international competition to hold the 1976 Olympics. Peter increased the fiction section of the magazine by publishing some of Hugh Garner's short stories,[18] and excerpts from novels by Whit Masterson, David Walker, and Elizabeth Peters. The book reviews grew livelier. Harry Bruce called Richler's *Cocksure* fresh and dirty. Many of the stories and novels were beautifully illustrated.

Critics, writers, and the editor himself agreed that Peter had greatly improved the magazine. On CFRB's *Time for Dialogue*, Pierre Berton argued that the new *Weekly* was the only Canadian magazine that knew where it was headed. *Time's* Canadian edition pointed out that Peter's *Star Weekly* bore as much resemblance to the old *Star Weekly* as *Valley of the Dolls* to *Little Women*. *Time* liked the sauciness of the magazine, especially the cartoon of Pierre Berton posing in psychedelic colour as Rodin's muscular *Thinker*. As far as Sylvia Fraser was concerned, Peter was at his best as editor of the *Weekly*. As an editor, he had a mission, Fraser argued in a *Toronto Life* article.[19]

—•—

Understandably, Peter was surprised and angry when the Honderichs, owners of the *Star* and the *Weekly*, folded the weekend supplement into *The Canadian.* The owners had no quarrel with the editor, but they could no longer afford to subsidize the magazine. Older readers had begun to cancel their subscriptions, and young adults, an audience that Peter had hoped to nurture, ignored it.[20] Beland Honderich paid Peter the equivalent of a year's salary, the not inconsequential sum of $35,000, which allowed Peter, Jennie, and their children to sail to England onboard the Soviet ship *Alexandr Pushkin.* The trip, Peter later claimed, was to nurse his wounds. It was probably also an attempt to patch up a marriage. He kept a diary for the first part of the trip until it declined into "melancholy scribbles, with more gin spilled on them than I'd like to recall." In a draft of his memoirs, he wrote "What a long time ago that seems, and how much all our lives have changed," but later crossed out that line, perhaps because he felt it too maudlin. In London the wounds remained open. Soon Jennie and the children flew back to Toronto. Peter wandered around London "like a soap opera," then flew back to Toronto two days later, because, he told Marci McDonald a few years later, he couldn't stay drunk all the time.[21] In an unpublished draft of what became his memoirs, Peter noted that Mordecai Richler, who was living in London, tracked Peter down, escorted him to various clubs, and introduced him to editors and agents.[22]

Back in Toronto, Peter wrote about the aborted trip. In "The Global Village Has Everything but Surprises," he didn't mention his drinking, nor the fact that his wife and children had abandoned him. "Beautiful, foggy, storied, civilized London," he wrote in *Saturday Night* in December 1968. He enjoyed the pubs, which, he thought, were "a more civilized way to drink." He loved the Sunday newspapers and the good and inexpensive theatre.[23] Did Peter really have the time and energy to explore London? Probably not. Instead, he apparently used his imagination to re-create the British capital. By mixing fact and fiction, Peter came up with a good travel article modelled on the literary journalism of Tom Wolfe and Hunter S. Thompson.

Soon after returning to Toronto, he continued to be interested in literary non-fiction. He headed down to New York to seek advice from

Clay Felker, founding editor of *New York*, a smart and sassy magazine that showcased the city's social scene, business, and politics, and provided consumer tips. In the early 1960s, in the manner of the *Star Weekly*, *New York* began as a supplement to the *Herald-Tribune* newspaper, but in 1968, Felker and co-founder Milton Glasser made the magazine into a stand-alone glossy publication that caught the eye of editors across North America. Among its roster of contributors were purveyors of literary journalism such as Tom Wolfe, who began to write for the magazine in 1962.[24] Peter figured that with former *Star Weekly* writers like Jack Batten, Harry Bruce, Bill Cameron, Margaret Daly, Sylvia Fraser, David Lewis Stein, and Walter Stewart, as well as Pierre Berton, Mordecai Richler, and Patrick Watson, he could emulate Felker's success in a magazine to be called *This City*. All he needed was about $400,000!

In November 1968, over rum and Coke atop the Park Plaza, Peter told the *Toronto Star*'s Martin Knelman that he had the necessary financial backing. He was so certain that *This City* would be successful that he had turned down three job offers, he told Knelman, including one from Ross McLean to replace Ken Lefolii on the television show *The Way It Is*.[25] Peter wanted to create a free-wheeling, open-ended magazine with a lively exchange of ideas and an insider's guide to Toronto. By May 1969, however, when he abandoned plans for *This City*,[26] he had lost a substantial sum of money. One problem Peter hadn't been able to overcome was the fact that Toronto already had a city magazine called *Toronto Life*, owned since 1967 by Michael Sifton. In December 1971, when Peter and Michael de Pencier bought the failing *Toronto Life* from Sifton, Peter's dream of being a part owner of a magazine about Toronto was realized.[27]

As well as the television job, Peter turned down a teaching position in Halifax and an offer to become the director of the School of Journalism at the University of New Brunswick in Fredericton.[28] Instead, he chose to continue freelancing. On the last Saturday in December 1968, Peter, who was identified as "one of Canada's leading magazine writers and editors," provided an overview of 1968 for the *Toronto Star*. "For me," he began, "the real story of 1968 can be summed up in two pictures from the Olympic Games." At the summer Olympics, held in Mexico City the previous October, two American runners, Tommie Smith and

John Carlos, raised their black-gloved fists on the medal stand during the playing of "The Star Spangled Banner" in protest against lack of civil rights and equality for African Americans. A gold medal gymnast from Czechoslovakia, who had tied for gold with a Russian competitor, refused to look at the flags of the two countries as a protest against the Soviet invasion of her country. Peter called these acts futile, for they didn't advance the cause of black Americans, nor did they loosen the Soviet hold on Czechoslovakia.[29]

In 1968, Peter and Jack Batten produced a ninety-six page picture book on the subject of skier Nancy Greene's rise to the top of the podium at the Grenoble Winter Olympics of 1968.[30] While researching and assembling the book, he played tennis with the gold medallist on a court near the Gzowski summer home. For weeks afterward, he sang the praises of Nancy to Jennie. When Jennie complained, Peter accused her of being rude. She punched him "right between the eyes," Peter later told Marci McDonald.[31]

In May 1969, *Saturday Night* published Peter's witty "How You Gonna Keep 'Em Down on the Farm After They've Said **** You." He was always good with opening lines. "Everything's going to pieces," he began. "Now the most celebrated and cherished of all the four-letter words has lost its value. What's left?" He reminded readers that he had managed to use the word, or at least to suggest it, in *Canadian Forum* in 1964.[32] The first time, he guessed, that the F-word had been used on CBC was on *Ideas* in 1967 when novelist Austin Clarke interviewed Piri Thomas, an African-American writer from New York.[33] Even before that, Peter recalled, when he was about fourteen, in other words in 1948, he was at a drive-in hamburger joint with a bunch of boys who were trying to pick up girls. One of the girls asked, "Do you guys ----?" Peter's uncertain reply, "Well, uh …well," brought the riposte "Well, ---- off." He was shocked. By 1969, however, the word had lost its power through overuse.

During the summer of 1969, while Peter Sypnowich, the *Toronto Star's* book reviewer, was on vacation, Peter took his place. On Saturday, July 5, he praised *The Strawberry Statement*, a collection of reports on the anti-war riots and student occupation at Columbia University that James Simon Kunen had sent to Clay Felker's *New York* during the autumn of 1968. A week later, on July 12, Peter reviewed Lillian

Hellman's *An Unfinished Woman*, which he thought made other memoirs about New York during the first half of the twentieth century seem "a little shallower and less adequate by comparison."[34] Like Kunen, Hellman was a rebel, and Peter may also have enjoyed her beguiling blend of fact and fiction. She was capable of turning a brief crossing of the Spanish-French frontier during the Spanish Civil War into firsthand experience with bombs and food shortages in Madrid. Perhaps Peter enjoyed Hellman's witty and caustic descriptions of writers such as Dorothy Parker and Ernest Hemingway, who could barely contain their mutual dislike during a dinner in Paris. He may have chuckled at Hellman's description of a New York party, which "seemed in the managerial hands of two brothers who, when they weren't kissing the gentlemen guests, were kissing each other."[35] The following Tuesday, July 15, 1969, Peter's topic was Arthur Hailey's *Airport*, which he liked so much that he chastised Helen Hutchison, who, in the *Star* a week earlier, had called the book nothing but "facts and titillations."

"Wouldn't it be nice," Peter asked rhetorically, "if people — especially reviewers — could just relax and appreciate [Hailey] for what he does so masterfully well?"

On Saturday, August 9, 1969, Peter reviewed James Laver's *Modesty in Dress*. While he didn't like the book itself — it was "random thoughts on striptease, fetishism and the see-through dress" — he did like "Laver's Law," in which the author claimed that a dress that is chic in its own time would have been thought daring one year earlier and indecent ten years earlier. Three years after being declared chic, it becomes dowdy, then amusing thirty years after its time, and downright beautiful a century and a half after its release. "The trouble is," Peter added, "like a lot of people who have one good idea in their lives, Laver won't let go." *Modesty in Dress* was his thirty-third book, and at least 10 percent of Laver's books were on fashion and "costumery."[36]

In early October 1969, Peter returned to full-time journalism as editor of *Maclean's*. The job had become available on September 12 when Charles Templeton, claiming management interference, suddenly resigned.

Templeton had been on the job for a mere seven months. Ironically, Peter was partly to blame. For Templeton he had been researching and writing a feature article critical of the Canadian news media. Peter had singled out Regina's *Leader-Post* for special opprobrium. When Ron McEachern received a telephone call threatening a libel case if *Maclean's* published the article, he ordered Templeton to kill it.[37] Templeton charged McEachern with editorial harassment. Furthermore, added Templeton, McEachern was attempting to turn the French-language version of *Maclean's* into a translation of the English-language version. *Le Magazine's* editor, Mario Cardinal, had resigned with Templeton. In Toronto ten staff members, among them Marjorie Harris, Walter Stewart, and Jon Ruddy, signed a letter of support for Templeton.[38]

Peter applied for the job left vacant by Templeton.[39] So did Philip Sykes, managing editor of the magazine, and Doris Anderson, editor of *Chatelaine*. On September 16, 1969, Ron McEachern addressed an envelope to Peter at 19 Alexandra Boulevard, northwest of Eglinton Avenue and Yonge Street. The letter inside announced that Peter was on a short list of candidates, and McEachern assured Peter that "personal incidents between us years ago, words then said or swallowed, feelings real or imagined have no relevance whatever to the choice and decision we must make."[40] On September 22, 1969, Harry Bruce wrote to Gerry Brander. "I would like to see Maclean-Hunter appoint Peter Gzowski the Editor of *Maclean's*," Bruce told Brander, for Peter would be "the best possible Editor for what's left of *Maclean's*."[41]

"I would have had that job in a flash," Doris Anderson claimed years later, "if I had been a man."[42]

"The main objection to you," Gerry Brander told Anderson, "is not that you're a woman, but that you can't represent the company publicly."[43] She continued as the esteemed editor of *Chatelaine*, but at a considerably lower annual salary than the $35,000 paid to the new editor of *Maclean's*.[44]

Before signing a contract, Peter met with management. He was assured that he would enjoy editorial freedom. On October 6, 1969, the *Toronto Star* announced that Peter had been appointed editor of *Maclean's*. A few days later, when Pat Annesley interviewed Peter, he was expansive and full of self-confidence. He ordered a coaster for the "young lady" who was about to place her coffee on his $6,000 desk. He looked, according to Annesley, like an "improbable shaggy Polish bear who wandered into Ralph Allen's old office by mistake." Peter appeared lost in so much elegance, wrote Annesley, and uncomfortable in his over-sized jacket, which she took to be "his Editor-of-*Maclean's*-Magazine outfit." Although he was, in Annesley's opinion, "one of the top talents in Canadian journalism," she wondered if the nonconformist Gzowski, who spent so much time in pool halls, would be able to live inside "the button-down world of Canada's largest publishing house?" Peter assured Annesley that he would be editor of *Maclean's* for a long time.

Immediately after taking up his new post, the new editor began to call upon old friends, who were happy to propose articles. "Israel: Oh Jesus Mordecai," Peter told the novelist in a letter dated October 31, 1969, "I just can't see what we could get out of that. Not right now any-way." Undaunted, Richler proposed that he be appointed the magazine's book columnist. Peter put him off. He did agree, however, that, if Richler insisted that Mavor Moore wasn't up to the standards of *Maclean's*, Peter would let him go. As for Larry Zolf, Peter couldn't understand what Richler liked about his writing.[45] A few weeks later Richler proposed a piece on Jean Drapeau, the mayor of Montreal, who had just opened Le Vaisseau d'Or, his own restaurant. Peter wasn't keen. "Every fuck-ing body has already done something about Drapeau's restaurant," he argued. Instead, Peter suggested an article on Robert Fulford, the editor of *Saturday Night*. "Here's this fantastic guy," Peter wrote, "who stays on in Canada, fighting all of the inside and outside battles that all of us fight, and he means so much to everything here …"[46]

Peter informed a reporter from *Time* that readers of *Maclean's* were far more sophisticated than readers of the *Star Weekly*, who moved their lips as they read. As the reporter from *Time* correctly noted, Peter was bright and aggressive, and if he chose to be, he could be quite charming.[47] Peter boasted that he would revitalize *Maclean's*, which for too long, he contended, "lacked any definable editorial image." Under his stewardship the magazine would become "tougher-minded and distinctly nationalis-tic" and "deeply Canadian." He wanted it to reflect Canada's excellence.

If Canada and Canadians were criticized in the magazine, it would be, in Peter's phrase, "as a lover criticizes his mistress." He planned to transform *Maclean's* into a truly national magazine. He would show Canada, which he described as a "bloody magnificent country," in all its diversity.

"Distinctly nationalistic"! "Deeply Canadian"! Like many other writers and editors of the late 1960s, Peter was becoming a Canadian nationalist.

During the 1960s, argues historian José Igartua, "English Canada shed its definition of itself as British and adopted a new stance as a civic nation … and erected this as the Canadian model." The process was so quiet, Igartua adds, that historians failed to notice.[48] Nationalists, in Canada and elsewhere, were inspired by the attempts of African and Asian nations to throw off European imperialism. In Canada the rise of Pierre Trudeau as justice minister and leading candidate to replace Lester Pearson as prime minister unleashed enormous pride of place. The intelligent and unconventional forty-eight-year-old bachelor promised to bring youth and energy to political life. He was a world traveller and spoke both official languages with ease. In February 1968, during the Liberal leadership convention, Peter was ecstatic. "The wild thing about it all," he had told Mordecai Richler, "is that Trudeau might *win*. Jesus! Pierre Trudeau as prime minister!" The very idea sent Peter into a tizzy of wild speculation: "Lefolii as head of the CBC! Fulford takes over culture! Richler becomes president of the Mount Royal Club! Concentration camps for westerners … the whole thing."[49]

Peter's ancestors would have found the idea of Canadian nationalism rather odd. For generations the Gzowskis and the Youngs, like most English-speaking Canadians, identified themselves as British. The Gzowskis had helped to found institutions such as the Queen's Plate and Ridley College, which were modelled on British institutions. Sir Casimir had happily accepted a knighthood from Queen Victoria. For the first three or four generations of Canadian Gzowskis, Canada wasn't so much an independent country as an important component of the British Empire. The young Peter inherited British-Canadian traditions. "Like everyone else who was born in English Canada when I was," Peter wrote in his memoirs, "or who came here as a child, I was schooled to be British."[50] Each weekday morning, along with schoolchildren everywhere in the empire, Peter joined his classmates in Galt in a rousing rendition of "God Save the King." Like most cities and towns in English Canada, Galt named its principal streets after British royalty. Peter's favourite hymn, "Jerusalem," was from the English canon, which in the 1940s and 1950s was as much as part of the (English) Canadian canon as Sara Jeannette Duncan, Stephen Leacock, and Morley Callaghan.

At the same time, Peter's generation was being drawn into the cultural orbit of the new imperial power to the south. When Peter was growing up, most of the feature films shown in movie theatres in Galt, St. Catharines, and Toronto were American. Hollywood stars were as well-known in Canada as in the United States. When Canada sold wartime bonds in order to defend the British Empire, it was stars like Shirley Temple who flew to Ottawa to help Prime Minister Mackenzie King with promotion. In spite of the existence of CBC Radio, most of the popular shows, from *Lux Radio Theater* to *The Lone Ranger*, emanated from the United States. "Eighty percent of the programs that were broadcast in Canada when I was a kid," Peter remembered, "were American." Except for hockey broadcasts and a few other Canadian shows such as *The Happy Gang, L for Lankey,* and *Sweet and Low* with Mart Kenney and his Western Gentlemen, Peter's generation found American popular culture overwhelmingly attractive. During the 1950s, American television culture in the form of *I Love Lucy* and *The Honeymooners* reinforced the idea that New York and Los Angeles were the capitals of culture and creativity for Canadians as well as for Americans.

Nevertheless, Peter's pride in Canada grew during the 1950s. While he was in Timmins in 1954, he began to realize that there could be such a thing as a Canadian identity. In his memoirs, he claimed that it was CBC Radio's *Stage 54* that made him appreciate Canadian writers and themes. The show was directed by Andrew Allan, who had founded the program in 1944 as *Stage 44*. Allan and his colleague Esse W. Ljungh produced international *and* Canadian radio plays. Peter listened to drama written by, among others, Lister Sinclair, Joseph Schull, Mavor Moore, W.O. Mitchell, Fletcher Markle, Tommy Tweed, and Len Peterson, and starring actors such as Jane Mallett, John Drainie, and

Don Harron. He was "entranced," he wrote in his memoirs more than three decades later, to discover that drama could emerge from experiences similar to his own. Canadians, he argued, "had something to say that was worth listening to." Thanks to the CBC, Peter slowly began to think of himself as a Canadian.[51]

There may have been some exaggeration in Peter's memory of this "Canadian" epiphany, for during the remainder of the 1950s, there is little evidence that he acted upon this idea that Canadians could tell their own stories, and that CBC Radio was the chief medium for disseminating those stories. His play *Christmas Incorporated*, written in Timmins, owes more to Hollywood and J. Arthur Rank than to any Canadian "tradition." As late as 1967, he wondered in a letter to Mordecai Richler if Canada should even be bothered creating and developing its own film industry. "Should we junk the [National] film board?" Peter asked the novelist.[52]

On the other hand, as editor of the *Star Weekly*, Peter had indicated his growing passion for things Canadian by promoting Canadian writers in some of his editorials such as "How to Be a Canadian." Of greater concern, arguably, was his fear that Canada was becoming a branch plant of the United States. In the March 1968 issue of the *Star Weekly*, Peter editorialized in favour of Mel Watkins, the economist who advocated greater Canadian control over American-owned subsidiaries in Canada.

Surely the tipping point for Peter and other evolving Canadian nationalists was Professor George Grant's *Lament for a Nation*, first published in January 1965. Grant's subtitle, *The Defeat of Canadian Nationalism*, provoked any Canadian who cared about the survival of Canada. A Red or Radical Tory who believed that the Canadian state should support Canadian institutions such as Medicare, publishing houses, and the CBC, Grant believed that Prime Minister John Diefenbaker, for all his weaknesses, had represented the last hope for Canada to stand up to the Americans. When Diefenbaker was defeated in 1963, Grant was appalled. Once in office, Prime Minister Lester Pearson agreed to install nuclear warheads in Bomarc missiles, and, later, signed an auto pact with President Johnson, thereby linking Canada's defence and a major part of its economy to its neighbour. The inevitable fate of Canada, Grant argued, was to be absorbed by the United States.

In 1965, so depressed was the philosopher that he was certain Canada had already ceased to be a nation.[53]

Grant had captured the unease of Canadians during the 1960s. Although Expo 67 had been a great critical and popular success, it had failed to erase concerns that Canada lacked a unifying narrative. Confederation had created a political entity but not a nation. Although the flag debate of 1964–65 had stirred up passions and debate, it was mostly English Canadians who were exercised.[54] During the 1960s, members of Canada's non-British and non-French communities began to argue that Canada was, and always had been, a multicultural nation, and some of them demanded special recognition.[55] As writer and broadcaster Laurier LaPierre put it, Canadians of the 1960s faced a dilemma. They were "seriously asked to define themselves as a people and to evaluate Canada as their *patrie*."The dilemma created a *crise de conscience*.[56]

Concerned Canadians began to search for homegrown roots. Small publishing houses such as House of Anansi, Coach House, and Jacques Hébert's Éditions du Jour were established to publish Canadian/ *Canadien* narratives. Writers such as Graeme Gibson, James Bacque, and Margaret Atwood, as well as Alice Munro, Timothy Findley, and Leonard Cohen were promoted by Robert Weaver on CBC Radio shows such as *CBC Stage*, *CBC Playhouse*, and *Anthology*. In 1959, Marie-Claire Blais's *La belle bête (Mad Shadows)* was critical of Quebec's church-dominated society. In the late 1960s, Michael Ondaatje worked with Stan Bevington and bpNichol of Coach House, as well as with Dennis Lee at Anansi, to write his prize-winning *The Collected Works of Billy the Kid* (1970).[57] *The Struggle for Canadian Universities*, a study by two professors at Carleton University, railed against the hiring of American professors in Canadian universities. Encouraged by reduced postage rates, Canadian magazines competed against American magazines. Small theatres, often located in abandoned downtown warehouses, began to develop plays on Canadian themes. Repertory movie houses attempted to interest Canadians in films such as *Winter Kept Us Warm, Nobody Waved Goodbye,* and *Goin' Down the Road*. In Quebec, directors such as Claude Jutras and Gilles Carle made films, and *chansonniers* and composers such as Gilles Vigneault, Luc Plamondon, and Monique Leyrac composed and sang music about their *pays* and its search for *liberté*. In all parts of the country, Canadians were searching for a nation.

As entertainment editor of the *Toronto Star*, Peter had taken note of the Canadian crisis of identity. On Saturday, December 17, 1966, his column was a review of a new study on the sorry state of Canadian cultural institutions. Ralph Allen considered the article so important that he had placed it on the front page. Under the title "Canada's Cultural Quandary," Peter commented on a thousand-page report on the woeful state of Canada's culture. Since May 1966, when it was completed, the report had lain dormant until the *Toronto Star* began to publish excerpts on the same day as Peter's piece on the report, which damned federal cultural institutions such as the National Library (understaffed), the National Film Board (antiquated distribution methods), and the National Gallery (muddled policies and poor leadership). The report, Peter noted, was especially critical of the CBC, which was incapable of or unwilling to clean its own house.[58]

Once appointed editor of *Maclean's*, Peter began to transform the magazine into a voice of the emerging Canadian nationalism. In the January 1970 edition, the first to show his editorial influence, he included a Terry Mosher (Aislin) cartoon of a rather dumpy Queen Elizabeth disdainfully observing a falling maple leaf. Canada, the cartoon proclaimed, was drifting away from Britain.[59] In the February 1970 issue, Courtney Tower's article on "The New Nationalism" surveyed the temper of the time when the interventionist government of Pierre Trudeau was promising tax incentives to increase Canadian investment in Canadian companies. James Richardson, Winnipeg capitalist and federal Cabinet minister, argued that foreign companies should be forced to permit Canadians to buy into them. Mel Watkins urged Canada to nationalize key industries. In his article, Tower singled out thirty-one-year-old Doug Ward, who had studied theology and was a member of the Students' Union for Peace Action. Ward, argued Tower, was typical of a generation that had grown up as worldly internationalist. "The late 1950s to the early 1960s," Ward told Tower, "was a time of internationalism, when nationalism meant defining other people as the enemy." Now that the word *nationalism*, which had once been associated with Adolf Hitler and the Nazis, had become a more positive word, Ward in turn became a Canadian nationalist.

Not all Canadian citizens, however, were willing members of Peter's version of Canada. One of his innovations was to increase reader input in the form of an expanded letters-and-opinion section. "I was extremely disappointed," wrote one Anglo Montrealer in a letter published in the April issue, "to find that you take an editorial stand supporting Canadian nationalism." The writer pointed out that while some nationalisms were worthy, Peter's version served no real purpose except to create in-groups.

Although Diefenbaker's northern vision, like the Avro Arrow, never got beyond the testing phrase, the vision inspired editors like Peter, who was one of the few Canadians who had seen northern Canada first-hand. In March 1970, *Maclean's* published a story called "Joe and Mariya in the Promised Land," written by Pamela Andres. "Each month," the editor explained, "*Maclean's* receives around 300 unsolicited manuscripts from would-be writers." All are read, he assured readers. Peter had developed an ability to absorb the essence of a manuscript by surfing it. "Joe and Mariya" had been mailed from northern Saskatchewan by the wife of a game warden. Pamela Andres was twenty-nine and lived alone for days while her husband patrolled for poachers over a large territory north of Prince Albert. The article described the settlement's Métis families and its "hermitlike bachelors," who lived by fishing, hunting, and raising mink.

Suddenly, Peter resigned from *Maclean's*. "Ronald A. McEachern's *Maclean's* is not the *Maclean's* I wish to edit," Peter stated in a letter of resignation, written on Thursday, April 23, 1970. Only a couple of months earlier, on February 17, Peter appeared to be on friendly terms with the same McEachern. On that day, Peter had told the Davey Senate Commission examining the mass media that, as editor, he was free "to edit and pursue topics in depth." As Peter spoke in a committee room on Parliament Hill, McEachern was seated beside him. When asked whether McEachern was doing any of the editing, Peter answered, "I'm doing it within the bounds normally prescribed."[60]

Two months later relations soured. McEachern had decided to suppress a cheeky article called "The Life and Times of Detective Inspector Greenberg," written by Mordecai Richler. Its subject was the first Jewish police inspector of Montreal during the heady days after the Second World War when the city was the speakeasy and striptease capital of Canada. It was to have been the first of six articles by Richler.[61]

On Monday afternoon, April 27, Peter delivered his letter of resignation to Donald Hunter, owner of Maclean-Hunter. He offered to make a "graceful and unpublicized exit from the scene" by leaking to the press that he had been offered a broadcasting job. Hunter accepted the resignation. Pat Annesley arrived at Peter's darkened office shortly thereafter. The office, that last Monday of April 1970, was dark and foreboding. The drapes were drawn, the lights were off, and the editor, his feet up on his rosewood desk, was staring at the narrow ray of light that dared to poke through the crack between the drapes. His eyes were red-rimmed. He looked as if he hadn't slept for days. As he mumbled into his telephone, he studiously ignored the young journalist who sat patiently on one side of his big desk where, once upon a time, Ralph Allen had edited Peter's articles at *Maclean's*.

"Would you mind if I set my coffee on your desk without a coaster?" Pat Annesley timidly asked.

"Go ahead and carve your initials on it," Peter mumbled as he slammed down the receiver.

"Here we've been putting out a magazine that's uninformative, boring, in bad taste, and Czechoslovakian," he reported to Annesley. "Why didn't they tell us?"

In fact, management had told Peter that it wasn't happy with the magazine, but only after he asked them for an assessment of his work as editor. Owners and managers were unhappy with what they called the "ego ramblings" of Harry Bruce, as well an article about a ship quarantined in Vancouver and an exposé of a Toronto land developer. Management was also unhappy with the expanded opinion section, which, it thought, gave too much space to letters from readers.

"I *am* hurt," Peter reiterated to Annesley. "I *am* angry, frustrated, and dispirited."

Annesley was sitting alone in a room with a man whose anger frightened her. He had been forced to resign. Annesley knew that he wanted sympathy, but somehow she felt more sympathy for Maclean-Hunter management. And she said so in the article.

Peter's colleagues also had misgivings about their editor. When Lefolii in 1964 and Templeton in 1969 had resigned, staff members followed suit. However, not one of Peter's journalists resigned in sympathy with him. There was discontent concerning Peter's dismissal of seven staff members. Some, like Horst Ehricht, were happy to see Peter go. On Christmas Eve 1969, Peter had tried to fire the respected director of photography, who had been with *Maclean's* since 1965. As Ehricht saw it, Peter preferred people who paid homage to him and who would play and drink with him on weekends. Ehricht wasn't a member of Peter's volleyball set.[62] Philip Sykes, managing editor of the magazine, as well as Douglas Marshall, didn't support Peter.[63] As Robert Fulford notes today, during Peter's few months as managing editor, he "hadn't established the kind of rapport with staff that would make people follow him out the door."[64]

Shortly after his resignation, Peter became involved with Patrick Watson, who was attempting to found a Canadian version of *I.F. Stone's Weekly*, with one satiric eye on Ottawa politics and the other on news and analysis of Canadian topics. Peter agreed to be editor. The magazine would deal with breaking news in the manner of *Radio Free Friday* and *As It Happens* and would emulate the edginess and satire of Stone's publication. According to Watson in his memoirs *This Hour Has Seven Decades*, Gzowski wrote most of the first and only issue, which no longer exists.[65]

To make money, Peter returned to freelance writing. In November 1970, his daring article "My Five Marijuana Problems: An Interim Report on the Non-Medical State of My Head" was published in *Saturday Night*. After months of hearings, the LeDain Commission on marijuana had just released an interim report, which recommended legal but controlled sale of marijuana, using the model of the provincial liquor stores. Since there was little or no proof that marijuana led to harder drugs, the commission recommended the decriminalization of possession of modest amounts of pot. Peter agreed, and one evening at home he persuaded Jennie to try pot. "Whether or not the first time I smoked marijuana was 'a trip,' I don't know," Peter wrote in the *Saturday Night* article. It was "nice," and both he and Jennie liked it. Jennie, however, saw the darker side of drugs and booze. "But it's marijuana," she protested, "And God knows there's enough trouble around this house with booze."

As the article came to a close, Peter also expressed doubts about the drug, especially since Andrew, the twenty-six-year-old dealer who had sold the pot to Peter, was subsequently found dead from a drug overdose, his body "crumpled at the bottom of a bridge." Did he want any of his own children to end up the same way? he mused. No matter what, Peter added, he believed that all parents should come clean with their children about their own pill popping and booze. And they should stop pretending to have all the answers.

It was a typical Gzowski piece, mixing confession, ambivalence, and whimsy. It was also a bold article for 1970. Growing, selling, and smoking the drug were indictable offences. Peter was also bold in his use of marijuana outside his home. According to a Toronto publisher who worked at the CBC in the late 1960s and early 1970s, no one was surprised by the smell of pot in a studio just vacated by Peter.[66]

— 8 —

Radio, Peter's Early Days,
1965–1971

*I may not always be as nice in private as I try to sound
on the radio — in private, in fact, I am more given to waspish
comments and pointed sarcasm than I ought to be.*

— *Peter Gzowski,* The Private Voice

One Friday evening in the summer of 1969, producer Doug Ward was
in a CBC Radio control room. Through soundproof glass he watched
as Peter Gzowski and Maggie Morris settled in for their show. Ward
began to cue up the theme music. Suddenly, he witnessed a strange
pantomime — Peter leaped from his chair, and Maggie made a dive
for the belt of his trousers. Ward ran from the control room into the
studio. "What happened?" he shouted. Soon he learned that, while
removing the plastic lid from a large container of scalding tea, Peter
had spilled the contents onto his lap. The long cast on his left arm,
whose purpose was to cure tennis elbow, had made it awkward for
him to manoeuvre the lid, and the container had flipped over. Maggie,
a trained nurse, reacted instinctively. In order to allow Peter's skin to

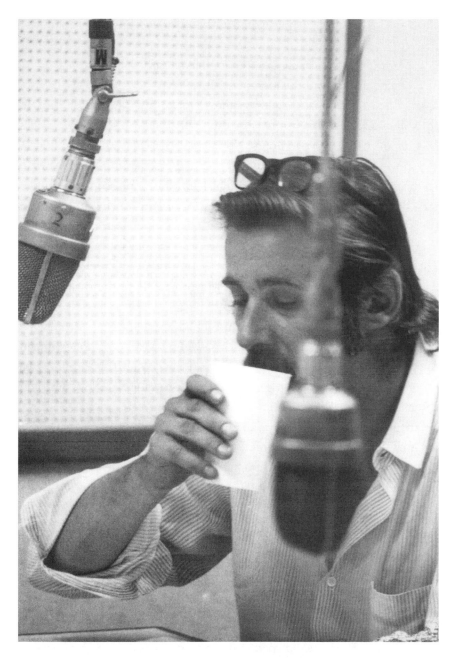

Peter and tea, circa 1969. Maggie Morris may be about to dive for his trousers.

(Courtesy CBC Still Photo Collection)

cool, she knew that his pants had to be removed quickly. Hence her dive for Peter's pants.

"Do you want to cancel the show, Peter?" Ward asked.

"Of course not" was the indignant reply. Ward returned to the control room. The theme music began to fade. Peter calmly introduced himself, then announced to his listeners in the Maritimes what they would be hearing over the next two hours. Not a single listener was aware that as the show rolled across Canada hour by hour, Peter sat in the Jarvis Street studio stripped from navel to toes as his skin slowly blossomed into blisters. By 1:00 a.m. Toronto time, as the last moments of the show drifted over Vancouver Island, he was in considerable pain. That evening what Ward admired most about Peter was his professionalism.[1]

The show was called *Radio Free Friday*, a name that celebrated the freedom of the weekend and the freewheeling style of the show and its host. Doug Ward and Peter also liked the implied send-up of *Radio Free Europe*,[2] a Cold War broadcast that preached liberty to people who lived behind the Iron Curtain. Each Friday evening Ward and Peter hoped to liberate the minds of listeners from St. John's to Fort St. John. It was an era of liberty, culminating in Woodstock in August 1969, when all things, even global peace, seemed possible.

By 1969 radio had long Canadian (and Newfoundland) roots dating from 1901 when Guglielmo Marconi experimented with radio signals from Cornwall to St. John's, and the following year from Glace Bay to Great Britain and Ireland. In 1923 Canadian National Railways established Canada's first radio network, which by 1926 extended from Atlantic to Pacific.[3] During the early 1920s, newspapers in Vancouver, Winnipeg, Toronto, and Montreal set up their own radio stations. The *Toronto Star*'s CFCA broadcast music and lectures each evening, as well as occasional afternoon concerts featuring what the *Star* called "many of the best known artists in the city." CFCA's range was wide, from Toronto to Port Elgin, Buffalo, Rochester, and even Ohio.[4] By 1928 more than sixty Canadian privately owned radio stations were licensed by Ottawa.

During the 1920s, American stations began to reach into Canada, and the *Toronto Star*, which apparently didn't fear the competition and perhaps recognized that readers wanted a choice of stations, printed a daily schedule of accessible American programs. The programming on those U.S. stations, including WJZ from New York City, featured classical music concerts with occasional breaks for news and stock market updates.[5] Canadians were also listening to radio shows emanating from American stations such as KDKA, Pittsburgh, and from privately owned Canadian stations such as CFRB, the Rogers station in Toronto.[6]

Some Canadians, especially an educated elite, grew concerned that more and more of their fellow citizens were listening to American stations and that U.S. networks had pre-empted the majority of frequencies. In 1929 the Aird Commission recommended a publicly owned, not-for-profit system modelled on British public radio. Accordingly, in 1932, the Canadian Radio Broadcasting Corporation (CRBC) was established with powers to regulate and control all radio broadcasting in Canada. Graham Spry, who, with Alan Plaunt, was the main lobbyist for a public system, argued that Canadians had a choice — the state or the States. One of the CRBC's first moves was to take over the Canadian National Railways radio network and production facilities,[7] though, because of economic constraints during the Depression, the CRBC never gained complete control of broadcasting in Canada as envisaged by the Aird Commission. By 1944 the CBC owned three networks, two in English and one in French. Meantime, Canadian-owned private stations, as well as American programs such as *Fibber McGee and Molly* and *Lux Radio Theater*, remained popular with Canadians, including the Brown household in Galt.

The launch in 1952 of CBC Television's visual appeal enticed companies to move their advertising budget from radio to TV. At that time, and into the 1970s, CBC Radio depended, in good part, on advertising income.[8] Frustrated by decreasing budgets, production staff and radio stars such as Wayne and Shuster and Don Messer and His Islanders began to defect to television.[9] Historian Sandy Stewart calls the period from 1954 to 1970 the dark age of radio,[10] even though there were many worthy CBC Radio programs such as *Preview, Assignment,* and *Anthology. Preview,* launched in 1957, was the first attempt to enliven early morning CBC Radio by reducing long, earnest weather forecasts, by extending the hourly newscasts, and by adding film and book reviews.[11] As late as 1970, a parliamentary commission on Canadian media chaired by Senator Keith Davey concluded that, while newspapers were "indispensable" and TV exciting and influential, radio in general was important only during emergencies and as a "source of background noise."[12] By that time, however, CBC Radio had begun to seek solutions to its falling ratings.

During the late 1960s, Doug Ward, a radio current affairs producer, and Peter Meggs, host of a radio show called *Concern*, a public affairs documentary series, were commissioned to explain why Canadians were disinclined to listen to CBC Radio. While the format of radio had remained fixed during the 1960s, listeners' needs and desires, the two men pointed out, had changed. Their report called for a major overhaul, including fewer Toronto-oriented shows, more listener participation, and greater flexibility of schedules. In order to encourage "more spontaneous and creative exchange,"[13] one of the major suggestions made by Meggs and Ward was to increase the number of intelligent and unscripted discussions heard on radio.[14]

Ward and Meggs had the backing of Margaret Lyons, acting head of current affairs at CBC Radio.[15] When she returned to Canada in the 1960s, after working for several years with the BBC in London, Lyons recognized that radio in Canada had become scripted and predictable. Some of the voices heard on CBC Radio were too crisp and formal. In April 1969, as *Radio Free Friday* was about to go on the air, Lyons explained to DuBarry Campau, a journalist with Toronto's *Telegram*, that, since the art of listening had become more casual, the style of radio had to become more conversational.[16]

Over the fifty years of radio broadcasting, the radio audience had radically changed. During the 1920s and 1930s when radios were so large that they sat on the floor, listening was usually a group or community activity.[17] In the 1940s, as radios grew smaller, they were placed on a shelf or table. Peter and his mother used to listen to *Lux Radio Theater* on their brown plastic Marconi radio in Galt. During the early 1940s on Saturday evenings, Peter was allowed to take that radio to his bedroom where he listened alone to *Hockey Night in Canada* narrated by Foster Hewitt.[18] In his room at Ridley College in the early 1950s, he listened to hockey broadcasts, perhaps with his roommate John Girvin.[19] During the 1950s and 1960s, lightweight portable transistor radios, as well as improved car radios, further splintered the listening audience.

In December 1964, someone, perhaps Peter himself,[20] had contributed an unsigned article to the review section of *Maclean's*. The subject was CBC Radio. "On the first of November," the article began, "the CBC reopened its FM network linking Ottawa, Montreal, Toronto and Vancouver, an indication that CBC brass and the politicians who rule them have at last recognized that radio is not dead, but has merely moved from the living room into the kitchen, the car and the street." The anonymous observer added that CBC Radio had once been the "backbone of Canadian unity" but was now considered "a backwater," ever since the mid-1950s when its audience and hence its sponsors had moved to television. However, there was hope, according to the article, because of a growing segment of the population — busy housewives and young mothers and their husbands on the way to work.[21]

The splintered audience forced radio stations to become less formal and more conversational. Peter helped to develop that more relaxed style, which happened to suit his own spontaneous, mischievous, and informal personality. For *Radio Free Friday*, Doug Ward and Margaret Lyons were seeking a host who could move back and forth from written material to intelligent, scintillating talk.

Lyons and Ward were somewhat acquainted with Peter, for they used to see him hanging around the CBC Radio offices on Maitland Street in Toronto whenever he was looking for contract work. They also knew him as a superb print journalist. They may have heard him from time to time on radio. He was an occasional guest on *Audio*, a CBC Radio talk show.[22] On Wednesday afternoon, April 21, 1965, Peter was a guest, with John Carroll,[23] a professor of English at the University of Toronto, on a show called *Speaking of Books*, a half-hour program broadcast on the new CBC-FM service. The book under discussion was Norman Mailer's *An American Dream*. The chat was amiable, and all three men liked the book. The novel, which mixes fact and fiction, begins with the line "I met Jack Kennedy in November, 1946." Both Stephen Rojack, the narrator, and Kennedy are war heroes who have just been elected to Congress. On a double date with Kennedy, Rojack meets the wealthy Deborah Kelly. They marry. Years later he strangles her. The novel is written in Mailer's characteristic boisterous, graphic style: "the arm around her neck leaped against the whisper I could still feel murmuring in her throat, and *crack* I choked her harder, and *crack*, I choked her again, and *crack* I gave her payment ..."[24]

One of Peter's questions had to do with legacy. "Will [Mailer] be classed eventually as one of the great American writers?" he wondered. Was Peter perhaps thinking of his own legacy? At that time, when he was attempting to make a living by writing sports columns for *Saturday Night*, as well as anonymous television reviews in *Maclean's*, there was little prospect of a Gzowski legacy.

Once the program was over, the host and guests adjourned to one of the nearby bars across Jarvis Street, perhaps the Four Seasons bar or The Celebrity Club, where CBC personalities gathered to drink and to play word and board games. In the bar, Fulford and Gzowski were joined by Norman DePoe, CBC-TV's irascible newsman and chief reporter. DePoe began to boast about acting as a child during the late 1920s in rural British Columbia. Not to be outdone, Peter announced that as a "boy reporter" he used to act, and that at the age of twenty-two, while editor of *The Varsity*, he had taken the leading role in *The Man Who Came to Dinner*.[25] His imagination inspired by martinis or by Rémy Martin, Peter began to blend fact with fiction in the manner of Norman Mailer. Never once had Peter acted at Ridley College. Nor had he ever been a "boy reporter," except at Ridley. He had indeed played the leading role in *The Man Who Came to Dinner*, but in Timmins, a couple of years before editing *The Varsity*. After enduring the debate "in glum silence," Fulford departed to attend a play.[26] The following September, Peter was still in battle mode: in *Maclean's* he declared DePoe to be a non-star.[27]

Peter returned to radio on November 22, 1966, on the third anniversary of the assassination of John F. Kennedy. This time he was the host of a discussion among three members of the Warren Commission, which had recently concluded that the assassination had been the work of Lee Harvey Oswald, a lone gunman. The show was pre-taped and broadcast on FM stations at 11:03 p.m. For nighthawks there were other, more appealing choices, including American talk-show television, and on Hamilton's CHCH-TV, Pierre Berton was interviewing Hollywood actress Celeste Holm. During the autumn of 1966 and early 1967 when he was entertainment editor at the *Toronto Star*, Peter hosted a radio panel show called *The Arts This Week*, broadcast each Thursday evening at 6:30 on CBL-740, the CBC's AM station in Toronto. In February 1967, he did a series of shows for CBC's *Ideas* on the subject of sportswriters such as George Plimpton and A.J. Liebling. Peter thought that Plimpton dealt too much with violence, pain, boredom, and failure in sports and not enough with "the sense of pleasure" that sports gives players and audiences.[28]

On Thursday, April 27, 1967, in the *Toronto Star*, Nathan Cohen announced that CBC Radio planned to air Peter's documentary *How The Beatles Changed the World* on May 9.[29] On May 6, 1967, Barbara Frum, the *Star*'s radio columnist, also reminded readers of the upcoming documentary. The Beatles show was produced by Geraldine Sherman, who had left her native Chatham, Ontario, for McGill University around the time that Peter had left Chatham for *Maclean's*. In 1966, Sherman had joined the CBC where she soon became "a very, very fine producer" who was "extremely good at getting a lot of good work out of an enormous variety of contributors." She quickly aquired a reputation for keeping the CBC in touch with the changing tastes of listeners.[30] If any one person should be given credit for Peter's first important step into radio, that person would be Sherman, who recognized that his magical voice and casual style were meant for the new, less formal radio. Perhaps Sherman agreed with her contemporary, June Callwood, who also admired Peter's broadcasting skills. "In those days," Callwood once explained, "a man who interviewed with empathy was rare."[31]

No doubt Sherman had read Peter's insightful article on Bob Dylan in the January 1966 issue of *Maclean's*. In it Peter had noted that The Beatles, like Dylan, were influenced by classical music. In fact, Peter was one of the first commentators in Canada to note the sophistication of The Beatles' music. When The Beatles appeared in Vancouver, William Littler panned them in the *Vancouver Sun*. Once he moved to Toronto in 1966, however, Littler began to recognize that The Beatles' music was inventive and complex.[32]

In his script for The Beatles documentary, Peter explained the Liverpool group's intelligent lyrics and complex rhythms, and he noted some of their influences, including Motown, Chuck Berry, soul, and East Indian music. He confessed that when he was seventeen Frankie Laine had been his idea of good singing and inspired lyrics. Now, however, Peter admitted he appreciated the intricacies of The Beatles' lyrics and rhythms.

To research the show, Peter interviewed a variety of people, from Malcolm Muggeridge, who didn't like the Liverpool Four, to Leslie Fiedler and Aaron Copland, who did. "Music has a sacred function … uniting man and honouring ancestors," a young Leonard Cohen told Peter, after which Judy Collins sang Cohen's haunting "Susanne," which was influenced, Cohen told Peter, by the unpredictable rhythms of Paul McCartney's "Yesterday." Near the end of the program "Yesterday" was played, with each line featuring a different group, from the Boston Pops to The Supremes and The Beatles themselves.[33] The show was ninety minutes of radio at its best. It was the first time that Elizabeth Gray, and no doubt many other listeners, heard Peter on radio. That evening Gray heard in his voice the same "mischief, the barely suppressed laughter, almost a schoolboy giggle, that had made working with him on *The Varsity* so much fun a decade earlier."[34]

When Ward and Lyons chose Peter for *Radio Free Friday*, they knew they had a good, if sometimes difficult, host. *Radio Free Friday* was to be broadcast on Friday evenings, beginning in April 1969. Its counterpart, *As It Happens*, which had begun the previous November, was broadcast on Monday evenings.[35] While *As It Happens* concentrated on current affairs, *Radio Free Friday* was to be a mix of entertainment and journalism, music and satire. "We tried to follow and advance the main news and current affairs stories of the day," recalls Doug Ward.[36] Both shows, Ward told journalist DuBarry Campau, marked a return to an oral tradition that had been interrupted by print. Peter would be, thought Ward, a village storyteller. Ward, it seems, had been reading his Marshall McLuhan and Harold Innis.

For *Radio Free Friday* and *As It Happens* to interview people across Canada and around the world, reliable long-distance telephone was indispensable. The telephone had, in fact, played a small role in radio as early as the 1930s when Alberta listeners, for example, were able to call Premier William Aberhart during live broadcasts of his *Back to the Bible Broadcast* from the Calgary Prophetic Bible Institute. Over those unreliable, fuzzy lines came voices from Camrose and Consort to tell "Bible Bill" about problems, spiritual and economic. For calling out, the telephone was used as early as the 1950s, but not as a regular feature. In 1956, *Assignment* called Budapest for an eyewitness account of the revolution. In October 1957, also on *Assignment*, Lister Sinclair conducted a transatlantic interview with a drama critic in London. Not until the 1960s, however, when telephone companies in North America built microwave towers, which reduced or eliminated the fuzzy sounds produced by the old copper wires, did the telephone become reliable enough to play a central role on radio. From its inception in 1966, the half-hour *World at Six* used the telephone.[37]

The use of the telephone for radio interviews was first developed in Germany in the mid-1960s. The idea was brought to Canada by CBC program director Alan Brown, who was acquainted with Germany through its writers, many of whom he had translated. Jack Craine, program director for CBC Radio, endorsed and encouraged the use of the telephone, for it helped him to solve a dilemma. The CBC's mandate was to cover the country, and, if it could, to unite it. At the same time, each region demanded some local programming. The telephone allowed *As It Happens* and *Radio Free Friday* to cover local, national, and international events without the expense and inconvenience of sending reporters across the country.

The structure and methodology of both *As It Happens* and *Radio Free Friday* were complex. Each show's broadcast time was two hours, but it took six hours to produce. In CBC parlance, the format was "rolling," and each of the four and a half time zones heard a slightly different version. Just after the 7:00 p.m. news in Toronto, the first hour was broadcast to the four Atlantic provinces. The first hour consisted of five or six phone-out interviews, some of them live, some of them prerecorded a few hours earlier. When hour one was finished, a story editor spent the next hour editing the tape for later use. Meantime, the second hour broadcast to the Atlantic provinces was heard as the first hour in Ontario and Quebec. The format of the second hour was identical to that of the first, and likewise the methodology — at the end of the second hour the tape was edited in preparation for upcoming hours farther west. At 9:00 p.m. in Toronto, Peter bid adieu to Atlantic listeners. At 9:05 he welcomed back Ontario and Quebec listeners, and welcomed listeners in Manitoba, and in the winter months, Saskatchewan.[38]

When the show reached the Prairies, Peter's role became slightly less hectic, for during hour three (Ontario, Quebec, Manitoba, and sometimes Saskatchewan), the best stories from the first hour were rebroadcast, along with perhaps two new stories that seemed specifically relevant to the West. For the story editors, too, the work was now less onerous, for there were only two new stories to consider for the two remaining time zones. At the beginning of hour four, Peter welcomed Alberta listeners, and in winter, listeners in Saskatchewan, and he welcomed back Manitoba listeners. Hour four consisted of the best stories from hour two, along with a couple of new stories. In hour five, Peter welcomed listeners in British Columbia, and welcomed back Alberta, and sometimes Saskatchewan. This fifth hour consisted of the best stories from hours one and three, along with one new story. As he bid adieu to listeners in Alberta and sometimes to those in Saskatchewan, it was midnight in Toronto. At the beginning of hour six, Peter welcomed back B.C. listeners, and the best stories from hours two and four, along with, sometimes, a new story, were broadcast. At 1:00 a.m. in Toronto, Peter said goodbye to West Coast listeners. The six hours had come to an exhausting conclusion.

Even with Peter's bountiful energy and determination, neither he nor the staff could have stood that pace five days per week. Gradually, Doug Ward and the story editors realized that all interviews could be captured by pre-taping them late Friday afternoon or during live interviews with the Atlantic provinces. And gradually Ward realized that, since most of the stories were of national and international import, there was no point in trying to tailor each hour to suit the tastes of each region. When Ward realized that it was no longer necessary to keep Peter and his on-air assistants in the studio until 1:00 a.m. Saturday morning, introductions and goodbyes for the final hour were pre-taped.[39]

Radio Free Friday was a window through which Peter and his listeners examined the passing scene at the end of the 1960s and the beginning of the 1970s — times of social and political upheaval. Peter interviewed Black Power advocate Stokely Carmichael, whom a producer discovered somewhere in Africa. Another Black Power figure, Eldridge Cleaver, was interviewed from Algiers, and John Lennon, along with Yoko Ono, were interviewed in bed while giving peace a chance in Montreal. In June 1970, Peter talked to Guy Bertrand, former candidate for the leadership of the Parti Québécois, who believed that the party should field candidates across Canada. One Friday evening in September 1970, the show broadcast part of an interview with Salvador Allende, who, it appeared, would become the first socialist leader of Chile. In November 1970, Peter talked to I.F. Stone about his new book *The Hidden History of the Korean War*. On the same evening, he interviewed Simone Chartrand about her husband, Michel, the labour leader who had been arrested during the October Crisis. In February 1971, Jack McClelland explained to Peter why he might be forced to sell his publishing company to Americans. One day producers arranged a debate with feuding fishermen who had been taking potshots at one another on the Bay of Fundy. As well as using the telephone to reach interviewees, Peter encouraged listeners to call him. Calls came from West Virginia, Fort McMurray, Labrador City, and even from a boat off Vancouver.[40]

Peter was always assisted by a co-host. During the first weeks of the show, he worked with Louise Delisle, who introduced the music, introduced and closed each segment of the show, and sometimes commented on interviews. As the introductory music died down, Delisle, in her soft, lilting Québécois accent, gave the name of the show. As it rolled across the country, she helped Peter to welcome each time zone, and she gave a preview of the next hour. In aged tapes located at the radio archives of the CBC in Toronto, one can sense the thrill and joy in Peter's voice as the show rolled across thousands of miles. No doubt listeners in 1969, still basking in the glow of Expo 67 and Trudeaumania, were as excited as Peter. Perhaps it was indeed true, as journalist Charles Taylor once argued, that George Grant, in predicting the demise of Canada, had inspired people to prove him wrong.

For Peter, hockey was the essence of Canada. On his first *Radio Free Friday* show, he discussed the sport, beginning with a brief introduction recorded at a hockey game for eleven-year-old boys. Accompanied by the sounds of shouting and pucks whacking into boards, Peter announced that he was a hockey father and was at an arena with his son, Peter. (During those early morning hockey practices, Peter himself was being observed by a young ticket collector at the North Toronto arena. Christie Blatchford, whose father was the arena's manager, loved Peter "madly." He was "cheerful and funny even at 5:00 a.m." Importantly, adds the *Globe and Mail* reporter, "They say you can judge people by how they treat those who can do them no good. Peter was lovely.")[41] Once the tape of the hockey game had ended, Peter announced that he was worried about hockey violence. His live guests were Brian Conacher, in the studio, and by telephone, Eric Nesterenko.

Peter was adept at moving from a hard-edged interview to the soft interview that followed with Moses Znaimer, future founder of CITY-TV. Znaimer had recently returned from Bosnia, then part of Yugoslavia, where he had discovered water that was guaranteed to increase male potency. By telephone, Znaimer told Peter that he had brought back two bottles of "sexy water," which he had purchased for forty cents. He had given one to Patrick Watson and kept one for himself. Unfortunately, his own bottle exploded before he had a chance to test its contents. Peter didn't inquire about Watson's potency levels.

One of Peter's first interviews on *Radio Free Friday* was with a woman in Vancouver whose husband had recently embarked on a round-the-world sailing trip. As the interview faded, Simon and Garfunkel's "Mrs. Robinson" started to play. While Patrick Scott of the *Toronto Star* recognized Peter's talent for radio, he expressed dislike for the host's taste in music, which often "sank" to the depths of the Edison Hotel and the Horseshoe Tavern, venues for country, western, and rock music in Toronto in the 1960s. Peter himself was really a glorified DJ, thought Scott.[42] What Scott didn't know was that the music was selected not by Peter but by Volkmar Richter.[43]

In June 1969, Maggie Morris, who perhaps had forgiven Peter for once calling her a non-star, became his sidekick. Like Louise Delisle, Morris introduced and closed each hour, commented on interviews, and sometimes asked for elaboration. Also she performed practical duties such as giving out the studio phone number for contests, like the one on June 27, 1969, to name Canada's new communications satellite. Peter wanted to name it "Leonard Cohen." Eventually, the satellite was called *Anik*.

When Peter introduced the topic of blue jeans with "Well! The dirty old Americans are doing it again," Maggie broke in with "Waddaya mean? Waddaya mean?" which allowed Peter to explain that Levi Strauss of San Francisco had just purchased Edmonton's Great Western Garment (GWG), whose overalls had helped to open the West. The theme of farming was pursued. Peter turned to the telephone. On a bad line to Saskatchewan, Peter talked to a wheat farmer about early frosts and low prices. On a better line, he talked to a Massey-Harris dealer, also in Saskatchewan, who reported slumping sales. When the interview was concluded, Morris introduced the next tune, Max Montgomery's "Road Song."

On Friday evening, August 15, 1969, Peter interviewed Rennie Davis, a leader of the American peace movement. The twenty-nine-year-old Davis was facing charges of inciting riots during the Democratic Party Convention in Chicago in August 1968. Davis, who had just visited North Vietnam, told Peter that, far from being defeated by American cluster bombs, North Vietnam was taking advantage of those bombs by locating vegetable gardens in bomb craters where residual nitrates acted as a fertilizer. Railways and bridges were being rebuilt, and the country had developed a lively underground system of factories, schools, and hospitals. Davis had spoken to Ho Chi Minh, premier of North Vietnam, who had told him that the North was prepared to continue the fight well into 1970.[44]

The war in Vietnam marked the beginning of the long, slow decline of the American empire, and with it, the rise of nationalism in Canada, which, since at least the 1930s, had been relatively content to be a cultural and economic member of the American empire. As early as the mid-1950s, however, some Canadians had become wary of growing U.S. control of the Canadian economy, and that wariness gave birth to a "New

Nationalism," so named in order to differentiate it from the nationalism and National Policy of Sir John A. Macdonald, a policy of protective tariffs that, with modifications and variations, had directed Canada's economy from the late 1870s into the 1930s.[45]

Peter's lament about "those dirty old Americans" taking over Canadian industry, and his sympathetic interviews with American dissidents, strongly suggest that he was influenced by the New Nationalism. Since the mid-1950s when Peter was a struggling university student, Walter Gordon had been advocating a moderate "national policy favouring domestic investment and management of the economy."[46] Gordon, in turn, influenced Jim Laxer and Mel Watkins, who, in turn, influenced Peter. Peter had met Laxer in the mid-1960s when the latter was a member of the New Left, so called to distinguish itself from the socialism of the 1930s, out of which had sprung the Co-operative Commonwealth Federation (CCF). To research and write "Crusaders of the New Left," published in *Maclean's* on November 15, 1965, Peter had attended a meeting of the New Left in St-Calixte, north of Montreal, and had come away with admiration for those peace activists whose roots, he surmised, lay among the radicals or "beatniks" of his own generation of university students. Whereas "beatniks" were "cool, withdrawn, and negativistic," the New Left was actively attempting to reform the 1960s. Unlike the Old Left of the 1930s, the New Left disdained politics, preferring instead to work with civil-rights groups and ban-the-bomb demonstrators.[47]

During the spring of 1969, Jim Laxer, his father, Robert, and Mel Watkins founded the Waffle movement, a name, according to Laxer *fils*, that came from a New Left member who supposedly said, "I'd rather waffle to the left than waffle to the right." The Waffle emerged out of frustration with the successor to the CCF, the New Democratic Party (NDP), whose leader, David Lewis, refused to take a strong stand against large unions, which were an important component in the coalition that had created the NDP.

The Waffle was also unhappy with the governing Liberals. In 1967, Mel Watkins had been commissioned, along with seven other university economists including Abe Rotstein, to draft a report that would advise Walter Gordon, finance minister in the Pearson government, on foreign ownership in Canada. The subsequent Watkins Report recommended moderate Canadianization of the economy. American-owned companies, for example, shouldn't be allowed to forbid Canadian branches from dealing with countries like Cuba and China. The Pearson government rejected the report.[48]

At the Waffle's founding meeting on April 29, 1969, the topic of discussion was "the position the NDP ought to take on American domination" of the Canadian economy.[49] American investment threatened Canada's independence, Waffle members argued. In its place, the Waffle movement called for government-controlled investment, the nationalization of Canadian industries, and "a democratic redistribution of decision making powers."[50] The founding meeting of the Waffle occurred just nineteen days after the launch of *Radio Free Friday*.[51]

James Laxer was a regular on *Radio Free Friday*. In order to satirize politics and the status quo, Laxer and Doug Ward created a character called Talleyrand, named after Charles Maurice de Talleyrand-Périgord (1754–1838), one of the most influential of all European diplomats. On *Radio Free Friday*, Talleyrand was Swiftian, and the character allowed Laxer to make astute and humorous observations on politics. On the first *Radio Free Friday*, Laxer/Talleyrand, known also as "Mr. X," observed that President Charles de Gaulle had pulled France out of NATO, and that he was planning to use Canada as a base for spying on the United States.

Peter was not, apparently, pleased with the Talleyrand concept, and Ward wondered if his aversion had something to do with the fact that he hadn't originated the concept. Margaret Lyons speculates today that Peter's displeasure was caused by Tallyrand's Waffle ideology. Rather than stating his reasons, Peter simply argued against Talleyrand on the grounds that the satire was so intellectual that it went over the heads of his listeners.[52]

Ward quickly realized that Peter had his own ideas on how the show should work, and, in fact, Ward concluded that Peter didn't really need a producer. He was a self-absorbed perfectionist, and it soon became obvious that he was a superb interviewer. He was quick to pick up the essence of books and articles, no matter what the topic. He demanded the best from himself, and he was well prepared for each interview.

Never a show-off, he reached out to each listener. On air he developed the persona that became his trademark, that of the shambling, stuttering, self-deprecating host. That persona, together with his voice of smoke and honey, so beguiled listeners, as well as guests, that they often failed to notice that his questions were laser-sharp. To paraphrase Finley Peter Dunne, Peter comforted the afflicted and afflicted the comfortable.[53] One of Peter's listeners was Michael Enright, who remembered Peter's interviews as "a fully charged and rounded conversation that had muscle and texture and vitality."[54] Patrick Scott may not have liked the music, but he did like Peter, who, according to Scott, had a "persistent way with an interview." Scott thought Peter was the show's greatest asset.[55]

Thus it must have come as a surprise to listeners and colleagues when, on Wednesday, April 1, 1970, Peter suddenly resigned, or so Patrick Scott reported in the *Toronto Star*.[56] Peter may have decided to devote more time to his work as editor of *Maclean's*. About three weeks later, however, he suddenly resigned from the magazine.[57] He returned to *Radio Free Friday*, and the show, with Peter as host, survived until August 1971.[58]

One of the most dramatic evenings was Friday, October 16, 1970. Before sunrise that same day, the federal government had resurrected the War Measures Act, which gave emergency powers to the federal Cabinet. The Front de libération du Québec (FLQ), which had kidnapped British diplomat James Cross and Quebec Cabinet minister Pierre Laporte, was outlawed, and a list of civil liberties were temporarily suspended. Immediately, the police in Montreal began to arrest anyone suspected of supporting the FLQ.

"This is *Radio Free Friday*" was Peter's introductory line that evening. Then he quickly added, "Not so free tonight." Neither Margaret Lyons nor producer Mark Starowicz, who had succeeded Doug Ward, knew exactly which civil liberties were curtailed or how much freedom of speech was allowed on the show that evening. The day was, according to Peter, "surely one of the most significant political occasions of our time," and almost beyond comprehension. "Our government," he added, "acting in our name, arrested and incarcerated people not for what they had done and been convicted of, but for what the government thought they *might intend* to do." The act was unwarranted, he argued, for there was no apprehended insurrection. And yet he could understand the dilemma faced by the prime minister. Pierre Laporte and Pierre Trudeau were friends.

On that Friday evening, the show was devoted to the crisis. Peter interviewed Laurier LaPierre on government intervention; Walter Tarnapolsky, dean of law at the University of Windsor, on the meaning of the War Measures Act; and three British journalists who were puzzled why the War Measures Act was invoked to deal with what seemed to them to be a minor threat. Dick Inwood reported from Montreal that troops weren't much in evidence, and Tom Earle reported that, in Quebec City, people made little fuss over the troops, and that Premier Robert Bourassa appeared calm when he explained to the press why his government had urged Ottawa to call in the army.[59]

The next evening, Saturday, October 17, 1970, Jennie and Peter were playing bridge with friends. Like most Canadians at the time, the four players kept one ear cocked to a nearby radio. "The announcements came in bursts," Peter remembered, "at first confused, rumours, hints confirmed, contradicted, reaffirmed ... and finally, correct and indisputable." The body of Pierre Laporte had been discovered in the trunk of a car. Once the bridge players realized the "obscenity" of the act, they ceased playing.

"Our world, our country had changed," Peter mused a year later. Most Canadians were horrified and shocked by this political murder in a country that had so far avoided the civil unrest in the United States and France.

After the October Crisis, Peter's nationalism grew more subtle. He became more interested in the cultural life of Canada in both official languages. His nationalism became more emotional,[60] which gave it broader appeal, for while most Canadians were lukewarm to the appeal of economic nationalism, a majority, it is fair to assume, agreed with Peter's sentiments expressed a year after the October Crisis: "If you had to boil down my love of this country to one word, that word would be 'hope' — hope for the future, hope that we can work things out here."[61]

Throughout the 1970s, economic nationalism declined[62] while emotional and cultural nationalism remained important, in one way or another, for most Canadians.[63]

During the summer of 1969, Peter had acted as substitute host for a morning radio show called *Gerussi: Words and Music for the Middle of the Morning*, launched in the autumn of 1967, with Alex Frame as its first producer, assisted by Diana Filer, who later became producer.[64]

Even before he filled in for Bruno Gerussi, and, in fact, before he became host of *Radio Free Friday*, Peter had been intrigued by the show. During the first months of 1968, while editor of the *Star Weekly*, he had commissioned the young journalist, Bill Cameron, to write a piece about the show. As he applied his pencil to Cameron's prose, the editor of the *Weekly*, no doubt, grew more and more interested in what his young staffer had discovered. In the article, published on April 6, 1968, Cameron noted that the show featured interviews, music, and poetry, some of it written by listeners, and on one occasion, by schoolchildren. The show "swings," Cameron concluded.

What Cameron especially noted was a new style of radio, more conversational, more relaxed.[65] At first Diana Filer found the prospect of two hours of unstructured radio a bit daunting. One day Barry Callaghan, a regular guest, told Gerussi that the structure of the show reminded him of hockey. While the show and the game appeared to be random, they were both highly structured. Hockey used an ice surface that was divided by painted lines and governed by rules; there were three periods, and two nets for scoring. For Diana Filer, who was listening from the control room, Callaghan's metaphor was reassuring. For each of the show's two hours, there was one regular guest. Callaghan, for example, discussed books; during the last five minutes before the 10:00 p.m. news, Nathan Cohen talked about theatre; Alan McFee[66] added his eccentric wit and naughty wisdom; and journalist Larry Zolf threw in what Cameron called "the odd zinger." Gary Dunford wrote topical poetry, Andrew Allan read beautifully crafted essays, and Marjorie Harris talked about books and other topics. Christina Newman was the specialist in politics, and Helen Hutchinson did weekly commentaries, mostly about literature.[67]

In addition to the regulars, there were guests. One morning a professor from York University inveighed against the hypocrisy of Canada's marijuana laws. On another morning, Weldon Hanbury[68] talked about the "sorrows of being a first-time novelist." In between regulars and guests, Gerussi had no trouble filling in the time with poetry, some of it pre-taped, and by reading newspaper articles upon which he commented. As Cameron watched, Gerussi referred to a long newspaper article about Pierre Trudeau, who was running for the leadership of the Liberal Party. "Wouldn't it be amazing if Trudeau got in?" the host commented theatrically. Gerussi moved on to an excerpt from a novel by George Bagby, after which he read an editorial called "How to Get Your Taxes Cut." Too much tax money was going to education, the editorial argued.

Gerussi, Frame, and Filer also welcomed the voices of ordinary people who, as Cameron pointed out in his article, had rarely been heard, at least on a regular basis, on radio. The new style of radio was democratic and participatory. One morning, for instance, one of Gerussi's guests was Sarah Sisson, a matriarch of Toronto's Cabbagetown, which in 1968 was just beginning to be transformed from a working-class area into a middle-class enclave.

As substitute host during the last week of July 1969, Peter interviewed Judge Little of York County, north of Toronto. The topic was, once again, marijuana, a subject much in the news because of the LeDain Commission. "There is overwhelming medical evidence from around the world," the judge told Peter, "that tobacco is a health hazard." However, the judge also brought Peter good news, that there was no such evidence for marijuana.[69] Peter was back as guest host in September. In the *Toronto Star* of September 18, 1969, Patrick Scott judged Peter a better interviewer than Gerussi, an opinion contested a few days later by a *Star* reader who thought that Peter as host "merely ventilated an infantile humour and a childish self-centredness."[70] However, no matter who thought what about his radio skills, Peter was still drawn to print journalism. He needed full-time employment, and he probably believed he had something to prove at *Maclean's*. On September 16, 1969, two days before Scott's review, Peter applied for the job as editor of *Maclean's*.

Even during his short second term at *Maclean's*, Peter was drawn to the Gerussi show as a freelance contributor. On November 17, 1969, he did a short piece on dressage at the Royal Winter Fair.[71] During the summer of 1970, after he was forced to resign at *Maclean's*, Peter returned as guest host on *Gerussi*, and was back in early March 1971. On March 3, one of his guests was A.C. Forrest, long-time and sometimes controversial editor of the *United Church Observer*, who, during the seven-day Middle East war of 1967, had dared to express sympathy for the Palestinians. Once again, in the summer of 1971, Peter substituted for Gerussi. Guests included Chester Ronning, the Canadian politician and diplomat who had flown to Hanoi in 1965 and 1966; Ontario Premier William Davis; and Hollywood director Dalton Trumbo, who had been blacklisted in the 1950s for his alleged membership in the American Communist Party. By 1971, Peter, like most intelligent broadcasters, was taking a stand against the American role in Vietnam. The interviews with Ronning and Trumbo, author of *Johnny Got His Gun* (1939), considered to be among the best of contemporary anti-war novels, were but two examples of the anti-war and anti-American sentiment that grew until the end of the war in the mid-1970s.[72] Like Patrick Scott, Blaik Kirby, media critic with the *Globe and Mail*, was impressed by Peter's talents on radio. On August 10, 1971, Kirby speculated that Peter might be more than suitable to replace Bruno Gerussi, who had accepted an offer to star in *The Beachcombers*. While Gerussi was theatrical on radio, Kirby noted, Gzowski, as summer replacement, was "less obtrusive, highly sensitive, admirably relaxed and amiable, and absolutely unaffected." Whenever Peter was host, the mail grew in volume and enthusiasm.

Alex Frame was an admirer of the Gzowski style. He watched the Gzowski radio persona develop whenever Peter had substituted for Gerussi. Frame realized how appealing Peter was, especially with a morning audience composed, for the most part, of women of all ages. What Frame liked was Peter's intimacy and vulnerability, and the fact that these qualities never sank to artifice or mere performance. In addition, Frame noted what Doug Ward, and later, Mark Starowitz, had heard on *Radio Free Friday*: Peter never allowed his astute journalistic skills to slip. His mind was always laser-sharp.[73]

The only nagging question was Peter's reliability. Alex was none too pleased one morning when Peter arrived late because he had missed the ferry from Ward's Island to the Toronto mainland. One day Alex asked Peter Meggs, head of CBC-AM programming, for his opinion on Gzowski as a permanent replacement for Gerussi.

"But Peter's an evening man, isn't he?" Meggs told Frame. "He won't succeed as a morning man."

Frame was determined. "There is something about the morning time slot that turns Peter on," he replied.

Shortly thereafter, Frame ran into Peter in the CBC cafeteria and offered him the job of host on a permanent basis. Because of the collapse of two television projects and his failure at *Maclean's*, Peter was in low spirits. He feigned indifference. Anyway, he told Frame, Mark Starowicz wanted him as one of three hosts for *As It Happens*.

"Look," Frame told Gzowski, "you have a choice, a safe show or a show that lives on the edge, that requires a host that is innovative, creative, and imaginative."

Peter thought about it. One day he and Peter Meggs were walking up Church Street. "I can't afford another loser," he mumbled to Meggs.[74]

— 9 —

Peter's Country in the Morning, 1971–1976

I'm a Barbara Frum fan unabashedly. Yes, I'd say she has some qualities that are supposed to be masculine — an ability to be tough-minded, not to take the easy answer and not to shrug it off. Barbara is just a bleepidy good interviewer; she has a superb quality of mind, a superb understanding of what's important. She won't let go until she's been told what's important. Now if these are masculine, aggressive qualities, then okay.

— Peter Gzowski, as Reported by Trent Frayne,
Toronto Star, *February 23, 1974*

In early October 1971, Peter and Alex Frame launched *This Country in the Morning*, which ran in each time zone from 9:13 a.m. until noon.[1] The four Atlantic provinces received the live version, and the other time zones heard the taped version. On one occasion, artist Greg Curnoe[2] used the F-word, which went live to the Atlantic provinces but was bleeped out for more sensitive ears in time zones farther west. The only problem was that technician Ron Grant bleeped out the wrong word, which left listeners from Quebec City to Qualicum wondering just what offensive word, obviously far worse than the F-word, had been expurgated.[3]

Peter was lucky to have a strong producer in Alex Frame, and they were both lucky that the two of them got along so well, for the relationship between producer and host is the key to a good show. Too often, a performer fails not for want of talent but for want of strong, sympathetic guidance. Like the masters of Ridley College, Frame guided Peter with a firm hand, which he always required in order to do his best. Frame was "highly intelligent and ambitious,"[4] and Peter enjoyed what he called Frame's "gleeful cockiness."[5] Perhaps they worked well together because they had little in common, except for a love of cigarettes and poor taste in clothing. Since they rarely met socially, they never grew tired of each other at work.

Early each weekday, Peter read the "greens,"[6] his carbon copy of the outline and questions for each interview prepared by the story producers who had talked to the guest a day or two earlier. Just before each interview, Frame and Gzowski spent about two minutes discussing the questions and strategy. Frame's purpose was to keep Peter focused during each interview. Once it began, Frame was in the control room within eyeshot of Peter though the large glass window that separated the control room from the studio where Peter worked. Frame communicated with Gzowski via facial gestures and by holding up large index cards — he sometimes used thirty for each show — on which he might write a word that suggested a new direction for the interview, or he might tell Peter to develop an idea from a previous part of the interview. Frame never let Peter go dry and never allowed him to feel abandoned.[7] One morning Harry Bruce observed the "almost spooky rapport" between the two men and compared their silent communication to "the way catchers talk to pitchers, with head movements, meaningful looks, secret signals."[8]

Today Robert Fulford gives Frame much credit for the development of the Gzowski style, an idea corroborated by one of the show's producers, who remembers that, at 11:00 a.m. each morning, once the last minutes of the show had been sent eastward to the Atlantic provinces, Frame and Gzowski listened to the show on tape. "See there, Peter," Alex might tell him. "You cut off that comment," or "Listen, Peter, you let that man meander." As Frame explains today, Peter was not so much interested in making himself sound better as he was in producing the best possible show.

Peter's trademark stammering and stuttering also developed under Frame. "I've loosened up a lot since doing *Radio Free Friday*," Peter told DuBarry Campau in 1970. "I used to try to be a real professional," he continued, "a Lloyd Robertson type ... Now I stumble or stutter and lose the thread of a thought half way through whatever I'm saying and I don't mind at all."[9]

Like any good executive producer, Frame was adept at one other important facet of broadcasting. He knew how to pry money out of the CBC, which resulted in a show that was better staffed than any other program at the time. Whereas the Gerussi show was put on air with a handful of producers, the staff of *This Country* numbered a dozen or more, all first-class, most of them young, and they developed what Robert Fulford calls "a wonderful esprit de corps."[10] Even though she was not a producer, Ruth-Ellen Soles was included in story meetings, and she was expected to contribute. Peter, she remembers, was an incredibly shy man who could become quite blustery if an interview did not meet his standards.[11]

Harry Bruce also noted the informal rapport among the staff. "Somebody was banging out the music's beat with a ballpoint pen. Somebody else started to dance. Affectionate wisecracks flew around the room."[12] Producer Bill Casselman was an occasional on-air commentator on the quirks of Canadian English. Krista Maeots, the show's managing director, and, according to Peter, "the most politically active staff member," was only in her mid-twenties when the show began. While she shared with her husband, Jim Laxer, the ideology of the New Left, Frame hired her because she was a strong, smart journalist.

Following the example of Gerussi's show,[13] the format of *This Country* was a mix of conversation, puzzles, games, essays, recipes, advice, music, nostalgia, contests, skits, arguments, and emotions. The loose structure of *This Country* allowed plenty of room for creativity. The day before each show, Frame, Gzowski, and producers discussed the next day's show. While some guests were interviewed by telephone, others came into the studio. Following the Gerussi model, when there was no guest available, Peter read and discussed newspaper clippings of current events. David Amer was in charge of the music. The day before each show, Amer chose a stack of vinyl LP records. By placing a paper across the record with an arrow pointing to the exact place on the record where the needle should be placed, he was able to select the correct song as accurately as one does with today's CD tracks. Peter scribbled ideas on scraps of paper and wrote essays or billboards to be read on the air, usually at the top of the show. His topics were varied, from flirting to the October Crisis to his rules for playing a civilized game of golf.

The first show, broadcast on Monday, October 4, 1971, was a good example of the mix of improvisation inside tight scheduling. It began with the shows upbeat theme music, a mix of country and rock. "This country in the morning, this country in the morning," the opening line, was followed by what sounded like "Wakin' up to be pa't of it," which emphasized the participatory nature of the show. Each morning the theme music inspired Christie Blatchford's mother-in-law's dog to bark.[14] The singers of the theme music continued with "Reachin' out to get hold of it … talkin' and listenin' … Things are gonna be so good …" Once the music faded, listeners in kitchens and cars across the country were ready to be informed about Peter's country in the morning. In the family laundry room in Ottawa, as a steam iron puffed and belched, young Shelagh Rogers listened as Mrs. Rogers ironed.[15]

On the opening show, the first nine minutes featured Earl Pomerantz,[16] TV critic for *This Country*. Peter and Pomerantz discussed *The Mary Tyler Moore Show*, a sitcom that had made its debut in September 1970. That show was groundbreaking — for the first time on television, an independent, self-supporting woman played the main role. At the end of the segment Joan Baez sang her rendition of "The Night They Drove Old Dixie Down," a song that had a Canadian angle, Peter told his listeners, for it was written by The Band, whose members were mostly Canadian.

By 1971, advertisers had been drawn back to CBC Radio. Between segments of the show, an insurance company, Eaton's, American Motors, Kentucky Fried Chicken, Molson beer, Eastern Airlines, Canadian Pacific Airlines, and others helped to bring *This Country* to air. The CBC also advertised itself. On *This Country*, there were ads for *As It Happens* and *The Max Ferguson Show*.

The next segment, which ran for seven minutes, was a dialogue between Helen Hutchinson and Peter on the subject of paperback books. The segment ended with the smooth and easy sound of "Nelson," who sang "My Old Desk." The following segment presented ordinary voices. On tape Lorne Saunders of Moosonee told listeners he had puked so hard "that he never remembered" what came up, and he promised to cure any woman who wanted to quit smoking by feeding her a plug of chewing tobacco.

Walter Stewart's *Shrug: Trudeau in Power*, a biography, occupied the next fourteen minutes. Trudeau, Stewart argued, hadn't managed the economy well, and he had created a centralized inner Cabinet that wielded far too much power. Yes, Stewart agreed, the book was angry, but he believed that more journalists should write with commitment and anger. On Quebec, Stewart disagreed with Peter that support for independence was dropping. Following the interview, the Toronto Mendelssohn Choir sang "The Old Maid's Song" from an LP of the choir's Newfoundland folk songs. The first hour concluded with the show's theme song, this time an instrumental version. The 10:00 a.m. news followed.

Hour two began with a short radio essay by Peter, who admitted that magazine writers had a habit of recycling old material. He referred to his article called "My Five Marijuana Problems," published in *Saturday Night* a few months earlier. His point, Peter told listeners, had been to show how scared he was that his children would use drugs, particularly because his oldest, Peter C., had just entered high school. Now, a year later, Peter wasn't so worried. "I guess the kids are a lot more grown-up now than some magazine writers," he concluded.[17]

After a musical interlude, Peter spent nine minutes with lawyer Aubrey Golden examining civil rights and the role of the police, an interview that was followed by the sounds of a whistling dentist from Vancouver. One minute was given over to a short poem read by Nova Scotia's Bill Howell. Helen Hutchinson interviewed Toronto psychiatrist Dr. Ben Geneen on female frigidity, following which she talked to Dr. Stanley Fefferman, a professor at York University, on the subject of his experimentation in Mexico with hallucinogenic plants. Peter spent eight minutes interviewing Don Shebib on his new film *Rip Off*, which followed his critically acclaimed *Goin' Down the Road*.[18] After Shebib, Bill Howell read more of his poetry.

Next came an eight-minute interview conducted by Danny Finkleman, who became one of the show's regular contributors. On that first episode of *This Country*, Danny interviewed Rummy Bishop, a stand-up comedian appearing at Starvin' Marvin's Burlesque Palace in Toronto. The informality of *This Country* suited Finkleman — he had no desk at the CBC and never attended production meetings. Finkleman just arrived and did his piece. Peter trusted Danny to come up with something interesting and amusing.[19] Immediately after the 11:00 a.m. news came a pre-taped interview, which took up the whole of the third hour, on the subject of the war in Vietnam. The guest was Jane Kennedy, who had spent fourteen months in prison for protesting the war.

Three days after the show's launch, Jack Miller, the new TV and radio critic for the *Toronto Star*, was pleased that Peter was "not turned on by a microphone the way the theatrical Bruno Gerussi used to be." Instead, according to Miller, Peter was "turned on by some of his guests."[20] Media critic Martin Knelman noted that, since Peter always lived for the moment and always sought instant gratification, the loose format brought out the best in him. *This Country*'s audience soon reached about one hundred and fifty thousand listeners.

Over the three years of the show, the list of guests and topics provide a snapshot of Canada at the time. In 1972, Helen Hutchinson interviewed Xaviera Hollander, a well-known hooker whose book *The Happy Hooker* provided details of her profession. That same year Hutchinson interviewed Jill Johnson on the latter's lesbianism, as well as sexuality in general, a topic that had rarely, if ever, been discussed on CBC Radio. Danny Finkleman spoke to Eric Margolis about the debate between natural and chemical cosmetics, and Peter interviewed Bryce Mackasey, who had recently resigned as minister of labour in the Trudeau Cabinet.

Peter and Alex Frame, sometimes to the consternation of Margaret Lyons, who was never sure where or when they were going, took the show to most corners of the country.[21] (Actually, Peter and Alex took great delight in annoying Lyons.)[22] "In three years," Peter noted, "we originated from nearly three dozen places from St. John's to Tuktoyaktuk."[23] In early September 1973, Peter was in Winnipeg, where he talked to Manitoba Premier Ed Schreyer about his political background and the fact that, at age twenty-two, he had been the youngest ever member of the Manitoba legislature.[24] Peter also travelled to Prince Albert, Saskatchewan, where he interviewed John Diefenbaker in front of the courthouse where the former prime minister had often acted as a defence lawyer. In Ottawa, Peter talked to Lester B. Pearson, not long before his death in December 1972, an interview Pearson's daughter greatly admired.

During the winter of 1972, the show journeyed to High River, Alberta, where, in the town's library, Peter interviewed W.O. Mitchell, his favourite Prairie writer. Mitchell was surprised when High River friends such as Grace and Charlie Clark, parents of future Prime Minister Joe Clark, emerged from behind bookshelves. Mitchell was always a good storyteller, and like Peter, he had a relaxed voice and style that suited the new, informal radio of the early 1970s. That morning he reminisced about transporting his grandmother across the international border, and of smuggling bananas from Hawaii into Canada.[25]

On October 23, 1972, in the Toronto studio, Peter interviewed Robertson Davies, whose novel *The Manticore* had just been published. It was the first time that Peter and Davies had met, though Peter claimed to be familiar with all of Davies's novels and plays. In fact, he thought Davies's *Leaven of Malice* was a "great novel," though there is no evidence in his articles during the 1960s that he had ever read it.[26]

Other well-known Canadians came into the studio for interviews: Celia Franca, founder of the National Ballet of Canada; actor Donald Pleasance; director Norman Jewison; and Leslie McFarlane, author of the Hardy Boys detective novels. Scott Young came by to talk about his famous son, Neil. When the Nashville-based singer Brenda Lee was in Toronto in early January 1973, she talked to Peter. The subject of one interview was James Bay Natives and their treaty rights. Another show featured a series of diary entries written by an expectant mother. One show examined the city of Belfast, where armed troops patrolled the streets.

During the autumn of 1972, Peter did a series of interviews on the fantasy lives of well-known people. Harry Bruce fantasized about becoming either a bartender or a chaplain aboard a corvette. He also fantasized that he would write great short stories in the style of Guy de Maupassant.[27] On Thursday, October 12, Adrienne Clarkson dropped by to reveal her fantasies. Even though she hated crocodiles, the host of *Take 30* could think of nothing better than to "penetrate" the mouth of a large tropical river, slowly, on a raft. How soothing, beautiful, and restful to be all alone, she explained, as one moved toward the heart of the river, yet never arriving.

"I have great fantasies about being a singer, being an opera singer," Clarkson told Peter, even though she confessed that her family, the Poys of Ottawa, used to bribe her not to sing. She imagined herself in a major role such as Violetta in *La Traviata*. At *Il Trovatore* in Stockholm the previous summer, she had fantasized that she was both the tenor and the soprano. She also admitted to standing in front of a mirror mouthing Peggy Lee songs, which she knew by heart. Perhaps "Fever"? Or "Is That All There Is?"?[28]

Letters were an important component of the show. Ellen Nygaard and Peter selected a few to be read on the air each day. When Marci McDonald interviewed Peter in February 1972, he showed her some of them. "They're pouring their guts out, getting involved, just wanting to talk things over," Peter told McDonald.[29] In a five-page letter, a woman described her first kiss at age thirteen. Someone wrote from Frobisher Bay (now Iqaluit) to tell Peter that, while on a camping and hunting trip on Baffin Island, she had listened to *This Country* at Ward Inlet, thirty-six miles from Frobisher. Letters often came in response to an interview or to one of Peter's essays. When Helen Hutchinson did a series on knitting, Peter received a letter with photographs from a retired railway engineer who had knitted 146 afghans for the Red Cross. Peter ran a contest on crafts, and a listener wrote a letter about how to build a bird feeder. One woman wrote about living in a caboose.

On Boxing Day 1973, a pre-taped show, Peter ran a contest called "The Worst Christmas Present," which drew many letters. On another show, Peter asked for letters of resignation. A woman in Saskatchewan announced her resignation from feeding the pigs, and a teacher in Ontario submitted letters of resignation written by her grade eleven English class. From Fort Smith, Northwest Territories, a woman resigned from Monday clothes washing. One contest asked for the definition of old age. Peter challenged listeners to complete the sentence that began with "A man is not liberated until ..." A contest on local jokes drew a response from Newfoundland about a passenger who wanted to get off the Newfie Bullet halfway to St John's. She was pregnant, she explained to the conductor, who told her she shouldn't have boarded in that condition. "I didn't," she replied. When Justin Trudeau was born on Christmas Day 1971, Peter ran a limerick contest, which elicited poems such as "There once was a baby named Justin / Who said I have parents I trust in / But I'm wondering why / Every time that I cry / The RCMP has to bust in." One day Peter asked for suggestions for a new winter holiday. He received a flurry of letters, including one that wanted a holiday called Chinook Day.

One of Peter's best interviews during that final season was with Pauline Julien, who, in words and music, was a strong supporter of Quebec sovereignty. In October 1970, during the October Crisis, Julien and her partner, poet Gérald Godin, had been among the four hundred or so Québécois who were locked up after the implementation of the War Measures Act. Julien was so emotional, Peter claimed in his memoirs, that she reached across the table and seized his hands.[30] She told Peter that he would never understand paternalism because, as a man and as an English Canadian, he was part of the power structure that kept women and French Canadians in chains.

This Country and Peter were much feted. At the second annual ACTRA Awards Dinner on Saturday, April 28, 1973, his peers in television and radio deemed him the best public affairs broadcaster over the previous year and a half. Runners-up were Barbara Frum and Pierre Berton,[31] who was one of Peter's fans. "I've been rearranging my schedule to give myself an extra half-hour's sleep in the morning," Berton told Peter in December 1973, "and so I am coming into town a bit later which gives me a chance to hear a good chunk of *This Country in the Morning*.... It's a hell of a program — ingenious, irreverent, witty and informative and I love every minute of it."[32]

Marci McDonald also liked the show. In the *Toronto Star*, she claimed that Peter was "the new darling of daytime radio." He had turned the three hours of morning radio into "three of the most vital, engaging and talked-about hours in any medium — and himself into one of the most vital, engaging and talked-to broadcasters this country has ever known." She thought that his voice was "just boyish enough to get away with a credible on-air guffaw, burnished with just enough living — to go with a face that looks like it's done a lot of living indeed."[33] On the other hand, some reviewers were unimpressed. Dennis Braithwaite of the *Toronto Star* disliked the "frightful music" and was fed up with Gzowski "phoning all over creation every morning of the week."[34]

The show and its chauvinistic host have rarely, if ever, been given credit for helping to advance the cause of women's liberation. Judging by the letters to Peter and to the editors of newspapers in Peter's defence whenever critics panned the show, the majority of listeners were female, many of whom appreciated the fact that the program provided them with intelligent book reviews and informed debates on current affairs. Women also appreciated the fact that Peter invited them to write or phone in their opinions "on controversial subjects" as they ironed, cleaned a floor, or sipped on coffee.[35]

"When *This Country* went on the air," Marjorie Harris once recalled, "the women's movement was tucked away in little corners all over Canada." Women's studies programs, she added, were just being launched, and feminists were labelled as bra burners. On *This Country* for twenty minutes each week, Harris discussed daycare centres, equal pay, and equal rights. Once Harris's radio essays began, women wrote letters accusing Peter of patronizing her and often chastised her for not retaliating. The series brought together ordinary women, both rural and urban, in ways that university lecturers never could. As the series progressed, Harris herself grew liberated. She even suggested housekeeping should be recognized as an occupation.[36] By the end of her series, Harris, with the compliance, not always willing, of Frame and Gzowski, had succeeded in using *This Country* to advance the cause of women's liberation.

—•—

On Wednesday, June 26, 1974, during the last week of *This Country*, Jack Miller, radio reviewer at the *Toronto Star*, visited its studios on Jarvis Street. Although the show seemed casual, Miller took note of how professional it had become. On one wall was a blackboard with a large graph of fifteen squares, one for each of the show's fifteen hours per week. In each square was the name of a person to be interviewed. The planning was done on one floor, and the show was broadcast from the floor below. "With maybe two minutes to spare," Miller reported, "Gzowski ambled into the matchbox-sized broadcast booth adjoining the control room and sat at one of the two microphones. Frame gave him a hand-wave signal and he was on the air." In the third square, which represented the third hour for that Wednesday, was the name of a writer and his book on alligators. When the author couldn't be reached by telephone, Frame played a twenty-minute tape of an interview with an alcoholic. The highlight of that day's show, in Miller's opinion, was Danny Finkleman's review of the Bolshoi Ballet, which, much to Finkleman's displeasure, had sent third-rate dancers to Toronto.[37]

On the final show, two days after Miller's visit, Peter spent the first seventeen minutes thanking his staff, his "incredible bunch of people, soft and strong" and always inspiring. They "fought, laughed, danced, giggled, drank, teased, tangled with each other … just like a family." He named them: Nancy Button, Sheilah White, Andrew White, Herb Watson, Betty McAfee, Bill Casselman, and Krista Maeots. He mentioned Hilary Armstrong, Bonnie Bisnett, and Judy Brake, his three story editors, and Frances Cardiff, Gary Katz, and Bob Rhodes. And finally, Alex Frame, whom Peter described as "kind, gentle, cute, cuddly … slim, hardworking, clever," which brought a guffaw from Frame.

The rest of that final show featured fiddle music and spoons; a Winnipegger who was following an ant around his home; an interview with W.O. Mitchell and Paul Hiebert; and during the third hour, a series of glimpses of that same week in 1954, twenty years earlier, including Marilyn Bell's swim across Lake Ontario, Hurricane Hazel, and Bill Haley's new music called rock and roll. In Rome, Pope Pius XII feared the "deep reaction" that TV was creating in people, though he did appreciate the fact that TV could bring the family together again. And Emily

Dionne, one of the five quintuplets, died of epilepsy in 1954. Live in the studio, Angèle Arsenault and Edith Butler sang.

During the final four minutes, Peter's voice cracked with emotion. He thanked the cast of the show. He thanked his listeners, many of whom were no doubt in tears. "I've learned that journalism, or whatever it is we do here, is a two-way street, and the people who taught me that are the people who listen to the program." He praised the quality of the letters, and after he announced his retirement, he was moved by the quantity of letters. "I'm going off the air now for a rest and a change, but I'll be back on CBC Radio."

Alex and Peter had always known that any show that demanded so much of Peter's energy could have only a limited run. At the end of three years the show had gone as far as it could go. Peter had wanted to quit at the end of the second year. "Too many shows ... go on after they've lost the energy, enthusiasm and freshness that made them successful," he told Marci McDonald a few weeks after the show ended.[38]

Charles Lynch felt sad and wished Peter the very best. He loved the program and Peter's style, so composed, relaxed, thoughtful, informed, and interested. Marci McDonald would miss Peter's "careless, guffawing charm that vibrates across the airwaves with a decidedly sexual quotient." She recognized that radio was the perfect medium for Peter, not only because he knew how to use it but also because it hid his nicotine-stained fingers, his hands that shook with energy, and his red-rimmed and pouched eyes. From Halifax, over the three years of the show, Harry Bruce listened to the "nice" voice and wondered how such a man, who wasn't always nice in person, could be so nice to strangers.[39] During those three years of *This Country*, Peter admitted, he had learned how little he knew. "Show me a man with a pat definition of what makes Canada," Peter had once said, "and I'll show you someone who doesn't know what he's talking about."[40]

As *This Country* was coming to its conclusion, Peter was plunged into what Ron Base of *Maclean's* called "a yearlong funk." He was depressed and "unsure of what to do next."[41] On Saturday night, June 22, 1974, six days before the show ended, he drove into a parked car on Mount Pleasant Road in Toronto. Charged with drunk driving, he lost his licence for three months and was fined $150.

Before *This Country* ended, the CBC had engaged Peter and Alex Frame to help develop new program concepts, to train people to emulate the Gzowski style, and in Jack Miller's words, "to come up with a new series for themselves, too." They were also helping to plan the CBC's coverage of the upcoming Olympics of 1976. In August, after a month of holidays, the two men moved into CBC offices at Bay Street and Yorkville Avenue in Toronto. Sid Adilman, who was close to Alex and Peter — the three of them enjoyed fishing trips together — was probably the first to report that they were already discussing with Peter Herrndorf, newly named head of CBC-TV's current affairs, the possibility of a television show. Jack Craine was hoping to have them back on a new radio show within a year.[42]

Peter was also busy putting together a book about *This Country*. On September 19, 1973, he had written to Mel Hurtig to tell him about a novel concept for a book that would publish recipes, stories, letters, and transcripts of interviews, including those with Lester Pearson, John Diefenbaker, W.O. Mitchell, and a woman who lived in a caboose. He wanted to include his interview with Howie Meeker on hockey, Pauline Julien on Quebec, hockey in Humboldt, Helen Hutchinson and Hugh Webster on second marriages, Danny Finkleman on the Stratford Festival, and so on. Then for the second volume, he announced exuberantly, a few Andrew Allan essays; Peter's memories of skating over ice-glazed fields; Harry Bruce on middle age; poetry, music, limericks; Arthur Vaile's advice on how to buy a schoolhouse; Bill Casselman's Canadian Quiz; and Adrian [sic] Clarkson's fantasy life, which, he assured Hurtig, didn't include Mel. Oh, Peter added, Harry Bruce wanted to be paid about $100, and Peter himself wanted a $2,000 advance.[43]

Hurtig liked the idea. In October 1973, Peter signed a deal. Hurtig paid him $1,000 on signing and promised another $1,000 for the completed manuscript. Betty McAfee and Nancy Button began to sort, select, and edit letters and interviews. When Peter finally began to examine hundreds of files, he was overwhelmed. Hurtig recommended that he hire Susan Kent, who had once been Hurtig's editor-in-chief. Mel Hurtig made it clear that it would be up to Peter to pay Kent. On January 16, 1974, Peter wrote again to Hurtig. Even though he was about to ask for a larger advance ($3,000), he began his letter by correcting Mel's misspelling of Peter's street. "Lytton," Peter explained, not "Litton."

Soon Susan Kent visited Peter at the CBC building on Jarvis Street where she found that the broadcaster's office was jammed with paper documents that spilled out into the adjacent hallway. Kent filled three or four boxes with scripts, letters, essays, recipes, songs, quizzes, and reports and took them to her house near St. Clair Avenue and Bathurst Street. After sorting the material into three piles labelled "Absolutely No," "Absolutely Yes," and "Maybe," she returned. Peter looked hurt. "You mean you don't like these?" he asked her as he riffled through the "Absolutely No" pile. He wanted to include almost everything. Reluctantly, Peter agreed with Kent's choices, but he still couldn't force himself to be ruthless. After more sorting, the two of them had what seemed like a manageable manuscript.[44] After copy-editing the manuscript, Kent sent it to Jan Walter, Hurtig's managing editor.

One day in the spring of 1974, Walter flew to Toronto, and with Susan Kent, she drove over to 98 Lytton.[45] The big and breezy house was alive with children running in and out of the living room, a large white Samoyed thumping after them. Above the marble fireplace mantel hung William Kurelek's *Poisoning Gophers*. The living room featured black and red leather box chairs. In the adjacent dining room, the Notman portrait of Sir Casimir loomed over the sideboard. As Walter and Kent stood in the living room, they weren't even vaguely aware of Jennie. She might have been cooking in the kitchen or trying to calm down the children and their dog.

"It's too long," Jan Walter announced to Peter.[46]

More editing and purging. Finally, on September 30, 1974, Walter wrote to Peter to inform him she was working on publicity in preparation for his promotional tour in October and November. In Toronto, she added, Peter's agent, Bev Slopen, was arranging the tour. Walter's letter contained a small cheque, what she called "pin money" to cover food and drink and other incidentals. At the end of the letter she added a PS: "Book just arrived! Fantastic! Super!! We are ecstatic!!!"[47] Already she understood Peter's need for reassurance and praise. Hurtig Publishers, Walter remembered years later, was genuinely excited by the book and its innovative format.

The book managed to capture the spirit of the radio show. Submissions to the Canadian alphabet contest ended up interspersed throughout the book. "A is for Avro / and Arrow and air / But too much was hot / and it never got there"; B was Dave Barrett, premier of British Columbia; E was for EH, "and to it we owe thanks / For whenever we say it, they know we're not Yanks"; H stood for hitchhiking across Canada; I was for Indians — "the original Reds / They've left warpath for courtroom to challenge the Feds." Over twenty of Peter's radio essays made it into the final version, as well as four of Andrew Allan's essays and four by Harry Bruce. Paul Hiebert contributed Christmas poems, and the book contained about a score of listeners' letters, as well as plot outlines from the Great Canadian Novel contest.[48] Although a rather dreadful satire of Edgar Rice Burroughs's Tarzan and Jane characters, narrated by Peter, with Danny Finkleman as Tarzan and Robert Fulford as Jane, made it into the book, the interview with Adrienne Clarkson wasn't, alas, included.

The book also published, verbatim, Peter's interviews with Jane Kennedy and Prime Ministers Diefenbaker, Pearson, and Trudeau, as well as probably the least successful portion of the book, Peter's interview with W.O. Mitchell, who recounted the story of how he accidentally soaked the crotch of his seersucker suit in a New York airport toilet. To dry it, he lifted himself onto a sink so as to be closer to a blow-dryer. He was observed by two men "smelling strongly of Brut," who had, Mitchell told Peter, recently visited Weyburn, Mitchell's birthplace.[49]

One of the best pieces from the radio show was published near the end of the book. In "Boxing Day Lament," future Tarragon Theatre artistic director and frequent *This Morning* commentator Urjo Kareda pilloried the conventions of Christmas and Boxing Day, deeming the latter "the most loathsome day of the year." Kareda told Boxing Day listeners: "But probably the thing that will have you feeling the dumbest today is the high lunacy of Christmas cards. By now, you're probably surrounded, like Custer with those Indians, by wall-to-wall kitsch." His solution? Mark on each one RETURN TO SENDER, along with a festive greeting, THE SAME TO YOU, FELLA.[50]

On October 19, 1974, the day when news of Peter's court appearance for drunk driving was published in the *Toronto Star*, the paper gave his "scrapbook" a favourable review, though Anita Latner, the reviewer, preferred the contributions of listeners, which she thought more genuine than Peter's "wholesomely casual" style, which she found at times a bit "trying."[51] Fans, however, had no such misgivings. By early November 1974, the first printing of twenty-five thousand was almost sold out. Mel Hurtig had ordered a second printing of fifteen thousand and was keeping his options open for yet another seven thousand copies. At a fundraiser for the Edmonton Symphony, while an autographed photo of Prime Minister Trudeau fetched $150, lunch with Peter was bid up to $225.[52] In November 1974 under the title "The Principality of Gzowski," the book was excerpted in *Maclean's*. "His *Country in the Morning* was more than a radio program," read the catchy lead. "It was a land where grandmothers played Black Jack, separatists joined the RCMP and housewives lived through February by studying the nature of door knobs."

Peter was rarely idle. In January 1975 at the St. Lawrence Centre in Toronto, he joined Robin Spry in a discussion of the filmmaker's National Film Board documentary *The October Crisis of 1970*.[53] Later that month Peter helped lead a walking tour along Harbourfront, which at that time was Toronto's derelict waterfront.[54] The following April he filled in for a vacationing Harry Brown as host of *Metro Morning*, Toronto's local early-morning talk show.[55] From time to time, Peter was substitute host of *As It Happens*. On Tuesday evening, July 29, 1975, his guests were Joey Smallwood and Farley Mowat, who called Smallwood a "little charlatan."[56] The following October, Peter hosted the awards ceremony of the Canadian Film Awards Festival held at the Shaw Festival Theatre in Niagara-on-the-Lake.[57]

On November 3, 1975, Peter returned to radio on a regular basis as host of a show called *Gzowski on FM*. Broadcast weekdays from 4:00 to 6:00 p.m., the program launched an eight-station FM network. The focus of *Gzowski on FM* was the arts, which allowed Peter to interview musicians, actors, painters, theatre critics, writers, and dancers. The Orford Quartet and other performers were invited into the studio to perform live. Sid Adilman, who visited the show to do a regular commentary on show business, never used a script, nor did he talk to Peter in advance about his subjects of the day. According to Adilman, during his commentary, Peter's hands shook, his body was in constant movement, and "his lips moved silently with what I was saying as if he was about to interrupt."[58]

Bronwyn Drainie liked Peter's "open, generous Everyman's view" of the arts. He only owned one expensive piece of art, Peter told Drainie, a William Kurelek, though he didn't apparently tell Drainie he had always felt uncomfortable in its presence. Peter did, however, tell her about his eclectic record collection, which ran from folk to classical music. He also let her know that he was a devotee of the mystery writer John D. MacDonald, whose Travis McGee novels, Peter had told listeners of *This Country*, were trash, but good and skillful trash. The detective novelist based in Florida was, according to Peter, "a total master of his craft, a storyteller, an enjoyer of people and of the senses, endlessly inventive, tirelessly imaginative." In other words, MacDonald reminded Peter of himself. It was perhaps those same qualities that Peter enjoyed in the novels of Arthur Hailey and W.O. Mitchell. "There is nothing in the arts I know a lot about," he admitted to Drainie, "except hockey." Peter was overly modest. The music on the show ran the gamut from Mozart to Roy Rogers. Each day, Drainie noted, Peter did a music review of his own favourite singers such as blues singer Leon Redbone.

Peter's interviews were probing, reflecting what Drainie called his "well-developed curiosity." From theatre director John Hirsch, Peter elicited a telling remark: taking charge of the CBC's drama department, Hirsch noted, was like "landing on the tip of the iceberg that sank the *Titanic*." When the novelist Susan Swan argued that Canada's own Barbara Ann Scott had captivated audiences by allowing a photographer to focus on her crotch during a jump, Peter maintained that "for him, Scott would always personify sexless perfection." As host, Peter was never glib nor superficial nor snobbish, Drainie contended, but some of his contributors, she noted, didn't meet Peter's standards of *politesse*, and she singled out novelist Sylvia Fraser who, on a phone-in portion of the show, told a young woman from Winnipeg that, if she wanted to find a publisher, she should pack up her typewriter and move to Toronto. Drainie was unaware that a producer had ordered Fraser to be abusive. What Fraser remembered from the show was that the host camouflaged his "incisive, sophisticated and informed side" in favour of "his folksy, sentimental side." She also noted that a letter of praise from a reader would make him beam while a letter of complaint would cause him to brood.[59]

Peter's friend Dennis Murphy was director of *Gzowski on FM*. "We made some radical radio," he remembered. One day, in an attempt to make radio more visual, Murphy brought in members of a circus, and on another day, the cacophonous Artists Jazz Band performed and chatted. In December 1975, Peter introduced a trade-in service. Listeners were encouraged to call the show with a list of items such as books, musical instruments, old magazines, or anything else that fell under the category of artistic. One listener called to offer his wife in exchange for anything of equal value.[60] On another show, broadcast on December 19, 1975, a quartet of guitar players located in Halifax, Ottawa, Winnipeg, and Vancouver managed to harmonize their music. It was one of the first examples of a cross-Canada live quartet.[61]

Surviving shows demonstrate what Bronwyn Drainie called Peter's "close to tour de force" performance. On February 3, 1976, Peter opened the show[62] by announcing that Jerry Elder, his guest in the second hour, had just received a telegram announcing that Mikhail Baryshnikov, because of an injury, would be bowing out of an engagement with the National Ballet of Canada. That announcement was followed by "Motorcycle Blues" by Jessie Colin Young, a blues piece with lines such as "I see you sittin' in the driveway / Shinin' in the sun." Peter's tastes were indeed eclectic.

After the music, the first hour featured a discussion about Nathan Cohen, the *Toronto Star*'s theatre reviewer, who, in March 1971, not yet fifty, had suddenly died. "He made Canadians aware of their theatre," Peter noted in his introduction. Peter's guests that day were Robert Fulford and Cliff Solway, who were in the Toronto studio, and Sean Mulcahy, theatre director at the Citadel Theatre in Edmonton, who talked via telephone from Montreal. Solway mentioned that Cohen, while formidable and testy, could be highly amusing. Peter intervened: "That's a side of him that not many people saw, the informal … um … Sean Mulcahy, was there anything you remember …?" After more discussion, a technician played an excerpt of a radio review by Cohen from the late 1950s of Shaw's *Pygmalion* at Toronto's Crest Theatre.

"That review was quintessential Cohen…. Oh, he cared, he *cared*," Peter noted with passion and emphasis, adding that he had been at two or three openings when Cohen had been in the audience.

To conclude, Peter said to Fulford, again in his halting conversational style, "And, uh, I don't know … can you summarize, Bob, his influence …?" Fulford did just that, and Peter finished the show with "He taught us something about ourselves, and I thank you all." A short piece of jazz featuring guitar and drums ended the show. As it faded, Peter announced that, after the news at 3:00 p.m., he would be talking to Jessie Elder about Baryshnikov. "I'll see you then," he said.

Once *Gzowski on FM* was over in June 1976, Peter joined Elizabeth Gray on CBC Radio to cover the Montreal Summer Olympics. Ever keen on emulating the literary journalist George Plimpton, Peter cast his eye on the Olympic pool. Were it not for his orthopedic doctor, who reminded him of an old back injury, Peter would have tested the ten-metre diving board.[63]

"I happen to believe," Peter once wrote in *Maclean's*, "that forbidding your kids to watch things you consider in bad taste is not the way to implant good taste in them. So I don't make any rules about what my youngsters can see." Even if one of his children wanted to watch *The Three Stooges*, which Peter thought "obscene," he didn't forbid it. On Sunday evenings in the 1960s, Peter had once written in another article in *Maclean's*, the Gzowski family ate the evening meal on trays in the living room while watching *Walt Disney Presents*, one of the few television shows "that both generations in our house can watch without at least one of them getting either bored or annoyed." He admitted that the family harmony created by Disney was "a rare interlude of togetherness in the grey-blue light."[64]

It must, therefore, have come as a complete surprise to his children when Peter announced one day during the summer of 1973 that the family would be giving up television for a whole week. Apparently, the idea had emerged from a contest on *This Country*, in which Peter had urged listeners to give up some well-ingrained habit. Always the journalist, Peter must have told Roy Bonisteel about his proposed television-free week. During the summer of 1973, Bonisteel, host of *Man Alive*, a CBC-TV show that dealt with the spiritual side of life, took a ferry over to the Gzowski summer home. The resultant television episode, which was broadcast on September 22, 1973, was called "Reflections on a Fun House Mirror."[65] Was television creating a world of illiterates, Roy Bonisteel asked in his introduction?

On *Man Alive* the contented television-free Gzowskis were shown playing cards. His long hair spilling over his ears and down his neck, Peter played the indulgent father and loving husband. Afterward, Bonisteel interviewed Peter, his arms casually outstretched over the back of an old couch. What about withdrawal symptoms? Bonisteel asked. No problem, Peter assured Bonisteel. Even his children, Peter pointed out, realized that television was full of misrepresentation, false images, invented and tailored images. "But is there anything that does give you a true picture of the world?" he mused. "Newspapers? Patently not. Radio?" His body language implied a negative response. "Do you give a true picture of the world yourself?" he mused. We see truth, Peter seemed to say, through a glass darkly. No medium, he implied, neither television nor radio nor print, and certainly not the human eye and imagination, was capable of understanding or conveying truth.

Bonisteel asked a final question: Would Peter recommend that other families give up television? "Yes," Peter replied, "if the answer is 'Yes' to the question 'Are we watching TV as a substitute for talking to each other?'"

That interlude of family happiness, manufactured for the television screen, didn't last long. As Peter became more involved in radio and with his colleagues at the top of the Park Plaza, he spent less time with his wife and family. Given the energy-sapping grind of early talk-show radio, perhaps it was inevitable that he would seek solace wherever he could. At least at the top of the Park Plaza he was far away from the stress of work and home.

There are signs, however, that he felt guilty for being away from home so much. In 1973, around the time he was awarded an ACTRA Award for his work on *This Country*, Peter did something odd — in the middle of the night, perhaps en route to the conjugal third-floor bedroom, he crept into Alison's bedroom. To the startled and sleepy teenager, Peter apologized for not having spent much time with his children. He asked her to think of something special to do the next day. So astounded was Alison that her first reaction the next morning was to ask her brother, Peter, if he had seen their father creep into her room. Or was it perhaps a dream? Peter C. had slept through it all. In any case, Alison couldn't think of anything that father and daughter might do together. "It just seemed too late," she wrote eleven years later. "I don't think he was a bad father," she continued. "I just think he didn't know how to do it."[66]

In the same article, Alison admitted to being afraid of her father during the few times she saw him at home. Mick tells a similar story. "To a certain extent," he explained, "my father was always a shared commodity." And he was "famously bad on the phone." Mick had no choice but to join the ranks of Peter's radio fans, passive and appreciative.[67] At 98 Lytton, as Peter's radio voice echoed through the house, Jennie found it frustrating that she had no opportunity to talk back to her husband. One day, when Alison was confined to bed, she heard her father's voice. Excited at the prospect that she might actually see her father in daylight, she raced downstairs, only to discover that someone had left a radio playing in the living room.[68] Radio was also the main method of communication between Peter and his father, who in a lonely room in Sutton, north of Toronto, was proud to listen to his son's voice.

Those who knew Peter well concluded that he himself was a lonely man. In an article that Peter deemed to be "by far the closest anyone has yet come to capturing me in print," June Callwood argued that it was Peter's "unfinished sorrows," combined with his "nimble bravado," that made him, on radio, a natural communicator. His clown-like exterior, she speculated, hid a great deal of melancholy and grief. "Clowns," she added, "are the most melancholy of men."[69]

— 10 —

Television, That Cruel Business, 1975–1978

What you see on the screen is not reality at all; it is television.

— *Peter Gzowski,* The Private Voice

"Oh, Christ," Peter lamented in a letter to Mel Hurtig on Thursday, May 12, 1977, "I wish I didn't have a show to start getting ready for in 20 minutes, because I'm really hungry to write this."[1] Peter was referring to a book about his parents called *Starting Out*, for which Mel Hurtig had paid him an advance of $9,000. What made Peter eager to write this book was the death of his father nine days before Peter wrote his letter to Hurtig. On May 3, Harold had suffered a heart attack. Next morning, Ernest Madden, husband of Peter's Aunt Joy, called to tell Peter that his father had "passed away." Peter hated euphemisms. "He's *dead*!" he wanted to shout into the phone. Three days later Harold was cremated, and his ashes were placed in the family vault at St. James cemetery on Parliament Street in Toronto. Someone, either Uncle Ernest or the man at the crematorium, gave to Peter all Harold's worldly possessions: scraps of paper from his wallet, $63 in cash and coin, a pair of glasses, a tube of toothpaste, and the Gzowski ring that the Colonel had given Harold on his twenty-first birthday. Peter had neglected his father to such an extent that he didn't even know the man's correct age. Harold was sixty-two, Peter claimed. He was really sixty-six.[2]

Peter cleared out the room where his father had lived alone, red-faced, shaky-handed, and forlorn in Sutton. At the Toronto-Dominion bank Harold's account held the grand sum of just over $1,000.[3] As Peter was writing the letter to Mel Hurtig, he was wearing his father's watch. It was the first time in years, he told the publisher, that he had worn one. All those watchless years, he speculated, were a protest against "the way my life is now cut into minutes and sometimes even seconds." According to Peter, the watch and Harold's heart had stopped on the same day.

The "show" that Peter referred to in his letter to Hurtig was *90 Minutes Live*, a television talk program that Peter and Alex Frame had conceived in the spring of 1974 on the last day of *This Country in the Morning*. After Peter's emotional farewell, Alex and Peter chatted. One of the things that struck them was the visual quality of many of their radio interviews. They wondered what it would be like to reveal on television the fiery, gesticulating Pauline Julien, or W.O. Mitchell's surprised look when confronted by friends in the town library of High River, Alberta.

By 1974, Peter, more than most reviewers except for specialists such as Marshall McLuhan, understood how television worked. For instance, he was aware of the role of the camera. On March 9, 1963, in *Maclean's*, he had reviewed *Inquiry*, a current affairs show that dealt with topics like the role of the press, politics, and censorship. Peter especially liked co-host Patrick Watson's "spark," his ability to connect directly with each viewer. According to Peter, Watson understood how to convey to viewers complicated national events such as the abrupt resignation of Defence Minister Douglas Harkness from the Diefenbaker government.[4] Peter also admired the simplicity and honesty found in shows such as *Singalong Jubilee* and *Let's Sing Out*, which emerged "straight and pure out of the television set and into our living rooms." What he disliked was "television's advancing artistry" such as fake sets, canned laughter, and odd camera angles, which only served to remind the viewer that he or she was watching "a set of flickering images on a sheet of curved glass."[5]

When he wrote those perceptive reviews in the mid-1960s, Peter's only experience on the medium had been as a minor player in an edition of *Explorations*, produced by Daryl Duke. The theme of "The Imperfect Machine," a three-part sub-series of *Explorations*, was crime and punishment. Its host was Knowlton Nash, assisted by Alan Millar. On the first of three shows, broadcast on March 29, 1961, there were four guests — lawyer Arthur Maloney and journalists Pierre Berton, Sidney Katz, and Peter.[6]

Peter surely wanted to forget a disastrous audition in August 1969 when he joined Alex Trebek and Vivian Wilson in an on-screen test of hosting skills.[7] The Saturday evening version of *Weekend*, a news and public affairs show scheduled to begin the following October, was looking for a co-host. "The job," Pat Annesley noted in the *Toronto Star* on September 6, 1969, was "the most important on-camera television slot ever created in Canada." Lloyd Robertson had already been chosen as one of the hosts. The three producers — Richard Nielsen, Neil Andrews, and Ian Murray — were looking for a second male host and either one female co-host or three rotating female co-hosts. Barbara Frum was one of the leading candidates. More than a hundred people were auditioned.

On August 23, 1969, Peter, Trebek, and Wilson sat tensely on stools as they awaited their audition. The cameras had already begun to roll. The trio had been given time to prepare for a discussion of the role of television in modern society. Peter, on the viewers' left, sported an ill-fitting jacket, as well as a shirt, slacks, and tie, the narrow half of which was hanging parallel to the wider half. Peter gave his nose a vigorous rub. He smoked nervously. He looked uncomfortable. As his Hush Puppies tried unsuccessfully to find a comfortable rung on his stool, Peter began by asking the other two about birth control and abortion. Wilson earnestly explained that she was against abortion. While she was answering his question, Peter gazed off to his right, away from the other two. Once again he rubbed his nose. Rising slowly from her stool, Wilson introduced a film clip on the "Troubles" of Northern Ireland.

Ian Paisley pontificated while Roman Catholics threatened to take up arms. The clip ended.

The camera returned to the three bored panellists who took turns peering off the set. Suddenly, Peter stated forcefully, "There's nobody who needs arms," and as if to emphasize *nobody*, he waved his right arm, the cigarette arm. His left arm was more difficult to wave, since it was sporting a rather weighty cast. He rose from his seat and moved rather tentatively to another stool. Keeping his eye on the camera, he almost missed the new perch. Now he looked even more embarrassed and angry. But once he had the stage to himself, he seemed more confident. He delivered a speech or essay, the kind that he later perfected on *This Country* and *Morningside*.

While he was a TV critic for *Maclean's* in the mid-1960s, he confessed, he had panned the first edition of *This Hour Has Seven Days*. Now, however, he better understood the nature of television — it wasn't analysis but experience. In other words, TV's role, from its inception, was to allow the viewer to be present at an event, and he gave the example of the Belfast riots. However, during the 1960s, the print medium had begun to emulate television. While traditionally the role of newspapers and magazines was to explain an issue or an event, the daily and weekly press had become more personal, more direct, thanks to journalists who put themselves into the story. He was thinking no doubt of the New Journalists, most of them based in New York City.[8] Now that print had caught up with television, Peter continued, television would have to change. It should continue to relate the moment, but it also needed to find a way to set things into the larger context. In other words, what he seemed to be saying, rather unclearly, was that print and television were exchanging roles.

Peter rejoined the other two. "I like men," Wilson announced with a lovely smile. Peter looked even more uncomfortable. Once again, he glanced off to his right. When Wilson announced that she also liked *Take 30*, for it stimulated the minds of stay-at-home women, Peter's Hush Puppies grew restless again. He puffed even more relentlessly.

After Wilson came Alex Trebek, who admitted he had given up reading years ago! He meandered, then announced that sadists always gravitated to the military or to the police, who had recently arrested a teenager for smoking under age. A judge had pronounced the teenager guilty. "Wait a minute," Peter broke in. Wilson, in the middle, seemed perplexed. "The judge was trying to make the point that if there's a law," Peter argued forcefully, "then it should be enforced." Furthermore, Peter added, television was incapable of teaching. It could only show, and thus it wasn't the right medium to teach laws.

Peter concluded by telling the other two that he allowed his children "to watch anything they want to, to play with anything they want to play with, do anything they like.... I do not presume to think that I'm smarter than they are." Then his final word: "It's a violent world, and TV reflects that world, which, I guess, is the role of TV we began this edition talking about." The screen faded to black. A ghostly voice mumbled, "I'm Peter Gzowski."

There was one man at the CBC who understood how best to use Peter on television. Glenn Sarty was executive producer of *Take 30*. When Adrienne Clarkson was absent, Peter often acted as guest host. Sarty admired Peter's relaxed style of interviewing and his uncanny ability to coax guests to reveal far more than they had intended. Peter and Glenn connected on many levels. They were about the same age, and both of them had risen by virtue of their talents. Sarty was a good writer who appreciated Peter's writing and editing talents. On a personal level, they had much in common. Each man guarded his private life, and each was complex. After watching them on a film shoot, Sarty's son, Roger, concluded that "they thought so much alike, they didn't even need to talk much. Two grumpy geniuses who somehow connected."[9]

In 1969, Sarty wanted to try a new kind of show that combined information and entertainment, which came to be called "infotainment." When Len Casey was appointed head of CBC-TV variety, Sarty made him a proposition: "Give me ten thousand dollars and I'll make you a pilot for the variety show of the future." What Sarty had in mind was a one-hour show to be broadcast each month from September to May. The show would focus on the arts, he explained to Casey, and it would showcase emerging stars. It would be a version of *The New Yorker* on television, covering topics such as "literary, art, music and dramatic subjects."[10] A Cape Breton native, Sarty was keenly aware of the regional talent overlooked by the Toronto-based CBC.

One day Sarty ran into Peter in the parking lot of the CBC studios on Jarvis Street. Would Peter like to host the pilot? Would he have the time? Peter wondered, and more importantly, would he be any good?

"I'll make you look good," Sarty replied, then explained that everything would be done on location, far from a studio. Importantly, he would use film. He would shoot more than needed and select the best bits. Peter remained skeptical.

Sarty was certain that the idea would grow on Peter. When he drew up a tentative story list, Peter grew excited. The two men and several cameramen flew to New York City where they met Mike McGrady and Harvey Aaronsen, the creators of the novel *Naked Came the Stranger*, a collaborative spoof on sex novels popular at the time. *Naked Came the Stranger* was badly written, deliberately so. The book became a bestseller, and the good-looking woman who fronted as the author became a popular talk-show guest. When the spoof was revealed, McGrady and Aaronsen also became celebrities.

Peter interviewed the two men and met the "author." Almost immediately he fell in love with the idea of filming interviews on-site, especially with such intriguing characters as literary con artists, who appealed to his creative, inventive side.

Early that evening, Sarty, Gzowski, and crew arrived in Cold Spring on the Hudson River, north of New York City, where next morning they met Pete Seeger, one of Peter's heroes, who with Joan Baez, Bob Dylan, and other folk singers was protesting the war in Vietnam. Seeger was also an environmentalist. His hair blowing in the gentle breeze as he stood on the deck of the schooner *Clearwater*, Peter asked Seeger, "How do you use music, your strongest weapon, to clean up pollution on the Hudson?" By staging concerts at venues along the river as he sailed northward, Seeger explained. The segment ended with a concert that evening back at Cold Spring.[11]

Once back in Toronto, Peter was convinced that Sarty's concept would work and that he could succeed as host. It was film, not live television, and Peter liked that. Film cameras were flexible, more mobile, and less intrusive than lumbering in-studio cameras. Importantly, film could be edited, and any mistakes, from poor questions to bad angles, could be removed. On film, especially if it was shot outdoors, Peter could remain informal. The only things that irritated him were cutaways and re-asks.[12]

Peter as host of the successful Gzowski pilots in 1969, directed by Glenn Sarty, who knew what to do with Peter on television. Too bad CBC management didn't have the foresight to allow Peter and Glenn to produce a series called Take 60, *with Peter as host*

(Courtesy CBC Still Photo Collection)

For the next segment, Glenn and Peter flew to St. John's and drove to Portugal Cove. From there a car ferry took them to Bell Island, the birthplace of Harry Hibbs, another of Peter's heroes. This segment of the pilot began with Harry and Peter standing at the tombstone of Michael Hibbs, Harry's father, who had been a miner and button accordion player. The camera moved to a lively party with Hibbs and his band playing and singing as Bell Islanders danced. A cameraman caught a group of boys peering through a window, looking slightly bemused.

Back in Toronto, Sarty arranged for Peter to interview Woody Herman and his band at the Palais Royale, a dance pavilion on Lake Ontario. Peter sported a bandana around his neck, as did Woody. Peter's short-sleeved shirt exposed the long cast on his left arm. His hair was parted irregularly on the left side. Peter seemed at ease as Woody explained that, by combining jazz and rock, he was attracting younger audiences. With his saxophone, he proceeded to the stage where he joined his band in "Baby, Won't You Light My Fire." The young, cool Toronto crowd, decked out in sideburns and bouffants, jived enthusiastically.

The weakest segment of the pilot was an interview with the rock group Edward Bear. The first shot revealed Edward Bear performing on a small stage in a CBC studio in front of a tiny audience of young people. Afterward, Peter joined the band on the stage. Only then, when he was forced to sit still, did he begin to look uncomfortable. His question about whether or not Canadian pop music had certain identifiable characteristics brought blank stares from the musicians.

In a final segment of the pilot, filmed inside a CBC studio, Peter interviewed Mike Mitchell and Willie Dunn, two Native Canadian musicians. Following the short introductory interview, a clip from Dunn's film *Crowfoot* was shown. The movie's soundtrack featured the two men singing "Why the sadness, why the sorrow / Maybe there'll be a better tomorrow." To conclude, Peter glanced at the camera and said, "And I'll bet you never thought of it quite that way. Good night."

Once the interviews were completed, Sarty filmed Peter introducing the overall theme of the series, that of popular music in all its variety. Sarty also filmed Peter introducing each segment. All this was done inside a television studio in Toronto. Sarty convinced Peter to dress smartly in a double-breasted jacket and trousers that actually fitted. His tie was fixed in place. And his hair, stylishly long, was combed back at the sides. He sported a moustache. He was fit, comfortable, and relaxed. He moved gracefully. And he smiled as if he were really enjoying himself. He looked directly at the camera. He had "spark." Sarty had him walk around a couple of cameras that sported large CBC logos or sit in the cameraman's seat way up on a boom. Sarty understood that television required movement, and that Peter was at his worst when sitting still.

In May 1970, when Jim Guthro, who had replaced Len Casey as head of variety at CBC-TV, viewed Sarty's pilot, he told him to take out "the biographical bits," leaving only the music. Guthro hated "infotainment." When Sarty gave Peter the news that there was to be no *Take 60*, he shrugged and mumbled, "What else is new?" He was accustomed to projects collapsing around him. (Only a few weeks earlier, Peter had quit, or was fired, as editor of *Maclean's*.)

All was not lost, however. The one-hour pilot was aired across Canada on June 3, 1970. Patrick Scott of the *Toronto Star* praised Peter's performance and hoped the pilot might develop into a "magazine-type series dealing with the lighter side of life … without a politician, an academic or an analyst in sight." Parts of the pilot were shown from time to time on *Take 30* in late 1970 when Peter was subbing for Adrienne Clarkson.

Unfortunately, Peter was drawn to talk-show television. In 1970 he was one of several hosts of a program produced by Ross McLean. Beginning in early November 1970, the pilots ran in Toronto on Thursday evenings over thirteen weeks. Patrick Scott wasn't impressed this time. Scott noticed that Peter was "uncharacteristically nervous" and that he allowed conversations to drag on until he was saved by the commercial breaks. On opening night, the only good interview, thought Scott, was with John Robarts, the hard-drinking Ontario premier (1961–71). In the *Saturday Star* of November 21, 1970, Scott was so unimpressed by Peter's performance that the critic placed him in a three-way dead heat, along with Barry Callaghan and Barbara Frum, in Scott's contest for the least attractive personality of the season. Even one of the production staff thought that both Peter and the show were "terrible, terrible."[13] Although McLean publicly defended the series and all its hosts,[14] Peter blamed his failure on McLean, who had expected Peter to learn by instinct.[15]

In 1974, about the same time as *This Country in the Morning* was concluding, Peter Herrndorf, newly appointed head of current affairs[16] at CBC-TV, was contemplating a late-night talk show to rival *The Tonight Show Starring Johnny Carson*. Herrndorf wanted Peter as host and Frame as executive producer. In late 1975, Peter told Bronwyn Drainie: "We want to try to bring the spirit of *This Country in the Morning* to television."[17]

Gradually, Herrndorf assembled a staff. His first acquisition was Nancy Oliver as director. She came highly recommended by Moses Znaimer, for whom Nancy had worked at CITY-TV from its inception in 1972 as head of variety programs. With her wealth of contacts with entertainers in Canada and the United States, Oliver was indispensable. One of the first people she hired was David Ruskin, a veteran of television.[18] In August 1975, Ruskin was given the task of directing three pilots that he hoped would impress viewers and CBC management. Peter liked Ruskin, and was comfortable with his direction.[19]

Oliver also hired Bob Ennis, who had worked at Channel 19, Ontario's educational network. Ennis, Oliver knew, was "a show business type" familiar with the latest Hollywood films, and with their stars and directors. Ennis knew Cathy Chilco, who was brought in to develop the entertainment and variety show component. John Martin, whose specialty was pop culture and new music, was hired because of his familiarity with British pop music. The youthful bandleader Jack Lenz was signed on to do the music. Actor John Kastner, along with Nancy Button and Val Ross, were hired as researchers. So was Selena Dack, who moved to the position of lineup editor in the second year of the show and also served as Peter's unofficial personal assistant. Gail Goldman, who had been Moses Znaimer's personal assistant, was hired to attract stars from Hollywood and New York. Anne Emin and Nancy Oliver organized a six-week training course for the current affairs department to teach them the latest in production skills. Emin also made sure that American and British guests got through customs. She booked hotel rooms, a complex job because each show featured five guests, which meant twenty-five guests each week, or one hundred per month. The logistics were made more intricate by the fact that the show was produced in about ten cities across Canada.

The staff of seventeen producers, researchers, and directors occupied space on the third floor of a CBC building at 790 Bay Street on the southwest corner of Bay and College Streets. According to one observer, the building, with sealed windows and poor air circulation, was toxic by mid-afternoon. By 3:00 p.m., performers and producers were forced to dash to the front door to get a breath of fresh Toronto air. Hugh Macmillan, paper chaser for the nearby Archives of Ontario, used to see Peter in the ground-floor drugstore where he bought his cigarettes, which no doubt contributed to the toxic miasma of the building.[20] Glenn Sarty, whose office was two floors above, was envious of the bonhomie of the crew of *90 Minutes*, who often gathered around the only pinball machine owned by the CBC.

90 Minutes seemed to be off to a good start, though Sarty wondered if the team-style management, which tended to subordinate individual creativity to bland consensus, would work. If any member of the *90 Minutes* team had asked him, Sarty would have explained that the most active participants in meetings tended to be "politically astute types who lived for meetings, but who were often the least effective in driving projects through." Sarty, who liked to be personally in charge of his television projects, created the parameters within which his stars' creative genius flourished. He was always noted for respecting, encouraging, and protecting hosts such as Adrienne Clarkson and Peter Gzowski. Unfortunately, no one on the *90 Minutes* team sought advice from Sarty, who with *Gzowski* and *Take 30* had already successfully brought literary and radio forms to television. Soon he would do so again with *the fifth estate*.[21] In fact, Sarty wanted Peter to join Adrienne Clarkson, as well as Moses Znaimer, on *the fifth estate*. Sarty understood that moving from radio to television took more than simply placing a couple of cameras in front of two or three talking heads. Peter probably would have succeeded on *the fifth estate*.

Ironically, Peter also understood that television had to be more than talking heads. In the mid-1960s, as television reviewer for *Maclean's*, he had been critical of CBC Television news, which, it seemed to him, was merely radio with pictures. And he understood why comedians Johnny Wayne and Frank Shuster were so successful on television. Unlike older comedians who had learned their trade in radio, and who on television simply stood in front of a microphone, Wayne and Shuster, Peter pointed out, made the cameras work for them. "The medium becomes part of their act," wrote Peter in his review. On one show, with the help of a camera, Wayne and Shuster created the illusion of walking down an infinite number of steps; on another they appeared to defy gravity while painting the Leaning Tower of Pisa.[22]

As a television reviewer in the mid-1960s, Peter didn't like talk shows. "Most of all, I find them embarrassing," he wrote. "A person appearing on a late-night conversation show suffers from some of the same conditions as an entry in a beauty contest: he is exhibiting not what he has learned to do or even practises doing, but what he *is*." As for the hosts, Peter wrote that they were "great know-nothings" because they could neither sing, act, or dance, and knew little about public affairs.[23]

During the long months of planning *90 Minutes*, Frame, Gzowski, and Oliver flew to London to see how the BBC managed its two live talk shows, *Nationwide* and *Panorama*, and especially how it blended satellite feeds from London to Manchester, Glasgow or Belfast. In Toronto dry runs using "guests" such as comedian Dave Thomas were carried out in a small studio on Maitland Street. In October 1975, for further practice, Peter hosted a local TV talk show called *24 Hours*, which didn't garner positive reviews. Peter was pushing himself. From November 1975 to June 1976, he hosted *Gzowski on FM* five days each week and occasionally filled in for Barbara Frum on *As It Happens*. He continued to smoke and drink excessively. One day while playing pinball, he collapsed and was rushed to hospital.

Even before the dry runs began in February 1976, opposition to the show inside the CBC began to grow. Since *90 Minutes* would cost about $1 million per year, producers and hosts of other shows feared that their own budgets would be frozen or reduced. Insiders at the CBC began to question the growing power of Herrndorf and his TV empire, which also included *the fifth estate, The Canadian Establishment,* and a long list of documentary specials.[24] The staff at *The National,* CBC's 11:00 p.m. newscast, was also upset, for it had been planning to extend its newscast from 11:15 to 11:25, now an impossibility, since *90 Minutes* would begin at 11:15. And affiliates and regional stations across the country were loath to broadcast *90 Minutes* when they could bring in greater advertising revenue from Hollywood movies.

There was also some personal antagonism. Many colleagues thought Peter was arrogant. He was "never gentle in conversation, he was always nervous, and he made many enemies by his frankness in stating objections to an idea or a guest," Robert Fulford points out today, while quickly adding that it was much better to work with Peter than with pleasant CBC hosts who weren't interested in their work and who did little if anything of distinction. One wonders if some of Peter's acerbic television reviews in *Maclean's* ten years earlier remained a sore point at the CBC. "One problem with *Seaway,* the most ambitious Canadian television series ever undertaken," Peter once opined in a review entitled "Rub-A-Dub: Seaway Floats a Flub," "is that it isn't a very good television series." Its script, he thought, was "atrocious."[25] And lines such as "Being a highlight of the 1965–66 television season is a little like being the best hockey player in North Carolina"[26] didn't endear Peter to actors, directors, and management.

During the last week of February and the first week in March 1976, the first pilot was broadcast from Halifax to Nova Scotia and Prince Edward Island. One of Peter's guests that evening was American pop star and war protester Freda Payne. While singing "Band of Gold," and "Feelings," her eyes started to run. "Did the lyrics really get to you," Peter asked, "or do you have a cold?" When Payne explained that she was allergic to the paint on the microphone, Peter was vaguely aware of stifled laughter. Apparently, the show's staff knew that Payne had been tippling in her dressing room.[27] In another segment, Peter dropped his index cards while interviewing General Nguyễn Cao Kỳ, former prime minister of South Vietnam and military commander during part of the Vietnam War. In a more successful interview, Gordon Pinsent talked about a new play and sang "Send in the Clowns."

The success of the Pinsent segment was due, in part, to the quality of the "greens" prepared by Selena Dack, whose first assignment on *90 Minutes* was to research Pinsent and to draw up a list of questions for Peter. Earlier that day, when she presented the greens to Peter, she was petrified. Peter was known for near-decapitation if the greens weren't up to his high standards. Selena waited. Nothing but the sound of pages turning for a couple of minutes, then, suddenly, Peter burst into a broad smile and announced loudly that Selena's work was among the best he had ever read.

The studio audience that evening in Halifax was enthusiastic, and feedback from television viewers was positive. On the second night, Tuesday, February 24, Peter talked to the mayor of Sydney, Nova Scotia, on the subject of a police strike. A professional groupie, after chatting with Peter, joined Miss Canada in selecting the winner of a Mr. Ninety Beauty Contest. Tommy Ambrose and Doug Riley performed blues songs, and Peter got soaked when he lost a log-rolling contest. On the third night, Wednesday, February 25, Theatre Pass Muraille and director Paul Thompson entertained with an excerpt from *The Farm Show*. On other nights, Sally Rand performed a fan dance, a local reporter talked to a detective about a Dartmouth robbery, and Carl Brewer spoke about the newly formed World Hockey Association. After dancing to *Swan Lake*, Les Ballets Trocadero de Monte Carlo reassured a suspicious Peter that they weren't female impersonators. Farley Mowat chatted about his move to Cape Breton, Shirley Eikhard sang "It Takes Time," and Mr. Nova Scotia gave Peter tips on bodybuilding.

After Halifax there was a break of several weeks until mid-April when a second dry run was scheduled for Vancouver, this time to be broadcast nationally. On the second night, Tuesday, April 19, 1976, Peter panicked when Mr. Justice Thomas Berger, who was just finishing two years of hearings on the controversial Mackenzie Valley Pipeline, didn't say what Peter had expected him to say. Jack Webster, another guest, was riled up and said so on his local radio show when he discovered that David Ruskin had planned a dangerous high wire act. What Webster didn't know was that Ruskin, by ordering an ambulance to stand by, made the act seem dangerous. Nor did Webster know that Ruskin had instructed Jay Cochrane to stumble once or twice.[28]

As the week wore on, Peter improved, and so did the show. On Thursday, April 21, two futurologists predicted climate change, and David Suzuki discussed "body farming," by which the dying might be kept alive so that others could benefit from their blood and organs. Jack Webster, considerably becalmed, talked about the upcoming ACTRA Awards; Debbie Brill demonstrated high-jumping skills; and Peter did the same, less effectively. "I've heard all about you. You're hot," singer Jaye P. Morgan announced to the embarrassed host. The next evening featured Frisbee tossing and a song about hogs. Red Kelly, coach of the Toronto Maple Leafs, explained how he used the power of pyramids on his players. All this left little time for David McTaggart to talk about his suit against the French government for blowing up a Greenpeace ship in a New Zealand harbour.

In *Maclean's*, on May 17, 1976, television critic Ron Base wasn't amused. "All too often the show deteriorated into the kind of late-night talk show hokum that sends viewers to bed." He especially disliked the segment in which Eartha Kitt cooed "Fifty Ways to Leave Your Lover" "while crawling all over Bruno Gerussi," and he didn't much like Craig Claiborne's review of Chinese restaurants in Vancouver — Claiborne liked them all. Base urged producers and Peter to avoid "overused, third-rate American performers such as Jaye P. Morgan."[29]

After the Friday evening show was completed at 9:00 p.m. local time, Peter partied in a downtown bar. On Saturday morning near noon, one of his staff knocked on the door of his hotel room. A sleepy Peter opened the door just enough for her to glimpse a pretty young woman in his bed. The staff member understood. The show provided Peter with a dozen good friends, but no one close enough for the intimacy he craved. She excused herself. Later, at the hotel's main desk, the same staff member overheard a second young blonde asking for Mr. Gzowski's room number. "Oh, I am so sorry to have to tell you," the staff member announced. "Mr. Gzowski checked out early this morning to catch a plane to Toronto."

Winnipeg, the third and last test-run city, was scheduled to begin the last week of June. Walter Stewart discussed the air controllers' strike, and a member of the Airline Pilots' Association took exception to some of his contentions. The producers, who had managed to arrange a telephone hookup with Beirut, allowed Peter to talk to a journalist about the civil war there. A Winnipeg writer spoke about her life and writing, and American singer Sherisse Lawrence sang "Love Will Keep Us Together." The highlight of the night for Peter was an interview with one of his heroes, Paul Hiebert, creator of Sarah Binks. Hiebert read a poem on the controllers' strike, and he and Peter discussed philosophy and religion, two subjects of Hiebert's forthcoming book *Doubting Castle*.

After the Winnipeg pilot shows, Martin Knelman wrote an ambivalent review in *Weekend Magazine* on June 26, 1976. Peter, he thought, was "the kind of man who always seems to be pulling himself out of a scrape." Knelman also believed that Peter's "air of extended adolescence" was a source of both strength and weakness. "It's what makes you want to shake him when he's coming on too much with his shucks-golly enthusiasms or getting silly in the manner of a bright juvenile who mistakes *New York Magazine* trendiness for deep ideas, but it's also what makes you root for him in spite of everything, because he projects the giddy nerviness of the amateur trying to pass himself off as an old pro." Knelman spotted why Peter and television weren't made for each other — on television, Peter's mischievous, boyish nature sometimes appeared petulant.

That Friday afternoon the staff gathered to await a call from Toronto. Finally, the phone rang. Herrndorf picked it up. Don Macpherson, vice-president of the CBC, announced that the show was a go. When Herrndorf conveyed the news to Peter and Alex, they and the entire staff wept for joy. (There was, however, one person who wasn't weeping for joy. Peter Yarrow, a member of the trio Peter, Paul, and Mary, had been booked to perform on Friday evening. Until told to get lost, he insisted on flirting with the statuesque Nancy Oliver.) That night, after the show, the crew celebrated at the Wellington Crescent home of Cynthia Wine, food critic and writer. Ten days later she announced to her husband that she was leaving him. She moved to Toronto and began a long career as one of Canada's media chefs. Her association with Peter lasted until the end of his life.

—•—

At 11:35 p.m. on Monday, November 29, 1976, the show began in earnest. David Ruskin, his tasks completed, was followed by a succession
of directors: Jack Sampson, Dennis Murphy, and Hank Pasila. Maureen
Forrester opened the first show with "It's a Quarter to Nine," then chatted about her career, following which the Rebounders performed a comic
act on a trampoline. Peter enjoyed a shiatsu massage, and Forrester, after
another song, discussed her Irish roots with David Suzuki, who earlier
had examined the morality of genetic engineering.

As the winter snow began to fall, it became obvious that talk-show
television didn't inspire Peter. Television made him appear fixed and
awkward. During the first months of the program, Peter sat on a chair
beside his guests. He crossed his legs away from them, which moved
his left shoulder around to a point where he appeared to be shunning
them. Sometimes he had difficulty finding the right camera. His large
horn-rimmed glasses, which reflected the studio lights, kept riding down
his nose. Nixon-like, his eyes made him seem slightly lost or longing to
be out on a golf course. He rubbed the index finger and thumb of his
left hand as if he were impatient with his guests' answers, or as if he
were craving another nicotine fix. Although the television camera enjoys
smiles, no matter how insincere, he rarely smiled. Peter hated makeup, as
well as his helmet-like hair. He was often visibly embarrassed by an unexpected comment such as when Mordecai Richler appeared on a show
from Halifax on December 16, 1976. Peter asked Richler to comment on
Anne Murray's contribution to Canadian identity and culture. "Who's
Anne Murray?" was Richler's apologetic response. Seated next to Richler
was Anne's brother, Bruce, who had just finished providing details of the
Murray clan. Anne herself had appeared on *90 Minutes* exactly a week
earlier, and Peter must have feared that she was watching that evening.

Whenever Peter attempted intimacy, he tended to look ridiculous.
Once with Lise Payette in person, Peter tried to cozy up to the attractive, full-figured woman of many talents — not only was she a politician
but she was also the successful TV talk-show host of Radio-Canada's
Appellez-moi Lise, who surely knew that Peter was floundering. As
he begged Lise not to quit Canada, Peter resembled the acne-covered
teenager trying to make love in a coach house in Galt, or the young city

editor trying to impress the assistant women's editor in the grain stubble near Moose Jaw. Payette politely but firmly rejected both host and federalism. On Valentine's Day 1977, Peter also had a contretemps with Ed Flemming, leader of a western Canada separatist party.

"Bullshit!" exploded Peter when Flemming attempted to explain why the West wanted to leave Confederation.

"Bullshit to you, too, then," replied Flemming.[30]

Some of the guests shocked Peter. "If I had to choose one moment to epitomize my discomfort on *90 Minutes Live*," he wrote in his memoirs a decade later, "I could scarcely do better than the night Craig Russell, the female impersonator, was on in Toronto. Men in dresses weren't my cup of tea …" One of the other guests that evening was the earnest feminist Laura Sabia, whom Russell called "Saura Labia." As Sabia scowled, Peter squirmed. Ten years too late, Peter realized that Carson would have played up the tension between Sabia and Russell.[31] Carson would also have known what to do with a guest like Malcolm Muggeridge, senior editor of Britain's satirical *Punch*, when he opined one night that Canada's absorption into the United States was "historically inevitable."

Anything connected with sex caused Peter discomfort. He seemed perplexed at *Monty Python* humour when the stars of the show appeared in drag. Peter admitted in his memoirs to being uneasy with the fact that at least one of the actors was gay. He might have been thinking about Graham Chapman, who, while in St. John's, was living with his limo driver in the Hotel Newfoundland. The irrepressible and youthful Rex Murphy claimed later that he himself was the only person on the show that evening who "could even pretend to normalcy."[32] On another show, this one from Vancouver, Peter asked a young blond therapist who used sex to unlock repressions, "So, are you a prostitute?" Nevertheless, Peter was capable of recounting raunchy, embarrassing stories. One night he accosted an exhausted Donald Sutherland with what Sandra Martin called "tasteless locker room stories about women."[33]

Peter was particularly embarrassed in March 1977 in St. John's when he interviewed a retired prostitute named Margo, an articulate woman of about forty, who was attempting to improve the lot of prostitutes, by, among other things, declaring St. Valentine's Day "Hookers' Rights Day." She was also trying to unionize prostitutes. Why prostitutes, Peter wondered, when sex was so easy to find at no charge? While Margo argued that prostitution was work like that of any other profession or vocation, Peter couldn't escape the idea that women who sold their bodies were immoral. Margo politely explained that prostitutes were selling not their bodies but their time. "All women should be paid for their time," she insisted, even housewives, who received only room and board for ninety hours of work per week. To Peter's question about the identity of customers, Margo explained that prostitutes dealt with politicians, truck drivers, television producers, and, in fact, all sorts of men.

How many people can one sleep with before getting married? Peter wondered. Margo answered that a recent report from the University of Washington in Seattle claimed that up to forty was just fine. Peter fell silent. Johnny Carson used to go silent, too, but his eyes always remained in control. Peter lowered his eyes as if he wanted to hide.

When Peter interviewed former world-champion wrestler Gene Kiniski on March 8, 1978, once again the guest took over the show. The big guy, dressed in a vibrant red suit, dwarfed Peter. Kiniski began by talking about his skills as a cook. Peter wanted, instead, to discuss wrestling as theatre. Kiniski wasn't about to agree that professional wrestling was scripted. "Your hands are shaking," noted the wrestler. "Something the matter?" Kiniski peered at his host. "Has anyone ever told you that you have beautiful blue eyes?" Peter appeared confused.

Singer Iggy Pop also created difficulties for Peter.[34] At one point Pop, busy cleaning his fingernails with his teeth, ignored one of Peter's questions. He grew irritated when Peter asked about punk rock. "Punk rock is a word used by dilettantes and heartless manipulators," he told Peter. It was a term "based on contempt … on fashion, style, elitism, and Satanism." Furthermore, he announced, he didn't like to hear such terms come out of anyone's mouth.

"What do you want it to come out of?" Peter asked with a snigger.

Iggy called Peter "sir" because, he claimed, he couldn't remember his name.

"At least I go with the one I was born with," Peter shot back.

"Are you happy to be popular?" asked Iggy.

"Sometimes," Peter replied.

In December 1977 Peter talked to Marshall McLuhan about the effect of the recently installed television cameras in the House of Commons. McLuhan explained why TV was such an unfriendly medium for people with inflexible bodies and personalities. Joe Clark, for example, McLuhan noted, played one role, that of Joe Clark, an earnest, well-intentioned, honest, but dull politician. TV, McLuhan predicted, would be the death of the leader of the opposition. Television demanded stars such as Pierre Trudeau, who changed personalities to suit the occasion. Trudeau could easily transform himself into an exotic Oriental. He could be arrogant or worldly or a Northern Magus. On television he commanded attention. Trudeau would therefore have a long and successful political career.[35] Surely, Peter knew that McLuhan was implying that Gzowski was Clark — honest, earnest, and one-dimensional. Peter's stiff body wouldn't allow him to metamorphose into different personae to suit the nature of each interview.

Executive producer Richard Nielsen wasn't surprised that Peter failed as a talk-show host. In 1969, after watching the dreadful audition with Alex Trebek, Vivienne Wilson, and Peter, Nielsen had rejected Peter for *Weekend*, even though, prior to the audition, Peter had been Nielsen's first choice. He was a known personality who could attract a large audience. He was bright, and Nielsen believed he could be made attractive on television. During the audition, however, Nielsen realized that the format of a live interview show could never demonstrate Peter's strengths. On television his method of circling around the guest to spot a weakness or elicit a confession took far too long.[36]

Allan Fotheringham, who was a semi-regular guest, witnessed the toll the show was taking on its host, and he was saddened to note that, in order to hide Peter's shaking hands, carpenters had built a riser in front of his desk. "I knew the end was nigh," Fotheringham wistfully remembered two decades later.[37]

—•—

While *90 Minutes Live* was deemed a failure by Peter himself and by most critics, many of its episodes succeeded because of what Alex Frame has called "smart risks," the right mix of guests and subjects. One show paired André Gagnon with ballerina Anne Ditchburn. Gagnon played the piano while Ditchburn danced, following which they talked to Peter about the art of music and dance. Another smart risk was uniting Veronica Tennant with Mikhail Baryshnikov, Shirley MacLaine, and Anne Bancroft, the stars of the movie *The Turning Point*. A clip of the film was shown, after which Tennant commented on the quality of the acting and the dancing. One evening David Clayton-Thomas sang "Spinning Wheel," his big hit from the early 1970s, after which he joined three other guests and Peter to examine crime, punishment, and prison reform. The two segments, music and discussion, complemented each other perfectly.

"Ladies of the Night" from St. John's, Newfoundland, was another example of good talk-show television. After the discussion of prostitutes' rights, Myra Maude Bennett, an eighty-six-year-old dressed in black oxfords with a matching purse draped over her left arm, strode onto the set. In 1921 Bennett had sailed from Southampton, England, to St. John's and then had travelled by train and boat to Daniels Harbour in the Northern Peninsula. She married and raised her family, all the while bringing the community's babies into the world. Bennett also made house calls to treat injuries and diseases. She had much in common with Margo, the retired prostitute. Nurse Bennett had been paid for her time. She, too, was a "Lady of the Night."[38] The visuals were lively, and the women were such a contrast in age and experience that Peter forgot his earlier embarrassment.

Not all reviewers were critical. At least, deemed Sandra Martin, Peter was "a real person asking — for the most part — questions that matter."[39] Ron Haggart, executive producer of *the fifth estate*, could never forget moving moments such as those when Peter debated "the future of the country" with Lise Payette.[40] "It was the most exciting experiment we have seen in late-night television in North America," deemed Morris Wolfe, television reviewer for *Saturday Night*. Today Diana Filer believes that if the show had continued for another year with Peter as host, it would have succeeded. Peter was getting better and better, and it must be remembered, Filer points out, that even Johnny Carson and Jack Paar hadn't been immediate successes as talk-show hosts.[41]

As *90 Minutes* plodded on, the staff managed to maintain a high level of camaraderie. After each show, they dined together. In Toronto, where the show was completed by midnight, the staff of about forty often retired to Sai Woo, one of the best Chinese restaurants in Toronto in the 1970s. There was one relationship, however, that didn't survive the show. Peter's once-symbiotic rapport with Alex Frame soured, and halfway through program's life the two of them had trouble communicating. As Peter Herrndorf put it years later, Alex tried in vain to find the clue to unlocking Peter's comfort level.[42]

There was a second relationship that didn't survive the show. As the television production went from bad to worse, the speakeasies and booze cans of College Street[43] and elsewhere, one of them above an art gallery, as well as the rooftop bar at the Park Plaza, grew more appealing. That rooftop bar looks much the same as it did when the Family Compact of Journalism adjourned there. Today, on the west wall, there is a rogues' gallery of famous drinkers, courtesy of the political cartoonist Andy Donato. Peter hangs next to Mordecai Richler, and above Graeme Gibson. Nearby are Adrienne Clarkson and June Callwood. Bartenders Joe and Harold, who served Peter over decades, remember him as "happy-go-lucky," "outgoing," and "easygoing," just one of the boys. He liked to bring up sports celebrities. One afternoon Eric Nesterenko of the Toronto Maple Leafs asked for a telephone. "We don't have a portable phone here," Harold told him. The hulking player rose from his seat and sauntered out to the foyer near the elevator where he yanked the pay phone from the wall and returned to the bar to be greeted with hoots of laughter from the bartenders, patrons, and Peter.

From the bar's north-facing windows, Peter could view the leafy city beyond Davenport Road and Upper Canada College, up past Eglinton Avenue to 98 Lytton where Jennie was at home cooking, cleaning, and counselling. "She belonged to a generation of Canadian women," Peter wrote several years after he and Jennie separated, "whose abilities the nation's economy, business establishment, and, far too often, their husbands, had ignored."[44]

Often the questions we ask of others reveal a good deal about ourselves. While researching *The Game of Our Lives*, Peter interviewed the wife of an NHL player. What was it like being a hockey wife who stayed at home when the good-looking, well-paid husband was travelling around North America? She cheerfully paid the bills, looked after the children, and ran "the whole show at home." It was her duty to keep her star organized. "It's like a successful businessman," she explained to Peter, "He needs a smart secretary." Certainly, the lonely wife had to respect "the camaraderie of the boys," for they needed to develop and maintain team spirit, and if a few beers did the trick, so be it. And yet, added the hockey wife, "it's so easy to become a shadow of your husband and live and die on how he's doing, live and die on how the team's doing." What about relationships with young women while on the road? Peter wondered. "There's a guy's world that you never ever enter into," the hockey wife explained. "I don't want to know anything about it."

Jennie had played a role not dissimilar to that of the typical hockey wife. Did she complain publicly? Never. When Marci McDonald visited the family during the summer of 1974, Jennie talked about herself as Peter's toughest editor. She told McDonald that she disapproved of Peter's monthly all-night poker games with Danny Finkleman, and Peter retorted, "But they help me keep sane." (In a sports column in *Saturday Night*, Peter had once argued that "the thrill of poker is in the gambling.... That's what keeps men up all night, throats crackling, eyes smarting.")[45] And furthermore, he told Jennie, as McDonald listened, wasn't it better than the old days when he used to drink after work with celebrity lady writers who had employed cleaning women to scrub their floors?

What about being married to "the sex symbol of the morning airwaves?" McDonald asked Jennie. Did it bother her that her husband received letters from women "pouring out their lives and loneliness" to him?

Jennie replied that she didn't have time to worry about "every damn letter." She insisted to McDonald that Peter's stardom hadn't affected her own life one iota.

In the introductory essay of *Peter Gzowski's Book About This Country in the Morning*, Peter mentioned a magazine editor, McDonald perhaps, who once asked Jennie, "with devastating sentimentality," if she was pleased that Peter was leaving *This Country*, for now she would see him more frequently.

"I don't think so," Jennie replied, for she had enjoyed the program.

"It's nice to have a fan who is also a friend and someone you love," Peter wrote. He apparently failed to see the corollary of Jennie's statement, that perhaps she might have liked the radio show to continue so that she wouldn't see so much of him during the day.

One evening in the spring of 1977, at the end of his first season of *90 Minutes Live*, Peter and Jennie brought the children together to announce that they were separating. Peter's writing is at its best in the section of his memoirs that deals with this moment. "Until I die, I will remember John, aged twelve, going upstairs to his room, fighting back silent tears," Peter wrote. "I remember, too, going up to console him, running my hand through his blond hair and trying to tell him in words what I felt in my heart but what, in his eyes, my actions must have been denying: that I loved him and would love him always." Peter concluded the scene by wondering if John believed him then, or had ever believed him. John has less dramatic memories of the incident.

While Peter's memoirs paint a picture of a rather peaceful parting, Sylvia Fraser reported in *Toronto Life* in 2002 that Peter told her, soon after the separation, that he had in the end been sacked. One of Peter's colleagues reported that Jennie had found a love note in the pocket of one of his jackets, apparently written by a producer with whom he had once had an affair. He knew, of course, that the person who took his jackets to the dry cleaner would find the note. Like many men in the late 1960s and 1970s, as divorce became easier, Peter probably wanted Jennie to make the first move. It wouldn't, after all, be manly to negotiate the end of a marriage. Negotiation implied equality. The planted note solved the problem. Peter was sacked, which allowed him to play the role of victim.

He moved into what he called "a furnished, glass-wrapped bachelor pad" at 11 Yorkville Avenue, which was really a dreary yellow-brick industrial building with no balconies and lots of neon lights. During the late 1960s after Prime Minister Pierre Trudeau and Justice Minister John

Turner made divorce easier, real-estate moguls set up furnished apartments for newly single men. One of these bachelor buildings was at 11 Yorkville Avenue. By 1977, the area had been transformed from a hippie and folkie haven, whose coffee bars had helped to launch the careers of Ian and Sylvia, Gordon Lightfoot, and Joni Mitchell, into a trendy urban village of art galleries, bistros, and bookstores.

One afternoon Peter ran into Sylvia Fraser and invited her to dine at 11 Yorkville. "The suite's unpalatable mess of soiled laundry, cigarette butts and unwashed dishes," Fraser wrote later in *Toronto Life*, "advertised depression if not self-loathing." After Peter removed dirty socks from the dining table, Peter and Sylvia ate takeout sandwiches, and adjourned to the nearby Brunswick House for some jazz. By that time, Peter was "drunk, lugubrious and overflowing with self-pity." While she began the evening feeling sorry for the lonely bachelor, as the evening wore on, she began to grow weary of his "mea culpa posturing." Later, at Fraser's apartment in the upscale Colonnade on Bloor Street, east of Avenue Road, Peter turned on "a repertoire of manipulations." Soon Fraser began to suspect that Peter wasn't quite as drunk as he pretended. Finally, she pushed him out the door.[46]

Before she moved back to Kingston to work at Queen's University, Cathy Perkins and Peter occasionally met for lunch in a Yorkville bistro, following which they strolled over to the bachelor pad that, according to Perkins, was sparsely furnished with a typewriter, desk, phone, and refrigerator where he kept ginger ale and soda. There was also a bed with "rather shoddy linen."

Jan Walter also witnessed the mess at 11 Yorkville. Peter had first met her in the spring of 1974 when Walter was managing editor at Hurtig Publishers in Edmonton. During the autumn of 1974, while Peter was in Edmonton to promote his book about *This Country in the Morning*, they met again. During the first season of *90 Minutes Live*, they also got together whenever the show was broadcast from Edmonton, as it was in early April 1977 when writer Myrna Kostash and politician Tom Hayden were guests.[47]

On Friday, April 8, when the program finished at 11:00 a.m. local time, Hayden and Kostash joined Jan and Peter atop the Château Lacombe Hotel. As the revolving restaurant provided the four diners with spectacular views of the bustling city and the university across the river, the conversation turned to the proposed Mackenzie Valley Pipeline. While the Berger Report wouldn't be released for two or three weeks, parts of it had been leaked to the media. The report was going to recommend a ten-year moratorium on the pipeline project, pending settlement of Native land claims. Hayden argued strongly that it was better to move oil via a pipeline than to ship it down the ecologically sensitive coast to an energy-hungry California. Jan, Myrna, and Peter concluded that a myopic Democrat was just as bad as a callous Republican.[48]

Once *90 Minutes* wound up its first year, Peter returned to Edmonton, where he spent the summer of 1977 with Walter in her house on Ada Boulevard near the Capilano Bridge. Weekdays, while she was at work as a public relations officer with Alberta Culture, Peter frequented the Northlands Raceway. One week he flew to Inuvik where bar patrons booed him for having pre-empted their favourite westerns.[49] Later Peter returned to Toronto. In the autumn of 1977, Walter, now employed by Macmillan of Canada, joined him in a third-floor flat in a Victorian farmhouse, once the home of the Bernard family, at 19 Bernard Avenue near Tranby Avenue. On the second floor lived John Saywell, a professor of history at York University.

Once having left Jennie, Peter was advised by his accountants, Arthur Gelgoot and Reg Adelman, to get a divorce, or at least a separation agreement, and perhaps even a separate bank account. Revenue Canada was keen that Peter pay thousands of dollars owed in back taxes. At tax time Peter arrived at his accountants' offices near the Park Plaza with a shoebox stuffed with bits of paper. "This is my life," he announced. Reg Adelman once noted that writers were "the most disorganized" of all his clients, even more disorganized than the forty or so rock groups whose taxes he calculated.[50]

Canadians eat their young, Peter noted a couple of years after the demise of his television show and marriage.[51] He was paraphrasing James Joyce, who thought the Irish, too, were unsympathetic to artists. Canadians are so short of national figures, Peter once wrote, that they adulate "anyone with the least bit of promise, and then, when there's nothing left to write about how well they're doing, we step on their fingers. And, as often as not, we step on them for getting too much publicity." Among his list of performers unjustly treated were Juliette and Anne Murray, as well as Adrienne Clarkson and Pierre Berton.[52] Peter was also, of course, thinking of himself. He once thought of writing a book on the theme of how Canadians chew up their heroes. "How fucking Canadian," he mused. "That's the kind of stuff we've got to grow out of."[53]

— 11 —

"They Don't Want Me Anymore,"
1978–1980

*The war we all fight, the beast we all battle, is the one that
lurks not so deeply within our own divided psyche.*

— *Rick Groen, "Dissecting the Monster Within,"*
Globe and Mail, *September 23, 2005*

In *Spring Tonic*, Peter reported on a game of golf played with his friend
Arnold Palmer. It was the spring of 1978. After years of lacklustre golf,
Peter was now at the top of his game. He had made it into the final
round with the champ. "Arnie" was amazed at Peter's golfing skills. He
was on his way to defeating the champ.

There was only one problem. Even though he had seen Palmer
playing golf a couple of times, Peter had never actually met the man.
Peter's game with Palmer took place in his imagination. "I *played* it, all
right," he explained in the introduction to *Spring Tonic*, "but the only
things that were real were the course, the weather, the clubs, the balls,
and me." In order to beat "Palmer," Peter had played with two balls, one
for himself and the other for the imaginary Palmer. Arnie always lost

because Peter declared that all short or wild shots belonged to Palmer.[1]

As an introduction to Peter's book about spring, the golf story was perfect, for the book's themes were hope, renewal, and dreaming. In 1978, when he began work on *Spring Tonic*, Peter was living in Rockwood, Ontario, near Guelph. In the spring of that year, Jan Walter and he had purchased a house, which, according to its previous owners, was haunted by a friendly ghost. While Peter was concluding *90 Minutes Live*, Jan drove over to Rockwood and signed the deal. They paid $76,000.[2] The house's thick walls were made of local stone. From the front, it looked tiny. At the back was a two-storey, wood-clad addition. The house, as Peter described it, "spilled down a hill and into a country kitchen, which had been modernized by the previous owners," Ian and Marc, restaurateurs the locals, according to Peter, called "Ian and Sylvia." In a *Toronto Star* column later that year,[3] he extolled the glories of the Rockwood area. "In the evenings," Peter told his readers, Jan and he would "light a fire of logs from the old black walnut that the people we bought the house from finally had to cut down, and put records on the stereo."

Peter needed a spring tonic, for he was deeply depressed. He deemed his television show a failure, and believed that the CBC no longer wanted him. He looked for gainful employment. On June 22, 1978, he wrote to Donna Logan, deputy managing editor with the *Montreal Star*, proposing a column called "Just Visiting" or "The Canada Beat." Peter was acquainted with Logan, who had volunteered as one of Peter's "spotters," his eyes and ears on events and ideas in Montreal during *This Country in the Morning*. In 1976, while Peter was doing radio commentary on the Olympics, the two of them often ran into each other at the Press Club. In the letter to Logan in 1978, Peter also wondered if he might contribute a column on television and radio. His only commitment, he told her, was to CBC Radio, "and even that could be broken." During his rambles across Canada over the previous seven years, he explained, he could not but note how little Canadians knew about one another. His proposed column would correct that ignorance.[4] Nothing came of this idea. In 1978 Peter turned down offers of teaching positions at both Conestoga College in nearby Kitchener and at the University of Regina.[5]

The "commitment" that Peter mentioned to Logan was CBC Radio's *Mostly Music*, a classical music show produced in Ottawa and broadcast in all time zones from 2:00 to 4:00 p.m. every weekday. In 1978, when Jane Forner, the program's producer, asked Peter to become the replacement host for one week, he was reluctant. "I don't know anything about classical music," he told her.

A few days before his stint began he ambled into the Ottawa CBC studios on the seventh floor of the Château Laurier Hotel and asked for a typewriter and an ashtray. On the Monday morning, he arrived early, isolated himself, and scribbled his introduction. He refused to go over the script with the producer and remained almost silent until thirty seconds before the show was scheduled to start, immediately following the news at 1:00 p.m. He lit up a cigarette and told the producer and technician to "Let 'er rip!"

"Good morning," he began. "This is *Mostly Music* and I'm Peter Gzowski, your host for this week." He continued by listing some of the music he was about to present. "On today's program, Kazuyoshi Akiyama conducts the Toronto Symphony in a program of Mozart, Mendelssohn, and Krzystof Penderecki." He pronounced the Japanese, German, and Polish names perfectly. "Well, my name is Gzowski, G-Z-O-W-S-K-I," he announced. "All my life, people have mispronounced and misspelled my name. This means that I know the importance of getting names right.[6] So, for the next week, we'll hear some good music, and I'll get the names right." Jane Forner was stunned and delighted by the transformation. On air Peter became "a happy person," the much-admired persona of *Radio Free Friday* and *This Country in the Morning*. He frolicked and cavorted as he enticed listeners to discover new shores.[7]

These short-term contracts, few and far between, left Peter with time to work on *Spring Tonic*. He convinced Mel Hurtig to publish it. It would surely make as much money as Peter's book about *This Country in the Morning*. Peter hired Selena Dack to manage the project.

Working on the book helped ameliorate his despair. "As the snow retreated" in the spring of 1978, he wrote in the introduction to the book, "so did the blues I'd been feeling for so long." Selena and Peter wrote to about two hundred community newspapers across the country, soliciting recipes, poetry, and memories. They commissioned thirty pieces from well-known writers and artists. W.O. Mitchell contributed a radio play about two Prairie towns competing to see which one could outdream

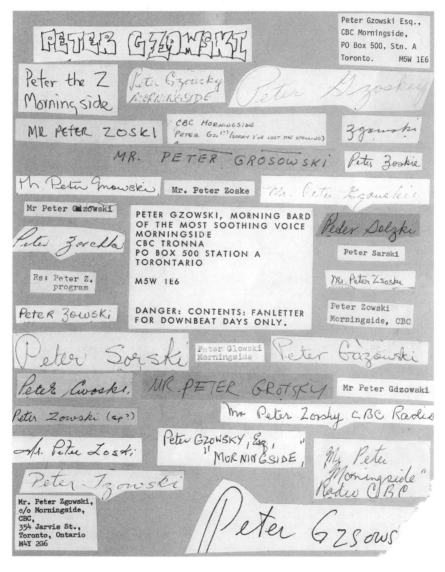

Not all of Peter's many letter writers knew how to spell his last name.

(Courtesy Trent University Archives, Gzowski fonds, 92–015, box 1, folder 32)

the other. Jack Hodgins wrote about dreaming of love, and Harold Town weighed in with spring from an artist's point of view.

Selena and Peter also included an essay by a Manitoba farmer about shearing sheep. They found a letter about homesteading in Saskatchewan written by a young girl to her grandmother in Ontario, and another by Catharine Parr Traill about the rigours of settling into Upper Canada. The book included articles about spring housecleaning and the first signs of spring in Dawson City and Toronto. Sheila Fischman wrote about spring in Quebec and concluded that winter was the most important season there. Harold Horwood described spring in Newfoundland.

Ken Lefolii contributed an essay called "The Sexual Imperative," in which he pointed out that spring is the "season for sex" for all creatures except human beings, who enjoy sex in any season. Alan McFee, Earle Birney, and Helen Gougeon were happy to provide pieces, and so, too, were Wallace Stegner, Paul Hiebert, and Harry Bruce. Don Harron, host of *Morningside*, sent an article about the satirical review *Spring Thaw*, which played at Toronto's Crest Theatre from 1948 to 1972. Harron pointed out that the 1967 version had received a nasty review from a certain Peter Gzowski.

Peter and daughter Alison drove to the farm of Margaret Atwood and Graeme Gibson in the Mulmur Hills northwest of Toronto. Peter complimented Atwood on her vast knowledge of blackflies and mosquitoes. When she said that her father had taught her about insects, Peter replied, "I never thought of him as really being an entomologist before."

Asked Peggy succinctly, "What did you think he was?"

It wasn't an altogether felicitous visit. Peter's tape recorder acted up, and Atwood had more important concerns — the previous night a fierce wind had wreaked havoc with the roof of the Gibson-Atwood barn.

In July 1978, while the *Spring Tonic* manuscript was in progress, Peter escaped to Poland. His trip was sponsored by an organization called Polonia, which was interested in the Polish diaspora.[8] In Poland, he told Jan in a postcard, he could avoid Canada and what he called "fame." In other words, no one greeted him in the street or stared in silence as he passed by. In a second postcard, he told Jan he had lost his jeans.[9] More importantly, he was in the "old country," in touch with the

"Polish resonance" he claimed from time to time to be meaningful to him, even though he was only one-thirtieth Polish (he usually claimed one-sixteenth) and much more English and Scottish (Young, McGregor, Williams, McCarthy, Bell, Miller, and Beebe).

Later that year in the *Toronto Star* he wrote about his trip. He had attended mass in Posnam and viewed a bust of Sir Casimir. One day he lost his way in Warsaw, which for many tourists is part of the joy of travelling, but not for Peter.[10] He loved to explore, but only in his imagination. While in Poland, he witnessed an archaeological dig and noted here and there evidence of Clan Gzowski, including what he took to be the family crest, a white ram rampant on a field of green. The animal, sporting a helmet decorated with five ostrich feathers, was covered in blood up to its ribs.[11] Bloodied but unbowed, the ram was a fitting image for the former host of *90 Minutes Live*. He sent a postcard to Selena Dack: "Szpring good here. Love P.G-Zowski."

Peter was back home in August 1978. In early December, the final version of the manuscript reached Edmonton, and on December 19, 1978, Hurtig sent Peter a cheque for $4,000, the final payment of his advance. The book was published in early 1979. Beautifully illustrated with drawings, cartoons, and colour photographs, the book covered more than three centuries of Canadian springs. Selena and Peter had commissioned John Reeves to take a photograph, which was published as a two-page colour spread at midpoint in the book. In the photo, Peter poses with Paul Soles, Barbara Hamilton, Dinah Christie, Patsy Gallant, Sandy Hawley, John Candy, Mendelson Joe, Karen Kain, and Abby Hoffman, all of them in flashy red tights. At age forty-four Peter looked fit and happy. His hair showed not a trace of grey. He still shaved, leaving only a tidy moustache.

Ken Adachi, book columnist for the *Toronto Star*, liked the book. "The sum of the selections," wrote Adachi, "suggests a sense of national culture, infinite with possibilities, mingling the heroic and the romantic, the traditional with the individual, the comic with the tragic."[12] Most reviewers, however, were unenthusiastic. "*Spring Tonic* is little more than a mind-boggling array of spring-inspired clichés and platitudes," wrote Claire Harrison of *Ottawa Revue* in April 1979. Brian Grant in the *Sunday Post of Canada*, published in Ottawa, found *Spring Tonic* uneven and Gzowski's interview with Atwood "profoundly boring." Even Peter admitted the book was "lousy."[13]

To promote *Tonic*, Peter travelled across the country, only to be met by apologetic bookstore owners. Although the book made it onto the Canadian bestseller lists, ever so briefly, it sold only a few thousand copies. In February, Peter lamented to "Pete" McGarvey of radio station CKEY in Toronto that Canadians weren't "celebratory" people and confessed that he found writing difficult, not just this book but his articles, too, because writing was, of necessity, so very lonely.

His book tour, however, wasn't without its lighter moments. While promoting the book in Fredericton, Peter ran into a member of the Canadian Brass in the lobby of the Beaverbrook Hotel. "You looked bored," said the horn player. He invited Peter to come with him to the home of Premier Richard Hatfield.

W.O. Mitchell was a frequent guest on most of Peter's shows, including here on 90 Minutes Live. *In fact, it might be argued that Peter ensured that Mitchell remained a public name long after the success of* Who Has Seen the Wind, *first published in 1947.*

"You sure?" Peter asked. "I don't want to be in the way."

Hatfield was happy to see Peter. "We were at *ease* with each other," Peter recalled a few months later. "We talked about politics and music, and religion and the premier's paintings, and sports and women and some things I'm not going to tell you, and the reason we got on so well, I think, is that we were speaking the same language." The day following the lobster dinner, Peter found his way to the premier's office where he dropped off a copy of *Spring Tonic*.[14]

Peter's joy didn't last long. On January 14, 1980, an annoyed Mel Hurtig reported that of 15,401 copies printed, he still had 10,223 on hand. He was "swamped with returns." In fact, over the previous six months, only sixty-six copies had sold while 3,751 were returned. He hoped that Peter and Jan were "well and happy" and also hoped they would meet again soon.

Fortunately for Peter, the book wasn't his only vocation. In the autumn of 1978, with the manuscript of *Spring Tonic* at the editing stage in Edmonton, he had accepted an offer from the *Toronto Star* to write a daily column. Today his articles provide a snapshot of a city emerging from decades of stuffiness and low self-esteem. Peter's columns are also a window on the mind of their author in the late 1970s when he, too, was dealing with issues of identity and self-confidence.

His first column appeared on October 9, 1978, on the subject of Thanksgiving dinner at the Salvation Army's Harbour Light Centre at Jarvis and Shuter Streets, at that time a down-and-out part of Toronto. The diners were men whose lives had taken a bad turn, men who reminded Peter of his father. On October 10, Peter wrote about visiting a punk shop on Queen Street East. The next day his subject was University College and a tour with daughter Alison, enrolled in first-year science, en route, Peter predicted, to becoming a medical doctor. The two of them, Peter imagined, "tried to pretend to each other we weren't looking at members of the opposite sex."

In October 1978, Krista Maeots, former staff member of *This Country*, committed suicide. She was, Peter wrote in the *Star* the day after her memorial service, "overwhelmed by troubles that those of us who knew her ... are still trying to understand ..." On October 16, Peter wrote about playing pinball with his youngest sons, John and Mick. The next day his topic was the gracious defeat of Doris Anderson, former editor of *Chatelaine* and Liberal candidate in a federal by-election in Toronto's Eglinton riding. Doris, wrote Peter, was the "right person in the wrong time and place." The government of Pierre Trudeau was at one of its low points in popularity, and the next year would lose a general election.

On October 20, Peter's topic was the "New Man," the liberated, sensitive male of the late 1970s, the urban, urbane male who owned a special pan to make a "mean omelet" with fresh cream and cheese, and who preferred, if you please, his own special mix of coffee beans. Furthermore, Peter wrote, the New Man no longer referred to gays as fags, though, mind you, the New Man didn't wish to admit that he knew any. Oh, and the New Man had given up smoking. In implying that he himself was a New Man, Peter's imagination was at its best. On October 23, he returned to the topic of Metropolitan Toronto's threat to destroy the remaining cottages on Ward's Island. He derided uncaring suburban politicians who, he guessed, had never once visited the islands to view the happy mix of residents and tourists. To battle the islanders, the Metro Toronto government had even hired Alan Eagleson, famous for his display of bad manners during the Canada-Soviet hockey tournament of 1972. "Peter Gzowski has no more need to live there than I do," Eagleson told the press one day. In advertisements directed at taxpayers of Toronto and its boroughs, Peter was pilloried. "Like all the other island residents," noted these ads, "the good life he lives on the island is subsidized by you, the municipal taxpayer."[15]

On October 25, Peter's column was illustrated by a Duncan Macpherson cartoon. The day before, they had researched topless bars in seedy hotels in the west side of downtown Toronto. In the House of Lancaster on Wellington Street, Macpherson sketched Gzowski and a waitress with fulsome breasts. Famous for skewering politicians, the highly acclaimed cartoonist for the *Toronto Star* captured Gzowski caught between his desire to size up the breasts and his shyness and sense of public propriety. "I am not opposed to human flesh and, given a choice, I prefer female," Peter wrote in his column the day after the visit. "I like *Playboy*, the *National Geographic* and Eaton's catalogue. But I'm not enthusiastic about bosoms in my soup."

Duncan Macpherson cartoon of Peter in October 1978 when the two men did some research on topless bars in west side Toronto hotels such as Lancaster House. The caption under the image reads "Peter Gzowski and (blush) waitress: He found it embarrassing."

The next day, October 26, Peter seemed a bit jealous of Peter Newman's good luck. Three major Toronto bookstores were attempting to outsell one another by drastically reducing the price of Newman's *Bronfman Dynasty*, which was thereby assured continued bestseller status. On October 27, Peter wrote about Mad John, a subway busker, and the next day, his topic was his preference for cash over credit cards. In other articles, he wrote about the death of Lela Parlow, a poet he had once interviewed, and about the estimated one hundred thousand cyclists in Toronto. He appealed for readers' comments on how to spend the last day of their lives; and he fulminated against the lack of English-language signs on an unnamed English-language bookstore in Montreal.[16]

Fran's restaurants, founded in 1940, were the subject of another of Peter's columns. Fran's had thrived in the old, bland Toronto. By the late 1970s, however, diners were experimenting with Continental and Asian cuisine, and the chain had become a bit passé. For Peter the restaurant had nostalgic value. In his column of December 6, 1978, he remembered that his "worldly wise cousin" (Wendy Gzowski?) used to take him, whenever he visited Toronto on weekends in the early 1940s, to the original ten-stooler on St. Clair Avenue. He smoked his first public cigarette at Fran's, he recalled. He liked the prose of the unchanging menu at Fran's: "hickory smoked" ham and "country fresh" eggs. In other columns, he wrote about the decline of hockey in Toronto, the increasing cost of insulin, and a production of *The Man Who Came to Dinner* starring R.H. Thomson, who would be, according to Peter, the next Donald Sutherland. He wrote about chicken at Swiss Chalet, and told his readers about three prominent American women living in Toronto: Jane Jacobs, Susan Fish, and Andrea Martin. In January 1979, his topics included Susan Musgrave's battles with mental illness, and the King Tut exhibition about to arrive at the Royal Ontario Museum. Other column topics included the dilemma of writing a letter of recommendation for someone you didn't admire, the need for a February holiday, Toronto Mayor John Sewell, Toronto's Chinese community, poet Irving Layton, and Pollution Probe. He examined boys' hockey and jobless white-collar men, and wrote sensitively about a blind and deaf man from Cape Breton who was managing to pay his own way in Toronto.

In February 1979, Peter devoted a column to a major collection of the architectural drawings of Kivas Tully.[17] Peter's imagination was once again at work. He claimed that Tully had designed Sir Casimir Gzowski's mansion, "The Hall," in 1854. Peter informed his readers that he and his daughter, Maria, would be attending the opening of an exhibition featuring the drawings at the Archives of Ontario in March. If father and daughter did actually attend the exhibition, they might have been puzzled by the absence of drawings of "The Hall." Tully, in fact, had had nothing to do with designing Sir Casimir's mansion, whose architect was Frederick Cumberland, better known for St. James Cathedral, University College, and the central section of Osgoode Hall.[18]

Peter's last column for the *Star*, his one hundredth, was published on March 23, 1979. He was anxious to return to magazines and radio, he told his readers. "Broadcasting may have taken over style," he argued, "but newspapers still own content." The problem, he explained, was that the creation of content required a lot of research, and he was tired of slogging through bad weather in order to dig up information for his stories. Although he himself often wrote about his reaction to events, Peter claimed to dislike reading articles by other journalists who did the same. Newspapers, he argued, should be reserved for what he called "reportage," by which he meant articles based on sound, accurate research. (Was he thinking of the sound research conducted on the architect of "The Hall"?) Personal reactions to events were fine on radio or television, but not in print. In February 1979, when interviewed by "Pete" McGarvey of CKEY, Peter added that he resigned from the *Star* before he grew "impressed by his own power."[19]

While he was primarily working in print journalism during this period, his radio voice was rarely silent. In 1979, Peter and writer-broadcaster Michele Landsberg were engaging each weekday in a supper-hour debate on current events. And on *Don Harron's Morningside*, Peter was giving a weekly sports report that allowed him, among other things, to report on his trip to Moscow that winter with a Canadian hockey team that lost to the Red Army club. "I was coaching minor hockey at the time," Peter recalled years later, "and I was given a chance to watch a practice in the Red Army boys' system." In Moscow he was "overwhelmingly impressed" by the rigorous Soviet training system. Early each morning for ninety minutes eleven-year-olds "wheeled through scrimmages and well-planned drills." He was particularly impressed by the fact that parents were banned from the arena. What didn't impress him as much was the drive, competitiveness, and elitism of the Soviet training regime. Some of his volleyball mates must have smiled at Peter's line that said "Winning *isn't* everything; playing is."[20]

Occasionally, Peter appeared on television. He made guest visits on shows, including the CBC's *Front Page Challenge*, an event he wrote about in his *Star* column of January 29. At the rehearsal the previous Friday evening he was surprised at how seriously Pierre Berton and Gordon Sinclair treated the show and themselves. The third regular panellist, Betty Kennedy, was in Peter's estimation a jaguar at heart who disguised her ruthlessness under a "lady-like" mask.

In 1979, Peter was a mystery guest on a CBC show called *Beyond Reason*. Hosted by Paul Soles, the program ran five afternoons each week.[21] It featured three panellists: an astrologer, a clairvoyant, and a palm reader, whose task was to identify mystery guests. The palmist was given an outline of the lines on Peter's palm; the astrologer was told the place, date, and time of his birth; and the clairvoyant used intuition, as well as a few of Peter's personal possessions. Like all guests, Peter was hidden from the panellists.

The astrologer was first. Peter's answers were rather revealing, though somewhat imaginary. Yes, he had a high degree of self-respect; yes, he had great respect for others; yes, he tended to bring out the best in his fellows; and, yes, he would never claw his way to the top. He denied that he was a good raconteur, but agreed he had writing ability and wasn't a stranger to television cameras. Yes, indeed, he had failed thus far to receive full recognition for his efforts.

The palmist began his questions. "Are you a very melancholy type?"
Peter answered, "No, I don't think so."
Palmist: "Peculiar?"
Peter: "Yes, aren't we all?"
Palmist: "Very sober?"
Peter: "At this time of the day."

Palmist: "Very restrained?"

Peter: "I don't think so."

Palmist: "Very wise?"

Peter: "Of course."

Palmist: "Very tall?"

Peter: "Yes."

Palmist: "Thin?"

Peter: "From time to time."

Palmist: "You take people apart?"

Peter: "No, I don't think I do."

Paul Soles interjected. "He does in a professional sense."

"What about nightmares?" the palmist asked.

"No," Peter said. A few minutes later he denied that he was prone to breaking bones. But he agreed he was impractical, and yes, he was rather withdrawn.

Based on hunches garnered during the previous questioning, Sandra, the clairvoyant, made her observations. The mystery guest was "an intensely serious person with a whole private world going on."

Peter agreed.

"You dwell on things a lot, connected with your career," Sandra guessed.

"I suppose, yeah, that I do," said Peter.

Did he have a comedic sense?

"I hope so," Peter answered.

"Sometimes you are so tense that a wall comes around you and you just back off from people," speculated Sandra.

"No," replied Peter.

None of the panellists was able to name the mystery guest. In his impeccably polite manner, Paul Soles introduced Peter and kindly promoted *Spring Tonic*. He also mentioned that Peter had worked for the World Hockey Association, doing the commentary for the Toronto Toros.

Around this time Key Porter Books hired Peter as an editor-at-large. The publishing company also hired Val Ross to write a travel guide to Ontario. One day Ross and Peter discussed the project over a boozy lunch. When Ross later turned in a "sloppy and snarky" first draft, Peter wrote a five-page, single-spaced critique that carefully and politely showed her how she might, in Ross's phrase, "engage in a conversation with the reader" rather than taking cheap shots at rural museums and restaurants. What Ross learned from Peter, she recalled years later, was a passion for the province and the country that Peter loved so dearly. And he taught her how to communicate that passion to the reader.[22]

Luckily, a book-length project came Peter's way. Brent Dyer and his sister-in-law, Donna Johnson, from Estevan, Saskatchewan, were looking for a writer who would provide a sympathetic account of an incident of cannibalism. During the spring of 1979, a Cessna 172 owned and piloted by Norm Pischke had crashed into a snow-covered mountain in Idaho. The plane, with Brent, Donna, and Donna's father, Don Johnson, onboard, was en route to Boise to pick up a West Highland terrier pup, a present to Donna from her father, who was the Southern fried chicken king of southeastern Saskatchewan. Don was killed on impact, and a badly injured Norm had wandered off, never to be seen again. To survive, Donna and Brent ate Don's flesh. When the media picked up the story, the young couple was embarrassed, even though it wasn't, by any means, the first time the consumption of human flesh had saved victims of plane crashes. In *Collapse*, his book about failed societies, Jared Diamond points out that cannibalism has always been an option of last resort for starving people.[23]

In June 1979, Brent and Donna consulted Dennis Ball, their lawyer in Estevan. Dennis, in turn, talked to his sister, Denise Ball, at that time the entertainment editor of Regina's *Leader-Post*. When she recommended McClelland & Stewart, Dennis called the publishing company. Not long after, Jack McClelland called from Vancouver, and a day or two later he touched down in Regina and drove to Estevan. Over martinis at Ball's country retreat, which was filled with Mission furniture, the two men talked. When a deer happened by, McClelland grew so agitated that Ball thought the publisher was going to succumb to a heart attack.[24] Upon his return to Toronto, McClelland presented the idea to Peter. In a few weeks, Peter provided McClelland with an outline of fifty pages. The strength of the book, he explained, would be in its wealth of real-life detail. "I think there's a book in here," he told McClelland. "I'm looking forward to writing it."

On August 10, 1979, Peter drafted a letter addressed to Brent and Donna, and to the lawyers on both sides. In pencil he wrote "I readily agree to give you control of matters of fact or of general taste. I cannot give you final editorial control." Then he crossed out those two sentences. In the end, according to Donna Johnson, it was the couple who retained control.[25]

On August 23, 1979, Jack McClelland wrote to Dennis Ball, enclosing Peter's outline. "Eighty percent of the authors' outlines that I have seen," McClelland explained, "bear little detailed reference to the final product." Writing, the publisher explained, was a creative process. "Concepts and ideas and even the juxtaposition of material are not constants and they all tend to change during the literary process." He wanted Ball to understand that Peter was a responsible writer, and a responsible human being who was "not out to write a lurid and sensational book."[26]

When the contracts were signed in late August, Donna and Brent were paid an advance of $5,000 and were guaranteed a share of the royalties. Peter agreed on an advance of $20,000, with a final payment of $5,000 on presentation of the completed work. The title caused some discussion. Peter wanted *The Gift of Love*. Brent objected. He had always imagined the consumption of his father-in-law's flesh and blood as the ritual consumption of the body and blood of Christ during Communion. *The Sacrament* was agreeable to all participants.

Not long afterward, Dennis Ball was surprised to see a stranger amble by the front window of his office in Estevan. Tentatively, the man pushed open the door and introduced himself as Peter Gzowski. The two men became friends, and Peter took up residence at the Ball residence on Lynd Crescent, while the Balls retreated to their nearby acreage. Surrounded by bottles of whisky and brandy, most of them soon empty, and by ashtrays full of cigarette butts and ashes, Peter wrote the first draft of the manuscript. From time to time, Dennis Ball took him to a workers' bar on the main street where Peter held court with a group of over-thirty amateur hockey players, who always found him engaging. One evening the Balls hosted a dinner to introduce Peter to a group of journalists from the *Leader-Post*. It was clear that they idolized Peter. It was also clear to Dennis Ball and to anyone else who got to know Peter in Estevan that he was suffering from the failure of his television show and from what he believed to be the CBC's rejection of him. Peter particularly admired Brent's father, Jim Dyer, who owned a car dealership in Estevan and who was a member of Alcoholics Anonymous. What Peter admired most in Dyer senior was the fact that he had a strong spiritual streak in him.[27]

For his research, Peter hired Marcia Kircher. She taped and transcribed interviews with participants, researched topics such as taboos, cannibalism, hunger, and parapsychology, and provided Peter with photocopies of articles and chapters from relevant books. Kircher also supplied Peter with a day-by-day, hour-by-hour synopsis of the plane's journey, its crash, the consumption of human flesh, the long walk from the plane, first contact with the outside world, and the reaction of the press. This "Fact Summary and Guide" for the period from May 6 to18, 1979, was based on two reports made by search-and-rescue units in Idaho and Montana. Kircher added weather reports and conversations with officials, who provided, among other things, details on the flight and the crash. She made certain that Peter assimilated the important facts. "If Sam were to stress anything to you, Peter," she wrote, "it would be that the type of flying is more important than the absolute number of hours." In other words, she explained, eight thousand hours over flat land doesn't prepare a pilot for mountain flying.[28]

Later, at their Rockwood home, Jan Walter, Peter acknowledged, "watched the manuscript evolve and offered suggestions and support." Peter saved the drafts, and thus one can see the book in evolution as Peter, the novelist *manqué*, employed the techniques of a fiction writer, from dramatic scenes to personification and metaphor. "The plane was struggling," Peter typed on one page. "The ice added to the Skylark's already heavy load, and violated the aerodynamics of its design."[29] He described the setting: "In summer, when the sun illuminates the pinks and blues and purples and browns … the mountains are staggeringly beautiful, and long before ~~Europeans~~ white men began to claw at the ~~rocks~~ minerals in their rocks, the Indians," he imagined, "would gaze on them with wonder." Those "fierce and terrible" peaks had "thrown back all but the hardiest pioneers who have tried to settle in their midst."

Perhaps at Jan's suggestion, Peter added by hand: "Pilots who fly them respect and fear them as the sailor respects and fears the sea." Like most good journalists and novelists, Peter was adept at appealing to the five senses and at creating a mood of suspense and foreboding. In early drafts, he tended to write baroque, complex sentences that he or his editors or perhaps Jan simplified in later drafts. When kept in check, Peter's figures of speech were graphic and poetic, as in "Downdrafts press like the hands of God." Peter's re-creation/invention of dialogue was, one supposes, derived from Donna and Brent's memories of conversations later preserved on tape. From there the novelist's imagination took flight, as in the sentence "In the seat beside Norm, Brent Dyer spoke over the squawking horns. 'Should those things be going off?'"

Jack McClelland believed he had a bestseller. McClelland told Ball he was hoping the manuscript might sell for up to $35,000 in the United States. Sid Adilman reported in the *Toronto Star* that McClelland had really been hoping to sell it south of the border for as much as $200,000.[30] Most American publishers weren't interested. However, McClelland did convince the Canadian Book-of-the-Month Club to make *The Sacrament* its main selection for one month. The book wasn't going to make anyone wealthy, McClelland lamented to Ball.

The reviews were mixed. In the *London Free Press*, Lynda Nykor wrote that Peter had treated cannibalism with "care and sensitivity," though she thought he had shown too much sympathy for Donna and Brent. Margaret B. Spittler in the *Chattanooga Times* in January 1981 liked Peter's speculation that the Christian rite of drinking the blood of Christ and consuming his body during Holy Communion was really a form of cannibalism. Robert Fulford called *The Sacrament* "a triumph of the reporter's art."[31] Bill Casselman, a producer of *This Country in the Morning*, thought the book "so expertly written it should be required reading in every Canadian journalism school."[32] On the other hand, Jim Christy in the *Globe and Mail* of September 27, 1980, found the book lacking in magic and its prose hackneyed and banal. Another reviewer found the book "occasionally too sentimental." Judith Timson disliked

Peter's "almost self-conscious attention to detail" and his "overly senti-mental writing style."[33]

At the end of September the book received the kind of publicity that most writers can only dream of — on four successive days, excerpts appeared in the *Toronto Star*.[34] In October and November 1980, Peter was on the road to promote the book. In the *Edmonton Journal* of October 11, 1980, Myrna Kostash described a "bristling" Gzowski, who was so excited at the prospect of spending a week in Jasper at the Edmonton Oilers' training camp that he had trouble sitting still during an interview. He was also exasperated with reviewers who had, he claimed, misread his book. Some of them, he announced to Kostash, even objected to the absence of judgment or critical insights. "I am one of this country's craftsmen, a journalist," he insisted. He objected to being called a per-sonality. "What I am is not important," he informed Kostash. "What I do is. And what I set out to do was not a book of reflection or judgment — my own judgment is of no interest; it's for the reader to make — but a reportorial work, a work of craftsmanship.... Here, write this down: I wrote a quartet and the critics were expecting a symphony." When Kostash told him that she agreed with reviewers who were put off by his "over-fastidious treatment" of cannibalism, Peter shot back, "You mean, why didn't I mention what human flesh tastes like?"

Once back in Toronto, Peter signed books at the University College Book Fair in November, and in December, in the company of seven-teen other writers, including Charles Templeton, John Fraser, and Jack Batten, he signed copies of *The Sacrament* at Edwards Books and Art on Queen Street West. Perhaps impressed by his interest in architecture and history, the Ontario Heritage Foundation appointed Peter to their board and paid him the agreeable sum of $85 per day plus expenses for advising on heritage sites and buildings.[35]

What Peter didn't tell Myrna Kostash was that the project had had its constraints from the beginning. Peter had been commissioned to write the book. In most if not all authorized projects, the author is constrained not only by the contract but by his own self-censorship, for he knows what will be acceptable to those who commissioned the work and he appreciates the paycheques. Although prior to publication, Donna and Brent asked for only a few minor changes in the manuscript, the pressure was on Peter to transform cannibalism into the central ritual of Christianity.

The other problem for Peter was his conflicted relationship with his own father. Like Brent and Donna, Peter had psychological "wounds to bind," to borrow a phrase from Peter's friends, Ian and Sylvia. *The Sacrament* was an act of contrition for three people. While writing the book, Peter was attempting to come to terms with the memory of his own father. In May 1977, when Harold Gzowski died, Peter didn't grieve. "I didn't cry, not then, not now," he told *Morningside* listeners years later. He always regretted that he had never been able to tell his father that he was proud of him for having fought hard and well during the war. Only after Harold's death was Peter able to steel enough courage to say on *Morningside*, "Sergeant Major, thanks for what you did."

As Peter aged, he was amazed by how much he gradually came to resemble his father. His own gestures, he thought, were replicas of his father's *"as if I had stolen them one by one*, sitting across the dining room table. Seeing me, on these infrequent visits, must have been as strange for him as it was for me, and we could eye each other warily, looking for the signs of similarity that others noted, *I at least soaking up every detail*, the sugar in the coffee, the Winchester cigarettes my mother also smoked, the strange, bold nose he had inherited from my grandmother *and passed on to me*, the eyes perhaps too close together."[36] Gestures stolen one by one. Details absorbed. The nose passed on from father to son. Although not literally, Peter, too, had consumed his father's blood and body. While Peter was able to help Donna and Brent come to terms with the ghost of Donna's father, he never did arrive at any reconciliation with a paternal ghost that haunted him for the rest of his life.

During his period of "exile" from Toronto, Peter began to dream of the glory days of the Gzowski clan, of their noble roots in Poland, and of Sir Casimir's illustrious career and impressive connections with elites in nineteenth-century Canada. On February 10, 1980, after he sent off the manuscript of *The Sacrament* to McClelland & Stewart, Peter wrote to Jack McClelland. His trip to Poland in 1978, he explained, had inspired him to write a book about his great-great-grandfather. He sent McClelland a first draft of a chapter. The book would be both scholarly and readable, he announced. He wanted an advance of $20,000. He was broke, "even down to the old income tax problem." Revenue Canada was pressing him for back taxes, and his accountants were pressing him to settle with Jennie. When it came to money, Sir Casimir and his great-great-grandson had little in common, for Sir Casimir had always preached "prudence and a determination to keep within our means ..."[37]

Peter had already written about Sir Casimir. On May 23, 1959, *Maclean's* published his article called "What's It Like to Have a Famous (but Forgotten) Ancestor?" No doubt Peter was inspired by *Sir Casimir Stanilaus Gzowski: A Biography*, also published in 1959, which painted an admiring portrait of the man who was made an honorary aide-de-camp to Queen Victoria in 1879, who was knighted in 1890, and who served a term as acting lieutenant governor of Ontario. The biography only hinted, ever so politely, at peccadilloes such as Sir Casimir's "adroit financial manipulation" and "maladministration."[38]

In his article in 1959, Peter added his own flourishes. He was correct in praising Sir Casimir for chairing the Niagara Falls Park Commission from 1885 to 1893, during which time the commission established the Niagara Parkway, one of Ontario's most beautiful parks, which today stretches along the Niagara River from Niagara-on-the-Lake to Fort Erie, where the International Bridge, whose chief engineer was Sir Casimir, joins Canada and the United States. However, Peter's imagination took over when he claimed that Sir Casimir had carried out the first survey of Yonge Street. Was Peter unaware that it was under the supervision of John Graves Simcoe in the 1790s that Yonge Street was surveyed from the Town of York to the lower end of Lake Simcoe? What Casimir had done more than a half century later was to supervise improvements on Yonge Street north of Toronto. In his *Maclean's* article, Peter also claimed that Casimir's plan for the Toronto waterfront in the 1850s would have transformed the lakeshore into a pedestrian-friendly esplanade of parks. Actually, Casimir was, in part, responsible for the fact that Toronto's waterfront was cut off from the downtown by railway lines. A major part of Casimir's plan provided the Grand Trunk Railway with an entranceway into the centre of Toronto along the lake between Spadina Avenue and the Don River.[39]

The article in *Maclean's* was illustrated by a photograph of Peter wearing "respectacles" and with his hands proudly folded over the scabbard of Sir Casimir's sword. Peter is seated in the nineteenth-century manner, while a standing Jennie holds baby Peter Casimir. All three pose in mock seriousness in front of the Notman portrait of Sir Casimir,[40] who had posed for the photographer in the court uniform of an aide-de-camp.

In 1978, in one of his columns in the *Toronto Star*, Peter again wrote about Sir Casimir. This time he recounted a story that may have been passed down through generations of Gzowskis. According to Peter, when Sir Casimir met Jan Paderewski, the Polish pianist, at Massey Hall in 1895, the old count wept because he couldn't converse in Polish with the pianist. The 1959 biography merely states that Sir Casimir "thanked the famous Polish pianist."[41] Furthermore, that biography states that Paderewski's concert was at the Toronto Pavilion in Allan Gardens and that it took place in 1892, which was a year before Massey Hall was opened.

Peter's model for his proposed biography of Sir Casimir was without doubt Donald Creighton's two-volume account of of Sir John A. Macdonald's life. In his magisterial biography of Canada's first prime minister, published in the 1950s, Creighton noted that, when Sir John A. lay in state in the Senate Chamber on Parliament Hill in June 1891, it was Sir Casimir who stepped forward on behalf of Her Majesty to place a wreath of roses on his friend's breast. It was a dramatic last act just before the doors of the Chamber were closed in preparation for the funeral cortège down Rideau Street to St. Alban's Church. To that brief description, which relies on a combination of sound scholarship and the imagination of Creighton, Peter added his own re-creation. The guards on duty, he wrote, "look anxiously" at the long lineup waiting to view the remains. Sir Casimir, "a solitary erect figure," moves toward the coffin, "his gait slowed by the dignity of age and the solemnity of the occasion." The mourners are impressed, and, of course, they all recognize the great Sir Casimir. "Heads turn. Way was made. The plume on his three-cornered hat rode above the crowd like a galleon over the seas. Even without the hat he would have been at six feet five inches, by far the tallest person in the ~~great quiet~~ room…. [Occasionally, Peter acted as his own editor by crossing out some of the excessive description.] He wore the scarlet tunic of the Queen's Volunteers. The blue-and-white cross of St. Michael and St. George glittered from the sash that crossed his breast, where Victoria herself had pinned it less than a year before. Rich mutton chops descended to his collar." His white moustache "bristled under his bold aristocratic nose."[42] The scabbard that sheathed his sword, Peter explained, bore the names of the battles in which Sir Casimir had fought in the name of Polish independence.[43] Sir Casimir laid the wreath "tenderly," then his eyes "misted, as if in memory of the struggles he had shared with his Scottish friend, and the toasts they had drunk together."[44]

The above is the kind of imaginative storytelling that would have elicited "Bullshit!" from Ralph Allen. Like Creighton, Peter knew how to set a scene, how to tease out its inherent drama. It was the kind of riveting, readable history that his colleagues Pierre Berton and Peter C. Newman were writing to much popular acclaim and to great academic disdain. Had a book resulted, reviewers would have noted a plethora of romanticizing and a dearth of scholarship.

Did Peter really inherit any of Sir Casimir's character and attitudes, as he liked to imagine? Is it possible that character traits and business methods can, in fact, be passed down from generation to generation? Perhaps yes, from grandfather to son to grandson, for two succeeding generations usually have personal contact and can therefore more readily emulate or absorb character. Does personality survive time and the mixing of genes over four or five generations? Not likely.

And yet, and yet, to use a favourite phrase of Peter's,[45] there are remarkable similarities between the two men. Like Sir Casimir, Peter was impatient with authority and management. He saw "Russian" overlords at the CBC and in any government that dared to rationalize spending. The younger Gzowski participated in an uprising at *Maclean's* in 1964 against overlords at Maclean-Hunter. During the late 1970s, he saw himself as an exile awaiting a call to return to greatness at the CBC. Eventually, like his ancestor, Peter would become a member of the Canadian Establishment, powerful and respected. Both Gzowskis enjoyed working and socializing with people who wielded power, and each man was happy to accept titles, orders, and honorary degrees. The two men even bear an uncanny physical resemblance to each other, especially in their eyes, merry and wary. Perhaps it is indeed possible that Peter inherited his ancestor's physical characteristics and personality, even though that ancestor formed no more than 4 percent of Peter's gene pool.

While the CBC didn't offer him a permanent contract during this period, he was certainly not unwanted or forgotten. In fact, he was never out of touch with Toronto, for he and Jan kept an apartment at 135 Crescent Road, just west of the bridge over Mount Pleasant Road. There they spent the colder six months of the year while they rented out their house in Rockwood. On August 2, 1978, Peter signed a contract to produce a CBC Radio show called *One to One — Poland Revisited*; and for one week in late September 1978, he filled in for Don Harron on *Morningside*.

The mail poured in. Jean begged him to return permanently to radio. She loved his "mellifluous voice," his great laugh, and his interesting guests. Diane wrote that "Yes — for you, hosting a radio show is like riding a bicycle. Your beautiful style — so smooth, so relaxed, so considerate, so comfortable.... Welcome home." A media colleague at a competing network told him: "You were superb ... comfortable and assured." On September 29, 1978, on the back of a postcard that featured a Karl Illini pen-and-ink drawing of the Kirkfield Lift Lock, a fan in Argyle, Ontario, wrote: "Dear Peter, Having been listening to you this week on *Morningside*, let me tell you how good it is to *hear* you again. Radio is your own medium. Thank you for redeeming yourself. Sincerely."[46] Two days earlier from her studio in Mount Carmel, Newfoundland, artist Mary Pratt wrote that she hadn't been able to listen to morning radio since Peter's departure in 1974. "Nobody else has quite 'the touch,'" she added. One group of listeners sent in a collage spelling out "Peter Very Special Old Friend ... come back" From British Columbia came "WOW! That voice ..." And from Regina: "No one makes pictures come out of the radio like Gzowski."

On Monday night, January 22, 1979, Peter looked relaxed on *Canada After Dark*, the continuation of *90 Minutes Live*, as he announced to host Paul Soles that the previous day he hadn't had a single cigarette, quite a feat for a man who usually smoked eighty per day. Peter was determined to give up the filthy habit. He had tried everything, he told Soles, from a hotline in Missouri to foot massage. Nothing worked, so he quit cold turkey at midnight the previous Saturday night. The following June, Peter was a guest on the noon-hour *Bob McLean Show*. Inside the studio at Cumberland Avenue and Bay Street, Peter taught McLean how to swing a golf club properly. Peter mentioned playing golf with George Knudson, and also with his son, Mick, age thirteen, who was planning, Peter announced, to study medicine at university.

Perhaps to keep fit for golf, Peter joined The Adelaide, a sports club located in the financial district of Toronto, where in February 1979 he was defeated in a game of racquetball by Jane O'Hara, a friend.[47] Later that month Peter was a member of a panel at the St. Lawrence Centre on the subject of women's liberation. "Women have changed the rules of the game and men are starting to react," read the ad in the *Toronto Star*.[48] In late February and early March, he was autographing copies of *Spring Tonic* at the big department stores in downtown Toronto.[49] In April 1979, he joined about a hundred other writers, among them Margaret Laurence, Barbara Amiel, Don Harron, Peter Newman, Charles Taylor, and Timothy Findley, at the Park Plaza as part of the National Book Festival.[50] During July, August, and September 1979, he was the summer replacement host of CBC Radio's 4:00 to 6:00 p.m. show in Toronto.[51]

While Peter's years at Rockwood were productive, he was unhappy and restive. He found the act of writing a book by himself a glum task. Like that young lad years before on the ice in Dickson Park in Galt, he worked best when he was surrounded by a backup team of cheering fans. Even magazine articles contributed to his depression. He "ground out an unsatisfactory piece for *Toronto Life*,"[52] and he suffered from writer's block. While Jan Walter commuted to Toronto, where she worked at Macmillan of Canada, Peter fretted. He drank heavily and watched daytime soap operas, talk shows, and *Jeopardy*, whose host, Alex Trebek, had learned the art of television. Peter missed his children. He had once been especially close to his namesake son with whom he used to play chess and engage in Marx Brothers gags. Now father and son saw little of each other. "There aren't too many things we have in common these days," Peter lamented. "We don't share a lot of intimacies." During a rare visit by Peter C. to Rockwood on a cold winter day, father and son skated "wordlessly over the dark ice."[53] One day an old Ridley College friend, Jack Barton, ran into Peter loping along Bloor Street, dishevelled, hunched over, and staring at the sidewalk. He reeked of alcohol. "They don't want me anymore," he mumbled to Barton. Robert Reguly also bumped into him one morning around this time and found him in a similar state.

Although Peter never wrote about the horrors of alcoholism, his friend Glen Allen did. "As I walk the streets, I wonder how all these people can be so happy with their coffee and their 'one beer and that's all,'" Allen once wrote. "People drink to change their feelings, to feel better. But some of us have a second, third, and thirteenth drink to make us feel better than the first drink makes us feel," Allen continued. Then he asked a question that Peter might have asked himself occasionally: "But why do we feel so bad in the first place?"[54]

During what he considered his period of exile, Peter fell into a deep depression. In all his writing, he provided few if any details. The novelist William Styron also once suffered from intense black depression, so much so that he contemplated suicide. Once recovered, he wrote about his problems in *Darkness Visible*. There are many parallels between Styron and Gzowski, beginning with the fact that they shared an artistic temperament that made them more observant, more sensitive to other people's reactions, prone to interpreting a sideways glace as disapproval and ready to take the blame for perceived failure.

Styron's subtitle is "A Memoir of Madness," and during his years at Rockwood, Peter showed all the symptoms described by Styron: black depression, self-hatred, debilitating anxiety, and lack of self-esteem. Styron believed he was doomed. Like Peter, Styron drank a great deal because alcohol stimulates the imagination while dulling overwrought senses. Each man developed what Styron calls a "fidgety restlessness."

The seeds of the illness, Styron speculates, lie in childhood, and one of the major causes is a "devastating loss" made worse by "incomplete mourning." Peter's great loss was that of his mother, and the picture of him at the funeral — quiet, aloof, controlled — suggests he couldn't grieve or that he refused to grieve. Styron's mother died when he was thirteen, and Peter's when he was sixteen. The death of a mother for a teenager can create "nearly irreparable emotional havoc," Styron explains. As adults, both men carried "an insufferable burden of which rage and guilt, and not only dammed up sorrow, are a part, and become the potential seeds of self-destruction." The death of his father in 1977 only added to Peter's woes. In both Peter and Styron, black depression resulted in withdrawal, self-pity, and dependence on alcohol.

— 12 —

"Is Pierre Berton a Canadian?"[1]
1980–1983

I suppose everybody who is a public character as well as a private one
has a kind of schizophrenia to overcome.

— *Northrop Frye to Peter Gzowski*, Morningside,
March 19, 1987

It was Peter's passion for hockey that put an end to his biography of Sir Casimir. In *God's Country and Mine*, Jacques Barzun claimed that, in order to understand "the heart and mind of America," one had to study baseball.[2] In order to understand Canada's heart and mind, Peter studied hockey. His first published piece on the game was in *Maclean's* on February 25, 1961. "Hockey has been called a game for brutes and Canadians," Peter began, but it is also "a game for heroes." Twenty-three-year-old Frank Mahovlich, the focus of the article, had "miner's hands, full-back's legs, dancer's hips, stevedore's shoulders and a sleepy, Slavic face." On Mahovlich's style, Peter was eloquent. "Other skaters stride, he swoops. They glide, he soars. They sprint, he explodes." As sometimes happened, Peter's style descended into hyperbole. In the very next line, he compared Mahovlich to a Super Continental train racing through Saskatchewan.[3]

In "The Highest Scoring Baritone in History" (*Maclean's*, September 22, 1962), Peter's hockey hero was the star of the Montreal Canadiens, Bernie "Boom Boom" Geoffrion, whose success in scoring, Peter explained, was due to his trademark slap shot. Once on CBC-TV, Boom Boom had sung about his hockey life with "baritone voice and muscular gestures" while moving "his square, manicured hands as if he were picking strands of a spider's web from in front of the camera." Away from the ice, he dressed "like an off-duty model for *Playboy* magazine." Ever observant, Peter noted Boom Boom's fingernails, "long enough to show beyond his fingertips." On the little finger of his left hand, he wore a "sparkling ring," a gift from his wife, who, Peter was pleased to report, was a daughter of hockey legend Howie Morenz. Geoffrion revealed little except that he smoked, drank, and swore minimally; that he thought the NHL and *les Canadiens* were "perfect"; and that hockey fans were "wonderful." In the March 23, 1963, issue of *Maclean's*, Peter N. Allison's "The 'Best' Player in Hockey" dealt with the twenty-two-year-old Davey Keon, star centre of the Maple Leafs and "one of the most indomitable checkers in the NHL, as quick and deadly as a rattlesnake with his poke-check."

During his brief stint as sports columnist for *Saturday Night*, Peter had written book reviews[4] and articles about hockey, including one in which he defended the exclusion of Vancouver from the expanded NHL.[5] In February 1965 in *Saturday Night*, his topic was the Soviet national team, which, the previous December, had played a series against Canada's national team at Maple Leaf Gardens. On January 29, 1966, in *The Canadian*, once again Peter noted that the Soviets were improving year by year.

For the *Star Weekly* in 1965, Peter wrote a series of freelance articles about the six teams that formed the NHL at the time. The first, published on January 30, 1965, was about the Chicago Black Hawks and the team's hulking blond Bobby Hull, whose zestful, swashbuckling style personified what Peter called "the Chicago Style." The novelist in Peter soon took over when he surmised that each team reflected its home city. Chicago, the team and city, was "a man's town" with great steaks and good jazz ... a Greenwich Village where you can tell the sexes apart ..."[6] The Boston Bruins, like Boston's shanty Irish immigrants, were scrappy and boisterous. In New York, he argued (February 13, 1965), the Rangers and hockey in general were mere bush league, a minority activity in a big city.

On February 20, 1965, the *Star Weekly* published Peter's "Les Canadiens sont là," in which he argued that the Montreal team represented the city's élan and excellence. The Habs "swoop and gambol," he wrote, "skating like fury and burning with zeal; they are somehow romantic, like Scaramouche or Cyrano or Jean Gascon."[7] In his earlier article on the Black Hawks, Peter thought the Montreal players were "as full of dash and élan as a Molière comedy by the Théâtre de [*sic*] Nouveau Monde." Jennie, Peter reported, found the Habs sexy. On February 27, 1965, *The Star Weekly* published Peter's "Golden Boys in a Gilded Cage," an article about the Toronto Maple Leafs. "There is scarcely a style of hockey," he wrote, "that is not exemplified by someone on the team, from the booming body checks of Bobby Baun to the dragonfly brilliance of Dave Keon." On March 6, 1965, in the *Star Weekly*, Peter wrote about the Detroit Red Wings. "Like its famous automobiles, Detroit's hockey team is finely engineered." The team was designed, Peter went on, "not to entertain but to win — and it does with great precision." He added that "it would be difficult to argue against the proposition that Gordie Howe is the greatest player the National Hockey League has ever known."

In March 1980, the Canada Council turned down Peter's hockey book proposal, even though he announced in his application that he planned to write "the best goddamn book on hockey."[8] What he had in mind was a book on the Stastnys, the Slovakian brothers who played for the Quebec Nordiques. The notes and drafts that Peter left behind, as well as one chapter on the Stastnys in *The Game of Our Lives*, a cloak-and-dagger espionage tale of how Anton and Peter were smuggled out of Austria, can only make readers wish he had pursued the topic.

Peter also considered writing a book on the Montreal Canadiens, which he believed would allow him to discuss the bilingual identity of Canada. At the same time he was aware that Wayne Gretzky, whom he had first met on *This Country in the Morning*, was by 1980 being compared to Gordie Howe. In July 1980, Peter called Gretzky, who agreed to a game of golf on July 15, 1980, at the Cutten Golf Club in Guelph. During the match, Wayne suggested that Peter ask Peter Pocklington for permission to write about the Edmonton Oilers.

"He's an amazing kid," Peter told Mordecai Richler in a letter written just after the golf game. Of all the important figures in hockey, Peter told Richler, only Gretzky was "totally new to my writing eye." In Peter's judgment, Wayne was "not very articulate (surprise!), but polite as hell, and he grows in poise every time I see him. Still painfully shy, as Howe was — but certainly not dumb."[9] Peter once asked Wayne if he feared that his early celebrity might provoke a hostile press reaction, exactly what Peter thought was happening to Pierre Berton. A puzzled Wayne asked, "Is Pierre Berton a Canadian?"[10]

The golf game resulted in an article, and ultimately a book. Peter wrote a profile of Gretzky, which was published in *Saturday Night* in November 1980. "Portrait of a Prodigy," which won a national sports-writing award, began with Wayne's derrière, which was the focus of a television commercial for GWG jeans. The commercial's theme song, sung to the tune of "Land of Hope and Glory," contained only one word — "bum." Later, *Inside Sports*, based in New York, published a version of the article under the title "The Great Gretzky."

Following the advice of Gretzky, Peter wrote a letter to Peter Pocklington. "I'm making the pretty arrogant assumption," Peter told the owner of the Oilers, "that through one of my various careers as writer, radio interviewer, TV host, or magazine editor, my name is familiar to you, because if it isn't I'm in heavy trouble with the proposal I'm about to make." Peter proposed writing a book on the Oilers. Pocklington and Glen Sather, the coach, general manager, and Oilers president, expressed reservations. They were averse to prying eyes and wanted, it seems, to control the final version. Peter refused restrictions. Sather and Pocklington relented, and in September, Peter joined the young team, which he followed throughout the 1980–81 season. Eventually, the players accepted him as one of their own. Like George Plimpton on football, Peter was allowed to view hockey from the inside.

To research the book, Peter observed games and talked to players, while his research assistant, Joan Dixon, collected newspaper articles about the players and read dozens of academic articles on sports, learning how players were able to conceptualize their game and how their bodies could endure long stretches of rugged play. As with all his research, Gzowski saved his notes. "Hockey was the centre of our winter lives, and its stars twinkled in a special heaven," he wrote on a yellow notepad one day in 1980, adding and crossing out "Each Saturday night, Foster Hewitt brought our dreams into our homes." On another sheet of paper, he wrote: "Is it a measure of the strength (or lack of it) of Western separation that the Oilers don't *reflect* a national aspiration the way the Canadiens do? Maybe it simply tells us that it's a different *kind* of alienation — economic as opposed to cultural. Cultural alienation gives us cultural heroes — Richard as well as Vigneault, Charlebois, etc. — economic alienation doesn't."

In one of his mischievous moods, Peter toyed with a title for the book. On foolscap he scribbled a list of about fifty titles, including "Hockey Wars," "No Place for a Nervous Person," "All the Young Animals," "Following Wayne, Following Howie," and a bilingual title, "The First Star, La Première Étoile." He must have suspected that no publisher would go for "The Fastest Fucking Game on Earth" or "You Cocksuckers."

While researching and writing the book, Peter was approaching fifty. Only those closest to him could understand how he could have so many doubts about himself. There was no guarantee, he knew, that Canadian readers would buy the argument that hockey was the Canadian soul. And there was even less guarantee they would buy a book expressing such a thesis. As he researched, he continued to despair. He wondered how hockey players handled fame. Those who lived in the spotlight were altered by it, he thought, and couldn't cope with fame. It had destroyed Howie Morenz, he noted, but it had made Gordie Howe. How you handled fame, Peter observed, had "much to do with 'middle-aged crisis'" when many men asked, "Is that all there is?"[11] Attempted suicide, alcoholism, and money problems weren't uncommon among hockey retirees. Not long before Peter began his research, a retired player had jumped from a bridge over the Perimeter Highway in Winnipeg. "This is tough stuff, tougher than I at first thought the book should be," he scribbled on a page of foolscap one day.[12]

Peter was also struggling with the meaning of his own fame and failure. "To do this stuff honestly," he wrote, "I have to deal up front with my own problems with television, etc." He wondered if there was a literature dealing with success. He would have to check with Dr. Kingsley Ferguson at the Clarke Institute in Toronto. "Whatever, my own experience applies," he concluded wistfully.

When *The Game of Our Lives* was published, Peter told Gordie and Colleen Howe that it was "the world's first really literate look at hockey from a fan's point of view." The dust jacket of the hardcover edition features a colour reproduction of a Ken Danby acrylic called *Lacing Up*, which shows a pair of muscular arms tugging at the laces of a skate. On the back jacket is an autographed photograph of the author dressed in an Edmonton Oilers uniform, stick on the ice, leaning forward, ready to face-off. Behind those horn-rimmed glasses is the boy who skated forever over fields of ice. Even the curmudgeonly Gordon Sinclair reported on CFRB radio that he couldn't remember being so struck by a dust jacket.

While the posed picture — it was taken by Joe Black, a professional photographer from Toronto[13] — makes Peter look a bit like a big Oiler, the truth was something else. After skating in wide arcs for a few minutes, Peter was drained of energy. "Sooner than I would have wished," he wrote, "a lifetime of cigarettes caught up with me, and I panted to the bench."[14] He had stayed on his skates just long enough to claim that he had played with Gretzky, albeit with a tennis ball rather than a puck. As he was completing the manuscript, the Oilers beat the Montreal Canadiens in the first round of the playoffs, and later came close to winning the Stanley Cup.

On Friday evening, October 29, 1981, *The Game of Our Lives* was launched at the Forum Hotel on 73rd Street in Edmonton. The Oilers were there, as well as Jack McClelland. During two hours, from 5:00 to 7:00 p.m., broadcaster Ted Barris, then the host of CBC Edmonton's *The Saturday Morning Show*, wove his way through the crowd, tape recorder in hand. Barris recorded the two Peters, Gzowksi and Pocklington, and the one Jack as they addressed the Oilers, who, as the liquor disappeared, grew more and more raucous. Wayne Gretzky thought the book was "fantastic" and "intriguing," and added, "Well, I think that people who read the book are going to be very impressed … it sent chills up my back …"[15] Had Wayne actually read the index-deprived book, he might have smiled at Peter's overwrought metaphors. In Peter's imagination, the Great One played hockey like a chicken hawk on the prowl, like a ballet dancer, a solemn squirrel, and a prancing reindeer.[16]

No one more than Peter enjoyed being one of the boys. He began that evening by responding to McClelland's short speech: "The son of a bitch thinks it's easy to write a book." He teased the players by claiming there were twenty-four tell-all books at $1,500 per book, and that unless there was a sellout on that edition, he would be reading it aloud the next evening at centre ice. He turned to the dedication. "For both my daughters and all my boys" netted not only his children but all the Oilers, of whom, he admitted, he had become fond and protective. "I would like to point out to Curt Brackenbury," he continued, referring to the big right winger, "that his inclusion by inference in the dedication, along with my two daughters, doesn't necessarily mean that he will ever get to meet one of those two daughters." Peter had been told, he added, that he could make a lot of money if only he would consent to "breed one of those daughters to Wayne Gretzky," a plan "discussed at some length" but rejected "on the grounds that … the offspring would skate like [Peter] and write like Wayne." The Oilers chuckled knowingly. Peter turned to Vickie Moss, Gretzky's girlfriend of the early 1980s. "So that plan, Vickie, has fallen apart, you may be delighted to know." More laughter.

The following evening, Peter was at centre ice in the Northlands Coliseum, standing tall with Gretzky, ready to give away the first of more than seventy-five hundred copies ordered by Pocklington for subscribers to Oilers home games. On three successive days the previous November, the *Toronto Star* had boosted sales by publishing excerpts of *The Game of Our Lives*.[17] By early December, the book made the non-fiction bestseller list. Before Christmas it had risen to number seven, ahead of David Lewis's autobiography *The Good Fight*. By the end of December, the book had fallen slightly to eighth, beaten out by Peter Newman's *The Canadian Establishment*, Pierre Berton's *Flames Across the Border*, and Mike Filey's *I Remember Sunnyside*. In early January, it was still number eight, just ahead of a biography of Elizabeth Taylor. Soon *The Game of Our Lives* moved up to fourth position, but by mid-March 1982 it had fallen to sixth, where it was squeezed between Margaret Trudeau's memoirs and Jane Fonda's workout book.[18] Peter's first royalty cheque, based on sales in 1981, paid him the not inconsiderable sum of $43,025.08,[19] a figure that would represent, some thirty years later, about $90,000.

Good reviews also inspired sales. *Alberta Report*'s reviewer, John Short, was positive about the book. *The Game of Our Lives* was full of "marvellously casual recollections," and its author managed to portray hockey gladiators as real human beings.[20] On November 28, 1981, the *Hamilton Spectator*'s Jim Ross wrote that "There's never been a better book about the game of our lives." Christie Blatchford, in the *Toronto Star*, called the book "a love story" without a single excess word. It was, deemed Blatchford, the Book of Peter's Life.[21] Jim Kernaghan wrote in the *London Free Press* on December 18, 1981, that he had never seen "a more accurate picture of what it is to be a hockey player."

At times Peter's writing in *The Game of Our Lives* is indeed lyrical and evocative. Often he touches the soul of the game. Peter begins one paragraph in the book with "There is an awesome, rushing beauty to this game," following which he describes the ebb and flow of the game as it emerges, fades, shifts, fades again, then reforms. In passages like these, Peter touched the essence of the sport.

In his hands, hockey becomes a metaphor not only for Canadian identity but also for the human quest for perfection, happiness, and immortality. There are no more beautiful descriptions of hockey than the following lines:

> But when Bobby Hull wheeled down the wing, his sweater bulging in the wind, we were there with him. We understood; we knew what it felt like. All that separated us from our true heroes was that they were better at something we all had done. They belonged to

Ewart and Audrey Whaley look on as Peter signs a copy of The Game of
Our Lives *at Audreys Bookstore in Edmonton on October 31, 1981, one of
the largest events at the store. Chaperoning Peter that day was McClelland
& Stewart's Edmonton agent, Sharon Budnarchuk, who refused to obey Peter
Pocklington's order that she cancel the last bookstore signing of the day so that
the two Peters could enjoy a drink before the Oilers game. The next day Peter
and Jack McClelland flew with Pocklington to Vancouver for the launch of the
second volume of Peter C. Newman's* The Canadian Establishment, *which
included a certain Peter Pocklington.*

us, as no other kind of hero ever could, at once more
celebrated and more approachable because of what we
shared. They were *of* us, playing the game of our lives.

Today, however, three decades after publication, reviewers probably
wouldn't be quite so kind.[22] There are far too many play-by-play accounts
of games that only meant something to fans in the early 1980s. Today

does anyone care that on March 28, 1980, on the first shift, Gretzky broke in alone on Larry Lozinsky, the Detroit Red Wings' goalie? Or that in early 1980, the Oilers lost momentum? Or that Ron Lowe asked that he be allowed to play with the farm club in Wichita, Kansas, to prepare himself for a return to the Oilers in the early 1980s? Or that Mark Messier was almost sent down to Wichita in February 1980? *The Game of Our Lives* is really a long magazine article, an extension of Peter's first-rate articles in *Maclean's* and *Saturday Night*. Magazine articles are transitory, while books are meant to last for at least a decade.

One also gets the impression that the book as published isn't the final draft. Like many writers, Peter thoroughly enjoyed the research. "I am having more fun in this year of travelling and living with the Oilers," he wrote in "A Fan's Notes," published in the Oilers program for their game against the Quebec Nordiques on February 13, 1981, "than I have ever had on a project I've undertaken before, and sometimes it is hard to realize this is the way I'm trying to earn my living."[23] However, he found writing a book onerous. And lonely. Like a marathon swim across a wide, dark, and cold lake, it takes enormous stamina to write a book. One writes for years, and the far shore never seems to get any closer. Having committed oneself to finishing, the swimmer/writer is too embarrassed and too proud to pull out.

Years later Peter admitted to Marco Adria that he was dissatisfied with *The Game of Our Lives*. When daughter Alison was planning to write a book about the Cowboy Junkies, Peter advised her to devote a chapter to each musician: chapter one from the drummer's perspective, chapter two through the eyes of the bass player, and so on. Suddenly, during an interview with Adria, Peter blurted out, "Goddamn it, that's what I should have done in *The Game of Our Lives*." He saw the structure he should have followed — every third chapter on Gretzky, and a chapter on the three Finns, in which he might have asked Jari Kurri for the name of the Foster Hewitt of Finland. He should have spent less time with Glen Sather, he realized. "I'm a bad reporter,"[24] he concluded.

—•—

The pity of *The Game of Our Lives* is that the book leaves so much out. It's far too respectful. When reviewing Frank Selke's book on hockey in the March 1965 edition of *Saturday Night*, Peter had chided the NHL for trying to cover up excessive drinking and other sins committed by hockey players. "This is the sort of bean-spilling the NHL now finds worse than heretical," Peter wrote, "because it wants to perpetuate the myth that players are superhuman."[25] Fifteen years later Peter was perpetuating the same myth. Why was he so protective of the Oilers? After all, unlike his contract for *The Sacrament*, he was under no restrictions. He was a journalist, he had told Sather and Pocklington. Therefore he sought the truth. Ironically, he censored himself.

His notes, however, are revealing, and much more interesting than the book itself. In those notes, Gretzky tells his teammates to "fuck off" when they complain that, while signing autographs at the team bus door, he is delaying their departure.[26] In the book, Gretzky is a pretty polite boy. And so are most of the other players as portrayed by Peter. Mind you, Doug Hicks did lead "an active bachelor life,"[27] and a few players, during a road trip to Montreal, "went to a bar whose chief feature was strip-tease dancers who came within body-checking range of the customers."[28] However, in the book Peter never reported on a "cocktail waitress into SM" and players "fucking in the bar."[29] In his notes, women who serviced the Oilers such as Vancouver Sally, Omaha Donna, and Chicago Shirley were quite adept at taking on several players simultaneously. In the book, the short and stout Shirley is almost as demure as a kindergarten teacher, her profession before plying her trade with testosterone-charged hockey players. While Peter does state in *The Game of Our Lives* that Shirley had "broken in rookies in all sports since the early 1960s,"[30] there is nothing in the book about Shirley's encounters with players such as Boom Boom Geoffrion, who, according to Peter's unpublished notes, gave Shirley "the best tongue." Nor anything about "the closet party" involving Ken Brown and Jack Norris. Nothing about "the girl who … sucked KB, fucked another guy & who had two dicks in her hand," following which, when she was washing herself, she "hid her breasts."[31]

In Peter's notes, the relationship between a beautiful Canadian and Mark Messier's troubled cousin, Don Murdoch, is sizzling. In the book, they merely go dancing,[32] perhaps at New York's Club 54. There is nothing in the book about the frantic phone conversations among the Mounties, the FBI, and upper echelons of government on the subject of cocaine possession and international borders.[33] In Peter's research notes, there is even mention of a naughty photograph taken by Murdoch as he lay on the floor while the young woman, scantily attired, danced above him.[34] Had Peter revealed these rather scurrilous details, he would have had to abandon the central hypothesis of the book — that hockey is the essence of Canada.

"I come from a generation that both socially and journalistically can easily be labelled 'prudish,'" Peter told students at the University of Guelph in September 1981. Therefore, he explained, he had removed from *The Game of Our Lives* the slang term for sexual intercourse because the way players used the word had no more meaning than *you know* and *like*.

Before television exposed and encouraged its violence, hockey seemed to be a sport of gentlemen. On radio, Peter's idol, Foster Hewitt, had portrayed hockey as almost bloodless.[35] In the book, Peter tried to perpetuate his innocent childhood fantasies of chasing that puck over the fields of ice surrounding Galt. *The Game of Our Lives* was a continuation of the invented goodness of Galt where the game, or so Peter claimed, "was one of elegant patterns and lingering rhythms."[36] It was as if he expected Messier and Murdoch, Lowe and Gretzky, to hop over the boards at Northlands Coliseum and skate joyfully across the fields of ice surrounding Edmonton, down to Leduc, past Red Deer, and on to Calgary. If players did take a whack at an opponent, it was no more harmful than when seven-year-old Peter accidentally cut David Graham's face. Or no more harmful than the day in 1945 when young Peter bled after being struck on the forehead by a stray puck.[37]

Peter knew very well that hockey had always been violent. In his article on Frank Mahovlich in February 1961, he had noted the "morass of violence" into which hockey was sinking, and he hoped Mahovlich would return hockey to its pure beauty, which, of course, existed only in Peter's imagination.[38] In *Maclean's* on March 21, 1964, in "The Maple Leaf Money Machine," Peter reported on a game between the Toronto Maple Leafs and the Chicago Black Hawks during which the two teams speared each other so viciously that Peter thought there was going to be a murder.[39] Years later, on *Morningside*, on Easter Monday, April 24, 1984, he told listeners "This is not the game I so publicly love ... It is not Ken Dryden's game and it is not the game I tried to teach my sons to play .... It is a game of intimidation and violence, of sucker punches like the one that felled a Montreal Canadien on Friday night — replayed and savoured by the TV crews — and triggered a brawl as ugly as a gang war." He was even critical of play-by-play commentators and sports journalists, including his friend Trent Frayne, all of whom, Peter regretted, admired a robust game. "It is their game now, and I am afraid they're welcome to it."[40]

In addition to his admiration for hockey players, Peter had great regard, too, for team owners Peter Pocklington and Nelson Skalbania. Pocklington had turned a used-car business into "an empire that turns over $1 billion a year,"[41] and he paid Skalbania for a half interest in the Oilers with a diamond ring worth at least $150,000 and a Rolls-Royce that had been used in *The Great Gatsby*, "a film," Peter wrote somewhat reverentially, "that had deep meaning for both the young millionaires."[42] He appeared to be unaware that the novel by F. Scott Fitzgerald and the movie based on it portrayed the shallowness of New York millionaires of the Roaring Twenties. Peter's description of Pocklington's "airy house" with its view over the North Saskatchewan River does seem to have been inspired by Fitzgerald's description of Gatsby's mansion on Long Island. "At dusk," Peter wrote of the Edmonton mansion, "sunlight would reflect off windows, and the house would be visible for miles." And Pocklington, like Gatsby, had important friends.[43]

Peter's unpublished notes, February 12–19, 1981, are more revealing. On Valentine's Day, Saturday, February 14, he had dinner with the Sathers. Glen Sather and Peter "talked about Messier and the drugs and how hard it is to get him going." After dinner "Peter Pocklington and Eva show up with their son Zachary and they have a couple of bottles of wine from a guy named Jack Petrone, who is involved some-how with the Drillers soccer team. It seems to be homemade wine and Peter [Pocklington] says it's 16% proof and they'll have a little glass of that and then we open another bottle and we all have another glass and it's a fairly late evening, sitting around talking about this and that and homosexuality." None of this, of course, made it into the book, nor did a rather strange story told by Sather, "about a guy coming after him in the dressing room in Houston and trying to touch his private parts." Given the high level of security surrounding hockey teams, it is difficult to believe that a stranger could wander into the Oilers dressing room. Even Peter had difficulty gaining access to the the team's dressing room. Or did Sather mean that it was an Oilers player who took a liking to his netherland?

The next day, Sunday, February 15, Peter was invited to "hear some piano players" at the Pocklington mansion. At 3:00 p.m. Peter arrived. There was more homemade wine. "When I arrive at Peter's house," noted Gzowski, "he's playing backgammon with a computer and colour TV which he obviously loves. The computer beats him and he curses a few times." One of the guests is Dr. Knut Vic, "who has exchanged paintings with Peter [P.], and now there's a Riopelle hanging in the Pocklingtons' dining room." Peter G. was impressed by the collection of two Renoirs, a Picasso, and other "priceless works of art." He especially liked their colours. In the Pocklington house, music was played and songs sung: tunes from *South Pacific* and other Broadway musicals, "Now Is the Hour," and "The Battle Hymn of the Republic." The highlight of the afternoon, according to Peter G., came when Pocklington mouthed the words for the Soviet anthem "The Internationale" while Frank Calder, a provincial civil servant, played it on an out-of-tune piano. Peter G. reported that Peter P. was fond of his million-dollar yacht, Rolls-Royce, Lear jet, and yoga teacher, a former Nazi. Eva Pocklington asked Peter G. if the Cohens, Leonard and Nathan, were related.[44] "One thing: I don't smoke for three hours," Peter G. noted.

Although Peter found the afternoon "pretty bizarre," he didn't lose his admiration for Pocklington. In April 1982, his "Great Expectations," a profile of the millionaire, appeared in *Saturday Night*. The man's profile graced the cover. "Peter Pocklington has the idea that you become what you believe," Peter G. noted. "Now that he's rich, he believes he could run the country." Peter G. mentioned Pocklington's collection of

Pierre-Auguste Renoir sketches purchased from the artist's grandson, whom Pocklington had set up in Edmonton in the cheese business.[45] In his office, Pockington displayed a "magnificent A.Y. Jackson," a few Emily Carrs, and a Cornelius Krieghoff, some of which risked being bleached by the intense sun streaming through Pocklington's office windows. Peter P., according to Peter G., was "marked by destiny," his chest was hairy, and his ice-blue eyes seldom blinked. In the middle of a conversation, Peter P. liked to insert a profanity, without malice, "like a child breaking wind." The Canadian Football League had a future, Pockington predicted, "as long as my dong." Peter G. didn't even seem to mind that, like economist Milton Friedman, guru of Ronald Reagan and Margaret Thatcher, Peter P. believed that government should withdraw from almost every aspect of society except for policing and the courts. Nor did Peter G. take umbrage at Peter P.'s urging that the government sell off the CBC and that Medicare be replaced by Mayo Clinics owned by doctors. Pocklington did acknowledge, most graciously, that the poor would always be with us, but, in order to "reinforce the welfare system," he would "shore up the family unit." Peter G.'s only reaction was to exclaim, "But, Peter, it's all just too simple."[46]

Although research and writing during this period took up a great deal of his time, Peter's voice was heard occasionally on CBC Radio. In June 1980, he was guest host on *As It Happens*. During the annual Conacher Sports Awards Dinner on June 5, he ran into Harold Ballard, owner of the Toronto Maple Leafs. A few days earlier Ballard had told Barbara Frum on *As It Happens* that "broads" had one purpose: to lie on their backs. When Peter told Ballard that he was going to substitute for Frum the following week and that he might like to call Ballard for a comment on his statement about the role of women, Ballard was incensed. "You can go fuck yourself, too," he huffed.[47]

Peter was always a welcome guest speaker and MC. In April 1979, he spoke at the Alberta Public Health Association's annual conference, which that year was called "Health Wise in the Eighties." In an upbeat mood, he talked about "Camp Gzowski," a pleasant health resort that only made "suggestions" about exercise and diet. He jested about trying to quit smoking. He even managed to allude to his problem with alcohol. "I'd run some clinics on decreased drinking, too. Again, not run by militants." While he would respect Alcoholics Anonymous in his imaginary camp, AA would be "as out of place as the WCTU."[48] In October 1980, he was MC at the fourth annual Authors' Awards Dinner in Toronto, and thus was among the august company of Timothy Findley, Robertson Davies, Robert Fulford, Margaret Atwood, and Sandra Gwyn. In September 1981, Peter was a visiting professor at the University of Guelph where he gave four lectures. His topic for one of these was the New Journalism. When young journalists attempted to emulate New Journalists such as Tom Wolfe, he told his audience, they often forgot the importance of research. While Wolfe placed himself somewhere near the centre of his stories, Peter pointed out, he always thoroughly researched his topic first.

Although he respected Wolfe's writing, Peter claimed he disliked most of the New Journalism for its self-indulgent, semi-fictitious style that paid small heed to facts.[49] In other words, after decades of writing literary non-fiction, Peter was still claiming to be a follower of Ralph Allen's factual journalism.

Near the end of 1981, once the publicity for *The Game of Our Lives* was winding down, Peter turned to horse racing, a passion as intense as hockey. The Gzowski connection with racing began with Peter's great-great-grandfather, who had been president of the Toronto Turf Club in 1860 when the first Queen's Plate was run in a dusty field beyond the western boundaries of Toronto. In 1883, to celebrate the first time the Queen's Plate was held at Woodbine Racetrack at the corner of Woodbine Avenue and Queen Street, Colonel Casimir Gzowski and his wife, Maria, escorted the Marquis of Lorne and Princess Louise to the Queen's Plate.[50] Peter admitted that Harold Gzowski had taught him to read *The Racing Form*, the Bible of racetracks, and "the purest form of fiction ever written," according to Ernest Hemingway.[51] At the University of Toronto, Peter had once shared a room with a student of Latin and English who taught him track vocabulary.[52]

Several of Peter's articles in *Maclean's* reflected his passion for horses and racing. To research "Anatomy of a Horse Race," published in *Maclean's* on September 10, 1960, Peter spent a week of fourteen-hour days at the New Woodbine northwest of Toronto. While trying to divine the characteristics of a winner, he focused on a horse called Anita's Son, as well as on its exercise boy, blacksmith, groom, jockey, and the horse's owners, Mr. and Mrs. M.J. Boylen. In "Horseback View of a Jockey" (*Maclean's*, June 17, 1961), Peter wrote about a new camera whose zoom lens and trigger made it possible to capture five images per second of a racing horse.

Peter also wrote an article about the Queen's Plate, which he attended faithfully every year after he returned to Toronto in September 1958. Beginning in June 1959, he and Ken Lefolii, with their wives, made the trek to Woodbine in Lefolii's battered Pontiac. Under a shade tree, they enjoyed a picnic lunch of barbecued chicken and martinis, the latter carefully camouflaged in a Thermos. Throughout the year Gzowski and Lefolii enjoyed the Woodbine bar where they listened to a sports reporter "tell Runyonesque stories of people and horses while he cheerfully sent in bets against his own predictions in the *Star*."[53]

In the *Maclean's* of June 20, 1964, Peter's "The Prettiest Event in Sports" dealt with the Queen's Plate of that year. On race day, the Lefoliis and the Gzowskis packed a picnic lunch and filled a Thermos again, this time with dacquiris. For club members such as Peter, dress was formal. In emulation of Ascot, women wore wide-brimmed hats, and a few men arrived in top hats and cutaway coats. On the other hand, Peter pointed out, the grandstand crowd, the ordinary folk, often removed jackets and loosened their ties, and women sometimes arrived in slacks!

Before the race, according to Peter, he and Jennie walked over to the paddock to view the horses. Peter pointed at what he thought was the favourite, E.P. Taylor's Victoria Park. "Look at the fire in those eyes," he explained to Jennie. "You can *tell* he's a champion."

"Isn't that Dittfach?" Jennie asked.

Yes, Peter agreed rather sheepishly. Possibly the dacquiris were having an effect.

The highlight of the day, aside from the race for the Plate, Peter explained, was the interval between the fourth and fifth races when the vice-regal couple — Governor General Georges Vanier and his wife, Pauline — entered the field in a landau, escorted by the Governor General's Horse Guards, all scarlet and plumed. When King George VI and Queen Elizabeth toured Canada in May and June 1939, the king had presented the King's Plate to the owner of the winning horse. Four-year-old Peter, held aloft, watched the royal limousine sweep along Queen Street East to the track.[54] In 1962, Queen Elizabeth, the Queen Mother, returned, to perform the honours.

When in Toronto, the Queen Mother usually stayed at the Bayview Avenue home of E.P. Taylor, whose son, Charles, Peter had known since the late 1950s when the younger Taylor was one of his stringers at *Maclean's*. A novelist, journalist, and historian, Charles Taylor is best known for his study of the Red Tory tradition in Canadian politics. In fact, in 1981, while Peter was doing research for *An Unbroken Line*, his book on horse racing, Taylor was completing *Radical Tories: The Conservative Tradition in Canada*, which was published in November 1982. Throughout the rest of the 1980s and into the 1990s, the book and Taylor himself would have a major influence on Peter's conception of Canada.

"For Charles Taylor and the radical Tories," Rudyard Griffiths explains in an afterword to the 2006 reissue of the book, "markets must be regulated, American power resisted at every turn, social and cultural institutions expanded, and the pre-eminence of democratic institutions defended against the courts and a rights-based political culture."[55] Red Tories, Taylor argued, preserve the best of democratic, parliamentary traditions while reforming society when necessary. They are, in Taylor's words, "conservatives with a conscience."[56] What Red Tories feared was the homogenization and internationalism that marked the political ideology of leaders, usually, but not necessarily, Liberal, such as Prime Ministers Mackenzie King, Lester Pearson, and Pierre Trudeau.

Until the early 1980s, Peter's political ideology had been ambiguous. In the early and mid-1960s, he had often been indifferent to Canadian cultural institutions such as the National Film Board and "Our Pet" Juliette. "No nation's identity," Peter had argued in 1965, "is going to stand or fall on the ability of its television stars to sing 'Mrs. Brown You've Got a Lovely Daughter.'" If the CBC really wanted variety shows, he once wrote, "let it buy old Andy Williams specials."[57] However, during the late 1960s and early 1970s, Peter was converted to the gospel of cultural nationalism, though he was perfectly capable of placing that ideology on the back burner, as he did in 1980 and 1981 while dealing with Peter Pocklington, for whom Canada had little meaning except as a place to park his Rolls.

Charles Taylor's idealogy was the polar opposite of Pocklington's. Peter admired the old-family elegance and wealth of Taylor. It was apparently Taylor who persuaded Peter that Radical Toryism was the only ideology through which Canada's culture and institutions could be preserved.[58] The two men must have talked about Red Toryism, perhaps at the track or on a flight to Maryland in Taylor's private plane. One wonders how much influence Peter had on Taylor and his book, whose first chapter deals with one of Peter's idols, Stephen Leacock. The subject of the fourth chapter of *Radical Tories* is the poet Al Purdy, a "folk" Red Tory who found evidence of his ancestors in the ruins of an old gristmill that had been built in 1842 in Loyalist country not far from Peter's grandfather's farm near Picton. Purdy's grandfather, a lumberjack and farmer, helped raise many a barn in Prince Edward County. Taylor saw in Purdy, and in all Red Tories, an echo of Edmund Burke, the ideological ancestor of conservatism. At the core of Burke's philosophy, insisted Taylor, is a belief in human continuity, from ancestors through to the living and "those who are about to be born." Burke, Taylor added, saw the state as a necessary partner of that human continuity.[59]

Like Purdy, Peter revelled in tangible evidence of his own ancestry — for instance, a "cathedral-like stone barn" near Rockwood that had been designed by Sir Casimir in the 1870s. Peter's "folk" Tory nature was also revealed in his love of folk and Celtic music. On July 1, 1979, when Peter hosted an afternoon radio show broadcast from Ottawa to celebrate the 112th birthday of Canada, most of the guests were folk artists such as fiddler Al Cherney and singer Stan Rogers.[60] For many years Peter was MC of the Winnipeg Folk Festival. In Toronto he was also part of a group that tried to found a folk festival in 1980.[61] Many of his friends, such as Murray McLauchlan and Ian Tyson, were folksingers. To counterbalance what one historian calls the "weightlessness" of modern technology,[62] Peter found roots in the music of ordinary people.

On the other hand, for Red Tories it was important to be able to claim several generations of property and prestige. As he walked over racetracks and visited horse owners' "gilded aeries" to research *An Unbroken Line*, Peter was haunted by the presence of Sir Casimir, his footsteps, and even by "echoes of his accented and distinguished voice." He found it difficult "not to feel the stirrings of ancestral pride as the royal landau sweeps down the stretch on Plate day."[63] Like other Red Tories, Peter "cherished his particular roots," which acted as a bulwark against Americanization and globalization.[64] The historian W.L. Morton, to whom Taylor devotes the third chapter of *Radical Tories*, contended that "a concern for ancestors and antecedents was one of the distinguishing marks of a conservative."[65] Or as Peter put it in 1979 in a *Toronto Star* column, "The more television and the other media shrink the world around us, the greater our need becomes to find some little corner that belongs only to us — or our families." In the midst of globalization and homogenization, Peter felt the need "to own my own hut in the Global Village."[66]

Occasionally, in his choice of metaphors, Peter implied empathy with Red Toryism. The Queen's Plate, he contended in *Maclean's* in June 1964, was "as much a part of our landscape as the Laurentian Shield." In that phrase, Peter was using a metaphor that was central to Radical Tory thinkers such as Harold Innis and Donald Creighton, both of whom believed that the Shield and its east-west river system had helped to create the political entity known as Canada. In the opening paragraph of his biography of Sir John A. Macdonald, Creighton places the country's first prime minister, "the man who made Canada,"[67] inside the "rocky formation of the Laurentian Plateau" that thrusts "a huge knotted fist southward" toward Kingston, the town that the young Macdonald called home.[68] In his unfinished biography of Sir Casimir, Peter was proud of the ties between Sir John A. and Sir Casimir and tried to make connections between Gregor Young and Macdonald. In *Radical Tories*, Creighton is second after Leacock in Taylor's list of men who created and perpetuated the Tory tradition that, according to Taylor, is the foundation of Canada, and its hope for survival. By using the metaphor of the Shield, Peter, even if unwittingly, was placing himself inside that tradition.

Horse racing, Peter believed, would help reinstate the name Gzowski as one of the oldest families in Canadian history, unbroken by loss of money and prestige during the first half of the twentieth century. If only Peter could be awarded the Queen's Plate, the Gzowski tale would find its worthy conclusion. Accordingly, on Tuesday, October 12, 1982, with "Charles Taylor smiling benignly from his perch in the Windfields delegation above us,"[69] Ken Lefolii and Peter became the proud owners of a racehorse they named Johnny Canuck. Peter then began to dream that Johnny might win the 1984 Plate. If so, the queen, who was coming to Toronto then, would be presenting the prized silver plate to Lefolii and Peter.

Peter would be ready. In *An Unbroken Line*, he imagined the conversation. "Thank you, Your Majesty,'" he replied to a royal compliment on his ability to recognize a good horse. "And you're a fine judge of horse-flesh too." Her Majesty asked something about the founder of the Queen's Plate. "Yes, he was my great-great-grandfather ... That's one of the reasons I called the book you spoke so highly of *An Unbroken* ... Yes, he did ... She knighted him, in fact ... Your great-great-grandmother ... Yes, ma'am, it is remarkable ..." Here was the great-great-grandson of a founder of the Queen's Plate deep in conversation with the great-great-granddaughter of the queen after whom the Plate had been named. The Windsors and the Gzowskis were old families whose lines, Peter implied, were unbroken.

In 1983, Peter's *An Unbroken Line* was published in hardcover, and in 1984, a slightly revised and illustrated paperback version was released. Excerpts from the best reviews of the hardcover version were printed on the back of the paperback version. "A loving look at an interesting world," noted the *Toronto Star*. "You don't need to know a fetlock from a forelock to appreciate what Peter Gzowski has done," commented the *Edmonton Journal*. And the *Globe and Mail* deemed Peter one of the best non-fiction writers in Canada.

Many of the reviews weren't so glowing. In fact, the one that appeared in the *Toronto Star* was actually a pan of the book. "There are no surprises in this book but it puts a lot of details together," noted John Brehl, who complained that Peter was too deferential "to specific big-wigs." The reviewer wondered why Peter, after winning several hundred dollars at the track, bothered to repeat Charles Taylor's rather silly joke. Whose picture, Taylor had asked Peter, was on the hundred-dollar bill? Your father's, replied Peter. And why, Brehl wondered, did Peter feel it was worth reporting "that Charles laughed just like everyone else at the table." And furthermore, Brehl noted, while Peter argued that the grand-stand is "the site of the real feel and smell of the racetrack," he was drawn much more to the clubhouse and trustees' lounge.[70]

A week later in the sports section of the *Toronto Star*, Jim Proudfoot was outraged at both Peter and his publisher. "We're forever being told McClelland & Stewart is Canada's greatest publishing house," he told readers. If so, he continued, why didn't someone correct Peter's errors in *An Unbroken Line*, including misspellings of prominent horse-racing people and his confusing of two prize-winning horses?[71]

"The game warrants more scepticism than Gzowski can muster," wrote sportswriter Dick Beddoes in the November 1983 issue of *Quill & Quire*. Beddoes did admit, however, that Peter was "on surer ground with his evocative scenes of a racetrack in the early morning." As another example of Peter's sometimes evocative style, Beddoes might have quoted the sentence: "But their profitable investments outweighed their losses and their pleasures outweighed their regrets,"[72] a beau-tifully balanced sentence that makes racing sound like love lost and regained. Peter's description of the flight taken with Charles Taylor to Maryland soars toward the sublime. "As the white jet floated over the lush greens of Maryland," the two men, gliding between earth and high heaven, discussed the immortal Northern Dancer.[73] Peter's style could be poetically lyrical.

Like *The Game of Our Lives*, *An Unbroken Line* contains too many details that were likely only of interest when the work was first pub-lished. Today, only aficionados of horse racing would appreciate Peter's explanation of betting procedures. "Unlike the triactor," he advised, "the Sweep Six is bettable only in two-dollar units. One horse in each race: two dollars." He added more details: "One horse in five races and two horses in the sixth: four dollars. But two horses in each race: two to the sixth power, or sixty-four dollars." Surely, nobody except Peter, and perhaps Charles Taylor, was interested in details such as: "Nevertheless, when Deputy Minister's owners sold half interest to Kinghaven Farms, Marko was dropped in favour of Kinghaven's more experienced trainer, John Tammaro."[74] Too much of *An Unbroken Line* is rooted in the daily grind of training and racing. Furthermore, bloodlines, whether equine or human, can become somewhat tedious and self-indulgent. Did readers really need to know that Peter's daughter, Maria, was named after Lady Gzowski or that Casimir, the middle name of his son, Peter, recalls his titled ancestor?

Johnny Canuck earned little more than a plugged nickel. Nevertheless, he did play an important role in Peter's life. As he noted in *An Unbroken Line*, "the track's financial inducements were a lesser allure than its sensory pleasures."[75] When the hardcover edition of *An Unbroken Line* was published in 1983, Peter thanked someone called Gillian Howard for her encouragement. In November 1983, when CKEY's "Pete" McGarvey interviewed Peter, McGarvey began by asking if the book wasn't the story of "a love affair … with thoroughbred racing." McGarvey's question bore no trace of irony, for he was unaware that the subtext of *An Unbroken Line* was, indeed, a love story.

Johnny Canuck served to introduce Peter to his third partner, a woman he would later call his "Partner for Life." Lefolii and Gzowski had hired Ian Howard as the trainer for Johnny Canuck. Gillian, Ian's sister, was handling publicity for the Jockey Club. At the annual Queen's Plate Ball and Banquet on June 25, 1982, a couple listed as "Mr. and Mrs. P. Gzowski," more accurately known as Peter Gzowski and Jan Walter, occupied table 41. At table 11 sat Gillian Howard, along with her parents, "Mr. and Mrs. J. Howard." Although Peter scribbled in the banquet's program that a Toller Cranston limited edition lithograph, *She Couldn't Dance*, fetched $675, he doesn't mention whether he took note of the good-looking woman at table 11. Gillian was the eldest of the four children of Jake and Nancy Howard. The Howard family was, according to Peter, "one of the track's most committed families." When

Jake Howard was elected a trustee of the Jockey Club, Peter wondered if there might be a drop or two of noble blood coursing through the family's veins. Perhaps they were related to the Duke of Norfolk? Maybe he was also thinking of Catherine Howard, one of the wives of Henry VIII. Jake Howard would have none of it and explained that he was descended from a house builder in Sarnia.[76]

Peter saved almost every piece of paper, from a parking ticket to scribbled notes of random thoughts. At Trent University Archives there is a volume of documents connected with his book on racing. In one of the folders there is a cryptic note: "1215 11 o'clock Bristol Place" At the top of the notepaper is the name "Gillian Howard." Unbeknownst to Jan, Peter and Gillian began to place bets both on and off the track. In room 1215 at the Bristol Place Hotel near Pearson International Airport, they could keep their affair private.

Mavis Gallant was writer-in-residence at the University of Toronto during the academic year 1983–84.[77] A couple of times Peter invited Gallant, along with Kathleen Davis, wife of Premier Bill Davis, to accompany him to the new Woodbine Racetrack near Pearson Airport. Kathleen Davis still smiles at Gallant's enthusiasm for racing and betting. The two women and Peter placed their bets, though Gallant's were modest while Peter's were reckless and not terribly lucrative. Gallant noticed that Peter paid a lot of attention to a young woman whom he asked to give Gallant and Davis a tour of the facilities. Gallant wondered about the young woman's identity. "Oh," someone explained, "that's Gzowski's new girlfriend."[78]

One day in 1983, Peter suggested to Jan that they take a one-month break to see if time might renew their relationship. Jan rented a room in a house owned by her friend Salena Dack on Roxborough Avenue in Toronto's Rosedale. During this time, Peter escorted Gill to a hockey game in Maple Leaf Gardens where the Oilers were playing the Maple Leafs. Glen Sather had arranged for Peter and Gill to sit in the gold seats next to the Oilers' bench. Gill was so shocked by the profanity, body odours, and what Peter described as "machine gun expectoration" emanating from the youthful players that she began to have second thoughts about Peter.[79]

The end of the relationship with Jan created tension at McClelland & Stewart where, since 1982, Jan was director of publishing and in charge of the editorial, design, and production departments. The detailed editing of *An Unbroken Line* was being handled by Charis Wahl, who was aware that Jan and Peter had ended their relationship. Jack McClelland also knew about the situation, and one day he tried to broach the subject with Jan, who was "at pains to appear coolly unruffled and in control at all times." She wanted to make certain that Peter could never complain that the breakup had hindered the success of his book. As it turned out, the book wasn't a commercial success, mostly because its subject matter didn't appeal to readers.

Four years later Peter had managed to airbrush Jan from his memory. "I like this city," he said of Edmonton in August 1987 when he opened the city's annual Fringe Theatre Festival. "I holed up here the summer between my two disastrous seasons of *90 Minutes Live* — and I have a number of friends here."[80]

"Holed up"? Peter was referring to the summer of 1977 when he lived with Jan in Edmonton.

— 13 —

Morningside: Canada Imagined, 1982–1997

He was a groundbreaking interviewer but preferred the homespun to the hard-hitting. He was a very meticulous overseer of his reputation as Mr. Canada. He was a very complex and, I sometimes think, lonely man.

— Michael Enright, January 8, 2009

J'adore son style radiophonique intimiste.… J'aime moins son côté Monsieur Canada.

— Nathalie Petrowski, La Presse, December 21, 1995

"I've been thinking about this moment for eight years. This is *Morningside*." That was how Peter introduced the first *Morningside* on Labour Day, September 6, 1982. When Don Harron had announced that the 1981–82 season would be his last, Nicole Bélanger, the show's executive producer, immediately thought of Peter.[1] Margaret Lyons, vice-president of English CBC Radio, who had never lost faith in Peter's radio abilities, was also in favour of offering the job to Peter. For Bélanger and Lyons, the choice was obvious.

Peter didn't hesitate to accept Bélanger's offer. Once he had signed a contract in the autumn of 1981, he began to ponder the role of radio. In his study in Rockwood on New Year's Day 1982, he wrote to Bélanger. He was thinking, he told her, of ways to make *Morningside* less formal, less preachy by diminishing the role of academics and journalists in favour of the voices of ordinary people who found themselves in the midst of an event such as a strike.[2] Rather than emulating print, whose strength was cold, clear analysis, he wanted the show to capture "radio texture," whose most important component was what he called "immediacy." Good storytellers worked well on radio, and Peter reminded her that celebrities such as Maureen Forrester, Yvon Deschamps, Tommy Douglas, and Gordie Howe, among others, could tell great stories. Not that he wanted to avoid analysis of current events, but radio, he believed, needed to show how things were changing as they changed. It should deal with topics such as the rise of anti-Semitism in Poland, the emergence of the New Right in Canada and elsewhere, and the loosening of the Soviet Union's grip on Eastern Europe. Radio should deal with the "tilt west": Alberta's prosperity, the Edmonton Oilers, and the "coming rise of Saskatchewan." Radio, he continued, should deal with the changing arts scene, aging women, booze, drugs, the new Quebec, and the struggle of Canadian publishers to survive.

"Radio is sharper, tougher, bitchier" than any other media, he added. And radio, he reminded Bélanger, had always been the centre of his life. "My marriage has gone, my kids are adults, my home is no longer in the city. But I'm still, I figured out in November if I hadn't been certain before, fucking good around a radio microphone, and I think it's wrong that I'm not there."

A few days later he penned another letter to Bélanger. In order to entice the listener, he liked teasers or billboards at the top of each show, a "tantalizing question" such as "why 100,000 Turks quit smoking" or a statement such as "We've got something really special today." Radio needed surprise, and Don Harron, in Peter's view, was rarely surprised or surprising. He wanted to create "some kind of town gathering of the nation" bringing people together across the country.

Above all he wanted to engage and respect his listeners one by one. The host, he once explained to his producers, shouldn't be talking only to the interviewee, and he should never ask questions such as "And what have you got for us today?"[3] Throughout the fifteen years of *Morningside*, Peter never forgot the listener. "The best radio writing ... doesn't sound like writing at all," he once noted. He wanted his introductory billboards to sound like the speech of ordinary people — long sentences followed by short sentences, with space for breathing and changing tone. "Journalese sucks on the radio," he contended. Once the guest is introduced, Peter maintained, a radio host should always respect the listener's intelligence by not repeating or reminding the listener about the guest's identity.[4]

Joey Slinger of the *Toronto Star* observed Peter as he prepared for his debut on *Morningside*. "Peter Gzowski is at home on the radio," wrote Slinger. Just before 6:00 a.m., Peter was "smashing away at a typewriter in an office that looked like it was waiting for Teperman.[5] He was chain-smoking, his glasses kept sliding down his nose, his hair was going every which way, too. The tail of his shirt hung out at the back, the seat of his trousers drooped, one shoelace was untied, he was talking to himself: 'Now what do I have to worry about? Everything!'"

As Slinger watched, Tina Srebotnjak, the show's first studio director, accompanied him to the broadcasting studio where voice levels were checked. The control room filled with staff, and a few seconds before the theme music began, Peter said, "Well, good luck to us all."

"To you, too," Srebotnjak replied

The theme music, "The Morningside March,"[6] rose and faded, then Srebotnjak gave Peter his cue.

"Hello, I'm Peter Gzowski. I've been thinking about this moment for eight years. This is *Morningside*."[7]

As he began *Morningside*, Peter must have hoped and perhaps even imagined that he was on the road to becoming the most famous and successful radio talk-show host in Canada, and one of the best anywhere else.[8]

The first show set the pattern for content — a mix of storytelling, music, and serious discussion. Peter and the producers understood their audience, a majority of them housewives and mothers, in addition to commuters, male and female, who listened on car radios. They wanted comfort and friendship mixed with information and light music. On the first day W.O. Mitchell told Peter about his summer vacation at Mabel Lake, British Columbia. Mitchell could always be counted on for a good story, and Peter, in return, helped to ensure that the novelist remained a public figure. Sylvia Tyson sang a labour song about "riding the hardest hard times we've known," and Fox Glove, a bluegrass group from Manitoba, also sang about the hard times faced by workers during the recession of the early 1980s. The erudite Paul Kennedy began a series of five shows on Harold Innis. One of the first Canadian nationalists, Innis had influenced Donald Creighton and Marshall McLuhan.

In hour two, after the 10:00 a.m. news, Peter introduced what became a favourite format — a dialogue in letters written by two listeners, in this case Grace, a widow Peter had met the previous summer at a magazine writers' conference in Regina, and Ann, a young feminist magazine writer from Toronto. Her grandfather, Grace wrote to Ann, was a Prairie homesteader, her mother was a university graduate, and one of her daughters was a lawyer. Ann wrote to tell Grace that she was an ex-American who had come to Montreal in 1970 during the October Crisis. By 1982, she was a stay-at-home mother. While Grace believed that conception and birth were absolutely necessary for the continuation of the human race, Ann was adamant that the decision to have a child should be the prerogative of a woman and her mate.[9] The exchange of letters — after Grace and Ann, there were other writing duets — became a regular feature each Friday.

Peter's next guest on that first show was Ken Dryden, goalie for the Canadian hockey team that ten years earlier had barely escaped defeat at the hands of a superior Soviet team. The Canadians had been overconfident, Dryden explained. Following a weather report and another labour song by Randy Bachman, Peter introduced the first of a series in which writers read one of their short stories. His initial guest was Elizabeth McGraw, a Newfoundlander whose work had appeared in *The New Yorker*. From its first day, the show promoted Canadian writing. During Peter's first week, one of his guests was Christopher Moore, who discussed his new book *Louisbourg Portraits*, which almost instantly became a Canadian bestseller.

In the third hour, the topics included the International Monetary Fund and the World Bank, whose representatives were meeting in Toronto; the one hundred thousand or so Canadians, mostly immigrants, who slaved at home making clothing for global industries; and the Convention of Little People, who were meeting in Vancouver. Between interviews folksinger Bob Ruzicka sang "Take the Money and Run."

The first political panel on that Labour Day in 1982 featured Doris Anderson, Roy Romanow, and Dalton Camp, who discussed the rampant inflation of the early 1980s and the Trudeau government's attempts to control it. "Can Lougheed be upset?" Peter asked the panellists. The premier of Alberta was about to call an election. No, thought Romanow. New Brunswick and Prince Edward Island were also preparing for elections. Camp believed that Premier Hatfield was growing in popularity. "Is B.C. going for an election?" Peter wondered.

By January 1983, Anderson and Romanow were replaced by Stephen Lewis and Eric Kierans, and the show was moved to Tuesday mornings. Their opinions tended to be in line with Peter's own Red Toryism. The debates between Camp, Kierans, and Lewis had chemistry and magic, noted Henry Mietkiewicz, the radio reviewer at the *Toronto Star*. In the autumn of 1984, Lewis left Toronto for New York where he acted as Canadian ambassador to the United Nations. Later Lewis told a reporter that the debates with Kierans and Camp, with the "certain spark" provided by Peter, were the most civilized and engaging conversations of his entire life.[10] "There may be sharp, dark corners in the private persona," Dalton Camp once speculated, "but as host of *Morningside* [Peter] was incurably civil. Peter's demeanour, Camp added, "was not an act but an art."[11] These political debates often inspired drivers to keep their radios running in parking lots in order to listen to the end at 9:25 a.m. each Tuesday morning.

During Peter's fifteen years at the helm of *Morningside*, the show was broadcast from many cities across the country. On one program from Saint John, New Brunswick, Freeman Patterson talked about his work as a photographer, while Pam Trecartin described her collection of nun dolls. Doug Hughes and Jack MacDougall announced the reopening of Saint John's Imperial Theatre, and Dr. Harry Flood spoke about being the oldest man to climb Mount Mera in Nepal. In 1997, Peter talked to Daniel Dugas of Moncton about his art gallery, The Trunk, which was operated out of a trunk he carried in his blue 1981 Chevy Citation.

Peter at the peak of his career in the mid-1980s as host of Morningside.

(Courtesy CBC Still Photo Collection)

There was no better interviewee than Timothy Findley, who often played the piano, sang, and delighted the radio audience with his smoke-and wine-infused laugh. Most listeners, it seemed, loved hearing Findley, even though a few expressed disappointment that his novels sometimes didn't live up to the quality of his interviews. One of Peter's favourite poets was Lorna Crozier, whose poetry literary producer Hal Wake thought "fabulous" and the poet herself "good value." A few listeners, however, grew tired of Crozier's poetry about the sex lives of vegetables. Another writer of good value for radio was poet and novelist Susan Musgrave, a close friend of Peter's, whose life was never dull, especially after she married bank robber Stephen Reid in his B.C. prison in 1986.

Occasionally, a quiet and obscure author made it onto the show. After Lake Sagaris was interviewed about her poetry, she had nothing but praise for Peter, who had read enough of her verse to ask intelligent questions. In 1991, Peter interviewed Ann Ireland, a young novelist who had just written about a childhood infatuation with Seiji Ozawa, former conductor of the Toronto Symphony Orchestra. As Ireland listened to Peter's rather convoluted opening question, she lost her nervousness, for she thought to herself, *I can speak better than Peter*. Another young novelist whose career was enhanced by an interview with Peter was Jane Urquhart, who later went on to write admired novels such as *The Stone Carvers*.

According to Peter, Stuart McLean was the show's "single most popular contributor."[12] Peter's Falstaff arrived each Monday with a human-interest story carefully crafted and scripted, though the two men made it sound as if McLean had just dropped by for a chat.[13] For a Monday show in 1986, McLean came into the studio with items he had purchased for about a dollar, including a cricket. Peter pointed out that it was dead; McLean argued that it was just sleeping. The two of them burst into prolonged fits of laughter. One listener was so pleased that she drew a picture of her house, located, she told Peter, not far from his childhood home at 24 Park Avenue in Galt. Unduly neglected is McLean's radio essay called "The Shocking Truth About Household Dust," which explained the fundamentals of dust and dust mites.[14]

The poet George Elliott Clarke was a frequent guest on *Morningside*. Like millions of other Canadians, Clarke was "intoxicated, seduced, and transfigured by [Peter's] voice as well as by the ideas, homely and cosmopolitan, that that inimitable voice conveyed." His first encounter with Peter was in January 1986, and the subject was the Afro-Canadian revival in Halifax. Although Clarke was at first somewhat intimidated, Peter put him at ease. The poet was bewitched, he later reported, by Peter's "gruffly dulcet voice, that blues-singer empathy and prime ministerial authority" of the man he called "the tribune of English-speaking Canada."[15]

Choosing guests as good as Clarke wasn't as easy as it seemed. Since the producers talked beforehand by telephone to any potential interviewee, rarely did Peter end up with a guest who didn't make good radio unless, of course, that guest was too important to ignore. Northrop Frye often answered Peter's sometimes convoluted questions with a scholarly yes or no. In the spring of 1987, Peter interviewed Frye on his latest book, *Northrop Frye on Shakespeare*. After reading a short introduction, Peter admitted, "Now I'm intimidated. I don't know how to deal with the fact of being intimidated in the presence of Northrop Frye. Are other people intimidated?"

Frye did his best. "Oh, yes. My wife used to say to them, 'You ought to see his baby pictures.'"

The line brought a nervous laugh from the host. "Your reputation is, in fact, a handicap for you, isn't it?" Peter probed.

Again Frye did his best. "Oh, yes, yes, it is."

Peter maintained the biographical trivia for a few more minutes. "I was just wondering ... I'm still somewhat in the same sentence ... in the same part of it," he continued. One wonders what the succinct critic was thinking as the host tied himself into verbal knots. "Perhaps we'd be less intimidated if we knew that ... Did you come to Toronto because you'd won a typing contest? Is that what brought you to this city?"

Peter's questioning technique — beginning with chit-chat, then some probing, followed by a surprising question designed to catch a guest off guard — worked with some people, but not with Frye, who explained patiently that he had come to Toronto not because he had won the contest but in order to compete. He came second, he quickly added.

"Who out-typed you?" Peter asked. "Do you remember?"

One can imagine the stern glare of the man who had come to talk about Shakespeare. Carefully, Frye explained that it was a young woman from Orangeville.

Finally, Peter arrived at the book, and the interview turned into an illuminating summary of Frye's thesis that, for each age, there is a Shakespearean play that suits the temper of the times.

Scientists were a difficult sale on *Morningside*, for like Frye, they answered Peter's questions literally without realizing he wanted them to chat over the backyard fence about the workings of the atom or the possibility of water on Mars. During Peter's stint on *Morningside*, he interviewed two Nobel Prize chemistry laureates: Gerhard Herzberg (June 1, 1984) and John Polanyi (May 20, 1987). Peter's technique of appearing ill-informed in order to encourage a guest to talk rarely worked with scientists, who just seemed to think he hadn't done his homework.[16]

Because he refused to play the interview game, Mordecai Richler was on Peter's list of least favourite interviewees. Whenever he realized that Peter knew the answer to a question, Richler refused to answer it. Other people on Peter's undesirable list were Martin Short, whom Gzowski found dreary; Betty Friedan, who once shouted, from Ottawa to Toronto that Peter was a chauvinist pig; Shirley MacLaine, who took her "visionary" experiences too seriously; Ray Hnatyshyn, who as minister of justice talked in political circumlocutions; and Mavis Gallant, who made Peter "feel stupid."[17]

Gallant was shocked to learn that she had such an effect on Peter. In 1982 Tarragon Theatre artistic director Urjo Kareda staged Gallant's *What Is to Be Done?* When Kareda and Gallant were walking out of the studio after an interview with Peter, Gallant turned to the director and said, "Wasn't that a good interview?" Kareda agreed. [18]

And what about Alexa McDonough? Did Peter consider adding her name to his list of least favourite interviewees? When she unexpectedly won the leadership of the NDP in October 1995, Peter seemed unprepared for the interview. Rather than dealing with leadership and policies, he asked her how it felt to be the second female leader in a row with the initials A.M.[19] McDonough informed Peter that he really wasn't prepared for the interview. "He was trivializing," McDonough maintains today. She feels he was implying, *Oh, no, here comes another woman as leader.*[20] In May 1997, during the election campaign that year, Peter was rude to McDonough. When she attempted to explain the need to spend money on daycare and unemployment, an annoyed Peter cut in with "I ask one question and you make a political speech."

Janice Gross Stein, an expert on the Middle East, was definitely not on Peter's bad list. Stein was a recurring guest on both *This Country in the Morning and Morningside.* Did she find him at all difficult? Yes, of course, but "he was worth it," she says. On radio, she believes, there was no one better.[21] After an interview about his book *An Anthropologist on Mars,* Dr. Oliver Sacks shook his head in astonishment and gratitude, according to Ian Pearson, literary producer at the time. "He put so much into it," Sacks told Pearson. "He made it so easy. He was so generous."[22]

Like Stein and Sacks, most interviewees retain good memories of their interviews. In November 1988, after the publication of his *New and Naked Land,* a study of Euro-Canadian perceptions of the Prairies, cultural geographer Ron Rees was a guest on *Morningside.* As he and Peter sat in the studio in Toronto waiting for the end of the hourly news, Peter was cordial. Rees's book appealed to him, for it dealt with a period of Canadian history when Sir Casimir Gzowski was an important player. The first Canadian Gzowksi had been acquainted with many of the businessmen and politicians who had opened the West to settlement. And, of course, Peter's recently published memoir dealt, in part, with his own perceptions of the Prairie landscape and of the artists who had painted it.

A year later, in November 1989, biographer John Ayre was featured on *Morningside.* While he waited for Peter, Ayre talked to Colin Henderson, the producer of that particular segment of the show. Peter arrived, Ayre recalls today, much like a "dominant gorilla beating his chest to intimidate lesser males." His main interest wasn't his guest but sales of *The Latest Morningside Papers.* From time to time, as if wondering who they were and why they were intruding on his territory, Peter stared at Ayre and Henderson. Soon Ayre was summoned to follow Peter to the studio, dark and reeking of smoke. Ayre was convinced the interview was going to be a grand failure, his second of the day, following a disastrous session with Shelagh Rogers at the CBC's Cabbagetown studio.

"As soon as Peter threw on the little red microphone switch, he transformed himself into Father Canada," Ayre remembers today. "He was gentle, flirtatious, and knowledgeable." What especially impressed Ayre, however, even more than the complete change of character, was the fact that Peter had read Ayre's biography of Northrop Frye and that he had absorbed most of it. His questions were intelligent, which brought out the best in the biographer. Afterward Ayre's publicist commented, "Boy, was *that* a good interview."

The novelist Scott Symons also made a good interview when Peter talked to him about his new novel, *Helmet of Flesh*, published in 1986. The book is a satire of the old, uptight, bland Toronto, and of English-Canadian society and culture. The main character, York Mackenzie, based on the author himself, believed that "the much vaunted 'Canadian identity' was a case of self-perfidy," and that modern Canada was "a self-willed failure," its literature nothing but "shallow tracts for the times."[23] Neither York Mackenzie nor Scott Symons fitted the image of Peter's apologetic Canadian.

"Are you mad at Canada?" Peter asked the novelist.

"Not mad but anxious and chagrined," replied the articulate Symons, who proceeded to explain that he admired French Canada because it had an identity. His writing, Symons explained, wasn't intended to "provoke" readers but to "convoke" contemplation of the true nature of Canadian identity. At the heart of that identity was bilingualism and mutual respect. When Peter asked if *Helmet of Flesh* was a gay novel, Symons answered, "You're unusually bright this morning, Gzowski." After Symons read an excerpt from the book, he mused that "life is not a quarrel, Peter, but a dance."

Interviews with Sylvia Fraser were occasionally somewhat tense. On Wednesday, September 23, 1987, Peter interviewed Fraser about *My Father's House: A Memoir of Incest and of Healing*. The weekend before, Peter had read the account. "Hit hard by Sylvia Fraser's book," he wrote in his diary. One of the characters, he surmised, was based on himself.

Peter opened the interview by "warmly acknowledging" his relationship with Fraser at the *Star Weekly*, after which he sensitively probed "the wounds and scars" caused by incest. Although Fraser was subsequently interviewed hundreds of times, she claimed that Peter's talk with her was "one of the classiest and most congenial." During the conversation, Peter kept returning to the scene in which he thought he had spotted himself. Afterward, according to Fraser, he blurted, "Is there anything in your book about me?" She denied his speculation.

However, after she left the studio, Fraser realized Peter was right. At certain points in the story, because of the sensitive nature of the memoir, she had covered "real-life events with a fictional overlay." And in one of those fictionalized scenes, she now recalled, she had indeed employed elements of an unpleasant encounter with Peter a decade earlier on *90 Minutes Live*. Peter was "a highly intuitive reader," Fraser concluded. "Probably his needle-sharp editorial eye, brightly threaded with some residue of regret or curiosity or amusement, made the connection."[24]

There was never any danger that Alice Munro would be anything but a first-rate guest. "He held you up for as long as you needed it," she reported a few days after his death, "so easily and gracefully and unobtrusively that it almost seemed as if he was learning to swim, too. Then, at some moment, he let you go, let you take you own direction, trusted you to do it right." Unlike Northrop Frye and Mordecai Richler, Munro happily played the interview game. Like any successful interview, what is implied is just as important as what is spoken. Alice and Peter were always at their flirtatious best, and the several interviews with Munro on *Morningside* are as fresh today as when they were first broadcast.

Among the many poets who appeared on *Morningside* was Ralph Gustafson when he was promoting the latest edition of the *Anthology of Canadian Verse*, which he had edited. The two men discussed the nature of poetry. "A poem should be heard," Gustafson maintained. "It's got to be heard … heard internally … in the inner ear."

F.R. Scott, poet and law professor, told Peter one morning, "I don't think you can build a good, free, democratic society on principles of competition." Scott, who had been a member of the group that had signed the Regina Manifesto in 1935, the founding document of the

CCF, expressed his admiration for J.S. Woodsworth. He also defended the invocation of the War Measures Act in 1970. The FLQ, he argued, was holding a gun to the head of the government of Quebec.

Peter's interviews with Margaret Visser, the engaging historian of everyday life, always sang, perhaps because they were both interested in ordinary material objects and daily rituals as, for example, the history of corn on the cob, its origins in prehistory, its uses in pipes, insulation, and nourishment, and the fact that its husks prevent it from propagating itself. Visser was, according to Peter, the "most popular occasional regular."[25]

Possibly because his son, John, was a musician, Peter also enjoyed the younger generation of musical talent. In 1991 he interviewed Barenaked Ladies, who were about to head west in a rented van. As often happened, Peter's endorsement of the band helped make them one of the best-known pop groups in Canada and elsewhere. Peter was also fond of the ragtime music of Catherine Wilson and John Arpin, whom he interviewed in April 1986 after the release of their album *Rags to Riches*. In 1985 the duo had composed and played the music for a *Morningside* drama called *Real Pearls*.[26] In March 1995, Peter's producers assembled five singers — Leon Dubinsky in Halifax, Connie Kaldor in Montreal, Bill Quinn in Winnipeg, and in the Toronto studio, Cindy Church and Ken Whiteley. They performed what listeners considered to be the greatest Canadian songs: Ian Tyson's "Four Strong Winds," which Peter deemed Canada's second national anthem; Dubinsky's "We Rise Again"; Oscar Brand's "Something to Sing About"; Bobby Gimby's "Ca-na-da"; "O Canada," sung that day by Church; and Gilles Vigneault's "Mon Pays," delivered movingly in a Radio-Canada studio in Montreal by Saskatchewan's Kaldor. It was Canada as Peter imagined it — a joyous, unified country with patriotic songs pulsating through its northern heart.

Perhaps because Peter had an eye for landscape, and maybe because he fancied himself an astute collector of Canadian art, he relished interviewing painters. In one of his introductory essays to *Morningside*, Peter talked about his collecting urges. During the 1960s, with the proceeds from a magazine article, he had purchased an oil painting by Claude

Breeze. After a few months, he returned it and the art gallery owner resold it at a higher price, with half the profits remitted to Peter. His appetite for art and easy profits whetted, Peter bought *Poisoning Gophers* by William Kurelek. Its vivid greens and "cruel, contorted figures" made him uncomfortable. Although he claimed that the Kurelek hung only "for a while" in the Gzowski household, Marci McDonald noticed it above the mantel in the Gzowski living room ten years later. Peter was more comfortable with a Prairie landscape by Wynona Mulcaster, purchased around 1975, which he was pleased to report had tripled in value. "For those of us who are willing to forgo the occasional vacation, or perhaps drive an older car," it was perfectly possible, he advised his listeners, to enjoy "the thrills of the rich and famous ..." The image of the informed but relatively impoverished art collector is somewhat precious. By his third season, Peter's annual salary had reached six figures.[27]

Nevertheless, his interviews with artists were lively and informative. "From time to time, it's my pleasure to talk to some truly great Canadians," Peter began an introduction to Jean-Paul Lemieux, who was waiting in a Radio-Canada studio in Quebec. "Why don't you like the colour blue?" asked Peter.

"Artists are a little crazy, you know," Lemieux offered.

On another show, A.J. Casson explained the difference between working in watercolour (you start with the lightest tones) and oils (you start with the darkest). At one point Peter accused Casson of cheating in his rendition of the town of Rockwood. "That's the village I've been living in for the last five years ... you moved it all around!" Peter's jocular remark inspired a chat about the nature of art and imagination.

With subjects such as philosophy, politics, history, and religion, Peter seemed at ease. Philosopher George Grant spoke with Peter about caring for society's underdogs. With NDP politician Stanley Knowles, Peter discussed raising the old-age pension. Tom Harpur, whose topic was religion, always made a compatible, companionable guest. So, too, did Desmond Morton and Rick Salutin, who once chatted about the famous First World War air ace Billy Bishop.

On *Morningside*, Peter even managed to focus on homosexuality: the killing of a gay man in Toronto's High Park; an interview with three gay men; and with Michele Landsberg and Hugh Segal, an examination of a gay scandal in Orillia, Ontario, in 1983. Peter also conducted several sensitive interviews with Regan Grant, an opera student at the University of Toronto, who after contracting AIDS, returned home to Melville, Saskatchewan, to die.[28] Other *Morningside* topics included abortion, abuse, assault, adoption, aging and the elderly, animal rights, and alcoholism. The Avro Arrow was the subject of one discussion; baldness and beards of another. Celibacy, censorship, charities, children, and the *Challenger* disaster of 1986 were also featured on *Morningside*. So were dieting, disabilities and extramarital affairs. (Affairs are wrong and always will be, wrote one listener, around the time Peter was having one of his own.) Farming, male friendship, and harems were discussed, as were the internment of Japanese Canadians during the Second World War, Jews in Alberta, pornography, poverty, the northern lights, and war memorials. Even acne came up one day. In 1993 Kelly Christensen, sitting in the studios of CBC Regina, joined two women in Toronto to talk about vegetarianism. Kelly told Peter that when he dropped meat from his diet, his acne cleared up.

"You cut out meat and your acne cleared up?" an astounded Peter asked.

"Yeah," answered Kelly.

"Wished I'd known that when ..."[29]

Beginning the second year of *Morningside*, Susan Rubes, head of radio drama at the CBC, revived the network's tradition of radio dramas, one that had begun in the mid-1920s when the CNR Radio Department broadcast Shakespeare and Canadian plays produced in Vancouver by Jack Gillmore.[30] On Labour Day, September 5, 1983, *Morningside* started a fifteen-minute daily serial as part of a six-month experiment. The first play, broadcast each morning over three weeks, was Linda Zwicker's award-winning *The Panther and the Jaguar*, which was about the tension-filled love affair between H.G. Wells and Rebecca West. Would the show's two hundred and fifty thousand listeners acquire a taste for drama? wondered Henry Mietkiewicz of the *Toronto Star*. And could they live for fifteen minutes without Peter's "comforting presence."

Panther began at 9:40 a.m.[31] Eventually, the radio dramas were broadcast during the last fifteen minutes of the third hour.

Peter Puxley, who had been an NDP researcher in Alberta, was drama producer. One *Morningside* playwright was Peter Gzowski himself. For his fifteen-minute drama called *Gouzenko*, Peter was paid $105.[32] During the last week of December 1987, a five-part play, *Get a Horse*, written by Marjorie Whitelaw, one of Peter's Maritime correspondents, dealt with women and aging. Other plays included *Wingfield's Progress* by Dan Needles; *Bananaman*, a tale about ethnic Toronto in the 1920s; *Sunshine Sketches of a Little Town*; and Frank Holden's one-man show *Judge Prowse Presiding* about an outrageous justice in Newfoundland.[33]

David Carley was a *Morningside* playwright. It was well-known among the production staff, Carley once revealed, that Peter wasn't fond of drama, though he did like anything by Linda Zwicker. His all-time favourite, according to Carley, was *The Last Flamingo* by Joan Fern Shaw. "We did badly crave his approval, like errant children," Carley notes today. "And we were very aware that he was delivering to us — in those last minutes of the morning — a massive, nationwide, and very intelligent audience."[34]

Peter's producers knew enough to avoid, if they could, the neo-conservative right-wing. Conrad Black was an exception, and so was Peter Pocklington. "I kinda like him," Peter told listeners on October 26, 1982, thereby explaining why Pocklington, a man who advocated selling off the CBC, was allowed into the inner sanctum of *Morningside*. "It's time you got commercials on radio, Peter," the head of Gainers Meats and Fidelity Trust advised Gzowski, who admitted in his introduction that he had stayed at Pocklington's house in Phoenix and had joined Pocklington on a fishing trip to Great Bear Lake.[35]

Some of the spokespeople for Black's and Pocklington's neo-conservatism felt ignored by *Morningside*. "Peter Gzowski's Canada is not my Canada," wrote newspaper editor and journalist Peter Worthington. David Frum wondered how anyone could build a country on Medicare, the CBC, and cheap university tuition. Michael Coren could never understand the great reverence for Gzowski, a privileged man who stammered as if he were attempting to be just one of the people. The Canada of *Morningside*, Coren contended, wasn't "the Canada of real people."[36] Gzowski's liberalism and nationalism, insisted Ted Byfield, owner of *The Alberta Report*, was fabricated by Toronto Yuppies during the 1960s.[37] Byfield had a point. As Stephen Aziz points out, the brand of nationalism that emerged after the Second World War and that gathered steam in the 1960s was predominantly a product of southern Ontario academics and "salaried professionals often in the public sector"[38] who pressured federal politicians to act on some of their ideas of protecting Canada from American control of Canada's economy and its sovereignty.[39]

"This country's structure," Peter argued during his *Morningside* years, "from its railways, its banks, its broadcast system, its support of the arts — its entire 'social network' in the common phrase — has been built by co-operation by people, as it were, huddling together against the cold."[40] His knowledge of Canadian history was selective. He failed to understand that the country's railways,[41] banks, and broadcasting system, except for the CBC and provincially owned television and radio stations, had been built and developed by private capital. And many of those capitalists had indeed contributed to the social fabric of Canada. While Canada lacked an Andrew Carnegie, Canada's capitalists have indeed supplied money for libraries (Bata), private schools (Gzowski), sports prizes (Mann), concert halls and theatres (Massey, Thomson, Winspear, Cohen, Appel, Taylor, Singer, Bronfman, Mirvish, and Cohn), art galleries (Walker, Mendel, Thomson, and Aiken), opera houses (Sharp), and hospitals (Ross, Flavelle, Elliott, Killam). Even the Canada Council had been founded with capitalist money.

Ironically, Peter himself inherited money accumulated during the railway boom from 1896 to 1913. When her estate was settled in 1979, his Great-Aunt Lady Mann left Peter about $4,000, money that had been generated by Sir Donald Mann.[42] For all of Peter's admiration for state enterprise, it might come as a surprise that in 1981 more than half of Peter's total income of $31,702 was derived from dividends from Canadian corporations.[43] Peter wasn't above investing in the stock market, that cesspool of capitalism. In January 1980, through his broker Barbara McDougall,[44] then with A.E. Ames, he bought shares in

Terra Mining & Exploration Ltd. for a total of $900 and sold them two months later for $1,500.[45]

Like Byfield and Worthington, William Gairdner held views about the role of the state that didn't coincide with Peter's. Gairdner argued that liberalism, Red Toryism, state intervention, and the welfare state had shallow roots dating only to the Great Depression. In books such as *The Trouble with Canada* (1990) and *The War Against the Family* (1992), he argued that the state had no business taxing Canadians in order to interfere in the management of families in the form of baby bonuses and education. He also argued against state subsidies for the CBC.

Keen to be interviewed on *Morningside*, Gairdner and his publisher mailed copies of his books to Peter. Then Gairdner started leaving telephone messages, about ten in all. Finally, a producer nibbled. Still no invitation. When *War Against the Family* reached bestselling status in 1992, even without a *Morningside* interview, Gairdner tried again.

Reluctantly, a producer set up an interview. When Gairdner was finally allowed into the precincts of *Morningside*, he was surprised to discover that the literary producer had set up not an interview but a debate with "some gay academic," who, according to Gairdner, had panned his book in the *Winnipeg Free Press*. "It was not an interview so much as a shouting match," Gairdner recalled years later. Peter intervened, but mostly on the side of "Chris," who was sitting in the CBC's studio in Winnipeg. After the interview, Gairdner offered to shake hands, but Peter didn't respond.[46]

While the public Gzowski, host of *Morningside*, was full of self-confidence, the private man was wracked with doubt and regret. In the summer of 1984, Peter rented a cottage on Lake Simcoe, close to Sutton. By returning to the area where his grandfather, the Colonel, had spent his summers, Peter thought he would be inspired to write a book about his parents. On July 13, 1984, he turned fifty. As often happens at that age, Peter began to understand his father. In notes for the book, he wrote, and edited: "I wish, now, I hadn't ~~been so bitter — er, if not bitter, so uncaring as to~~ just let him slide out of the word [world] like that. I've been thinking a lot about Harold a lot this summer. Partly, this may be because I'm here at the lake myself, not far from where he spent his last days, and many of the people I meet say they knew my father.... A lot of them seem to have liked him ..." Like Harold, Peter was sprouting hair on his back. He even had a mole on his left chest at exactly the same spot as Harold's. "I can never think of Harold as old," wrote Peter. "I saw the signs, of course, the dark hair turning grey and, towards the end, beginning to thin, the tremor in his hands, the halting walk.... Even in his last, sorry days of his life, when the blue veins stood out on his white calves and the tremor of his hands made it difficult for him to hold a bridge hand, my father never seemed old to me." At least Harold had stood erect to the end, Peter noted, whereas his son at age fifty had already begun to emulate his mother's slouch.[47]

One guest on *Morningside* guessed correctly that Peter was a profoundly shy and insecure man. Creative people are often pseudo-extroverts, Bruce Little, a professor of psychology at Carleton University, once explained on *Morningside*. As such, Little continued, they are friendly while signing autographs or when making a speech, or when hosting a radio show, but afterward they want to be alone. To be a skillful pseudo-extrovert, Little said, one must be a good actor. Introverts who pretend to be extroverts fool listeners who begin to believe that the radio persona is the real person. Little added that alcohol, which depressed the central nervous system, was a tool of pseudo-extroverts.

"I spend all day talking to people," Peter once said to Knowlton Nash. "I don't want to go out after work and talk to people.... I want to go home."[48] Not surprisingly, when fans and colleagues met Peter in person, they often found him distant and sometimes rude. One Saturday morning, Munroe Scott, author and filmmaker, ran into Peter at The Highlander restaurant in Sutton, Ontario. Peter was hunched over coffee.

"How are you, Peter?" Scott asked ebulliently.

"I want to be alone, Munroe," Peter replied.[49]

There is a Gzowski story that hints that Peter went to great lengths to ensure his privacy. One day in the early 1980s, Toronto police raided a bawdy house in downtown Toronto where Madame X, as she was known to her clients, played Bach on a piano near the front door as her employees plied their trade with customers, many of whom were

On January 28, 1986, Peter was more interested in his hors d'oeuvre than in listening to the Honourable Marcel Masse's story, to which Margaret Atwood and Graeme Gibson gave their undivided attention. As minister of communications from 1984 to 1986, Masse argued during negotiations on free trade that Canadian culture must be protected, an argument that endeared him to the likes of Peter, Atwood, Gibson, and most other creative minds in Canada.

(Courtesy Trent University Archives, Gzowski fonds, 92-016, box 1, folder 7)

prominent Torontonians. When Madame X was taken to court, she mentioned that one of her clients was a man called Gzowski. Mind you, she informed the judge, he rarely if ever turned up to listen to her version of *The Goldberg Variations*. Instead, he would call up Madame X and ask her to send a "girl." When the women returned from Peter's furnished suite at Mayfair Mansions[50] on Avenue Road, south of St. Clair Avenue, they reported that Client Gzowski had merely talked. Was Peter so lonely that he needed someone to talk to? Who else but a call girl could he rely on for a visit in the middle of the day? As P.K. Page once wrote in *Brazilian Journal*, she could learn to like people, really like them, if she knew she never had to see them again. When the story of Madame X's testimony broke, Peter's name, thanks to Robert Reguly, was kept out of the press.[51]

On radio, however, Peter was usually affable, gregarious, charming, and sweet. What was it that made him a first-rate broadcaster? The closest Peter came to describing his interviewing skills was his attempt in *The Game of Our Lives* to define the hockey genius of Wayne Gretzky, who had the ability to imagine the entire ice surface and the position of each player. And not just the particular formation of any given play. Gretzky could visualize hundreds of on-ice formations. According to Peter, psychologists called these hundreds of patterns "chunks of memory," which allowed Gretzky to predict subconsciously where he should shoot the puck to make it land where a teammate would be located a few seconds later. What Gretzky lacked in physical power, he made up for in accuracy of shot, which Gzowski compared to the precision and sharpness of a surgeon's needle. And the Great One did all this with what Peter called "an unhurried grace."

Wayne played with time. "In front of the net, eyeball to eyeball with the goaltender," Peter said, Gretzky held on to the puck for an extra split second, thus "upsetting the anticipated rhythm of the game," just as a ballet dancer seems to extend time during a long leap. Sometimes, to fool the goalie, he released the puck a split second early. Gretzky was a combination chess player, jazz musician, and superb athlete.

Like Gretzky's, Peter's mind worked in chunks or patterns. Out of that brain, he could pull hundreds, perhaps thousands, of combinations and permutations of interview styles and personal memories. Peter's mind was as sharp and accurate as a surgeon's needle. He circled around a guest until he saw an opening. In order to score his goal, Peter might surprise an interviewee by leaving the most important question to the end. As politician and businessman Frank McKenna noted, Peter's questions were unexpected, "disarming you and peeling away your defences and getting to your most secret thoughts." McKenna always felt he had given away too much, but he never minded, for Peter infused his deft questions with warmth.

"Would that we all had his easygoing urbanity, his genuine curiosity, his fair-minded decency," wrote Douglas Marshall in 1986.[52] Although his radio shows sounded extemporaneous, Joey Slinger noticed they were always well planned. "The important thing," Slinger explained, "was to *sound* extemporaneous, and this was where Gzowski shone." Peter, argued Slinger, had "a rare ability to *sound* as if everything he encounters is a discovery, and he can do it *without sounding* naive, *without sounding* like a dope. He *sounds* fascinated by hydroponic gardening, for God's sake, and this *sound* is central, is the key, because when a sloppy old joker like Gzowski comes on this way, the rest of us don't have to feel self-conscious about *being* this way and we relax and listen and sail along with him."[53]

Many people agreed with McKenna, Marshall, and Slinger. In 1986, for his contributions to broadcasting and to his country, Peter was appointed an Officer of the Order of Canada. Three years later he was presented with the John Drainie Award.[54]

During those fifteen years of *Morningside*, Peter attempted to compensate for something missing in the late twentieth century, what Tristram Hunt in *The Guardian Weekly* called "the inherited ties that once bound people to their pasts," ties such as social class, an active faith, a unified labour market, a "culture of storytelling," and powerful political movements.[55] Stephen Leacock's *Sunshine Sketches of a Little Town* is a portrait of the last great age of shared values. It was published in 1912, two years before the outbreak of a war that contributed to the cynicism and distrust that grew with the century.

Peter tried to correct that cynicism. In a country with few if any commanding narratives,[56] he was creating what he believed was a national mythology. While *Morningside* did deal with spousal abuse and drugs, massacres and suicides, hockey violence, poverty, and political tensions, Peter apparently believed problems could be solved with quiet discussion and renditions of "O Canada" or "Four Strong Winds." With help from the state and the generosity of fellow Canadians, Canadians would survive adversity. So went the mythology.

In speeches and articles, Peter told audiences and readers that Canadians were quite a nice people. They didn't brag, and they were fond of apologizing. Martin O'Malley apologized after someone rode over his foot with a golf cart. When Peter burst into a coughing spell during the taping of an interview with Northrop Frye, the William Blake scholar mumbled, "I'm sorry."

"When Lester Pearson won the Nobel Peace Prize in 1957," Peter once said, his reaction was "Gee, thanks." When Paul Henderson scored his famous series-winning hockey goal against the Soviets in September 1972, he thanked his teammates ... and God. After Anthony Burgess announced on *Morningside* that Robertson Davies should be awarded the Nobel Prize for Literature, Davies replied, "Goodness gracious, I'm sure I don't deserve it." Peter believed that the expression "Not bad, eh?" should be Canada's national motto.[57]

On *Morningside*, Robertson Davies once told Peter that Canadians liked to think of themselves as "a sort of Honest John, who you could trust with anything.... It's not the American myth," he added, "which is the myth of success, and the clever guy, and the fellow who makes it big in the world." Canadians, Davies suggested, tended more to "the sincere, good, honest, decent person whose word is his bond." Of course, he admitted, myth and reality were often two different things. Nevertheless, he concluded, Canadians continued to imagine themselves as sincere and honest peacekeepers.[58]

Karen Armstrong reminds us in *A Short History of Myth* that:

> We need myths that will help us to identify with all our fellow-beings, not simply with those who belong to our ethnic, national or ideological tribe. We need myths that help us to realize the importance of compassion, which is not always regarded as sufficiently productive or efficient in our pragmatic, rational world.[59]

Although many listeners might not have articulated the reasons for their enjoyment of *Morningside*, intuitively they knew what they liked, and for most it was the comfort derived from membership in a community of fellow Canadians from coast to coast to coast. They liked the depth of Peter's unhurried questions, the breadth of his guest list, his skill and subtlety in concluding an interview to allow for the hourly newscast. "He had a lovely way of guiding the interview," noted Erin Lemon, "so that the guest could answer his last question without rushing, and he made it seem easy, as though any Canadian could go on the radio and shape a thought that gracefully filled the last twenty-three seconds before the ten o'clock news." How painful, Lemon added, to listen to a host who stops a guest in mid-thought.[60] Even worse, a host who asks a question and promptly orders that the answer must be brief, because "we're outta time."

The near-perfect radio persona, with its winning hesitation in the middle of a question, appealed to a large number of listeners. In 1993 a Bureau of Broadcast Measurement (BBM) survey reported that 1,228,200 people were tuned in to *Morningside* for at least fifteen minutes once a week.[61] The number of people who listened to all or a good part of the show was an estimated 350,000.[62] At 9:12 a.m. in each of the five Canadian time zones, members of the clan gathered. In Newfoundland an artist called Mary listened to the show in her studio, as did Sheila in St. Andrews, New Brunswick, on a radio quietly playing near the cash register in her shop on Water Street. Eveline, a potter near Caraquet in the Acadian Peninsula, listened as her wheel spun, and Lawrence from North Wiltshire, Prince Edward Island, was listening to the same segment of the show. As the program wound down in the Atlantic Provinces, in Quebec, Aline, artistic manager for Pauline Julien and other Québécois artists, was learning that English-speaking Canada wasn't an empty stage. At his farm in the Eastern Townships, where he retreated between films, Donald Sutherland had hooked up an antenna so that he wouldn't miss a word of *Morningside*.[63]

In the same time zone in Ottawa, Maggy, an empty Tim Hortons paper cup sitting on a bench beside her, was listening to the second hour wind down. As he was driving between appointments in the Ottawa Valley, Charlie, a shy speech therapist, was also enjoying the closing moments of the second hour. So, too, Bruce, a bookseller in the High

Park area of Toronto, and Toni, a young mother in the Niagara Peninsula. In Peterborough, Brennan, a painter and decorator, was listening as he hung wallpaper. Not far away at Trent University, Gene, a groundskeeper, was listening on his truck radio as the second hour slipped away. In Argyle, an hour northwest of Peterborough, a graduate student who was tending to a dying parent was also listening and silently thanking Peter for saving his sanity. On her radio in suburban Detroit, Joyce, one of Peter's many American fans, was learning about Canada, the ancestral homeland of her husband. In Stoney Mountain Penitentiary, north of Winnipeg, an inmate placed in solitary confinement was enjoying the end of hour one, especially if the topic was politics or justice or aboriginal affairs. As Robin, a supervisor of teachers in federal penitentiaries, was driving alone for hours across the Prairies, he found *Morningside* an informed companion.[64]

Meantime, in Regina, Jeanie eagerly awaited Linda Zwicker, and Eric Kierans, Dalton Camp, and Stephen Lewis. At the same moment Lyn, heading out of Regina to visit a Little Theatre group on behalf of the Saskatchewan Arts Board, was listening on her car radio to the end of the first hour. Near Hanna, Alberta, a grain farmer was catching up on news and books by listening to Peter on his radio-equipped tractor.[65] In Fort Smith the whole town, it seemed, listened to Peter, for *Morningside* played on radios in homes, government offices, a coffee shop, a gift shop, and a grocery store.[66] Even farther north at Shingle Point on the Beaufort Sea, an Inuit family was listening.[67] In Vancouver, Rauld, a building contractor, and in Whitehorse, Valerie,[68] waited in anticipation for those magical words: "Good morning. I'm Peter Gzowski and this is *Morningside*."

— 14 —

Morningside: Behind the Scenes

We frequently love our icons, even, perhaps especially, from a distance,
with physically chaste but erotically charged possessiveness.

— *Gale Zoë Garnett, "Oh, He Was More Than a Contender,"*
Globe and Mail, *January 10, 2009*

Peter was the star of *Morningside*. However, the discipline and content of the show were the result of the hard work of a staff of about ten producers, a script assistant, a studio director, an executive producer, a letters person, and a personal assistant. In addition, network producers from St. John's to Vancouver "pitched" local stories to the senior producer of *Morningside*. Each day about a dozen pieces were "voiced" on *Morningside*, from interviews to letters, games, and quizzes. The programs were planned with military precision. A large white magic-marker board was divided into squares for each segment. Janet Russell made sure of the exact timing of each segment down to the second. David Amer's music was also planned in advance and timed by Russell with a stopwatch. Little was left to chance.

Although all producers were "generalists" — Peter's description in his introduction to the first *Morningside Papers* — they each had their specialities. In the 1980s, Richard Handler produced science and medical interviews, Jim Handman was in charge of theatre, Tina Srebotnyak handled Quebec and Newfoundland, and Talin Vartanian did fashions and fads, as well as the weekly political debates.[1]

Glen Allen, who joined *Morningside* as a producer in 1986, dealt with anything from history to health. Like the other producers, he pre-interviewed guests and tried to weed out cranks as well as vainglorious or boring folk. Soon after he joined the team, he talked by telephone to a man from Windsor who gave every promise of a strong interview on the subject of Canada's governors general. After selling the story to fellow producers and to Peter, Allen booked the man for thirteen minutes. However, after four minutes of yes-and-no answers, accompanied by a rumbling stomach so loud that it could be heard from Charlottetown to the Queen Charlottes, Peter began to make slashing motions across his throat. Allen attempted to redeem himself by setting up an interview on the premenstrual cycle, and though the debate was lively, Peter started to squirm.[2]

From 1982 to 1989, Hal Wake, the literary producer,[3] was in constant touch with publishers across Canada in order to be the first to learn about upcoming books. Because there was no better place to gain publicity than *Morningside*, publishers were always happy to accommodate Wake, who often read the work first in eight-by-eleven-inch galleys, the penultimate stage of the publishing process. Although Peter was a speed-reader, he counted on Wake's more careful reading and analysis of scores of books whose authors made it onto *Morningside* each year.

Wake prepared what Peter called "thoughtful background essays" about proposed books and authors, along with a road map showing how he thought each interview would unfold. The literary producer took these background papers to story meetings, held at the end of each show, by which time Peter was understandably exhausted. Even if he said little during those meetings, Peter's opinions were evident. He was known to kill an idea, even before the producer in question had a chance to develop it, saying *"Boring!"* or "Why are we *doing* this?" Wake knew which authors Peter liked to interview.

When a proposal was accepted by a majority of producers and Peter, Wake began the task of writing an introduction to be read by Peter on the air, then composed fifteen to twenty questions. Wake tried to ensure that each question evolved organically out of the previous answer. He became particularly good at preparing questions that brought a certain kind of answer, which in turn led to the next question. Furthermore, since he had already talked to the guest during the previous week, he knew what was uppermost in the guest's mind.

However, if the guest veered off the track that had been laid out, Wake knew Peter was good at juggling questions, of asking number eight if number four didn't follow the answer for number three. If Peter went dry, the producer in charge wrote a new question on a large piece of bristol board and waved it to catch Peter's attention. Later, after moving to the new broadcast centre in the 1990s, messages in large print were quietly sent from the control room to the host via notebook computers.

Wake also kept Peter up-to-date on breaking literary news. At two minutes before seven on Tuesday evening, December 1, 1987, Peter noted in an unpublished diary that his phone rang in his condo in Market Square. It was Wake with news of the suicide of poet Gwendolyn MacEwan. Little more than three weeks earlier, on Sunday evening, November 8, Peter had introduced MacEwan to a small audience at the BamBoo Club on Queen Street West. Those in attendance had gathered to raise money for *Canadian Forum*. The show featured readings by Carol Bolt, Margaret Visser, Katherine Govier, and MacEwan. Bob Rae, NDP opposition leader at Queen's Park, was there with his wife, Arlene Perly, whom Peter didn't recognize, even though the children's fiction author had been a guest on *Morningside* several times. At the BamBoo that evening MacEwan had read three poems to the sparse audience. Although she used a microphone, few people could hear her soft, withdrawn voice until the end of the reading when she shouted, *"Fuck Mulroney!"* At the time the prime minister, in order to deal with debts and deficits, had cut grants to the CBC and to Canadian books and journals, including *Canadian Forum*. The morning after McEwan's suicide *Morningside* paid tribute to her.

—•—

One of the most important players in the production of each day's show was the studio director. Gary Katz, Heather Matheson, Susan Perly, and Bruce Steele were followed, from 1990 to 1997, by Marieke Meyer, who compared her role to that of an orchestra conductor. "Someone else has written the score and someone else was playing the instruments, but it was my job," she explained, "to make it come alive." By using a pre-taped interview, she solved unexpected problems such as the no-show or late guest, or a poor telephone connection. If a tape or CD skipped or broke, or a big news story occurred, it was the studio director who found a way to cope without, of course, distracting the host. Once the show began, the studio director was all-powerful, and even the executive directors asked her permission before entering the studio where Peter was doing the program. Meyer kept in touch with Peter via earphones and a small microphone. She also communicated with him via computer screens. Meyer cued him on the next piece of music, reminded him of the names of guests, suggested questions beyond what the producers had written into the scripts, and relayed information from producers. As each interview unfolded, Meyer decided whether to cut it short by a few minutes or to let it progress longer than planned, and she made sure there was never any dead air between interviews.

For more than seven years, Gzowksi and Meyer worked together, first in the old Jarvis Street studios of *Morningside*, and, beginning on Monday morning, December 7, 1992, in the new Broadcast Centre on Front Street West, a building that failed to inspire Peter.[4] He trusted Meyer never to betray a confidence. Even more importantly, she wasn't afraid to challenge Peter, who got along best with people who didn't defer to him. Her comments and criticism, Peter knew, could only improve the program. If he wanted to let off steam, Meyer was there to listen.

Each weekday morning from September to May, Meyer rose shortly after 4:00 a.m. in order to arrive at the CBC headquarters by 5:30 a.m. By that time, *Morningside* was more or less ready to go. Her first task was to put on the coffee. On Peter's desk, she arranged the greens and checked the storyboard. Even though Peter already had a good idea of the structure of each morning's program before he arrived at 6:00 a.m., Meyer gave him a verbal preview of the greens. They spent most of the following hour carefully reading the scripts, checking content and themes, eliminating errors, and deciding on correct pronunciations.

When Peter needed some obscure piece of information, such as a line from the Old Testament about Mount Taber for an interview about the shooting of high school students in Taber, Alberta, he turned to Meyer. At about 6:45 a.m., while Marieke and Peter took a short break for coffee, and for Peter, another cigarette, the production assistant collated the greens according to the order of the interviews, checked the links to studios across the country where guests would soon be arriving for interviews, and discussed any possible problems with sound technician Tim Lorimer.

At about 7:00 a.m., an hour before the show began, Meyer and Peter met again to smooth out any wrinkles noted in the previous hour, after which Peter spent a few minutes thinking about his introduction, his opening billboard. At about 7:45, Peter summoned Meyer to his office where he read his opening essay to her. She commented on timing and content.

The two of them walked from his office to the studio in preparation for the live broadcast. Peter entered his studio, which was separated by a wall and a soundproof picture window that revealed the control room where Meyer stood watching near the sound technician and production assistant, as well as the producer of each segment, all of them seated. Always in Peter's view, Meyer gave him her undivided attention. He carefully gauged her reaction to each interview as an indication of the response of listeners. Meyer learned how to stifle a yawn.[5]

"Peter was a man who never used a cliché," she recalls today, "and his turns of phrase" were "both original and brilliant." She enjoyed his interviews with well-known people, but even more admired the interviews that were just plain fun, such as the one with a grandmother who did moose calls. "Peter was endlessly curious — and that's what made him such a great radio host."

Les MacPherson, a journalist with Saskatoon's *StarPhoenix*, was one of two Saskatchewan correspondents. Every third Wednesday for about eight years he rose early and walked to the CBC studios in downtown Saskatoon. "What impressed me most about Gzowski," he recalled after Peter's death, "was his relentless professionalism. He never stopped working hard to make it sound easy." The preparation for the fifteen-minute Saskatchewan report was elaborate. Two days before the interview a producer in Regina and MacPherson drew up four or five possible topics, which the next day were reduced to two or three by a producer in Toronto. After a teleconference call involving the Toronto producer, MacPherson and the correspondent in Regina, were faxed the script and briefing notes, which Peter also read. However, according to MacPherson, Peter never followed the script, yet the conversations always succeeded, anyway.[6]

Although photographs published in *The Morningside Years* show a collegial staff, there were inevitable disagreements, especially in 1987 near the end of Gloria Bishop's first tenure as executive director.[7] "I feel privately in constant tension with some of my producers," Peter told Adrienne Clarkson, the president and publisher of McClelland & Stewart, on May 19, 1987. "I sometimes think they're less fair, that their political biases show," he continued. "So I battle with them and the battle wears me down."[8]

Peter might have been thinking about one particular producer. During an interview on the subject of the Chinese army, Peter strayed from the greens prepared by this producer because he began to sense the conversation was growing stale. He started to panic and sought help by looking into the control room. The producer made no response. Desperate, Peter wrapped up what he called an "unengaging interview."

Later Peter confronted the producer, who informed the host that he shouldn't have strayed from the greens. They exchanged words. Peter stalked off to his office. On his old Remington typewriter, he wrote: "I shouldn't (a) snap at you when you want to charge me with going off the green and thereby weakening a piece — I have done so and will no doubt do so again — or (b) lean so hard on you over such matters as the 'myth' discussion,[9] and I apologize for having done both today. It's probably much tougher on you than I intend it to be (one thing that has always bothered me about *Morningside* is the way criticism of an *idea* is taken as criticism of the *person*; it's not. Certainly if it were I'd have been blown out of this profession about thirty years ago, when

Ralph Allen used to kick the living shit out of stuff I had proposed, written or edited. That's how I began to learn.

"The other thing I want to say," Peter continued, "is that, perhaps contrary to what you've come to think, I do not always think I'm right. I have a lot of good ideas and a lot of opinions. Some of them are good; some of them suck." In fact, he told the producer, he enjoyed being challenged as long as it led to "mutual enlightenment." He continued at some length. "I've spelled this out in some detail because I don't leave greens as frequently as you probably think. I follow the line of the producer because, most of the time, I am convinced the producer has thought about the piece a lot — and I catch his drift (or hers) and want to use my skills to make that drift work…. But when I'm just presented with a set of questions whose logic I cannot see and which is not evident from the background (the book) I feel much less constrained. So what I mean by don't be condescending is if you want me to follow your line of thought rather than that which crops up from a reading of the background I think you should take the trouble to show me how and why you've reached the position you have. The way to get what you see as the right radio onto the air is to make me — so long as I am the last link between the stuff and the listener — your *ally*. You can't do it by just writing down a bunch of questions that don't seem to suit the internal logic…. I think curiosity is our stock in trade — we use *our* facilities, brains and opportunities, as well as gifts, to satisfy questions that arise in the listeners' minds."

Peter concluded his letter with: "Sorry. I've run on and on with this. But I don't like edgy and unsatisfactory discussions any more than you do, and sometimes find that pounding the typewriter for a while can help."

As early as the 1960s, Peter had considered personal letters to be an integral part of a magazine or a radio program. On *Morningside*, so important was mail that one person was put in charge, first Eve McBride, who was hired in the autumn of 1982. Early each morning she read as many as fifty letters, after which she separated the memorable from the unreadable. She then divided the letters she liked into various themes.

Each morning, before the light broke through the window of his studio in the old Jarvis Street building, Peter settled in to read the mail. Twice a week McBride joined Peter to read some of those letters on air.[10]

Listeners, of course, were never aware of the complicated process of dealing with the letters, whose numbers grew with each succeeding year. Letters' editors — after Eve McBride came Glen Allen for a year, then Shelagh Rogers — kept track of which letters were to be read on the air with the code "ROA." Almost every one of the thousands of letters preserved in the Gzowski Papers at Trent University Archives has at least one comment in the margins. A big "NO" meant rejection. The letters often went through many hands, each reader adding a comment.

In early September 1987, Peter did a piece on favourite things. One listener sent a list of what she liked about autumn. The letter was marked ROA for "Read on Air." For the song "It Might As Well Be Spring," another listener wrote new words: "I've a list of books I've read and found exciting / And a list of porno flicks I want to see ..." On a Post-it note, Shelagh Rogers wrote: "I like this but am (sorry) uncomfortable with 'the list of porno flicks I want to see' — kinda gives me the creeps! SR." The letter didn't get read on the air. Other lists of favourite things included short stories whose predominant mood was horror, and lists of clichés such as "I can't believe I ate the whole thing." Peter and Rogers thought a letter from Salmon Arm, British Columbia, was suitable for reading on the air, which they did on October 16, 1987. It was a list of the ten best hours the letter writer wished to spend, including one drinking coffee with Margaret Laurence in the kitchen of Morag Gunn, the main character in *The Stone Angel*. At the top of the letter in Peter's scrawl are the words "nice — yes!"

On March 17, 1994, Angela Clark wrote to Peter. "I belong to 'Tea and Empathy' — a fledging group of 10 women, ages 28 to 60. We meet once a month to let our hair down with conversation ranging from the hilarious to the serious." The previous month, she went on, the group decided it would discuss fantasies at the next meeting. Angela's fantasy was to watch the creation of *Morningside* early one morning. Two weeks later Shelley Ambrose called to invite Angela to *Morningside*, but she warned, "Don't speak to Peter" and "Tell your group this will never happen again."

Early on the morning of April 22, 1994, Angela arrived at the Broadcast Centre. "Fulfillment of a dream," she wrote in a journal. She observed the Newfoundland fisherfolk choir, whose members invited Peter to join them in singing, but he declined on the grounds that he "couldn't carry a note in a basket"; she met political activist and feminist Judy Rebick; and she listened to a discussion about the intelligence of dogs and another on Canada's own durum wheat. At the end of the show Shelley Ambrose presented Angela with a sweatshirt and a mug. "We couldn't turn down a dream," Ambrose told Angela.[11]

Most letters were, like Angela's, favourable and admiring. On November 28, 1989, an expatriate American living in Toronto wrote to see if a visiting U.S. friend who listened to *Morningside* on shortwave could meet Peter on Friday, December 8, to obtain an autograph for *The Latest Morningside Papers*. At the top of the letter someone, perhaps Peter, wrote "Call! Yes sign-yes meet-no. Left message on machine"

A former New Yorker was lonely after moving to Canada in 1985, she told Peter. Lonely, that is, until she discovered *Morningside*. Peter made her feel listened to, cared about, and loved. She had once attended one of Peter's readings. As Peter began to talk, the letter writer closed her eyes, and "knew that you were the person I loved." One woman wrote to Peter offering a weekend at her cottage during which, she promised, she would cure him of his nicotine habit! One of Peter's producers estimated there was a club with about five thousand women members across Canada, all of whom were madly in love with the man who hosted *Morningside*. One of them named her dog "Gzowski."[12]

One of Peter's greatest fans never wrote him a letter. Maggy lived on Bank Street in Ottawa where she begged for money outside a busy office tower. One morning in 1994, Michael O'Malley stopped to give her change. He was surprised to learn that she planned to buy batteries for her transistor radio.

"No time to chit-chat," she told O'Malley. "Peter's on in ten minutes."

"Why Gzowski?" O'Malley asked.

"Because he speaks to me like I am smart," she announced as she headed off to a nearby Tim Hortons for a triple-triple. Each morning she listened to *Morningside* in a Bank Street mall.[13]

Not all letters were so full of accolades. From Vancouver Island on November 9, 1987: "Dear Peter Luddite (alias Gzowski). Does your health suffer from the contradiction that you are living? On the one hand you despise technology, and on the other make your living by it." On April 8, 1988, a Halifax listener thought that Peter was "developing further" into himself "and thereby encouraging in your guests a form of stumbling, repetitive speech which is at once most annoying and, in fact, grammatically wrong." The following October a crusty listener wrote: "You are affable, you are charming, you are fun to talk with, but unfortunately you are a lightweight…. Heaven forbid that you should even ask a question that may be viewed as provocative, or that may bruise somebody's feelings." On May 3, 1988, Professor Michael Bliss wrote: "Do the opponents of Meech Lake get equal time to reply to Senator Lowell Murray?"

Riled, Peter scribbled comments all over the letter, and then on May 11, he replied to Bliss, "Michael, Jesus! One of the reasons Senator Murray was on is that we were growing concerned about the volume of anti-Meech Lake arguments we've been carrying."

A listener who had complained about the accent of a francophone commentator received a chastising letter from Peter, which was edited by someone, probably Shelley, before being typed and mailed. "Dear Ms. ____, ~~Perhaps you shouldn't be listening to CBC radio, after all,~~" wrote Peter. ~~I don't think anyone~~ I'm sorry that when Carole Beaulieu had to pause for a moment to translate her thoughts into English, you ~~didn't get~~ missed the point of her comments on the French debate. Next time, I'll urge her to simply express herself in French. Since French is also an official language of this country," continued Peter, "since francophone taxpayers join you in your support of the CBC and since you obviously understand this basic fact about Canada, I'm sure you'll appreciate our decision. Yrs sincerely."[14]

One afternoon, in April 1987, Shelley Ambrose burst into Peter's office on Jarvis Street. *Excuse me!* Shelley shouted as she waved a letter telling Peter to fuck off.

"The last thing you do with people like that is to quarrel with them," Peter calmly told her.[15]

Another letter that was discarded was from a proud new Canadian. When C. arrived in Toronto from the United States in 1982, he knew little about Canada. One morning he happened upon *Morningside*. Peter became C.'s beloved teacher. For five years C. rarely missed an interview. Then along came the Ontario election of 1987, called by Premier David Peterson, who wanted to convert his minority into a majority. C. volunteered as a scrutineer for the NDP in the Fort York Riding of the poll at Market Square, where Peter would be voting. Naturally, C. was looking forward to saying hello to his hero. He waited all day, but no Peter. He checked the voters' list to see if perhaps Peter had voted in an advance poll. But, no, Peter's name wasn't crossed off the list of eligible voters. In the Ontario election of 1987, Peter, apparently, didn't vote. C.'s opinion of Peter declined, and he told Peter so in a letter.[16]

None of the contrary letters made it into any of Peter's *Morningside Papers*. To produce what became five volumes of *Morningside Papers*, Peter reverted to the collaborative method of creating a book. In 1985 the first *Morningside Papers* was published. Peter and his chief editor, Edna Barker, with assistance from Gill Howard, Alison Gzowski, and others listed in the acknowledgements, sifted through transcripts and letters and divided the book into themes suggested by the radio program. For instance, on *Morningside* Peter had once read an essay on moving from country to city, so he asked listeners to send him their own stories on the subject. That theme became the first chapter of the book. The remaining twenty-four chapters included commissioned exchanges of letters between listeners, Glen Allen's diary on alcoholism, memorable meals, listener-composed verse, a journal of a Canadian in Nicaragua, and so on. The book soon climbed into the bestseller lists for non-fiction, and reviewers generally liked it. Henry Mietkiewicz of the *Toronto Star* was rapturous. The book, he pronounced, captured "the mood of a certain group of people — in this case, average Canadians reflecting on the pleasures and heartaches of life in the 1980s." How refreshing it was, noted Mietkiewicz, "to be privy to the feelings of people who do not pretend to be VIPs or celebrities or experts — just a bunch of literate folks with something interesting to say."[17]

To assemble the second *Papers*, Peter had the help of Glen Allen. In an undated letter in reply to one from Glen dated May 2 [1987], Peter typed on his ancient typewriter: "I just read Herb at 2,700 words, and like it very much. I'm pleased to have it in the book." Like Allen, Herb Nabigon, a member of the Mobert Reserve near Thunder Bay, was a recovered alcoholic. Herb had been interviewed on *Morningside*, and his long piece appeared in the second volume of *Papers*, immediately followed by an update by Allen on his own recovery program.

At McClelland & Stewart, Jan Walter was now vice-president of publishing. It was to her that Peter sent notes on the progress of the book. "The following print-out is of *unedited* adoption letters," he wrote on May 4, 1987. "We are still cutting, in number and length.... This is here only to give you an indication of this chapter's scope and flavour. PG. (I guess, come to think of it, Scope *is* a flavour.)" Later Peter wrote to Jan, enclosing his only copy of an unpaginated draft of the chapters. Edna Barker was trimming some of the sections, he reported, including the sixth one on the theme of adoption. "I have lists of chapters — boy, do I have lists of the chapters — but if someone drops one and the pages go awry .... hoo boy! Dangerous stuff." He concluded with "I have a brutal schedule this week, but wouldn't mind a call if you have time ... PG"

In September 1987, a second *Morningside Papers* was released. It followed the successful formula of volume one, alternating between the light-hearted — for instance, letters on the origin of the expression "Keep your fork, Duke. There's Pie" — to the inspired ("Where I live where I live"), as well as a selection of short short stories written by *Morningside* listeners.

This time not all reviewers were happy. On October 3, 1987, in "Gzowski Toots His Own Horn in Latest Literary Knockoff," Craig MacInnis, the radio reviewer for the *Toronto Star*, called Peter "the eminence grise of avuncular radio journalism" who introduced chapters "with anecdotal asides and a sense of assurance bordering on the self-reverential." Furthermore, MacInnis railed, "do we need to read the precious purple passages of amateur Thoreaus and would-be Leacocks from sea to shining sea?" He did like some pieces, including Gertrude Adema's memory of a painful childhood Christmas. MacInnis also liked Timothy Findley's tribute to Margaret Laurence, but he considered Stuart McLean's visit to a chicken factory "fairly fatuous." Much of the book, MacInnis continued, "may have been good radio, but as reading it is little more than a homely diary, frequently spoiled by the exasperating conceits of its editor (whose grinning puss is plastered on the front cover)." Listeners would lap it up, MacInnis admitted, but he wondered "who gets the royalties?"[18]

As Oscar Wilde once observed, the only thing worse than being talked about is not being talked about. MacInnis's review served to alert Peter's fans that the book was for sale. By December 1987, it had rocketed to number one in non-fiction ahead of Pierre Berton's *Vimy*. Peter's book remained supreme into January 1988, though Berton, in the number two slot, was breathing down Peter's neck.[19]

In 1989, *The Latest Morningside Papers* (volume three of the series) was published by McClelland & Stewart. Peter's team this time consisted of about eight people, including Edna Barker, Gill Howard, Shelagh Rogers, and Shelley Ambrose, as well as Lynne Reilly of Shelburne, Ontario, who was paid $836.25 for "inputting original letters;" and Debby Seed of Toronto, who earned $1,900 for copy-editing. Once again, the collaborative process was at work. For chapter eight, "The *Morningside* Book of Lists," Peter scribbled a note: "Let's ask Gill to have a go here — the file from Edna is complete — but Shelley could read it too." Note from Peter: "SENTIMENTAL JOURNEYS: Since I've made a *lot* of changes here (with much consultation with Gill, who read many of these entries in the first place), it's important to note that without the work Edna put in in the first place, this task would have been impossible." Note from Edna Barker: "Then there are three chapters I really want you to read please please — I think they are ready but they await your approval. (Shelagh & Conch saw two on women & liked them. No one but me has seen 'travelling.')"[20]

In this third volume of *Papers*, Peter and his team chose to include the transcript of Peter's interview with Elly Danica, an artist who lived in penury in a clapboard church in small-town Saskatchewan. As a child, she had been abused by her father, and like Sylvia Fraser not long before, Danica had written about it in *Don't — A Woman's Word*. Chapter six of the third *Papers* was devoted to memories of folksinger Stan Rogers, who had been killed a few years earlier in a plane fire. In chapter nineteen, Richard Osler, one of Peter's esteemed business panellists, wrote about a day in his broadcasting and stockbroker's life. The following chapter was devoted to the sightings of blue cows.

The Fourth Morningside Papers, published in 1991, was introduced by Peter's long meditative essay "Whistling Down the Northern Lights," which begins with his description of a game of golf he and a score of friends,

On August 30, 1989, to celebrate the reissue of Pierre Berton's The Mysterious North, *four McClelland & Stewart authors flaunt their latest books. While Peter and Pierre hang on dearly to their own books, Don Harron has somehow got hold of Sylvia Fraser's* My Father's House, *and Sylvia holds the Common Bible, published in 1986.*

(Courtesy William Ready Division of Archives and Research Collections, McMaster University Library, Pierre Berton fonds, Box 386, Env. 56a)

including Cynthia Dale, Colleen Peterson, Shelley Ambrose, Colin James, former Edmonton Oiler Randy Gregg, and Sheree Fitch, played on the ice at Pond Inlet, Baffin Island. From 1989 to 1991, Canada appeared to be breaking up. With the rejection in June 1990 of the Meech Lake Accord, which would have granted Quebec some form of special status, Quebec was threatening to separate. The policy of official multicultural- ism, Peter argued, only served to emphasize differences, and in the West, Preston Manning's Reform Party, he contended, had risen on a wave of resentment against Quebec. Perhaps as an antidote to all the gloom, Peter recommended that Canadians get to know the Far North.

In the fourth volume, Peter printed letters from his favourite cor- respondents, including Krista Munroe. "It's been almost a year! How are you?" wrote the woman from Medicine Hat. "The last time I wrote, I was just getting over that awful miscarriage." Peter and his assistants included poetry written by his favourite *Morningside* poets such as Maxine Tynes, Patrick Lane, Susan Musgrave, and Sheree Fitch. Another chapter included letters written in response to the shooting of fourteen female engineering students at l'École Polytechnique de Montréal in December 1989. One chapter dealt with snow fleas while the next included let- ters in response to the deaths of Morley Callaghan and Northrop Frye, including a delightful letter from Gale Zoë Garnett.[21]

Even before the fourth volume had been published, Peter and Douglas Gibson of McClelland & Stewart had begun to make deals for the next installment. In March 1991, Gibson wrote to Peter, reminding him that his advance on the current book, the fourth, was $30,000. For the next volume, Gibson was offering $40,000. In addition, Peter was to be paid $5,000 to cover permission fees, as well as research and editorial costs.[22]

As the manuscript moved toward publication during the late summer of 1994, Gibson wondered why Peter was taking so much time. "Dear Doug," Peter faxed Gibson. "This won't do." McClelland & Stewart wasn't giving the Gzowski book team enough time, only one weekend, to get page proofs back to the publisher, especially since "new errors have been inserted," including a comma after "Latest" in the first sentence of the preface. Peter complained that M&S editor Dinah Forbes had sat on the manuscript for two weeks, that she had wiped one computer disk clean, and that a chapter was missing from the first galleys on July 18. "I still haven't seen what you propose for the front cover," Peter added, "and, as I think of what you had for the *Fourth Papers* at that year's CBA [Canadian Booksellers Association trade show], I cringe with concern."

To add to Peter's woes, in her introduction, Shelagh Rogers was telling readers what they already knew about the personal letter. "Please, please," Peter told Edna Barker, "no one else write that the art of letter-writing isn't dead." Peter and Barker revised the piece, removing in the process Rogers's faux pas about petards being hoisted.[23]

The fifth volume featured several of Peter's *Morningside* billboards, including homages to Barbara Frum, who had died in March 1992; one to A.J. Casson, who had died the month before Frum; and one to cartoonist Duncan Macpherson, who had died in May 1993. The fifth *Morningside Papers* also contained a whole chapter on faux pas — a veterinary in Saskatoon confessed to having tried to spay a male cat, and Peter admitted he had once messed up John F. Kennedy's famous line about doing good for your country. One chapter was a journal of living with a spouse's cancer, part of which had been read on *Morningside* from 1992 to 1994. Michael Kusugak's journals of living in Rankin Inlet formed another chapter. There were recipes for butter tarts and Rice Krispie squares, as well as letters both cheery and sad about Christmases past. Like all previous volumes, number five sold briskly.

Peter's book tours were adventures. In Edmonton in 1994, he was interviewed by Daryl Richel at the University of Alberta's radio station CJSR. After touring the station, Peter recorded a station identification. "Hi, I'm Peter Gzowski. You're listening to CJSR. When I like to rock, I listen to CJSR." After he finished what Richel had written for him, Peter said, "Okay, I'm now going to do my own." His own was "Hello, I'm Peter Gzowski of *Morningside*. CJSR plays appalling music, but if you like it, keep listening."[24]

On Friday, October 30, 1987, Peter was due to travel to Kingston to publicize the second volume of the *Morningside Papers*. That morning his interview with Joan Didion was bruising, he reported in his diary, for she was "just not into conversation at all." In the early afternoon, he set off on his signing tour. There are two versions of the trip. Peter's diary mentions that he drove his 1978 BMW eastward to Belleville and Kingston. He was greeted by bagpipes and a town crier at W. and R. Greenley Bookstore in front of which he left the engine running as he signed books inside. Afterward, he got back into his car and proceeded to Kingston for a second signing.

A second version of what may have been the same trip provides slightly different details. He was driven in a limo hired by M&S. With him was the company's marketing manager, who watched in alarm as Peter consumed a bottle of Rémy Martin. However, once Belleville appeared on the horizon, Peter rose to the occasion, greeting with his usual shy charm each book buyer at W. and R. Greenley and later in Kingston at A Printed Passage.

In his diary, Peter noted: "Kingston — dinner with Glen at Piggy's[25] … booze." In his published memoirs: "Dinner with Glen Allen. A rare pleasure." While Peter drank double Scotches, Glen sipped soda. Peter became introspective. "What makes *Morningside* unique?" he asked Allen, who explained his theory of Eros-Thanatos. Eros was love, as well as "humour, play, healthy eccentricity, nostalgia, and information…." On the other hand, Thanatos represented death, gloom, pessimism, and tragedy. Most media favoured Thanatos. While *Morningside* didn't overlook Thanatos, it was best at Eros, and perhaps that was why at the end of three hours, listeners felt elated to be a member of a national tribe presided over by their friend and chief.[26] Peter and Glen also talked about alcohol and its abuse, including Peter's own "occasionally scary history," about their uncomfortable relationship with their fathers, the prose of A.J. Liebling, and the politics of *Maclean's*. And also about a woman in Montreal to whom both Glen and Peter had once been attracted.

Not surprisingly, Peter tossed and turned all night at the Hochelaga Inn. The next day President John Stubbs and Trent University, whose buildings soared "from the imagination of Ron Thom," wrote Peter in *The Private Voice*,[27] honoured him with a degree at the autumn convocation. At some point, perhaps at this convocation, Stubbs convinced Peter to deposit his papers at the Trent University Archives.[28]

Publishers' agents, as well as marketing managers and literary agents, are unsung heroes in the quest to sell books. The local agent plays many roles, from meeting the author at the airport or train station to driving him or her to television and radio studios and newspaper offices for interviews.

In Regina the agent hired by M&S was Donelda Thomas. She drove to the airport where she noticed a tall, dishevelled man shuffling toward the luggage carousel. "Are you Peter Gzowski?" she asked.

"No," Peter replied.

As Thomas began to apologize, it dawned on Peter that this polite woman was his agent in Regina. It was late afternoon on a holiday Monday. Rather than leaving him at his hotel, Donelda took him home where she and her husband, a General Motors executive, entertained him at dinner. Eventually, fifteen-year-old Alicia Thomas, dressed only in a post-shower bathrobe and a towel wrapped around her head, wandered into the living room.

"I have a daughter your age," Peter told Alicia, "and she's pitch perfect."

Alicia looked puzzled, for she had no idea who Peter was. When the evening ended, Peter had consumed a bottle of Scotch. The Thomases offered him a second, which he took back to the hotel. The next morning, when Donelda arrived at the hotel to escort him to his first interview, Peter was raring to go.[29]

In the mid-1990s as Peter's health began to deteriorate, his exhaustion started to show on *Morningside*. When Peter interviewed Ezra Schabas in 1995 on the subject of his biography of Sir Ernest MacMillan, Schabas was convinced that his host hadn't read the book, or if he had, that he wasn't interested in MacMillan. Or possibly that he was just too tired even to appear interested.[30] An interview with Ted Barris in October 1995 on the subject of *Playing Overtime*, Barris's book on old-timers' hockey, left Barris with the same feeling. The producer had set Peter up with three men who continued to play hockey. While Barris waited in the studio across the table from Peter, Peter talked by telephone to the old-timers, all of whom were included in Barris's book. When it came time to talk to Barris, Peter kept his head down, as if Barris, too, were a voice on a telephone. Was Peter tired? Had he not had time to prepare for that segment of the show?

Peter in the Great White North at Cambridge Bay, Northwest Territories.

Some listeners grew impatient. On January 21, 1993, an old fan complained about Peter's "staid, conservative attitudes, constant stutters, misreads" and his "pointless comments." The listener advised Peter to "let someone who still has the willingness to listen, not just be listened to, take over; someone who doesn't yet feel *he* is a Canadian cultural institution."[31] Another listener was tired of hearing Peter whine about cuts at the CBC and suggested he consider cutting back on discussions about female pornography with Pamela Wallin. One listener used the uppercase to order Peter to stop interrupting guests.[32]

In the early 1990s, Peter's voice was losing much of its resonance and range. The old interviewing methods were no longer working. The hesitancy, the mumbling, the pretense of ignorance had for several years been declining into too many *uh-huhs* and *hmmms* to the point where his relaxed, intelligent style was often soporific. More than one listener renamed the show *Boringside*.[33] Another, who returned to Canada in 1992 after several years in Key West, noticed that the stuttering and hesitation, which had worked well in the 1980s, had become self-parody.

Peter must have been particularly hurt when he read the letter from a once-faithful listener, an artist in Edmonton. "From time to time I get this empty feeling that the magic has been lost," wrote Dan on January 8, 1997. After more than a decade of gruelling work that might have killed other broadcasters, and after a half-century of cigarettes, booze, and sleep deprivation, Peter's body was wearing out.

He also suffered from producer sycophancy. Gone were the days of strong producers who, like Ridley College masters, provided strict parameters within which Peter's creative genius always flourished. Gone into CBC management was Alex Frame, Peter's masterly executive producer on *This Country in the Morning*, and gone, too, was the strong direction that had kept Peter creative in the earlier days of Morningside. To a great extent, during the last half of *Morningside*, what Peter wanted, he got. And rare was the producer who was strong enough to advise him that perhaps Wayne Gretzky's genius on ice didn't guarantee a good radio interview.

—•—

On the morning of May 30, 1997, Peter ended his fifteen-year run of *Morningside*. At the urging of fans in Moose Jaw, Saskatchewan, he finished his tenure in the place, he reminded his audience, where his career had begun forty years earlier. On that morning in 1997, as he sat in front of a microphone in the Temple Gardens Mineral Spa Resort Hotel, he fondly recalled his halcyon days at the *Times-Herald* in the city with the underground tunnels he had been too busy, he claimed, to explore in 1957. (In fact, the tunnels had only been "discovered" in 1985.)[34] This last show featured Stuart McLean, Connie Kaldor, and Colin James.

"All Canadian writers are indebted to you, Peter," said an ailing W.O. Mitchell from his sickbed in Calgary.

"Well, I'll tell you something," Peter replied. "Every Canadian is indebted to you ... you showed us ourselves. You inspired other people, you lifted our hearts, you described the landscape."[35]

Among the 250 teary members of the audience that day was a fan dressed in a white bathrobe, hair curlers, and fuzzy slippers shaped like moose heads. She shouted at Peter, "You're the only thing that helped me stay sane when I was home with the kids."[36] Also in the audience was Mary Grant, mother of Regan, who a few years earlier had died with AIDS. Former Premier Grant Devine said he had just "climbed off his tractor" to come by for the show. Eleanor Romanow, wife of Roy, the premier defeated by Devine in 1982, was also there. So, too, was Elly Danica, who had talked to Peter about sexual abuse. In the audience was Deb Thorn, whose recently deceased mother, Connie Wilson, along with Barry Gray, had helped to convince Peter and Gloria Bishop to do the last show in Moose Jaw.[37]

Many of the Canadians, and no doubt some of his American fans, listened to that final broadcast with great emotion. A young woman in Muskoka would miss the man who had kept her company in her kitchen for the past eleven years when she was raising her child.[38] A woman in small-town Alberta told Peter he had been just like a member of her family, and that one of her partners used to be jealous as his voice filled their little cabin.[39] On Vancouver Island, as Peter signed off, a husband and wife, self-employed commercial fishermen, hugged each other as tears streamed down their faces.[40] Across Canada listeners gathered in small groups in some twenty locations — at Bookers Bookstore in Oakville, Ontario, for instance, and at The Remarkable Bean in Toronto.[41] In a retirement home in Edmonton, residents were listening. One of them penned a note to Peter: "Thanks for being the voice that's kept Canada human, warm & caring! For me, you defined what we really are as a country & I liked what I heard."[42]

Retired Prime Minister Brian Mulroney opined that Peter brought to radio "a unique understanding that reflects some of the realities of all parts of Canada. Peter's voice, his approach and his attitude, was one of the country's strands of cohesion. He brought a sense of genuineness about his affection for Canada." Knowlton Nash compared the Gzowski style to a warm bath, while Don Harron maintained that Peter "made his listeners feel important." Critic Geoff Pevere agreed with Peter's admirers that *Morningside* was like a large dinner table with guests gathered around from Victoria to St. John's. "But it's a question of who the program invites to the table and what it serves," Pevere added. "I would say, in terms of the national family, it's had a small table and a pretty narrow range of nutritional goods to offer." For this and other derogatory comments from Pevere, Steve Paikin of TVOntario's *Studio Two* called Pevere "a puissant," presumably an attempt at an insult, though the rather archaic word really means "mighty, potent, and powerful."[43]

Some critics, Glen Allen noted not long after Peter's final broadcast, called Peter yesterday's man, a rustic figure celebrating a country long gone, a country full of Celtic music and pickle recipes, while, at the same time ignoring the new Canada that was increasingly multi-hued. Critics claimed that Peter's stories were cute, Allen continued, and that his approach was too middling and moderate, too lulling and calm. Allen would have none of that, for he believed Peter was "brilliant and cerebral." He had pushed his producers to find harder stories, ethnic stories, and it wasn't his fault if they didn't. So what if he was moody off the air? He was a shy man, Allen insisted, "with a complicated childhood." He was uncomfortable with fame. Yes, Peter was often self-referential, Allen admitted, and too often, perhaps, he talked about his love of horse racing, his fear of snakes, and his great cause, literacy. Granted, some topics such as animal rights were beyond him, he was "slow to judge others," and he believed that even the worst could be redeemed, not perhaps a realistic attitude during the latter part of the twentieth century.[44]

In November 1997, a couple of months after Glen Allen's article appeared in *The New Brunswick Reader*, Hal Wake wrote to Peter. "Everything I know and understand about radio," he told Peter, "I learned at *Morningside*: that good radio is an intimate relationship between listener and the program, that radio has the power to help build communities like no other medium, that all good pieces start with questions, not answers, that at our best we provide a forum for discussion, debate, the exchange of ideas and the sharing of wisdom, that a good host has to be a great listener."[45]

Last day of Morningside *on May 30, 1997, in Moose Jaw — Peter, left; Shelley Ambrose, glasses; executive produce Gloria Bishop with head turned; network producer Sean Prpich; senior producer Willy Barth on phone; and technician, seated, possibly Tim Lorimer.*

(Courtesy Trent University Archives, Gzowski fonds, 92-015, box 4, folder 5/photograph by Don Hall)

— 15 —

"I Don't Know Who I'll Be When I'm No Longer Peter Gzowski"

There are things I remember which may never have happened
but as I recall them so they take place.

— *Anna in Harold Pinter's* Old Times

Although radio was his principal vocation from 1982 to 1997, Peter did return to television occasionally. In 1982 he became the host of *Fighting Words*, a revival of a CBC-TV show hosted by Nathan Cohen during the 1950s. Cohen used to throw out a quotation at the beginning of each show, and after the panellists guessed its source, they debated its significance. His panel of regulars and guests included Rabbi Abraham Feinberg, Morley Callaghan, and Ralph Allen. Occasionally, Robert Fulford was a guest panellist, as was William F. Buckley, Jr., and his ideological opposite, Sir Isaiah Berlin.

Peter's version of the show was taped at CHCH-TV in Hamilton, Ontario, four sessions at a time, and he was paid $1,000 per show.[1] From 1982 to 1984, the shows were broadcast on Thursdays at 8:30 p.m. Among his panellists were Barry Callaghan, son of Morley; Irving

Layton, who had also been part of the earlier version; Barbara Amiel, journalist, broadcaster, and former researcher for Adrienne Clarkson's *Take 30*; and the irascible Gordon Sinclair, one of the stars of *Front Page Challenge*. For the *Fighting Words* of October 14, 1982, Peter read a line from anthropologist Margaret Mead: "Women want mediocre men." When the panellists failed to guess the source, Peter provided clues that led Callaghan to Mead. The ten-minute discussion was lively. Even though he was certain that none of his wives had considered him mediocre, Layton agreed with Mead. "Men in the twentieth century," Amiel opined, "have had their virility bred out of them." Gordon Sinclair asserted that women married for money. Amiel mentioned something about pink shirts. "And what's the matter with pink shirts?" asked an uncomfortable Peter, who managed to regain control of his panel by ringing a bell.[2] During the 1983–84 season, panellists included Hugh Segal, Jim Laxer, Mel Watkins, Elizabeth Hardwicke of *The New York Times Review of Books*, and Jill Johnston of *The Village Voice*. Stephen Lewis and Leslie Fiedler also made appearances.[3]

"Cohen's ghost haunts his successor," noted Jim Bawden of the *Toronto Star*, who wondered why Peter couldn't be as relaxed as the host of *Morningside*. While Nathan Cohen, in order to maintain control of his version of the show, had used asides, facial grimaces, and chuckling, as well as a "formidable presence," Peter seemed overwhelmed.[4] Or as Joey Slinger had once noted, Peter "took to television the way a duck takes to an oil spill."[5] Nevertheless, some observers liked Peter's work on *Fighting Words*, for in March 1985 he was nominated for an ACTRA Award for best host of an entertainment show.[6]

In the right hands, however, Peter and the television camera worked well together. In 1985, Peter had the good fortune to work once again with Glenn Sarty, who persuaded him to do a television show called *Gzowski & Company*, a series of informal half-hour interviews with Canadian artists, actors, musicians, dancers, and singers. The show's mandate was "to make the arts seem less formidable to Canadian viewers."[7] In order to showcase talent from all regions of the country, Sarty hired David

Gerrard, a British producer with a literary background, to locate and mentor talent across Canada.[8] Sarty let Peter keep his beard, if trimmed, and his relaxed dress code. Little makeup was applied, and because Sarty employed two cameras, with one constantly on Peter, the show's host didn't have to ask questions twice.

But why, Henry Mietkiewicz asked Peter, did he consent to return to television? "Unquenchable curiosity," Peter explained. The new show, he believed, would be "*Morningside* with pictures,"[9] which is exactly how he had conceived of *90 Minutes Live*, a program that was to have been *This Country in the Morning* with pictures. Apparently, Peter still didn't understand how to transcribe radio format to television. Sarty, however, did.

During the summers of 1985 and 1986, Peter and Glenn did interviews across the country. As he had done with the old *Gzowski* show fifteen years earlier, Sarty edited hours of film to make about twenty-six minutes of good television. During interviews with Mary Pratt, Angèle Dubeau, and dozens of other artists and actors, Peter was relaxed, interested, and congenial. In other words, Sarty managed to re-create the radio Gzowski on television. Importantly, Sarty had long understood that Peter worked best on television when he was moving and that the medium demanded movement. Thanks to a Canadian-invented camera, which even at high speeds maintained a level image, Sarty was able to film Peter close up as he rode a chuckwagon near Calgary. When he interviewed Alexina Luie, he strode beside the roller-blading musician in Toronto's High Park. Peter's interview with H. Gordon Greene, a chicken farmer in Quebec, was conducted, in part, as Peter and Greene wandered amid cackling hens. An interview with Mike Duffy took place as the two men walked on a beach in Duffy's native Prince Edward Island. Peter ambled with Evelyn Hart through Assiniboine Park, and later, in a downtown studio of the Royal Winnipeg Ballet, they danced a pas de deux. Unrecorded on film was a taxi ride from the park to the studio. As they rode down Portage Avenue, Peter put his arm around Hart's shoulders and told her "Gee, you're really great."

"He was like a big teddy bear," Hart remembered with a big smile.[10]

On one show, Moses Znaimer told Peter he wanted his television empire to become national. Douglas Cardinal talked about his innovative buildings, including the Canadian Museum of Civilization. For a show with k.d. lang, Peter visited Consort, Alberta, where he talked to the singer's mother.

In total, Sarty and Gzowski did fifty-two interviews over two years. Although Peter began to appreciate TV, he still believed it could never achieve the "real spontaneity" of radio. Even though the show faced stiff competition from popular American shows such as *M*A*S*H*, *Entertainment Tonight*, *Murder, She Wrote*, *Wheel of Fortune*, and *Cagney & Lacey*, the number of viewers rose from an estimated 200,000 to 632,000. However, during the 1986-87 schedule, numbers fell to 250,000.[11] Jim Bawden was vexed at the CBC's decision to cut the show at the end of its second year, for Peter, he argued, had been improving.[12]

The voice that made Peter so successful on radio was in demand to narrate television shows such as *Stanley Knowles: By Word and Deed*, a television biography. "Knowles nagged and prodded and shamed every government since Mackenzie King's," Peter's voice informed viewers, "until such programs as the old-age pension and Medicare were enacted…. He believes that man is good but society can be made good."[13] On October 30, 1989, Peter was the narrator and probably also the scriptwriter[14] for a TV show called *Degrassi Between Takes*,[15] a thirty-minute retrospective of the popular television show *Degrassi High*.[16] As the half-hour program opened, Peter began his narrative. "On a downtown Toronto street, the everyday world of Canadian teenagers meets the never-never land of network television. Here fantasy collides with teenage realities of the eighties, from AIDS to zits."[17]

Peter was frequently invited to participate in literary events. In October 1982 in Toronto, he joined a hundred other writers, including Richard Gwyn, Ken Adachi, Michele Landsberg, Alice Munro, Kildare Dobbs, Charles Templeton, Pierre Berton, Margaret Trudeau, and Maureen McTeer, to raise money for the Writers' Development Trust.[18] Later in

October, with Barbara Frum, Robert Fulford, Peter Hernndorf, Sylvia Fraser, Jack Batten, Sid Adilman, and others, he attended the launch of Alan Fotheringham's *Malice in Blunderland* at the Rosedale mansion of his friends, Michael and Honor de Pencier.[19] In October 1987, he acted as chair for a panel discussion on "Neo-Colonialism and the Writer" at Harbourfront in Toronto. "No one knows what the hell it's all about," he noted in his diary. "Can't find Nurrukic Farrah from Somalia ..."[20] In 1988 he served as writer-in-residence at Trent University, and the same year he served as narrator for the Toronto Symphony Orchestra's evening of Inuit folk legends.[21] He was also constantly autographing books and attending fundraising dinners for writers.[22]

In July 1992, Peter participated in the Georgina Festival of Stories at Jackson's Point, Ontario.[23] And in November that year he and the Brampton Festival Singers presented at Mayfield Secondary School in Brampton "a tour of Canada through words and music," with proceeds going to Frontier College's literacy programs.[24] A few days later Peter played a character called "Mr. Gzowksi," a member of a TV panel show, on CBC's *Street Legal*.[25] In March 1993, Peter and what the *Toronto Star* called his "celebrity pals" campaigned for the ABC Canada Literacy Foundation at Toronto's Winter Garden Theatre.[26] In May 1993, Peter flew to Montreal to act as MC for a Mordecai Richler Roast.[27] In November of the same year, he participated in a Scrabble tournament in Toronto to raise funds for the Canadian Give the Gift of Literacy Foundation.[28] In December 1995, he was part of the Huron Carol Benefit Concert, which each Christmas raised funds for Toronto's food banks and soup kitchens.[29]

While performing these public functions, Peter did his best to keep in touch with his growing family and called his children on their birthdays. On his own fiftieth birthday, July 13, 1984, he wrote in a journal: "I am fifty today, and have gathered the kids to help me celebrate, and cannot get my father out of my mind."[30] On Friday October 23, 1987, Peter wrote in a diary: "Mick calls about dinner. I tell him, as we chat, I'm thinking 'about a job in ____.' I say I'm sick of being a 'personality.' Mick replied: "You could always come & play in my band. Then no one would notice you."[31]

In 1986, on his fifty-fourth birthday, the children were invited to dinner, but they chose to eat with their mother. It was, after all, her birthday, too. "Am I jealous?" Peter asked himself. "Probably a little, even though I know there's no reason." Gill plied him with gifts, which didn't help him forget what he interpreted as a subtle slight from his children.[32] In December 1993, Peter was making his last round of Christmas shopping at upscale Holt Renfrew on Bloor Street. This time it was he who was buying for Gill. He ran into Cynthia Dale from whom he received a warm hug, after which Peter enlisted her to try on what an observant reporter from the *Toronto Star* called a "giftie garment."[33]

Despite the fact that Harry Bruce occasionally wrote articles that revealed the darker side of Peter's nature, the two men remained friends for years. In 1964 they had celebrated FOTT, the Festival of Turning Thirty, by drinking for five days straight. They had hoped to celebrate FOTS, the Festival of Turning Sixty, in July 1994. Even if they had managed to get together, it is doubtful they could have managed to drink for five days straight. In February 1996, when Bruce learned that Peter was in hospital, he wrote to him, attributing his ill health to his having missed FOTS. The surgery, explained Peter, was "the old Triple A ... Abdominal, Aortic and Aneurism. They snip out a bit of your biggest artery and replace it with Dacron. Knocks you down for a bit. My advice, if you need any, is don't go to a doctor in the first place." Except for one nurse, Peter continued to Bruce, "a ditzy *Morningside* fan who made her rounds on line skates and found me sleepless in my room at 4:00 a.m., and suggested I go down for a cigarette — 'it's part of your creativity,' she said — most people in the, ahem, medical community, seem to think smoking, not missing FOTS, was a cause of my downfall. What do they know?"[34]

How did he manage to remember dates and deadlines, including family birthdays? By means of detailed lists, Shelley Ambrose kept Peter on schedule. Her list of events in early 1990 is typical of all such Ambrosean lists:

Write: *Canadian Living column — deadline <u>Tuesday</u>*
            <u>*February 27*</u>

Think: *Mordecai Richler introduction* — <u>*Tuesday February 27*</u>

Think: *Country Estate reception — few words —* <u>*Wed. February 28*</u>

Think: *Ottawa Golf Meeting —* <u>*Thursday March 1*</u> *with Bonnie*

THINK: *ABC MEETING* <u>*Thursday March 1*</u> *(take file)*

WRITE: *ABC Kick-off — few words —* <u>*Friday March 2*</u>

WRITE: *commentary — Vncvr tv — 1½ mins on literacy:* <u>*March 2*</u>

WRITE: *Picton speech — window — see file — Saturday* <u>*March 3*</u>

WRITE: *newsletter for all gold committee members*

WRITE: *Fulford piece — deadline* <u>*Thursday March 8*</u>

THINK: *U. Of Vic. reading —* <u>*Friday March 9*</u>

THINK: *Victoria Golf meeting in Vncvr w/Linda Mitchell —* <u>*March 10*</u>

WRITE: *Literacy speech — Vncvr —* <u>*Saturday March 10*</u>

WRITE: *Convocation speech — Open Univ. — see file —* <u>*March 10*</u>

THINK: *Saltspring Reading - Saturday* <u>*March 10*</u>

WRITE: *Arctic mag — 850 words — literacy and feelings about the north — deadline* <u>*April 1*</u>

WRITE: *Enroute — Canadian flag — see file — deadline* <u>*April 2nd*</u>

ALSO: *Invite the Shuffle Demons to the Briars, Tom Cochrane, David Crombie, and Dewar — cartoonist for Ottawa: Clarke Davey — re: Ottawa tourn.*[35]

On May 19, 1987, Peter wrote to Adrienne Clarkson, president and publisher of McClelland & Stewart. The next day, he told her, he would be treating his producers to a day at Woodbine Racetrack where he would decide whether to continue as host of Morningside. "That decision, I think — the moment at which I make it — would be the perfect point at which to begin my diary," he told Clarkson. The diary would lead to a memoir, which he wanted M&S to publish. And what did he want to discuss in his memoir?

> CBC politics (a major shuffle in the radio bureaucracy has just begun this week). CBC *policies* (I think it's time they killed the sports department). How programs work ... and sometimes why they don't (we've just had to kill a very expensive panel discussion we recorded on the Queen Charlottes because the sound wasn't good enough — we lost the only Haida voice). Internal struggles, external fame. Guests who show up the worse for booze in the morning, or with speech impediments or not at all. Guests who arise from the mail and turn into friends. Why we can't get Anne Murray, why Francophones are better on the radio than we are.

Peter wanted also to write about things he couldn't say on radio such as coming out against capital punishment and an explanation about why Patrick Watson almost lost his job at the CBC for doing so. Also "how I deal with people I don't like; whether I really *do* read all those books." He wanted to write about the real meaning of free trade and about the amusing things that had happened behind the scenes at *Morningside*, which, he told Clarkson, was becoming too routine. "I'm scared that some morning," he continued, "I'll look at a lineup with one more Manitoba report than I can handle."

He asked Clarkson for an advance of $30,000 by the end of the month so that he could finish his cottage on Lake Simcoe. And, of course, he wanted the usual royalties. "My divorce is even closing in on me — which means I need the cottage more than ever. (Goodbye, city house.)"[36] Clarkson promised the money — during her brief time at M&S, she acquired a reputation for generosity to authors — and told him to proceed.

Soon after his visit to the racetrack, Peter began to keep a diary of the show. Meantime, events such as the death of Ross McLean on

June 1, 1987, the departure of Robert Fulford from *Saturday Night*, and a chat over dinner with June Callwood triggered his memory, and the autobiographical side of the book grew. By early January 1988, Peter and Douglas Gibson agreed that the manuscript was long enough. After several more drafts and a title suggested by Peter Sibbald Brown,[37] *The Private Voice* was published in the autumn of 1988.

In the book's introduction, Peter claimed that the book was about honesty and "truth." Like Ralph Allen, he explained, he believed that "the writer of non-fiction … has an unspoken contract with his reader to report only what he has witnessed. To do otherwise is to assume for himself the totally different licence of the novelist …" In other words, Peter was distancing himself from literary journalism and its blend of fact and fiction. He complained that "the priests of New Journalism" would argue that a story was true "if it *could* have happened, if it fits with what is known about character and situation."[38]

Peter was being rather ingenuous. While it is true that Ralph Allen had taught Peter to write well and clearly and to report only on events he had actually witnessed, the truth of the matter is that Peter was much more influenced by writers who wrote prose that seamlessly blended fact with imagination. Robert Fulford, who, along with Harry Bruce, best understood Peter, argued that Peter was influenced by the literary non-fiction vogue that was sweeping New York during the 1950s and 1960s. In 1965, in a review of Joseph Mitchell's *Joe Gould's Secret*, Fulford placed Peter among a group of writers who positioned themselves inside the story they were reporting. The other members of the group, according to Fulford, were John Updike, Rebecca West, A.J. Liebling, and Joseph Mitchell, all of whom invested factual material "with the properties of mythology," thereby turning fact into a kind of literature.[39] Or as David Remnick noted in his introduction to *Just Enough Liebling*, "one of the commonplaces of feature writing at the time was a tendency to embroider…. Details were embroidered, colours heightened, dialogues faked."[40] One of Peter's favourite books was *An Unfinished Woman*, the first volume of the memoirs of Lillian Hellman, a writer who never let a fact spoil a good memoir. Peter admired journalists like Calgarian Bob Edwards, whose satiric newspaper *The Eye Opener* excoriated the peccadilloes of politicians and businessmen. In November 1997, at the twenty-third annual Bob Edwards' Luncheon in Calgary, Peter quoted Edwards: "Some men spoil a good story by sticking to the facts."[41] In most of Peter's writing, there is no clear line dividing fact from fiction.[42]

By nature, Peter had always thought like a literary journalist. In Galt one day, when a reporter from the *Reporter* dropped by to take a picture of Peter's touch football team, Peter had pasted Band-Aids across his nose and chin to "look as tough as possible."[43] While he might have stuck to the so-called facts when he reported on crime for Toronto's *Telegram* in 1953–54, soon thereafter he began to dabble in a form of literary journalism. In Timmins, Peter's staging of the photograph of the burning tree is a blend of fact (a major forest fire) and imagination (on a tree he joined together two signs, one on the dangers of forest fires and the other on the dangers of smoking. When the tree refused to burn, he set it on fire and took the photograph).

Throughout his writing career Peter was greatly influenced by literary journalism. In 1968 he flew to New York City to talk to Clay Felker, editor of *New York* magazine, which published many of the purveyors of literary non-fiction such as Tom Wolfe. Peter had in mind a Toronto version of the magazine, which would publish writers like Sylvia Fraser and Harry Bruce. Years later Bruce recalled the influence of New York literary journalism on Peter and himself, especially the work of Gay Talese,[44] whose *The Kingdom and the Power* (1966) was a study of the *New York Times* and its owners and editors. In lines such as "After Clifton Daniel had finished his dictation, Miss Riffe stood up and, with that nice hip motion she has when she walks, left his office,"[45] Talese was artfully blending fact and imagination.

Another literary journalist Peter admired was E.B. White, one of whose books Harry Bruce sent to him in 1996 during his convalescence after a triple bypass operation.[46] "I sometimes amuse myself by bringing Henry Thoreau back to life and showing him the sights," wrote White in *The Points of My Compass*, first published in 1954. "I escort him into a phone booth and let him dial Weather.... I take the celebrated author to Twenty-One for lunch, so the writers may study his shoes.... I doubt that Thoreau would be thrown off balance by the fantastic sights and sounds of the twentieth century."[47] In 1996, Robert Fulford's post-operative gift to Peter was a book by A.J. Liebling, another literary journalist greatly admired by Peter.[48] "My old friend looked at me with great respect," Liebling wrote, in an article about dining in Paris. "He was discovering in me a capacity for hypocrisy that he had never credited me with before."[49]

In fact, the perceptive Robert Fulford had noted that one of the important influences on Peter's writing style and technique was the novel. In writing *The Sacrament*, noted Fulford in a review of the book in 1980, Peter had absorbed lessons taught to him by novelists, especially in re-creating small-town Prairie life.[50] Although Fulford didn't name these novelists, he may have been thinking of W.O. Mitchell and Margaret Laurence. Another novelist also saw the influence of novelists in *The Sacrament*. In a review, Leo Simpson, whose novel *Kowalski's Last Chance* had been published around the time of *The Sacrament*, noted Peter's sensitivity for characters and landscape and his blending of fact with the techniques of fiction.[51] In other words, Simpson implied that Peter had written a non-fiction novel, whose model might have been perhaps Norman Mailer's *An American Dream* or Truman Capote's *In Cold Blood*.

In *The Private Voice*, Peter became the main character in a non-fiction novel whose hero, a man called Peter, was balanced, gently self-mocking, and avuncular. He had been orphaned at the age of fourteen. He missed his saintly mother still. He wished he had understood his father. Oh, he hadn't been the perfect husband and father, and he now regretted the evenings when he returned home late and lifted the lids of pots to see just what Jennie was keeping warm for him. He had negotiated the end of his marriage. He had been a failure, poor man, on talk-show television. However, he had done it his way. Affairs? None to speak of. *Private Voice* is what writer and cartoonist Lynda Barry calls today "autofictionography."

One wonders if another autofictionographer didn't have some influence on Peter's blend of diary and memoir. Was Scott Symons's *Helmet of Flesh*, published in 1986, a subconscious influence on *The Private Voice*? At almost the same time that Peter began his memoir he had read the Symons's novel in preparation for his interview with the author.

Like Peter's *The Private Voice*, *Helmet* combines diary and autobiography. Indeed, if Symons had called his hero Scott Symons rather than York Mackenzie, the similarities between *Helmet* and *Voice* would be even more striking. Like Symons's journals, Peter's diary is incorporated into the memoir more or less as he wrote it. Peter even uses the word *plot* to describe the structure of his memoir. His memoir's plot, he explained, had emerged "unbidden from the events of the year,"[52] which is how novelists and short-story writers sometimes explain the origins of their fiction. Even his settings are novelistic. "Rain drenches the cottage as I write," he writes, "pounding on the clerestory high above my head, running in torrents down the new pine siding. On the screened verandah overlooking Hedge Road, the skylights leak prodigiously; puddles deep enough for tadpoles to shine on the floor."[53]

On November 7, 1988, shortly after *The Private Voice* was published, Robert Fulford sent Peter a note. He deemed pages 61 to 327 to be f---ing wonderful. Why? Perhaps the line on page 62 in which Peter speculates that, after he publicly criticized CBC policies, Margaret Lyons might have wanted to drive a dessert fork through his larynx? And why, one wonders, did Fulford not include pages 1 to 60 in his commendations? Perhaps he didn't like page 17 on which Peter defines the verb *to Fulford* as "to be so determined to share your own delight in something that you spoil other people's pleasure." He was referring to Fulford's habit of revealing the ending of a movie or a book to anyone who hadn't seen or read it.

Fulford's letter to Peter continued. He wanted to dispatch one reviewer to the glue factory.[54] On November 5, Harry J. Boyle, former chair of the Canadian Radio-television and Telecommunications Commission, had written a perceptive review entitled "The Secret Fears of Radio's Superstar." Given the fact that he was an enormous success on radio, why, Boyle wondered, did Peter insist on dwelling on failures?[55]

Most reviewers, like Boyle, were respectfully disappointed. "For most memoirists," wrote the novelist John Bemrose, "the first 20 years of life are the source of their richest insights. But for Gzowski, that period is clearly a minefield to be avoided."[56] In *Saturday Night*, George

Galt thought that the book suffered from some of the same flaws as *Morningside*: Peter's "aw-shucks bonhomie" could be winsome, but also "maddeningly hollow" when used to skirt issues that invite criticism.[57] While David Olive, a senior writer at *Toronto Life*, admired Peter's courage in dealing with his troubled relations with his father and with his ex-wife, he lamented the fact that the book projected "an image of Canada that is safe, unprovocative — rather like the pieces of Eskimo art we're so fond of giving to distinguished visitors from abroad."[58] The reviewers were right — like many, perhaps most memoirs, *The Private Voice* was "torn between the desire to confess and the need to obscure," as Tim Gardam said about Günter Grass's memoir *Peeling the Onion*.[59]

Peter's fans had no such reservations, and Christmas was approaching. By mid-December *Voice* was number six on the *Toronto Star*'s non-fiction bestseller list, though trailing Pierre Berton's *The Arctic Grail*.[60] By early January, *Voice* had moved up to number four.[61] The memoir continued to sell briskly throughout the winter and spring of 1989. And in February 1989 it was nominated for the Ontario Ministry of Culture's Trillium Award.[62]

On page seven of the March 1987 issue of *Tiger*, Ridley College's alumni magazine, there appeared a short article called "Gzowski Requests Your Company," and beside it a photograph of a pensive Peter, his left hand cupping his bearded chin and left cheek. "I'm delighted to announce some plans for a book that will celebrate the school's first hundred years," he wrote. Until he was engaged to write the book, Peter had expressed little or no interest in his alma mater.[63]

The project cost the college $150,000, which included printing costs and salaries for Peter and his designer, Peter Sibbald Brown. Gzowski recommended a printing of three thousand copies, which would result, he explained, in a profit of $30,000 for the college, provided all books were sold. In addition, he suggested the publication of an additional two hundred deluxe copies to be sold at $275 each, thereby adding a further $55,000 to the college's coffers. Judge Stewart Kingstone, chair of centennial celebrations, was persuaded that the book would be a bestseller.

Paul Lewis, the college archivist, ransacked the institution's archives and hired a U-haul to drive the documents up to Peter's Lake Simcoe cottage.[64] Responding to Peter's appeal in the *Tiger*, actor Hume Cronyn mailed a photograph of the large cast of *Scenes from Pickwick*, including the young Cronyn hidden under an enormous judicial wig. John Stubbs provided Peter with his grade thirteen report card, showing the future president of Trent University rather weak in ten of fourteen subjects. From the archival collection, the two Peters chose photographs of sports teams and the chapel, as well as reproductions of letters written to parents. Peter G. and Peter S.B. even included the last seating plan, dated September 1949, of the old dining room, replaced soon thereafter by the present Great Hall. On that seating plan Peter Gzowski's name is visible at table 2a.

Because of space limitations, Hedge Road Press, owned by the two Peters and by Lucinda Vardey, removed much of the text dealing with the 1970s, thus omitting almost entirely Headmaster Richard Bradley, who immediately set to work with Paul Lewis on *Ridley: A Canadian School*, published in 2000. Since only about two thousand copies of Peter's book were sold, the project lost money for the college, though not, apparently, for Hedge Road Press. Peter quickly lost interest in Ridley.[65]

Perhaps because much of Stephen Leacock's writing focuses on a less complicated world that may have existed during the earlier part of the twentieth century, Peter was always drawn to the man and his writing, so much so that he invented, or so it appears, a connection between the famous humorist and McGregor Young. According to Peter, his grandfather Young was a "good friend of Stephen Leacock," and the proof was Leacock's autograph, "To Greg from Stephen," found in Leacock's books in Young's library. However, Peter was never able to locate those autographed books, and in David Staines's edition of Leacock letters, there is no evidence of any Young-Leacock correspondence.

In 1992, Peter wrote a short piece called "Leacock's Smile," based on a 1941 photograph by Yousuf Karsh of Ottawa. What, Peter wondered, made one of the most famous humorists in the world smile so fetchingly for Karsh? "For those of us whose pleasure in his company is limited to the words he left behind," Peter wrote, "the smile is hard to read." On the front cover of the attractive booklet is the Karsh portrait of Leacock. On the back is a photograph of a smiling Peter Gzowski. Both smiles are hard to read.[66] In 1994, Peter wrote the afterword for a short publication of Leacock's "A Lesson on the Links," taken from the humorist's *Short Circuits*. In the afterword, Peter did his best to link Leacock with golf.[67] He wondered if Leacock had ever played the game at the Briars, a highly unlikely event given Leacock's essay called "Why I Refuse to Play Golf."[68]

Also in 1994, Peter was guest speaker at the annual Leacock Award banquet near Orillia. The chair of the evening, fellow broadcaster "Pete" McGarvey, wondered how the well-liquored Peter would get through his talk. Even though McGarvey had announced that smoking wasn't allowed, Peter chain-smoked at McGarvey's table while fidgeting and scribbling notes. As usual his speech was witty and appropriate, though it did reinforce Peter's misconception that Leacock was a kindly humorist. In truth, from time to time Leacock painted the darker side of small-town Canada, such as the suicide of the young mining speculator Fizzlechip in "The Speculations of Jefferson Thorpe," one of the stories in *Sunshine Sketches of a Little Town*.[69]

In 1995, Peter narrated an introduction for a taped version of two rare recordings of the voice of Leacock. In fact, like many other English Canadians, Peter had thought that the real voice of Leacock was that of actor John Drainie. Peter knew, he said in the introduction, that the great humorist liked to listen to radio.[70] But could Leacock do Leacock? wondered Peter. Of course, he could, and the proof was in two recordings.[71]

Beginning in 1989, Peter contributed monthly columns to *Canadian Living* on the subject of homey, throwaway topics such as "The Joys of Sissie Scrabble," "Summer Memories, Winter Dreams," and "John: A Couple of Grey-haired Grandfathers." In 1993, when these articles, short, personal, and not of the quality of his magazine articles of the 1960s, were published under the title *Selected Columns from Canadian Living*, the book quickly rose to number one in paperback non-fiction, beating out Stuart McLean's *Welcome Home* and John Ralston Saul's *Voltaire's Bastards*.[72] In 1998, when *Friends, Moments, Countryside*, the second of two collections of his *Canadian Living* articles was published, it, too, was enthusiastically received by his fans. During this period of his life, he contributed to almost a dozen books.[73]

As well as for broadcasting and writing, Peter wanted to be remembered for something altruistic. In 1986 he founded an annual golf tournament, the PGI (Peter Gzowski Invitational), which over the ensuing fifteen years raised millions of dollars for literacy. The idea first arose in Peter's mind, it seems, from a series of talks by Charles Haines during the 1984–85 season of *Morningside*. Every Monday morning the professor of English at Carleton University informed Peter about the abuses of the English language, which Haines blamed on the high level of "functional illiteracy" in Canada, as high as 40 percent. "A functional illiterate," Haines told Peter, "has difficulty reading brand names in supermarkets, and greater difficulty writing an address on an envelope that even a case-hardened postal clerk can read."[74]

Peter never acknowledged Haines's contribution. Instead, he attributed the idea to himself, Gill Howard, and John O'Leary. In 1985, Peter and Gill purchased a cottage on the first fairway of the Briars Golf Glub near Sutton. With the precision of a novelist, Peter always remembered the exact moment when the idea for a tournament was conceived. As he contemplated "a challenging six-iron into the eight green and revelled in the summer air and the sound of the birds," he began to wonder about holding a tournament for a few of his friends. "If I did it right," he recalled thinking, "I might even raise a little money." Peter needed a cause. His mind went back to an interview on *Morningside*, not with Haines but with a Palestinian woman who had become literate only after moving to Canada.[75] Meantime, John O'Leary of Frontier College, which had been established at the turn of the twentieth century to teach literacy to lumberjacks and miners, requested help with fundraising for literacy. The marriage of *conjoncture* and epiphany proved irresistible, and *voilà!* Peter had his cause.[76]

The first PGI took place on Thursday, June 5, 1986. Each of the eighty players paid $200, and the proceeds, about half from fees and the other half from corporate sponsorships, were turned over to Frontier College.[77] For that first tournament, Ontario Premier David Peterson arrived by helicopter to join Ken Dryden, Scott Young, Joey Slinger, Diane Francis, Lorne Rubenstein, and Michael de Pencier. Peter appointed Dennis Lee poet laureate of the first PGI, and each participant received a copy of the first volume of Peter's *Morningside Papers*, as well as a radio donated by Canadian Tire.[78] Within five years the tournaments had spread from coast to coast to coast. In 1990, Peter launched the first of the Red Barn evenings, which were held at the historic barn-cum-theatre[79] at Jackson's Point. Most of the entertainers in 1990 and subsequent years were friends from *Morningside*.[80] The logistics of each PGI were complicated.[81] A good deal of the revenue came from private firms such as Mother Parker's Tea Company, Scott's Chicken Villa, Coles Books, Superior Propane, Inc.,

At the first PGI, Peter, Ontario Premier David Peterson, and publisher Jack McClelland carry on an animated conversation.

(Courtesy Trent University Archives, Gzowski fonds, 92-015, box 1, folder 34)

Hillebrand Estates Winery, Loblaw's President's Choice, Labatt, David Geller Associates, and the New Zealand Lamb Co., Ltd.

Until he became too ill to travel, Peter attended all PGIs across the country. In 1991 he was in Charlottetown. For the "night before" entertainment, Don Harron and Norman Campbell wrote *Pete of Green Gables* in which Peter played Matthew Cuthbert, capably assisted by Cynthia Dale and Peter Mansbridge, Mike Duffy and Catherine McKinnon. By that year, the PGIs had grown so large that Grant Fleming was hired as PGI's first full-time employee.[82]

There was one "celebrity" who was apparently not impressed by the tournaments. In 1996, in spite of being personally solicited by Peter — "We've put you in a good spot, I think — right near the end, after Cassandra Vasik and just before Ben Heppner"— Pierre Berton had cancelled his appearance and therefore didn't swing clubs with Lorne Elliott, Rick Mercer, Jan Wong, Brent Carver, and Marjorie Harris.[83] The next year Shelley Ambrose tried to entice Berton to attend the 100th PGI, and with it, the evening of entertainment at the Red Barn. She listed many of the celebrities, from Murray McLauchlan to Ambrose's husband, C. David Johnson, Holly Cole, Tom Cochrane, Michael Burgess, and again Ben Heppner. Berton's response was a noncommittal "I'll go if I can, but what do they want me to do?"[84]

Did Peter's tournaments lower the rate of adult illiteracy in Canada? In an article in *Maclean's* in May 1961, Barbara Moon estimated that there were two million illiterate Canadians, or about 10 percent of the population.[85] Since the criteria for calculating numbers vary from year to year, it is difficult to make comparisons among rates in 1900, 1961, and 2002.

Importantly, literacy was a safe cause. Throughout his career Peter carefully chose his causes. Through PEN Canada he attempted to alleviate oppression of writers around the globe. In October 1983, he joined other journalists on the Polish Journalists' Aid Committee to assist journalists who had lost their jobs when martial law was imposed in Poland in 1981.[86] Two months later Peter and several of his NHL heroes laced up skates to raise money for the champion cyclist Jocelyn Lovell, who had been paralyzed in a road accident.[87] Peter also campaigned on conservation and environmental causes.[88]

Peter's fans would be forgiven for assuming that he always supported worthy causes. There was, however, one group of people he was loath to support. In 1975, when John Damien, retired jockey and member of the Ontario Racing Commission, was fired for being gay, Peter was called upon to help rectify a gross injustice. Many of his colleagues and friends such as Marie-Claire Blais, Pierre Berton, Patrick Watson, Barbara Frum, John Robert Colombo, Allan King, Jane Rule, Jack Batten, Margaret Gibson, Andreas Schroeder, and Brian Linehan signed a petition that made public their support for Damien. In addition, Margaret Atwood, Mordecai Richler, and June Callwood, as well as Claude Jutras, Gordon Pinsent, Doris Anderson, Kate Reid, and Charmion King, lent their names and their photographs to the cause. Although he was well aware of the mistreatment of Damien, Peter's name wasn't among the list of petitioners.[89]

Whether the golf tournaments lowered the illiteracy rate or not, they did succeed one way — they gave Peter a chance to play the role of celebrity. In Regina, after observing Peter on the links and later during the evening of entertainment, Dennis Ball wondered how much of the tournaments was for literacy and how much was for self-aggrandisement.[90] Over the years, some of Peter's colleagues and friends had also noticed his yearning for fame. In 1980, for instance, Martin O'Malley reported that an unnamed critic in attendance that day said that Peter "spent a lot of time trying to be famous." O'Malley agreed and said so in a column in the *Toronto Star*.[91]

Celebrities, Richard Nielsen once pointed out, often lead anxious lives. Behind their masks of self-confidence lurks massive insecurity, for they know their elevated status can be withdrawn at any moment by their fans. Hollywood stars such as Marilyn Monroe had recognized the fragility of fame. "In this celebrity age," Peter C. Newman once noted, "shelf lives are measured by the span of new moons."[92] In an article entitled "The Dark Side of Saint Peter," published in March 1997, Dave

In Whitehorse, Yukon, June 1991, Peter and friends, including C. David Johnson, Vicki Gabereau, Alison and Tom Jackson, and Shelley Ambrose during another PGI. Gzowski and Jackson shared a common destiny as chancellors of Trent University.

(Courtesy Trent University Archives, Gzowski fonds, 01-004, box 1, folder 2)

Cameron wondered if there was any connection between Peter's off-air truculence and "the enormous self-doubt and need for acclamation that comes from being a celebrity."[93] Peter himself was never unaware of the fragility of status. "We made gods of them," he wrote of hockey heroes such as Bobby Hull. "And then, when they were thirty-five or forty ... we took it all away from them at once."[94] Peter had warned radio and television host Vicki Gabereau how quickly stars are forgotten once they leave "the prime-time fray."[95]

There were signs of anxiety at one PGI. One evening David Morton and his wife, along with Murray McLauchlan and Bonnie Patterson, president of Trent University, arrived at the Gzowski-Howard compound. When Gill opened the door, she looked worried. They found Peter in his study with a drink in one hand and a cigarette in the other.

Apparently oblivious to the house full of guests engaged in animated conversation, he was staring out at the lake. After much persuading, David, Bonnie, and Murray finally convinced him to join his own party.[96]

In order to gain prestige and publicity for themselves, and at the same time to honour an achiever, universities are always pleased to grant honorary degrees. In total, Peter was so honoured by twelve post-secondary institutions. He received a doctor of letters from the University of New Brunswick on Thursday, May 24, 1984. Walking just behind Peter in the procession to the Aitken Centre, Premier Richard Hatfield showed Peter how to hide one last cigarette up the sleeve of a gown.[97] "This

En route to the Aitken Centre where Peter was about to be granted an honorary degree from the University of New Brunswick, Fredericton, May 24, 1984. On Peter's right is James Downey, president and vice-chancellor. Richard Hatfield, just behind, had just taught Peter how to hide a burning cigarette in the sleeve of his gown.

(Courtesy Trent University Archives, Gzowski fonds, 92-015, box 1, folder 7)

degree is the greatest single honour of my life," Peter told 1,055 graduates, parents, and faculty. His beard was shaved, he explained, because
the Edmonton Oilers had just won the Stanley Cup.[98] In 1987, when
the University of Windsor bestowed an honorary degree, Peter told his
audience that "I stay up late at night reading books whose frequently
over-interviewed and occasionally hungover authors I must try to make
sound fresh in the morning."[99]

Queen's University in Kingston honoured Peter on June 2, 1990.
Cathy Perkins wrote the citation, which was addressed by Principal
David C. Smith to Chancellor Agnes Benidickson:

> Madam Chancellor, by authority of the Senate, I have
> the honour to present to you, that he may receive at your
> hands the degree of Doctor of Laws, *honoris causa*, Peter
> John Gzowski, Officer of the Order of Canada; godfa-
> ther of Confederation; and great-great-grandson of a
> pioneering nation-builder; groundbreaking journalist,
> magazine maven, influential, and acclaimed broadcaster,
> bestselling author, passionate hockey fan, and genial
> circuit-rider for Canadian publishing; the CBC's uncer-
> emonious master of ceremonies, who has earned many
> doctorates for taking this country's pulse most mornings
> for two decades and become a 'master of letters' — as
> his *Morningside Papers* clearly attest; whose curios-
> ity stretches from sea to shining sea and whose voice,
> whether public or private, is the voice of this country
> in the morning, speaking straight to the hearts of his
> '*Morningside* Million' and tapping wellsprings of patrio-
> tism, humanity, and zesty individualism; who is our avid
> ally in the teaching of arts, science, and medicine and
> who brings Canadian history, geography, politics, and
> current affairs to vivid life and lively debate on farms
> and fishing boats, in urban kitchens, classrooms, truck
> cabs, and wilderness camps; whom we especially salute
> in this International Year of Literacy for his innovative

raising of awareness, workers, and resources for the cause in Canada and who, in his recent Arctic tournament, took the sport of golf to new latitudes and longitudes; who is, in summary, an uncommon Canadian, a national treasure, whose personal and journalistic ideals strike a deep chord within a university that shares his dedication to serving the community, the nation, and the community of nations.[100]

Peter's address that day was on the subject of media herding. Imagine, he invited his audience, if all media were located on an island and someone shouts, "News! News!" Every reporter stampedes to the same beach. When coverage reaches the saturation point, a scout shouts "News!" from another place, and the island nearly tips when all the media rush to the new spot. What was missing was perspective and balance.[101] The speech owed something to Gay Talese, who once wrote that "journalists travel in packs with transferable tension and they can only guess to what extent their presence in large numbers ignites an incident, turns people on.... Nobody knows whether people make news or news make people.... When the press is absent, politicians have been known to cancel their speeches ..."[102] In 1995, thanks to Professor Michael Bliss and others, Peter received an honorary degree from the University of Toronto. A year later Acadia University, too, granted Peter an honorary degree.

In October 1995, along with Denys Arcand, Anne Murray, and Maureen Forrester, Peter was awarded a Governor General's Award for the Performing Arts.[103] A week after he concluded his fifteen-year run of *Morningside*, Peter flew to New York where he received a Peabody Award, named for the American capitalist George Foster Peabody. Given annually since 1940, the award was one of the most prestigious anywhere.[104]

There was one advantage for Peter in not being on the air five days a week. In June 1999, Peter Goddard, the *Toronto Star*'s radio reviewer, noted that "with Peter Gzowski's retirement from *Morningside*, Gzowski-bashing seems to be on the wane."[105] On the wane, yes, but not completely banished. Later that year Geoff Pevere, inspired by the movie *Being John Malkovich*, imagined a Canadian movie called *Being Peter*

Gzowski, in which "a skid full of remaindered McClelland & Stewart books is moved to reveal a hole leading directly to the world according to Canada's most beloved public broadcaster. Travellers find themselves engaging in cozy conversations with like-minded Canadian institutions, struggling to keep honorary titles straight, and taking lots of naps to cope with [the] sheer pressure of holding the country together."[106]

— 16 —

"Oh, Stop Being Mavis Gallant,"
1997–2002

Fundamentally, all writing is about the same thing:
it's about dying, about the brief flicker of time we have here,
and the frustrations that it creates.

— *Mordecai Richler,* Quoted in Time, *May 31, 1971*

"Oh, stop being Mavis Gallant," Peter blurted out to one of his two breakfast companions. In September 1997, Peter and Bonnie Burnard flew to Paris where they joined Mavis Gallant to choose the five finalists from the sixty-five novels submitted for the Giller Prize. The year before, Burnard's *The Good House* had won, beating out the odds-on favourite, Timothy Findley's *Pilgrim*. Mavis and Peter were replacing Carol Shields and David Staines, the previous year's judges.[1] (Later, on November 4, at the Giller Prize Gala, Peter, as chair of the jury panel, would announce the winner, Mordecai Richler's *Barney's Version*.)[2]

Peter seemed ill at ease in Paris. Apparently, he refused to explore the city by himself. In an inebriated haze, he spent much of his time in his hotel room. The Luxembourg Gardens and Montparnasse Cemetery were but a short walk away, and the Seine and Notre Dame not much farther. In fact, the whole of central Paris was at his feet. One day Burnard offered to take him anywhere he wanted to go. "I want to see the Seine," he announced. So Burnard led him there. He looked up and down the river. "Now I want to go home," he told Burnard.

One morning over breakfast Peter grew petulant when he discovered that Gallant, quite by chance, had ordered exactly what he was having — sausage, eggs, and toast. Normally, the short-story writer started her day *à la Parisienne* with a piece of baguette and strong coffee. Unaccustomed to large breakfasts, she was constantly hungry. Over espresso one day on the top floor of the Village Voice Bookshop near Boulevard St-Germain, the three judges were chatting amicably when Peter suddenly ordered Gallant to "stop being Mavis Gallant." Gallant was shocked. What on earth did he mean? "Oh, probably something about being too intuitive," the writer speculated a few years later. Did Peter worry that he was becoming a character in one of Gallant's short stories? Did he think she was going to dissect him as deftly as she did most of her characters, for instance, a male artist in "Speck's Idea"?

> An artist's widow was bound to be suspicious and adamant. She had survived the discomfort and confusion of her marriage; had lived through the artist's drinking, his avarice, his affairs, his obsession with constipation, his feuds and quarrels, his cowardice with dealers, his hypocrisy with critics, his depressions (which always fell at the most joyous seasons, blighting Christmas and spring); and then — oh justice! — she had outlasted him.[3]

In that description of a male artist, Gallant might well have been depicting someone like Peter. Since Gallant is to Paris what Christopher Isherwood was to Berlin, each of them cameras whose lenses have captured the essence of those two European cities at two points during the twentieth century, Peter may have suspected he was being captured and analyzed.

Peter, so it would seem, had always feared becoming a character in someone else's imagination. He was always uncomfortable if he thought he was being analyzed. In his article on volleyball, published in 1966 in *Saturday Night*, he expressed relief that, among the volleyball players who gathered each summer weekend to play near their Toronto Island cottages, there were "no novelists or psychologists around taking notes."[4]

His unusual reaction to the male protagonist in Sylvia Fraser's *A Casual Affair* bespoke Peter's dread that someone might intuit a deep hurt or trait of character he wanted to keep secret. On Thursday night, March 23, 1978, as the second season of *90 Minutes Live* was winding down, Peter had talked to Fraser about her new novel. Three times he popped into the makeup room to tell Fraser how happy he was that she was on the show. A few minutes later, as the two of them sat waiting to go live to Newfoundland and the Maritimes, Peter blurted out, "Is your book about me?" Fraser stared at him. Was he daft? she wondered. Seconds after the cameras began to roll, Peter turned to Fraser, smiled, and announced, "We used to call girls like you mmmm-breakers."[5]

The "eye" of a camera often made Peter uncomfortable. "With television," he once noted, "the subject becomes something different ... the presence of an observer changes the condition of the observed ..."[6] When Don Hall, at the request of one of Peter's producers, arrived at the Regina studios of the CBC in May 1997 to photograph Peter's last visit to the city as host of *Morningside*, Peter put up quite a ruckus. Only after much cajoling did he consent to have his picture taken.[7] A human eye made him even more uncomfortable. In December 1978, in one of his *Toronto Star* columns, he wrote about dropping into Fran's Restaurant near Yonge and College Streets in Toronto, probably for coffee or breakfast before proceeding to an early-morning shift at the CBC. In the restaurant, he was made uneasy by what he called "the gaze of the tinselled men who used to make Fran's the last of their late-night rounds."[8] Even a curious child could make Peter uncomfortable. In 1991 while dining in a bistro on Yonge Street at the western edge of Toronto's Rosedale, Peter became aware of a four-year-old boy who sat nearby with his parents. The little boy began to stare at Peter. Perhaps the child was fascinated by his beard? Finally, Peter rose from his table, shuffled over to the table of his observer, and ordered his parents, "Tell your son to stop staring at me!"[9]

A portrait artist's perceptive eye once made Peter testy. In June 1996 when Elaine Goble was commissioned to paint Peter, she discovered how irritated he could become when he was being closely observed. She arrived at the CBC Broadcasting Centre and waited in what she described as a tiny office smelling of cigarettes, damp wool, and pencil erasers. Peter walked in, and according to Goble, "checked the time on his watch, raised his eyebrows, and said nothing." Goble introduced herself. Peter said nothing for a few minutes. "Finally," Goble recalled later, "he crossed his arms, leaned tiredly against his chair, and asked, 'Where do you want me?'" When she asked for a smile, Peter responded, "I don't *do* smiles." As Goble was taking photographs of Peter, he shouted, "Shelley, get me that file *now!*" Soon Goble packed her bag and departed.[10]

Once back in Toronto from Paris, during the autumn of 1997, Peter began to invent details of his visit there in "Paree, Oui, Oui," a brief article published in the *Globe and Mail*, then republished as "Memoirs of a Boulevardier" in *Canadian Living* the following January. He extolled the virtues of Paris, a city that was, he claimed, one of his favourites. "Whenever I go to Paris, I like to stay at an unpretentious but comfortable and friendly hotel close to Montparnasse," he told his readers. "As all experienced Paris hands know, you should walk everywhere you can in Paris." He listed the Seine, Notre Dame, and the Louvre. And it was *de rigueur* to dine at the Dôme. Peter was, it seems, positioning himself among the literati of Paris, including Ernest Hemingway, Jean-Paul Sartre, and Simone de Beauvoir, as well as Mordecai Richler and Mavis Gallant, all of whom had dined and sipped wine and engaged in political and literary discussions at the Dôme and the nearby Deux Magots. In other words, Peter's version of his visit to Paris, an artful blend of fact and fiction, mostly the latter, was literary journalism at its best.[11]

—•—

In the autumn of 1997, in order to take advantage of Peter's enormous popularity as host of *Morningside*, McClelland & Stewart published *The Morningside Years*, which included a CD of what Peter considered to be his best interviews. Stuart McLean's episode with the dead cricket was given a reprise, as was an interview with Roberta Bondar and fellow astronauts, though Bondar's comment to Peter that he would make a good astronaut because he wasn't wearing shoes or socks that day isn't preserved on the CD.[12] Also reproduced was an interview with Marilyn Bell and the other women who had conquered Lake Ontario; Robertson Davies and a new opera called *Jezebel*; the school principal who ate a worm; Prime Ministers Mulroney and Chrétien, who defended their policies; Margaret Atwood, who spoke in plosive *p*'s to tell Peter about her children's book *Princess Prunella and the Purple Peanut*; and Ben Heppner, who sang "O Canada" during the final few minutes of the Red River Rally, which raised relief money in the wake of the great flood of 1997.

The book included transcripts of interviews with Alice Munro, whom Peter called "the first important writer I ever tried to interview on the radio"; Robertson Davies, who in his eighties was "at the height of his gracious and erudite conversational powers"; W.O. Mitchell ("one of a kind"); Margaret Atwood ("always a delight"); Margaret Laurence ("I was touched by her"); and Timothy Findley ("And, may I say, simply a lovely guy to talk to"). Between these transcripts were the inevitable recipes (peanut butter squares and easy chocolate cake), "Letters Home" from Nairobi and Bhutgan, and some of Peter's cherished letters on topics such as galoshes and whistling anaesthetists. Peter and his editors also included the *Morningside* drama *Mourning Dove* by Emil Sher, a play loosely based on the story of Robert Latimer, who had ended the life of his severely handicapped daughter. Also reproduced was *Morningside*'s trial of Louis Riel, Peter's interviews with four scientists, Nancy Huggett's journal of life with her handicapped daughter, and "Voices from the North." Some of Fred McGuinness's "Letters from Section Seventeen," his *Morningside* reports from near Brandon, Manitoba, were also incorporated. *The Morningside Years* was illustrated by black-and-white photographs, including three shots of the finale in Moose Jaw, and by cartoons of Peter, some of them by Terry Mosher. It concluded with "A Fond Farewell" from Robert Fulford, who, evoking Marshall McLuhan and Pierre Berton, contended that *Morningside* had "burrowed so deeply into our lives" that it was "intimately linked with national dreams and disappointments."[13]

At about the same time Peter and chef Virginia Careless developed a proposal for a cooking show that would demonstrate historic Canadian recipes. They approached Norflicks, a film company owned by producer Richard Nielsen. *Cooking the Old-Fashioned Way* was to be shot during the winter and spring of 1998 for broadcast in the autumn of 1999. Norflicks offered to pay Peter $5,000 per show, and there was even talk of publishing a cookbook. Not a single television network was interested. Peter did manage, however, to make an appearance in late 1997 on *This Hour Has 22 Minutes*. After discussing Canadian identity in bars and a tattoo parlour in Halifax, Peter and the show's Rick Mercer ended the episode in a jail cell in Dartmouth.[14]

Peter remained an esteemed guest and host. In late October 1997, Professor Michael Peterman invited him to participate in a dinner in the Great Hall of Champlain College at Trent University to honour Timothy Findley. "Peter's job," Peterman recalled, "was to say a few words about Tiff, to oversee a reading by Margaret Atwood, and to introduce performances by Sylvia Tyson, Joe Sealy, Peter Togni, Veronica Tennant, and Erin and Donnell Leahy." At the head table a forlorn-looking Peter scribbled a few words on a napkin. When he rose to speak, however, Peter "found his rhythm immediately and," Peterman recalled, "sailed through the evening." Two years later Peterman invited Peter to be the guest speaker at the first annual fundraising dinner of the Friends of Bata Library. He talked about libraries, writers, and artists, and about his mother's days at the Carnegie Library in Galt. When Peter departed at eleven o'clock, Peterman marvelled at his stamina and admired his "commitment to institutions and individuals he loved and valued," as well as his ability "to communicate that love."[15]

Gzowski in Conversation was Peter's last television series. Mary Young Leckie, a production manager and line producer for CBC, NBC, and TVOntario, was a great fan of *Morningside* and its host, and identified with what she later called "Peter's vision of Canadian identity." Almost immediately after the end of *Morningside*, Young persuaded the slightly reluctant Peter to do a series of informal conversations with successful Canadians. Peter insisted on a full hour, though during the second year of the show he agreed that a half-hour program worked better. The shows were shot in Toronto and Montreal. When a teleprompter was suggested, Peter resisted, but soon changed his mind. The show was live-to-tape and allowed for editing.[16]

Gzowski in Conversation was broadcast on CBC-TV over two summers, beginning the last week of April 1998 when the guests were the Nielsen brothers — Erik the politician and Leslie the actor. Other guests on subsequent shows were Steve Smith, Rick Mercer, and Bruce McCulloch, who explained and demonstrated the components of good comedy. Two talented fiddlers, the classically trained Angèle Dubeau and the Celtic-style Donnell Leahy, were paired on another show. Gordon Lightfoot, Murray McLauchlan, Diana Krall, Jann Arden, and Brent Carver, who at the beginning of the show reached forward to give Peter a reassuring pat on the arm, were featured on other programs. In Montreal, Luc Plamondon, well-known in Quebec and Paris for his opera *Starmania*, and the politician and scholar Jacques Parizeau, talked to Peter about music and politics. Evelyn Hart and Donald Sutherland focused on dance and film, while Natalie MacMaster, Conrad Black, and Doris McCarthy discussed their specialties, music, the media, and art.

In June 1998, Peter wrote about *Gzowski in Conversation* in *Canadian Living*. He was pleased that the show had "no band, no studio and no glaring lights — as little HMU[17] as I can get away with." The set, he noted, was hung with Canadian art, some of it his own. He had made some concessions to wardrobe — "snazzy new shoes" and socks long enough "to hide my unglamorous shins."

At the end of its second summer, in 1999, the show wasn't renewed by the CBC. Later that year Analekta produced a CD called *Gzowski in Compilation*, which included an introduction by Peter, whose thin, reedy voice must have shocked his fans. There were also contributions from *Gzowski in Conversation* guests such as Jann Arden, Natalie MacMaster, and Kate McGarrigle, the last with her equally talented offspring, Rufus and Martha. Peter himself sang a rather embarrassing version of "I Want to Be Seduced."

During his post-*Morningside* years, Peter did three series for CBC Radio. One was called *Radio Cabaret* and began in September 1998. Recorded live at theatres across the country, the show replaced Stuart McLean's *Vinyl Café* once a month. The music was eclectic, from jazz to classical to country. One of the programs recorded at the Red Barn Theatre was a blend of rural humour by Marsha Boulton and music by Cindy Church.[18] On *Gzowski's Forum*, broadcast Friday evenings at 8:05 p.m., starting in January 1998, Peter interviewed Dalton Camp, Chantal Hébert, Robert Mason Lee, Judy Rebick, Bob Rae, Frank McKenna, and others on politics, society, and economics. His last radio show, *Some of the Best Minds of Our Time*, was aired on summer Sundays from 1998 to 2000 as the third hour of *This Morning — The Sunday Edition*. Some of these best minds belonged to Malcolm Gladwell and Chief Justice Beverley McLachlin, as well as to scientists, philosophers, poets, economists, and authors.[19] On August 2, 1998, perhaps to answer critics who claimed the host of *Morningside* had personified a Canada that had ceased to exist, Peter interviewed Soushima Datt, the founder of Canada's first East Indian radio station.

He was, it seems, always writing. In 1998 he penned the foreword to Rick Mercer's *Streeters: Rants and Raves from This Hour Has 22 Minutes*. Peter was also asked to write a foreword for *Total Gretzky*, published in 1999 to celebrate the life and art of the Great One as he prepared to face the challenges of retirement from active hockey.[20] In a beautifully written mood piece, Peter summarized his long relationship with Wayne, from the first time they talked on *This Country in the Morning* to his last interview with Wayne a quarter-century later on *Gzowski in Conversation*. When Wayne first met Peter, the thirteen-year-old soprano called him "sir." Peter predicted Gretzky, who reminded him of a squirrel, would eventually make a million dollars. When Wayne was playing major junior hockey in Sault Ste. Marie, Peter and his film crew drove to the Soo to interview him for *90 Minutes Live*. It was Wayne, Peter reminded readers, who had urged Peter to contact Peter Pocklington for permission to write a book about the Edmonton Oilers. Over time Wayne moved from "sir" to "Peter" to "Gzowsk," which signified perhaps that Peter had become a member of Gretzky's inner circle. It was the same name used by the boys at Ridley College, once they had accepted Peter as one of their own. In the article about Wayne, Peter informed readers that he sometimes called Wayne "Gretz." During hockey scrums, Wayne occasionally winked at Peter as if to signify he was keeping a secret known only to him and Peter. Once, in Boston, a nervous Wayne had asked Peter to accompany him early in the morning to NBC's studios where he was to make his debut on American network TV on *The Today Show*. "I was happy to oblige," Peter wrote in the foreword to *Total Gretzky*. A few years later in July 1988, Peter was unable to accept an invitation to Wayne's wedding, though he did watch on television twenty-four days later as Wayne wept at the news that Peter Pocklington was selling him for US$15 million to the Los Angeles Kings. Later Peter worried that Wayne had "gone downtown" in the big city, a term that implied too much sophistication and a diminution of manliness. Years later Peter was relieved to receive one last opportunity to interview his favourite hockey player on *Gzowski in Conversation*, and his only regret was that the young woman at the office of Mary Young Leckie hadn't greeted Wayne with "How do you do, sir?"

In 2000, along with Mordecai Richler, Jack Granatstein, Alison Gordon, Anne Kingston, and Catherine Annau, Peter contributed a chapter called "Watch Me, 1968 to 1974" to the *Trudeau Albums*, a picture-book tribute to Pierre Trudeau.[21] Like the article on Gretzky, Peter, ever the skilled literary journalist, placed himself inside the story that traced his relationship with Trudeau from the first interview in 1961 in Outremont to the final *Morningside* interview with the retired prime minister. The beautifully illustrated and carefully nuanced article, which discussed the October Crisis of 1970 and the National Energy Policy of the mid-1970s, as well as Trudeau's sometimes difficult private life, proved that Peter's skills as a magazine writer hadn't diminished since his days at *Maclean's* in the 1960s.

From late 2000 to his death, Peter wrote a weekly column for the *Globe and Mail* on identity, politics, and language. On January 6, 2001, he wrote in praise of the CBC and Radio-Canada's television show *A*

People's History, a series on Canadian history. "The national *public* broadcaster," he told his readers, "has never been more important to the survival of our national identity."[22] On April 28, 2001, Peter scorned Canadian Alliance leader Stockwell Day's publicity gesture the previous year when he jet-skied on Okanagan Lake.[23]

Peter also wrote three columns for *FiftyPlus* magazine, which was (and still is under its new name *Zoomer*) aimed at boomers, seniors, and retirees. In October 2001, he wrote about the complications of new technology, from computers to VCRs to beeping wristwatches. In December 2001, his topic was unforgettable historic moments such as Pearl Harbor, the assassination of John F. Kennedy, and the recent destruction of the World Trade Center towers. He also wrote a short piece describing his irritation at the pseudo-friendliness of strangers such as a parcel courier, a pharmacist, and a policeman, all of whom, at one time or another, had called him "Peter" rather than the old-fashioned "Mr. Gzowski" or "sir." A week before his death he called the magazine's editor, Bonnie Baker Cowan, and asked for an extension on an article he was attempting to do for the April issue.[24] In place of the unwritten piece, Baker Cowan wrote an article about Peter, illustrated by a photograph of "Peter's fantasy dinner" with ten women considered by him to be the most interesting women in Canada. The women — Dr. Mary-Wynne Ashford, Alice Munro, Maude Barlow, Nellie Cournoyea, Evelyn Hart, Dinah Christie, Debbie Brill, Barbara McDougall, Margaret Somerville, and lawyer Dulcie McCallum — had been invited to Peter's fifty-sixth birthday party on July 13, 1990.[25]

Peter's final book was a collection of his favourite pieces, all previously published in magazines, newspapers, his memoirs, and other books. *A Peter Gzowski Reader*, which appeared in hardcover in 2001 and in paperback soon after his death, took Peter on an autobiographical journey that included his boyhood in Galt, Ridley College, Labrador, Timmins, *The Varsity*, Moose Jaw, *Maclean's*, his near-death experience while sailing off Antigua in 1984, and his article about his smoking cure, published in *FiftyPlus* in June 2001.

—•—

Since 1986, Peter had been an Officer of the Order of Canada. In 1999 Governor General Roméo LeBlanc appointed him Companion, the highest of the Order's three rankings. Now he was the equal of Pierre Berton, who had been a Companion of the Order since 1986. Also in June 1999, Peter was installed as chancellor of Trent University.[26] He asked for his own office and was given one down the hall from the president's on the ground floor of Bata Library. On investiture day, someone asked Peter about the role of a chancellor. "I run the joint" was his answer.[27] Although increasingly infirm of body, so much so that a Trent staff member drove him around the campus in a golf cart, he never missed graduation ceremonies, held under an unforgiving sun. President Bonnie Patterson usually managed to persuade him to wear socks for the occasion. Tim, a coffee wholesaler from Omemee near Peterborough, was at one graduation ceremony to witness his nephew accept a degree from Chancellor Gzowski. "I just want to tell you how much I have enjoyed you over the years," Tim told him.[28]

Chancellor Peter Gzowski at his first Trent University convocation, May 1999.

(Courtesy Trent University Archives, Photo Collection, "Gzowski")

Like many of his other friends, President Patterson, or "Bonnie" as she was called at Trent, attempted to dissuade him from smoking. One day during the summer of 1999, the chancellor and the president were dining on salmon at the Peterborough Golf and Country Club. Peter lit up his first cigarette, even though he knew Bonnie had a mild allergy to smoke. "I am enjoying this smoked salmon," the president told him with a grin. "Smoked salmon is the best kind," Peter replied with his own grin. Because he couldn't smoke inside Bata Library, he ambled past the archives where most of his papers were stored, down a corridor, and out to the loading dock where he smoked in clear view of the university's archivist.

In early 2000, Peter entered a detoxification clinic, and, of course, wrote about the experience: "At 9:30 on the morning of February 7, 2000, I pulled into the parking lot of a four-storey building in the suburbs of Toronto, rolled down the window of my ashtray on wheels, and flicked the butt of my last Rothmans into a snowbank." As he shuffled toward the main entrance of the West Park Health Centre, he thought to himself that his heavy drinking of the past few years, a family trait, was enough to qualify him to enter the clinic.

After several weeks, he was off both cigarettes and booze. Some of his friends wondered if it had been worth the agony. A few months later he developed a chest infection, which turned into chronic emphysema. His closest non-human companions became an oxygen tank and a walker.[29] More than a year after his sojourn in the clinic, Peter wrote about life on oxygen. Either Gillian Howard or he had to call ahead to restaurants to make sure the toilets were on the main floor, and in hotels his room had to be close to an elevator. Immobility brought one benefit — he had more time, if not as much energy, to read and write.[30]

No matter how tired Peter felt, he presided over Trent's Chancellor's Evenings, which were sponsored by Quaker Oats, no doubt thanks to Peter's friendship with David Morton, the company's president. One session in March 2000 dealt with the topic of the brain drain. Featured guests were Heather Reisman, CEO of Indigo Books; John McCallum, vice-president and chief economist of the Royal Bank; and John Helliwell, professor of economics at the University of British Columbia. When

Robert Pritchard, president of the University of Toronto, cancelled his appearance, Harry Kitchen, a professor of geography at Trent, stepped in. As the four panellists discussed the topic and answered questions from the audience, Peter sat in the middle, playing the moderator, sometimes bemused, other times earnest or slightly bored. Later that year the topic of a Chancellor's Evening was "Why Study the Liberal Arts?" On another occasion, Rob Winslow, artistic director of the 4th Line Theatre at Millbrook near Peterborough, was on a panel to discuss Canadian culture. Over dinner beforehand, Winslow had told Peter he would be honoured to have the former *Morningside* host as an honorary member of 4th Line. "Why don't you appoint me chancellor of Millbrook?" replied Peter. Later, in his introductory remarks, Peter spoke highly of 4th Line Theatre and called Winslow one of his heroes for promoting Canadian culture.

"It was an odd night for me," Winslow recalls today, "as I was a last-minute addition since Peter had originally planned to speak solo and then changed his mind and requested a panel discussion on Canadian culture, which included Leah McLaren and writer Andrew Pyper. They were both much more articulate and speedy in their responses than I was, being on Millbrook rhythm, and I remember Peter looking to me to defend Canadian culture ..." Arguing that too much Canadian culture dwelt on rural themes, McLaren and Pyper failed to see the value of Winslow's specialty, that of discovering "strange and interesting tales of all kinds" in "the twilight of our rural and village way of life."[31] When Winslow mentioned theatre in Saskatchewan, Peter congratulated him for his correct pronunciation of the Prairie province.[32]

Peter also felt it his duty to accept invitations to official dinners. In 2001, in a wheelchair and accompanied by his oxygen tank and tubing hooked to his nose, he arrived at a banquet at Otonabee College to honour Trent financial donors. Peter managed to give a short talk on the importance of the liberal arts to Canada. If they were important, one member of the audience asked him, why was Trent, along with most other universities, investing so much money in the sciences.[33]

—•—

President Bonnie Patterson had been hired in 1998 by a board, assisted by a finding committee composed of businessmen,[34] most of whom believed the university would be better off financially without its Victorian houses near the centre of town. In fact, Bonnie and her board probably had little choice, according to one observer at the time, who was certain the university, after enduring a couple of faculty strikes, was on the verge of bankruptcy.[35] Bonnie and her board managed to keep the university running, but many professors and students objected to centralization and rationalization. The old ties with the folk of Peterborough, they argued, not to mention the vision of Trent's founding president, Tom Symons, would be forever lost. The dissidents wanted to perpetuate the college-centred system, with its small classes and intimate tutorials, and they believed that the president and her board weren't open to discussion on those and other issues. However, unlike a couple of her predecessors, Bonnie stood her ground, and in the process earned eternal rebuke from a good portion of her faculty, three of whom hired a lawyer to prevent the sale of the century-old buildings.

In January 2000, when Peter was called by a reporter from the *Toronto Star*, he explained that he understood the concerns of professors and townspeople, but he was "also sensitive to financial imperatives." He added that he thought it possible "that what we all want to achieve can be achieved on the new campus." He would be sorry to let the old campuses be sold off, but he thought it "exciting that we can build on the new one."[36]

Throughout 2000, debates grew more heated. One evening Peter was a dinner guest of Tom and Christine Symons. Also invited were several Trent students. Peter listened to one student's concerns about the threatened closing of Traill College. A few weeks later at convocation, while shaking hands with the same student, the chancellor mentioned the Symons dinner.[37]

At a meeting of the Board of Governors on February 16, 2001, at which the board approved an update of the master plan of centralization on the Symons Campus, a student warned that she and others were tired of having their opposition to centralization fall on deaf ears. She mentioned something about "a less polite strategy and warned that things would get 'messy.'"[38]

At 9:30 a.m. on Monday, February 26, 2001, things indeed got messy when eight students occupied the office of Vice-President (Academic) Graham Taylor. They ordered Taylor's staff to leave, and with the help of more than a dozen supporters in the hallway outside, barricaded themselves inside. Surrounded by filing cabinets that contained material of a personal nature, they wouldn't budge. President Patterson paid them a visit. "When you're ready to negotiate," they told her, "you can come back and discuss it."[39] The next day the student newspaper, *Arthur*, published an opinion piece entitled an "Open Letter to Chancellor Peter Gzowski," in which the writer asked Peter to "help us reclaim our voices, the voices of Trent University." President Patterson talked to the police. Armed in riot gear, they broke into the office through an outside window at 3:00 a.m. on March 1. The eight women were taken to jail and strip-searched.

On March 17, 2001, an article by Peter appeared in the *Globe and Mail*. Its title, "The Trouble Is Everyone Loves Trent Too Much," quickly entered the lexicon of the university, and today one can hear it quoted to explain the mood of discontent that lingers almost a decade later. Peter had always found all sides in the dispute quite agreeable, he wrote, from the divided faculty and student body to the president, whom Peter described as a "decent, fair-but-tough-minded leader who has been unfairly and personally attacked (and deeply wounded) by some of her opposition." In no way, Peter argued, was the president responsible for the strip searches.[40] In typical *Morningside* fashion, Peter believed that, if only opposing sides could sit down for a good discussion, the dissonances could be bridged.[41]

The article, which was meant to pacify ill feelings, sparked resentment among some staff members and students, especially those who worked, lived, and studied at Catharine Parr Traill and Peter Robinson, the two downtown colleges under threat. A librarian at one of those colleges detected a whiff of condescension in the article. "Trent has always had a tradition of student dissent," she explained one day, adding that she remembered, during a previous occupation, walking by the office of President John Stubbs, who was standing outside his office and pleading with occupiers to hand over a folder required for a meeting. Never, during previous occupations, had the police been called. Perhaps never had the university been so polarized nor the mood so bitter as it was in February 2001.[42] In *Arthur*, Peter was chastised for his support of the president. For months the mood at Trent remained querulous. A few months later when John Milloy, the master of Peter Robinson College, challenged the chancellor's views, Peter called him "the most dangerous man in Canada."[43] To some colleagues, Master Milloy had pointed out a certain lack of consistency in the chancellor's ideology. The Red Tory host of *Morningside* had become a neo-conservative, an ideology he had once despised.

Most of us change our minds several times over a lifetime, so perhaps it is unfair to note that Peter had once admired independent-minded university students. At Memorial University in the mid-1960s he had praised his audience of students by telling them that they and their contemporaries at universities across the country were "tougher minded, better versed" than students of his generation. In December 1969, when the *Financial Post* asked Peter for his favourite book published that year, he named several, including *The Strawberry Statement* by James Simon Kunen, because, he explained, Kunen was "one of the few of his generation who can take his cause seriously but himself not seriously at all."[44] The book dealt with an occupation of the office of the president of Columbia University in protest over the administration's support of the war in Vietnam. What Peter especially liked was the fact that Kunen told the story in a cheeky, humorous manner. "At about 8:30 A.M. we hear that the cops are coming," wrote Kunen. "One hundred seventy-three people jump out the window.... That leaves twenty-seven of us sitting on the floor, waiting to be arrested"[45]

In 1969 in the *Financial Post*, Peter also included among his favourite books *The Catcher in the Rye* and Lillian Hellman's *An Unfinished Woman*. For most of his life, Peter had had a decided affinity with rebels. More than once he had railed against CBC and Maclean-Hunter management. Now, in his sixties, Peter defended the status quo at Trent University. At McMaster University, Gill Howard agreed with Peter — they frequently talked by telephone. No university could allow eight young women to take control.[46]

—•—

During the last year of his life, the telephone became Peter's most important method of communication. Soon after the World Trade Center was destroyed on September 11, 2001, he called Selena Forsyth in Port Hope, Ontario, to express concern about her son, who had been inside one of the towers. Peter also used the telephone to talk to Cathy Perkins in Kingston, Edna Barker, editors at the *Globe and Mail* and *FiftyPlus*, and many others.

Peter's last year wasn't a happy one. Shelley Ambrose, who by that time was an assistant to Pamela Wallin in New York City, reported to a visiting Canadian that Peter had taken up smoking and drinking again and that he railed against his body for letting him down. There were rumours of domestic unease.

On Peter's last New Year's Eve, he and Gillian Howard celebrated with Stuart McLean and Sheila O'Brien, as well as with Murray McLauchlan, his wife, and their young son, who rode Peter's chair lift up and down the stairs to the recreation room of Peter and Gill's home in Don Mills. During the evening, Peter talked about how rewarding he was finding the chancellorship at Trent. He was dressed, a somewhat surprised McLauchlan recalled, in a new sweater and creased slacks, and despite the constant need for strong oxygen, was in fine fettle. At midnight, while the others headed for the deck to sip champagne and to light sparklers, Peter sipped mineral water. When McLauchlan turned to look, Peter attempted to straighten up while waving a sparkler to welcome 2002.

Peter never lost his interest in people and language. On January 2, 2002, he called Kathy Stinson, a writer he had met at the first annual Stratford Book Festival on November 25, 2001, when Kathy gave him a copy of *King of the Castle*, her latest novel for young people. The book's hero, Mr. Elliot, is a school caretaker who learns to read. Later, when Kathy met Peter at his book table, she explained why she had "snuck" her novel to him while he was drawing tickets for door prizes.

"Tut-tut. You can't say *snuck*," Peter retorted. "The word is *sneaked*."

Back home, Kathy's *Canadian Oxford Dictionary* informed her that *snuck* was perfectly acceptable. A few days later she emailed Peter, asking if he had ever met Elijah Allen, the caretaker in Inuvik who had inspired her to write her novel. On January 2, 2002, Peter called Kathy to talk about Elijah, as well as his brother, Abe Ookpik.

"I'll never forget what a thrill it was," Kathy recalled, "to sit in my home office with Peter's unmistakable voice coming through my telephone, and also just what a lovely pleasure, to have a private and relaxed — yes, relaxed, because that was one of Peter's amazing gifts, wasn't it, to put people at ease — conversation with him." At the end of the call Peter read the following line from Kathy's novel: "Mr. Elliot liked being a caretaker. Every day he hoisted the flag in front of Jessie Lucas Public School as proud as can be."

On Saturday, January 5, 2002, three days after his call to Kathy, Peter's article "Say 'Sofa' All You Like — I'll Always Be a 'Chesterfield' Man" appeared in the *Globe and Mail*. He recounted the story of meeting Kathy at the book festival, and wrote about Elijah Allen. "In 1967," Peter continued, "Abe was given the job of replacing 'Eskimo numbers' our government had imposed on people. Their traditional nomenclature had no need for surnames, but modern administration did." Peter still owned a copy of the eastern Arctic telephone book from the late 1960s, just after Abe began his work. In that book the listings consisted of first names and an initial followed by the government-assigned numbers, as in PETER E5-3170.

In the next paragraph of the *Globe and Mail* article, Peter returned to the word *snuck*, which he deemed "an ugly little word, uglier even than its better-bred cousin 'sneaked' ..." He had discovered in his *ITP Nelson Canadian Dictionary* that the word was of nineteenth-century American origin, a fact that caused him to rise to patriotic heights. Throughout his radio career, and especially during his *Morningside* years, Peter argued, he had been a Canadian cultural nationalist who adhered to what he thought was the Canadian version of spelling and linguistics.[47]

He went on to list Canadian words such as *shit-disturber, beer parlour, humidex, crokinole,* and *bloody Caesar*, as well as *moccasin* and *First Nations*. And he reminded his readers that the Canadian term was *reserve*, not *reservation*. "We rest in our 'Muskoka chairs' when we sit outdoors (at least in the summer)," he continued, "and on our steadfast 'chesterfields,' as opposed to 'couches' or 'sofas,' when we move indoors." As a grand finale, he declared *storm-stayed*, a term that had been the subject of discussion a few years earlier on *Morningside*, the "loveliest of Canadianisms I know." And if it wasn't a Canadian term, he would declare it so. The column was typical Peter Gzowski. He had begun with *snuck* and soared to a lesson on language, with two or three human-interest stories *snuck* in for good measure.[48]

During the last couple of weeks of his life, Peter became a character, a radio interviewer called "Peter Gzowski," in a play produced at Toronto's Theatre Passe Muraille. *Walking to Russia*'s main character was a retired chemistry professor from Winnipeg obsessed with saving the environment. "Peter" first emerged in the play as a voice. Later "Peter" appeared in person. Theatre director and reviewer Richard Ouzounian was unimpressed. What we got, Ouzounian argued, wasn't Peter Gzowski. "It isn't even Shelagh Rogers. It's more like Mr. Rogers."[49]

About a week after Ouzounian's review appeared in the *Toronto Star*, Peter was rushed to North York General Hospital. As his diminished body gasped for air, what was he thinking? Was he skating forever over fields of ice? Was he pumping ink at Ridley College? Was he beating Arnold Palmer at golf? Was he interviewing Her Majesty Queen Elizabeth II? Or was he recalling, through his morphined memory, the conclusion of *Who Has Seen the Wind*, one of his favourite novels? Something about the day greying, "its light withdrawing from the winter sky …"? Something about a train whooping in the night, "the sound dissolving slowly"? Or did A.E. Housman's "When Smoke Stood Up from Ludlow" drift through his fading memory?

> Lie down, lie down, young yeoman;
> The sun moves always west;
> The road one treads to labour
> Will lead one home to rest,
> And that will be the best.

Did Peter have time to remember a letter written to him in late 1996 after a show on which he had defended cigarette sponsorship of music festivals, including the DuMaurier Jazz Festival in Montreal. Without cigarette sponsorship, his son, John, would have had a hard time performing, he told listeners. "Exactly one week prior to the announcement" that tobacco advertising at music festivals would soon be phased out, Elaine Lillico-Carter told Peter: "My husband, age forty-six, died of lung cancer.... So next time you are tempted to discuss addiction and the 'cost' to a community in losing advertising dollars, look at your son and picture him in a bed, perhaps unable to lift his hand, unable to play his music, and imagine the true cost of advertising."[50]

Or maybe on his deathbed what flashed through Peter's mind was a column that appeared in the *Toronto Star* on November 10, 1978, in which he had told readers how he would spend the last day of his life.[51]

> For myself, I'd get up early. I know this sounds strange for someone who likes sleeping in as much as I do, and who has trouble getting to the office by 9. But among the many jobs I've had, there have been a couple for which I've had to get up when the rest of the world was asleep, and I've liked that.
>
> There's a sense of anticipation in the dark and cool of early morning in the city, a feeling of limitless possibilities and even if you knew you were going to realize only one or two of the possible things, the excitement would be rewarding on its own.
>
> I'd make a pot of Earl Grey tea and — good heavens — I think I'd shave my moustache off. I put the exclamation in there because I honestly didn't know I'd want to do that until I started thinking about it.
>
> Maybe it's a symbol of living the way other people expect you to.
>
> Maybe, come to think of it, I'll shave it off anyway one of these days. It's almost 10 years old now and ...
>
> You can see what I mean about the pleasures of this fantasy.

I'd put the Pachelbel Canon on the record player. The version done by the Pro Arte Musica of Munich. This is kind of strange, too. I'm a Beatles freak, and an unreconstructed 1960s folkie. And there's a lot of country and western I like. But on a day I was devoting to self-indulgence, I'd play my own favourite recording of a glorious old classical war-horse.[52]

I'd call up my kids. I'd ask them to go to the island with me. I'd want to throw a ball around. We could cook something outdoors — hamburgers, I think, with tomatoes and big slices of raw onion and mayonnaise on the buns. I'd crack open a bottle of a good raw Italian red wine. Valpolicella. I'd smoke a big cigar.

When the announcement of Peter's death reached Canadians on Friday morning, January 25, 2002, he was mourned across the country. At Stoney Mountain Institution north of Winnipeg, some of Canada's most hardened criminals sat around quietly discussing their favourite *Morningside* interviews.[53] Upon hearing of Peter's death, Kathy Stinson could only hope that her book had given Peter "some small fraction of the pleasure" he had given to her "through his writing, his radio interviews, and through his very presence across our vast Canadian landscape."[54]

Of course, a good many English Canadians, the nineteen million or so who didn't listen to Peter, didn't grieve. That the media of French Canada also appeared indifferent brought reproach from a Toronto journalist. Ironically, no other English-language broadcaster had reached out to Quebec so passionately as did Peter. Among those he had interviewed was Nathalie Petrowski, an arts reviewer for both *Le Devoir* and *La Presse*, who once bragged on *Morningside* that if she were going to read a novel in English, she would choose an American one. And who was Margaret Laurence, anyway?[55] Peter's intimate friendship with Mordecai Richler, a critic of Quebec nationalism, had done nothing to endear him to the Québécois, nor did his claim that he had made a star out of Patsy Gallant, who was considered a traitor in Quebec for her Americanized disco version of "Mon Pays," Gilles Vigneault's anthem to his country. Had any Québécois read *The Morningside Papers*, they would have been annoyed by the fact that one of Quebec's most prominent *chanteuses* suffered a name change from "Dufresne" to "DuFreme."[56] And unlike Peter Jennings, whose death a few years later was greeted with genuine sorrow on Radio-Canada,[57] Peter didn't speak French well enough to conduct an interview in that language.[58]

Nevertheless, the claim made by *Destinies*, a survey history of Canada, that Peter was "virtually unknown" among francophone Québécois is somewhat of an exaggeration. Surely, Louis Lemieux, host of *Matin Express Week-End*, broadcast to viewers across Canada, wasn't the only francophone fan of the cool, relaxed Gzowski style, so untypical, Lemieux points out, of the more formal style of CBC English broadcasters.[59] Other journalists such as Chantal Hébert, who appeared for years on *Morningside*, were aware of Peter's role in Canadian broadcasting. In the Gzowski Papers, there is an occasional letter from a Québécois listener.[60]

Two memorial services were held on Monday, January 28, 2002, at Frontier College near Yonge Street and St. Clair Avenue in Toronto, the first in the morning for his family and the second in the afternoon for close friends. During the first week in February, there were two public memorial services, one at Convocation Hall where Vicki Gabereau could barely contain her emotions, and Susan Aglukark could not. On February 2 at a memorial service at Wenjack Theatre, Trent University, W.O. Mitchell's son played an excerpt from an interview from *Morningside*. Molly Johnson sang her signature tune "My, Oh My," and Peter, on tape, sang his off-key version of "I Want to Be Seduced." The talented Leahy family from nearby Lakefield fiddled a couple of moving laments, and two Trent students read commemorative messages. President Bonnie Patterson expressed her loyalty to the man who had remained loyal to her. The service was over at last, and the audience filed out into the raging blizzard that blurred lines and margins. "And then the winter darkness fell," wrote Silver Donald Cameron a few months later, "and we couldn't find him any more."[61]

As the snow slowly turned her grey hair white, one member of the audience, one of Peter's most devoted fans — each morning his voice filled all corners of her art-filled farmhouse near Lindsay, Ontario — was so moved that she smoked her last cigarette just outside the theatre. The woman was about Peter's age, and she, too, had abused her lungs for more than a half-century. She died a few weeks later, but not before she found a tape of "I Want to Be Seduced," which she played at high volume as she drove at illegal speeds to her final bridge games in Lindsay.

Even as the memorial services were taking place, however, misgivings began to set in. Peter, Richard Gwyn argued in the *Toronto Star*, personified the optimism of Canada during the two decades following Expo 67. *Morningside*'s host, Gwyn noted, believed that all problems, from Quebec nationalism to Native resistance, could be solved "by reason, by dialogue, by goodwill, by listening to the other side." Peter's Canada of small towns and essentially good-hearted white people had long ago been replaced by a cosmopolitan, polyglot urban nation. His Canada, Gwyn continued, was "an unsustainably intimate Canada because too many of those who took part in the program were nationalists and liberals like Gzowski."[62] Outsiders often bring fresh perspectives to their adopted country. The Welsh-born Gwyn wasn't alone in suggesting, ever so politely, that what Peter represented was nostalgia for a self-confident, decent, and compassionate Canada that had all but vanished, except in the memory of many of his listeners.

Epilogue:

A Secret Long Guarded

There is this mother who's been deserted by her man,
or lost her man in some way, and the child is crying
for his father, and yet the woman knows that the child's
grief compared to hers is ... well, like a fire in the sun.

— *Peter Gzowski, "Dylan: An Explosion of Poetry,"*
Maclean's, *January 22, 1966*

To end Peter's biography, there is the story of an attractive, intelligent young woman, a child, and the child's father. The child was Peter's third, born in early 1961, about two and a half years after Peter C., more than a year after Alison, and about six months before Maria. The mother guarded the secret for decades because she respected and loved Peter.

The child was conceived the night of Ralph Allen's retirement party in late April 1960. The Lord Simcoe Hotel once stood in misnamed splendour[1] at the corner of University Avenue and King Street, a few blocks south of the headquarters of Maclean-Hunter at University Avenue and Dundas Street. Oil company executives, whose headquarters were nearby, as well as journalists, editors, and newspaper magnates, rented suites in the hotel, whose bellboys, house detectives, and maintenance men were privy to one of Toronto's best-kept secrets: the hotel helped the city protect its facade of Toronto the Good. Inside the suites Toronto the Naughty carried on with full-frontal impunity. *Maclean's* rented a room at the Lord Simcoe, to which writers and editors sometimes retreated for tough editing assignments. Allen's retirement party was held in a larger, more elegant suite.

Cathy Perkins had first seen Peter in a photograph. When he was editor of *The Varsity*, she worked for Queen's University's *Journal* as editor of Canadian University Press (CUP). She selected news stories from college newspapers across the country to be reprinted in the *Journal*. Cathy admired Peter's style of writing, his opinions, his insights, and his mischievous sense of humour. One day she noticed a photograph of Peter supervising his *Varsity* reporters. She was intrigued. They occasionally exchanged notes, and Cathy became Peter's one-member fan club at Queen's. When Peter left *The Varsity* in March 1957, Cathy missed him. "I felt we somehow knew each other, even though we had never met in person," she remembers today.

In May 1959, after graduating from Queen's, Cathy moved to Toronto where she worked as the first editorial researcher of the *Star Weekly*. Because she read *Maclean's*, she knew that Peter was back in Toronto. No doubt she had read Peter's first feature article, published in January 1959, on the subject of university newspapers. In the spring of 1960, Cathy and Peter met in person at the Lord Simcoe Hotel during a press conference called to announce the arrival in Toronto of the stripper Cupcake Cassidy. Knowing that Cathy would be the only other woman present and that she would provide quite a contrast to the buxom stripper, John Clare, the crusty editor of the *Star Weekly*, sent Cathy as a joke. When Cathy spotted Peter's name on his press pass, she reminded him that they had corresponded during his year at *The Varsity*. People remarked that Cathy was a taller version of Jennie, and just as good-looking. The two of them headed over to the nearby Toronto Press Club where Peter surprised everyone by playing some pretty good jazz on the club piano.

Cathy Perkins in 1960, the year she met Peter. With her is "Ragtime" Bob Darch, after whom Cathy named her son.

(Courtesy Cathy Perkins)

Although Peter wasn't looking for the comfort of women, the situation at home made it easier for him to have feelings for Cathy. Jennie was preoccupied with two young children, born in close succession in 1958 and 1959, and Alison had trouble swallowing food and keeping it down. Peter felt useless, and he resented the time that Jennie devoted to the children. While Peter was full of sexual energy, Jennie was drained at the end of the day. After busy days at *Maclean's*, Peter often spent evenings drinking with colleagues in the rooftop bar of the Park Plaza.

Like many women, Cathy found Peter attractive. He wasn't good-looking like Errol Flynn or the young Marlon Brando. In fact, he was spindly, untidy, and pimply. Acne had pockmarked his face and back. What he did have was the charm and charisma of a Richard Burton, whose acne scars also bore testament to teenage embarrassment and hurt. Furthermore, Peter was witty, and like Cathy, he loved word games. "What's the singular of *martini*?" he would throw into a conversation. Or "How about a *coffus*?" And, oh, those eyes that flirted almost constantly!

Eyes that always paid attention to any woman whose ideas and person they found attractive.

Cathy and Peter began to meet for drinks high above the city at the Park Plaza, and sometimes at Cathy's apartment on Eglinton Avenue. Between meetings they carried on a lively correspondence. On the day before Ralph Allen's retirement party, Peter took out a piece of *Maclean's* stationery and wrote:

> Cathy sweet: Bloody frustrating week! Last night was asked to stay for a quick — quick! — meeting with Blair and Ken Lefolii that ended up with a drinks (drinx) and then dinner at the Northcliffe and then another drinks at the Park Plaza and then coffee (two coffi) — how about coffus? — at the Concerto or one of those darling places and then Lefolii driving me home and then some heel-taping (rye, wine, vermouth, God!) and more coffee and the dawn. Oh quiet flowed the dawn.
>
> So I'm dead this ayem, as we cablers say and have no excuse for not going right home this eve (up and adam) and tomorrow evening whoopee is the party to drink a toast to Ralph Allen and that will go till all hours whereupon I no doubt, drunky, will phone sleepy you.

Peter concluded the letter by telling Cathy "for goodness' sake I miss you." He signed the letter "Yours, James Joyceingway, to judge by the styles," overtop of which he scrawled a large "P."

The following evening, once Ralph Allen and celebrants had departed, a well-lubricated Peter called Cathy: "Why don't you come down here and keep me company? The place is empty."

Birth control pills weren't available in Canada until 1961. Until then it was generally up to the male to use condoms. A month later, when Cathy told Peter that she was pregnant, he assumed she would have an abortion. As a Catholic, she never considered such an idea.[2] Cathy carried on with her research job at the *Star Weekly* where her severe morning sickness was the subject of speculation, though no one, not even the crusty John Clare or the perceptive Sylvia Fraser, guessed the reason.

As the pregnancy progressed, Peter grew scared to death of losing Jennie. He was greatly relieved when Cathy decided to give birth in England, far from her conservative family in small-town eastern Ontario, and a long way from the chattering classes of Toronto. In the 1960s, single motherhood was a scandal. Peter's job at *Maclean's* might have been jeopardized, and one can only imagine how difficult it would have been to rise through the ranks of the Canadian media had it become known he had fathered an "illegitimate" child. Had Jennie discovered the pregnancy, Peter's marriage would surely have ended abruptly.

In August 1960, Cathy sailed from Montreal to London. She figured that National Health in Britain would help with delivery costs and that adoption proceedings could be kept secret. McKenzie Porter, Peter's colleague at *Maclean's*, arranged a room with his wartime landlady in Sussex Gardens near Paddington Station. One day Charles Taylor, who was writing novels in his West End flat in a building owned by Sigmund Freud's daughter, rang Cathy. They had known each other at Queen's. Taylor invited Cathy to meet him at BBC headquarters. From there they went over to a posh Piccadilly restaurant where Taylor introduced Cathy to scampi. Taylor called occasionally to see if Cathy was in good health, and she always lied that she was fine. She sensed that he was uncomfortable with her pregnancy. "I'm pretty sure that I never mentioned Peter to him," Cathy recalls today, "except in the context of *Maclean's*. I didn't want Charles's sympathy at the expense of his regard for Peter."[3]

Meantime, Peter wrote to encourage Cathy to write short pieces for the "Preview" section of *Maclean's*, which would earn her some money. However, since she suffered from morning sickness that lasted twelve hours each day, she managed only one article. In *Maclean's* "Preview" section of December 17, 1960, she wrote about Charles Taylor's father, E.P., and Roy Thomson, who were investing in British brewing (Taylor) and British newspapers and television (Thomson). The latter, Cathy reported, was attempting to introduce five-pin bowling to Britain. The game had been invented in 1909 by Thomas J. Ryan, a Torontonian.[4] The fee earned from the short piece was only enough to pay for three weeks' rent at Sussex Gardens, and Cathy had no choice but to move into a state-run mother-and-baby home in Hammersmith.

On February 3, 1961, Robert Lawrence Perkins was born a few days overdue in Queen Charlotte's Hospital, the biggest maternity hospital in the British Commonwealth. Peter had forbidden the use of any of his three names. "I had to shame myself into writing 'Father Unknown' on the birth records," Cathy recalls today. She named the baby after "Ragtime" Bob Darch, an American friend who often played in Toronto and who sent Cathy money for music research in London. The baby's second name came from another benefactor, Lawrence Earl, a native of Saint John, New Brunswick, and Cathy's first boss at the *Star Weekly*. His novel *Yangtse Incident* had been published in 1950, and in 1953 he had been awarded the Leacock Medal for Humour for *The Battle of Baltinglass*. In London he was editor of *John Bull*, a weekly magazine that caught the essence of the swinging city of The Beatles, Twiggy, and a growing consumer society.

By February 1961, Peter was the Quebec editor of *Maclean's*. At the very moment of his son's birth, he later told Cathy, he was sharing a cab with Mordecai Richler, who was back in Montreal to see if it was tolerable enough to live there. Years later, when Rob became a voracious reader of Richler's novels, Peter whimsically attributed his son's predilection to that taxi ride.

In England it was generally the rule that babies couldn't be surrendered for adoption until they were six weeks old. That was long enough for Cathy to fall in love with her son. She sent word about the baby to her Roman Catholic family in eastern Ontario and asked them for airfare. Then she informed Peter that she wouldn't be giving up their son for adoption.

In March 1961, when Rob was five weeks old, he and his mother flew to Toronto. While Cathy looked for work, the two of them lived with writer Gwen Beattie on Heath Street. Soon Cathy found an editorial job with *Canadian Homes*, part of the family of Maclean-Hunter magazines. Meantime Peter signed a legal agreement to pay $30 monthly child support, an overly modest sum that Cathy agreed to only because she didn't want to diminish the Gzowski household budget too much.[5] Peter's compliance was desultory at best, though he never seemed short of money for drinking and gambling. Sometimes when he won at poker he would show up at Cathy's door with a bag of groceries. After observing the sleeping baby for a few minutes, he would softly cry. It was enough to keep Cathy from taking him to court or pressuring him in any other way to pay regularly. She was always short of money, but she didn't want to harm Peter's reputation. Furthermore, she says today, "I did not want to hurt Jennie." To compensate for Peter's shortcomings, Eric Hutton of *Maclean's* kept young Rob in expensive toys. Once, in order to supplement Cathy's income, Peter wrote a short piece on Canadian football and gave it to Cathy to sell. "Put your own byline on it," he told her.[6]

Until Rob was three, and thus old enough for daycare, Cathy placed him with a foster family from Monday to Friday so that she could work hard at improving her income as a senior editor for *Canadian Homes*, whose offices were in the Maclean-Hunter building a few floors below Peter's office at *Maclean's*. If they found themselves alone in the elevator, they held hands up to the floor where *Maclean's* was located, after which she descended alone to her office. When *Canadian Homes* folded, Cathy worked as a senior editor and writer for *Liberty*. Eventually, she ended up back in the Maclean-Hunter group as an editor-writer with the *Financial Post*. By that time, Peter and colleagues had resigned from *Maclean's*.

While Rob was a toddler, he spent weekends with Cathy in her modest apartment on Jameson Avenue in west Toronto. He missed the children at the foster home, so on sunny days Cathy often took him over to the Toronto Islands where there were lots of other children. For a single mother of little means, it was the perfect way to spend part of a day. The ferry ride on the *Kwasind* was free, and there were slides, swings, and teeter-totters at the island amusement park. Cathy had no idea that Peter and Jennie's summer home was nearby. One day she ran into Harry Bruce, who was supervising his son, along with Peter C. and Alison Gzowski. Rob began to play with his half-siblings, whom he knew only as new friends.

On another occasion, Cathy ran into Peter. As they watched the children play, they chatted. The relationship between Cathy and Peter remained amicable. They talked by telephone about mutual interests, including Gzowski family medical history. Three or four times a year they met for lunch or a drink. And they made love without ever planning it.

In 1968, after an exhausting stint as editor of *Canadian Travel* and *World Travel*, Cathy accepted a job with Queen's University as public relations and publications officer. With seven-year-old Rob, she returned to Kingston. In 1972, when Rob was eleven, a nun at his school thought it was time for sex education. She taught the grade six class new words to a Burt Bacharach song: "What do you get when you fall in love?" The answer? "You get a sperm to make a baby." At the end of the school day Rob ran home to confront his mother. "I *do* have a father," he insisted. "I *must* have a father. Why didn't you tell me?"

Cathy called the host of *This Country in the Morning*. Peter was prepared. A year or so before, he had told Cathy that some day he must tell his son that he was, indeed, his father. Up to that time, Peter was known simply as a friend who, from time to time, dropped by, and who once gave his son CBC pens and other memorabilia.

"Now is the time, Peter," Cathy told him by telephone.

Later that month Peter drove to Kingston. Rob was excited. Both mother and son took the day off because their friend Peter was coming for lunch. As Peter parked his car down the street, a buoyant Rob flew off the porch and ran along Barrie Street, near the Queen's campus. The two of them hugged and walked back to the house like old buddies. Peter hemmed and hawed and talked about the way that he and Cathy, once upon a time, had loved each other very much.

"You're my father!" exclaimed Rob.

"Yes," said Peter. "And have you anything to say about that?"

"Congratulations, Rob!" shouted the boy. The three of them burst into laughter.

Rob took Peter to his school. They shot baskets for more than an hour, each of them delighted that the other was an athlete. Later Rob and his parents dined at Chez Piggy where the "men" couldn't stop talking sports. When Peter was leaving, he and Rob hugged each other long and hard, and Peter assured his son that he would always listen to his worries or troubles. The following Christmas, Rob was thrilled to receive a box of gifts delivered right to the door. Peter's presents included a

Buffalo Sabres hockey jersey autographed by Rick Martin. A few years later Peter asked Rob to be part of the audience of *90 Minutes Live*. Invited by her father to meet a young man called Rob, Alison was in the audience that evening. Afterward, Peter introduced Rob and Alison to guests, including the writer Tom Wolfe. Never once did Peter divulge that the two teenagers shared a father.

When in Kingston for lectures and readings, Peter treated Rob to meals at the Fontainebleu or the Fireside Inn. Until Rob was old enough to drive, his mother took him to these rendezvous. From 1974 to 1979, when she was unhappily married to a man who was jealous of Peter, she didn't dare stay to share even a glass of wine. In 1977, Peter bought Rob his first car, a used Toyota. He also sent the teenager first editions of his books, autographed "With love, Dad." Peter always joined Rob and Cathy for a drink after his Kingston events, and father and son sometimes breakfasted together the next morning. When Rob and his first wife separated, Peter helped with the rent deposit.

In Rob today, one can imagine Peter. The parallels between the two are astounding, right down to three partners or wives, a passion for gambling and sports, and the gene for alcoholism.[7] Even their voices are similar — when Rob speaks or laughs in public, fans of Peter often turn their heads. Like his father, Rob is a talented, comical master of ceremonies much in demand. He is also a writer of short stories that demonstrate a good ear for dialogue.

It hasn't always been easy. Rob was upset when he read in *The Private Voice* that, when they turned twenty-one, Peter's children by Jennie, "in keeping with a family tradition that goes back to our distant Polish ancestry," were presented with signet rings bearing the Gzowski coat of arms.[8] Rob wasn't so honoured. When he read that line, he threw down the book. Why Peter bothered to send Rob the book with the offending line in it still puzzles Cathy. Had Rob read the first *Morningside Papers*, he would have noted that there, too, he was overlooked. He hadn't been a bad father, Peter surmised, and the proof was "five living, handsome" offspring.[9]

One evening in 1988, Cathy was a member of a standing-room-only audience at Kingston's Grand Theatre when Peter read from his memoirs. At one point Peter was searching for a particular passage. "It's about *90 Minutes Live*," he told the audience.

From where she was standing, Cathy quietly told him, "It's on page 173."

With a smile in her direction, Peter told the audience, "That's Cathy Perkins, one of my oldest friends."

The news came as a surprise to Cathy's Queen's colleagues. She smiled her thanks. Later, in Cathy's copy of the book, Peter inscribed: "To Cathy, who knows, among other things, this book better than I do."

In early June 1990, when Peter received an honorary doctorate at Queen's, Cathy was special assistant to Principal David Smith, with responsibility, among other things, for the care and feeding of honorary graduates. "You know Peter Gzowski from your old Maclean-Hunter days, don't you, Cathy?" the principal asked one day. She smiled and said yes. She was embarrassed but didn't know how to decline. She called Peter to explain. He understood and said that there would be no awkwardness because neither Gill nor his children planned to attend the ceremony.

The evening before the convocation Peter was at a party that celebrated the end of another *Morningside* season, which meant that he couldn't be an overnight guest at the principal's residence, Summerhill, where Cathy was live-in hostess. When Peter arrived early on the morning of June 2, he was exhausted. As he scribbled notes for his convocation address, Cathy was on her knees with a wet cloth, trying to scrub spots off his trousers and add some shine to his dusty shoes.

Rob had just started a new job and had to work that Saturday, but he called before the convocation to congratulate his father and to invite him to drop in on his way back to Toronto to see baby Caitlan. Peter didn't drop in that day or any other day. Cathy has tried to explain Peter's decision to Caitlan: her grandfather knew that if he ever met Caitlan, he would have to add her to the people he loved, and he simply wasn't very good at loving. Today the granddaughter he never met keeps an eye posted for Peter's books and CDs. She studies his books and saves photographs of Peter on her computer. Among the collection is the only photograph ever taken of her grandparents together — at the Summerhill luncheon on June 2, 1990.

Rob Perkins in 1991 with his daughter, Caitlan, the grand-daughter Peter never met.

(Courtesy Cathy Perkins)

Cathy and Peter remained friends — loving friends — until Peter's death. Theirs was an ideal kind of love, unencumbered by the daily inconveniences of housekeeping, grocery shopping, sickness, and all those other aggravations that bedevil shared lives. Peter sent flowers on special occasions such as Cathy's retirement in 1995, and she phoned on his birthdays. She always found him alone, free to chat.

In 2001, during Peter's last visit to Kingston, he gave the sixteenth annual MacClement Lecture. Afterward, Peter, Cathy, Rob, and his wife, Tracey, met for a hug and a chat before the sponsors of the lecture swept Peter away. By that time, Peter was visibly ill. He invited "Cath," as he always called her, to meet him later at the Donald Gordon Centre. He seemed so alone. When Cathy arrived at the reception desk of the Gordon Centre, Peter was still with the lecture committee. After leaving him a note and the most recent issue of *Journey*, her church paper, she continued on to her home on Wolfe Island.

"I wish you had stayed," he told Cathy by telephone message the next day. Before leaving Kingston, he left two more messages. He just wanted to say goodbye, he told her. To this day, Cathy regrets that she missed his calls. She had a premonition that he was saying goodbye for good.

Now, almost a decade after his death, Cathy thinks of Peter every day. "I could love him happily," she explains, "as long as I never was in a position where I had to trust him." Because his support of baby Rob was sporadic at best, Cathy knew that Peter was unreliable. Furthermore, she adds ruefully, "being the other woman teaches you that there will be other women." She carefully saved every letter Peter wrote to her, including one written in 1959 before they had actually met in person, in which he told her that he was happy to discover *Winnie-the-Pooh* by reading it to his first-born son at bedtime.[10]

Peter and Cathy did talk one last time — by telephone. Cathy told Peter that if he needed her, she would move back to Toronto. A long

Peter and Cathy Perkins, June 2, 1990, when Peter was awarded an honorary degree from Queen's University, Kingston.

(Courtesy Cathy Perkins)

silence was followed by audible weeping. "I'm fine, really," Peter assured her. "I'm looked after and I am loved. I love you."

"This was not romantic, mind you," Cathy reflects today, "only old and very affectionate friends who shared something important."

Perhaps love really is two solitudes that "protect and touch and greet each other."[11]

As Peter was dying at North York General Hospital, Gillian Howard called to ask Cathy to relay the news to Rob. Peter died too quickly for a last visit from his son in Kingston. Cathy wasn't invited to the memorial service at Frontier College. Nor was she, a career writer and editor and lifelong friend, asked to contribute to *Remembering Peter Gzowski*.

Had she not received a telephone call from Peter's biographer one Sunday afternoon in October 2006, asking about an article published in the "Preview" section of *Maclean's* in 1960, Cathy would have carried her story to the grave.[12]

Notes

Introduction

1.   Peter Gzowski, introduction to an interview with Michael Bliss, *Morningside*, March 22, 1984.

2.   Peter Gzowski [untitled] in Arlene Perly Rae, ed., *Everybody's Favourites* (Toronto: Viking, 1997), 145–46.

3.   Another variation has the boys stickhandling down the frozen Grand River, which runs through Galt. For one version, see Peter Gzowski, *The Game of Our Lives* (Toronto: McClelland & Stewart, 1981), 106. The final telling of the incident, in print at least, was in Peter Gzowski, "How to Quit Smoking in Fifty Years or Less," in Lorna Crozier and Patrick Lane, eds., *Addicted: Notes from the Belly of the Beast* (Vancouver: Greystone Books, 2001), 57.

4.   Peter claimed that the phrase was Scottish. No, *verglas* is French, and it is often heard in winter weather forecasts on Radio-Canada. Peter's French was shaky. In an article in *Maclean's* (November 16, 1963, 54), he explained that he had learned French in construction camps in Québec and Labrador, and thus he had less trouble "with worker-*joual* than with Montréal cabdrivers." In 1997 in Paris, he spoke so little French that he had to have menus translated by Mavis Gallant. On the other hand, his friend Cathy Perkins has related that he could order beer in Montreal bars *sans effort*.

5.   Peter Gzowski, *The Private Voice, A Journal of Reflections* (Toronto: McClelland and Stewart, 1988), 105.

6.   *Toronto Star*, April 20, 1982, A2.

7.   Peter Gzowski, "And Even, Sometimes, Lying," in Peter Gzowski, ed., *Friends, Moments, Countryside, Selected Columns From Canadian Living, 1993–98* (Toronto: McClelland & Stewart, 1998), 126–29.

8.   "I don't know if television will ever be able to recapture the kind of magic radio held for us then," Peter mused in 1982, a few months before he became permanent host of *Morningside*. He was referring to the 1940s when he used to take the family radio to bed to listen to hockey games (TUA, Peter Gzowski fonds, 92-015, box 12, Peter Gzowski, "A Fan's Notes," in the Edmonton Oilers program for February 19, 1982). Radio may have played a key role in developing many impressionable imaginations. The filmmaker Donald Brittain used to listen to radio at the family home in Ottawa, including hockey games narrated by Foster Hewitt. In his imagination Brittain transformed the family basement into Madison Square Garden, where he played basketball against himself with a tennis ball and restaged on-ice fights with a tough neighbour. See Brian Nolan, *Donald Brittain: Man of Film* (DigiWire, 2004), 11. Television leaves so little to the imagination.

9.   Peter Gzowski, "Skating," in *Peter Gzowski's Book About This Country in the Morning* (Edmonton: Hurtig Publishers, 1974), 171.

10. Although the line is often attributed to Peter, it was penned in 1972 by Heather Scott, a young woman from Sarnia, in response to Peter's first contest on *This Country in the Morning*. See Peter Gzowski, *The Morningside Years* (McClelland & Stewart, 1997), 330.

11. Sylvia Fraser, "Peter Peter," *Toronto Life*, April 2002, 106.

12. Email from Michael Enright, January 8, 2009.

13. The reference to the Greek sculptor from the fourth century B.C. bears a whiff of pretense. Peter borrowed the name, he later admitted, from a Chicago society columnist who in the 1960s had described Bobby Hull as "a statue by Praxiteles come alive from the Golden Age of Greece" (TUA, Gzowski fonds, 92-015, box 16, folder 3, rough drafts of his "Fan's Notes").

14. See eg. TUA, Peter Gzowski fonds, 92-015, box 12, Peter Gzowski, "A Fan's Notes," in the Edmonton Oilers program for December 23, 1981, 67. Peter repeated the phrase in his description of Messier that opens *The Game of Our Lives*, 13.

15. TUA, Peter Gzowski fonds, 92-015, box 20, folder 28, notes on *Morningside*, in preparation for his first *Morningside Papers*, where his notes, in part, appear on page 228–29.

16. His boys, as Peter liked to call them, wore well-cut suits that showed "slim hips." On airplanes, they "expressed themselves physically, wrestling, tugging, patting, slugging each other on the arm, and wrapping a fellow's neck in the crook of an arm...."

17. Peter N. Allison, "Life in Eaton's Catalogue, or How I Wrestled My Uncle Ernest in My Medium-Weight Thermal Underwear," *Maclean's*, April 20, 1963, 24–26.

18. The show pitted two families against each other to see which family could guess the "correct" answers to questions posed by the host. The correct answer had nothing to do with anything called truth. Instead, the answer was based on a survey of one hundred people, who arbitrarily chose what they thought *should* be the correct answers. The family that guessed the greatest number of answers could win up to $25,000.

19. Alison Gzowski, "Dad and Me," *Quest* (June/July/August 1984), 41.

20. Alan McGlashen to Lawrens van der Post in *Night of the New Moon* (London: Hogarth Press, 1970), 33. I wish to express my gratitude to Richard Osler for this line.

21. TUA, Peter Gzowski fonds, 92-015, box 2, folder 2.

22. Peter Gzowski, "Too-Big Daddy from the Ponderosa," *Maclean's*, June 5, 1965, 47.

Chapter 1: "Some Drastic Shaking Up, Early in Life"

1. Mavis Gallant, preface in *The Selected Stories of Mavis Gallant* (Toronto: McClelland & Stewart, 1997), xv.

2. Peter's contribution to the English language, in imitation of the sound of skates on ice.

3. For one version, see Peter Gzowski, sports column, *Saturday Night*, December 1965, 42–43, 45–46. For another, simpler version, see Peter Gzowski, *The Game of Our Lives* (Toronto: McClelland & Stewart Limited, 1981), 82.

4. Most of the information on James McGregor Young comes from the University of Toronto Archives (UTA), Department of Graduate Studies Records, A73-0026/531(70).

5. Trent University Archives (TUA), Marco Adrea fonds, Adrea interview with Peter Gzowski, April 28, 1987. Macdonald's relatives in Kingston and area were the Macphersons, Shaws, Grants, Clarks, and Greenes, none of them, apparently, related to the Youngs. For Sir John A's relatives, see Richard Gwyn, *John A, the Man Who Made Us: The Life and Times of John A. Macdonald*, Volume One: 1815–1867 (Toronto: Random House Canada, 2007), 41. Young graduated from the University of Toronto in 1884 and for three years was a junior member of the law firm of Blake, Lash & Cassells. In 1887 he founded his own firm, Young & McEvoy. In 1893 he began lecturing in law at Osgoode Law School, and in 1900 he was appointed professor of constitutional law, history, and international law at the University of Toronto, a position he held until 1913. His office was in the cloisters of University College. In 1908 he was made king's counsel, and in the 1920s, Ontario's Official

Guardian, whose role it was to oversee abandoned or abused children. In the 1930s, when he returned full-time to the practice of law, his offices were in the financial heart of Toronto.

6. Mackenzie and Mann made small fortunes by building bridges and snow sheds for the Canadian Pacific Railway in the Selkirks of British Columbia during the 1880s. From the late 1890s to 1917, they owned their own railway, the Canadian Northern, whose greatest monument is Winnipeg's Union Station. Mackenzie was president of the street railways of Winnipeg and Toronto for about thirty years, beginning in 1891. He was also president of Brazilian Traction.

7. My thanks to Mabel's son, Tony Griffin, and his wife, Kitty, for showing me Mabel's autograph book and the poem.

8. Her records at St Andrews and at the University of Toronto give her birth year as 1909. Peter, and perhaps Margaret, always claimed 1910 as her birth year.

9. Peter Gzowski, "How to Quit Smoking in Fifty Years or Less," in Lorna Crozier and Patrick Lane, eds., *Addicted: Notes from the Belly of the Beast* (Vancouver, Greystone Books, 2001), 56.

10. Later, in 1937 she did indeed obtain a bachelor of library science from the University of Toronto, and there is a record for that.

11. Pat Annesley, "Peter Gzowski: Growing up means never having to say you're perfect," *Chatelaine*, November 1972, 94.

12. In 1932, Young and his family, including Margaret, lived at 177 Balmoral Avenue, between Avenue Road and Poplar Plains Avenue. The next year the City of Toronto Directory lists McGregor Young as owner of a house at 97 Dunvegan Road near Timothy Eaton Memorial Church, in the posh St. Clair Avenue and Avenue Road district. At his death in 1942, he was living at 177 St. Clair Avenue East.

13. Interview with Kitty Griffin, November 2, 2006.

14. Interview with Neysa Mitchell, August 31, 2007. Her mother was living in the same nursing home at the same time. In a speech at the summer home of Stephen Leacock in the summer of 1989, Peter added further confusion. His mother and his grandmother Young, he told his audience, were crossing the Atlantic in October 1929 when the stock market crashed. Since Maude Young was out of touch with her brokers, Peter explained, much of the Young family fortune vanished, as if somehow his grandmother Young, had she been in Toronto, could have saved the family fortune. Peter also claimed, that evening in Orillia, that Margaret was on her way to enrol at St. Andrews in late October 1929. In his memoirs, published the year before the Leacock Festival speech, he had claimed that his mother had obtained her M.A. at age nineteen from St. Andrews. Since he believed that she was born in November 1910, Peter's version that evening would mean that she graduated soon after enrolling at St. Andrews. Margaret was most likely not on her way to enrol at St. Andrews in October 1929. See Peter Gzowski, "My Grandfather

Leacock," in Edna Barker, ed., *A Peter Gzowski Reader* (Toronto: McClelland & Stewart Ltd., 2002), 9; and Gzowski, "First Splashes of Printer's Ink," in *Ibid.*, 38). Peter's inventions may be attributable, in part at least, to the fact that his customary method of speech making was to scribble a few notes on the back of an envelope while waiting to speak. Nevertheless, part of the confusion of details seems deliberate, and Margaret herself may have been the source of the camouflage in order to account for missing years. As Peter once said, he would never let a few facts stand in the way of a good story.

15. The Colonel's grandfather, Sir Casimir, was legitimately a colonel, but the title isn't inherited. However, lieutenant-colonel or major doesn't have quite the ring of colonel.

16. The street was named after Colonel Joseph Wells, a decorated veteran of the Napoleonic wars, whose Georgian mansion, Davenport, though torn down about 1913, bequeathed to Toronto the name of one of its longer avenues.

17. Peter Gzowski, *Peter Gzowski's Book About This Country in the Morning* (Edmonton: Hurtig Publishers, 1974), 14.

18. Peter Gzowski, *The Morningside Papers* (Toronto: McClelland & Stewart), 276.

19. He probably rode the rails. Apparently he worked as a miner at Red Lake, Northern Ontario, as a newspaper reporter in New Orleans, and he picked grapefruit, perhaps in Florida.

20. UTA, Department of Graduate Records, A2007-004/004, Librarians' Course, 1936–37. Margaret's records at the University of Toronto, 1936–37, give her address as 63 Wells Hill Avenue.

21. UTA, Department of Graduate Records, A73-0026/531(70), Young, James McGregor.

22. Her grades at library school were not remarkable, all in the 60s and 70s.

23. Gzowski, "My Grandfather Leacock," in Barker, ed., *A Peter Gzowski Reader*, 10.

24. Marci McDonald, "What Does a Guy Who Quits a Winner Do for an Encore?" *Homemakers*, vol. 9, issue 5, September 1974.

25. Around the same time, Sir Frederick Banting was seeking a divorce. He hired detectives to spy on his wife, only to have the whole thing blow up in the headlines when reporters discovered that Banting himself was having an affair with a Canadian writer well known at the time. Fortunately, Margaret and Harold, neither of whom had discovered or invented anything except stories, kept their divorce proceedings out of the headlines — old families have a habit of guarding family secrets.

26. Gzowski, "How to Quit Smoking in Fifty Years or Less," 58.

27. Instead, Peter claimed that when he was about five, in other words in 1939, his mother married Reg Brown. City of Galt Directories and Assessment Rolls for 1940 show Reg Brown living by himself at 26 Rose Avenue. And in the autumn

of 1939, Margaret was still working in the book department of Eaton's. (See TUA, Peter Gzowski fonds, 01-004, box 1, file 17, Jack Young to Peter Gzowski, January 29, 1996.)

28. The war was good news for Harold, as it was for most unemployed men. Finally he had found steady, albeit dangerous, work, with a regular pay cheque, as a sergeant in the Royal Canadian Engineers. He was in charge of laying Bailey bridges across rivers in Sicily and up the boot of Italy. In the wedding announcement, Harold's second wife was listed as Mrs. Raikes. It was not her first marriage either. She had connections — her aunt, Countess Hollender, was in attendance. In a television review in *Maclean's* in 1965, Peter recalled that, during the late 1940s and 1950s, he often heard his father and his buddies reminiscing about the war, mostly about "good times: girls, parties, gifts from Italian villagers — and so on." (See Peter Gzowski, "Smile Boys — It Never Was Worthwhile," *Maclean's*, December 15, 1965, 51.) Once back in Toronto, Harold and three war buddies operated the Red Patch Delivery and Shopping Service whose motto was "If you're ill, busy, tired or just too lazy — we're not." Customers called in orders for anything from party dresses to baby sitters, wedding cakes, and house painters, all of which Harold and his partners purchased or hired, and delivered. (See *Toronto Star*, May 4, 1977, B10.)

29. UTA, Department of Graduate Records, A73-0026/132 (20). Lady Mann died five years later, in 1945. Sir Donald Mann, born in 1853, had died in 1934.

30. At 161 St. George today sits a 1950s-style apartment block.

31. Gzowski, *Peter Gzowski's Book About This Country in the Morning*, 104.

32. Gzowski, *Peter Gzowski's Book About This Country in the Morning*, 59.

33. Since the Waterloo County Board of Education has destroyed Peter's records, the exact day of his enrolment is unknown.

34. Peter Gzowski, *The Fourth Morningside Papers* (Toronto: McClelland & Stewart, 1991), 203–06.

35. Peter Gzowski, "Smile Boys," *Maclean's*, December 15, 1965, 51.

36. TUA, Peter Gzowski fonds, 01-004, box 4, folder 9.

37. Peter Gzowski, "The Pleasure of Guns," in Gzowski, *Peter Gzowski's Book About This Country in the Morning*, 215.

38. Russell Baker, "Life with Mother," in William Zinsser, ed., *Inventing the Truth: The Art and Craft of Memoir* (Boston: Houghton Mifflin, 1998), 26.

39. Peter Gzowski, *The Morningside Years* (Toronto: McClelland & Stewart, 1997), 2–5. During the 1930s and 1940s, homosexuality was more or less tolerated, if not generally, at least in the military and secret service. In 1951, after the homosexual British double agent Guy Burgess, along with Donald Maclean, fled London to live in Moscow, gays in Britain, and no doubt elsewhere, were equated with treachery and dishonour, and the full force of sodomy laws was used to prosecute gays. This

may be part of the background of Alice Munro's story of Poppy Cullender. See Miranda Carter, *Anthony Blunt, His Lives* (New York: Farrar, Straus and Giroux, 2001), 355.

40. A car without a back seat, but often with a rumble seat over the trunk, which could be pulled open for al fresco seating. The inside seat could hold two adults and a child. The term is derived from *coupé*, French for "cut" or "cropped."

41. Peter Gzowski, *The Fourth Morningside Papers* (Toronto: McClelland & Stewart, 1991), 29.

42. See *www.ourkids.net/camp/images/media/434_eBrochure.pdf* for a history of the camp.

43. Peter Gzowski, "First Splashes of Printer's Ink," from *The Private Voice*, reprinted in Barker, ed., *A Peter Gzowski Reader*, 38.

44. Alice Munro, *Open Secrets* (Toronto: McClelland & Stewart, 1994), 35 and 51.

45. TUA, Gzowski fonds, 01-004, box 1, folder 17, Jack Young to Peter Gzowski, January 29, 1996.

46. Strabo (Peter Gzowski), "What Disney Does to One Man's Family," *Maclean's*, February 20, 1965, 47.

47. Gzowski, "How to Quit Smoking in Fifty Years or Less," 57–58.

48. Its director was James Onley, father of Tony, well-known today for his impressionist sea- and landscapes of B.C.

49. Gzowski, "How to Quit Smoking in Fifty Years or Less," 56.

50. Peter N. Allison's "Life in Eaton's Catalogue, or How I Wrestled My Uncle Ernest in My Medium-Weight Thermal Underwear," *Maclean's*, April 20, 1963, 24–26.

51. Interview with Tom Brown, February 23, 2005.

52. TUA, Gzowski fonds, 92-015, box 20, folder 28.

53. Peter Gzowski, "Gordie Howe, Hero," *Maclean's*, December 14, 1963, 54.

54. TUA, Gzowski fonds, 92-015, box 12, Peter Gzowski, "A Fan's Notes," February 25, 1981; Gzowski, "A Fan's Notes," in *Playoff Magazine*, spring 1981, 67; and Gzowski, *Game of Our Lives*, 82. Peter wrote a regular column for the program that was published whenever the Oilers played on home ice. When the team was at home during the playoffs, in the spring of 1981, the program acquired the name *Playoff Magazine*.

55. Baker, "Life with Mother," 26.

56. Manoly Lupul, seven years older than Peter, grew up in Willingdon, near Edmonton. In his memoirs, he recounts listening to many of the same radio programs, including *Lux Radio Theatre*, and *Hockey Night in Canada*. Lupul, *The Politics of Multiculturalism, A Ukrainian-Canadian Memoir* (Edmonton Toronto: Canadian Institute of Ukrainian Studies Press, 2005), 8–9.

57. As a child, this biographer could never figure out what Hewitt meant by "His zone zone." Slowly, it became clear that Hewitt was saying "His own zone."

58. In an article in Moose Jaw's *Times-Herald* on May 25, 1957, Peter claimed that he had actually helped Hewitt to describe the game. In the *Times-Herald* piece, Peter added that, each time he listened to Hewitt on radio, subsequent to his visit to the Gardens, he bragged to his chums about having assisted Hewitt. Peter was always a great storyteller.

59. While Sir Casimir Gzowski spoke English with a Polish accent, it is doubtful if the Colonel, who was born in Toronto, son of a Canadian-born man, would have spoken with anything but a rather posh Ridley accent whose origin was somewhere in the mid-Atlantic.

60. William Burrill, "Gzowski Was a Bootlegger at 13," *Toronto Star*, April 20, 1982, A2. Peter's addiction to golf lasted well into the 1960s when he took the cure, only to fall off the wagon in the mid-1980s. See Peter Gzowski, sports column, *Saturday Night*, May 1966, 55 and 57. The metaphors are those of alcoholism: "I was hooked," "compulsive golfer," and "I'm clean. I haven't touched a golf club in three years."

61. Peter Gzowski, "1961: Summer of the Angry Forest Fires," *Maclean's*, September 9, 1961, 19.

62. Strabo (Peter Gzowski), "What Disney Does to One Man's Family," *Maclean's*, February 20, 1965, 47.

63. A rather excessive putdown. By contrast, in 1949, not long after Peter heard someone read Drummond in Galt, the *Dalhousie Review* called Drummond's language "freshened" and "renewed"; and in 1978 poet and critic Louis Dudek credited Drummond for loosening "the straitjacket of literary puritanism" in Canadian literature.

64. TUA, Gzowski fonds, 01-004, box 1, folder 8.

65. Gzowski, "How to Quit Smoking in Fifty Years or Less," 52.

66. On the other hand, Robert Fulford never let academic failure stop him. Fulford failed grade ten, as well as some grade twelve subjects. As Fulford says in his own memoir, "There are people for whom school simply never acquires meaning." See Robert Fulford, *Best Seat in the House*, (Toronto: Collins, 1988), 24. In fact, some of the most successful adults were bored by the education system's often meaningless discussions, essays, and examinations.

67. "Peter Gzowski's Remarkable Teachers," *Professionally Speaking*, December 1998, 25. My thanks to Paul Lewis, Ridley College Archives, for pointing out this article.

68. TUA, Gzowski fonds, 92-015, box 21, folder 3.

69. TUA, Gzowski fonds, 01-004, box 1, folder 2.

70. TUA, 01-004, box 4, folder 9, Cambridge *Reporter*, February 2, 2002, a reprint from *Canadian Living* by Peter Gzowski about growing up in Galt.

71. Elizabeth Renzetti, "Slinkers, Jailers, Soldiers, Lies," *Globe and Mail*, October 4, 2008, R1 and R18.

72. TUA, Gzowski fonds, 92-015, box 1, folder 7.

Chapter 2: "Don't Try to Be Something That You're Not"

1. Although the ballpoint pen was invented in the 1880s, the first serviceable and affordable ballpoints weren't available until 1952. The pens are still sometimes called "Bic" in memory of France's Marcel Bich, who made the concept practical.

2. J.D. Salinger, *The Catcher in the Rye* (Boston: Little, Brown, 1991), 4. Since *The Catcher in the Rye* was published in 1951, more than a year after Peter's departure from Galt, it is unlikely that Peter could have emulated its fictional hero in 1949. It is also unlikely that the young Peter had encountered Holden Caulfield in stories or excerpts that appeared in *Collier's, Saturday Evening Post*, and *The New Yorker* when he was only ten years old. More likely, since the novel was a favourite of Peter's, it influenced the way he remembered his flight from Galt.

3. Peter Gzowski, *Peter Gzowski's Book About This Country in the Morning* (Edmonton: Hurtig Publishers, 1974), 14.

4. Peter Gzowski, ed., *A Sense of Tradition* (St. Catharines, ON: Ridley College and Hedge Row Press, 1988), 15. The lion is no longer to be seen by the millions of motorists who use the road each year. A few years ago, it was removed in the name of progress and the automobile. The road required widening and salt was damaging the monument and its lion. The Queen Elizabeth Monument was partly the work of two sculptors, Frances Loring (the lion) and Florence Wyle (the crown and relief medallion of the King and Queen). The monument now sits in nearby Sir Casimir Gzowski Park, Lakeshore Boulevard West, Toronto. See Elspeth Cameron, *And Beauty Answers, The Life of Frances Loring and Florence Wyle* (Toronto: Cormorant, 2007), photographs between 324 and 325. In his history of Ridley, Peter claims that there were two lions. He was probably confusing the one large lion on the Queen Elizabeth Monument with the two smaller lions at either end of the bridge over Martindale Pond in St. Catharines.

5. His birthplace, Toronto, was burned during the same war, but unlike the booming provincial capital, the Niagara Peninsula has memorialized the war by preserving battle sites and forts and by erecting statues and monuments. Toronto did rebuild Fort York.

6. "Peter Gzowski's Remarkable Teachers," *Professionally Speaking*, December 1998, 25.

7. Peter Gzowski, *The Private Voice: A Journal of Reflections* (Toronto: McClelland & Stewart, 1988), 63.

8. The library also held the British *Dictionary of National Biography*, all fourteen volumes, *Portrait of Britain, 1851–1951*, and Trevelyan's *English Social History*, as well as an excellent collection of records, including Rachmaninoff's "Rhapsody on a Theme of Paganini," Brahms's "Hungarian Dances," and works by Mozart, Grieg, and other masters.

9.   Given Peter's love of theatre and performance, it is surprising not to find his name among the list of actors and directors at Ridley. In 1947, a couple of year before Peter arrived, Darcy McKeough, later a Cabinet minister under Premiers William Davis and John Robarts, had starred in *The Ghost Train*, dressed smartly in a lady's hat, suit, and sensible shoes; and in 1949, Bill Glassco, later artistic director of Tarragon Theatre in Toronto, starred as a rather demure maid in *Ridley Onward* in 1949. Since at that time Ridley barred girls, female characters were played by males. While Peter was at Ridley, Anton Chekhov's *The Marriage Proposal* was produced but without Peter.

10.   In the early 1950s, a few years before the rock-and-roll revolution, Peter and his fellows may have listened to Jo Stafford's "You Belong to Me," Vaughan Monroe's "Ghost Riders in the Sky," Gogi Grant's "The Wayward Wind," and any number of Frank Sinatra tunes. They may also have chosen Canadian music played by Oscar Peterson or Moe Koffman. There were Canadian singers at the time, such as Terry Dale and Norma Locke, but they performed on radio and television without being much recorded. For a survey of Canadian music, see Alex Barris and Ted Barris, *Making Music: Profiles from a Century of Canadian Music* (Toronto: HarperCollins Canada, 2001).

11.   Peter Gzowski, "How to Quit Smoking in Fifty Years or Less," in Lorna Crozier and Patrick Lane, eds., *Addicted: Notes from the Belly of the Beast* (Vancouver: Greystone Books, 2001), 60. Shortly after Peter's death in January 2002, Harry Bruce wrote a piece about Peter for the *Globe and Mail*. He had talked to John Girvin, who recounted a slightly different version of the bar story, one that places Peter at the middle of the tale. Peter was given the ultimate punishment, a caning "for arranging bus rides for his classmates to Niagara Falls, New York." Peter turned eighteen in July 1952, a month after graduating from Ridley, so even by American standards he was drinking under age. Not surprisingly, there is a third version, that while Peter helped organize the excursion, the ringleader was a boy named Weaver, who was killed in a car accident a few years after graduating from Ridley. There's even a fourth version, as recounted by Peter in that article in *Maclean's* in 1961. The excursion took place the year after the ink fight, which seems to have occurred sometime between January and June 1950, shortly after his arrival at Ridley. In this version, Peter was sixteen or seventeen. "Everyone in the class took his monthly movie leave the same Friday evening," Peter explained. "We chartered a bus and went to a nearby town where we could drink." In this version, Peter did not mention crossing into the States. They returned to Ridley, he remembered, quite late, "broke and singing or broke and sick, but full of beer and satisfaction and comradeship." The rule-breakers were severely caned. In the article in *Maclean's*, Peter explained that caning was actually considered an achievement. The only member of the class not to participate in the drinking was

E. Abelard Shaw, who was accused of squealing. In 2001, Peter wrote about the incident for the last time. This time the bus was "secretly" chartered, and it was his entire grade twelve class that quietly slipped out of the college. Their noisy return, however, alerted the masters to the misdeed, and the boys were caned.

12. Chicago-born Julian Street was a novelist, playwright, and travel writer who wrote for *Acta Ridleiana in the 1890s*. Subsequently, he was the drama critic for New York's *Mail and Express* and wrote for *Saturday Evening Post*.

13. Most if not all high schools at the time held cadet training each autumn. Students dressed in khaki uniforms with puttees and army boots, and marched around the sports field of the school each afternoon in preparation for a final march past. Cadets, no longer a feature of high schools today, may have been the tail end of the standing army of "Volunteers" that posed so proudly for photographs in the nineteenth century.

14. Out-of-date Eaton's catalogues were often the only paper in outhouses of yore.

15. Peter Gzowski, *The Game of Our Lives* (Toronto: McClelland & Stewart, 1981), 55.

16. Interview with Scott Symons, October 30, 2008.

17. Harold Averill and Gerald Keith, "Daniel Wilson and the University of Toronto," in Elizabeth Hulse, ed., *Thinking with Both Hands: Sir Daniel Wilson in the Old World and the New* (Toronto: University of Toronto Press, 1999), 176–77; and emails from Harold Averill, July 21–22, 2009. The house, which was known as the University College Men's Residence when Peter lived in it, was torn down during the summer of 1953 to make way for the Sir Daniel Wilson Residence, officially opened in December 1954.

18. The house on Tranby has survived. In fact, most of the Annex has survived and is/was home to Jane Jacobs, Adrienne Clarkson, and Margaret Atwood, as well as to thousands of other well-heeled folk who in the last two or three decades of the twentieth century opted to live amid the splendours of nineteenth-century Toronto.

19. Letter from John Girvin, nd (circa June 2005).

20. Perhaps he was inspired by an article in *Acta Ridleiana* published in the Midsummer issue of 1952. In "Railway to Labrador," Ridley Old Boy A.A. Wright advised young men who were considering a career in civil engineering to spend a summer in Labrador, northern Manitoba, or at Kitimat. "He will learn much — even perhaps ... that he is temperamentally unsuited for work of this type," Wright advised.

21. In 1953, CBC-TV didn't reach Kitimat, and of course this was long before the days of video movies.

22. Trent University Archives (TUA), Peter Gzowski fonds, 95-008, folder 16. Although Peter gives 1952 as the year, it was 1953, for he had just written his first-year examinations at the U of T.

23. Email from Harold Averill, July 21, 2009.

24. TUA, Peter Gzowski fonds, 92-015, box 20, folder 28.

25. The university directory for that year does not list a Peter Gzowski. In his memoirs, he claimed he did enrol, but that his pride was wounded when one professor told him that he couldn't write. In *Homemakers*, September 5, 1974, Peter told Marci McDonald that he had quit university that autumn because he had gambled away his money. This version ties in with a story he recounted in March 1957 to Cathie Breslin, a journalist at *The Varsity*. He had made $1,000 in Labrador, but had lost it in Montreal. Gambling? Alcohol? Peter also told Breslin that, once back in Toronto, he had made $250 in a crap game, and that he worked as a grease monkey in a gas station, perhaps the one owned by his grandfather Gzowski. He tried writing, he told Breslin, but all he ever earned were rejection slips.

26. Robert Reguly is remembered today as the man who found Gerda Munsinger, in Munich, where she had retreated after "lunching" with George Hees and Pierre Sévigny, Cabinet ministers in the government of John Diefenbaker. The Reguly dictation incident appeared first in Peter's *The Private Voice*, 65, and was later reprinted in Edna Barker, ed., *A Peter Gzowski Reader* (Toronto: McClelland & Stewart, 2001), 40.

27. Interview with Robert Reguly, November 4, 2007.

28. Peter never did learn the difference between *so* and *so that*. Come to think of it, the difference is rarely acknowledged today by his CBC colleagues, nor by his successors at *Maclean's*. At this time, and for a few more years, Peter used the American spelling of words such as *colour* and *favourite*.

29. Interview with Robert Reguly, November 4, 2007, and with Chris Salzen, November 7, 2007.

30. Gzowski, *Peter Gzowski's Book About This Country in the Morning*, 59–60.

31. Gzowski, *The Private Voice*, 67–68.

32. Peter Gzowski, "The Global Village Has Anything but Surprises," *Saturday Night*, December 1968, 33.

33. Interview with Chris Salzen, November 7, 2007. The character Sheridan Whiteside was a malicious representation of the New York City drama critic Alexander Woollcott. My thanks to Jeanie Wagner for pointing out this detail.

34. Email from Chris Salzen, November 12, 2007.

35. Alas, the building, the pride of Timmins, was torn down a few years ago.

36. My thanks to Chris Salzen for straightening me out on the two radio stations in Timmins at that time (email November 27, 2007).

37. Gzowski, *The Private Voice*, 105.

38. Robert Fulford, *Best Seat in the House: Memoirs of a Lucky Man* (Toronto: Collins, 1988), 58. See also Robert Fulford fonds, William Ready Division of Archives and Research Collections, McMaster University Library, box 5, file 43, Peter Gzowski

— article by him for *Maclean's*, rough draft, December 29, 1986 TMs(copy) 41 pp. not published, 2–3.

39. Donald Sutherland was but one of several actors who during the 1950s acted at Hart House Theatre under directors such as Leon Major and Robert Gill. Other actors at Hart House were William Hutt, Charmion King, Kate Reid, and the Davis brothers, who with their sister, Barbara Chilcot, founded the Crest Theatre on Mount Pleasant Road in 1954.

40. Peter saved the entire run of *The South Shore Holiday* but left the copies at 98 Lytton Boulevard when he quit the family home in 1977. Spring housecleaning took care of the weeklies, and perhaps only one copy remains, in the Gzowski fonds at Trent University Archives.

41. Interview with Judy (Brodie) Burton, November 21, 2005.

Chapter 3: Not Paris Nor London, but Moose Jaw and Chatham

1. Interview with John Burbidge, September 22, 2008. Burbidge sat on the Student Administrative Council (SAC) as a representative of one of the four colleges that made up the University of Toronto. Scott Symons had been a member of SAC, representing Trinity College, and his brother, Tom, was chair of SAC, when Peter was elected editor, though the chair had no say in the selection.

2. Later Elizabeth Gray.

3. Wendy Michener was the daughter of Governor General Roland Michener. She and Peter met again at *Maclean's*.

4. The Bobby Darin version of "Mac the Knife" wasn't released until August 1959.

5. The Reverend Iain Macdonald in Edna Barker, ed., *Remembering Peter Gzowski: A Book of Tributes* (Toronto: McClelland & Stewart, 2002), 29.

6. Peter Gzowski, *Maclean's*, January 31, 1959, in Trent University Archives (TUA), Peter Gzowski fonds, 92-015,box 3, folder 3.

7. Interview with Professor Tom Symons, June 20, 2006.

8. Breslin went from Toronto to New York where she continued to work as a journalist. Around 1960, when Peter was Previews editor at *Maclean's*, Breslin wrote feature articles for the magazine.

9. According to Patsy Pehleman, Elizabeth Gray told a variation of this story — the young Peter "could make a trip to the laundromat sound like an adventure." (See Patsy Pehleman in Barker, ed., *Remembering Peter Gzowski*, 77.) Gray, no doubt, had read Breslin's article.

10. Not quite. Pierre Berton probably holds the record. At twenty-one, he became city editor of the Vancouver *News-Herald*. Peter was about a year older when he went to Moose Jaw. See A.B. McKillop, *Pierre Berton, A Biography* (Toronto:

McClelland & Stewart Ltd., 2008), 139.

11. Peter Gzowski, postscript added in 2001 to "The Editorial That Changed My Life," in Barker, ed., *A Peter Gzowski Reader*, 55.

12. TUA, Peter Gzowski fonds, 92-015, box 1, folder 18. The correspondent's memory seems precise. Often Peter commented in the margins of letters, especially if he disagreed with their content. There is nothing in the margins of this letter.

13. "Speck's Idea," *The Selected Stories of Mavis Gallant* (Toronto: McClelland & Stewart, 1996), 474.

14. Colm Tóibín, *The Master* (Toronto: McClelland & Stewart, 2004), 333. In later life, Peter was careful to hide any spiritual or religious life. In fact, on one occasion he made fun of miracles and other manifestations of faith. One day in the early 1970s when his friend Cathy Perkins was in Toronto, the two of them met for coffee at the Four Seasons Hotel across from the CBC building on Jarvis Street. At the time Peter was on crutches, thanks to an injured joint. As he hobbled in, he was hailed by a table of colleagues. He headed to their table, dramatically threw down his crutches, raised his eyes heavenward, and cried out, in the manner of evangelical TV preachers of the day, "Praise the Lord! I'm c-c-c-c-c-cured!" (Email from Cathy Perkins, September 8, 2008). And yet there are hints that Peter did indeed believe in something beyond the physical and material. At Ridley College in March 1952, the Lord Bishop of Niagara confirmed Peter and twenty-three other young men, after which they listened to the Right Reverend Walter E. Bagnall explain that "Confirmation commits a person to God and God will see them through all the hard times which may arise." At Ridley he loved attending services in the college's chapel where he and fellow choir members sang his favourite hymn, William Blake's "Jerusalem," whose words speak of revival and utopianism. Peter's radio play written in Timmins in 1954 denounced materialism and implied that there was indeed a world of faith. He told readers of the *Toronto Star* of October 18, 1978, that on his trip to Poland in the late 1970s he had attended mass in Posnan. In May 1992, he told Marco Adria that he was "touched by mystery, ritual, and faith." Thus he enjoyed the Polish pope's visit to Canada in 1984, for which he did the colour commentary for CBC-TV. His faith wasn't necessarily tied to a god. In Wayne Gretzky's gracious and stylish goals, he claimed to find mystery and faith.

15. Was the horseshoe motif common to city editors? In William Weintraub's *Why Rock the Boat* (1961), the city editor of a large Montreal newspaper also sits behind a big horseshoe desk. See William Weintraub, *Why Rock the Boat* (Toronto: McClelland & Stewart, 1961), 61; and interview with William Weintraub, September 25, 2006, who pointed out that the horseshoe shape allowed staffers to sit on three sides of the editor.

16. According to a contributor to Warren Clements's column on words in the *Globe and Mail*, February 4, 2006, D14.

17. The Tommy Douglas government had also invested in fish, shoes, paper boxes, lumber, and wool blankets without remuneration, and in potash, which eventually became profitable. "Saskatchewan blankets" kept many a Canadian knee warm during hockey games played in cold arenas in the 1950s.

18. Peter Gzowski, "Report from the Heartland of Canada," *Maclean's*, July 25, 1964, 29. In 1959, Ross Thatcher became the Liberal opposition leader in Saskatchewan and premier in 1964.

19. Where he would meet his future wife, JoAnn. And the rest is history and biography.

20. The *Times-Herald* also kept readers informed of the world at large. At Little Rock, Arkansas, in 1957, African Americans were confronting the state governor and his enthusiastic police dogs over the issue of integrated schools. In early October, the Soviet Union surprised the West by lobbing *Sputnik* into space. In July the Festival Theatre opened at Stratford, Ontario, and Queen Elizabeth II and the Duke of Edinburgh paid a four-day visit to Canada in October.

21. Interviews with Murray Burt, March 15, 2006, and May 24, 2007.

22. Interview with Louise Brennan, March 17, 2006. The car was immobilized on Monday evening, September 16, 1957, when a second car driven by Shirley Avery of Second Avenue ran into Joseph Kennan's parked car on Grafton Avenue, not far from Peter's apartment. The news appeared on the city page, September 18, 1957, under the headline "Parked Car Hit on Grafton Ave." This biographer regrets that Louise hasn't lived long enough to read about herself and Peter.

23. Not quite true. Canadian television went on the air in 1952, the year Peter turned eighteen, and before that, Galt was close enough to the American border to pick up television signals from Detroit, though it must be noted that the Brown flat seems not to have had a television set when Peter lived there until Christmas 1949. Nor apparently did Ridley College during Peter's years there.

24. Sylvia Fraser, quoted by Marci McDonald in "What Does a Guy Who Quits a Winner Do for an Encore?" *Homemakers*, vol. 9, issue 5, September 1974.

25. Interview with Sheila Phillips, January 15, 2005.

26. Now the home of the Snowbirds.

27. Email from Lyn Goldman, September 16, 2008.

28. Interview with Cal Abrahamson, April 2, 2006.

29. Peter Gzowski, *The Private Voice: A Journal of Reflections* (Toronto: McClelland & Stewart, 1988), 40.

30. The *Toronto Star* reported on November 30, 1962, that Reg Lissaman had been retained on the board of Manitoba Hydro.

31. Card, October 2, 2005, from "Jennie" Lissaman Gzowski to author. Peter usually spelled his wife's name as "Jenny." Her middle name is Anne.

32. Peter Gzowski, "The Awesome Cult of the Utterly Trivial," *Saturday Night*, June 1965, 16.

33. Interviews with Margaret McBurney, April 16, 2005, and November 10, 2007.

34. Gzowski, "Report from the Changing Heartland of Canada," *Maclean's*, July 25, 1964, 10.

35. During the summer of 1957, movies such as Michael Todd's *Around the World in 80 Days* and Cecil B. DeMille's *The Ten Commandments* played in Regina and Moose Jaw. Deborah Kerr and Cary Grant starred in *An Affair to Remember*, and Elvis Presley in *Loving You*. In Moose Jaw, the Capitol Theatre on Main Street, a former vaudeville house, was a popular place for movies. The *Ten Commandments* played there in September, and *The Delicate Delinquent* with Jerry Lewis in October. At the Golden West Drive-in, Frank Sinatra and Debbie Reynolds starred in *The Tender Trap*.

36. Interviews with Margaret McBurney, April 16, 2005, and November 10, 2007. Murray Burt has confirmed that, during Peter's brief sojourn in Moose Jaw, the city was no prize. Since then it has transformed itself, with a little help from gambling and Al Capone mythology, into today's attractive, viable city.

37. In 1958, for instance, Peter attended Murray's wedding in Regina.

38. Although often hard on capitalists, fiscal conservatives, and anyone who valued black ink, Peter usually defended Roy Thomson, who, Peter contended, never interfered with content unless it threatened to lower sales. Raymond Giroux, a journalist with Quebec's *Le Soleil*, once told the biographer the same thing about Conrad Black, that paper's then owner.

39. Peter Gzowski, *Peter Gzowski's Book About This Country in the Morning* (Edmonton: Hurtig Publishers, 1974), 15.

40. When Peter was hired, the managing editor was Ray Munro, who had held the position since February 1957. Munro followed in the footsteps of Richard Doyle and Clarke Davey, two first-rate journalists and editors. Expectations were high, and when Munro didn't meet them, he was fired. In his memoirs, Peter claimed that the dismissal was punishment for attempting to "transform" the paper by making it more lively and positive. Other witnesses weren't so kind. On March 19, 1958, the paper reported that Munro was suing the *Daily News* and Thomson Company Ltd.

41. TUA, Peter Gzowski fonds, 01-004, box 4, folder 17.

42. Soon after Maria's birth, in August 1961, Peter reported to Mordecai Richler that "Jennie girled again." See Mordecai Richler fonds, Special Collections, University of Calgary, MsC 36.7.40.31, Gzowski to Richler, nd.

Chapter 4: The Dangerous Temptation of Prediction

1. The novels included a war story (1946), *The Chartered Libertine*, a satire on the

CBC (1954), and *Peace River Country* (1958), which Blair Fraser called "a serious and major contribution to Canadian literature." See Blair Fraser, "Ralph Allen and *Maclean's*: An Unfinished Story," *Maclean's*, May 7, 1960, 87. Fraser had just taken over from Allen as editor. Allen had been in the Italian campaign of the Second World War as a correspondent for the *Globe and Mail*. Afterward, he joined *Maclean's* as assistant editor.

2. Peter Gzowski, "The Editorial That Changed My Life," in Edna Barker, ed., *A Peter Gzowski Reader* (Toronto: McClelland & Stewart, 2001), 55.
3. Peter Gzowski, *The Private Voice: A Journal of Reflections* (Toronto: McClelland & Stewart, 1988), 109; and cited in Marco Adria, *Peter Gzowski: An Electric Life* (Toronto: ECW Press, 1996), 80.
4. Gzowski, *The Private Voice*, 104.
5. Some examples of what his stringers sent Peter: "Preview" for June 20, 1959, quoted the president of Foothill Products Pipe Line, Ltd., on the possibility of shipping coal to wood through large pipes over long distances by using pressurized water. In the next issue, two weeks later, "Preview" contained seven short articles, one of which was a new idea on how an ex-smoker might deal with nervous hands. The solution was "Conversation Beads" that two businessmen were marketing at $2.98. One contributor to "Preview," perhaps Peter himself, predicted that CBC Radio would soon have an FM radio network. In subsequent issues, "Preview" predicted that Barkerville, British Columbia, would snare tourists with its historic re-creation of a gold-mining town, that Canadians would soon be driving on rubberized roads, and that lighthouse keepers would soon be as rare as blacksmiths. In September 1959, "Preview" predicted the next bestsellers, including Ralph Curry's biography of Stephen Leacock, and Pierre Berton's *Just Add Water and Stir*, a collection of his *Toronto Star* columns.
6. Interview with Murray Burt, May 24, 2007.
7. Ironically, it was Quebec that led the way toward less censorship, but in 1958 few people could have believed it possible in a province run by Premier Duplessis and the Roman Catholic Church.
8. Was Peter implying that Ross McLean was gay? If so, in 1960 he had to suggest homosexuality in code, for at that time most gays lived in dark closets. Colleagues of Ross McLean don't remember him as gay. Later he married, which, of course, proves nothing.
9. Peter may have been thinking of New York photographs by Alfred Stieglitz and movies such as *An Affair to Remember*.
10. Was the Modigliani his *Nude*, painted in 1917, and part of the collection of the Guggenheim? The large oil depicts a sensuous female draped over a couch in full pubic glory, her eyes closed, her arms resting behind her head.
11. Abstract Expressionism, an art movement that developed in New York after the Second World War, used spontaneity to discover and express the subconscious.

Peter might have been looking at a Jackson Pollock, who laid his canvases on the floor and dripped paint on them; or a Mark Rothko, who painted blocks of colour on canvas; or a Barnett Newman, who used bold, primary colours. In 1962 the school was promoted and encouraged in Canada when Clement Greenberg, a New York art critic, was invited to teach at the Emma Lake School of Fine Art in Saskatchewan. Among Canadian Abstract Expressionists encouraged by Greenberg were William Perehudoff, Jack Shadbolt, and Ronald Bloore.

12. Peter Gzowski, "The Global Village Has Everything but Surprises," *Saturday Night*, December 1968, 33. Nothing was surprising in New York in 1968, deemed Peter. He had seen it all in the movies. Nor was he impressed by the fact that Dylan Thomas had written *Under Milk Wood* in the men's room of the White Horse Tavern. In fact, his only surprise was that *all* the tables in the Algonquin Hotel were round.

13. In 1950, with Gérard Pelletier and others, Pierre Trudeau had founded the journal *Cité Libre*, which published articles by Quebec intellectuals opposed to Premier Maurice Duplessis and also to excessive nationalism.

14. Jacques Hébert became better known for *Deux innocents en Chine rouge* (1960), co-written with Pierre Trudeau, with whom he had travelled to China and the Soviet Union. Hébert also worked at *Cité Libre* and Radio-Canada and was president of Éditions du Jour publishing house. He was appointed to the Canadian Senate in 1983.

15. The Vanier Cup, named for Governor General Georges-Philéas Vanier, was awarded for the first time five years later in 1965 for the champion university football team.

16. Mordecai Richler fonds, Special Collections, University of Calgary, MsC 36.7.40.31 and 33, Gzowski to Richler, June 21, 1961, and July 11, 1961.

17. Peter claimed he was one of the founders of *Le Magazine Maclean*, whose first suggested title was the not very French *Le Magazine Maclean's*.

18. The terminology used in this narrative is mostly borrowed from the period in which it was used — the 1960s. *French Canadian* was the usual term to refer to what in French was *Canadien*, which evolved into *Canadien français* and *Québécois*. The term *separatist* was used only in English, for Quebec nationalists preferred *indépendentiste*. In an address to a conference at the University of Alberta in September 1977, Camille Laurin, Quebec's minister of state for cultural development, claimed that "Quebec does not want to be separated any more than any other healthy country would want to be," and thus *les Québécois* didn't accept the term *separatist*. See Manoly R. Lupul, ed., *Ukrainian Canadians, Multiculturalism, and Separatism: An Assessment* (Edmonton: University of Alberta Press, 1978), 13.

19. In a separate and short piece on the same page, Peter pointed out the irony that, among the militants, were several anglophones: Peter White, president and founder of the Laval Conference; and Michael Meighen and Brian Mulroney,

two of its vice-presidents. Even the editor of the Laval student newspaper was an anglophone. All spoke fluent, unaccented French. Two of them, probably Meighen and Mulroney, hoped to become MPs. Peter predicted that all three would achieve "prominence in public life before they're much older."

20. On *The Best of Morningside*, Friday evening, May 1, 1988, Peter and his political panel were discussing the origin of the term *quiet revolution*. Peter surmised that it had been a reporter from Toronto's *Telegram* who had first coined it. In Powell River, British Columbia, Brian Upton was listening that evening. Three days later he wrote to Peter to claim that it was he who first employed the phrase while reporting for the *Montreal Star* in 1961 from Quebec City. Not until 1969 did Upton join Toronto's *Telegram*. In his "Quebec Report" of May 5, 1962, Peter announced that he was no longer going to use quotation marks around the term because it had become ingrained in daily Quebec life. While Peter didn't invent the phrase, he did make it a part of our lexicon. In 1967, Jean Lesage confirmed that the phrase was first used by English-speaking newspapermen who "wanted to give their readers a short and imaginative expression to describe the energy and initiative that had suddenly taken hold of all of Quebec's population." (LAC, Paul Yuzyk fonds, MG 32, C-67, vol. 18, file 9, Lesage's address to the Canadian Jewellers Association, Montreal, May 8, 1967). Lesage may have been thinking of Upton.

21. *Les insolences du Frère Untel* sold more than one hundred thousand copies, while Marcel Chaput's book sold thirty-five thousand copies, figures that made English-language publishers drool. Even history books such as *La Crise de la conscription* and a history of theatre in Quebec sold well.

22. Jean Lesage's Liberals, who first came to power in June 1960, won the election of 1962 but were defeated by Daniel Johnson and his Union Nationale in June 1966.

23. Because Blair Fraser was a friend of the Trudeau family and a subscriber to *Cité Libre*, he might have informed Peter about one of the rising stars of Quebec intellectual and political life. See John English, *Citizen of the World: The Life of Pierre Elliott Trudeau, Volume One: 1919–1968* (Toronto: Knopf Canada, 2008), 230, 311, and 329–30.

24. Peter Gzowski, "Portrait of an Intellectual in Action," *Maclean's*, February 24, 1962, 23, 29–30. A decade later Prime Minister Trudeau made multiculturalism official (1971). When he talked to Peter, Trudeau's term was *multinationalism*. The term *interculturalisme* is used in French Canada today.

25. Michael Gauvreau, *The Catholic Origins of Quebec's Quiet Revolution, 1931–1960* (Montreal and Kingston: McGill-Queen's University Press, 2005), 11.

26. Interview with William Weintraub, September 25, 2006.

27. Charles Taylor, *Six Journeys: A Canadian Pattern* (Toronto: House of Anansi Press, 1977), 203–05. Unlike Peter, Scott Symons was fluent in French. Whether or not

Meet with a certified technician and get personalized recommendations for your PC.

Plus, we will also:

- Boost speed and performance
- Check for spyware and viruses
- Optimize your hard drive

Schedule an appointment today.

Peter talked to Symons before Peter left Toronto for Montreal in November 1961, or whether he was even aware of Symons's twenty-five articles in *La Presse* on what became known as the Quiet Revolution, Peter never said.

28. Mordecai Richler fonds, Special Collections, University of Calgary, MsC 36.7.41.14, Gzowski to Richler, December 6, 1963. In Peter's papers at Trent University Archives, there is no evidence of a book on Quebec.

Chapter 5: "You're Taking Too Much Goddamn Time"

1. Peter Gzowski to John Millyard during a golf game, circa 1964.
2. Harry Bruce on Peter, *Globe and Mail,* January 25, 2002, A17; and interview with Harry Bruce, October 24, 2007. When Bruce expressed similar sentiments in an article in *Weekend Magazine* in 1973, Peter took exception to Bruce's description of his sideways, distasteful appearance. Years later, however, Gill Howard told Bruce that he had hit the nail on the head, for she remembered that same expression one night when *90 Minutes Live* was being broadcast from Charlottetown.
3. Mordecai Richler fonds, Special Collections, University of Calgary, MsC 36.7.40.52b-c, Gzowksi to Richler, December 16, 1962.
4. The letter provides a glimpse of the housing market in Toronto at the time. To buy the house on Washington, Peter figured he would need $30,000, with a 25 percent down payment. Banks preferred to provide mortgages for the new, suburban houses in Don Mills, Etobicoke, and Scarborough. The land, then as now, was the most important factor, at least in the downtown area where about two-thirds of the cost of a house was the land on which it sat. Peter was astounded to discover that a house on Prince Arthur Avenue near the Park Plaza was selling for the astronomical sum of $53,000. (By 1970, that same house was probably nudging $100,000.) Peter warned Richler that the east end of Toronto was full of Orangemen!
5. Peter might have added that Radio-Canada, beginning in 1952 when Canadian television went on the air, played an important role in destroying the colonial mentality of French Canadians. Satirical sitcoms starring actors such as Dominique Michel, *téléromans* re-creating/inventing golden ages, and serials such as *Les Plouffe* helped to forge a nation. Nor does Peter mention that inside Montreal's smoke-filled *boîtes-à-chanson*, *chansonniers* like Pauline Julien sang their protests to young, intellectually engaged Québécois. The five bombers named aren't so well-known today, overshadowed as they are by their successors, Paul and Jacques Rose and others, who moved from bombs to kidnapping and murder in October 1970.
6. The poll was carried out by *Maclean's* and *Le Magazine Maclean*, together with the CBC-TV show *Inquiry* and *Le Groupe de recherche sociale* at l'Université de Montréal.

7.   The idea of running candidates in federal elections wasn't part of the questionnaire. That the survey was conducted while Marcel Chaput, leader of the largest *indépendentiste* party, was on a hunger strike, may have helped to make independence more appealing for some of the one thousand people surveyed.

8.   There were, Peter noted, more and more translations of books such as *Les insolences du Frère Untel.* The *Globe and Mail* now had bureaus in Quebec City and Montreal. French-Canadian entertainers now performed in Toronto nightclubs, and Toronto galleries held exhibitions of French-Canadian artists. No French-language newspaper sent reporters to the rest of Canada, Peter pointed out. No English-Canadian play had ever been shown on Radio-Canada. Mordecai Richler's novels could be read in French in Paris, but not in Montreal. And Peter C. Newman's *Renegade in Power* was available in English only.

9.   John Chaput, "Thomas Shoyama, Civil Servant and Teacher 1916–2006," *Globe and Mail*, December 30, 2006, S9. When Peter was researching and writing the article, about seventy of these bright, young bureaucrats, no longer appreciated by the new Liberal regime of Ross Thatcher, were moving to Ottawa. Eventually, Shoyama became federal deputy finance minister.

10. The restaurant Peter liked in Regina was probably l'Habitant, a tiny bistro with about four tables on Lorne Street near 14th Avenue. One reviewer deemed its pea soup the best in Canada. Gene Ciuca, the owner of l'Habitant, also owned the city's first pizza restaurant, its first coffee house, the "Fourth Dimension," and its first Kentucky Fried Chicken franchise (email from David Wessel, January 1, 2007, with an addition by Jeanie Wagner, March 17, 2007). Saskatchewan residents today are no doubt aware that in 1964 it wasn't difficult to meet the dining standards of Toronto, whose meat-and-potatoes cuisine was only just being challenged by pasta, shish kebobs, and coq au vin.

11. Peter Gzowski, "Last Chance to Head Off a Showdown with the Canadian Indian," *Maclean's*, July 6, 1963, 4; and "This Is Our Alabama," July 6, 1963, 20–21, 46–49. It was as honest an account as any journalist could have written in 1963. To his credit, Peter was the first journalist to alert Canada to the growing alienation of its First Nations people. In fact, today Donald Smith, noted historian of Native history, gives Peter the credit for awakening historians to this black mark in Canadian history (Email from Donald Smith, January 25, 2006). Peter's honesty is all the more remarkable when one recalls that a decade later Pierre Berton gave nary a thought to how the Canadian Pacific Railway, our "National Dream," had helped to dispossess First Nations in the 1880s and 1890s.

12. In 1886 the Caughnawaga Reserve became known for high-steel construction when members worked on a Canadian Pacific Railway bridge into Montreal. To pursue the trade, Horn's father moved the family to Brooklyn, New York, where Audrey, Horn's given name, and her siblings lived until their father was killed in

a work accident. Audrey then enrolled at Concordia University, worked in Paris, travelled in Europe, and became an activist at home. Although Horn may have told Peter that she was twenty-two in 1964, Bennett McCardle in "Horn, Kahn-Tineta" in *The Canadian Encyclopedia*, second edition, vol. 2, 1007, gives Horn's birth date as 1940. McCardle claims Horn was born in New York City, while Horn seems to have told Peter that, until age seven she lived on the reserve near Montreal. In the 1960s, Horn dumped rats onto a table during a government meeting. She later became a bureaucrat with the Department of Indian Affairs.

13. Peter N. Allison's "Life in Eaton's Catalogue, or How I Wrestled My Uncle Ernest in My Medium-Weight Thermal Underwear," *Maclean's*, April 20, 1963, 24–26.

14. TUA, Gzowski fonds, 92-015, box 9, folder 6.

15. *Maclean's*, January 4, 1964, 4.

16. Peter Gzowski, "The Hottest Little Horse in Canada, the Best Foot Race All Winter," *Maclean's*, February 22, 1964, 46.

17. Mordecai Richler fonds, Special Collections, University of Calgary, MsC 36.7.41.14, Gzowski to Richler, December 6, 1963; and MsC 36.7.41.16, Gzowski to Richler, December 20, 1963.

18. As it turned out, Ken Lefolii liked the article, and the short piece, called in Richlerian fashion "Anyone with a Thick Accent Who'd Steal Milk Money from Little Children Can't Be *All* Bad," was published on April 4. In it the novelist scorned stage and screen clichés such as the one about all sensitive men being lean, or that all scientists smoked pipes, or that all writers wore tweed jackets and smoked pipes. He was also cross that all upper-class women were portrayed as having the hots for working-class men. (He might have had a film like *Room at the Top* in mind.) Richler wasn't an admirer of Irving Layton's poetry, but admitted that at least Layton added colour to the otherwise grey Canadian landscape, as did Charlotte Whitton, the long-serving mayor of Ottawa.

19. Mordecai Richler fonds, Special Collections, University of Calgary, MsC 36.7.41.18, Gzowski to Richler, February 4, 1964. In 1964 it was common to jest about homosexuality. In the March 7, 1964, issue of *Maclean's*, Sidney Katz's "The Harsh Facts of Life in the 'Gay' World" lamented the fact that most homosexuals couldn't be converted, and thus their only option was shame, agony, and fear.

20. W.O. Mitchell fonds, Special Collections, University of Calgary, 19.8.12.21, Mitchell to Gzowski, March 11, 1964.

21. In *Canadian Forum*, October 1964, reprinted as "A Hockey Writer's Last Stand at *Maclean's*," in Edna Barker, ed., *A Peter Gzowski Reader* (Toronto: McClelland & Stewart, 2001), 130–35. Floyd Chalmers's Canada Council metaphor comes from this article (133).

22. The other two articles, by Peter C. Newman and Mordecai Richler, did manage to get published in the yellow pages under "Reports and Reviews." Newman, the

magazine's Ottawa editor, had been critical of the new Liberal government of Lester B. Pearson; and Richler had panned a memoir by Rabbi Abraham Feinberg of Toronto. (The rabbi's book was neither good nor even readable, nor was it troubled "by originality and insight," wrote the acerbic novelist. See Richler, "New Books: The Trouble with Rabbi Feinberg Is He's Just Too Palatable," *Maclean's*, July 25, 1964, 46.) According to the *Globe and Mail*'s report on the imbroglio, an editorial on Medicare and the Canadian Medical Association may also have been killed. But it was Harry Bruce's article on the strike that broke management's back.

23. Interview with Harry Bruce, October 24, 2007.

24. Interviews with Harry Bruce, October 24, 2007, and February 15, 2008. A receptionist across the hall witnessed Ronald McEachern's error and reported it to Bruce.

25. A large bowl or goblet, or in this case, a very large wine bottle. According to the *Oxford English Dictionary*, the word *jeroboam* seems to have gone out of use during the late nineteenth century.

26. Peter Gzowski, *The Private Voice: A Journal of Reflections* (Toronto: McClelland & Stewart, 1988), 56.

27. Edmund Wilson, *O Canada: An American's Notes on Canadian Culture* (New York: Farrar, Straus and Giroux, 1965), 4; and cited in Marco Adria, *Peter Gzowski: An Electric Life* (Toronto: ECW Press, 1996), 88.

28. Gzowski, "A Hockey Writer's Last Stand at *Maclean's*," in Barker, ed., *A Peter Gzowski Reader*, 133.

29. Adria, *Peter Gzowski: An Electric Life*, 91–92. One wonders how aloof Peter could possibly remain when it came to writing about corporate giants like Peter Pocklington, whose profile by Peter appeared in *Toronto Life* in April 1982. In it Peter claimed that the man, whom most colleagues found shrewd and calculating, was actually rather naive, and that he knew less about the realities of the Canadian political system than he did about geophysics. How much was Peter was influenced by the blandishments of Pocklington, including a return flight on his private jet from Edmonton to Yellowknife. On another occasion, the private jet took the two Peters north for a six-day fishing trip (TUA, Gzowski fonds, 92-015, box 1, folder 19, memo from Pocklington to Gzowski, July 5, 1983). Peter liked to claim that he was always wary of close links between journalism and broadcasting, on the one hand, and business on the other. "There is something questionable, surely, about the man who reads the evening news on the national network," Peter argued in 1965, "also pleading the merits of a particular brand of toothpaste or a particular kind of car." His main objection was that the newsreader was part of the CBC, which gave him "an aura of fairness and incorruptibility that the national news itself carried." He was perfectly willing to allow an announcer "to take any commercial assignments he can get," but he should never be allowed to

continue reading the news. See *Toronto Star*, February 18, 1970, 10; and Strabo (Peter Gzowski), "How TV Is Spoiling All the Fun," *Maclean's*, April 17, 1965, 46.

30. TUA, Gzowski fonds, 92-015, box 2, file 4: Speeches and Lectures, 1965.

31. *Toronto Star*, December 30, 1965, 3.

32. Harry Bruce, *Globe and Mail*, January 25, 2002, A17.

33. Email from Dennis Murphy, January 29, 2007.

34. Interview with John Millyard, May 25, 2005. A provisional ball assumes a count of one for the original shot, a second for returning the "lost" ball to the playing lie, and a third when the player strikes the ball.

35. Peter Gzowski, sports column, *Saturday Night*, May 1966, 58.

36. Email from John Millyard, October 10, 2007. The real Millyard didn't have a home course, and the match wasn't the finals but the semis. Since Millyard won, he went on to play another winner, Lloyd Hodgkinson, a vice-president at *Maclean's*, at the latter's home course, the Credit Valley Club.

37. Harry Bruce, note to author, October 15, 2007.

Chapter 6: A Sharp Eye on the World of Entertainment

1. Harry Bruce fonds, private collection, R.A. McEachern to Harry Bruce, July 31, 1964, just before Borden Spears was named editor of *Maclean's*.

2. The article was co-written with Shirley Mair, one of three assistant editors at *Maclean's*, the other two being Harry Bruce and David Lewis Stein.

3. Peter Gzowski, "Arnie Recruits His Canadian Army," *Maclean's*, September 19, 1964, 44.

4. Peter Gzowski, *The Private Voice* (Toronto: McClelland & Stewart, 1988), 109.

5. The name seems to have been a Latin term used by the Romans to describe anyone whose eyes were distorted or crossed. Hence the squinting. The term was also used to describe a Sicilian with vision so good that he could clearly see distant objects.

6. Knowlton Nash, *The Microphone Wars: A History of Triumph and Betrayal at the CBC* (Toronto: McClelland & Stewart, 1994), 334.

7. Strabo (Peter Gzowski), "Why the Real Sports Fans Stay Home," *Maclean's*, March 6, 1965, 46.

8. Strabo, "Why No Spoof Can Ever Kill 'UNCLE'," *Maclean's*, March 20, 1965, 46–47.

9. Strabo, "The Only Comics Who Use TV Right," *Maclean's*, April 3, 1965, 46.

10. Strabo, "How TV Is Spoiling All the Fun," *Maclean's*, April 17, 1965, 46.

11. Strabo, "Why TV's Bad Guys Are All White," *Maclean's*, May 1, 1965, 66.

12. Of course, the anonymous writer admitted, *Seven Days*, unlike *Bonanza*, had no commercial breaks to allow for visits to the bathroom; and, of course, on Sunday

evenings many people went to bed at 10:00 p.m. when *Bonanza* ended, and therefore were finished using the bathroom.

13. Strabo, "The Stealthy Comeback of the Quiz Show," *Maclean's*, July 3, 1965, 54. Alex Trebek didn't become the host of *Jeopardy* until September 1984.

14. Strabo, "Do TV Admen Watch Their Own Product?" *Maclean's*, June 19, 1965, 54.

15. Strabo, "Reruns? OK — But Why Bad Ones?" *Maclean's*, July 24, 1965, 48.

16. Strabo, "What TV Really Does to Our Kids," *Maclean's*, September 4, 1965, 46. The corollary, it seems, is that while television made stars seem ordinary, radio, though more intimate, maintains a distance between listener and host, thereby perpetuating the star quality that it helped to create. Unfortunately, Peter never went on to explain this role of radio.

17. Peter (Strabo) Gzowski, "Wow! Count Those Stars on the CBC," *Maclean's*, September 18, 1965, 63–64.

18. Peter Gzowski, "See Dick, See Jane, See CTV," *Maclean's*, October 2, 1965, 51–52.

19. Peter Gzowski, "At Last — A Hero Who Even Lies," *Maclean's*, November 15, 1965, 63.

20. Peter Gzowski, "Mr. MP — A Winner by Acclamation," *Maclean's*, December 1, 1965, 51.

21. Peter Gzowski, "Smile, Boys — It Never Was Worthwhile," *Maclean's*, December 15, 1965, 51. During the Persian Gulf War of early 1991, Peter revisited the subject of how TV could trivialize a serious situation. See Peter Gzowski, *The Fourth Morningside Papers* (Toronto: McClelland & Stewart, 1991), 190–206.

22. Peter Gzowski, "Winners of One Kind or Another," *Maclean's*, January 1, 1966, 47.

23. Peter Gzowski, "Countdowns Are Counted Down and Out," *Maclean's*, January 22, 1966, 49.

24. Peter Gzowski, "The Sheer Boredom of CBC's News," *Maclean's*, February 5, 1966, 43.

25. Peter Gzowski, "Seaway's Unsinkable Miss Samuels," *Maclean's*, March 19, 1966, 67. Colour TV was introduced to Canada on July 1, 1966, but not until 1974 did CBC broadcast fully in colour.

26. Contestants had been given correct answers in advance of shows like *The Sixty-Four Thousand Dollar Question*.

27. Peter Gzowski, "The Joys of Something for Nothing," *Maclean's*, April 2, 1966, 47.

28. Peter Gzowski, "Some More on the Joys of Color TV," *Maclean's*, April 16, 1966, 51.

29. Peter Gzowski, "Who Needs Real Live Hockey?" *Maclean's*, May 2, 1966, 49.

30. Peter Gzowski, "7 Days: Let's Take It Slowly, from the Top," *Maclean's*, May 16, 1966, 45–46.

31. Peter Gzowski, "How Success May Come Under Any Other Name," *Maclean's*, June 4, 1966, 49.

32. Peter Gzowski, "The Vietnam War: TV's Epic Eastern," *Maclean's*, June 18, 1966, 55. Later the protesters won the day and attracted the eye of television. The situation in 1966 is reminiscent of the lack of publicity given to protests against the wars in Iraq and Afghanistan forty years later.

33. Peter must have been familiar with Marshall McLuhan's *Mechanical Bride* (1952), his assessment of the effect of ads, comics, movie posters, magazine and book covers, and other examples of popular culture on readers' conception of reality; and *The Gutenberg Galaxy* (1962), McLuhan's analysis on how the printing press helped to standardize culture and make the eye the dominant sense. One of Peter's earliest references to McLuhan and his theory of hot and cool media was in an article published in 1966. See Peter Gzowski, "Dylan: An Explosion of Poetry," *Maclean's*, January 22, 1966, 23: "Dylan's poetry is, I think, what Marshall McLuhan would call a cool medium: the songs themselves are the message."

34. Peter Gzowski, *Peter Gzowski's Book About This Country in the Morning*, 14; and Gzowski, *The Private Voice*, 109. It is difficult to understand why Geneviève Bujold wouldn't have liked the article, for it is nothing but complimentary. Peter noted her "trim if unmemorable figure," and he quoted her as saying that she was just as comfortable in Toronto as in Montreal, surely not an inflammatory statement. As an actress, Peter pointed out, she was much admired in both Canada and France, where she and Yves Montand were being directed by Alain Resnais in *La guerre est finie*, a film that turned out to be less memorable than Resnais's masterpieces, *Hiroshima mon amour* and *L'Année dernière à Marienbad*. The photographs accompanying the article — Bujold strolling down a city street, the attractive twenty-two-year-old posing for Toronto sculptress Ursula Hanes, and Bujold with Montand at a café in Paris, served to enhance her beauty and talent.

35. Obviously, some of Peter's predictions and assessments were inaccurate.

36. Canada's national game, of course, is lacrosse.

37. Peter Gzowski, "Epilogue: The Changing Styles of Watching and Playing," in *Great Canadian Sports Stories: A Century of Competition* (Toronto: *Weekend Magazine*/McClelland & Stewart, 1965), 120–25.

38. Interview with Horst Ehricht, July 24, 2007. Ehricht's images of well-known figures, including Bobby Hull, Marshall McLuhan, Gordon Lightfoot, Bob Dylan, Pierre Trudeau, Ian and Sylvia, and Robertson Davies appeared in prominent magazines.

39. Peter Gzowski, sports column, *Saturday Night*, October 1965, 47.

40. A high compliment. H.L. Mencken (1880–1956), the Baltimore journalist who satirized American culture, and William S. Burroughs (1914–1997), who wrote autobiographical novels such as *Naked Lunch* (1959), were expert stylists.

41. Peter Gzowski, sports column, *Saturday Night*, November 1966, 68–69.

42. Peter Gzowski, sports column, *Saturday Night*, January 1966, 36–37, 39.

43. Peter Gzowski, sports column, *Saturday Night*, February 1966, 36–38.

44. Peter Gzowski, sports column, *Saturday Night*, March 1966, 50–51.

45. Peter Gzowski, sports column, *Saturday Night*, June 1966, 45–46.

46. For $2,700 (*Toronto Star*, November 4, 1978, C3).

47. Years later, when the Amers split, Peter said to at least one of the volleyball players, "My God, if they're coming apart, what chance do the rest of us have?" (Interview with David Crombie, October 27, 2008.)

48. Interview with David Crombie, October 27, 2008. A few years later the Crombies lived not far from the Gzowskis in North Toronto, and Shirley and Jennie used to take walks together. Like everyone who knew her, Shirley had nothing but the highest regard for Jennie.

49. Peter Gzowski, sports column, "Volleyball for Pete's Sake," *Saturday Night*, July 1966, 41–42; and Harry Bruce, "The Most Competitive Man I've Ever Known," in *Each Moment As It Flies* (Agincourt, ON: Methuen Publications, 1984), 153, a reprint of "How Can the Most Competitive Man I've Ever Known Be So Nice to Strangers?" *Weekend Magazine*, May 19, 1973, in Trent University Archives (TUA), Peter Gzowski fonds, 92-015, box 1, folder 3, "Articles About Peter Gzowski." Robert Fulford (email, October 8, 2007) did his best to identify the players. Peter was equally aggressive when it came to Monopoly. One day, eight competitors — Peter and Jennie, Harry and Penny Bruce, David and Liz Amer, and Harry and Anne Malcolmson — began to play the game at noon. The Bruces dropped out early. The last three players, David Amer, Harry Malcolmson, and Peter, made deals on the side. The mood turned sour. The winner (name unknown) was declared at 8:00 p.m. that evening (interview with Harry Bruce, October 24, 2007).

50. Ironically, for someone with a Polish surname, Peter never once mentioned the attack on the Royal Commission on Bilingualism and Biculturalism mounted by some leaders of ethnic organizations, including Senator Paul Yuzyk, who used the commission to draw attention to what he called the Third Force or Element of Canadian society, composed mostly of Eastern Europeans who had arrived in Canada after Confederation. See Laura Weir, "The Making of a Multicultural Imaginary: The Ukrainian Canadian Community's Role in Redefining the Nation During the Royal Commission on Bilingualism and Biculturalism," Department of History, Carleton University, Ottawa, 2009. Peter represented perhaps the majority of descendants of migrants to Canada in that he wanted to be Canadian first and Polish or "Old Country" second. In fact, by his generation, the fifth, that old country, whether it be Scotland, France, or Poland, is but a racial memory overlain by nostalgia and bad songs.

51. *Toronto Star*, December 30, 1965, 3.

52. Email from Dennis Murphy, January 29, 2007.

53. Kildare Dobbs, *Running the Rapids: A Writer's Life* (Toronto: Dundurn Press, 2005), 182–83; and emails, January 10 and 11, 2007.

54. Interview with William Littler, August 16, 2007.
55. *Toronto Star*, November 19, 1966, 13. In addition, Peter wrote an article about the CBC for *The Nation*, a New York magazine. In the article, published on July 11, 1966, he argued that the CBC was the main counterforce east and west to the north-south lure of the United States. See TUA, Peter Gzowski fonds, 92-015, box 3, folder 3.
56. A few months later the Sunday edition of the *New York Times* proclaimed Peter "a close observer of the Detroit music scene," a claim that Robert Fulford, in his own column, edited and approved by Peter, thought much exaggerated, given the fact that Peter had only spent eight hours in Detroit and had only written one story. See *Toronto Star*, November 30, 1966, 43.
57. In 1965–66, 138 Canadians were charged with possession of marijuana. In truth, Peter stood little chance of being caught and charged with possession of pot. As Marcel Martel points out, the Royal Canadian Mounted Police simply didn't have the human resources in the late 1960s to pursue pot smokers. Although the official figure was low, the LeDain Commission of Inquiry into the Non-Medical Use of Drugs estimated that "about 1.5 million Canadians had used marijuana at least once by the end of the sixties." See Marcel Martel, "'They Smell Bad, Have Diseases, and Are Lazy': RCMP Officers Reporting on Hippies in the Late Sixties," *The Canadian Historical Review*, vol. 90, no. 2 (June 2009), 218–20. See also Marcel Martel, *Not This Time: Canadians, Public Policy and the Marijuana Question, 1961–1975* (Toronto: University of Toronto Press), 2006; and Catherine Carstairs, *Jailed for Possession: Illegal Drug Use, Regulation, and Power in Canada, 1920–1961* (Toronto: University of Toronto Press), 2006.
58. Peter Ludlow, "In Defence of Pot, Confessions of a Canadian Marijuana-Smoker," *Saturday Night*, October 1965, 28–29, 32. The yacht in question was probably the derelict ketch that Peter and Ken Lefolii once purchased from a member of the National Yacht Club in Toronto. It was so full of holes that, first time out, it began to sink into the filthy waters of Toronto's harbour. Lefolii, in charge of the steering wheel, drove the watery ketch shoreward at full throttle. Harry Bruce, on the bow, tried to cushion the inevitable crash with his legs. As the ketch approached the dock of the yacht club, Lefolii failed to slow down the motor. Bruce, thrown backward, was badly bruised. (Interview with Harry Bruce, February 15, 2008.)
59. Actually, Tyson was hired to sing, and Cohen to write. The hosts were Douglas Leiterman, Patrick Watson, and Laurier LaPierre, as well as Robert Hoyt and Larry Zolf. Peter Reilly joined the staff after moving back to the CBC from CTV. The show, whose executive producer was Daryl Duke, ran on Sunday evenings from 10:00 to 11:00 p.m., November 1966 to April 1967.
60. *Toronto Star*, October 22, 1966, 1.

61. Harry Bruce, introduction to *The Short, Happy Walks of Max MacPherson* (Toronto: Macmillan Company of Canada, 1968), v–x. In the introduction, Bruce thanks Peter "for inventing Max's beat." The book was reviewed favourably by Kildare Dobbs on September 19, 1968, 27, in the *Star*.

62. Gzowski, *The Private Voice*, 109.

63. TUA, Peter Gzowski fonds, 92–015, box 3, folder 3.

64. Gzowski, *The Private Voice*, 108–09.

65. TUA, Peter Gzowski fonds, 92-015, box 3, folder 3.

66. Nathan Cohen could be exacting: in 1964 he had called a production of *Hamlet* in Toronto an "unmitigated disaster," and its star, Richard Burton, not much better.

67. Peter Gzowski, "Revelations in a Sheep Meadow," *Saturday Night*, June 1967, 22–24.

68. Peter was overlooking French Canada, which, thanks to playwrights such as Gratien Gélinas and Marcel Dubé, was able to see itself on the stages of Montreal and Quebec City. Peter was also overlooking the plays of Robertson Davies, Joseph Schull, W.O. Mitchell, and others writing for the English-Canadian stage at the time. A few years later, in the early 1970s, English-Canadian theatre was thriving with homegrown playwrights and directors, from George Ryga to David French, Paul Thompson, Rex Deverell, and Erika Ritter, many of whom Peter welcomed to *Morningside* in the 1980s.

69. Email from Kildare Dobbs, January 10 and 11, 2007, and conversation over a non-alcoholic lunch, January 15, 2007. Dobbs admitted that dates aren't his forte. The editing episode took place, he thought, in 1966 or 1967. It was probably during the first half of 1967 when Peter was in need of work. In the small world of Toronto journalism, the feud didn't last long. The two men worked happily at *Saturday Night* not long afterward; Peter mentioned Dobbs without negative import in a letter to Mordecai Richler, and years later, Peter interviewed Dobbs on *Morningside* on the subject of his *Ribbon of Highway*, a travelogue of Dobbs's trips by bus across Canada.

70. Sylvia Fraser, "Girl, Must Be Accurate," *Toronto Life*, November 1996, 155–56.

71. Interview with June Callwood, January 13, 2005.

Chapter 7: "How Come We Can't Talk to Each Other Anymore?"

1. From "Song for Canada," lyrics by Peter Gzowski, music by Ian Tyson.

2. Sylvia Fraser, "Girl, Must Be Accurate," *Toronto Life*, November 1996, 155.

3. Harry Bruce fonds, private collection, Harry Bruce to F.G. Brander, September 22, 1969.

4. Robert Fulford email, November 12, 2006.

5. Email from Dennis Murphy, January 29, 2007.

6. In other words, this was Peter's maiden letter to Mordecai Richler. The term, with its sexual overtures of "maidenhead," comes from the world of horse racing, where "he broke his maiden" means "he won his first race." For Peter's use of the term in a book, see Gzowski, *An Unbroken Line* (McClelland & Stewart, 1983), 209.

7. Peter spelled his wife's name as "Jenny," while she spells it as "Jennie" (Card from Jennie Lissaman Gzowski to biographer, October 2, 2005).

8. Mordecai Richler fonds, Special Collections, University of Calgary, MsC 36.12.43.4a-4b, Gzowski to Richler, August 25, 1967.

9. Richler fonds, MsC 36.18.43.1, Gzowski to Richler, 23 October; and MsC 36.12.43.11, November 10, 1967.

10. It appears not to have been published.

11. Richler fonds, MsC 36.12.43.14a, Gzowski to Richler, November 20, 1967.

12. Richler fonds, MsC 36.12.43.2, Gzowski to Richler, February 21, 1968.

13. Since Mordecai Richler's letters are missing from this correspondence, the novelist's words must be inferred.

14. Richler fonds, MsC 36.12.43.25, Gzowski to Richler, March 7, 1968.

15. Richler fonds, MsC 36.12.43.2, Gzowski to Richler, nd, though an archivist at the University of Calgary has penciled in "May 1968?"

16. Harry Bruce confirmed that Peter did his best to increase circulation and advertising revenue and all other aspects of "the grim business side of that finally hopeless operation." In his letter of September 1969 to Gerry Brander of *Maclean's*, Bruce added that "we editorial idealists were not used to hearing one of our own reciting regional circulation statistics, ad rates per page, and so on" (Harry Bruce fonds, private collection, Bruce to F.G. Brander, September 22, 1969).

17. Richler fonds, MsC 36.12.43.28, Gzowski to Richler, June 4, 1968.

18. *Toronto Star*, February 21, 1968, 38.

19. Sylvia Fraser, "Peter, Peter," *Toronto Life*, April 2002, 108. Later, in the 1980s, when Peter Gzowski became a star and a commercial commodity, Fraser believed that he lost the "gregarious charm," the charm that had inspired so many writers from Cathy Breslin and Liz Binks at *The Varsity*, Murray Burt at the *Times-Herald* in Moose Jaw, and Harry Bruce, Sylvia Fraser, and Mordecai Richler.

20. Trent University Archives (TUA), Peter Gzowski fonds, 92-015, box 3, file 3, comments by Bob Bossin.

21. Marci McDonald, "What Does a Guy Who Quits a Winner Do for an Encore?" *Homemakers*, vol. 9, issue 5, September 1974, in TUA, Peter Gzowski fonds, 92-015, box 3, folder "Articles About Peter Gzowski."

22. Robert Fulford fonds, William Ready Division of Archives and Research Collections, McMaster University Library, copy of the draft that Peter sent to Fulford on December 29, 1986, 8.

23. Peter Gzowski, "The Global Village Has Everything but Surprises," *Saturday Night*, December 1968, 33–34.

24. Norman Sims, ed., *The Literary Journalists* (New York: Ballantine Books, 1984), 87; and Lily Hindy, "Magazine Publisher [Felker] Cultivated the 'New Journalism,'" *Globe and Mail*, July 4, 2008, S8. Tom Wolfe's "Radical Chic: That Party at Lenny's," published in 1970, is considered one of the magazine's most influential articles. In 1974, Felker (1925–2008) bought *The Village Voice*.

25. The show, which combined current events with entertainment, ran from September to June 1967–68, and 1968–69. Its executive producer was Ross McLean, one of its story editors was Barbara Amiel, and its host was John Saywell, who was supported by interviewers and reporters, including Warren Davis, Percy Saltzman, Peter Desbarats, Patrick Watson, Moses Znaimer, and Ken Lefolii, who was also the show's executive editor.

26. *Toronto Star*, November 6, 1968, 33; and May 29, 1969, 33.

27. *Toronto Star*, December 18, 1971, 55; Marci McDonald, *Toronto Star*, February 12, 1972, in TUA, Peter Gzowski fonds, 92-015, box 3, folder "Articles About Peter Gzowski"; and interviews with John Macfarlane, June 16, 2009, and with Michael de Pencier, June 18, 2009.

28. Silver Donald Cameron in Edna Barker, ed., *Remembering Peter Gzowski: A Book of Tributes* (Toronto: McClelland & Stewart, 2002), 17–18.

29. *Toronto Star*, December 28, 1968, 5.

30. Jack Batten and Peter Gzowski, *Nancy* (Toronto: Toronto Star Limited, 1968).

31. McDonald, "What Does a Guy Who Quits a Winner Do for an Encore?" *Homemakers*, vol. 9, issue 5, September 1974.

32. The first time Peter used *fuck* was in *Maclean's*, about six months before his article in *Canadian Forum*.

33. If so, that would have been two years after *fuck* was first heard on BBC-TV (1965) and two years after President Lyndon Johnson used it in conversation with the Greek ambassador. It wasn't until 1971 that the word may or may not have been heard in the House of Commons when Prime Minister Trudeau may have said "fuddle duddle."

34. Later that year, when asked about books that had recently impressed him, Peter named *The Strawberry Statement* and *An Unfinished Woman*, as well as Joe Namath's memoir *I Can't Wait Till Tomorrow, Cause I Get Better Lookin' Every Day*. When he finished reading each book, Peter explained, he felt as if he were saying goodnight "at the end of an enthralling evening, still savoring [sic] the pleasure of the author's company." Each of the three writers was a genuine, visceral human being, he added. He liked Namath because he was multi-dimensional, and furthermore, Peter commented, "any man who hates sportswriters can't be all that bad." In 1969, Peter reread *The Catcher in the Rye* for the seventeenth time, and he had discovered J.R.R. Tolkien and Kurt Vonnegut, Jr. See *Financial Post*, December 6, 1969, 15.

35. Lillian Hellman, *An Unfinished Woman: A Memoir* (Boston: Little, Brown, 1968), 50 and 78.

36. Peter later contributed freelance reviews to the *Toronto Star*. On Saturday, November 6, 1971, his review of two sports books appeared on page 51. In *The Plastic Orgasm*, Laverne Barnes, wife of Canadian Football League player Emery Barnes, exposed the hardships of football, the pains, pills, girls, and wicked owners. Peter thought the book a bit snarly. In the same review, he discussed Bernie Parrish's *They Call It a Game*, which looked at American football and its stingy owners, gambling, and racism.

37. Peter's article on the *Leader-Post* seems not to have survived.

38. *Globe and Mail*, September 13, 1969, 5.

39. *Toronto Star*, February 13, 1970, 8, for Ron McEachern's testimony to the committee.

40. TUA, Gzowski fonds, 92-015, file 1, box 30, McEachern to Gzowski, September 16, 1969.

41. Harry Bruce fonds, Bruce to F.G. Brander, publisher of *Maclean's*, September 22, 1969.

42. Doris Anderson as quoted by Sandra Martin, "Doris Anderson, Journalist and Political Activist 1921–2007," *Globe and Mail*, March 3, 2007, S9.

43. *Toronto Star*, November 3, 1996, D2.

44. It was, in part, thanks to the good work of Borden Spears that Maclean-Hunter could afford to pay Peter such a handsome salary. In 1968, in order to meet the competition from the Canadian edition of *Time*, Spears had adopted the smaller format used by the American magazine, and at the same time, *Maclean's* began to publish once, rather than twice, a month. Its advertising revenue rose by 17.5 percent, and Spears managed to move the magazine, for the first time in years, into the black. By comparison, young secondary school teachers were making just over $7,000 that year.

45. Richler fonds, MsC 36.7.41.44a, Gzowski to Richler, October 31, 1969.

46. Richler fonds, MsC 36.7.41.46, Gzowski to Richler, February 9, 1970. My thanks to John Ayre, who explained that Mordecai Richler, who was living in England where he was "trying desperately to finish *St. Urbain's Horseman*," had an assignment from Peter to write about the Rockies (email from John Ayre, January 15, 2008).

47. University of Toronto Archives (UTA), Peter Gzowski clipping file, A1973-0026/132(22), *Time*, October 17, 1969. The *Globe and Mail*, September 13, 1969, reported on the Charles Templeton resignation and the connection with Peter.

48. José E. Igartua, *The Other Quiet Revolution: National Identities in English Canada, 1945–71* (Vancouver: University of British Columbia Press, 2006), 1 and 5. It might also be argued that the process had begun during the latter stages of the Great War in 1917 and 1918. Colonial soldiers left Canada and the other

so-called "White Dominions" to defend their empire and returned home with increased pride in their native land. Nevertheless, the older imperial nationalism survived the Great War, as well as the war that followed.

49. Richler fonds, MsC 36.12.43.2, Gzowski to Richler, February 21, 1968.

50. Peter Gzowski, *The Private Voice* (McClelland & Stewart, 1988), 69.

51. Gzowski, *The Private Voice*, 73–74.

52. Richler fonds, MsC 36.12.43.6, Gzowski to Richler, September 21, 1967.

53. George Grant, *Lament for a Nation: The Defeat of Canadian Nationalism* (Montreal and Kingston: McGill-Queen's University Press, 2005), 85.

54. Igartua, *The Other Quiet Revolution*, 164–92.

55. See Senator Paul Yuzyk's maiden speech in the Senate, March 4, 1964, published in Paul Yuzyk, *For a Better Canada* (Toronto: Ukrainian National Association, Inc., Canadian Office, 1973).

56. Laurier L. LaPierre, "The 1960s," in J.M.S. Careless and R. Craig Brown, eds., *The Canadians, 1867–1967* (Toronto: Macmillan of Canada, 1968), 545.

57. See Michael Ondaatje, "'I Had to Invent Billy from the Ground Up,'" *Globe and Mail*, August 23, 2003, R1 and R15. All this literary activity was observed by Northrop Frye, who noted a few years later that the old "yawning" literature of Canada gave way, after 1960, to what he called a "real" Canadian literature in both official languages. He added that, after 1960, Canadian literature gained international attention and admiration. See Northrop Frye, "Across the River and out of the Trees," in W.J. Keith and B.Z. Shek, eds., *The Arts in Canada: The Last Fifty Years* (Toronto: University of Toronto Press, 1980), 3–4. In this article, Frye modestly neglects to state that he himself played a role in the creation of that literature. At Victoria College at the University of Toronto he inspired the new generation of writers from Margaret Atwood to Jay Macpherson and many others.

58. Peter Gzowski, "Canada's Cultural Quandary," *Toronto Star*, December 17, 1966, 1–2.

59. The new attitude toward the monarchy was in contrast to the magazine's reverence for Her Majesty a few years earlier when *Maclean's* named the queen the most outstanding Canadian of 1964 for having "walked unafraid among her people, in full awareness that her life might be in jeopardy." She had braved threats from detractors in Quebec City on October 10, 1964, a day that the magazine called "Black Saturday." See *Maclean's*, January 2, 1965, 7. On the other hand, historians in Quebec today claim that the visit served to rekindle the embers of *indépendentisme*.

60. *Toronto Star*, February 18, 1970, 10.

61. Richler fonds, MsC 36.7.41.48, Gzowski to Richler, April 15, 1970. Peter's expression "cheered me *for one of* no end" should read "has cheered me *to* no end."

62. Interview with Horst Ehricht, July 24, 2007. It was Ron McEachern who annulled Peter's decision to fire Ehricht.

63. *Toronto Star*, February 20, 1970, 8. Back in February 1970 when Peter told the Senate committee in Ottawa that Charles Templeton had overemphasized management interference, Philip Sykes and Doug Marshall had fired off a telegram to Senator Davey. There had indeed been management interference during Templeton's tenure as editor, Sykes and Marshall explained to Davey. Furthermore, it was only because of Templeton's resignation that Gzowski had enjoyed so much editorial freedom.
64. Robert Fulford email, November 12, 2006.
65. Patrick Watson, *This Hour Has Seven Decades* (Toronto: McArthur & Company, 2004), 320.
66. Interviews with Barry Penhale, February 18, 2004 and November 22, 2007.

Chapter 8: Radio, Peter's Early Days

1. Doug Ward in Edna Barker, ed., *Remembering Peter Gzowski: A Book of Tributes* (Toronto: McClelland & Stewart, 2002), 36–37. Ward doesn't give the exact month, but Peter wore the same cast while Glenn Sarty filmed the pilots of the television show called *Gzowski*, sometime during the summer of 1969, and the cast can be seen in the audition for *Weekend*, filmed on August 23, 1969. Peter told a version of this story in Moose Jaw in May 1997. He seems to have claimed that he dropped his trousers without help from Maggie. Robert Currie, a Moose Jaw poet who wrote a poem about Peter's last visit to Moose Jaw, may have heard Peter mention the incident, which he included in his poem "Gzowski in the Heartland." Poem courtesy the poet, December 2004.
2. Email from Doug Ward, February 1, 2008.
3. For the early history of Canadian radio, see Frank W. Peers, *The Politics of Canadian Broadcasting, 1920–1951* (Toronto: University of Toronto Press, 1969); and Frank W. Peers, "Broadcasting, Radio, and Television," in *The Canadian Encyclopedia*, second edition, vol. 1 (Edmonton: Hurtig Publishers, 1988), 283. Also see G.R. Stevens, *History of the Canadian National Railways* (New York: Macmillan, 1973).
4. See *Toronto Star*, July 14, 1922, 7.
5. *Toronto Star*, August 12, 1924, 21.
6. My thanks to Bruce Rogers (email, July 9, 2008) for enriching my knowledge of pioneer radio. Rogers (no relation to cable magnate Ted Rogers) also explained the importance of a station being a clear channel, which meant that it broadcast on a frequency unavailable to other stations in North America. KDKA Pittsburgh was a clear channel with a wattage of fifty thousand plus and was therefore heard throughout most of North America.
7. Stevens, *History of the Canadian National Railways*, 326–27, 329.

8.   For decades, until the 1970s, CBC Radio depended on advertising revenue from private corporations.

9.   Paul Rutherford, "Radio Programming" in *The Canadian Encyclopedia*, second edition, vol. 3, 1819.

10.   Sandy Stewart, *From Coast to Coast: A Personal History of Radio in Canada* (Montreal: CBC Enterprises, 1985), 148–63.

11.   Stewart, *From Coast to Coast*, 149–50.

12.   *Toronto Star*, December 10, 1970, 3.

13.   Bruce Rogers's phrase, email July 9, 2008. As Rogers explains, there were news editors who resisted unscripted interviews, perhaps because they had begun their careers in print journalism. By about 1962, however, those editors who refused to go to unscripted interviews had little input or influence on news production or current affairs programming.

14.   Stewart, *From Coast to Coast*, 165–66. As Bruce Rogers points out, CBC news was already unscripted, in part at least. On-air interpretation and commentary of major news stories was a style used in the 1950s by the CBC's James M. Minifie in Washington, D.C., and Patrick Keatley in London. The on-air style can be traced to wartime broadcasting by Matthew Halton, and before that, to the Moose River Mine Disaster in April 1936 when J. Frank Willis took his microphone to the mine head and talked to people in the town. The fiery crash of the *Hindenburg* in New Jersey in May 1937 was reported on-site in a similar manner (emails from Bruce Rogers, December 27, 2007, and July 9, 2008). The Springhill, Nova Scotia, coal-mining disasters of the 1950s were covered in a similar live fashion.

15.   Margaret Lyons deserves much credit for her innovations and risks at CBC Radio. In the *Toronto Star*, April 8, 1984, C5, Ellie Tesher recognized her achievements, which began soon after she and her husband, Ed, had returned from eleven years in London, where they had lived during the 1950s. "The little lady is a powerhouse," wrote Tesher. Lyons hired Mark Starowicz when he was only twenty-one. As head of current affairs, Lyons also promoted voices such as Barbara Frum's on *As It Happens*, and, of course, Peter's on *Radio Free Friday* and *This Country in the Morning*. Peter Herrndorf, who appointed Lyons managing director of radio (later, in 1982, she became vice-president of English-language radio), called Lyons a "risk-taker of real proportions — she bet on a lot of young journalists others were nervous about or ignored." Lyons, according to Herrndorf, believed that presentation was as important as content, a heretical notion in the late 1960s. Although accused of trivializing and popularizing, she successfully gestated *Sunday Morning*, *As It Happens*, *Quirks and Quarks*, and *Morningside*. "Her commitment to national workaday audiences was very real," Herrndorf reported to Tesher.

16.   Trent University Archives (TUA), Gzowski fonds, 92-015, box 3, folder 2, clippings.

17. When Peter was growing up, he was no doubt part of that group activity. In 1936 his grandparents, parents, aunts, and uncles, and perhaps even two-year-old Peter, had surely joined millions of other members of the British Empire around floor-model radio sets to listen to King Edward VIII announce that he was about to give up the throne for the woman he loved. At exactly the same moment in the lobby of the Bessborough Hotel in Saskatoon, Stephen Leacock joined hotel guests to listen to the same speech. Likewise, people gathered around sets to hear declarations of war or the sound of a big band coming from the Royal York, Hotel Vancouver, or the Waldorf Astoria.

18. TUA, Peter Gzowski fonds, 92-015, box 12, Peter Gzowski, "A Fan's Notes," in the Edmonton Oilers program for February 19, 1982. Peter seems also to have "smuggled" that radio into his bedroom, or so he suggested in Gzowski, *The Morningside Papers* (Toronto: McClelland & Stewart, 1985), 162.

19. Peter Gzowski, "Why Dave Keon Is the 'Best' Player in Hockey," *Maclean's*, March 23, 1963. In the article, Peter claimed he was listening one evening when Foster Hewitt introduced his son, Bill, to the airwaves as his assistant hockey commentator. Peter doesn't give the date, but it was probably 1951 when Bill became sports director of CKFH, Foster's radio station. Actually, Foster had introduced Bill Hewitt to radio audiences when Bill was eight, in other words in 1936. On that occasion and in the years following, Foster allowed his son one minute of radio time once a year on a show called *Young Canada Hockey Night*. In 1936, Peter was two, and thus probably didn't hear Bill Hewitt the first time he was introduced to radio listeners. Therefore, 1951 is the more likely year.

20. *Maclean's*, December 2, 1964, 53. The article was published not long after Peter had joined Ken Lefolii, Robert Fulford, and others in their walkout from *Maclean's*. Borden Spears, the new editor, may have wanted to keep Peter's name out of the magazine. At the same time Spears was negotiating with Peter to write a regular column on television, which began in February 1965.

21. According to Bruce Rogers, the CBC was also aware in the early 1960s that a goodly number of university students were solitary listeners (email from Rogers, July 9, 2008).

22. Interview with Ron Grant, July 10, 2008.

23. John Carroll (1929–1989) lectured at the University of Toronto from 1958 to the mid-1970s. His specialties were the eighteenth-century novelist Samuel Richardson and the twentieth-century novelist F. Scott Fitzgerald.

24. Norman Mailer, *An American Dream* (New York: Vintage, 1999), 31. The novel was first published in 1964.

25. Robert Fulford, "A Day in the Life," *Toronto Star*, April 22, 1965, 23.

26. Some, perhaps many, of these programs never made it into the CBC Archives. Some of them may have been taped over or were taken home by producers or stars.

27.   Peter (Strabo) Gzowski, "Wow! Count Those Stars on the CBC," *Maclean's*, September 18, 1965, 63–64.

28.   Library and Archives Canada (LAC), 170422, A1 2005-11-0010, CBC *Ideas*, "Style in Sports," February 6, 1967.

29.   TUA, Gzowski fonds, 92-015, box 20, file 26.

30.   Margaret Lyons, "Geraldine Sherman of *Soundings*," *CBC Times*, June 21–27, 1969, 10. "Gerry" Sherman also produced a show called *This Is Robert Fulford*, the host of which she later married.

31.   Interview with June Callwood, January 13, 2005.

32.   Interview with William Littler, August 16, 2007.

33.   The reel-to-reel tape of the show is at TUA, Gzowski fonds, 92-015, folder 26. According to Ken Puley, there is another copy at the CBC Radio archives.

34.   *Toronto Star*, January 27, 2002, in TUA, Gzowski fonds, 92-015, box 20, folder 26.

35.   *As It Happens'* first host was Phillip Forsyth, assisted by Harry Brown. The following April in 1969, when *Radio Free Friday* was launched, the hosts of *As It Happens* were Harry Brown and artist William Ronald.

36.   Email from Doug Ward, January 28, 2007.

37.   It was, in fact, the news department that launched the regular use of the telephone at the CBC. When the current affairs department adopted the technique, it also absorbed some of the budget of the news department, much to the latter's consternation and resentment.

38.   Whose clocks, indifferent to daylight saving time, remain the same year-round. Saskatchewan is therefore on the same time as Manitoba in the winter and Alberta in the summer.

39.   I want to thank Doug Ward, emails August 3 and 8, 2008, for taking so much time to sort out the rolling format.

40.   Donnalu Wigmore on television and radio, *Chatelaine*, November 1969, 12.

41.   Email from Christie Blatchford, February 9, 2008. In April 1972, *Toronto Life* published Peter's "How 31 Kids Taught Me Hockey: My Life and Times as a Neighbourhood Hockey Coach," 32, 52–54. When it came to parental pressure and lack of humour, Peter thought that mothers were worse than fathers.

42.   *Toronto Star*, May 29, 1969, 32.

43.   Email from Doug Ward, February 1, 2008.

44.   *Toronto Star*, August 16, 1969, 7.

45.   Stephen Azzi, "Foreign Investment and the Paradox of Economic Nationalism," in Norman Hillmer and Adam Chapnick, eds., *Canadas of the Mind: The Making and Unmaking of Canadian Nationalisms in the Twentieth Century* (Montreal and Kingston: McGill-Queen's University Press, 2007), 65–67.

46.   Denis Smith, *Gentle Patriot: A Political Biography of Walter Gordon* (Edmonton: Hurtig Publishers, 1973), 40.

47. During the 1960s, Peter, along with Peter Flemington, had acted on a voluntary basis as eyes and ears for the Ontario CCF (interview with Peter Flemington, August 27, 2008).

48. Azzi, "Foreign Investment and the Paradox of Economic Nationalism," 72.

49. James Laxer, *In Search of the New Left: Canadian Politics After the Neoconservative Assault* (Toronto: Viking, 1996), 148. See also "Whither Waffle," in Philip Resnick, *The Land of Cain: Class and Nationalism in English Canada, 1945–1976* (Vancouver: New Star Books, 1977), 229–32.

50. John Bullen, "The Ontario Waffle and the Struggle for an Independent Socialist Canada: Conflict within the NDP," *Canadian Historical Review*, vol. 64, no. 2 (1983), 188.

51. Nationalism was in the air. On September 17, 1970, the Committee for an Independent Canada (CIC) was founded. Less radical than the Waffle, and therefore more inclusive, the CIC's intent was to promote Canadian economic independence, and with it, the country's cultural institutions. The idea of such a committee was conceived by Abe Rotstein, Peter C. Newman, and Walter Gordon. CIC's first co-chairmen were Jack McClelland and Claude Ryan, editor of *Le Devoir*. Although Peter's name doesn't appear on the steering committee, the list includes prominent colleagues such as Pierre Berton, Max Ferguson, Doris Anderson, and Adrienne Clarkson, as well as historians W.L. Morton and Ken McNaught, and Tom Symons, founding president of Trent University. The list also includes names such as Lloyd Axworthy, Earle Birney, Molly Lamb Bobac, Chris Chapman, Keith Davey, Peter Desbarats, George Grant, Mel Hurtig, J.R. Kidd, Judy LaMarsh, Laurier LaPierre, Hugh MacLennan, Farley Mowat, Alden Nowlan, John C. Parkin, Al Purdy, Laura Sabia, Denis Smith, Harold Town, and Jack Webster. In 1981, having achieved many of its goals, the CIC was disbanded. See Resnick, *The Land of Cain*, 224–28; and Roger Rickwood, "Committee for an Independent Canada," in *The Canadian Encyclopedia*, second edition, vol. 1 (Edmonton: Hurtig Publishers), 465.

52. Email from Margaret Lyons, July 19, 2008. I am grateful to Margaret, who, in several emails, and during two telephone conversations, added texture to the narrative.

53. I am grateful to Doug Ward for spending time in explaining the workings of *Radio Free Friday* during a telephone interview, January 7, 2007, and in subsequent emails. It was Doug who found the source of the phrase about comforting the afflicted.

54. Michael Enright in Barker, ed., *Remembering Peter Gzowski*, 40.

55. *Toronto Star*, May 29, 1969, 33.

56. *Toronto Star*, April 2, 1970, 69. Patrick Scott added that Robert Fulford would be hosting the show two days later, and that Doug Ward, who had moved to television, would return to host the show on the following Friday evening.

57. Coincidentally, Maggie Morris departed from the show around the same time as Peter, and Patrick Scott wasn't sure why. CBC chief announcer John Rae had hired

Maggie during the summer of 1969 when she began work on *Radio Free Friday*, but, claimed Rae, her accent and voice became "precious" after Christmas of that year, and that listeners had complained. Morris was unaware of the complaints, and one day Rae dismissed her. See *Toronto Star*, April 2, 1970, 1; and April 3, 1970, 26. Maggie's fans, who were legion, concluded that the CBC just didn't like her English accent. Petitions to reinstate her were circulated, but to no avail.

58.   According to radio logs, the show ended on Friday, August 9, 1971 (email from Ken Puley, March 14, 2008), with Peter as host to the end (see Jon Ruddy, *Toronto Star*, October 9, 1971, 71). In October 1971, *As It Happens* subsumed *Radio Free Friday*, and, with Colin MacLeod as producer, and alternating hosts Barbara Frum and William Ronald, *As It Happens* assumed its current format of five evenings per week. The exhausting rolling format continued on *As It Happens* during its first year, which is why the show required alternating hosts. In its second year as a Monday to Friday show, *As It Happens* ran from 6:30 to 8:00 p.m. in all times zones, and Barbara Frum became the host, though always with an assistant (interviews with Doug Ward, Margaret Lyons, and Mark Starowicz, March 4, 2008). The term *executive producer* wasn't used at the time. (See also Stewart, *From Coast to Coast*, 166–67; and Jack Miller, *Toronto Star*, September 2, 9, 31). During his time as host of *Radio Free Friday*, Peter did freelance work. On January 15, 1971, he and Warren Davis, along with journalist Hugh Winsor, conducted a twenty-minute interview with Kenneth Kaunda, president of Zambia. Kuanda was in Singapore at the Commonwealth leaders' conference. He wasn't pleased that Prime Minister Edward Heath of Great Britain was supplying the apartheid government of South Africa with weapons, and the Zambian leader wouldn't have been unhappy to see Great Britain leave the Commonwealth (*Toronto Star*, January 16, 1971, 2).

59.   Information on these *Radio Free Friday* shows comes from printouts of the detailed index of each show, courtesy Ken Puley, CBC Radio Archives.

60.   For an inside view of Peter's nationalism, I am grateful to Alex Frame (interview June 16, 2008). Based on Peter's interviews on *Radio Free Friday*, his biographer believes that Peter was indeed an economic nationalist who, more or less around the time of the October Crisis, became what Frame witnessed on *This Country in the Morning* — a cultural and emotional nationalist.

61.   Peter Gzowski, *Peter Gzowski's Book About This Country in the Morning* (Edmonton: Hurtig Publishers, 1974), 33–34. Quebec *nationalistes* also talk about hope, but hope for the survival of *la nationalité québécoise*.

62.   It was given its last rites in the free trade policies of the late 1980s.

63.   Pierre Trudeau had never been a nationalist of any sort (see Taylor, *Radical Tories*, 185), and only passed the Foreign Investment Review Agency (FIRA) in 1973 to maintain the support of the NDP (see Azzi, "Foreign Investment and the Paradox of Economic Nationalism," 78). Because Trudeau was reduced to a minority of seats

in 1972, he was forced to govern with the support of the NDP until 1974 when the Liberals won a majority.

64. Of Italian parentage, Bruno Gerussi was born in Medicine Hat, Alberta, in 1926. When Diana Filer heard that Harry Boyle was seeking a host for a new morning radio show, she recommended Gerussi, who had been working at a small radio station in Toronto. He was also a respected actor at the Shakespeare festival in Stratford, Ontario, and in Toronto at theatres such as the Crest. Once he left CBC Radio, he was well-known as the star of *The Beachcombers*, a television show that ran from 1972 to 1990. Perhaps because he wrote no memoirs, his contribution to radio has been largely overlooked.

65. The relaxed style noted by Bill Cameron wasn't novel. In fact, from its inception in the 1920s, radio had fostered the illusion of intimacy. A voice on radio created what historian Len Kuffert has called "the illusion of presence," as if the host were casually chatting to each listener in his or her living room, kitchen, or automobile. Radio reduced distances and created new neighbours. See Len Kuffert, "'To Pick You Up or to Hold You': Intimacy and Golden-Age Radio in Canada," a paper delivered at the Canadian History Association annual meeting at York University, May 29, 2006.

66. After Alan McFee died in December 2000, Peter mused, "He was very much his own guy, the model rebel who was a legend for his bad behaviour, but he was always extremely kind and generous to me." Peter also admitted that when he sat in for Bruno Gerussi he was in awe of McFee. See *Toronto Star*, December 16, 2000, N9.

67. Interview with Diana Filer, February 1, 2008.

68. Weldon Hanbury did, eventually, make it into print. In 1982, *A Surfeit of Love*, a collection of poetry, was published by Toronto's Coach House Press.

69. *Toronto Star*, August 2, 1969, E8.

70. *Toronto Star*, September 18, 1969, 32; and September 23, 1969, 6.

71. LAC, 1763361: A1 2005-11-0011, *Gerussi*, November 17, 1969, Peter Gzowski on the Royal Winter Fair.

72. In Canada books such as *The New Romans: Candid Opinions of the U.S.* (1968) and *Close the 49th Parallel: The Americanization of Canada* (1970) expressed growing distrust of the empire to the south.

73. Interview with Alex Frame, June 16, 2008.

74. Interview with Peter Meggs, January 31, 2008.

Chapter 9: Peter's Country in the Morning

1. The narration for *This Country in the Morning* emerged from several sources: the CBC Radio Archives — tapes, a database, and an index card system; Peter Gzowski, *Peter Gzowski's Book About This Country in the Morning* (Edmonton: Hurtig Publishers)

1974; Sandy Stewart's history of CBC Radio; newspaper articles about the show; interviews with Alex Frame, Danny Finkleman, Robert Fulford, Mark Starowicz, and Bill Casselman, as well as with others who observed and listened to the show, including Bruce Rogers, Diana Filer, Margaret Lyons, and Peter Meggs; and last, but certainly not least, Peter's large collection of papers at Trent University Archives. From time to time, Peter also mentions the show in his memoirs, Peter Gzowski, *The Private Voice: A Journal of Reflections* (Toronto: McClelland & Stewart, 1988).

2.   Gzowski, *The Private Voice*, 306.

3.   Gzowski, *Peter Gzowski's Book About This Country in the Morning*, 12. See also Jon Ruddy, "CBC Radio's Dramatic Shuffle Displaces Old Favourites," *Toronto Star*, October 9, 1971, 71. The expanded morning show was but one of several changes made by Jack Craine, managing director of CBC Radio, to broaden and democratize the appeal of the network. *Radio Noon* was expanded to two hours, with less emphasis on farm news and more on urban issues. The 4:00 to 6:00 p.m. slot was given over to a drive-home show aimed at urban commuters who wanted light discussion mixed with traffic reports and weather. Max Ferguson and his salty sidekick, Alan McFee, were in charge of the afternoon slot from 2:30 to 4:00 p.m. Ferguson's largely unscripted style and genius at imitating voices of well-known Canadians suited the new and informal style of CBC Radio. The long newscast, *The World at Six*, with its shorter morning counterpart, *The World at Eight*, continued as before, with hosts such as Bruce Rogers and Russ Germain.

4.   Email from Robert Fulford, November 12, 2006.

5.   Peter Gzowski, "TV Dream Dies Amid Bitter Regrets," *Toronto Star*, January 3, 1979, A3.

6.   So named for the colour of the paper. There were multiple copies of the instructions, Peter's always being green. On *Morningside*, there were five copies, each a different hue. Other copies were read by producers and other members of staff. To make multiple copies, several sheets of thin carbon paper were necessary, and so were strong fingers on the typewriter, so that the last copy would be legible. Today the idea of carbon copies seems to belong to the age of dinosaurs. (My thanks to Margaret Lyons for reminding me about the carbon paper, email June 21, 2009.)

7.   Interview with Alex Frame, June 16, 2008.

8.   Harry Bruce, "The Most Competitive Man I've Ever Known," in *Each Moment As It Flies* (Agincourt, ON: Methuen, 1984), 159–60, a reprint of "How Can the Most Competitive Man I've Ever Known Be So Nice to Strangers?" *Weekend Magazine*, May 19, 1973, in TUA, Peter Gzowski fonds, 92-015, box 1, folder 3, "Articles About Peter Gzowski."

9.   DuBarry Campau, *Homemakers* [late May 1970], in TUA, Peter Gzowski fonds, 92-015, box 3, folder "Articles About Peter Gzowski." The clipping service removed the title and date.

10. Email from Robert Fulford, November 12, 2006.

11. Interview with Ruth-Ellen Soles, October 11, 2008.

12. Bruce, "The Most Competitive Man I've Ever Known," 159–60.

13. Peter claimed that the show had no model (Gzowski, *Peter Gzowski's Book About This Country in the Morning*, 12), which wasn't true.

14. Email from Christie Blatchford, February 9, 2008.

15. Shelagh Rogers, "Reading with Peter," in Peter Gzowski, *The Fifth (and Probably Last) Morningside Papers* (Toronto: McClelland & Stewart, 1994), 9.

16. The year before, Earl Pomerantz had been one of several Canadian actors in a CBC-TV film called *That's Show Biz*. His later career in Hollywood was more stellar.

17. In May 1972, the LeDain Commission on the medical use of drugs recommended the abolition of penalties for the use and possession of marijuana and hashish.

18. A film about two Maritimers who drive to Toronto for money and good times and end up turning to robbery.

19. Interview with Danny Finkleman, January 31, 2008.

20. Jack Miller, *Toronto Star*, October 7, 1971, 33.

21. Interview with Margaret Lyons, November 26, 2007.

22. Interview with Donna Logan, October 19, 2008.

23. Gzowski, *Peter Gzowski's Book About This Country in the Morning*, 12.

24. I am grateful to Ken Puley, CBC Radio archivist, for locating interviews such as this one. His Honour Edward Schreyer remembered another interview with Peter on Manitoba's Hutterites (interview with Schreyer, January 7, 2008).

25. Barbara and Ormond Mitchell, *Mitchell: The Life of W.O. Mitchell, the Years of Fame, 1948–1998* (Toronto: McClelland & Stewart, 2005), 269.

26. In 1969, when he was asked about his favourite books, Robertson Davies's *Leaven of Malice* wasn't mentioned, nor even, for that matter, W.O. Mitchell's *Who Has Seen the Wind*. J.D. Salinger's *The Catcher in the Rye* topped Peter's list of favourite novels.

27. Harry Bruce, "On Things He Never Got to Do," in Gzowski, *Peter Gzowski's Book About This Country in the Morning*, 25.

28. Adrienne Clarkson never explained how one could float lazily upriver without the assistance of a noisy motor! About a year later the Clarksons split up.

29. Marci McDonald, "The New Darling of Daytime Radio," *Toronto Star*, February 12, 1972, 61.

30. Peter claimed that it was the mention of Pierre Trudeau's name that raised Pauline Julien's wrath. However, in the taped version of the interview, she never once mentioned Trudeau's name. Throughout the talk she remained so remarkably cool and collected that it was sometimes difficult to hear her.

31. TUA, Gzowski fonds, 92-015, box 1, folder 1, program for ACTRA Awards, April 1973.

32. Pierre Berton fonds, William Ready Division of Archives and Research Collections, McMaster University Library, Group G, box 188, F.10, "General Correspondence," Pierre Berton to Peter Gzowski, December 10, 1973.

33. McDonald, "The New Darling of Daytime Radio," 61.

34. *Toronto Star*, January 25, 1972, 9.

35. Letter to the editor, *Toronto Star*, January 7, 1975, C5, in response to Dennis Braithwaite's "*This Country* from Bad to Bad," December 27, 1974, E5. Braithwaite was commenting on the show after Michael Enright took over as host, but he also took a swipe at Gzowski.

36. Marjorie Harris, "Marjorie Harris on People's Liberation," in *Peter Gzowksi's Book About This Country in the Morning*, 100–04.

37. Jack Miller, "Gzowski Ambles Off the Air," *Toronto Star*, June 29, 1974, D6.

38. Marci McDonald, "What Does a Guy Who Quits a Winner Do for an Encore?" *Homemakers*, vol. 9, issue 5, September 1974, in TUA, Peter Gzowski fonds, 92-015, box 3, folder "Articles About Peter Gzowski."

39. McDonald, "What Does a Guy Who Quits a Winner Do for an Encore?"

40. Peter Gzowski, "Newfoundland," in Gzowski, *Peter Gzowski's Book About This Country in the Morning*, 160.

41. Ron Base, "Comeback of the Year," *Maclean's*, December 15, 1975, 64.

42. Miller, "Gzowski Ambles Off the Air"; and Sid Adilman, "Eye on Entertainment," *Toronto Star*, October 17, 1974, E12.

43. TUA, Gzowski fonds, 92-015, box 9, folder 1, Peter Gzowski to Mel Hurtig, September 19, 1973.

44. Interview with Susan Kent, October 20, 2005; and email from Susan Kent Davidson, May 29, 2009.

45. At Carleton University in her hometown of Ottawa, Jan Walter had edited the yearbook *The Raven*. She was a cousin of Mel Hurtig's first wife, Eileen Walter, and with that connection and a good deal of talent, she worked for two summers at Hurtig's big bookstore on Jasper Avenue in Edmonton. When she graduated from Carleton, she moved to Edmonton to work for Hurtig Publishers.

46. Interviews with Jan Walter at various times during the research for this book, the first being in Kingston on April 16, 2004.

47. TUA, Peter Gzowski fonds, 92-015, box 9, folder 18, Jan Walter to Peter Gzowski, September 30, 1974.

48. Inspired by Robert Fulford and Lister Sinclair, who one morning on *This Country* wondered it there ever would be a great Canadian novel. Harry J. Boyle's ambitious novel *The Great Canadian Novel*, published in 1972, was perhaps an inspiration for the contest.

49. Gzowski, *Peter Gzowski's Book About This Country in the Morning*, 24. W.O. Mitchell's biographers claim that it was Merna Mitchell who told the story

(Barbara and Ormond Mitchell, *Mitchell*, 246–47). In the transcript as published in Peter's book, Merna merely introduced it, but it was W.O. who told the story. Incidentally, the Mitchell story might have made good radio in 1972, but not all good radio makes good print. Perhaps, for that very reason, an interview with Joey Smallwood, always a good raconteur, wasn't included in the book.

50. Urjo Kareda, "Boxing Day Lament," in Gzowski, *Peter Gzowski's Book About This Country in the Morning*, 225–26.

51. *Toronto Star*, October 19, 1974, H7.

52. *Toronto Star*, October 19, 1974, A4; and November 5, 1974, E7.

53. *Toronto Star*, January 11, 1975, F6.

54. *Toronto Star*, January 30, 1975, E12.

55. *Toronto Star*, April 25, 1975, E12. Harry Brown followed Bruce Rogers, who was the first host of the early-morning show aimed at the Greater Toronto area. Bob Rhodes was *Metro Morning*'s first producer.

56. *Toronto Star*, July 31, 1975, E8.

57. *Toronto Star*, October 4, 1975, H10; and October 13, 1975, D5. *The Apprenticeship of Duddy Kravitz* was named the best film of the year; Michel Brault won for best director, and his film *Les Ordres*, on the subject of the October Crisis, was declared best picture.

58. *Toronto Star*, January 29, 2002, D8.

59. Bronwyn Drainie, "Comeback of the Year," *Maclean's*, December 15, 1975, 64; and Sylvia Fraser, "Peter, Peter," *Toronto Life*, April 2002, 106. Patrick Watson also mentions the show in *This Hour Has Seven Decades* (Toronto: McArthur & Company, 2004), 353–54.

60. *Toronto Star*, December 11, 1975, E22.

61. *Toronto Star*, December 18, 1975, E13; and email from Dennis Murphy, January 29, 2007.

62. LAC, 337097, A1 2005-01-0072, *Gzowski on FM*, February 3, 1976.

63. LAC, 276262, A1 2005-11-0017, *Olympic Magazine*, July 31, 1976; and LAC, 276263, A1 2005-11-0018, *Olympic Magazine*, July 31, 1976. Peter claimed that he had been an Olympic buff since at least the Melbourne games of 1956 but that it was the Montreal Games that had made him an addict.

64. Strabo (Peter Gzowski), "What Disney Does to One Man's Family," *Maclean's*, February 20, 1965.

65. LAC, 216675 VI 9510-0034, *Man Alive*, September 22, 1973.

66. Alison Gzowski, "Dad and Me," *Quest* (June/July/August, 1984), 41.

67. Mick Gzowski in Edna Barker, ed., *Remembering Peter Gzowski*, 183. Mick refers to the period after his parents separated, but one can only wonder if brusque telephone calls weren't customary, even before Peter moved out of 98 Lytton Boulevard.

68. Alison Gzowski, "Dad and Me," 40. Alison, born in 1959, gives her age as nine. However, in order to hear her father on daytime radio, she may have been slightly older. It was probably *This Country in the Morning*, which began when she was eleven, that she heard from her bedroom. In any case, the story's essence is true.

69. June Callwood, "The Informal Peter Gzowski," *Globe and Mail*, January 19, 1976, 8.

Chapter 10: Television, That Cruel Business

1. Trent University Archives (TUA), Gzowski fonds, 92-015, box 1, folder 26, Peter Gzowski to Mel Hurtig, May 12, 1976.

2. TUA, Gzowski fonds, 92-015, box 20, folder 28, probably a draft of *Starting Out*. Harold Gzowski was born on February 19, 1911. In May 1977, therefore, he was sixty-six. In the letter to Hurtig, it was the man at the crematorium who turned over Harold's few worldly possessions. In the draft of 1984, it was Uncle Ernest who gave these items to Peter.

3. TUA, Gzowski fonds, 92-015, box 1, folder 12, estate of Harold E. Gzowski. Once legal fees of $100 were paid and a cheque for $174.67 was issued to Gerda Friedricks, Peter received a cheque for $782.35.

4. Peter Gzowski, "'Inquiry': The One Show That Shouldn't Be Sacrificed to the Politicians," *Maclean's*, March 9, 1963, 64.

5. Strabo (Peter Gzowski), "The Sunny Simplicity of 'Singalong,'" *Maclean's*, August 7, 1965, 46.

6. Library and Archives Canada (LAC), "The Imperfect Machine," March 29, 1961, 74886, V1 85-1-0047; and *Toronto Star* March 16, 1961, 36. *Explorations* was known as the CBC's "semi-educational" series.

7. LAC, 9166, V1 8403-0122. *CBC Weekend*, August 23, 1969.

8. He was surely thinking of Norman Mailer, Tom Wolfe, George Plimpton, and Hunter S. Thompson, who, as purveyors of what came to be called New Journalism, placed themselves at the centre of the story, and who often imagined details that enhanced the theme and mood of the article. In 1965, Bob Bannerman, a book reviewer at *Maclean's*, wrote about Wolfe and his first book, *The Kandy-Kolored Tangerine-Flake Streamline Baby*, a collection of his newspaper and magazine articles. At that time the young Wolfe was just becoming known (*Maclean's*, August 21, 1965, 46). By 1969, he was well-known.

9. Email from Roger Sarty, July 22, 2009.

10. For this inside information, I am greatly indebted to Glenn Sarty's unpublished memoirs, which he generously made available to me. I also appreciate the time that Sarty spent with me by email and telephone.

11. LAC, 21042, V1 8405-0002, "Personalities, Gzowski, Music in Canada," June 3, 1970.

12. Cutaways were shots that showed the reaction of the crowds or the person being interviewed. They made editing easier. Re-asks, as Glenn Sarty explains in his memoirs, were "questions repeated in close-up to underscore the mutual nature of the exchange."

13. Email from Dennis Murphy, January 29, 2007.

14. *Toronto Star*, March 13, 1971, 43. Ross McLean explained that each show was designed to suit the tastes of the several hosts — after Peter, hosts included Fred Davis, Gene Lees, John O'Leary, Bruce Rogers, and Helen Hutchison. Dennis Murphy (email January 29, 2007) recalled another host, Alan Thicke, who mostly interviewed his wife, Gloria Loring.

15. Peter Gzowski, *The Private Voice: A Journal of Reflections* (Toronto: McClelland & Stewart, 1988), 22. According to Peter, the only advice Ross McLean had given him was to emulate the witty and sophisticated Dick Cavett, who was enjoying success as the late-night host of *The Dick Cavett Show*, which had made its debut a few months earlier. Peter's criticism of McLean is at odds with his interpretation of the man in his article in *Maclean's* in January 1960. At that time Peter painted a picture of a controlling producer who scripted every word spoken by his on-air hosts.

16. Peter Herrndorf was appointed head of CBC current affairs in 1974. He had joined the network in 1965 as a reporter and editor in Winnipeg, and later in Edmonton. In 1967 he moved to Toronto where he produced the CBC current affairs show *The Way It Is*. In 1970 he was appointed assistant to the vice-president of the CBC and general manager of the English network. In 1979 he became vice-president and general manager of English Radio and Television Networks. Later he was publisher of *Toronto Life* and chair of TVOntario. Today he is president and CEO of the National Arts Centre in Ottawa.

17. Bronwyn Drainie, "Comeback of the Year," *Maclean's*, December 15, 1975, 64.

18. During the mid-1960s, David Ruskin had worked as studio director on *This Hour Has Seven Days*, and on a lesser known show called *Compass*, broadcast Sunday mornings during the summers of 1965 and 1966. As station manager during CITY's first hectic years, he had managed to keep the channel on the air.

19. Interview with Peter Herrndorf, January 30, 2007.

20. Not all observers recall the toxicity. Perhaps only the non-smokers, who were in the minority then. Glenn Sarty, whose offices for *the fifth estate* were two or three floors above, did remember the toxicity.

21. Email from Roger Sarty, July 24, 2009.

22. Strabo (Peter Gzowski), "The Only Comics Who Use TV Right," *Maclean's*, April 3, 1965, 46.

23. Strabo (Peter Gzowski), "TV's Flood of Late-Night Small Talk," *Maclean's*, August 21, 1965, 46.

24. On the subject of Henry Ford, Lord Beaverbrook, the October Crisis, organized crime, aviation in Canada, and a thirteen-part series on John Diefenbaker.

25. Peter Gzowski, "Rub-a-Dub-Dub: 'Seaway' Floats a Flub," *Maclean's*, October 16, 1965, 69.

26. "Welcome Back 7 Days, All Is Forgiven," *Maclean's*, November 1, 1965, 71. In 1965 it was unthinkable that North Carolina would have an NHL franchise, let alone win the Stanley Cup.

27. Gzowski, *The Private Voice*, 167.

28. Interview with David Ruskin, September 25, 2005.

29. Ron Base, *Maclean's*, May 17, 1976, 66.

30. Sandra Martin, "Gzowksi's Problem Is That He Isn't Slick. Hamel's Problem Is That He Is," *Maclean's*, March 7, 1977, 65.

31. Gzowski, *The Private Voice*, 134.

32. Rex Murphy in Edna Barker, ed., *Remembering Peter Gzowski* (Toronto: McClelland & Stewart, 2002), 103.

33. Martin, "Gzowski's Problem," *Maclean's*, March 7, 1977, 65.

34. John Martin had booked Iggy Pop and David Bowie for March 11, 1977. Not long before the show was due for broadcast from the CBC studio at Yonge Street and Marlborough Avenue, Martin was informed that Pop and Bowie wouldn't be able to perform in Toronto since they were members of the British Musicians' Union but not of its North American counterpart, the American Federation of Musicians, which controlled all performances in Canada. A representative of the American union hovered over the set that evening to make sure that neither Iggy nor Bowie burst into song. The show came close to being blacked out. Peter had to make do with an interview with Iggy. Much to the disappointment of some of the staff, David Bowie never did show up.

35. According to John English, Marshall McLuhan had long been intrigued by Pierre Trudeau, whom he called the made-for-television "Man in the Mask." The two men became friends, and Trudeau often dropped by McLuhan's Toronto home unannounced. See John English, *Citizen of the World: The Life of Pierre Elliott Trudeau, Volume One: 1919–1968* (Toronto: Knopf Canada, 2008), 257. "It is the paradox of politics in a mass-media age," Rex Murphy once observed, that "style, even dark and rough, will beat character every time." Murphy was thinking particularly of television. See Rex Murphy, "'Nice' Is a Killer for Dion," *Globe and Mail*, September 22, 2007, A25.

36. Interview with Richard Nielsen, February 2, 2007.

37. Allan Fotheringham, "Like the CPR, Gzowski Tied Us Together," *Maclean's*, June 16, 1997, 68.

38. Today the late Nurse Bennett, a cultural icon of Newfoundland, lives on as the main character of *Tempting Providence*, a play by Robert Chafe.

39. Martin, "Gzowksi's Problem," *Maclean's*, March 7, 1977, 65.

40. Frank Jones, "Why Canada After Dark Died," *Toronto Star*, January 7, 1979, A4.

41. Interview with Diana Filer, February 1, 2008.

42. Interview with Peter Herrndorf, January 30, 2007.

43. See Murray McLauchlan, *Getting Out of Here Alive: The Ballad of Murray McLauchlan* (Toronto: Viking, 1998), 230–31. Around the period of *90 Minutes Live*, McLauchlan used to see Peter, as well as Ian Tyson and several unnamed visual artists, at booze-cans such as the one operated by Gary LeDrew, who ended up with a fine art collection. "Pretty well everybody of any note in town would pass through Gary's of an evening," noted McLauchlan.

44. Peter Gzowski, *An Unbroken Line* (Toronto: McClelland & Stewart, 1984), 182. While he was writing about Nancy Howard, mother of his third partner, he may also have been thinking of Jennie, who was almost of the same generation as Nancy Howard.

45. Peter Gzowski, sports column, *Saturday Night*, January 1966, 37, 39.

46. Sylvia Fraser, "Peter, Peter," *Toronto Life*, April 2002, 108.

47. On Wednesday, April 6, Myrna Kostash had joined Dalton Camp, Newfoundland fiddler Rufus Guinchard, Tom Rolston (director of the Banff School of Music), and singer Tom Waits to talk to Peter. The following Friday evening, Hayden had talked about his wife, Jane Fonda, his political activism during the 1960s, and his trial as a member of the Chicago Seven, the radical leaders who helped to disrupt the Democratic Party Convention of 1968.

48. This Edmonton section is woven together from interviews with Myrna Kostash and Jan Walter, from a description of the city provided by Kenneth Munro, and from the CBC Archives' index to *90 Minutes Live*.

49. TUA, Peter Gzowski fonds, 92-015, box 12, Peter Gzowski, "A Fan's Notes," in the Edmonton Oilers program for December 19, 1981, 67.

50. Brenda Zosky, "How Larry Zolf Found Shelter," *Toronto Star*, March 4, 1979, D1.

51. *Toronto Star*, January 3, 1979, A3.

52. Peter Gzowski, "Pierre Berton Earned All the Praise," *Toronto Star*, March 1, 1979, A3.

53. TUA, Peter Gzowski fonds, box 1, folder 26. Peter was thinking of himself and also of Debbie Brill, the Canadian high jumper, who at the Montreal Summer Olympics of 1976 failed to win a medal. The Canadian media weren't impressed. Afterward, Brill and Peter talked for two hours.

Chapter 11: "They Don't Want Me Anymore"

1. Peter Gzowski, "Some Notes on the Recipe for This Book," in Peter Gzowski, *Peter*

Gzowski's Spring Tonic (Edmonton: Hurtig Publishers, 1979), 9–11.

2. The house went on the market in the summer of 2005 for $479,900, and no doubt climbed even higher until the real-estate bust in 2008.

3. Peter Gzowski, "Do You Have a Retreat?" *Toronto Star*, December 29, 1978, A3.

4. Trent University Archives (TUA), Peter Gzowski fonds, 92-015, box 1, folder 31, Gzowski to Donna Logan, June 22, 1978; email from Donna Logan, October 1, 2008; and interview with Logan, October 19, 2008.

5. TUA, Peter Gzowski fonds, 92-015, box 1, folder 27.

6. Ironically, Peter himself had difficulty pronouncing New Canadian names at the CBC such as that of Jian Ghomeshi, lead singer with Moxy Früvous and now host of CBC Radio's *Q*. Interview with Ghomeshi, December 5, 2005. On *Q*, Ghomeshi has distinguished himself as a first-rate interviewer who is, this biographer predicts, the next Peter Gzowski. Or perhaps he has already attained that level of quality.

7. Jane Forner in Edna Barker, ed., *Remembering Peter Gzowski: A Book of Tributes* (Toronto: McClelland & Stewart, 2002), 37–39.

8. It was a heady time to be Polish. There were signs that the long winter of communism was about to end, though it wasn't until two years later that a strike at the Lenin shipyards in Gdańsk set Poland on a rapid path of liberation. In October 1978, Polish Cardinal Karol Wojtyła was elected Pope John Paul II, and in March 1979, Peter devoted an admiring column in the *Toronto Star* to the new pontiff. In 1984 when the pope visited Canada, Peter did the colour commentary for CBC-TV.

9. TUA, Peter Gzowski fonds, 92-015, box 1, folder 35, Peter Gzowski to Jan Walter.

10. In 1981, Peter admitted that he was as frightened as he had ever been while lost in Warsaw with no knowledge of Polish (TUA, Gzowski fonds, 92-015, box 12, Peter Gzowski, "A Fan's Notes," in the Edmonton Oilers program for November 23, 1981, 67).

11. Ludwik Kos-Rabcewicz-Zubkowski and William Edward Greening, *Sir Casimir Stanislaus Gzowski: A Biography* (Toronto: Burns and MacEachern, 1959), 173.

12. Ken Adachi, "Gzowski Tidbits Fight Misery," *Toronto Star*, D7.

13. TUA, Peter Gzowski fonds, 01-004, box 4, folder 17, Gzowski to Nancy Southam, nd.

14. TUA, Peter Gzowski fonds, 92-015, box 20, folder 28.

15. *Toronto Star*, June 17, 1981, A3; and June 19, 1981, A18.

16. Probably Double Hook Book Shop or Paragraphe Bookstore, the result of Camille Laurin's Bill 101, which gave prominence to the French language on signage. Like many English Canadians, Peter had trouble understanding the fear of disappearance that has haunted *Canadiens* from at least 1759–60. Double Hook, now closed, was owned by Judy Mappin, daughter of E.P. Taylor and sister of Peter's friend, Charles Taylor.

17. Peter Gzowski, "How I Discovered My Roots in a Victorian Inkwell," *Toronto Star*, February 26, 1979, A3.

18. See Lucy Booth Martyn, *Toronto: 100 Years of Grandeur* (Toronto: Pagurian Press, 1978); and William Dendy and William Kilbourn, *Toronto Observed: Its Architecture, Patrons, and History* (Toronto: Oxford University Press, 1986).

19. "Pete" McGarvey fonds, private archives, interview with Peter Gzowski by McGarvey, February 1979. My thanks to "Pete" McGarvey for making available two of his interviews with Peter Gzowski, this one and another in November 1983.

20. Peter Gzowski, "Canada's Olympic Promise," *Maclean's*, February 6, 1984, 24–25.

21. The show had begun in 1977 as a summer replacement for *Front Page Challenge*. It proved so popular that it continued five days per week during the winter from 1978 to 1980. It was taped at the National Theatre Centre in Winnipeg, as well as in studios across the country.

22. Val Ross in Edna Barker, ed. *Remembering Peter Gzowski: A Book of Tributes* (Toronto: McClelland & Stewart, 2002), 31.

23. Jared Diamond, *Collapse: How Societies Choose to Fail or Succeed* (Toronto: Penguin Canada, 2006), 120, 132, 134, and 151–52. During the eighteenth century, residents of the South Pacific island of Mangareva fought civil wars and ate the enemy for protein. Easter Islanders and the Donner Party, the latter caught in a mountain pass during the winter of 1846–47, also ate their fellows in order to survive. So, too, did the residents of Stalingrad during the long German siege in the Second World War. Piers Paul Reid's book *Alive* dealt with sixteen Uruguayans who ate human flesh to stay alive for ten weeks in the Andes after a plane crash. Mordecai Richler once attempted a book about Martin Hartwell, who resorted to cannibalism after a plane crash in the Canadian Arctic.

24. Interview with Judge Dennis Ball, October 3, 2008.

25. Interview with Donna (Johnson) Coulter, December 7, 2005.

26. TUA, Peter Gzowski fonds, 92-015, box 11, folder 17, Jack McClelland to Dennis Ball, July 3, 1979.

27. Interview with Judge Dennis Ball, October 3, 2008.

28. TUA, Peter Gzowski fonds, 92-015, box 11, folders 1–12.

29. Later an editor, or editors, probably Don and Billie Dewar of Salmon Arm, British Columbia, cut "The ice added to the Skyhawk's already heavy load, and violated the aerodynamics of its design." The editor(s) argued: "We know it, and the violated aerodynamics are awkward."

30. Sid Adilman, "Eye on Entertainment," *Toronto Star*, January 16, 1980, B1.

31. *Canadian Reader*, volume 21, no. 10, which was a publication of the Book-of-the-Month Club. The reviews are located in TUA, Peter Gzowski fonds, 92-015, box 11, folder 19.

32. William Casselman, "A Song of Moral Sympathy," *Toronto Star*, September 27, 1980, F13.

33. Judith Timson, "Survival on Faith and Human Flesh," *Maclean's*, October 6, 1980, 60–62.

34. *Toronto Star*, September 23, 1980, A15, and also September 24–26. The Casselman review was timed to appear on the day following the last excerpt.

35. *Toronto Star*, November 6, 1980; December 11, 1980; and April 10, 1981. Perhaps by that time Peter had had time to read Lucy Booth Martyn's book on Toronto architecture, which would have straightened him out on the name of the architect of "The Hall."

36. TUA, Peter Gzowski fonds, 92-015, box 20, folder 28, draft of *The Private Voice*. The biographer has italicized three phrases for emphasis.

37. *The Jubilee Volume of Wycliffe College* (Toronto: Wycliffe College and University of Toronto Press, 1927), 72. Colonel Gzowski was speaking as chair of the board of Wycliffe College at a convocation on May 22, 1884. He was more than pleased to announce that the college owed not a farthing and that its endowment had "steadily increased."

38. Kos-Rabcewicz-Zubkowski and Greening, *Sir Casimir Stanislaus Gzowski*, 63 and 77. Three decades later historian Viv Nelles was less indulgent. Most of Casimir Gzowski's life, Nelles wrote, was "quite prosaic; some of it verged upon the scandalous. But it began dramatically and ended well, and that is what he would be primarily remembered for." See H.V. Nelles, "Gzowski, Sir Casmir Stanislaus," in *Dictionary of Canadian Biography*, vol. 12, 1891 to 1900 (Toronto: University of Toronto Press, 1990, reprinted 1997), 389–96.

39. J.M.S. Careless, *Toronto to 1918: An Illustrated History* (Toronto: James Lorimer & Company and National Museum of Man, National Museums of Canada, 1984), 94; and email from David Bain, September 24, 2005. In 1818 the Toronto waterfront had been set aside as an esplanade (hence Esplanade and Front Streets today). In the 1850s, railway companies began to fill in the lakeshore, pushing the waterfront southward. In 1854, Casimir Gzowski was contracted to build a new esplanade on the newly filled land. However, he lost the contract in 1855 when it was discovered that he was planning to run a railway through the new esplanade. Peter's argument that, if his great-great-grandfather's plans had been carried out, Toronto would have had a large lakefront park, is untenable.

40. Gradually, Sir Casimir became better known. On March 5, 1963, a commemorative stamp was issued by the Post Office Department on the occasion of the 150th anniversary of his birth. The park named after him in West Toronto on the lake has also kept his name alive.

41. Kos-Rabcewicz-Zubkowski and Greening, *Sir Casimir Stanislaus Gzowski*, 126. The tears of which Peter spoke may have been the embellishment of Polish

Canadians in the 1930s, who, according to Viv Nelles, seized upon Sir Casimir as "one of their own who had won the complete acceptance they themselves sought." For these often shunned immigrants, Gzowski "embodied the ideal of Polish resistance, fortitude, and accomplishment." Ironically, Sir Casimir showed little interest in his homeland, preferring instead to identify with Canada and the empire, whence came his cherished honours. He even converted to the Church of England and identified with the ideals of Canada's imperial-nationalists, including the dissemination of Ontario ideals to the emerging Prairies, even if military force was required. In 1885 he concluded a talk at Wycliffe College by referring to the good news of the surrender of Chief Poundmaker during the North-West Rebellion, especially since, he noted, three Wycliffe students were with the Queen's Own Battalion, which was helping to restore imperial and Ontario order in the territories. Sir Casimir had also helped to establish Ridley College, which perpetuated the ideals of empire. Did Sir Casimir weep at not being able to thank the Polish pianist in Polish in the 1890s? More likely, he was pleased to show off his imperial uniform and medals, which signalled a life well lived in Canada and the British Empire.

42. TUA, Peter Gzowski fonds, 92-015, box 1, folder 15.

43. In 1990 in the *Dictionary of Canadian Biography*, Viv Nelles put it more tentatively: Sir Casimir Gzowski was "most probably" among troops that "temporarily halted" the Russian army in 1831; and Gzowski "was said to have suffered a minor wound" during a battle in front of Warsaw.

44. Of course, there is nothing about patronage or the fact that at the time of the Pacific Scandal, Sir Casimir Gzowski was a trustee of a trust fund of $66,576, established to provide Sir John A. Macdonald with what Viv Nelles calls "a dignified, regular income commensurate with his position."

45. For one example of Peter's use of the phrase, see Gzowski, *The Morningside Papers*, 178. Peter claimed that he had borrowed the phrase from Mordecai Richler (see Gzowski, *The Morningside Papers*, 18).

46. TUA, Peter Gzowski fonds, 92-015, box 1, folder 17, R.B. Fleming to Peter Gzowski, September 29, 1978. The italicized words were underlined in the original.

47. Peter Gzowski, "Women Are Taking Over Our Hangouts," *Toronto Star*, February 22, 1979, A3.

48. Advertisement for the Forum, *Toronto Star*, February 23, 1979, C8.

49. At that time The Bay, Simpson's, and Eaton's, where Peter's mother once worked, had book departments. See *Toronto Star*, February 26, 1979, B12; March 1, 1979, A16 and D16.

50. Ken Adachi, "NDP Book Policy Has Familiar Ring," *Toronto Star*, April 5, 1979, D8.

51. TUA, Peter Gzowski fonds, 92-015, box 1, folder 21.

52. Peter Gzowski, "Farewell and Hello to Television," *Toronto Life*, October 1978, 62–63, 76.

53. TUA, Gzowski fonds, 92-015, box 12, Peter Gzowski, "A Fan's Notes," in the Edmonton Oilers program for February 6, 1981, 67.

54. Peter Gzowski, *The Morningside Papers* (Toronto: McClelland & Stewart, 1985), 174.

Chapter 12: "Is Pierre Berton a Canadian?"

1. Wayne Gretzky to Peter Gzowski over lunch in Edmonton, circa 1981, Peter Gzowski, *The Private Voice* (Toronto: McClelland & Stewart, 1988), 138.

2. Quoted by Peter Gzowski, "Graceful Runs Through the Sports Reruns," *Toronto Star*, October 15, 1966, 36, which was a review of a book on baseball. The book referred to Jacques Barzun.

3. Peter also threw in rather odd comparisons with Billy the Kid and Mazo de la Roche.

4. *Saturday Night*, March 1965, 47. The books were Henry Roxborough's *The Stanley Cup Story* and Frank Selke's *Behind the Cheering*.

5. Peter Gzowski, sports column, *Saturday Night*, April 1966, 43. April's column defended the expansion of the NHL to American cities like St. Louis, even though Vancouver hadn't been included in the larger league. After all, Peter argued, American teams had been included as early as 1924, and furthermore, Vancouverites would still be able to watch the NHL on television.

6. Obviously, Peter hadn't forgotten his shock, when Jennie and he visited Greenwich Village in 1960, that it was difficult to distinguish the men from the women!

7. A respected actor from Quebec who acted and directed at the Stratford Shakespeare Festival where Peter may have seen him playing Cyrano de Bergerac or in a Molière comedy.

8. This was the second rejection by the Canada Council, which had turned him down for a biography of Sir Casimir.

9. Mordecai Richler fonds, Special Collections, University of Calgary, MsC, 582/95.20, box 19, folder 94.1, Peter Gzowski to Mordecai Richler, [July 1980].

10. Peter Gzowski, *The Private Voice* (Toronto: McClelland & Stewart, 1988), 138; and Peter Gzowski, foreword in Steve Dryden, ed., *Total Gretzky: The Magic, the Legend, the Numbers* (Toronto: McClelland & Stewart, 1999), 8. Peter was being a bit unfair. Gretzky was probably typical of most Edmonton Oilers, and indeed of most hockey players. "Few of them would read," Peter reported. "The front section of the newspaper meant little to them," and "much time was spent staring at television in their rooms" See Peter Gzowski, *The Game of Our Lives* (Toronto: McClelland & Stewart, 1981), 15 and 18. Having been born in 1961, Wayne

was too young to have been interested in watching Pierre Berton standing on a cowcatcher while narrating the television version of *The National Dream*.

11. Like Adrienne Clarkson, Peter must have been a fan of Peggy Lee.

12. TUA, Gzowski fonds, 92-015, box 14, folder 27. In January 1981, *Saturday Night* published Peter's "Broken Life of Billy Heindl," 61–62. Heindl's attempted suicide took place in September 1979.

13. The inside back flap of the dust jacket states that the photograph was by Joseph Black/Graphic Artists, Toronto. Did Peter pose in Toronto for the photograph?

14. Gzowski, *The Game of Our Lives*, 248.

15. Ted Barris fonds, tape of Barris interview with Wayne Gretzky et al. at the Forum Hotel, Edmonton, October 30, 1981.

16. Gzowski, *The Game of Our Lives*, 35, 118, 164, 174, and 233.

17. Some readers might have found those excerpts a pleasant reprieve from the ongoing discussions among the premiers and the prime minister concerning the patriation of the Canadian constitution. See *Toronto Star*, November 3, 1981, A1.

18. *Toronto Star*, December 26, 1981; and March 13, 1982.

19. On the other hand, for the same calendar year, *The Sacrament* earned only $22.14.

20. *Alberta Report*, November 20, 1981, 38.

21. *Toronto Star*, November 14, 1981, H11.

22. In fact, in one of the latest articles on hockey literature, while Ken Dryden's *The Game* is hailed as "a remarkable book," Peter's *The Game of Our Lives* isn't once mentioned. See Michael Bérubé, "Of Ice and Men," *The Common Review*, vol. 7, no. 4 (Spring 2009), 12.

23. TUA, Peter Gzowski fonds, 92-015, box 12, Peter Gzowski, "A Fan's Notes," in the Edmonton Oilers program for February 13, 1981, 67.

24. TUA, Marco Adria fonds, Adria interview with Peter Gzowski, May 26, 1992.

25. Peter Gzowski, sports column, *Saturday Night*, March 1965, 49–50. In June 1963, Peter had criticized owners of hockey and baseball teams who controlled what their players could say in print. Eric Nesterenko of the Chicago Black Hawks and Jim Brosnan of the Cincinnati Reds of baseball's National League had been reprimanded by owners for publishing articles about the darker side of their games, Nesterenko on hockey violence and Brosnan on pitchers' block. The real issue was freedom of speech, Peter wrote in 1963. See Peter Gzowski, "Brosnan's Fight for Literary Freedom in Big League Baseball," *Maclean's*, June 1, 1963, 63.

26. TUA, Peter Gzowski fonds, 92-015, box 17, folder 1.

27. Gzowski, *The Game of Our Lives*, 28.

28. Gzowski, *The Game of Our Lives*, 18.

29. TUA, Peter Gzowski fonds, 92-015, box 15, folder 9.

30. Gzowski, *The Game of Our Lives*, 64.

31. TUA, Peter Gzowski fonds, 92-015, box 15, folder 9. Ken Brown, a retired goalie, was the local Foster Hewitt in Edmonton. He did the colour commentary for a privately owned radio station. One day in Edmonton, after Peter told his story of skating endlessly on *verglas* in and around Galt, Brown, not to be outdone, told a story of playing shinny on spilled milk one Prairie winter's day (Gzowski, *The Game of Our Lives*, 106). Jack Norris, too, had been a goalie — with three NHL clubs, with the World Hockey Association, and with the American Hockey League. His career had begun in the early 1960s with the Estevan Bruins of the Saskatchewan Junior Hockey League and ended in 1976 when he retired from the Phoenix Roadrunners. He was a native of Saskatoon. See *www.legendsofhockey.net*. I thank Ted Barris for tracking down information on Jack Norris.

32. Gzowski, *The Game of Our Lives*, 47.

33. See Earl McRae, "Coke on Ice, Don Murdoch's Crime Was Not Being Caught — It Was Getting Caught in Public," *The Canadian*, October 14, 1978, 5–10a. During the 1978–79 season, Murdoch had been suspended from the New York Rangers, his team before he joined the Oilers, for possession of cocaine and for attempting to carry it across the American-Canadian border.

34. TUA, Peter Gzowski fonds, 92-015, box 15, folder 9.

35. Once the games began to be broadcast on television in 1952, the eye witnessed what Foster Hewitt had denied to the ear. Hewitt's gondola was perhaps too far above the play for him to witness blood. Only on television did viewers see and understand that hockey was/is a rather brutish game. Of course, it might have been the advent of television, with its thirst for drama and blood, that encouraged more violence.

36. TUA, Peter Gzowski fonds, 92-015, box 12, Peter Gzowski, "A Fan's Notes," in the Edmonton Oilers program for November 9, 1980, 67.

37. Peter Gzowski, sports column, *Saturday Night*, December 1965, 17.

38. Violence has always have been at the heart of hockey. In 1894, for instance, Lady Aberdeen was appalled at the brutality of a hockey game played at Rideau Hall; in the 1930s during a game, Eddie Shore almost killed Ace Bailey of the Toronto Maple Leafs. See email, Alastair Sweeney to H-Canada, February 15, 2007; email Jason Ellis to H-Canada, February 14, 2007; and Gzowski, *The Game of Our Lives*, 121. See also Dave Seglins, "'Just Part of the Game': Violence, Hockey, and Masculinity in Central Canada, 1890–1910," M.A. thesis, Queen's University, 1995; and Stacy L. Lorenz and Geraint B. Osborne, "'Talk About Strenuous Hockey': Violence, Manhood, and the 1897 Ottawa Silver Seven–Montreal Wanderer Rivalry," *Journal of Canadian Studies*, vol. 40, no. 1 (Winter 2006), 125–56. The two authors show that "a number of early twentieth-century hockey players used their sticks and fists to inflict severe, intentional blows on their opponents …" (150).

39. Peter's attitude to hockey violence was ambivalent. He had once admitted that his hero, Gordie Howe, always had a "penchant for cruelty." When he wrote about

Howe in *Maclean's* on December 14, 1963 ("Gordie Howe, Hero"), Peter noted that Howe had once shattered the nose of Lou Fontinato of the New York Rangers. In a sports column for *Maclean's* on May 2, 1964, Peter wrote that violence was an integral part of the game and a mark of team spirit. He had no sympathy for mothers who complained that their young sons were encouraged to be violent. "If someone knocks my son's friend down," Peter wrote, "I rather hope my son will knock the bully down — in hockey or in whatever else he chooses to do with his life." In *Saturday Night* in January 1965, Peter's article "A Father's Defence of Rough Play in Sports" defended hockey violence: "Violence ... is as natural a part of some young males' lives as playing harmonica is of others," he argued, "and what's wrong with it?" He added that in Galt he had learned not only how to be a good sport but "how much fun it is to knock somebody down." When he played football at Ridley College, Peter noted, he took pleasure in ramming his elbow into the belly of an unsuspecting opponent during a scrum (Peter Gzowski, "A Father's Defence of Rough Play in Sports," *Saturday Night*, January 1965, 17). As he grew older, however, Peter's attitude changed. In a column for the *Toronto Star* in 1979, he raged against hockey bullies and quoted Foster Hewitt, who claimed that the success of the bullies on the Philadelphia Flyers, who were winning Stanley Cups at the time, diminished the "scientific" aspect of hockey as it used to be played.

40. TUA, Peter Gzowski fonds, 92-015, box 20, folder 28, notes on *Morningside*, in preparation for his first *Morningside Papers*, where his notes, in part, appear on pages 228–29.

41. TUA, Peter Gzowski fonds, 92-015, box 12, Peter Gzowski, "A Fan's Notes," in the Edmonton Oilers program for October 23, 1981, 67. Some of Nelson Skalbania's business deals in Vancouver didn't draw rave reviews (interview with Joan Banks, December 2, 1991).

42. Gzowski, *The Game of Our Lives*, 67.

43. Gzowski, *The Game of Our Lives*, 70. One of Peter Pocklington's friends, apparently, was Paul Newman. Strangely enough, Newman's obituaries failed to mention his friendship with Pocklington. Race cars were probably the only thing the two men had in common. In addition to being a fine actor, Newman was a man of character, a political activist, and a philanthropist (Brian Baxter, "Paul Newman," *The Guardian Weekly*, October 3, 2008, 46).

44. TUA, Peter Gzowski fonds, 92-015, box 15, folder 11, typed notes that seem to have been transcribed from a tape recording, probably made by Peter after returning to his hotel room that evening. See also TUA, Peter Gzowski fonds, box 17, folder 14, for more on the afternoon at the Pocklingtons.

45. The cheese business, alas, is no more. Pierre-Auguste Renoir's grandson operates a Paris-style bistro called La Table de Renoir near Churchill Square in downtown Edmonton.

46. Peter Gzowski, "Great Expectations," *Saturday Night*, April 1982, 19–26.
47. TUA, Peter Gzowski fonds, 92-015, box 14, folder 12; and Richler fonds, MsC, 36, 582/95.20, box 19, folder 94.1, Gzowski to Richler, [July 1980]. During the awards evening, Peter was told of Ballard's horizontal dancing with girls on the Zamboni at Maple Leaf Gardens. When Ballard told a racist joke about African Americans, Peter confessed that everyone, including himself, laughed.
48. TUA, Peter Gzowski fonds, 92-015, box 1, folder 2, address to the Alberta Public Health Association, April 16, 1980. WCTU, the Women's Christian Temperance Union, was once an important organization that preached abstinence from alcohol.
49. *Guelph Daily Mercury*, September 16, 1981.
50. From 1860 to 1882, the race had been held in cities and towns around Ontario.
51. Quoted by Ian Brown, "Male Jeanius," *Globe and Mail*, July 7, 2007, L5.
52. Peter Gzowski, *An Unbroken Line* (Toronto: McClelland & Stewart, 1984), 170–71.
53. Gzowski, *An Unbroken Line*, 171–72.
54. Gzowski, *An Unbroken Line*, 119. Peter claims that he saw the royal couple as the royal limousine "made its way along Carlton Street." If he was talking about the procession to the race trace, he was probably on Queen Street.
55. Rudyard Griffiths, afterword in Charles Taylor, *Radical Tories: The Conservative Tradition in Canada* (Toronto: House of Anansi Press, 2006), 219.
56. Taylor, *Radical Tories*, 115.
57. Strabo, "Let's Quit Subsidizing Music Shows," *Maclean's*, May 15, 1965, 64–65.
58. Charles Taylor's papers haven't yet been released to the public.
59. Taylor, *Radical Tories*, 87–89.
60. Radio and TV schedule, *Toronto Star*, June 30, 1979, G10. The year before, when he hosted the "Great Canadian Birthday Party," the emphasis was also on folk music performed by Sneezy Waters and Duke Redbird. See radio and TV schedule, *Toronto Star*, June 29, 1978, C5.
61. TUA, Peter Gzowski fonds, 92-015, box 1, folder 14. Since Peter had co-signed to guarantee a loan of $48,000, the Toronto City Savings Credit Union, Inc., insisted that Peter and the other co-signers each pay back $2,012.80, a sum that in 1980 he had difficulty raising. The Toronto festival never took off. It did, however, allow Peter, who was an MC for many of the shows, to rub shoulders with folk groups and individual performers such as Stringband, Odetta, Nancy White, Valdy, Salome Bey, and Willie P. Bennett. The Toronto festival needed to attract twenty thousand people just to break even. With so much competition — there were folk festivals in most parts of Canada, and competition from the Mariposa Folk Festival, which by that time had moved from its original venue, Orillia, to Toronto — Peter's venture failed, and he, along with others, including the singer John Allan Cameron, lost their investments. See Peter Goddard, "Folk Festival Going for a New Crowd," *Toronto Star*, July 25, 1980, B1.

62. For a discussion of this quest for the "folk," see Sharon Wall, "Totem Poles, Teepees, and Token Traditions: 'Playing Indian' at Ontario Summer Camps, 1920–1955," *The Canadian Historical Review*, vol. 86, no. 3 (September 2005), 517; and the same article, slightly revised, as the sixth chapter in Sharon Wall, *The Nurture of Nature: Childhood, Antimodernism, and Ontario Summer Camps, 1920–55* (Vancouver: University of British Columbia Press, 2009), 216–50. The historian of "weightlessness" is T.J. Jackson Lears, *No Place of Grace: Antimodernism and the Transformation of American Culture, 1880–1920* (Chicago: University of Chicago Press, 1981); and the "quest for the folk" comes from Ian McKay, *Quest for the Folk: Antimodernism and Cultural Selection in Twentieth-Century Nova Scotia* (Montreal and Kingston: McGill-Queen's University Press, 1994). Each is quoted by Sharon Wall.

63. TUA, Peter Gzowski fonds, 92-015, box 19, folder 11.

64. See Taylor, *Radical Tories*, 179.

65. Taylor, *Radical Tories*, 52.

66. Peter Gzowski, "How I Discovered My Roots in a Victorian Inkwell," *Toronto Star*, February 26, 1979, A3.

67. The subtitle of the latest biography of John A. Macdonald by Richard Gwyn.

68. Donald Creighton, *John A. Macdonald: The Young Politician* (Toronto: Macmillan Company of Canada, 1974), 1.

69. Gzowski, *An Unbroken Line*, 199.

70. *Toronto Star*, November 6, 1983, G09.

71. *Toronto Star*, November 15, 1983, F02.

72. Gzowski, *An Unbroken Line*, 198.

73. Gzowski, *An Unbroken Line*, 161.

74. Gzowski, *An Unbroken Line*, 187, 193, and 236.

75. Gzowski, *An Unbroken Line*, 172.

76. Gzowski, *An Unbroken Line*, 176.

77. Mavis Gallant's term as writer-in-residence began in November 1983 and ended in April 1984. She lived at Massey College and had an office at New College. Although her position at the University of Toronto ended in April 1984, she remained at Massey College until August of that year. My thanks to Harold Averill of the University of Toronto Archives for sending me a synopsis of articles on Gallant from *University of Toronto Bulletin*, October 24, 1982, 7; *The Varsity*, November 9, 1983, 8–10; *Globe and Mail*, March 15, 1984, and July 27, 1984.

78. Author interviews with Mavis Gallant, December 30, 2005, and with Kathleen Davis, April 7, 2007.

79. Gzowski, foreword in Dryden, ed., *Total Gretzky*, 8.

80. Gzowski, *The Private Voice*, 115.

Chapter 13: *Morningside*: Canada Imagined

1. As early as June 1981, Peter's name was being bruited around Toronto as a possible substitute for Barbara Frum, who was leaving *As It Happens* for the new television show called *The Journal*, set to begin in September 1981. Sid Adilman, who usually had the scoop on Peter, also pointed out that Bronwyn Drainie and Patrick Martin were leaving *Sunday Morning*, the radio newsmagazine show, for a year in Greece. In other words, there were posts to be filled, and Adilman knew that Peter would make a first-rate host. After all, he was, Adilman pointed out, "a relaxed, informed and popular radio presence" (*Toronto Star*, June 19, 1981, A18).

2. The idea, of course, had been introduced by Bruno Gerussi during the late 1960s, and developed by Peter on *This Country in the Morning*. Did Peter think that the more formal style was creeping back in?

3. TUA, Peter Gzowski fonds, 01-004, box 1, folder 8, Peter Gzowski to Nicole Bélanger, January 1, 1982, and January 5, 1982.

4. TUA, Peter Gzowski fonds, 01-004, box 2, folder 3, Peter Gzowski memo, September 13, 1988, perhaps directed at his producers or perhaps notes for a talk.

5. Teperman was a company that tore down buildings in Toronto in preparation for redevelopment.

6. Email from Dave Thompson, December 13, 2005. "The *Morningside* March" was written by Thompson, who had performed on Don Harron's *Morningside* as a cabaret pianist. The music was commissioned by Alan Guettel, music producer of *Morningside*, who wanted a short piece that began as gently as "a summer morning off-shore breeze," with a break for the host to introduce himself and the show. The music continued for a few more bars, then faded out as the host began his short introductory essay or "billboards." In order that they would fit the pattern of the music, they were usually forty-nine seconds long. In addition, Thompson was asked to create short segments that would allow the show to move to station breaks, newscasts, announcements, and so on. And, of course, there had to be a few sombre bars to introduce a show that might follow the death of a pope, a monarch, or a prime minister. The only instruments used were Yamaha synthesizers, a grand piano, and drums. Thompson played everything except the drums, which were played by Marty Morel.

7. *Toronto Star*, September 7, 1982, A2.

8. The BBC's John Peel, who died in 2004 at age sixty-five, also had a talent to make listeners feel they were "hearing from a friend" (Simon Garfield, "Unfinished Symphony," review of Peel's autobiography *Margrave and the Marshes*, *The Guardian Weekly*, November 4–10, 2005, 24. Charlie Rose, host of PBS's *Charlie Rose*, also camouflages astute questions under a cloak of neighbourliness.

9. Peter Gzowski, *The Morningside Papers* (Toronto: McClelland & Stewart, 1985), 107–14.

10. *Toronto Star*, October 10, 1984, B02, Henry Mietkiewicz on "Radio."

11. Dalton Camp, foreword, in Peter Gzowski, *The Morningside Years* (Toronto: McClelland & Stewart, 1997), ix.

12. Peter Gzowski, *The New Morningside Papers* (Toronto: McClelland & Stewart, 1987), 25. Today Stuart McLean remains popular enough to fill small theatres across most of the country and in some of the northern states.

13. Stuart McLean, introduction in *The Morningside World of Stuart McLean* (Toronto: Penguin Canada, 1995), [ii].

14. McLean, *The Morningside World of Stuart McLean*, 231.

15. George Elliott Clarke, "Who Listens to Us Now?" *Journal of Canadian Studies*, vol. 37, no. 1 (Spring 2002), 8–9.

16. For these several interviews with scientists, and others, I am grateful that Peter, or someone among his staff, made cassette recordings, which ended up in his papers at Trent University Archives.

17. TUA, Peter Gzowski fonds, 92-015, box 12, folder 12.

18. Interview with Mavis Gallant, December 30, 2005. In Peter's diary, he used the word *stupid*, but in his memoirs, Gallant merely intimidated him.

19. Alexa McDonough succeeded Audrey McLaughlin, who was NDP leader from 1989 to 1995.

20. Interviews with Tony Fry, September 20, 2008, and with Alexa McDonough, November 3, 2008.

21. Interview with Janice Stein, December 20, 2005.

22. Ian Pearson in Edna Barker, ed., *Remembering Peter Gzowski: A Book of Tributes* (Toronto: McClelland & Stewart, 2002), 75.

23. In fact, one wonders if Scott Symons might have believed that *Morningside* had helped to create and perpetuate the blandness that he so detested in English-Canadian culture. What may have convinced Peter to interview Symons was the fact that Charles Taylor had dedicated *Radical Tories* to Symons. Peter was a fan of all things Taylor.

24. Sylvia Fraser, "Peter, Peter," *Toronto Life*, April 2002, 109; TUA, Peter Gzowski fonds, 92-015, box 20, folder 1; and *Toronto Star*, September 27, 1987, A22.

25. Peter Gzowski, *The Private Voice: A Journal of Reflections* (Toronto: McClelland & Stewart, 1988), 153.

26. My thanks to Catherine Wilson's mother, Maria Wilson, for sending me tapes of the interview and of the drama.

27. Peter Gzowski, "Passion Play: One Man's Fixated Love Affair with Canadian Painting," *Canadian Art* (Summer 1987), 86–87; and Gzowski, "Private Passions," in *The New Morningside Papers* (Toronto: McClelland & Stewart, 1987), 95–98. Peter was no longer impoverished. In his second year, 1983–84, his salary was a respectable $90,000. On August 30, 1984, he signed a contract that paid him

$105,600 for the 1984–85 season. Later, for the 1989–90 season, Peter was paid $165,000, and $185,000 for the 1990–91 season. By that time, his contract stipulated that his air travel and accommodation would be first-class. (See TUA, Peter Gzowski fonds, 92-015, box 1, folder 8; and box 1, folder 25). At the same time his income from stocks, royalties, speaking fees, and occasional television appearances was considerable. On April 27, 1990, for instance, Douglas Gibson of McClelland & Stewart sent Peter royalty cheques totalling close to $40,000, mostly from sales of the various *Morningside Papers* (see TUA, Peter Gzowski fonds, 01-004, box 2, folder 5). The radio essay read on *Morningside*, and its two reprints in Peter's second *Morningside Papers* (1987) and in *Canadian Art* (1987), leave the impression that he wanted to fashion himself into a connoisseur of good Canadian art, perhaps just like his great-great-grandfather, whose collection, Peter once claimed, contained thirty-four paintings by Cornelius Krieghoff (see *Toronto Star*, February 26, 1979, A3). What had become of Sir Casimir's Krieghoffs, Peter didn't know. Strangely enough, there are no Krieghoffs in any of the photographs of the art hanging in Sir Casirmir's "The Hall." And a search at the Art Gallery of Ontario archives for the provenance of the gallery's Krieghoffs turned up no one by the name of Gzowski.

28. Transcripts of *Morningside* interviews are found at TUA, Peter Gzowski fonds, 92-015, box 7, folder 1. For the Grant correspondence, see TUA, 01-004, box 4, folder 20. One of the last interviews with Regan Grant and his mother, Mary, was published in Peter Gzowski, *The Fifth (and Probably Last) Morningside Papers* (Toronto: McClelland & Stewart, 1994), 209–19.

29. My thanks to Kelly Christensen for sending me a tape of his interview.

30. Howard Fink, "Radio Drama, English Language," in *The Canadian Encyclopedia*, second edition, vol. 3 (Edmonton: Hurtig Publishers, 1988), 1817–18. The first radio series was Merrill Denison's *Romance of Canada*, produced in Montreal. Another series of radio dramas during the 1930s was produced and broadcast from the University of Alberta. Beginning in 1932, when the Canadian Radio Broadcasting Commission took over the CNR broadcasting network, program director Eric Bushnell increased the number of radio dramas. When Andrew Allan was appointed national drama supervisor in 1943, he placed renewed emphasis on Canadian themes, and in 1944, established the weekly *Stage 44* series, based in Toronto. It was Allan's series that made Peter even more aware of radio drama. In Timmins he had listened to *Stage 54* and *Stage 55* where he heard plays by international playwrights as well as those written by Canadians such as W.O. Mitchell, Joseph Schull, Mavor Moore, Lister Sinclair, and Len Peterson.

31. Henry Mietkiewicz, "Epic Radio Drama Broadcast as Serial," in *Toronto Star*, September 3, 1983, F10.

32. TUA, Peter Gzowski fonds, 92-015, box 1, folder 25.

33. *Toronto Star*, February 4, 1989, F8; February 18, 1989, H10; March 11, 1989, F4; November 18, 1989, G8.
34. Email from David Carley, May 15, 2008. Peter even played a character in a play broadcast on June 4, 1983, on CBC-FM's *Saturday Stereo Theatre*. His role was that of the "good" cowboy in *Dynamite Trail*, a radio play by veteran writer George Salverson, produced by another veteran, Fred Diehl, whose idea it was to cast Peter, who was joined by actors Murray Westgate, Sheila Moore, and Mavor Moore. "It's a 'good' part, no cameo walk-past-the-mike stuff," commented CBC Radio drama chief Susan Rubes. One unnamed insider told Peter's friend Sid Adilman that, before the taping, Peter seemed nervous, "as might be expected ... but he really came through." See Sid Adilman, "Radio Vet Gzowski Makes Acting Debut," May 3, 1983, C1.
35. During the summer of 1983, Peter Gzowski remained friendly with Peter Pocklington when the two of them flew on the millionaire's private jet from Edmonton to Yellowknife for another week of fishing. See TUA, Gzowski fonds, 92-015, box 1, folder 19.
36. LAC, 317871, A1 2005-11-0021, CJRT's *On the Arts* with Tom Fulton, Wednesday Edition, May 7, 1997.
37. TUA, Marco Adria fonds, Professor Marco Adria interview with Peter Gzowski, and with Ted Byfield, February 23, 1993.
38. Stephen Azzi, "Foreign Investment and the Paradox of Economic Nationalism," in Norman Hillmer and Adam Chapnick, eds., *Canadas of the Mind: The Making and Unmaking of Canadian Nationalisms in the Twentieth Century* (Montreal and Kingston: McGill-Queen's University Press, 2007), 77 and 87 n64. Azzi's source for his contention concerning the middle-class Ontario origins of the New Nationalism is Resnick, *The Land of Cain*, 167. In February 1974, when interviewed by Peter Gzowski on *This Country in the Morning*, Prime Minister Trudeau pointed out that the West was alienated in both a business and a cultural sense. "In the West they don't recognize Toronto productions as something expressing their desire for their own culture. When we have the Canada Council or other cultural agencies, the Film Board, the CBC and so on, making decisions that seem good from the point of view of those who make them, people out in Vancouver or in Edmonton say, well, you know, these are made down in Toronto or Montreal ..." See Peter Gzowski, *Peter Gzowski's Book About This Country in the Morning* (Edmonton: Hurtig Publishers, 1974), 52, where most of the interview is printed.
39. For an overview of Canadian economic nationalism from Sir John A. Macdonald to Brian Mulroney, see Azzi, "Foreign Investment and the Paradox of Economic Nationalism," 63–88.
40. For a version of this line, see Gzowski, *The Morningside Years*, 328.

41. Sir Casimir Gzowski would have smiled at his great-great-grandson's enthusiasm for state enterprise. While all railways received state assistance in some form, often as land grants, the only completely state-owned railway was the National Transcontinental, built through northern wilderness by the government of Sir Wilfrid Laurier, in order to give the privately owned Grand Trunk Pacific an eastern line to the Atlantic. The National Transcontinental was a grand failure. For the first two years, the Canadian Pacific Railway was owned by the Dominion government, which in 1880 was more than pleased to hand it over to a corporate syndicate headed by William Van Horne. From the Canadian Pacific to the Canadian Northern and the Grand Trunk Pacific, railways were private concerns, with governments playing regulatory roles by setting construction standards and attempting to regulate freight rates. It was only during the First World War that the national government under Sir Robert Borden, in order to preserve confidence in Canadian financial institutions and save the credit rating of the country, was forced to create Canadian National Railways, which included most railways except for the CPR.

42. TUA, Peter Gzowski fonds, 92-015, box 1, folder 2. Peter was speaking to the Alberta Public Health Association at Banff Springs Hotel on April 16, 1980. Peter even disparaged this same great-uncle on at least one occasion by naming Sir Donald Mann, along with his partner Sir William Mackenzie, as one of the principal crooks in the Beauharnois Scandal. In fact, neither man had anything to do with the scandal, in which the company building the canal near Montreal had lined the pockets of federal Liberals in return for business favours. Peter had confused two of Ralph Allen's articles in *Maclean's*, each one an excerpt from Allen's book *Ordeal by Fire*. The first, "The Princely Beggars, Mackenzie and Mann," published in August 1961, accused the two railway barons of being swindlers between 1896 to 1913; and the second, published the following month, was on the much later Beauharnois. For more on the Beauharnois Scandal, see T.D. Regehr, *The Beauharnois Scandal: A Story of Canadian Entrepreneurship and Politics* (Toronto: University of Toronto Press, 1990).

43. TUA, Gzowski fonds, 92-015, box 1, folder 18.

44. Yes, the same Barbara McDougall, later a Cabinet minister in the government of Brian Mulroney, and also sister-in-law of the CBC's Michael Enright.

45. TUA, Gzowski fonds, 92-015, box 1, folder 40. There was also a whiff of hypocrisy in Peter's attitude to social programs such as Medicare, which surely is supposed to treat all Canadians on a more or less equal basis. However, in 1980–81 he reported, without censure, that Brett Callighen of the Edmonton Oilers was able to leap over a six-month waiting list to have a cataract removed by a Calgary specialist See Peter Gzowski, *The Game of Our Lives* (Toronto: McClelland & Stewart, 1981), 56–57.

46. Interview with William Gairdner, March 2, 2006.
47. TUA, Peter Gzowski fonds, 92-015, box 20, folder 28.
48. Knowlton Nash, *Cue the Elephant: Backstage Tales at the CBC* (Toronto: McClelland & Stewart, 1996), 262.
49. Interview with Munroe Scott, June 25, 2005. Shelley Ambrose, who for years watched Peter handle and mishandle people off the air, noted that if people rushed up to him to tell him what a great star he was, he was at a loss for words. On the other hand, if a fan approached him at an airport or on the golf course with an opinion on a specific topic that he or she had heard on *Morningside*, Peter was usually willing to listen for a few minutes (interview with Shelley Ambrose, May 16, 2005). Peter's CBC colleagues weren't exempt from his coldness. For years Russ Germain arrived at about 5:00 a.m. to prepare for *World Report*. Germain and Gzowski often crossed paths in the Barbara Frum Atrium. "I guess he saved his cozy side for his listeners," Germain reported years later without blame (email from Russ Germain, June 15, 2005). On one occasion at the ACTRA Awards, Peter met his match. He and Terry Campbell, the impeccable and affable host of *Stereo Morning*, were in competition for best radio host. Peter won. At the end of the evening Peter ambled over to Campbell. "Ah, Terry," he mumbled consolingly, "it's better to have run and lost." His eyes twinkled. "No, it isn't," Campbell snapped. "Winning is everything. And don't be so smarmy about it." Campbell, like Gzowski, had a carefully honed radio persona that showed none of his sharp angles (interview with Terry Campbell, April 16, 1999).
50. TUA Peter Gzowski fonds, 92-015, box 1, folder 6. This may be the apartment that Peter rented after he left the bachelor apartment in Yorkville. At Mayfair Mansions, which during the 1970s and 1980s, provided short-term leases of furnished flats, he wrote some of his *Toronto Star* columns in the late 1970s. Apparently, he kept this suite fairly secret. His partner of that period had never heard of it.
51. Email from Robert Reguly, November 21, 2007.
52. *Toronto Star*, January 17, 1986, B2.
53. *Toronto Star*, September 7, 1982, A2.
54. TUA, Peter Gzowski fonds, 01-004, box 2, folder 5; and *Toronto Star*, July 1, 1986, A1.
55. Tristram Hunt, *The Guardian Weekly*, July 14–20, 2006, 20. For a further discussion of the loss of community, see Michael Valpy, "Is This the End of the Age of Social Cohesion?" *Globe and Mail*, August 29, 2009, A21.
56. At least not in the disparate, multicultural English Canada. French Canada may be a different story.
57. TUA, Peter Gzowski fonds, 92-015, box 2, folder 5.
58. Gzowski, *The Morningside Years*, 62.
59. Karen Armstrong, *A Short History of Myth* (Toronto: Knopf Canada, 2005), 136–37.

60. Erin Lemon in Barker, ed., *Remembering Peter Gzowski*, 69–70.
61. TUA, Peter Gzowski fonds, 01-004, box 4, folder 19; email from Craig Kayama, March 18, 2009; and email from Mark Cannon, March 18, 2009. The BBM measures radio listenership using the diary methodology. Roughly seventy-five thousand randomly selected households fill in a diary that lists seven days divided into fifteen-minute periods. Each participant is asked to list the radio station listened to in each segment and the location of the radio (car, work, home, et cetera). The survey is carried out twice a year. The figure of 1,228,200 for 1993 is an extrapolation based on the sample of seventy-five thousand or so households. Although this figure may have been a peak in numbers of listeners — it is difficult to tell because neither the CBC nor the BBM places a priority on answering a researcher's queries about the figures over fifteen years of *Morningside* — Peter liked to imply that the program usually enjoyed more than a million listeners.
62. *Toronto Star*, February 2, 1996, A21.
63. *Toronto Star*, December 23, 1991, C8.
64. Interview with Robin Quantick, March 23, 2009.
65. *Toronto Star*, October 14, 1991, A13. The unnamed farmer told a travelling committee on constitutional reform that he had "picked up most of his information about Ottawa's new constitutional proposal by listening to Peter Gzowski as he finished harvesting."
66. Pat Buckna in Barker, ed., *Remembering Peter Gzowski*, 45.
67. Shelagh Rogers, "Reading with Peter," in Gzowski, *The Fifth (and Probably Last) Morningside Papers*, 15.
68. Rauld Liset and Valerie Loewen in Barker, ed., *Remembering Peter Gzowski*, 55 and 58 respectively.

Chapter 14: *Morningside*: Behind the Scenes

1. Peter Gzowski, *The Morningside Papers* (Toronto: McClelland & Stewart, 1985), 7–9.
2. Trent University Archives (TUA), Peter Gzowski fonds, 99-015, box 2, folder 2, clipping of an article by Glen Allen, *The New Brunswick Reader*, May 24, 1997, on working with Peter Gzowski.
3. After Hal Wake came Larry Scanlan, Peter Kavanagh, Ian Pearon, and Paul Wilson.
4. *Toronto Star*, January 22, 1993, D16. The old building had so much resonance and so many memories, Peter told Michele Landsberg of the *Toronto Star* when she asked if the new building "affected the feel of a program well-loved for its homey informality." The new building appeared cold. "Look — nobody on the street. Like

Stalingrad after the siege," Peter cracked. Time didn't mellow his aversion to the new building. In 1996 he called it "our awful building downtown." See TUA, 01-004, box 2, folder 3, Peter Gzowski to Jane (Gordon) Glassco, November 24, 1996.

5.   My thanks for Marieke Meyer, who in a series of emails in May 2005 explained her role. See also Marieke Meyer in Edna Barker, ed., *Remembering Peter Gzowski: A Book of Tributes* (Toronto: McClelland & Stewart, 2002), 70–71.

6.   Les MacPherson in Barker, ed., *Remembering Peter Gzowski*, 55–57. The tightly scripted *Morningside* wasn't, however, welcomed by all producers — David Amer for one. One day in the late 1980s, Amer told Peter that he missed the spontaneity, adventure, and good fun of *This Country in the Morning*. Now, Amer told Peter, tension replaced fun and producers were no longer encouraged to follow their instincts. Even worse, Amer contended, *Morningside* relied far too much on specialists because they could be counted upon to be brief and succinct. No longer were ordinary voices welcomed. The criticism worried Peter. Nevertheless, he believed that listeners were better served than in 1974. *Morningside* had fewer self-indulgent, meandering interviews. In 1985, Henry Mietkiewicz, who wrote about radio in the *Toronto Star*, implied much the same sentiments as Amer. While the early to mid-1970s were "an era of freshness, dynamism and innovation," radio in the 1980s, Mietkiewicz argued, had become much more complicated, like a Rubik's cube, which was "square and solid and uniform, without much allowance for creative non-conformity." See TUA, Peter Gzowski fonds, 92-015, box 2, folder 8; and *Toronto Star*, February 23, 1985, F3.

7.   See Peter Gzowski, *The Private Voice: A Journal of Reflections* (Toronto: McClelland & Stewart, 1988), 256.

8.   TUA, Peter Gzowski fonds, 01-004, box 3, folder 1.

9.   The "myth" discussion was the producer's proposal for a series on myths, a proposal that Peter called "a disconnected set of statements."

10.   Peter Gzowski, *The Morningside Papers*, 1985, 11.

11.   Note to author from Angela Clark, February 5, 2009, copies of the letter to Peter, and her notes made after the visit to *Morningside*; interviews with Angela Clark, February 13, 2009, and March 7, 2009; and with Bryan Clark, February 18, 2009.

12.   Interview with Jim McGivern, August 13, 2009.

13.   TUA, Peter Gzowski fonds, 01-004, box 4, folder 9, Michael O'Malley to Peter Gzowski, June 26, 1996, and March 28, 1997. The second letter was to report the death of Maggie.

14.   TUA, Peter Gzowski fonds, 92-015, box 27, file 12.

15.   TUA, Marco Adria fonds, Adria interview with Peter Gzowski, April 28, 1987.

16.   Interview with C., April 8, 2008; and emails from C. in January 2009. What C. couldn't have known was that exactly thirty years earlier when Peter first voted, he told readers of Moose Jaw's *Times-Herald* that he looked forward to exercising his

franchise "in many more elections" when he would feel "some of the same thrill that tingled today" when he first cast a vote.

17. *Toronto Star*, October 27, 1985, G10.
18. *Toronto Star*, October 3, 1987, F3.
19. *Toronto Star*, December 27, 1987, E18; January 3, 1988, A16; and January 24, 1988, A20.
20. TUA, Peter Gzowski fonds, 01-004, box 23, folder 2.
21. Gale Zoë Garnett wrote about the evening of Morley Callaghan's last book launch when, to prevent people from calling Northrop Frye "Professor Frye," a title he disliked, Garnett gave Frye a red clown's nose that, when in place, encouraged his fans to call him what he preferred — just plain "Norrie."
22. TUA, Peter Gzowski fonds, 92-015, box 23, folder 2, Douglas Gibson to Peter Gzowski, March 5, 1991.
23. TUA, Peter Gzowski fonds, 95-008-01, folder 26, Peter Gzowski to Douglas Gibson, [August? 1994].
24. Interview with Daryl Richel, May 25, 2007.
25. "Piggy's" was Chez Piggy, owned by former rock star Zol Yanoski.
26. TUA, Peter Gzowski fonds, 99-015, box 2, folder 2. In his diary, Peter attributes the theory to Glen Allen, and Allen verifies that it was his theory, in a clipping from the same file, which is an article by Allen for *The New Brunswick Reader*, May 24, 1997. While Peter was an excellent editor of other writers' work, he sometimes made mistakes that went uncorrected by his own editors. In his memoirs, he incorrectly attributes the theory to *Max* Allen (Gzowski, *The Private Voice*, 272).
27. Gzowski, *The Private Voice*, 274. Who knows what Peter might have thought of Trent's Gzowski College, whose yellow exterior is admired by few.
28. Peter's biographer has done his best to follow Peter's narrative. The diary is sometimes at variance with *The Private Voice*. In the memoir version, Peter claims that "as soon as the program finished in Toronto this morning, I jumped into the car and headed down the 401 towards Belleville ..." The entry in the memoir is for Saturday, October 31, 1987, at 1:00 a.m. By "this morning," he may mean Friday morning. If so, why not say "yesterday morning"? He adds "Peterborough tomorrow," by which he may mean "today." See Gzowski, *The Private Voice*, 270–71.
29. Interview with Donelda Thomas, July 25, 2006; and with Alicia Thomas, July 4, 2009.
30. Interview with Ezra Schabas, June 18, 2007.
31. TUA, Peter Gzowski fonds, 01-004, box 4, folder 18.
32. TUA, Peter Gzowski fonds, 01-004, box 4, folder 23.
33. For one such comment, see TUA, Peter Gzowski fonds, 01-004, box 4, folder 7. One listener renamed the show *Peter Exhausted and Boringside*.
34. In 1957 the myth of the tunnels and of Al Capone's association with them hadn't yet been invented. For more on the Moose Jaw tunnels, see Brian S. Osborne,

"Moose Jaw's 'Great Escape': Constructing Tunnels, Deconstructing Heritage, Marketing Places," *Material History Review* (Spring 2002), 20–21. Osborne speculates that the "tunnels" may have been storage areas, conduits, or basements.

35. The taped interview with W.O. Mitchell is reported in Barbara and Ormond Mitchell, *Mitchell: The Life of W.O. Mitchell — The Years of Fame, 1948–1998* (Toronto: McClelland & Stewart, 2005), 400.
36. *Toronto Star*, May 31, 1997, A32.
37. Peter Gzowski, *The Morningside Years* (McClelland & Stewart, 1997), 324.
38. TUA, Peter Gzowski fonds, 01-004, box 4, folder 9.
39. TUA, Peter Gzowski fonds, 99-015, box 2, folder 2.
40. TUA, Peter Gzowski fonds, 01-004, box 4, folder 9.
41. *Toronto Star*, May 27, 1997, F6.
42. TUA, Peter Gzowski fonds, 01-004, box 2, folder 3.
43. *Toronto Star*, May 30, 1997, A1 and A4.
44. TUA, Peter Gzowski fonds, 99-015, box 2, folder 2, clipping of Glen Allen in *The New Brunswick Reader*, May 24, 1997, on working with Peter Gzowski.
45. TUA, Peter Gzowski fonds, 01-004, box 4, folder 9, Hal Wake to Peter Gzowski, November 5, 1997.

Chapter 15: "I Don't Know Who I'll Be When I'm No Longer Peter Gzowski"

1. Trent University Archives (TUA), Peter Gzowski fonds, 92-015, box 1, folder 13.
2. Thomas Fisher Library Archives, University of Toronto, Ms. Coll. 337, Cameron, E. Papers, box 40, Layton, cassette tape #19; and email from Elspeth Cameron, March 29, 2009. The second quotation of the show was even more treacherous: "I believe in White supremacy until the Blacks are educated to a point of responsibility." No one guessed that the line came from actor John Wayne. Since all but one of the tapes of the show have vanished from CHCH-TV, the only way now to "watch" Peter's version of *Fighting Words* is to listen to the audiotapes of the show, located in the Elspeth Cameron fonds, Fisher Library Archives. Cameron collected the tapes while preparing her biography of Irving Layton. These tapes make good radio.
3. *Toronto Star*, June 3, 1983, D1.
4. *Toronto Star*, December 5, 1983, D1.
5. *Toronto Star*, September 7, 1982, A2.
6. *Toronto Star*, March 19, 1985, E1. During the second season of *Fighting Words*, the show almost lost its host. Peter and Gill, along with Peter C. and Heather Black, went sailing off Antigua, and as Peter told it in *Toronto Life*, December 1984, the mast broke and they were tossed about *sans merci* in heavy seas.

7. *Toronto Star*, March 26, 1987, F1.

8. Email from Roger Sarty, July 24, 2009.

9. *Toronto Star*, September 1, 1985, G1.

10. Interview with Evelyn Hart, September 3, 2005.

11. *Toronto Star*, January 21, 1987, D1.

12. *Toronto Star*, March 26, 1987, F1.

13. Library and Archives Canada (LAC), V1 2005-11-0108, *Stanley Knowles: By Word and Deed*. The old-age pension was really a program instituted in 1927, not by Knowles but by James King, Prime Minister Mackenzie King's minister of health and veterans' affairs. At the time the Liberal Party had a majority government.

14. Interview with Melinda Sutton, assistant to Linda Schuyler, who conceived and developed the Degrassi shows, February 25, 2009. There is no name on the script, but the style is Gzowskiesque.

15. LAC, V1 2005-11-0108, *Degrassi Between Takes*.

16. Over its long run the show had three names: *The Kids of Degrassi Street*, *Degrassi Junior High*, and *Degrassi High*.

17. LAC, 2000687651, October 30, 1989, *Degrassi Between Takes*; and interview with Toni Wrate, November 9, 2008, whose husband Eric was one of the editors on the Degrassi series. In early 1992, Peter narrated a two-part show called *Country Gold*, shown on CBC Television over two evenings. It subject was Canada's country music from the early days to the early 1990s. According to the *Toronto Star*, Peter narrated the show "with obvious affection." See *Toronto Star*, February 1, 1992, J3.

18. *Toronto Star*, October 2, 1982, A2.

19. *Toronto Star*, October 18, 1982, D3.

20. TUA, Peter Gzowski fonds, 92-015, box 20, folder 1.

21. *Toronto Star*, January 30, 1988, G3.

22. In June 1991, in the George Ignatieff Theatre at the University of Toronto, Peter joined Michael Ondaatje, Linda Griffiths, and others in a tribute to the late poet Bronwen Wallace (*Toronto Star*, June 13, 1991, F4). In early November 1991, along with June Callwood, Elizabeth Baird, Bill McNeil, Morley Torgov, and other writers, he attended the opening of a branch of The Book Company in midtown Toronto (*Toronto Star*, November 6, 1991, F3). Later that month Peter attended one of a series of cross-Canada dinner parties that raised money for the Writers' Development Trust. The largest was held at Sutton Place Hotel on November 14. Along with Peter were Ken Dryden, Robert Fulford, Don Harron, Knowlton Nash, Rick Salutin, and others (*Toronto Star*, November 15, 1991, D20). A few days later Peter was signing copies of the fourth volume of *Morningside Papers* at The Book Company at Toronto's Yorkdale Mall (*Toronto Star*, November 20, 1991, B4). He concluded his busy year by writing an article in the *Toronto Star* on how to

reduce the trauma of entertaining by barbecuing scalloped potatoes outdoors (*Toronto Star*, December 1, 1991, G1).

23. *Toronto Star*, July 22, 1992, B1.

24. *Toronto Star*, November 5, 1992, MS4.

25. *Toronto Star*, November 12, 1992, C12.

26. *Toronto Star*, February 15, 1993, B4. Peter's pals included Oscar Peterson, Karen Kain, Murray McLauchlan, Mordecai Richler, Cynthia Dale, Molly and Taborah Johnson, Rebecca Jenkins, Shirley Eikhard, Prairie Oyster, Tom Jackson, Jane Siberry, Moxy Früvous, Valdy, and Michael Kusugak.

27. *Toronto Star*, May 10, 1993, C4.

28. *Toronto Star*, November 3, 1993, F2.

29. *Toronto Star*, November 30, 1995, F3.

30. TUA, Peter Gzowski fonds, 92-015, box 20, folder 28.

31. Peter deliberately left blank the name of the place.

32. TUA, Peter Gzowski fonds, 92-015, box 2, folder 8, notes made in 1988, in preparation for his memoirs.

33. *Toronto Star*, December 26, 1993, E3.

34. Harry Bruce fonds, Peter Gzowski to Harry Bruce, February 25, 1996. Five years later when Peter wrote about this incident, the nurse was no longer "ditzy," and he added a detail not in the letter to Harry Bruce — he had refused the nurse's offer because he didn't want to join "the gaggle of people outside every hospital who lean on their IVs, bare bums exposed to the winds, as they suck on the toxin that put them there in the first place." See Peter Gzowski, "How to Quit Smoking in Fifty Years or Less," in Lorna Crozier and Patrick Lane, eds., *Addicted: Notes from the Belly of the Beast* (Vancouver: Greystone Books, 2001), 64. In 1996, he could have smoked inside the hospital, for it wasn't until the Smoke-Free Ontario Act of May 31, 2006, that all smoking was banned inside hospitals. The 1994 Ontario Tobacco Control Act didn't prohibit indoor smoking in hospitals. My thanks to the Ontario Ministry of Health Promotion for these details, and to the helpful member of that ministry who didn't wish to be acknowledged.

35. TUA, Peter Gzowski fonds, 01-004, box 1, folder 2.

36. TUA, Peter Gzowski fonds, 01-004, box 3, folder 1, Gzowski to Adrienne Clarkson, May 19, 1987.

37. *Toronto Star*, July 10, 1988, A19; and see also Peter Gzowski, *The Private Voice* (Toronto: McClelland & Stewart, 1988), 1–7.

38. Gzowski, *The Private Voice*, 2, 7, and 301.

39. Robert Fulford, *Toronto Star*, December 23, 1965, 11.

40. David Remnick, introduction in A.J. Liebling, *Just Enough Liebling: Classic Work by the Legendary* New Yorker *Writer* (New York: North Point Press, 2004), xvi–xvii.

41. TUA, Peter Gzowski fonds, 01-004/2/9.

42. Indeed, following the example of biographical novels such as Colm Tóibín's *The Master* or Tomás Eloy Mártinez's *The Perón Novel*, there were times when this biographer wondered if a novel called *Peter Gzowski: Master Storyteller* might better portray Peter.

43. Peter Gzowski, "A Perfect Place to Be a Boy," as reprinted in Edna Barker, ed., *A Peter Gzowski Reader* (Toronto: McClelland & Stewart, 2002), 4.

44. Interview with Harry Bruce, October 24, 2007.

45. Gay Talese, *The Kingdom and the Power* (New York: World Publishing Company, 1969), 46.

46. TUA, Peter Gzowski fonds, 01-004, box 4, folder 8, Peter Gzowski to Harry Bruce, February 25, 1996.

47. E.B. White, *The Points of My Compass: Letters from the East, the West, the North, the South* (New York: Harper & Row, 1962), 23–24.

48. TUA, Peter Gzowski fonds, 01-004, box 4, folder 8, Peter Gzowski to Harry Bruce, February 25, 1996.

49. A.J. Liebling, "At Table in Paris," in Liebling, *Just Enough Liebling* (New York: North Point Press, 2004), 16.

50. *Canadian Reader*, vol. 21, no. 10, which was a publication of the Book-of-the-Month Club. The reviews are located in TUA, Peter Gzowski fonds, 92-015, box 11, folder 19.

51. *Hamilton Spectator*, November 15, 1980.

52. For Peter's use of the word *plot*, see Gzowski, *The Private Voice*, 5.

53. Gzowski, *The Private Voice*, 9.

54. TUA, Peter Gzowski fonds, 01-004, box 1, folder 2.

55. *Globe and Mail*, November 5, 1988, C19.

56. John Bemrose, "King of the Airwaves," *Maclean's*, November 7, 1988, 67.

57. George Galt, "The Hungry Ego," *Saturday Night*, November 1988, 88.

58. *Toronto Star*, November 11, 1988, M11.

59. Tim Gardam, "Playing Hide and Seek with His Past," *The Guardian Weekly*, July 13, 2007, 34. In fact, few members of what Alan Fotheringham once dubbed the Family Compact of journalism and broadcasting in Toronto have ever dared to reveal the inner workings of the Compact except perhaps for McKenzie Porter, who once outed members of Pierre Berton and Jack McClelland's Sordsmen Club, a cabal of male journalists and publishers who invited well-known women — Dinah Christie and Adrienne Clarkson, among others — for dining, drinking, and seduction; and Knowlton Nash, whose *Cue the Elephant* moved in and out of the lives of his CBC colleagues, though Nash does treat Peter with kid gloves. Even so, when Geraldine Sherman reviewed Nash's book, she scolded him for revealing that Peter was a grump. See A.B. McKillop, *Pierre Berton: A Biography* (McClelland & Stewart, 2008), 443 and 734–35 (fns. 75–85); and *Toronto Star*, November 30, 1996, L17.

60. *Toronto Star*, December 17, 1988, M7.
61. *Toronto Star*, January 7, 1989, M7.
62. *Toronto Star*, February 18, 1989, M7; February 28, 1989, F4; and March 25, 1989, M7.
63. Email from Paul Lewis, August 13, 2009.
64. Peter was one of those rare researchers who were important enough to have an archive come to him, which is even better than the singular honour bestowed on Adrienne Clarkson, who while researching the life of Dr. Norman Bethune was given a room of her own at Library and Archives Canada.
65. Email from Paul Lewis, August 13, 2009.
66. Peter Gzowski, "Leacock's Smile," with an afterword by David Staines (Orillia, ON: Leacock Museum in association with Frontier College, 2003). Yousuf Karsh published several versions of his session with Leacock, one of which graces the cover of Alan Bowker, ed., *On the Front Line of Life: Stephen Leacock — Memories and Reflections, 1935–1944* (Toronto: Dundurn Press, 2004).
67. Peter speculated that the young Stephen Leacock might have gazed from the garden of the Leacock farm near Sutton, Ontario, onto the land upon which the Briars golf course would be built decades later. In "Life on the Old Farm," Leacock wrote that the farm was located four miles to the south of Lake Simcoe and "out of sight of it." See Leacock, "Life on the Old Farm," in Bowker, ed., *On The Front Line of Life*, 51.
68. Stephen Leacock, "Why I Refuse to Play Golf," in Leacock, *Over the Footlights and Other Fancies* (London: John Lane The Bodley Head, 1923), 251–59. The essay, of course, shouldn't be taken too seriously, but there is no evidence of Leacock's love of the game. Beginning in 1908, Leacock spent his summers on Brewery Bay near Orillia, not an easy drive to Sutton, a town for which he had "no use." Leacock to his sister, Margaret; his brother, George; and his mother, Agnes, June 4, 1907, in David Staines, ed., *The Letters of Stephen Leacock* (Toronto: Oxford University Press, 2006), 35. For details of the life of Leacock, see Margaret MacMillan, *Stephen Leacock* (Toronto: Penguin Canada, 2009).
69. Stephen Leacock, "The Speculations of Jefferson Thorpe," in Leacock, *Sunshine Sketches of a Little Town* (McClelland & Stewart, 1965), 47.
70. Since Leacock died in 1944, he had the good fortune to live without television.
71. *The Voice of Stephen Leacock*, introduced by Peter Gzowski and produced by David Lennick, with copyright held by the Stephen Leacock Museum, Orillia Ontario. The first of the two recordings of Leacock's voice was called "Professors and Their Life Work," in which Leacock poked fun at the oddities and pretenses of university professors, including Sir Daniel Wilson, his old professor at the University of Toronto.
72. *Toronto Star*, November 20, 1993, J17.

73. *Hooray for Canada* (1989); *More Than Words Can Say* (1990); *Cabin at Singing River* (1991); *Touring Prose* (1992 and 1993); *Writing Away* (1994), a PEN Canada travel anthology; *Dandelions Help* (1995); *Images of Waterloo County* (1996). In 1997, Peter contributed to three publications: *Gorillas on the Dance Floor and Other Poems from the First 100 PGIs* (1997); Sheree Fitch's *If You Could Wear My Sneakers*; and *Everybody's Favourites*, a collection of articles by more than one hundred Canadians on the subject of books that changed their lives. Peter's choice was *The Catcher in the Rye*. The Constance Rooke book was a fundraiser for PEN Canada, which was organized in November 1984 as part of PEN International, founded in 1921 to defend the free speech of writers. PEN is an acronym for poets, playwrights, editors, essayists, and novelists.

74. Professor Charles Haines, as quoted in Peter Gzowski, *The Morningside Papers* (Toronto: McClelland & Stewart, 1985), 320.

75. Peter told the story about the origins of the PGI many times, including in Peter Gzowski, "Beyond Statistics," in Canadian Organization for Development Through Education, *More Than Words Can Say* (Toronto: McClelland & Stewart, 1990), 85–93.

76. Although he claimed that his tournaments had made literacy "fashionable," Peter was scarcely the first Canadian to deal with illiteracy. As early as 1859, the Kingston, Ontario, YMCA began to teach young men the fundamentals of reading, spelling, and grammar. See *Toronto Star*, May 9, 1992, G7; Jody Lundrigan, ed., *Beyond the Book: Learning from Our History* (Toronto: Ontario Literacy Coaltion, 2009), 50–51; and Carol Goar, "Milestone for Literacy Movement," *Toronto Star*, March 4, 2009, A23.

77. TUA, Peter Gzowski fonds, 01-004, box 1, folder 25. In 1987, Labatt Breweries donated $5,000 while Hiram Walker gave $2,000; other sponsors over the years included Quaker Oats, PetroCanada, Superior Propane, Air Canada, Famous Players, McClelland & Stewart, the Royal Bank of Canada, Canada Post, and Manulife, which raises the question of how careful Peter and his *Morningside* producers had to be when dealing with topics such as alcoholism, pollution, banking charges, and homelessness.

78. *Toronto Star*, June 15, 1986, A18.

79. And, alas, destroyed by fire in April 2009.

80. Among the entertainers in 1991 were Timothy Findley, W.O. Mitchell, June Callwood, Dinah Christie, Mary Lou Fallis, Murray McLauchlan, Tom Cochrane, Hagood Hardy, and Veronica Tennant, with whom Peter kicked up his heels. In 1992 the Grievous Angels, Katherine Govier, Scott Young, Alison Gordon, Cynthia Dale, Kenneth Welsh, Gail Zoë Garnett, Peter Mansbridge, Wendy Mesley, and Premier Bob Rae were among the entertainers who read, sang, and played the piano. The 1994 Red Barn event featured Frank Shuster, Molly Johnson, Catherine O'Hara,

Graham Greene, Sylvia Tyson, Quartette, Thomas King, Sara Botsford, Don Ross, Lorne Elliott, Stuart McLean, Bruno Gerussi, Quartetto Gelato, and others. TUA, Peter Gzowski fonds, 92-015, box 24, folder 1; LAC, Frank Shuster fonds, R4610-0-3-E (MG31-D251, vol. 30: File: "Special Events, PGIs Play the Red Barn"; LAC, Frontier College fonds, R35584-0-0-E (MG28-1124), vol. 389; and interview with Judge Dennis Ball, October 3, 2008.

81. The logistics of these large annual events was complicated. Coordinated by Jenny Marcus, preparations began each year in January. Brochures were printed, a budget was drawn up, and limousines were rented. Prizes were solicited from corporations, and letters were mailed to previous participants, including Beland Honderich, Allan Burton, Wayne Gretzky, Paul Godfrey, Alan Eagleson (!), Barbara McDougall, David Crombie, and so on. Someone was required to organize the volunteers, someone to direct traffic into the parking lot, and two people to register golfers. To make sure that everyone was happy, five or six volunteers mingled with the crowd. Someone called Sarah was in charge of the media. Volunteers had to ensure that each golfer knew to which foursome he or she belonged. Other volunteers organized the display of prizes and set up the display for Frontier College. For tournaments in other provinces, Peter had contacts. Dennis Ball, chair of the Saskatchewan Literacy Foundation, was that province's representative.

82. *Toronto Star*, May 9, 1992, G7. Also in 1991, Peter appeared in *Kipinnguijautiit*, a television documentary of a PGI played on the ice and snow of Yellowknife. It also featured Cynthia Dale, Randy Gregg of the Vancouver Canucks, Sheree Fitch, and singers Colin James and Colleen Peterson. There were scenes of Peter listening to youngsters singing, of his watching native dancing, and of his attempting to join in. There was also throat singing and drumming.

83. Pierre Berton fonds, William Ready Division of Archives and Research Collections, McMaster University Library, Group G, box 312, F.10G, Peter Gzowski to Pierre Berton, May 2, 1996; and Berton fonds, G-312-F.10G, Shelley Ambrose to Pierre Berton via Elsa Franklin, June 5, 1996. Was Pierre Berton, perhaps, smarting from the treatment given to him in Peter's memoir? "I am bothered by Pierre's lack of self-questioning," wrote Peter in 1988, "his insistence on being right all the time" (Gzowski, *The Private Voice*, 138). Or by the fact that, on *Morningside*, Peter once had asked Pierre whether it seemed wrong that he had become famous "largely by writing about the famous"?

84. Pierre Berton fonds, William Ready Division of Archives and Research Collections, McMaster University Library, Group G, box 340, F.8, unidentified to Elsa [Franklin], April 15, 1997; and Shelley Ambrose to Pierre Berton via Elsa Franklin, June 9, 1997, with Berton's handwritten note at top.

85. Barbara Moon, "Illiterates: Canada's Obsolete Tenth," *Maclean's*, May 6, 1961, 23–24, 45–48.

86. *Toronto Star*, October 22, 1983, "Fund Launched for Polish Journalists," A12.

87. *Toronto Star*, November 22, 1983, F03; November 25, 1983, A02; and Roy MacGregor, "The Peter Gzowski Principle in Mind, I Gave It My Best Shot," *Toronto Star*, December 16, 1983, A2. The game pitted the Flying Fathers, a hockey team composed of athletic priests, against a team of NHL old-timers (Gordie Howe, Yvon Cournoyer, Frank Mahovlich, Paul Henderson, and the Drydens, Ken and Dave), assisted by Roy MacGregor, Ken Danby, and Warren Allmand, former Cabinet minister in the government of Pierre Trudeau.

88. *Toronto Star*, June 17, 1984, A3; and June 24, 1984, A4; *Toronto Star*, February 3, 1988, B2 and February 8, 1988, D14; and *Globe and Mail*, July 4, 2009, M1 and M2. In June 1984, Peter continued his campaign to stop the destruction of the 250 remaining homes on the Toronto Islands, including his own. In June 1984, in the company of Olympic skier Steve Podborski, poet Earle Birney, former mayor John Sewell, city councillor Jack Layton, and broadcaster Jan Tennant, Peter led a bicycle tour of Ward's Island. (In 1993 the Ontario government, led by Peter's friend Premier Bob Rae, passed a bill that gave long-term leases to homeowners like Peter.) In February 1988, Peter was the MC for a jazz concert featuring Moe Koffman to raise money for more than 250 conservation organizations, including one that was attempting to stop clear-cutting in Ontario's Temagami area. Later, after he was weaned off cigarettes, Peter took to the airwaves to preach against smoking.

89. TUA, 92-015, Peter Gzowski fonds, box 19, folders 7 and 8. The name of the magazine is missing from the clipping. The fact that Peter kept a detailed file of the Damien case proves he was well aware of the situation.

90. Interview with Dennis Ball, October 3, 2008.

91. Martin O'Malley, "Ah, Fame, It's Time You Were Humbled," *Toronto Star*, June 15, 1980, A13.

92. Peter C. Newman, "Tough-Guy Iggy: The Grits Are on Their Way to Being a Contender," *Globe and Mail*, March 19, 2009, A13.

93. Dave Cameron, "The Dark Side of Saint Peter," *Ryerson Review of Journalism*, March 1997.

94. Peter Gzowski, *The Game of Our Lives* (Toronto: McClelland & Stewart, 1981), 206.

95. *Toronto Star*, May 2, 1987, E2. Ironically, during the last years of his life, Peter had to share the limelight with his son, John, who was becoming a prominent musician. John's name was mentioned in newspaper articles as frequently as his father's.

96. This story came from both David Morton and President Bonnie Patterson.

97. TUA, Peter Gzowski fonds, 01-004, box 4, folder 17, Gzowski to Nancy Southam, nd.

98. TUA, Peter Gzowski fonds, 92-015, box 21, folder 3, clippings.

99. TUS, Peter Gzowski fonds, 01-004, box 3, folder 1.

100. My thanks to Cathy Perkins, who sent me the citation by email on September 19, 2008.

101. Again my thanks to Cathy Perkins, who recalled from memory Peter's speech (email September 22, 2008). According to Queen's University Archives, the speech hasn't been preserved. Peter probably made it from a few scribbled notes on the back of an envelope.
102. Talese, *The Kingdom and the Power*, 1.
103. *Toronto Star*, October 14, 1995, J13.
104. *Maclean's*, May 26, 1997, 58.
105. *Toronto Star*, June 5, 1999, J8.
106. *Toronto Star*, December 3, 1999, D3.

Chapter 16: "Oh, Stop Being Mavis Gallant"

1. *Toronto Star*, May 13, 1997, E6; and email from David Staines, April 20, 2009.
2. Mordecai Richler's novel was selected over Michael Helm's *The Projectionist*, Shani Mootoo's *Cereus Blooms at Night*, Nino Ricci's *Where She Has Gone*, and Carol Shields's *Larry's Party*. See *Toronto Star*, October 2, 1997, E6.
3. Mavis Gallant, "Speck's Idea," *The Selected Stories of Mavis Gallant* (Toronto: McClelland & Stewart, 1996), 486.
4. Peter Gzowski, sports column, "Volleyball for Pete's Sake," *Saturday Night*, July 1966, 42.
5. Sylvia Fraser, "Peter, Peter," *Toronto Life*, April 2002, 107; and CBC Video Archives, index to *90 Minutes Live*. Who knows what Peter might have thought of Elizabeth Hay's character, Harry Boyd, in *Late Nights on Air*? The novel is set, in part, in a mid-1970s Yellowknife radio station during the Berger hearings on the issues surrounding the possible construction of the Mackenzie Valley Pipeline. In Hay's novel, Harry is forty-two, Peter's age in the mid-1970s. On *90 Minutes Live*, Berger had been one of Peter's first guests. Harry finds his element early on, writes Hay, "and then makes the mistake of leaving it — radio for a television talk show, where he'd bombed." Like Peter, Harry's personal life fell apart, and "rumours rose up and settled down." See Elizabeth Hay, *Late Nights on Air* (McClelland & Stewart, 2007), 4. There are too many parallels for the main character of Hay's novel not to have been based, in part at least, on Peter. Since Hay's Giller Prize–winning novel was published five years after Peter's death, he was denied a chance to query its author, on air or off. Nor did Peter have the chance to ask Robert Rotenberg about the true-life identity of the crime novelist's murderer, a Gzowski look-alike, in *Old City Hall* (2009).
6. Peter Gzowski, *The Private Voice: A Journal of Reflections* (Toronto: McClelland & Stewart, 1988), 243.
7. Interview with Don Hall, August 25, 2009.

8.   *Toronto Star*, December 6, 1978, A3. His assumption that these observers were gay may have added to his discomfort.

9.   Interview with Michael Morse, December 10, 2008.

10.   Trent University Archives (TUA), Peter Gzowski fonds, 01-004 box 4, folder 19.

11.   And, in a way, he admitted as much, because the first half of the article is a send-up of travel writing. Nevertheless, most readers surely believed that their favourite radio host had strolled around Paris, *un vrai boulevardier* who sipped Bordeaux at a table on the Boulevard St-Germain while taking notes on the passing scene.

12.   Interview with Roberta Bondar, June 2, 2009. In space, astronauts don't stand on their feet.

13.   Robert Fulford, "A Fond Farewell," in Peter Gzowski, *The Morningside Years* (Toronto: McClelland & Stewart, 1997), [335–36]. The piece is a reprint from *Toronto Life*, June 1997. Fulford may have been thinking of Peter's moving and near-brilliant billboard the morning after Ben Johnson won and lost a gold medal at the Seoul Summer Olympics.

14.   Rick Mercer in Edna Barker, ed., *Remembering Peter Gzowski: A Book of Tributes* (Toronto: McClelland & Stewart, 2002), 110–12.

15.   Michael Peterman, "At Home with Peter," *Journal of Canadian Studies*, vol. 37, no. 1 (Spring 2002), 10–11.

16.   Interview with Mary Young Leckie, June 13, 2007.

17.   Hair and Makeup.

18.   *Toronto Star*, June 27, 1998, M4.

19.   TUA, Peter Gzowski fonds, 01-004, box 2, folder 3; and email from Ken Puley, February 7, 2009.

20.   Peter Gzowski, foreword in Steve Dryden, ed., *Total Gretzky: The Magic, the Legend, the Numbers* (Toronto: McClelland & Stewart, 1999), 6–11.

21.   Peter Gzowski, "Watch Me," in Karen Alliston, Rick Archbold, Jennifer Glossop, Alison Maclean, and Ivon Owen, eds., *Trudeau Albums* (Toronto: Penguin Studio, 2000), 66–88.

22.   *Globe and Mail*, January 6, 2001, A16.

23.   *Toronto Star*, May 5, 2001, J15. Commenting on Peter's article, Philip Marchand of the *Toronto Star* pointed out that "when Peter Gzowski, the ever-amiable soul of Canadian broadcasting, openly sneers at a Canadian politician, you know the man is dead."

24.   Bonnie Baker Cowan in Barker, ed., *Remembering Peter Gzowski*, 20.

25.   Bonnie Baker Cowan, "How Do You Edit the Man Who's Known as Jcanuck? Gently, Very Gently," *FiftyPlus*, April 2002, 63–64; and interview with Jayne MacAulay, senior editor of *Zoomer*, May 1, 2009. In her tribute to Peter, Baker Cowan pointed out that, like most if not all writers, he needed a good editor. A draft of his article on the mysteries of new technologies had been completely

rewritten by David Tafler, publisher of *FiftyPlus*. While a somewhat irritated Peter rejected the rewrite, he was moved to rework the entire piece himself. Later he called Tafler to thank him for the inspiration to do the rewrite.

26. The dearly held belief that Peter naively believed he was becoming chancellor of John Stubbs's Trent University isn`t tenable.

27. Bonnie Patterson, "Remembering Peter Gzowski," *Journal of Canadian Studies*, vol. 37, no. 1 (Spring 2002), 11.

28. Interview with Tim Fleet, August 21, 2007.

29. Peter Gzowski, "How to Quit Smoking in Fifty Years or Less," in Lorna Crozier and Patrick Lane, eds., *Addicted: Notes from the Belly of the Beast* (Vancouver: Greystone Books, 2001), 65–69.

30. Peter Gzowski, "Life After Smoking," in Edna Barker, *A Peter Gzowski Reader* (Toronto: McClelland & Stewart, 2002), 269–271.

31. Email from Rob Winslow, December 3, 2008.

32. Interview with Rob Winslow, October 5, 2008. The final syllable of Saskatchewan is pronounced correctly not as *wan* but as *won* or *one*.

33. Interview with Robin Quantick, March 23, 2009.

34. Interview with Bryan Graham, one of the search committee members, July 16, 2009.

35. Another observer, a member of the history department, scorned the idea of bankruptcy, pointing out that no government of Ontario would ever allow one of the province's universities to disappear.

36. *Toronto Star*, January 26, 2000, A4.

37. TUA, Peter Gzowski fonds, 01-004, box 3.

38. TUA, Board of Governors Open Session Minutes, Trent University Board of Governors, February 16, 2001.

39. TUA, *Arthur*, February 27, 2001.

40. Nor should Bonnie Patterson be blamed for the fact that the police used helmets and other riot gear. The argument that there were twenty-five police and only eight women neglects to mention the students waiting just outside the office.

41. Peter Gzowski, "The Trouble Is Everyone Loves Trent Too Much," *Globe and Mail*, March 17, 2001, A9-A10.

42. At her retirement in June 2009, President Bonnie Patterson was given a rousing and sympathetic reception in the Great Hall of Champlain College.

43. Interviews with John Milloy, September 15, 2008, and February 12, 2009. Peter made the remark to Milloy's research assistant, who relayed it to the master of Peter Robinson College, as perhaps Peter had expected her to do.

44. *Financial Post*, December 6, 1969, 15.

45. James Simon Kunen, *The Strawberry Statement: Notes of a College Revolutionary* (New York: Random House, 1969), 24.

46. Interview with Gillian Howard, February 4, 2004.

47. He failed to mention that during the 1950s and 1960s, he and most of his fellow Canadian journalists, by dropping the *u* in words ending with *or*, such as *labor*, had opted for the American spelling.

48. Emails, telephone conversations, and an interview with Kathy Stinson at Chapters in Newmarket, Ontario, November-December 2004. And further emails in January 2009.

49. *Toronto Star*, January 14, 2002, E4.

50. TUA, Peter Gzowski fonds, 92-015, box 3, series C: folder 3, letters 1996, Elaine Lillico-Carter to Peter Gzowski, nd.

51. Peter Gzowski, "Tell Me How You Would Spend the Last Day of Your Life," *Toronto Star*, November 10, 1978, A3.

52. Peter wasn't as classically illiterate as he liked to claim. While playing chess, he liked to sip wine and listen to Mozart. See Peter Gzowski, *The Morningside Papers* (Toronto: McClelland & Stewart, 1985), 178. No doubt he claimed musical illiteracy in an attempt to be one of the boys, especially one of the Edmonton Oilers' boys. His appreciation for good music may have developed as he aged.

53. Interview with Robin Quantick, December 10, 2008.

54. Kathy Stinson, email January 31, 2009.

55. Ironically, Peter himself left a lasting impression on Nathalie Petrowski — on March 27, 2009, in an article in *La Presse* about the CBC's financial difficulties, Petrowksi referred to an interview between former Prime Minister Jean Chrétien and Peter. See Nathalie Petrowski, "Un peu de mémoire, S.V.P.," *La Presse*, March 27, 2009, "Arts and spectacles," 1. That she could use the name Peter Gzowski without identification suggests that Peter was not as much unknown in francophone Quebec as some journalists and nationalists liked to believe.

56. Gzowski, *The Morningside Papers*, 284.

57. When Canadian-born Peter Jennings died in August 2005 at the same age as Peter Gzowski and from the same cause, the cursed cigarette, Radio-Canada replayed a long interview with Jennings, conducted by his friend Pierre Nadeau. Even though most of his career was in New York City, Jennings spoke French. Ironically, unlike Gzowski, Jennings made no attempt to explain Quebec to anglophones either in the United States or Canada.

58. Even the death of Walter Cronkite in July 2009 attracted more attention on Radio-Canada newscasts than did the death of Peter Gzowski in January 2002.

59. Interview with Louis Lemieux, March 27, 2009.

60. TUA, Peter Gzowski fonds, 01-004, box 1, folder 12.

61. Silver Donald Cameron, in Barker, ed., *Remembering Peter Gzowksi*, 19.

62. *Toronto Star*, January 27, 2002, A13.

Epilogue

1. Lieutenant-Governor John Graves Simcoe, the best-remembered founder of the Town of York, later the city of Toronto, was never a lord.

2. A brave choice. Most single mothers at the time gave their babies up for adoption. Joni Mitchell, for instance, gave up her "Little Green," baby Kelly, in February 1965. For years she, too, kept the secret.

3. Email from Cathy Perkins, September 24, 2008.

4. The British had only recently become accustomed to playing the slower ten-pin bowling introduced in 1959 by film mogul J. Arthur Rank to make use of some of his increasingly empty movie theatres. The origin of American nine- and ten-pin bowling, Perkins pointed out, was in the old British game of skittles, imported into the United States in the eighteenth century and brought back to Britain by Rank.

5. Even in 1961, $30 was meagre. In 1961 Peter's salary at *Maclean's* was at least $6,000 per year or $500 per month.

6. Ironically, in *Maclean's*, on September 22, 1962, around the time that Peter wrote the article for Cathy, he reported that hockey player Andy Bathgate of the New York Rangers had been fined $500 for placing his name on a ghost-written article published in *True* magazine.

7. Rob Perkins is now cured.

8. Also in Peter Gzowski, *An Unbroken Line* (Toronto: McClelland & Stewart, 1984), 174, Peter noted that his second daughter, Maria, received her ring on her twenty-first birthday in August 1982. Rob had turned twenty-one the previous February, with no ring.

9. Peter Gzowski, *The Morningside Papers* (Toronto: McClelland & Stewart, 1985), 269.

10. Email from Cathy Perkins, September 19, 2007.

11. The phrase, first penned in a letter written in 1904 by the German novelist and poet Rainer Maria Rilke, that love was two solitudes that "protect and touch and greet each other," inspired Hugh MacLennan to write *Two Solitudes*, which has become a metaphor, albeit simplistic, for the two predominant cultures of Canada.

12. Thanks to an aggrieved ex-wife of Rob Perkins's, the story did leak out once — to *Frank Magazine*. Since few people admitted to reading *Frank*, the story never made headlines elsewhere.

Appendix:

An Essay on
Peter Gzowski's Publications

Peter Gzowski's list of publications is impressive and extensive. This appendix is meant to serve as an impression, not a definitive list, of the scope and depth of the man's written work.

Articles

Peter's earliest known published work was written while he was a student at Galt Collegiate, where he reported on sports for his grade ten class. At Ridley College several of his short pieces appeared in the college's yearbook, often about one sport or another. His literary and journalistic talents developed during his eight months as editor of *The Varsity* when his subjects were sports, politics, and theatre. In both Moose Jaw's *Times-Herald* and Chatham's *Daily News*, where he was city editor, his talents began to develop as he covered theatre, both local and in Detroit, the politics of the time, including the rise of John Diefenbaker, and city events such as strikes. His first short anonymous articles for *Maclean's*, probably sent to Ralph Allen while Peter was in Moose Jaw and Chatham, can only be determined by style and subject matter.

Once he reached *Maclean's* in September 1958, more and more of his pieces bore a name, especially his feature-length articles. However, even in *Maclean's*, he wrote under several names, including Peter N. Allison, Strabo, and Peter (Strabo) Gzowski, as well as just plain Peter Gzowski. His first long articles in *Maclean's* were on the familiar subjects: university newspapers, including *The Varsity*; and Sir Casimir Gzowski, his once-famous ancestor. Peter's passion for hockey can be seen in feature articles on NHL stars such as Dave Keon, Frank Mahovlich, and Gordie Howe.

His big breakthrough in terms of subject matter was during his one year in Montreal in the early 1960s when his eyes were opened to the Quiet Revolution (which he always spelled lowercase), a subject that English-speaking Canadians little understood before Peter's articles on Quebec were published. He wasn't, it must be said, the first English-speaking Canadian to delve into the emerging Quebec. The novelist and cultural historian Scott Symons had already written on the subject, but in French for *La Presse*.

Until his resignation from *Maclean's* in 1964, Peter wrote on a variety of subjects, including a couple of groundbreaking articles on the plight of Canadian Natives, and always, articles on sports. He was interested in television as a medium, and many of his most perceptive articles were written under the name Strabo, a nom de plume that hid his real identity from the owners of *Maclean's* after his resignation in September 1964. He also wrote a pivotal article on the music of Bob Dylan (January 22, 1966). His skills as an editor shone during his few months in 1967–68 as editor of the *Star Weekly*. When he returned to *Maclean's* as managing editor for a few months in 1969 and 1970, his interest had turned to Canadian nationalism in its various manifestations. For the rest of his life, he wrote occasional articles for *Maclean's*, including "The Best in the World" in April 1999, which was about Wayne Gretzky, one of his favourite hockey players and the subject of several articles.

Canadian Forum

Peter's most controversial article for *Canadian Forum* dealt with his resignation from *Maclean's* and the corporate sponsorship of magazines ("Time the Schick Hit the Fan," October 1964).

Saturday Night

After his resignation from *Maclean's* in 1964, Peter published several feature articles, as well as a regular sports column, in *Saturday Night*, including one anonymous piece, "In Defence of Pot: Confessions of a Canadian Marijuana Smoker" (October 1965), under the name "Peter Ludlow." He was still contributing to the magazine in the early 1980s when he wrote about Wayne Gretzy and Peter Pocklington ("Great Expectations," April 1982).

Toronto Life

For the magazine about the social and cultural life of Toronto, a magazine in which he had a small financial interest, Peter published several articles, including "How 31 Kids Taught Me Hockey: My Life and Times as a Neighbourhood Hockey Coach" (April

1972), "Farewell and Hello to Television" (October 1978), and "High Wind Off Antigua" (December 1984).

Toronto Star

Scores of Peter's articles were published in the *Toronto Star* when he spent several months as entertainment editor during the mid-1960s and when he was a columnist at the newspaper during the late 1970s. His main topic was the city that was emerging from decades as the rather stuffy Toronto the Good. He also wrote freelance articles for the paper, including a three-part series on marijuana.

Edmonton Oilers Home Games Programs

When he was researching and writing *The Game of Our Lives* in 1980 and 1981, Peter wrote short pieces called "A Fan's Notes" for the Edmonton Oilers' programs whenever they played on their home ice in Northlands Coliseum.

Canadian Living

Peter wrote a series of whimsical short articles throughout the 1990s for *Canadian Living*, most of them human interest, and most of them remembrance of things past in his long career. The best were published in two volumes in 1993 and 1998.

Canadian Literature

Peter's interview with Thomas King ("Peter Gzowski Interviews Thomas King on *Green Grass, Running Water*") was published in the academic journal *Canadian Literature*, Summer/Autumn 1999.

Globe and Mail

For more than a year until his death in 2002, Peter wrote a frequent column for the *Globe and Mail* on anything that struck his fancy, from language to books to his term as chancellor at Trent University ("The Trouble Is Everyone Loves Trent Too Much," March 17, 2001).

FiftyPlus (now called Zoomer)

For the magazine aimed at so-called seniors, Peter wrote three articles and had a fourth in mind when he died.

Appendix: An Essay on Peter Gzowski's Publications

Excerpts, Forewords, and Introductions Published in Larger Works

From 1978 until his death, Peter's written work was included in other publications in many forms, from excerpts of an article or a book to forewords and introductions. The following is a sampling of those books.

1. Excerpt from "This Is Our Alabama" in Clery, Val, ed. *Canada from the News-Stands: A Selection from the Best Journalism of the Past Thirty Years.* Toronto: Macmillan of Canada, 1978.

2. Excerpt from *The Game of Our Lives* in Davies, Richard, and Glen Kirkland, eds. *Dimensions: A Book of Essays.* Toronto: Gage, 1986.

3. Excerpts from *The Private Voice* in *Hooray for Canada.* Toronto: A Canadian Living Publication and Telemedia Publishing, Inc., 1989.

4. "Beyond Statistics" in Canadian Organization for Development Through Education, *More Than Words Can Say.* Toronto: McClelland & Stewart, 1990.

5. Introduction in Czajkowski, Chris. *Cabin at Singing River.* Camden East, ON: Camden House, 1991.

6. Foreword in Rubenstein, Lorne. *Touring Prose: Writings on Golf by Lorne Rubenstein.* Toronto: Vintage Books, 1993.

7. Introduction in Southin, Gwendolyn, and Betty Keller, eds. *The Great Literary Cookbook.* Sechelt, BC: Festival of the Written Arts, 1994.

8. "Up the Liard by Magic Carpet" in Rooke, Constance, ed. *Writing Away: The PEN Canada Travel Anthology.* Toronto: McClelland & Stewart, 1994.

9. Foreword in McBride, Eve. *Dandelions Help.* Montmagny, QC: Shoreline Press, 1995.

10. Introduction ("A Perfect Place to Be a Boy") for *Images of Waterloo County* (1996).

11. Untitled piece in Rae, Arlene Perly, ed. *Everybody's Favourites.* Toronto: Viking, 1997.

12. "Introduction" in *Gorillas on the Dance Floor and Other Poems from the First 100 PGIs.* Toronto: ABC Canada, 1997.

13. Foreword in Fitch, Sheree. *If You Could Wear My Sneakers.* Toronto: Firefly Books, 1998.

14. Foreword in Dryden, Steve, ed. *Total Gretzky: The Magic, the Legend, the Numbers.* Toronto: McClelland & Stewart, 1999.

15. "Watch Me" in Alliston, Karen, and Rick Archbold, Jennifer Glossop, Alison Maclean, and Ivon Owen, eds. *Trudeau Albums.* Toronto: Penguin Studio, 2000.

16. "How to Quit Smoking in Fifty Years or Less" in Crozier, Lorna, and Patrick Lane, eds. *Addicted: Notes from the Belly of the Beast.* Vancouver: Greystone Books, 2001.

17. "Pierre Trudeau: Intellectual in Action" in Benedict, Michael, ed. *Maclean's People.* Toronto: Penguin Canada, 2002.

PETER GZOWSKI

Booklets

Early in his career during his university days, Peter wrote what he called a booklet for Christie Bread of Toronto. He also wrote an article published in a booklet called "Leacock's Smile." Orillia, ON: Leacock Museum in association with Frontier College, 2003.

Book Reviews

Peter wrote up to a score or more of book reviews, mostly on books about hockey, for instance, in *Saturday Night*, March 1965, on *The Stanley Cup Story* by Henry Roxborough, and Frank Selke's *Behind the Cheering*. He also reviewed James Simon Kunen's *The Strawberry Statement* (*Toronto Star*, July 5, 1969); Lillian Hellman's *An Unfinished Woman* (*Toronto Star*, July 12, 1969); Arthur Hailey's *Airport* (*Toronto Star*, July 15, 1969); and James Laver's *Modesty in Dress* (*Toronto Star*, August 9, 1969).

Tape

Introduction to *The Voice of Stephen Leacock*.

Books (Listed by Order of Year Published)

Gzowski, Peter, and Trent Frayne. *Great Canadian Sports Stories: A Century of Competition*. Toronto: *Weekend Magazine*/McClelland & Stewart, 1965.

Gzowski, Peter, and Jack Batten. *Nancy*. Toronto: Toronto Star Limited, 1968.

Gzowski, Peter. *Peter Gzowski's Book About This Country in the Morning*. Edmonton: Hurtig Publishers, 1974.

____. *Spring Tonic*. Edmonton: Hurtig Publishers, 1979.

____. *The Sacrament: The Incredible Story of Brent Dyer and Donna Johnson*. Toronto: McClelland & Stewart, 1980.

____. *The Game of Our Lives*. Toronto: McClelland and Stewart Limited, 1981.

____. *An Unbroken Line*. Toronto: McClelland & Stewart, 1983.

____. *The Morningside Papers*. Toronto: McClelland & Stewart, 1985.

____. *The New Morningside Papers*. Toronto: McClelland & Stewart, 1987.

____. *The Private Voice: A Journal of Reflections*. Toronto: McClelland & Stewart, 1988.

____. *A Sense of Tradition: An Album of Ridley College Memories, 1889–1989*. St. Catharines, ON: Ridley College and Hedge Row Press, 1988.

____. *The Latest Morningside Papers*. Toronto: McClelland & Stewart, 1989.

_____. *The Fourth Morningside Papers.* Toronto: McClelland & Stewart, 1991.

_____. *Selected Columns from Canadian Living.* Toronto: McClelland & Stewart, 1993.

_____. *The Fifth (and Probably Last) Morningside Papers.* Toronto: McClelland & Stewart, 1994.

_____. *The Morningside Years.* Toronto: McClelland & Stewart, 1997.

_____. *Friends, Moments, Countryside: Selected Columns from Canadian Living, 1993–98.* Toronto: McClelland & Stewart, 1998.

_____. *A Peter Gzowski Reader.* Edited by Edna Barker. Toronto: McClelland & Stewart, 2002.

Select Bibliography

Archival Sources

Marco Adria fonds, Trent University Archives.

Peter Gzowski fonds, Trent University Archives.

Pierre Berton fonds, William Ready Division of Archives and Research Collections, McMaster University Library.

Robert Fulford fonds, William Ready Division of Archives and Research Collections, McMaster University Library.

Mordecai Richler fonds, Special Collections, University of Calgary.

W.O. Mitchell fonds, Special Collections, University of Calgary.

Elspeth Cameron fonds, Thomas Fisher Library Archives, the University of Toronto.

Gzowski clipping files, photographs, and university records, University of Toronto Archives and Records Management Services.

Gzowski files and photographs, Ridley College Archives.

Gzowski radio and TV shows and photographs, CBC Radio and Television Archives, and CBC Still Photography Archives.

Gzowski clippings and assessment rolls for Galt, City of Cambridge Archives.

Gzowski art, Archives of the Art Gallery of Ontario.

Gzowski tapes and booklets, Stephen Leacock Museum and Archives.

Gzowski clippings and city directories, City of Moose Jaw Library and Archives.

Gzowski clippings, newspapers, Saskatchewan Archives Board, Regina.

Duncan Macpherson cartoon, *Toronto Star* Archives.

Records of Margaret Young, Archives of the University of St Andrews, Scotland.

Records of Jennie Lissaman, University of Manitoba Archives.

Reg Lissaman clipping file, Legislature Library of the Province of Manitoba.

The fonds of Frank Shuster, Frontier College, Robertson Davies, and Glenn Sarty, as well as tapes, audio and visual, of CBC shows such as *Gzowski on FM*, *Olympic Magazine*, *Gzowski*, *Gerussi*, *Man Alive*, *Explorations*, *Stanley Knowles: By Word and Deed*, *Weekend*, *Degrassi Between Takes*, and *Gzowski & Company*, Library and Archives Canada.

Harry Bruce fonds, private collection.

Ted Barris fonds, private collection.

"Pete" McGarvey fonds, private collection.

Primary Sources (Published)

Directories

City of Galt Directories and *Assessment Rolls*, 1940.

Henderson's Moose Jaw Directory. Winnipeg: Henderson Directories, Ltd., 1957.

Toronto City Directories, 1900–1980.

Articles

Adachi, Ken. "NDP Book Policy Has Familiar Ring," *Toronto Star*, April 5, 1979.

_____. "Radio Vet Gzowski Makes Acting Debut," *Toronto Star*, May 3, 1983.

Adilman, Sid. "Eye on Entertainment," *Toronto Star*, January 16, 1980.

Allen, Glen. Article re *Morningside* in *The New Brunswick Reader*, May 24, 1997.

Annesley, Pat. "Peter Gzowski: Growing Up Means Never Having to Say You're Perfect," *Chatelaine*, November, 1972.

Averill, Harold, and Gerald Keith. "Daniel Wilson and the University of Toronto." In *Thinking with Both Hands: Sir Daniel Wilson in the Old World and the New*. Edited by Elizabeth Hulse. Toronto: University of Toronto Press, 1999.

Azzi, Stephen. "Foreign Investment and the Paradox of Economic Nationalism." In *Canadas of the Mind: The Making and Unmaking of Canadian Nationalisms in the Twentieth Century*. Edited by Norman Hillmer and Adam Chapnick. Montreal and Kingston: McGill-Queen's University Press, 2007.

Baker, Russell. "Life with Mother." In *Inventing the Truth: The Art and Craft of Memoir*. Edited by William Zinsser. Boston: Houghton Mifflin Company, 1998.

Baker Cowan, Bonnie. "How Do You Edit the Man Who's Known as Jcanuck? Gently, Very Gently," *FiftyPlus*, April 2002.

Base, Ron. "And Now, He-e-ere's Peter!" *Maclean's*, May 17, 1976.

_____. "Comeback of the Year," *Maclean's*, December 15, 1975.

Baxter, Brian. "Paul Newman," *The Guardian Weekly*, October 3, 2008.

Bemrose, John. "King of the Airwaves," *Maclean's*, November 7, 1988.

Bérubé, Michael. "Of Ice and Men." *The Common Review*, vol. 7, no. 4 (Spring 2009).

Braithwaite, Dennis. "*This Country* from Bad to Bad," *Toronto Star*, December 27, 1974.

Brown, Ian. "Male Jeanius," *Globe and Mail*, July 7, 2007.

Bullen, John. The Ontario Waffle and the Struggle for an Independent Socialist Canada: Conflict Within the NDP." *Canadian Historical Review*, vol. 64, no. 2, 1983.

Burrill, William. "Gzowski Was a Bootlegger at 13," *Toronto Star*, April 20, 1982.

Callwood, June. "The Informal Peter Gzowski," *Globe and Mail*, January 19, 1976.

Cameron, Dave. "The Dark Side of Saint Peter," *Ryerson Review of Journalism*, March 1997.

Camp, Dalton. Foreword in Peter Gzowski, *The Morningside Years*. Toronto: McClelland & Stewart, 1997.

Casselman, William. "A Song of Moral Sympathy," *Toronto Star*, September 27, 1980.

Chaput, John. "Thomas Shoyama, Civil Servant and Teacher 1916–2006," *Globe and Mail*, December 30, 2006.

Clarke, George Elliott. "Who Listens to Us Now?" *Journal of Canadian Studies*, vol. 37, no. 1 (Spring 2002).

Fink, Howard. "Radio Drama, English Language" in *The Canadian Encyclopedia*, second edition, vol. 3. Edmonton: Hurtig Publishers, 1988.

Fotheringham, Allan. "Like the CPR, Gzowski Tied Us Together," *Maclean's*, June 16, 1997.

Fraser, Sylvia. "Girl, Must Be Accurate," *Toronto Life*, November 1996.

_____. "Peter Peter." *Toronto Life*, April 2002.

Fulford, Robert. "A Day in the Life," *Toronto Star*, April 22, 1965.

_____. "A Fond Farewell" in Peter Gzowski, *The Morningside Years*. Toronto: McClelland & Stewart, 1997.

Galt, George. "The Hungry Ego," *Saturday Night*, November 1988.

Gamel, Irene. "Papa's Changeable Feast," *Globe and Mail*, August 22, 2009.

Gardam, Tim. "Playing Hide and Seek with His Past," *The Guardian Weekly*, July 13, 2007.

Garnett, Gale Zoë. "Oh, He Was More Than a Contender," *Globe and Mail*, January 10, 2009.

Goar, Carol. "Milestone for Literacy Movement," *Toronto Star*, March 4, 2009.

Griffiths, Rudyard. Afterword in Charles Taylor, *Radical Tories: The Conservative Tradition in Canada*. Toronto: House of Anansi Press, 2006.

Groen, Rick. "Dissecting the Monster Within," *Globe and Mail*, September 23, 2005.

Gzowski, Alison. "Dad and Me," *Quest*, June/July/August 1984.

Hindy, Lily. "Magazine Publisher Cultivated the 'New Journalism,'" *Globe and Mail*, July 4, 2008.

Jones, Frank. "Why Canada After Dark Died," *Toronto Star*, January 7, 1979.

Katz, Sidney. "The Harsh Facts of Life in the 'Gay' World," *Maclean's*, March 7, 1964.

LaPierre, Laurier L. "The 1960s." In *The Canadians, 1867–1967*. Edited by J.M.S. Careless and R. Craig Brown. Toronto: Macmillan of Canada, 1968.

Leacock, Stephen. "Why I Refuse to Play Golf." In Stephen Leacock, *Over the Footlights and Other Fancies*. London: John Lane The Bodley Head, 1923.

Lorenz, Stacy L., and Geraint B. Osborne. "'Talk About Strenuous Hockey': Violence, Manhood, and the 1897 Ottawa Silver Seven–Montreal Wanderer Rivalry," *Journal of Canadian Studies*, vol. 40, no. 1 (Winter 2006).

Lyons, Margaret. "Geraldine Sherman of *Soundings*," *CBC Times*, June 21–27, 1969.

Martel, Marcel. "'They Smell Bad, Have Diseases, and Are Lazy': RCMP Officers Reporting on Hippies in the Late Sixties," *Canadian Historical Review*, vol. 90, no. 2, June 2009.

Marshall, Douglas. "On Your Behalf," *Toronto Star*, March 16, 1985.

Martin, Sandra. "Doris Anderson, Journalist and Political Activist 1921–2007," *Globe and Mail*, March 3, 2007.

_____. "Gzowski's Problem Is That He Isn't Slick. Hamel's Problem Is That He Is," *Maclean's*, March 7, 1977.

McDonald, Marci. "The New Darling of Daytime Radio," *Toronto Star*, February 12, 1972.

_____. "What Does a Guy Who Quits a Winner Do for an Encore?" *Homemakers*, vol. 9, issue 5, September 1974.

Macfarlane, David. "Hockeyland," *The Walrus*, June 2010.

MacGregor, Roy. "The Peter Gzowski Principle in Mind, I Gave It My Best Shot," *Toronto Star*, December 16, 1983.

McRae, Earl. "Coke on Ice, Don Murdoch's Crime Was Not Being Caught — It Was Getting Caught in Public," *The Canadian*, October 14, 1978.

Mietkiewicz, Henry. "Epic Radio Drama Broadcast as Serial," *Toronto Star*, September 3, 1983.

Miller, Jack. "Gzowski Ambles Off the Air," *Toronto Star*, June 29, 1974.

Moon, Barbara. "Illiterates: Canada's Obsolete Tenth," *Maclean's*, May 6, 1961.

Murphy, Rex. "'Nice' Is a Killer for Dion," *Globe and Mail*, September 22, 2007.

Nelles, H.V. "Gzowski, Sir Casmir Stanislaus." In *Dictionary of Canadian Biography*, vol. 12, 1891 to 1900. Toronto: University of Toronto Press, 1990, reprinted 1997.

Newman, Peter. "Tough-Guy Iggy: The Grits Are on Their Way to Being a Contender," *Globe and Mail*, March 19, 2009.

O'Malley, Martin. "Ah, Fame, It's Time You Were Humbled," *Toronto Star*, June 15, 1980.

Ondaatje, Michael. "'I Had to Invent Billy from the Ground Up,'" *Globe and Mail*, August 23, 2003.

Osborne, Brian S. "Moose Jaw's 'Great Escape'; Constructing Tunnels, Deconstructing Heritage, Marketing Places," *Material History Review* (Spring 2002).

Patterson, Bonnie. "Remembering Peter Gzowski," *Journal of Canadian Studies*, vol. 37, no. 1 (Spring 2002).

Peers, Frank W. "Broadcasting, Radio and Television." In *The Canadian Encyclopedia*, second edition, vol. 1. Edmonton: Hurtig Publishers, 1988.

"Peter Gzowski's Remarkable Teachers." *Professionally Speaking*, December 1998.

Peterman, Michael. "At Home with Peter," *Journal of Canadian Studies*, vol. 37, no. 1 (Spring 2002).

Petrowski, Nathalie. "Un peu de mémoire, S.V.P.," *La Presse*, March 27, 2009.

Remnick, David. Introduction in A.J. Liebling, *Just Enough Liebling: Classic Work by the Legendary* New Yorker *Writer*. New York: North Point Press, 2004.

Renzetti, Elizabeth. "Slinkers, Jailers, Soldiers, Lies," *Globe and Mail*, October 4, 2008.

Richler, Mordecai. "New Books: The Trouble with Rabbi Feinberg Is He's Just Too Palatable," *Maclean's*, July 25, 1964.

Rickwood, Roger. "Committee for an Independent Canada." In *The Canadian Encyclopedia*, second edition, vol. 1. Edmonton: Hurtig Publishers, 1988.

Ruddy, Jon. "CBC Radio's Dramatic Shuffle Displaces Old Favourites," *Toronto Star*, October 9, 1971.

Rutherford, Paul. "Radio Programming." In *The Canadian Encyclopedia*, second edition, vol. 3, Edmonton: Hurtig Publishers, 1988.

Timson, Judith. "Survival on Faith and Human Flesh," *Maclean's*, October 6, 1980.

Tower, Courtney. "The New Nationalism," *Maclean's*, February 1970.

Valpy, Michael. "Is This the End of the Age of Our Social Cohesion?" *Globe and Mail*, August 29, 2009.

Vickery, Amanda. "Not Just a Pretty Face," *The Guardian Weekly*, March 21, 2008.

Zosky, Brenda. "How Larry Zolf Found Shelter," *Toronto Star*, March 4, 1979.

Secondary Sources (Published Books)

Adria, Marco. *Peter Gzowski: An Electric Life*. Toronto: ECW Press, 1996.

Armstrong, Karen. *A Short History of Myth*. Toronto: Knopf Canada, 2005.

Barker, Edna, ed. *Remembering Peter Gzowski: A Book of Tributes*. Toronto: McClelland & Stewart, 2002.

Barris, Alex, and Ted Barris. *Making Music: Profiles from a Century of Canadian Music*. Toronto: HarperCollins Canada, 2001.

Bliss, Michael. *Northern Enterprise: Five Centuries of Canadian Business*. Toronto: McClelland & Stewart, 1987.

Bowker, Alan. *On the Front Line of Life: Stephen Leacock, Memories and Reflections, 1935–1944*. Toronto: Dundurn Press, 2004.

Bruce, Harry. *Each Moment As It Flies*. Toronto: Methuen, 1984.

____. *The Short, Happy Walks of Max MacPherson*. Toronto: Macmillan Company of Canada, 1968.

Budrewicz, Olgierd. *Polish-Canadian Profiles*. Warsaw: Interpress Publishers, 1981.

Cameron, Elspeth. *And Beauty Answers: The Life of Frances Loring and Florence Wyle*. Toronto: Cormorant Books, 2007.

Careless, J.M.S. *Toronto to 1918: An Illustrated History*. Toronto: James Lorimer & Company and National Museum of Man, National Museums of Canada, 1984.

Clarkson, Adrienne. *Heart Matters*. Toronto: Viking Canada, 2006.

Creighton, Donald. *John A. Macdonald: The Young Politician*. Toronto: Macmillan Company of Canada, 1974.

Crowley, David, and Paul Heyer. *Communication in History: Technology, Culture, Society*. New York: Longman, 1991.

Dendy, William, and William Kilbourn. *Toronto Observed: Its Architecture, Patrons and History*. Toronto: Oxford University Press, 1986.

Diamond, Jared. *Collapse: How Societies Choose to Fail or Succeed*. Toronto: Penguin, 2006.

Dick, Philip K. *I Hope I Shall Arrive Soon*. Edited by Mark Hurst and Paul Williams. London: Victor Gallancz, 1986.

Dobbs, Kildare. *Running the Rapids: A Writer's Life*. Toronto: Dundurn Press, 2005.

Edinborough, Arnold. *The Enduring Word: A Centennial History of Wycliffe College*. Toronto: University of Toronto Press, 1978.

English, John. *Citizen of the World: The Life of Pierre Elliott Trudeau, Volume One, 1919–1968*. Toronto: Knopf Canada, 2008.

Fotheringham, Allan. *Birds of a Feather: The Press and the Politicians*. Toronto: Key Porter Books, 1989.

Frayne, Trent. *The Tales of an Athletic Supporter*. Toronto: McClelland & Stewart, 1990.

Fulford, Robert. *Best Seat in the House*. Toronto: Collins Publishers, 1988.

Gallant, Mavis. *The Selected Stories of Mavis Gallant*. Toronto: McClelland & Stewart, 1996.

Gauvreau, Michael. *The Catholic Origins of Quebec's Quiet Revolution, 1931–1960*. Montreal and Kingston: McGill-Queen's Press, 2005.

Grant, George. *Lament for a Nation: The Defeat of Canadian Nationalism*. Montreal and Kingston: McGill-Queen's University Press, 2005.

Gwyn, Richard. *John A., the Man Who Made Us: The Life and Times of John A. Macdonald, Volume One, 1815–1867*. Toronto: Random House Canada, 2007.

Hay, Elizabeth. *Late Nights on Air*. Toronto: McClelland & Stewart, 2007.

Hellman, Lillian. *An Unfinished Woman: A Memoir*. Boston: Little, Brown, 1968.

Igartua, José E. *The Other Quiet Revolution: National Identities in English Canada, 1945–71*. Vancouver: University of British Columbia Press, 2006.

The Jubilee Volume of Wycliffe College. Toronto: University of Toronto Press, 1927.

Kos-Rabcewicz-Zubkowski, Ludwik, and William Edward Greening. *Sir Casimir Stanislaus Gzowski: A Biography*. Toronto: Burns and MacEachern, 1959.

Kunen, James Simon. *The Strawberry Statement: Notes of a College Revolutionary*. New York: Random House, 1969.

Laxer, James. *In Search of the New Left: Canadian Politics After the Neoconservative Assault*. Toronto: Viking, 1996.

Leacock, Stephen. *The Letters of Stephen Leacock*. Edited by David Staines. Toronto: Oxford University Press, 2006.

____. *Sunshine Sketches of a Little Town*. Toronto: McClelland & Stewart, 1965.

Leonard, John. *Smoke and Mirrors: Violence, Television, and Other American Cultures*. New York: The New Press, 1997.

Liebling, A.J. *Just Enough Liebling*. New York: North Point Press, 2004.

Lundrigan, Jody. *Beyond the Book: Learning from Our History*. Toronto: Ontario Literacy Coalition, 2009.

Lupul, Manoly R. *The Politics of Multiculturalism: A Ukrainian-Canadian Memoir*. Toronto: Canadian Institute of Ukrainian Studies Press, 2005.

Mailer, Norman. *An American Dream*. New York: Vintage, 1999.

Martel, Marcel. *Not This Time: Canadians, Public Policy and the Marijuana Question, 1961–1975*. Toronto: University of Toronto Press, 2006.

Martyn, Lucy Booth. *Toronto, 100 Years of Grandeur: The Inside Stories of Toronto's Great Homes and the People Who Lived There*. Toronto: Pagurian Press Limited, 1978.

McKillop, A.B. *Pierre Berton: A Biography*. Toronto: McClelland & Stewart, 2008.

McLauchlan, Murray. *Getting Out of Here Alive: The Ballad of Murray McLauchlan*. Toronto: Viking, 1998.

McLean, Stuart. *The Morningside World of Stuart McLean*. Toronto: Penguin Canada, 1995.

MacMillan, Margaret. *Stephen Leacock*. Toronto: Penguin Canada, 2009.

Mitchell, Barbara, and Ormond Mitchell. *W.O.: The Life of W.O. Mitchell, Beginnings to Who Has Seen the Wind, 1914–1947*. Toronto: McClelland & Stewart, 1999.

____. *Mitchell: The Life of W.O. Mitchell, the Years of Fame, 1948–1998*. Toronto: McClelland & Stewart, 2005.

Munro, Alice. *Open Secrets*. Toronto: McClelland & Stewart, 1994.

Nash, Knowlton. *Cue the Elephants*. Toronto: McClelland & Stewart, 1996.

____. *The Microphone Wars: A History of Triumph and Betrayal at the CBC*. Toronto: McClelland & Stewart, 1994.

Newcomb, Horace, ed. *Television: The Critical View*. 7th ed. New York: Oxford University Press, 2007.

Newman, Peter. *Here Be Dragons*. Toronto: McClelland & Stewart, 2004.

Nolan, Brian. *Donald Brittain: Man of Film*. Toronto: DigiWare, 2004.

Ondaatje, Michael. *Divisadero*. New York: Knopf, 2007.

Peers, Frank W. *The Politics of Canadian Broadcasting, 1920–1951*. Toronto: University of Toronto Press, 1969.

Pinter, Harold. *Old Times*. London: Eyre Methuen, 1972.

Resnick, Philip. *The Land of Cain: Class and Nationalism in English Canada, 1945–1976*. Vancouver: New Star Books, 1977.

Rutherford, Paul. *The Making of the Canadian Media*. Toronto: McGraw-Hill Ryerson, 1978.

Salinger, J.D. *The Catcher in the Rye*. Boston: Little, Brown, 1991.

Sims, Norman, ed. *The Literary Journalists*. New York: Ballantine Books, 1984.

Skene, Wayne. *A Requiem for the CBC*. Vancouver: Douglas & McIntyre, 1993.

Smith, Denis. *Gentle Patriot: A Political Biography of Walter Gordon*. Edmonton: Hurtig Publishers, 1973.

Spears, Borden. *Borden Spears: Reporter, Editor, Critic*. Edited by Dick MacDonald. London and Markham, ON: School of Journalism, University of Western Ontario/ Fitzhenry & Whiteside, 1984.

Stewart, Sandy. *From Coast to Coast: A Personal History of Radio in Canada*. Montreal: CBC Enterprises, 1985.

Stevens. G.R. *History of the Canadian National Railways*. New York: Macmillan, 1973.

Stouck, David. *As for Sinclair Ross*. Toronto: University of Toronto Press, 2005.

Styron, William. *Darkness Visible: A Memoir of Madness*. New York: Vintage, 1992.

Talese, Gay. *The Kingdom and the Power*. New York: World Publishing Company, 1969.

Taylor, Charles. *Radical Tories: The Conservative Tradition in Canada*. Toronto: House of Anansi Press, 2006.

———. *Six Journeys: A Canadian Pattern*. Toronto: House of Anansi Press, 1977.

Tessier, James. *A History of St. Joseph's Parish, 1901 to 2001*. Moose Jaw, SK: Grand Valley Press, 2001.

Tóibín, Colm. *The Master*. Toronto: McClelland & Stewart, 2004.

Wall, Sharon. *The Nurture of Nature: Childhood, Antimodernism, and Ontario Summer Camps, 1920–55*. Vancouver: University of British Columbia Press, 2009.

White, E.B. *The Points of My Compass: Letters from the East, the West, the North, the South*. New York: Harper & Row, 1962.

Williams, Raymond. *Raymond Williams on Television: Selected Writings*. Edited by Alan O'Connor. New York: Routledge, 1989.

Toye, William, ed. *The Oxford Companion to Canadian Literature*. Toronto: Oxford University Press, 1983.

Vincent, David. *The Rise of Mass Literacy: Reading and Writing in Modern Europe*. Malden, MA: Blackwell Publishers, 2000.

Watson, Patrick. *This Hour Has Seven Decades*. Toronto: McArthur & Company, 2004.

Weintraub, William. *Why Rock the Boat*. Toronto: McClelland & Stewart, 1961.

Secondary Sources (Unpublished Books)

Kuffert, Len. "'To Pick You Up or to Hold You': Intimacy and Golden-Age Radio in Canada."

Sarty, Glenn. "Memoirs."

Acknowledgements

I owe an enormous debt of gratitude to Jeanie Wagner. In written comments on each chapter and during telephone conversations, she gave wise advice that has resulted in a critical but fair biography. Also I am grateful for Lois Smith-Brennan's act of generosity. When the Canada Council for the Arts and the Ontario Arts Council discovered that their cupboards were bare, Lois acted as patron of the arts.

Thanks goodness for archives and archivists. Bernadine Dodge and Jodi Aoki of Trent University Archives, home of the Peter Gzowski Papers, made my weekly research visits in 2004 and 2005 enjoyable and enlightening. Janice Millard, Bernadine's successor, continues to make researchers welcome. Archivists at the University of Calgary (Apolonia Steele and Marlys Chevrefils) and McMaster University (Carl Spadoni and Rick Stapleton) were most helpful in photocopying Gzowski correspondence in various collections.

Other archivists also deserve thanks: Jim Quantrell of the City of Cambridge Archives; Loryl MacDonald and Harold Averill, the University of Toronto Archives; Paul Leatherdale and Susan Lewthwaite of the Law Society of Upper Canada Archives; Fred Addis of the Stephen Leacock Museum; Ken Dalgarno of the Moose Jaw Public Library; Susan Millen and Tim Novak of the Saskatchewan Archives Board; Paul E. Lewis of the Ridley College Archives; Wendy Watts and Joanne MacDonald of TorStar Syndication Services; Elaine Cartwright, Alumni Relations Officer, University of St Andrews, Scotland; Brian Hübner and Lewis St. George Stubbs of the University of Manitoba Archives; Rick Machowick of the Legislative Library of Manitoba; Paul Banfield of Queen's University Archives. At Library and Archives Canada, Rob Fisher, Michelle Lillie, Catherine Hobbs, Daniel Potvin, Dan Somers, and William Russell located documents and videos. Andrew Rodger kept me up-to-date on photographs and documents related to Peter Gzowski, and directed me to Andrea Kunard and Sue Lagasi at the National Gallery of Canada where Sue Legasi and France Beauregard made available the Lutz Dille photograph published in this biography. At the archives of the Art Gallery of Ontario, Blythe Koreen, Parin Dahya, and Greg Humeniuk researched the provenance of the gallery's collection of Cornelius Krieghoff oils.

Thank goodness, as well, for libraries and librarians. The staff at the Toronto Metro Library, including members of the Baldwin Room, were always obliging. In Lindsay, Mary Callaghan, Julie Lynch, Phyllis Gray, Heidi Long, Georgia Robinson, and Linda Kent worked the interlibrary loan system and provided me with "Pages of the Past." As a research associate of the Leslie Frost Centre at Trent University, I enjoyed long-term borrowing privileges at Bata Library. For a copy of a wedding photograph of Peter and Jennie, I turned to Brianne Sloane of the Chatham-Kent Public Library.

At the CBC, Mark Mietkiewicz, Catherine Jheon, Vivian Moens, David Thompson, Margaret Fitzgerald, Robert Campbell, Mark Cannon, Brenda Carroll, and Roy Harris facilitated my research. Ken Puley of the CBC Radio Archives was unfailingly friendly and helpful. Other CBC people were also helpful, including June Callwood, Russ Germain, Bill Casselman, Ron Grant, Gloria Bishop, Hal Wake, Shelagh Rogers, Philip Ditchburn, Sue Campbell, and Barry Penhale. Dennis Murphy recounted tales of his decades-long friendship and working relationship with Peter Gzowski. Bruce Rogers and Diana (Baillie) Rogers enriched my knowledge of CBC Radio during the 1960s and 1970s. Mareike Meyer's explanation of her role as studio director of *Morningside* from 1990 to 1997 was invaluable. Through his writing, Glen Allen told me about his relationship with Peter. Shelley Ambrose offered memories of Peter and helped to identify several photographs. Donna Logan, program director of the English-language section of CBC Radio, recalled her connections with Peter. Paul Soles talked about his acquaintanceship with Peter, and directed me to his sister, Ruth-Ellen. Also at the CBC, Fred Langan introduced me to Patsy Pehleman. Diana Filer talked about her role as producer of the Bruno Gerussi radio show, and commented on the chapter dealing with *This Country in the Morning*. Doug Ward and Margaret Lyons, who were always forthcoming when I pestered them about Peter's early radio days, read several chapters with insight and sensitivity. In addition, Doug Ward helped me to understand the rather complicated "rolling" format of *Radio Free Friday*. Other CBC people who talked to me include Michael Enright, Mark Starowicz,, Peter Meggs, and Danny Finkelman. Nancy Oliver of *90 Minutes Live* connected me with David Ruskin and Alex Frame, who during several conversations patiently explained the Gzowski genius on radio. Peter Herrndorf provided insights into *90 Minutes Live*. Roger Sarty put me in touch with his father, Glenn, arguably Peter's most sympathetic and talented executive producer on television.

Other contributors include Mark Rothman, Mary Young Leckie, Horst Ehricht, Eric Reguly, Robert Reguly, Chris Salzen, Elspeth Cameron, Hugh Grant, Serge Cipko,

Acknowledgements

Peter Wardlaw, Courtney Garneau, Jason Bane, Bruce Corcoron, Dave Benson , Nancy Granada, Bruce Pratt, Irene White, Angie Clark, Don Hall, and Gary Ross. Lloyd Johnston connected me with Colleen Macdonald, who put me in touch with Cathy Perkins, who led me to Rob Perkins. Christie Blatchford reported on Peter the hockey dad. Margot Fawcett explained how Margaret Brown turned her into a bibliophile. I can't thank John Ayre enough for putting me in touch with documents and archivists connected with Peter and Mordecai Richler. Thanks to John, I enjoyed an hour's transatlantic telephone conversation with Mavis Gallant in December 2005.

Others who contributed were Richard Osler, Greg Oliver, Gene Kiniski, Amina Beecroft, Robert Bringhurst, Rob Winslow, Robin Quantick, Robert Fulford, Harry Bruce, John Macfarlane, Michael de Pencier, David Crombie, Christopher Moore, Jayne MacAulay, Bonnie Baker Cowan, Vanessa Allen, Mary Pratt, and Kildare Dobbs. Kenneth Munro cast light on Edmonton during the late 1970s and early 1980s, as well as on Frank Ferguson, one of Peter's Galt teachers. Steve Budnarchuk, co-owner of Audreys Books in Edmonton, kindly identified a photograph of Peter signing books at Audreys in 1981. Gillian Howard agreed to answer questions about Peter, and Peter C. Gzowski was unfailingly polite whenever I asked biographical questions. Peter's cousin, Jack Madden, provided first-hand memories. Lyn Goldman connected me with Cal Abrahamson, who described Jennie Lissaman's intelligent set design for the Regina Little Theatre in 1957. Jan Walter shared memories of Peter and directed me to Susan Kent and to Selena Forsyth, who was generous with her time over the course of this biography.

Also helpful were Babs Tancock, Ken Tancock, Leslie Pearl, Ed Mannion, Lloyd Robertson, Richard Nielsen, Janice Stein, James Adams, Fred Carmichael, Miki Carmichael, Governors General Adrienne Clarkson and Ed Schreyer, Luba Goy, Premiers William Davis and David Peterson, Brian McKillop, Munroe Scott, Toni Wrate, Eric Wrate, Linda Schuyler, and Melinda Sutton. John Millyard described a tense golf game with Peter and explained the rules of match play, as did Marg Evans and Charlotte Empringham. Murray Burt was more than generous and colourful in sharing memories of Peter. Louise (Brennan) Beler, Ray Christensen, Kelly Christensen, Margaret McBurney, Peter Sibbald Brown, Ross McKerron, and Mel Simmons also contributed.

To enrich my knowledge of Galt during Peter's boyhood, I talked to Reg Brown's nieces, Phyllis and Shirley, as well as to Charles Wilson, Jeanette Chippendale, Michael Johnson, Dafi Gilad, and Mardi New. Tom Brown, Peter's old schoolmate, showed me around Galt. Moose Jaw residents were particularly helpful. Yvette Moore, of Yvette Moore Gallery, gave me permission to use her beautiful rendition of the old Temple Gardens Dance Hall; and Doug Marr, Joyce Walters, Sheila Phillips, Yvonne Pearson, Barry Gray, Nancy Gray, Ray Belt, Earl Bush, Deb Thorn, and Robert Currie provided details of Peter's time in Moose Jaw in 1957 and 1997. For Peter's role in Leacock events in Orillia, I turned to "Pete" McGarvey and Jean Dickson. "Pete" was also kind enough to give me tapes of two interviews conducted with Gzowski at radio station CKEY in Toronto.

Staff and administration of Trent University were always forthcoming. They include President Bonnie Patterson, Michael Peterman, John Milloy, John Wadland, John Burbidge, Ashley Horne, Jennifer MacIsaac, and Chancellor Roberta Bondar. Tom Symons, founding president of the university, recalled Peter's days as editor of *The Varsity*. Professor Symons is a member of many boards, including those of the Symons Trust Fund and the Ontario Heritage Trust, both of which have been generous to me and to this biography. For his kindly influence, I wish to thank him.

Ron and Diana Rees read chapters, and as usual their comments and encouragement, as well as their friendship, are remembered and appreciated. I can't thank Ted Barris enough for encouragement, as well as for tapes of interviews with Peter, and a rare, perhaps unique tape of the launch in Edmonton of *The Game of Our Lives* in October 1981. Marco Adria made available two taped interviews with Peter Gzowski, as well as two other interviews, one with Mel Hurtig and the other with Ted Byfield. Marco's biography *Peter Gzowski: An Electric Life* was indispensable. Ridley College old boys who remembered Peter were Norris Walker, Jack Barton, Darcy McKeough, Jim Chaplin, Andre Dorfman, and especially John Girvin. For the Chatham period, I turned to Winn Miller and Darcy McKeough.

I want to thank many others, including Evelyn Hart, Terry Campbell, Sheila Whitney, John Imrie, Madelyne Imrie, Donald Smith, Wayne Scott, Jim Harris, Audrey Brooks, Ken Luffert , Myrna Kostash, Jennifer Weber, Maria Wilson, Ginette Saint-Jules, Patricia Morley, Pat Boyle, D'Arcy Jenish, Douglas Frayn, Doug Cole, Will Hawking, Peter Flemington, Judge Dennis Ball, Tony Fry, Alexa McDonough, Michel Gaulin, Scott Symons, Aline Houghton, Chris Raible, Chris Guly, David Morton, Jennie Marcus, John Gray, Elizabeth Gray, John Court, Douglas Richardson, Robert Thacker, Owen Cooke, Donna Coulter, Alex Hewlitt, Donelda Thomas, Valerie Hewlitt, Alicia Thomas, Sandra Howland, Ken McGoogan, Alan Bowker, Carolyn Bowker, Bill Bolstad, William Weintraub, Dorothy Macpherson, Michael Kesteron, Charlie Bellerby, David Wessel, Christine Merrikin, Carole Munden, Steve Kurtz, Edie Kurtz, Judy Burton, Kathy Stinson, Hugh P. Macmillan, Muriel Macmillan, Tony Griffin, Kitty Griffin, Joyce Horne, Bruce Steinman, Daryl Richel, Deb Quaile, Ferne Burkhardt, Lake Sagaris, Toni Sinclair, Eleanor Burton, Ian Campbell, Steve Campbell, Joyce Campbell, Neysa Mitchell, Barbara Fleming, John Fleming, Nancy Walsh, John Sabean, Diane Mooney, Frances Daunt, Lilianne Plamonden, and Stephanie Suitor.

At Dundurn Press I enjoyed working with Kirk Howard and the staff of the publishing company, especially Associate Publisher and Editorial Director Michael Carroll and the design department headed by Jennifer Scott.

I would be remiss if I didn't thank, once again, my parents, without whose hard work in the Argyle General Store I wouldn't be able to afford the luxury of writing. During her three years of retirement from 1984 to 1987, my mother listened to *Morningside*. During her final fifteen weeks of life, *Morningside* was her caregiver's salvation.

Acknowledgements

Finally, I want to thank the Symons Trust Fund for Canadian Studies, Trent University, for contributing to the cost of this book's illustrations, and also to the cost of obtaining permission for the quotations used in this biography.

Index

Index

Index

Index